MANAGEMENT AND BEHAVIOURAL PROCESS

Prof. H. R. APPANNAIAH
Dean, Surana P.G. Centre, Bengaluru,
Former Director, SRN Adarsha College, Bengaluru,
Former Principal, P.A. College, Tiptur,
Founder President, Federation of Teachers' Councils of Commerce and Management in Karnataka

Dr. M. MUNINARAYANAPPA,
M.Com., M.Phil., Ph.D., MLI.Sc., MBA (D.Litt.)
Reader in Commerce,
Dept. of Post Graduate Studies in Commerce,
Bangalore University.

Dr. DINKAR
B.E., M.Tech., MBA, M.Phil., Ph.D.,
Professor & HOD, Rajarajeswari College of Engineering,
Dept. of Management,
Bengaluru.

Himalaya Publishing House

MUMBAI • NEW DELHI • NAGPUR • BENGALURU • HYDERABAD • CHENNAI • PUNE
LUCKNOW • AHMEDABAD • ERNAKULAM • BHUBANESWAR • INDORE • KOLKATA

First Edition : 2010

Published by : Mrs. Meena Pandey
for **HIMALAYA PUBLISHING HOUSE PVT. LTD.,**
"Ramdoot", Dr. Bhalerao Marg, Girgaon, **Mumbai - 400 004.**
Phones: 2386 01 70/2386 38 63, Telefax: 022-2387 71 78
Email: himpub@vsnl.com
Website: www.himpub.com

Branch Offices:

New Delhi : "Pooja Apartments", 4-B, Murari Lal Street, Ansari Road, Darya Ganj, New Delhi - 110 002. Phone: 011-23270392/23278631, Telefax: 011-23256286

Nagpur : Kundanlal Chandak Industrial Estate, Ghat Road, Nagpur - 440 018. Phone: 0712-2738731/3296733, Telefax: 0712-2721215

Bengaluru : No. 16/1 (Old 12/1), 1st Floor, Next to Hotel Highlands, Madhava Nagar, Race Course Road, Bengaluru - 560 001. Phone: 080-22281541/22385461, Telefax: 080-22286611

Hyderabad : No. 3-4-184, Lingampally, Besides Raghavendra Swamy Matham, Kachiguda, Hyderabad - 500 027. Phone: 040-27560041/ 27550139, Mobile: 09848130433, Telefax: 040-27560041

Chennai : No. 85/50, Bazullah Road, T. Nagar, Chennai - 600 017. Phone: 044-28344020/32463737/42124860

Pune : No. 527, "Laksha" Apartment, First Floor, Mehunpura, Shaniwarpeth, (Near Prabhat Theatre), Pune - 411 030. Phone: 020-24496323/24496333/32326733

Lucknow : Jai Baha Bhavan, Church Road, Near Manas Complex and Dr, Awasthi Clinic, Aliganj, Lucknow - 226 024 Phone: 0522-2339329/4068914, Mobile: 09305302158, 09415349385, 09389593752

Ahmedabad : No. 114, "SHAIL", 1st Floor, Opp. Madhu Sudan House, C.G.Road, Navrang Pura, Ahmedabad – 380 009. Phone: 079-26560126, Mobile: 09327324149, 09314679413

Ernakulam : No. 39/104 A, Lakshmi Apartment, Karikkamuri Cross Rd., Ernakulam, Cochin – 682011, Kerala. Phone: 0484-2378012/2378016, Mobile: 09344199799

Bhubaneswar : 5 Station Square, Bhubaneswar (Orissa) - 751 001. Mobile: 09861046007, E-mail: orissa@himpub.com

Indore : Kesardeep Avenue Extension, 73, Narayan Bagh.Flat No. 302, IIIrd Floor, Near Humpty Dumpty School, Narayan Bagh, Indore (M.P.) – 452 007 Mobile: 09301386468

Kolkata : 108/4, Beliaghata, Main Road, Near ID Hospital, Opp. SBI Bank Kolkata - 700 010. Mobile: 09910440956, E-mail: nkmitra@himpub.com

DTP by : Elite-Art, N.S. Marg, Daryaganj, New Delhi - 110 002, Mobile: 09911297688

Printed by : Bengaluru

PREFACE

Today's business world is facing many challenges. The world recession of 2008-2009 had heavy impact on developed economies of the world. Main contributor for this worldwide recession was the USA. Accumulated economic malpractices of the USA, bursted in 2008. The impact of economic imbalance in the USA spread to all other countries. Many countries in the world suffered the impact of American recession. One of the main reasons for recession is managing irrationally the economy in general and the corporate world in particular. Although the countries initiated corrective measures to come out of this situation, sound management system can give a permanent solution to this major disaster.

The economic recession has taught one lesson to the business world. In global and domestic business, without maintaining world-class quality in operations and without practicing ethical aspects of business, the survival of business is a difficult task. At macro and micro level, business managers who are the drivers of their business, have to have solid training in managerial aspects. Besides understanding the basic principles of management, managers at micro level should also know the behavioural aspects of their workforce and of themselves. In this backdrop, this title "Management and Behavioural Process" is placed in the hands of readers.

This work has an integrated approach of management, blending both principles and behaviour in a workplace. The book is divided into two sections, *viz.*, (i) Management and (ii) Behavioural process.

The first section contains principles and process of management. This section has 12 chapters which discuss management issues such as planning, organizing, leadership, communication, motivating and controlling. Initial chapter contains the overview of management and the role of managers.

The second section is on behavioural process and contains 13 chapters covering, the issues of individual behaviour, group behaviour and organisational behaviour.

All the chapters in both the sections have been carefully designed to provide the information on the chapter theme and written in a simple language for an easy understanding of the readers. Each chapter contains learning objective, text, summary and questions for self-study. This comprehensive book on management provides small cases for easy understanding of the concepts wherever necessary.

— Authors

ACKNOWLEDGEMENT

We fondly remember the encouragement given by late Sri D.P. Pandeyji in all our writing endeavour.

We thank Sri K.N. Pandeyji, Sri Anuj Pandey, Sri Niraj Pandey, Sri Vijay Pandey for their continuous encouragement in our writing activity and for readily accepting to publish this work.

We thank Sri H.R. Ramanath, Professor, East-West College of Management Studies, Bengaluru for his assistance in reading the manuscript and giving suggestions to make the book qualitative.

We also thank Sri N. Manjunatha, Faculty, Department of Management Studies, Rajarajeswari Engineering College, Bengaluru for his assistance in composing some chapters of this title.

We also thank, Smt Nimisha Kadam, Production executive, HPH and staff of HPH for their co-operation in bringing out this textbook on time.

— Authors

CONTENTS

SECTION I:

MANAGEMENT

1

MANAGEMENT — OVERVIEW

LEARNING OBJECTIVES

After reading this chapter, you should be able to know;

- The Concept of Management
- Nature, Purpose and Functions of Management
- Managerial Skills
- Factors Influencing Managerial Success

INTRODUCTION TO MANAGEMENT

Today's business management practices demand an integrated management approach considering prime factors such as ethics, global environment and quality, which are really challenging for modern managers. Managing the business in real time, is more an amazing and learning experience from the theoritical aspects that may be understood from studying some management related material. But basic principles of management have to be studied to undersand the domain of management. This domain focuses on the subfunctional management areas such as production, finance, marketing, HRD and other general management issues.

In the present-day industrial world, management has become universal. With the increase in the complexities of management of business concerns, the importance of 'management' has increased enormously. The principles of management are being applied not only for managing business concerns, but also to manage various other institutions like hospitals, educational and social institutions and government. Management occupies such an important place in the modern world that the welfare of the people and the destiny of the country are very much influenced by it. Marshall E. Demock has rightly stated that "The management is not a matter of pressing a button, pulling a lever, issuing an order it is the power to determine what shall happen to the personalities and happiness of the entire people, the power to shape the destiny of a nation and of all the nations which make up the world."

Peter F. Drucker, considered as the *"Father of Management"*, in his book *"Management: Tasks, Responsibilities and Practice"* states three vital tasks of management.

(i) "to determine the goals and mission of the organisation,
(ii) to make work productive and the worker achieving,
(iii) to take care of social impacts and responsibilities."

Of these three tasks, second task assumes priority. Human resource of the organisation is the real resource. This resource has to a be effectively managed to achieve high productivity from this. Managers have to co-operate with human elements in and out of the organisation. They have to coordinate each human element to attain the organisational goals.

MANAGEMENT - MEANING

Unlike other subjects like philosophy, psychology and economics, management is a relatively a new subject. The principles and techniques of management are still in a developing stage and the definitions of management given by different scholars emphasise different aspects of management. The following are a few of the important definitions of the term 'management.'

"Management is a distinct process consisting of planning, organising, actuating and controlling performanc to determine and accomplish the objectives by the use of people and resources"

- *George R. Terry*

"Management is concerned with seeing that the job gets done, it tasks all centre that on planning and guiding the operations to it are going on the enterprise." **- *E.F.L. Brech***

"Management is simply the process of decision making and control over the actions of human beings for the express purpose of attaining predetermined goals." **- *Stanley Vane***

"Management consists of getting things done through others. Manager is one who accomplishes the objectives by directing the efforts of others." **- *S. George***

"Management is that function of an enterprise which concerns itself with the direction and control of the various activities to attain the business objectives." **- *William Spriegel***

"Management embraces all duties and functions that pertain to the initiation of an enterprise, its financing, the establishment of major policies, the provision of all necessary equipment, the outlining of general form of organisation under which the enterprise is to operate and the group of officials in primary control of an enterprise is referred to as the management."

- *Kimbail and Kimball*

"Management is the art of getting things done through and with people in formally organised groups. It is the art of creating an environment in which people can perform as individuals and yet co-operate towards the attainment of group goals. It is the art of removing blocks to such performance, a way of optimising efficiency in reaching goals." **- *Harold Konntz***

The first definition of management is that it is an economic organ of industrial society. It means taking action to make the desired result to pass. **- *Peter. F. Drucker***

From these definitions, it is clear that nanagement consists of getting things done through others by directing their efforts in an integrated and co-ordinated manner in order to attain business objectives. It is a process consisting of functions such as planning, organising, actuating and controlling business operations in such a manner as to attain the predetermined goals. It also involves securing men, money, materials and machinry needed for the achievement of business objectives and putting all of them into operation and checking their performance in order to ensure the productive use of the material resources. It consists of resource and all of organisational activities that involve goal formation and accomplishment, performance appraisal and the development of an operating philosophy that ensures survival of the organisation.

(i) "to determine the goals and mission of the organisation,
(ii) to make work productive and the worker achieving,
(iii) to take care of social impacts and responsibilities."

Of these three tasks, second task assumes priority. Human resource of the organisation is the real resource. This resource has to be effectively managed to achieve high productivity from this. Managers have to co-operate with human elements in and out of the organisation. They have to co-operate each human element to attain the organisation goals.

THE NEED FOR MANAGEMENT

The concept of "Management" nas been fully explained in previous paragraphs. Accordingly,

(i) Management is a Process
(ii) Management is a discipline, in the sense that "it is an accumulated body of knowledge" that can be learnt and
(iii) Management is a career.

The third aspect "Management as a career" is mainly considered here to show how a manager can manage an organisation. If one is a successful manager, one will have a good career. Many a time we make some statements about known 'people who have performed well as administrators or managers. "Mr. Bhaskar is functioning well as Purchase Manager after holding several positions ever since he joined Elite Engineering Company." "Mr. Abraham has a fine career as H.R.D. Manager in Tata Pharmaceuticals." "Mr. Viswanath is doing well as Chief Marketing Manager in Rallies India Ltd." These statements speak of the performance of individuals working for an organisation taking "Management as a career." These managers devote cheir time to co-ordinate the activities their functional areas and "lives to the process of management progress through a sequence of new activities and, often new challenges." Today the business world is highly competitive in character and the persons involved in business units to run an effective show (manager), should dedicate themselves to their work, develop an identity with their activities and organisations. Only then, they can perform as good managers.

Therefore the need for management or effective management is highly emphasised. Every business unit is facing stiff competition and the persons holding key positions in these units should have certain qualities to become effective managers. The needs that force the management to have an effective managerial process are;

(i) The competition faced by the organisation;
(ii) The behaviour of consumers towards the product or service of that organisation;
(iii) The market conditions or behaviour which keep the organisation on toes to adopt certain strategies to overcome the situation which affects the organisational growth;
(iv) The policies of the government favouring or affecting the organisation growth;
(v) Expansion of the organisation for a better result;
(vi) Diversification of activities to utilise the unexploited resources of the organisation.

NATURE AND CHARACTERISTICS OF MANAGEMENT

An analysis of the definitions of management indicates that the management has the following characteristics:

1. Management is an activity. Management *is* a process of organised activity which is concerned with the efficient use of resources of production. Resources include materials, money and people in the organisation.

2. It is a purposeful activity. It is concerned with the achievement of an objectivity through its functions such as planning, organising, staffing, directing and controlling. Objectives may be explicitly defined or implicit.

3. It is concerned with the efforts of a group. According to Appleby, management is concerned with the management of people and not the direction of things. It inspires and motivates workers to put forth their efforts to the maximum extent.

4. Management is getting things done. According to Koontz and O'Donnell, management is the art of getting things done through and with people in formally organised groups. In other words, a manager does not do any operating work himself but gets it done through others.

5. It applies economic principles. According td Dr. Kimball, management is the art of applying the economic principles that underlie the control of men and materials in the enterprise under consideration.

6. Involves decision-making. Management involves decisions relating to various aspects of management. It is said that management is the decision-making process and the decisions are involved in all the functions of management.

7. It co-ordinates all activities and resources. It is concerned with the co-ordination of all activities and resources through its various functions to attain the stated objectives.

8. It is an universal activity. Managers, irrespective of the enterprise in which they are working and their place in the organisation structure, make use of the management principles. It means that the techniques and tools of management are universally applicable.

9. It is an integrating process. It integrates men, machines and materials for carrying out ihe operations of an enterprise and for achieving the stated objectives. It is said that the task of business management is the responsibility for welding into a single working force of the three factors — men, methods and machinery.

10. It is concerned with direction and control. It is concerned with the direction and control of the various activities of the enterprise to attain the business objectives. It deals particularly with the active direction of the human effort.

11. It is intangible. It is abstract and cannot be seen with the eyes. It is evidenced by the quality of the organisation and the results such as increased productivity and increased morale of the subordinates, etc.

12. Management is both a science and an art. It has developed certain principles and laws which are applicable to any group activity. It is also an art, because it is concerned with the application of knowledge for the solution of organisational problems.

13. It is a profession. Gradually, it is becoming a profession. Because there are established principles of management which are being applied in practice.

14. It is an interdisciplinary approach. Management as a body of discipline which takes the help of other social sciences like psychology, sociology, anthropology, engineering, economics, mathematics, etc.

15. It is an economic resource. There are five factors of production, *viz.,* land, labour, capital, management, and entrepreneur. The entrepreneur establishes the organisation as owner and it is the management which transforms these various resources into productive processes. Peter Drucker has observed that "whatever rapid economic and social development took place after World War II, it occurred as a result of systematic and purposeful work on developing managers and management." The inputs of labour, capital and material do not by themselves ensure growth; they require the catalyst of management to maximise results.

16. It is a system of authority. As the management is a process of directing men to perform a task, authority to extract work from others, it is implied in the very concept of management.

17. It is dynamic, not static. Management adapts itself to the social changes and also introduces innovation in methodology.

MANAGEMENT – THE SCOPE

Management includes the following aspects:

1. Subject-matter of Management. It consists of various management functions such as planning, organising, staffing, directing and controlling.

2. Management is an interdisciplinary approach. For the correct and effective application of the principles of management, a study of various other subjects such as economics, sociology, mathematics, psychology, behavioural science, statistics, etc., is required.

3. Principles of Management are of universal application.

4. Management also includes scientific methods, human relations, and quantitative techniques.

FUNCTIONAL AREAS OF MANAGEMENT

It consists of the following functional areas:

(i) *Financial management:* It includes cost control, budgetary control, financial planning, management accounting, standard costing etc.

(ii) *Personnel management:* It includes aspects such as recruitment, training, transfers, promotions, retirement, industrial relations, social security, etc.

(iii) *Purchasing management:* It consists of purchasing of raw materials, maintaining of records, materials control, issuing relations, social security, etc.

(iv) *Production management:* It deals with aspects such as producrion planning, quality control and inspection, production control techniques, etc.

(v) *Marketing management:* It includes marketing of goods and services, price determination, market research, sales promotion, advertisement, publicity, etc.

(vi) *Office management:* It is concerned with office layout, staffing, equipment of office, etc.

(vii) *Maintenance Management:* It relates to the proper care and maintenance of the building, plant and machinery etc.

(viii) *Transport Management:* It includes packing, warehousing, transportation by rail, road, air etc.

MANAGEMENT - THE ROLE

Management plays a vital role in modern society. It regulates man's productive activities by organising factors of production. Drucker observes that without the leadership provided by management, the resources of production remain mere resources and never become production. The well-being of society is largely dependent upon the quality of management. By making the facfors of production perform better, management enables society to get a better and increased supply of goods and by this, it promotes the welfare of society. Urwick and Brech have rightly observed that no ideology, no 'ism', no political theory can win a greater output with less effort from a given complex of human and material resources. And it is on such greater output that a higher standard of life, more amenities for all must necessarily be founded.

The running of a modern business has become a complex matter due to numerous factors such as the size, structure, ever-changing trends of consumers' tastes and needs, ceaseless competitive drive, new techniques of production, government regulations, social responsibility of business, etc. Because of these, 'management which consists of scientific thinking, accurate planning and meticulous control' plays a vital role in the running of a modern business. Management enables the enterprises build up its competitive strength and develop and expand its assets and profits. Drucker has rightly observed that "management, which is the organ of society specially charged with making resources productive, with the responsibility for organised economic advance, reflects the basic spirit of the modern age."

Management is needed not only for business concerns but also for social organisations like educational, religious, charitable and other non-business institutions. Further, governments of all types need management as much as others, perhaps, more than all other social organisations. The late President Roosevelt of the USA aptly said that "a government without good management is a house built on sand." In short, management is an essential accompaniment of all social organisations and everywhere it is found as a distinct, separate and dominant activity.

MANAGEMENT AND RESOURCES

Every business or non-business organisation has to assess itself about the various assets available to manager and the institution. It should also know as to how these assets are to be effectively used. The assets or resources include both human and non-human factors. These organisational resources may be explained as labour, capital, land and entrepreneural skills. These resources are coordinated and final products or services are produced.

Of the two main resoures-human and non-human, human factor plays a key role. It is the human element that can coordinate other human work in the firm such as the equipment and other resources. Human resources possess skills and knowledge. These are to be effectively used by human element, otherwise called managers. Managers have to effectively utilise capital, labour and other resources to bring out final output. Waste of resources lead to increase in cost of production. This finally reduces the profit. Therefore, cost effectiveness will be a focal point in good maangement.

The companies like Infosys, Wipro, etc. which are run on sound lines will have the following managing techniques :

- **Sound Decisions:** Well managed companies take sound decisions. Their decisions will be such that the operations have to be more cost-effective and avoid wastage in the production process.
- **Customer Relation:** The excellent companies like Tata Group, Toyota-Kirloskar, TVS and various other companies which are run on excellent lines, learn from customer feedback. They care for the opinion of customers. Many innovative companies got their best product ideas from customers. Companies close to the customer do well.
- **Freedom to Workers:** Excellently run companies allow their workers try and try on operation, allow them to commit more mistakes, take risks to improve the quality of product or operations. These companies foster many innovators thorughout the organisation. These organisations donot look like corporations. They will be a sort of loose network of laboratories in which restless inventors and dauntless entrepreneurs work to convert their imagination into reality. The management supports these innovators to invent new things, inspite of many mistakges they commit in the process of inventing. This freedom to innovators is given to see that company becomes an excellent one.
- **Using Human Potential to the Core:** Excellent companies make their human resources to give out their best to the company. Each worker will be respected to extract his potential to the core for increasing the overall productivity of the organisation. The good management will consider each indvididual as a "Source of ideas and not just a pair of hands"
- **Result Orientation:** Best managed companies look to their achievements, rather than various other inputs such as technology and other resources. Although these are provided, their aim is to get best results through quality, service, cleanliness and value.

- **Managing the Fundamentals :** Well managed companies never forget their base. They do the business that they know. They never run the business that they donot know. The fundamental principle here is that they sould stick to the business they should know.
- **Flat and Simple Organisational Structure:** Managing a company on sound lines, need an effort which will be cost-effective. This means the organisations should appoint less number of staff who are highly skilled. It should be a flat organisation with minimum managerial levels.
- **Decentralisation and Delegation :** Better management lies in decentralisation. There may be centralised organisations which are excellent one. But most of the well-managed compaines decentralise their activities and delegate authority with accountability and responsibility to make sure that workers develop organisational identity.

This information provides a base as how an organisation has to use its resources to run "effectively" and "efficiently".

"Effectiveness" implies the extent to which the management achieves its organisational objectives. Managerial effectiveness measures the degree of organisation's resource utilisation to achieve the goals of the firm. It also measures the strength of the manager in achieving the goals. (To do right things)

Efficiency, measures the extent to which organisational resources are used in production process. (To do things right). This indicates the contribution of resources to the production.

ADMINISTRATION AND MANAGEMENT

The terms 'administration' and 'management' are used in different senses by different writers. Broadly, there are three different types of views expressed by different schools of thought which are given below.

According to some writers (like Drucker, Fayol and Newman), there is no distinction between the terms 'administration' and 'management' and both of them are synonymous and used interchangeably. According to these writers, running of a business or social institution, or a government office requires specialised skill and this specialised skill is called 'management' in business and 'administration' in government and other social institutions. In other words, executive functions in business are referred to as 'management' whereas the executive functions of other institutions like government and public bodies are termed 'administration.'

Henry Fayol who is regarded as the real originator of management has pointed out that there is only one administration or management science which can be applied equally well to the public and private affairs. He has stated: "All undertakings require planning, organising, command, co-ordination and control and in order to function properly. All must observe the same general principles. We are no longer confronted with several administrative sciences, but with one which can be applied equally well to public and private affairs." (Thus, according to him, both the terms are synonymous and any distinction between them is misleading.)

According to another school of thought, administration and management are different functions. According to this school, administration is a top level function, which centres round the determination of major policies and objectives of a business enterprise (*i.e.,* thinking function), while management is a lower level function involving the execution of policies and directing the operations to attain the objectives laid down by the administration (*i.e.,* doing function). This view is supported by eminent writers like Oliver Sheldon, William R. Spriegel, G.W. Milward and others and we quote here the concepts of these writers.

Oliver Sheldon: Administration is the function in industry concerned with the determination of the corporate policy, the co-ordination of finance, production and distribution, the settlement of the compass (structure) of the organisation under the ultimate control of the executive. Management, according to him, "is the function in industry concerned with the execution of policy within the limit set by the administration and the employment of the organisation for the particular objects set before it."

William R. Spriegel: "Administration is that phase of business enterprise that concerns itself with the overall determination of institutional objectives and the policies necessary to be followed in achieving those objectives. Administration predetermines the specific goals and lays down the broad areas within which those goals are to be attained. Administration is a determinative function; management, on the other hand, is an executive function more which is primarily concerned with the carrying out of the broad policies laid down by the administration."

G.E. Milward: "Administration is primarily the process and the agency used to establish the object or purpose which an undertaking and its staff are to achieve; secondarily, administration has to plan and stabilize the broad lines or principles which will govern action. These broad lines are in their turn usually called policies. Management is the process and the agency through which the execution of policy is planned and supervised."

Thus, according to this school of thought, administration and management are not synonymous and they have different functions to perform. If we accept this view, the differences between 'administration' and 'management' are as follows:

1. Administration is concerned with policy-making while management is concerned with the implementation of policy.
2. Functions of administration are legislative and largely, determinative, whereas functions of management are executive and largely, governing.
3. Administration is a thinking function and management is a doing function.
4. Administration relates to the apex and top level management whereas management relates to middle and lower level management.
5. Administration needs administrative rather than technical ability but management requires technical ability more than administrative ability.

Another viewpoint which has been expressed by E.F.L. Brech and others interprets management as a comprehensive generic term which includes administration. Brech, the renowned management expert, regards management as a comprehensive generic function, embracing the entire process of planning, policy-making, co-ordination of activities, maintaining of moral and discipline as well as controlling the operations so as to attain the best possible results. Administration, according to him, signifies certain aspects of management functions (*viz.,* planning and control) and it is interpreted as a branch of management. On the basis of this concept, the management function has been divided into two categories: (1) administrative management and (2) operative management. The upper level of management is usually called administrative management and the lower level is known as operative management. From Fig. 1.1, we can know the scope of administrative management and operative management.

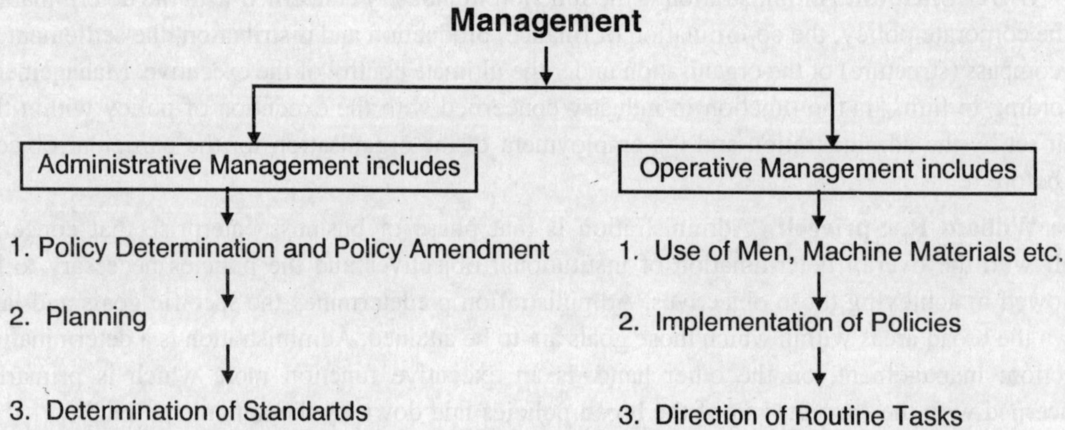

FIG. 1.1. Administrative Management and Operative Management.

We may sum up our discussion by stating that different interpretations of the terms 'administration' and 'management' have been given by different schools of thought. Fortunately, this controversy of the meaning of these two terms is not to be seen nowadays and the term 'management' is generally used for the whole process of managing.

Is Management a Science or an Art?

Science is a systematised body of knowledge acquired by making through observation and experimentation based on certain principles capable of general application. Art, on the other hand, is concerned with the application of skill or knowledge so acquired. If this idea of science and art is applied to managerial activity, it is clear that management is both science and an art. The term 'management' involves providing a body of principles or laws for the solution of specific management problems and the objective evaluation of results. Further, the analysis of the functions of management has led to the development of certain principles which are useful for solving concrete business problems in future. On the other hand, the art of management is concerned with applying of skills and knowledge for accomplishing an end through deliberate efforts. Thus, we find that management is both a science and an art. The American Society of Mechanical Engineers has rightly stated that "management is the art and science of preparing, organising and directing human effort applied to control the forces and utilise the materials of nature for the benefit of man."

Is Management a Profession?

Before drawing any conclusions regarding whether management can be regarded as a profession, it is necessary to know the characteristics of a profession and of management so that we can know whether management meets the characteristics of a profession or not. The characteristics of a profession are:

1. There must be an organised and systematised body of knowledge, principles, and techniques.
2. Conscious acquisition of that knowledge.
3. Entrance into a profession is restricted by standards established by an association of that profession.
4. Existence of an organisation to regulate the behaviour of the members of the profession.
5. Prevalence of ethical standards to guide the activities of the members of the profession.
6. Spirit to the society should receive priority over economic considerations.

The characteristics of management are as follows:

1. It is an organised and systematised body of knowledge, principles and techniques. According to A.P.M. Fleming, "Modern management has a technique quite apart from the technology of the particular works concerned."
2. There is a formal method of acquiring knowledge and principles of management through professional schools of business management.
3. Existence of management associations.
4. The growth of professional management consultants.
5. The growing emphasis on the ethical standards of managerial personnel.
6. The growing emphasis on social responsibility of a manager.

An analysis of the characteristics of management indicates that it does not possess all the essential characteristics of a profession. Like other recognised professions, such as medicine and law, management does not have norms of managerial behaviour, common rules, uniform code of conduct and organisation or licensing. Further, it does not restrict the entry of people into managerial jobs with a special academic degree. In the light of this analysis, we can conclude that management cannot be called a profession. However, we may state that there are certain trends which indicate that the management is moving in the direction of a profession. For example, it is increasingly becoming not only desirable but also essential to acquire the knowledge of management, if one has to become a successful manager in a business. There is also a growing emphasis on formal training of managers and managers who are trained in management institutions are fast replacing the self-made ones. Further, various management organisations which have come into existence have been taking increasing interest in guiding the behaviour of individual managers. Management has been identified as a crucial social activity. Further, there is a growing emphasis on the ethical conduct of management personnel as their social responsibility. All these trends indicate that management is moving in the direction of a profession.

LEVELS OF MANAGEMENT

The process of dividing authority and responsibility among the various executives is called the creation of levels of management. In other words, it is concerned, with the classification of

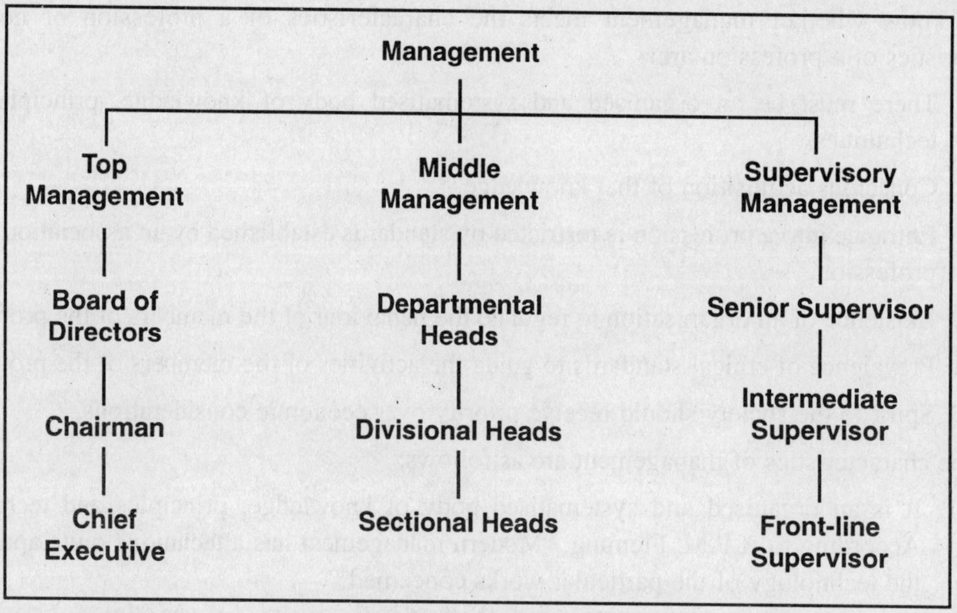

FIG. 1.2. Levels of Management

superior-subordinate relationship in an organisation. There is no-fixed number of management levels prescribed for particular organisation and this depends, to a certain extent on how they are defined and classified, the nature of organisation, size of enterprise, etc. Further, there is no unanimity among the writers in this respect. Keith Davis has classified various management levels as trusteeship management, general management, departmental management, middle management and supervisory management. Piffner and Shorword have classified management levels into fours parts, *viz.,* corporate management, top management, middle management and supervisory management. Koontz, O'Donnell and Brech have classified the levels into two, *viz.,* top-level management and supervisory-level management. Joseph Litterer has suggested three supervisory levels, *viz.,* institutional level, general management and departmental management. Prof. J.B. Batty has classified management and department into five levels, viz., top management, upper middle management, middle management, supervisory management and operating force. Thus there is no unanimity among the writers.

For the convenience of study, the levels of management may be classified into three groups: 1. top management, 2. middle management and 3. lower or supervisory management. The various positions which are included in each level of management may be seen in Fig. 2.

1. Top Management

Top management is at the head of the organisation. It consists of the Board of Directors and its Chairman, the Chief Executive (e.g., Managing Director or General Manager) and the Senior Executive (viz., Deputy General Manager). In the operation of the enterprise, top management is the ultimate level of authority.

Functions of Top Management. The main functions of top management are as follows:

(a) Determine objectives for the organisation. Objectives may relate to profit, business growth, survival, prestige, competitive pricing, marketing method, widening the area of sales, relations with workers, customers, public etc.

(b) Frame the Policy. To frame the policies and chalk out the plans to carry out the objectives and policies. Policies may relate to different aspects of the organisation. For example, production policy deals with the quality, product variety, scheduling of production to meet the market demand etc. Marketing policy deals with such matters as advertising and sales promotion techniques, pricing the product, channel of distribution, commission, discounts, placement, training, remuneration, promotion, appraisal of performance etc. of the personnel. Financial policy relates to the procurement of funds, source of finance, management of earning etc.

(c) Organisational Framework. Top management determines the organisational structure for the purpose of executing the plans that have been laid down. Execution of plans is necessary to carry out the objectives and policies.

(d) Assemble the Resources. For the purpose of executing the plans, the resources of men, machines, materials and money have to be assembled. This again is the task of management.

(e) Control the Operations through Organisation. Top management also controls operations through budget, cost, and statistical quality control and accounting devices.

2. Middle Management

Middle management consists of departmental, divisional or sectional heads and other executive officers attached to the different departments. This level of management is responsible for implementing the policies and plans decided by the top management. Middle management comes between the top management and the supervisory management. According to Mary C. Niles, middle managers have pressures from the corners, viz., (a) from above by his chief in the top management with whose ideas, policies and attitudes he must agree; (b) from below by the supervisors who press for counsel, guidelines, decisions etc. and (c) sideways by colleagues whose departments or functions or activities are interrelated with his own.

Functions of Middle Management: According to Mary C. Niles, middle management acts with and under the top management to accomplish the following broad objectives of administration:

(i) To execute the various functions of organisation so that the top management gets enough time to look after their responsibilities.

(ii) To co-operate among themselves, with the top management and the supervisors so that the organisation functions smoothly.

(iii) To understand the interlocking of departments in major policies.

(iv) To achieve co-ordination between the different parts of the organisation.

(v) To develop and train employees in the organisation for better functioning and for filling up vacancies that may arise in future.

(vi) To build company spirit where all are working to provide a product, or service wanted by the public.

3. Supervisory Management (Lower Level Management)

Supervisory management consists of senior supervisors, intermediate supervisors and frontline supervisors. Supervisory management is above the operatives but below the middle management in the organisation. The executives at this level are in direct touch with the rank and file of workers and have to see that the work is properly carried out. The personnel employed at this level play an important role in the organisation. The effective implementation of the plans and policies, the quality of workmanship, quality of output and-overall success of the organisation very much depend on the hard labour, discipline and loyalty of the personnel at this level of management. Further, this level of management represents the workers before the higher management and the higher echelons of management to the workers.

As the supervisor is the immediate boss of the workers, the workers look to him for orders, policies, instructions, guidance, encouragement, increased pay etc. The success of the supervisor depends on the preference of the workers, their co-operation, their ungrudging effort, their satisfaction and their loyalty to him. The supervisor in turn look to his superior in middle management for orders, policy information, help and guidance.

Functions of Supervisors

The various functions of a supervisor are as follows:

(i) To issue orders and instructions to the workers and to supervise and control their work.

(ii) To plan the activities of his section.

(iii) To classify and assign jobs to the workers.

(iv) To direct and guide the workers about work procedure.

(v) To arrange for the necessary tools, equipment, materials etc for the workers.

(vi) To arrange for providing on-the-job training to the workers.

(vii) To look after the proper maintenance of tools, machinery etc.

(viii) To solve the problems of workers.

(ix) To inform the management about the problems of workers which are not solved at this level.

(x) To advise middle management about the working environment and to act as liaison between the middle management and the rank and file workers.

(xi) To maintain discipline among the workers and to develop in them the right approach to work.

(xii) To maintain good human relations.

(xiii) To build a high group morale among the workers.

Effective Supervision

Effrctiveness of a supervisor is judged by how he is contributing to his organisation by his work for achieving the organisational objectives. Some of the important elements of effective supervisory practices are: (a) leadership, (b) closeness of supervision, (c) employee orientation of human relations, (d) group cohesiveness, (e) delegation, (f) satisfying the needs of subordinates for promotion and recognition, (g) providing work-centered benefits to subordinates, (h) providing on-the-job training to the subordinates, (i) informing the subordinates about their duties and relevant organisational matters, and (j) presenting model behaviour to the subordinates.

Due to the increased complexity in business operations, today we notice the mix of both horizontal and vertical systems and a blended system is in operation in many of the complex organisations. The following chart exhibits this blended system :

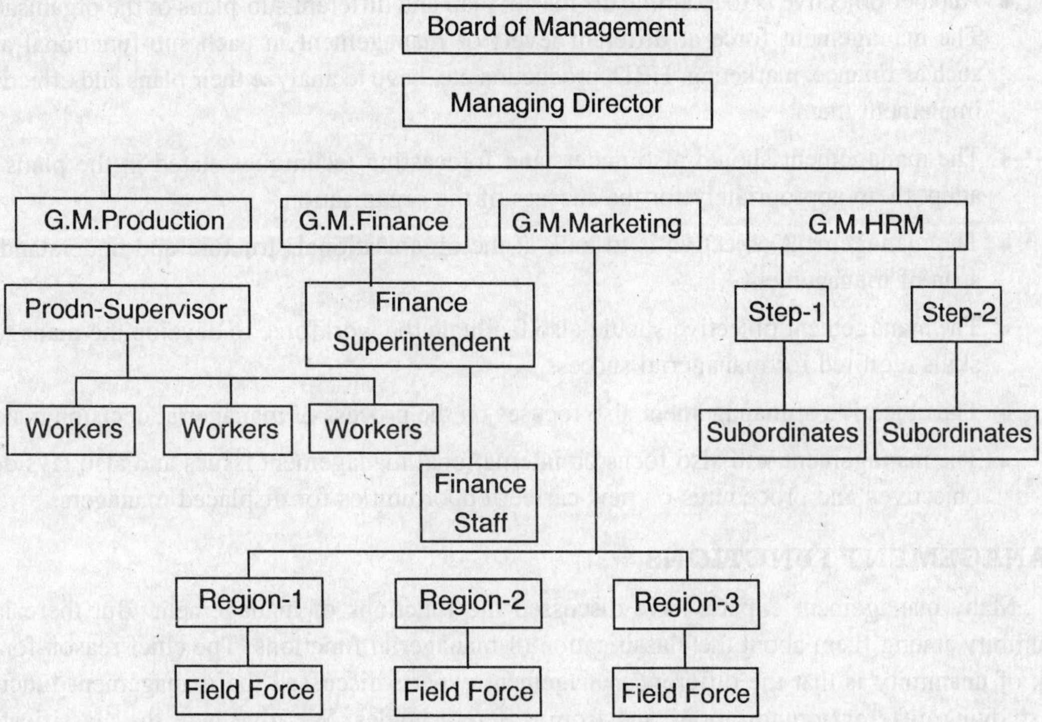

FIG. 1.3. Horizontal-Vertical System

MANAGEMENT - THE PURPOSE OR OBJECTIVES

The Prime Minister of India, The Governer of a State, the Chairman of Metro or Family Mart, The Vice-Chancellor of an University are all managers and leaders. Managers preside over organisations as diverse as Vishweshwaraiah Technological University, the Wokhard. Hospital or any hotel of your town.

Organisational success of any type of business or NGO depends open effective management. You examine any business failure or failure of a state development. You find that poor quality management will be one of the main reasons for failure. The problem starts with the top management. The Board of Directors and Chairman accept the reports status quo. They never examine the reports and simply accept them and believe their consultants and draw plan after plans. But, who has to execute it? And adopt corrective measures to set the operations right. Again, if top brass is sensible and sound, they suggest corrective measures to the report to make the organisation successful. Here the role of management, right from chief executive officer-CEO to the last-person in the heirarchy have to play their roles in the a organisation. In this context we can list out the **purpose or objectives** of the management.

- The main objective is to look at how a company can create a competitive diffrentiation.
- The management has to examine mission statements and corporate objectives to find out whether they can implement successfully.
- Another objective is to examine the master plan and different sub-plans of the organisation. The management force at different levels of management in each sub-functional areas such as finance, marketing, HRD, production etc. have to analyze their plans and effectively implement them.
- The management should also understand forecasting techniques stated in the plans and adopt them appropriately for the success of the organisation.
- The management objective is to look at the organisational structure and understand the span of management.
- The management objective should also facilitate the workforce to develop the managerial skills required for managerial success.
- The objective of management also focuses on the process of managerial decision making.
- The management will also focus on international management issues and also lays down objectives and procedures on new carreer opportunities for displaced managers.

MANAGEMENT FUNCTIONS

Many management experts have discussed the functions of management. But there is no unanimity among them about the classification of managerial functions. The chief reason for this lack of unanimity is that the different management experts discussed the management functions by studying different organisations and from different angles. We give here the classifications given by some of the writers.

Henri Fayol, the father of principles of management, has classified managerial functions as follows:

(a) Planning, including forecasting, (b) Organising, (c) Commanding, (d) Coordinating, and (e) Controlling.

Gulick and Urwiik have classified management functions into seven. They coined the word *'PODSCORB'* to describe the functions of management. Each letter of this word denotes the initial letter of management functions, namely:

(a) Planning, (b) Organising, (c) Directing, (d) Staffing, (e) Coordinating, (f) Reporting, and (g) Budgeting.

According tc R.C. Davis, there are three management functions, viz., (a) planning, (b) motivating, and (c) controlling, whereas G.R. Terry classified management functions into four, viz., (a) planning, (b) organising, (c) activating. and (d) controlling.

Koontz and O'Donnell have classified management functions into five. They have stated that "the most useful method of classifying managerial functions is to group them around the activities of planning, organising, staffing, directing, and controlling." Thus, according to them, there are five functions of management.

From the above study, we can state that the functions vary from three to eight and there is unanimity only in respect of three functions, viz., planning, organising and controlling. The functions of directing which is concerned with the directing of human behaviour for getting things done has been called by various authors as commanding, motivating or communicating. Some authors have introduced staffing functions by splitting the social aspect of organisation. Thus, the functions of management may be classified as:

(a) Planning,

(b) Organising,

(c) Staffing.

(d) Directing, and

(e) Controlling.

Some authors consider "co-ordinating" as a separate function. But as the basic objective of all managerial functions is to achieve co-ordination in organised human efforts, co-ordination is the essence of management and it cannot be considered as a separate function.

Koontz and O' Donnell have stated that, in practice, it is not always possible "to place all managerial activities neatly into these categories since the functions tend to coalesce."

According to Professor Haimann, it is helpful to think of these managerial functions as a continuous circular movement (see Fig. 1.4). They flow into each other and at times, it is difficult to know where the one ends and the other begins.

Considering all these views on management functions, it may be said that management involves the following functions:

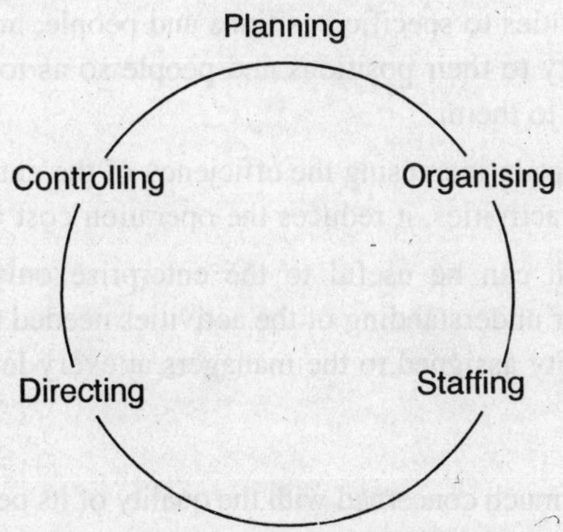

FIG. 1.4. Management Process

PLANNING

Planning is concerned with the determination of the objectives to be achieved and the course of action to be followed to achieve them. Before starting any action, one has to decide how the work will be performed and where and how it has to be performed. Thus, planning implies decision-making as to what is to be done, how it is to be done, when it is to be done and by whom it is to done. Planning helps in achieving the objectives efficiently and effectively. Planning involves selecting of objectives and strategies, policies and programmes and procedures for achieving them.

Planning function is performed by managers at every level because planning may either be for the entire enterprise or for any section or department thereof. Planning pervades the entire gamut of managerial activity, and also it is continuous and never-ending. While the managers at the top level devote more time on planning, the managers at the lower level follow the policies, programmes and procedures laid down by the top management.

For any business activity, planning is a prerequisite for doing anything and also to ensure the proper utilisation of the resources of the business concern to achieve the desired goals. Plans can be classified into standing plans and single-use plans. Standing plans include objectives, policies, procedures, methods and rules and single-use plans include budgets, programmes, strategies and projects.

ORGANISING

According to Fayol, "to organise a business is to provide it with everything useful to its functioning — raw materials, tools, capital and personnel." Thus, organising involves bringing together the manpower and material resources for the achievement. of objectives laid down by the enterprise. Organising involves the following process:

(a) determining and defining the activities involved in achieving the objectives laid down by the management;
(b) grouping the activities in a logical pattern;
(c) assigning the activities to specific positions and people; and
(d) delegating authority to their positions and people so as to enable them to perform the activities assigned to them.

Organising function helps in increasing the efficiency of the enterprise. Further, by avoiding repetition and duplication of activities, it reduces the operation cost of the enterprise.

But organising function can be useful to the enterprise only when there are clear and verifiable objectives and clear understanding of the activities needed to achieve the objectives and clear definition of the authority assigned to the managers at every level.

STAFFING

Every enterprise is very much concerned with the quality of its people, especially its managers. The staffing function is concerned with this aspect of management. According to Harold Koontz and Cyril O'Donell, "the managerial function of staffing involves manning the organisational structure through proper and effective selection, appraisal and development of personnel to fill the roles designed into the structure." Thus, the staffing functions involve:

(a) proper selection of candidates for positions;
(b) proper remuneration;
(c) proper training and development so as to enable them to discharge their organisational

(c) proper training and development so as to enable them to discharge their organisational functions effectively; and

(d) proper evaluation of personnel.

Staffing function is performed by every manager of the enterprise as he is actively associated with the recruitment, selection, training and appraisal of his subordinates. For example, the Board of Directors of the enterprise undertakes the staffing function by selecting and appraising the Chief Executive who, in turn, performs these functions in relation to his subordinates like divisional heads or departmental heads of the enterprise. Similarly, departmental heads or their subordinates also perform the staffing function.

Staffing function is a difficult managerial function because it is concerned with the selection of persons who are properly qualified and mentally will-adjusted to the situations.

Directing is one of the important functions of management and is the art and process of getting things done. While other functions like planning, organising and staffing are merely preparations for doing the work, the directing function actually starts the work.

Directing is concerned with actuating the members of the organisation to work efficiently and effectively for the attainment of organisation goals. Directing involves the manager telling the subordinates how they have to perform jobs assigned to them. It is concerned with guiding, supervising and motivating the subordinates for achieving the enterprise objectives. According to Joseph Massie, "Directing concerns the total manner in which a manager influences the action of his subordinates. It is the final action of a manager in getting others to act after all preparations have been completed."

Directing consists of the following four sub-functions:

1. Communication or issuing of orders and instructions to subordinates. A manager has to instruct the subordinates what to do, how to do it and when to do it.
2. Guiding, energising and leading the subordinates to perform the work systematically and also building up among workers confidence and zeal in the work to be performed.
3. Inspiring the subordinates to do work with interest and enthusiasm for the accomplishment of the enterprise's objectives.
4. Exercising supervision over the subordinates to ensure that the work done by them is in conformity with the objectives that are determined.

CONTROLLING

Controlling is related to all other management functions. It is concerned with seeing whether the activities have been or being performed in conformity with the plans. According to Haimann, "Control is the process of checking to determine whether or not, proper progress is being made towards the objectives and goals and acting if necessary to correct any deviation." Koontz and O'Donnell have defined controlling "as the measurement and correction of the performance of activities of subordinates in order to make sure that enterprise's objectives and the plans devised to attain them are being accomplished." Thus, controlling involves the following sub-functions:

(a) Determination of standards for measuring work performance.

(b) Measurement of actual performance.

(c) Comparing actual performance with the standards.

(d) Finding variances between the two and reasons for variances.

(e) Taking corrective actions to ensure attainment of objectives.

For control to be effective and fruitful, it must be based on a plan; there must be measurement of actual performance to ascertain deviations and to take action to remedy the deviations.

MANAGEMENT FUNCTIONS AND MANAGERIAL LEVELS

We have stated above the various functions of management. A manager has to perform these functions, irrespective of the position in which he is placed or the objectives of the enterprise. But the mix of management functions which are to be performed by a manager would depend on the organisational level (viz., top, middle or lower level) at which he is working. In the Fig. 1.5, we have given the relationship of management functions at the various levels.

At the higher levels, a manager's major task is planning, organising and staffing functions are not of much importance while the other two functions, viz., directing and controlling, are least important. At the middle level of management, the manager is concerned with a mix of all the basic functions of management. At the lower levels, directing and controlling are of much importance while organising and staffing functions are of less importance and planning function is only of a short-term nature.

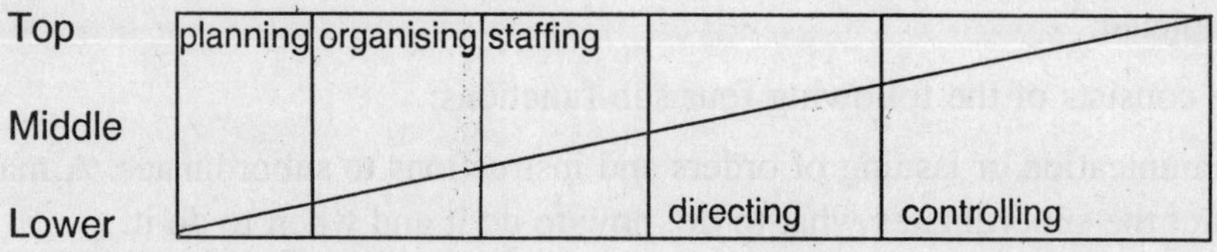

FIG. 1.5. Relationship of Management Functions at Various Levels

It is asked in some quarters which management function is more important. All management functions have equal importance and no one is more important than the others. All these functions are necessary for accomplishing the enterprise objectives but their mix would depend on the organisational level and nature of task.

PRINCIPLES OF MANAGEMENT

We have observed that the management has to perform a number of functions such as planning, organising, co-ordinating, directing, controlling etc. for the purpose of achieving its aims of operational efficiency, financial economy, and profitable return on investment. In order to perform the management functions effectively so as to enable the business concern to achieve its aims, there is need for the business concerns to observe certain principles of management. Henry Fayol who is regarded in responsible quarters as the real father of management science, has evolved fourteen principles of management, which may be briefly stated as follows:

1. Division of work

The object of division of work is to derive benefits from the principle of specialisation. The various functions of management like planning, organisation, co-ordination control, etc., cannot be performed efficiently by a single proprietor or by a group of directors on their own and they have to be entrusted to specialists in the related fields. Division of work in the management process produces more and better work with the same effort.

2. Authority and responsibility

As management consists in getting the work done through others, it implies that the manager should have the right to give orders and the power to exract obedience. Thus, the manager gives orders to his subordinates to perform the job as per his diretion. A manager may exercise his official authority and also his personal authority. Official authority is derived from his official status, while personal authority is compounded by intelligence, experience, moral worth, ability to lead, past service etc. Authority is closely related to responsibility, and it arises wherever authority is exercised. An individual to whom authority is given to exercise power must also be prepared to bear the responsibility to perform the work.

3. Discipline

Discipline is absolutely essential for the smooth running of business. By discipline, we mean obedience to authority, observance of rules of service and norms of performance, respect for agreements, sincere efforts for completing the given job, respect for superiors, etc. The best means of maintaining discipline are: (a) good supervisors at all levels, (b) "clear and fair agreements between the employer and the employee, and (c) judicious application of penalties.

4. Unity of command

This principle requires that the employee should receive orders from one superior only for any action or activity. It means workers in a department are required to be accountable to one superior for complying with the orders for performing a job. If two superiors wield authority over the same person or department, it causes uneasiness, disorder, indiscipline among employees and undermining of authority. Further, for the same job, if the workers have to report to more than one superior, they will be confused and it will be difficult to pinpoint responsibility on anyone.

5. Unity of direction

It means that there should be one head and one plan for a group for activities having the same objective. While unity of command is concerned with the functioning of personnel, unity of direction is concerned with the functioning of the body corporate, the departments and sub-departments comprising the business concern. For every category of work, there should be one plan of action and it should be executed under the overall control and supervision of one head or superior.

6. Subordination of individual interest to general interests

In a business concern, the interest of one employee or group of employees should not prevail over the common interest or should not block the fulfilment of general goals of the business concern. If there is disagreement among two superiors on any matter, the management should reconcile the differences so as to conduct the overall operation of the enterprise smoothly.

7. Remuneration

The remuneration that is paid to the personnel of the firm should be fair and as far as possible, afford satisfaction both to the personnel and the tirm. Employees who are paid decent wages or salary will have a high morale and their efficiency will be high. Further, contented staff is an asset to the firm and also there will be good relationship between the management and the employees. The rate of remuneration paid should be based on general business conditions, cost of living, productivity of the concerned employees and the capacity of the firm to pay.

8. Centralisation

If subordinates are given a higher role and importance in the manage ment and organisation of the firm, it is decentralisation whereas if they are given less role and importance, it is centralisation. Management has to decide the degree of centralisation and decentralisation's decisive authority on the basis of the nature of circumstances, size of undertaking, the type of activities and the nature of organisational structure. The objective should be the optimum utilisation of faculties of the personnel.

9. Scalar chain

Scalar principle exhibits the chain of superiors or the line of authority from the highest executive to the lowest one for the purpose of communication. It states superior-subordinate relationship and the responsibility of superiors in relation to subordinates at the various levels. According to this principle, order or communications should pass through the proper channels of authority along the scalar chain. But in case there is need for swift action, the principle of scalar chain (proper channel of authority) may be reconciled with due respect for the line authority by making direct contact with the concerned authority instead of going through the proper channel. A diagrammatical explanation of Scalar Chain is given. This diagram consists of double ladders and we find a hierarchy of authority from A to E and A to P. If section D wants to communicate with section O, the file should go up the ladder from D to A and then descend to O, stopping at each section. This involves a lengthy procedure and is time-consuming. In case there is need for

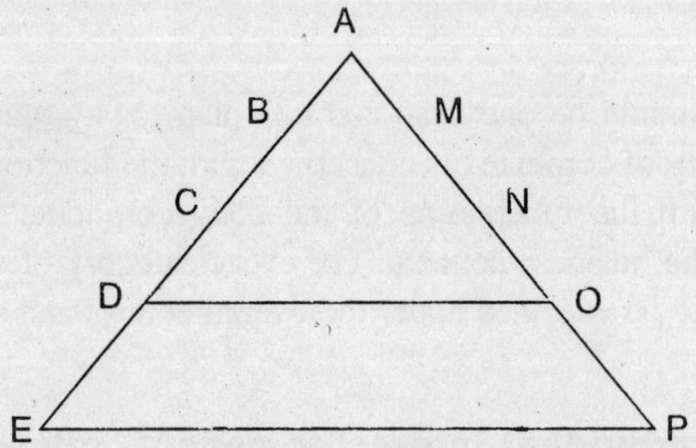

FIG. 1.6. Scalar Chain and Gang Plank

swift action or urgent contact, D and O may be authorised by their respective superiors (viz., C and N) to have direct contact to settle that matter. By this method, the scalar principle is safeguarded and at the same time, the subordinate officers are enabled to take swift action.

10. Order

Management should obtain order in work through suitable organisation of men and materials. The principle of "right place for every thing and for everyman" should be observed by the management. To observe this principle, there is need for scientific selection of competent personnel, correct assignment of duties to the personnel and good organisation.

11. Equality

Equality means fair dealings, equality of treatment and accommodative or co-operative attitude among the personnel in the undertaking. Equality results from a combination of kindness and justice. Employees expect equity from the management. The application of equity requires good sense, experience and good nature on the part of the manager. The managerial treatment of the subordinates should be free from the influence of prejudices and personal likes or dislikes. Equity ensures healthy industrial relations between management and labour which is essential for the successful working of the enterprise.

12. Stability of tenure of personnel

In order to motivate the workers to show keener interest in their work, enterprise, initiative and turn out of better work, it is necessary that they should "be assured security of job by the management. If they have fear of insecurity of job, their morale will be low and they cannot turn out better work. Further, they will not have a sense of attachment of the firm and they will always be on the lookout for a job elsewhere. Hence, the management must ensure stability of tenure of personnel.

13. Initiative

Initiative means freedom to think and execute a plan. The zeal and energy of employees are augmented by initiative. Innovation which is mark of technological progress is possible only where the employees are encouraged to take initiative. According to Fayol, "initiative is one of the keenest satisfactions for an intelligent man to experience" and hence, he advises managers to give its employees sufficient scope to show their initiative. Employees should be welcomed to make any suggestions regarding the fomulation of objectives and plans and they should be encouraged to turn out better work with maximum versatility.

14. Esprit de corps

Since 'union is strength', the management should clrear a team spirit among the employees. Only when all their personnel pull together as a team, there is scope for realising the objectives of the concern. Harmony and unity of the staff of a concern is a great source of strength to the undertaking. The management should not follow the policy of 'divide and rule' and it should strive to maintain unity among the staff. If there are any differences or misunderstandings or symptoms of distrust, the management should take

MANAGEMENT — UNIVERSAL APPLICATION

Management principles are universal in nature. They can be applied to all types of organisations. In an ever changing world, many new types of organisations emerge. But the basic principles of management; viz., planning organising, staffing and controlling are to be adapted for the success of the organisation. But all these principles are not implicity applied. Every organisation is guided by the philosophy of the promoters and accordingly management principles are adapted. Basic management process is observed in all types of organisations. But they are driven by personal qualities of the top management.

MANAGEMENT — TOMORROW

Business organisations today have their own culture called "corporate culture". Each organisation has its own language, history, heroes and villains. Society's demands are exceeding supply and a permanent avenue is created to new organisations to emerge, whether, it is old or new national or global, the cultural aspects of these entities are changing. As said in the beginning of this chapter, quality, ethics and global environment are dominating the corporate scene. Customers are more demanding than ever before. They decide the fate of the business organisations. It is not the command of managers nor the loyalty of workers in the organisation that provides security, stability and continuity for the organisation. But the loyality of the customer that does.

As satisfaction of the customer is the key factor for organisational growth, tomorrow's managers and employees, besides working hard, should stay close to the customer, be flexible in operations, reduce non-value-adding overhead and respond quickly to new situations. Management should have an integrated approach for growth and sustainability.

SUMMARY

1. Concept of Management has become universal and no organisation can survive without it. Management consists of getting things done through others by directing their efforts in an integrated and co-ordinated manner for achieving the business objectives. It is a process consisting of functions such as planning, organising, actuating and controlling the business operations in such a manner as to attain predetermined goals.
2. Important characteristics of management are:
   (a) It is a organised and purposeful activity.
   (b) It is concerned with the efforts of a group.
   (c) It is the art of getting things done through and with people.
   (d) It applies economic principles.
   (e) It involves decision-making.
   (f) It co-ordinates all activities and resources.
   (g) It is an universal activity.
   (h) It is an integrating process.
   (i) It is concerned with direction and control.
   (j) It is intangible.
   (k) It is an inter-disciplinary approach.
3. Includes various management functions such as planning, organising, staffing, directing and controlling and also functional areas of management such as financial management, personnel

management, purchasing management, production management, marketing management and office management.

4. Different interpretations of the terms 'administration' and 'management' have been given by the different schools of thought. But this controversy of the meaning of these two terms is not seen nowadays and the term 'management' is generally used for the whole process of managing.

5. Management is both a science as well as an art.

6. There is no unanimity among management experts on the classification of managerial functions. However, the following list of managerial functions is followed: planning, organising, staffing, directing and controlling. Each of the managerial functions is an exercise in co-ordination and hence, co-ordination is treated as the essence of management and is not considered as a separate function.

7. The management process involves the following:
   (i) Planning is concerned with the determination of objectives to be achieved and the action to be taken to achieve them,
   (ii) Organising involves bringing together the manpower and material resources for the achievement of objectives,
   (iii) Staffing involves manning the organisational structure through proper selection, appraisal and development of personnel to fit the role designed into the structure,
   (iv) Directing is concerned with actuating the members of the organisation to work efficiently for attaining the organisation goals,
   (v) Controlling is concerned with seeing whether the activities have been or being performed in conformity with the plans.

8. Management does not possess all the characteristics of a profession and hence it cannot be called a profession. There are, however, certain unmistakable trends towards the professionalisation of management.

9. There are no fixed levels of management. Further, there is no unanimity among writers in this respect. For the convenience of study, the levels of management may be classified into three groups: (a) top management, (b) middle management and (c) lower or supervisory management. Top management consists of the Board of Directors and its Chairman, the chief executive and the senior executives. Middle management consists of departmental, divisional or sectional heads, and other executive officers attached to the different departments. Supervisory management consists of senior, intermediary and frontline supervisors. Top management decides the plans and policies, middle management is responsible for implementing the plans and policies and the supervisory management has to see that the work is properly carried out.

10. A manager has to perform managerial functions irrespective of the position in which he is placed. But the mix of management functions which are to be performed by a manager would depend on the organisational level (viz., top, middle or lower level) at which he is working.

11. For performing the management functions effectively, there is a need for the business concern to observe certain principles of management. Henry Fayol has evolved 14 principles. They are:
   (i) Division of work,
   (ii) Authority and responsibility,
   (iii) Discipline,
   (iv) Unity of command,

(v) Unity of direction,
(vi) Subordination of individual interest to general interests,
(vii) Remuneration,
(viii) Centralisation,
(ix) Scalar chain,
(x) Order,
(xi) Equity,
(xii) Stability of tensure of personnel,
(xiii) Initiative, and
(xiv) Esprit de corps.

STUDY QUESTIONS

1. What is management?
2. What is administration?
3. What is operative management?
4. Name three levels of management which are in practice.
5. Expand PODSCORB.
6. Name any four well-known thinkers on management.
7. What do you mean by division of work?
8. What is unity of command?
9. Give the meaning of unity of direction.
10. What is scalar cliain?
11. What do you mean by 'Equity'?
12. What is "Esprit de corps"?
13. Name the four major functions of management.
14. Name any four well-known thinteen on management.
15. Analyse the nature and characteristic features of management.
16. Give a note on scope of management.
17. Analyse the role of management in modern corporate activity.
18. Distingiuish between administration and management.
19. Analyse whether management is a Science or an Art or Profession.
20. Analyse the concept - "management process".
21. Give a brief note on the need for "Principles of Management".
22. Analyse the inter-dependence of planning and control.
23. Give a note on the functions of supervisors.
24. Briefly explain on to how important is the management function to (i) the organisation, (ii) the workers in the organisation and (iii) the society.
25. Briefly explain the relationship between the four functions of management described in this chapter.
26. Briefly explain the resources that drive an organisation.
27. Give an explantory note on objectives of management.
28. What are the managerial functions which help the growth of an organisation? Explain.
29. Give an explanotory note on the role of
    (i) Top management, (ii) Middle management and (iii) Supervisory level.
30. Briefly explain the nature, scope and advantages of management.

2

MANAGER

LEARNING OBJECTIVES

After reading this chapter, you should be able to know;

- Manager - The Concept
- Need for Manager
- Managerial Skills
- Managerial Success
- Global Awareness
- Non-Manager
- Managerial Roles
- Personal Characteristics
- Social Responsibility of Managers
- Global Managers

Management process denotes the sequence in which a manager normally functions in an organisation. These functions are repetitive in character. They are contained within each other. Management process involves creating, planning, . organising, motivating, communicating, controlling etc. Again planning process involves all these functions. Similarly any other function involves all other functions in the managing process. Therefore all functions can be considered as subfunctions of each other. Which management function is vital? Each function is vital by itself. But none of the functions is more important than the other. The importance of each function depends upon the management task and varies from task to task. All play their own role in attaining organisational objectives. They are interactive (repeatitive) in nature. In this backdrop, the viewpoints of writers on management functions that are to be followed by managers are already analyzed in previous chapter. In this chapter, the focus is on the managers and their roles.

MANAGER — THE CONCEPT

Today's business is more complex in nature. Evry big business group will have many business units which may be related, allied or unrelated. A steel manufacturing firm may produce different types of steel and may install and operate three to four plants. This is called allied business. However, the business group, besides steel production of various types, can also establish and run textile unit, which is unrelated. In this type of business, how many managers are to be appointed to run the business units? Each plant will have production manager, general manager etc. As many hierarchy are there in each business unit run by the conglomorate such many managerial positions exist and each is occupied by a manager. Therefore, the manager is positioned in such a manner that he has to execute his task to achieve managerial efficiency. If the managers fail, the overall productivity of the organisation fails and ultimately the business fails.

Manager is the key person in discharging the task assigned to a sub-unit of business. Thus, "Manager" can be understood as the "person who is in charge of business task and executes effectively to achieve the objectives or goals of the organisation." To put it in simple words, "Manager is one who manages one's task effectively and efficiently."

Some Definitions

1. "A manager is the person responsible for planning and directing the work of group of individuals, monitoring their work, and taking corrective action when necessary."
   – F. Jhon Reh, A Management Thinker.
2. "A manager is a person who directs, manages and controls our organisation, an industry, a shop or a task." ***– Dictionary Meaning.***

These definitions cleary explain the tasks to be performed by a manager. He has to design the task, develop, direct and control a tasks for achieving an organisational goal. He is an individual who is in charge of a certain group of tasks. He will have the staff often report to him.

NON-MANAGER — THE CONCEPT

In the traditional management system, middle managers were essential as the organisations were tall and were having a long heirarchy. But in modern times, organisations are becoming flatter due to:(i) development of computer technology, (ii) information explosion, (iii) reduction of costs to meet the challenge of global competition and (iv) change in business environment.

This development has caused the abolition of middle management levels in many organisations, particularly in small and medium enterprises. After reducing the hierarchy, the workers of middle positions are trained and empowered to make decisions. They are given continuous training to efficiently handle many jobs. Organisations while recruiting the employees focus on the strength of these prospects, whether they can run the business taking decisions well within the authority delegated to them. Analysing their strength, competent workers are appointed and placed in required positions. This new type of workers have replaced middle management positions in organisations and perform to satisfy the goals of the organisation. These are called "Non-managers".

"Non-managers are the ones who are newly recruited workers with authority to take decisions or the ones who are already working in the line with experience, to whom the authority is delegated to perform the task without taking the permission from any immediate boss". These non-managers can take quick decisions and perform the task effectively and quikly. Therefore, the advantages derived from these non-managers are:

(i) Better time management

(ii) Quick decisions

(iii) Performing the task efficiently and effectively

(iv) Improved motivation and morale in the organiation.

These new non-managers who are emerging on the business scene ask questions, listen, and guide their fellow workers and facilitate their co-workers. The result of that is, the work is now organised around teams rather than individuals. These teams are self-managed teams - SMT. In otherwords, these SMTs have a new method of structuring, managing and implementing the work. These teams which are empowered to design, develop and implement the required task are also called **non-managers**.

The team of workers should possess creative thinking, ready to meet challenging situations, should possess several skills and cross trained persons who have responsibility and authority to cary out well-defined function. These teams are self-regulating and function without direct supervision. They distribute the tasks to be performed within themselves, by deciding who will work on which tasks (This is called workchoice decision). They also know the method of addressing interpersonal difficulties within in the group. They are adept in resolving the problems that may crop up in the team.

In the traditional system, middle managers were gathering information and were sharing with their fellow workers. But this activity in modern times is taken care of by information technology, the tool being computers and internet. Actually this technology has replaced middle management level. The organisations are becoming more horizontal than vertical. This has resulted in the emergence of task-based, self-managing teams which are called **"non-managers".**

PERSONAL CHARACTERS

The features clearly indicate that men with **creativity, vision** and **courage** can only handle the situations in organisation and steer them towards attaining organisation goals. They should also possess certain other qualities to manage the organisation effectively.

"Productivity" of the organisation is measured by the input-output relationship. How the inputs are efficiently managed? and How the expected output is also obtained? need to be answered. The answers to the questions are given by managers and his workforce. In all organisational problems, human element plays a vital role. Particularly, the persons co-ordinating the various activities (managers) put in their efforts to solve problems. One concept of productivity takes cognizance of the efficiency of workforce involved in the production process. In any organisation achieving goal or "effective performance" will be achieved only when human force (manager) works honestly and discharges the assigned duties. With reasonable work environment and with good leadership of the persons in charge of the tasks, the efficiency or productivity will be attained. The real input and real output relationship measures the productivity of an organisation.

The real input refers to the human and non-human (technological and financial) resources used in production process. The co-ordinator (Managers) of inputs should be tactful and honest. These co-ordinators design and operate the non-human resources. They establish work flow charts, make purchases, put raw materials in the production activity, produce goods or service, sell them, receive revenue and earn money or lose in the process. Thus, managers make the organisation effective. If they skillfully manage, the organisation survives.

Successful manager should have certain qualities. A study conducted in 1984 by Harbridge House, an American consultancy firm, has recognised the following qualities of a manager, which is applicable to any production unit, irrespective of size, or to any service sector organisation.

1. Goal setter: A qualitative manager establishes goals and standards for the organisation as a whole. Not only he/she sets the goal for himself/herself, goals and tasks for all the groups that work in the organisation. While setting the group or individual goals, the manager involves all concerned in the organisation.

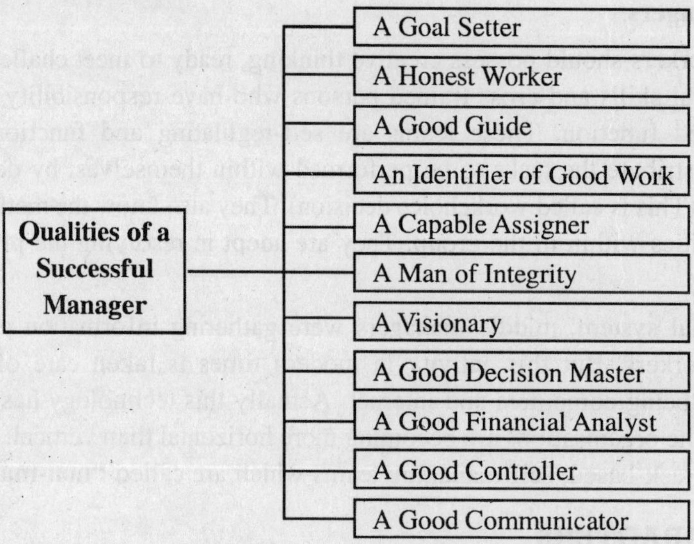

FIG. 2.1. Role of a Quality Manager

2. Honest worker: "People want straight information from their bosses and managers establish a climate of openness and trust." This statement in the report of the study of Harbridge House says that managers should be open and honest in their operation and dealing with fellow men in the organisation, They should be unprejudiced and be realists in their thinking and mode of work. Managers being the link between work force and top brass, should convey the facts to top management.

3. A Good Guide: The manager guides and will be helpful to his fellow workers in the organisation. The report says "that one of the aspects of Collective Leadership" is found in managers. They will be supporting the fellow workers whenever workers' genuine issues come before the top management. Thus he is identifier of good work.

4. Good Identifier: The Study reveals that "Most managers don't realise how much they criticise they do it to be helpful, but positive recognition is what really motivates people." According to this, the manager should recognise his fellowmen with a positive approach. Good work of the employees should be identified and honoured. Quality in work of the co-workers can be brought in by the manager, if he rewards quality performance.

5. Capable Assignor: He should be capable of placing right people on right jobs. Appropriate tasks have to be assigned to each employee according to this ability to perform.

6. Integrity: He should be honest and a man of integrity and should exhibit integrity on a high profile.

7. Visionary: He should be a man of vision and creative ideas. He must be capable of introducting innovative works and encourage workers who gives innovative ideas regarding work flow.

8. Good Decision master: He should not be an indecision master. He must give instructions and take decisions in very clear terms. "Employees want a say in things, and the best managers know when that lime comes." Therefore, the managers should be good decision-makers and make decision at appropriate times.

9. Good Financial Analyst: A good manager should be a good financial analyst too. This means, whenever he takes decisions, he should be capable of understanding financial implications of such decisions.

10. Good Controller: A qualitative manager practices good control systems, he educates his fellow workers about the control system in operation and makes them to work within the framework of these systems.

11. Good Communicator: Manager should communicate will with this employees.

When we look at the organisation, we observe that every organisation will have different levels of management, each level has to be headed by a person called manager. If the size of the business unit is small, there will be one manager and many subordinates. But in medium and large sized units where the operations are more and the levels are many, more than one manager will have to exist to conduct the operations. The following chart shows single manager operations.

QUALITY AND PERFORMANCE EXCELLENCE

A successful manager should possess the various traits and attributes stated in previous paragraphs. The quality of work and performance excellence of a manager is measured by different yardsticks. Situational aspect-plays or major role in measuring the performance of managers. Although the managers possess required traits and attributes, taking round decision at the appropriate time is governed by his intellectual calibre and emotional intelligence. The quality of decision is measured by the strategy one adopts at each time of making decision for the success of the organisation. His vision, Creativity empathy, organizational identity and such other traits and moral and ethical aspects direct him/her to take quality decisions. He/she excells in performance, where these traits along with appropriate strategy required in the situation over considered for decision-making. Quality manager takes quality decisions to drive the organization on a sound track. Generally speaking, quality of a manager depends upon ones good traits and the situations one would face at the time of taking decisions.

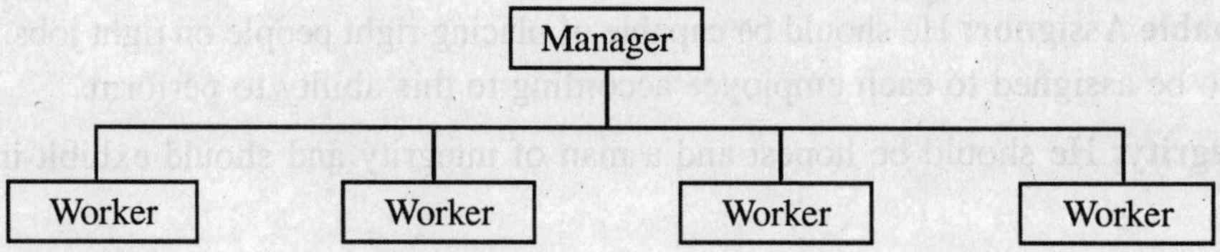

FIG. 2.2. Single Manager and many workers.

This type of organisations are many in number. All small sized business units have single manager system. In this system all the activities of the organisation are carried out by one head with his subordinates. When the operations increase, work will be distributed to different levels of management and managers. Because of increased operation and evolution in business unit, vertical expansion takes place. Two or three levels will be created vertically. The following chart will show this expansion.

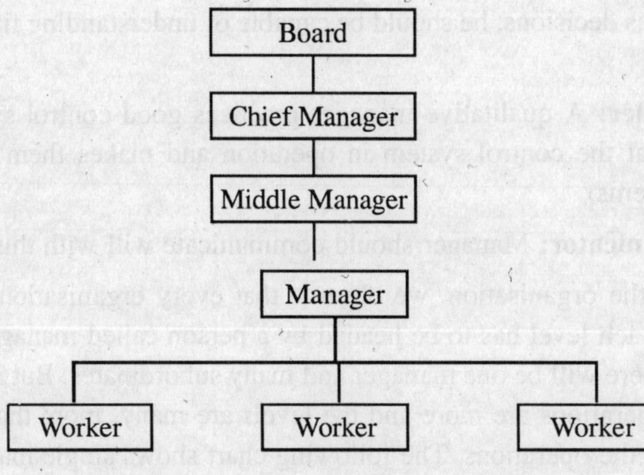

FIG. 2.3. Vertical expansion of Hierarchy

In this type of expansion, interim level is created to carry out work smoothly. Chief manager shares his responsibility with middle level manager and a joint effort will make management easy. There will be smooth flow of management process.

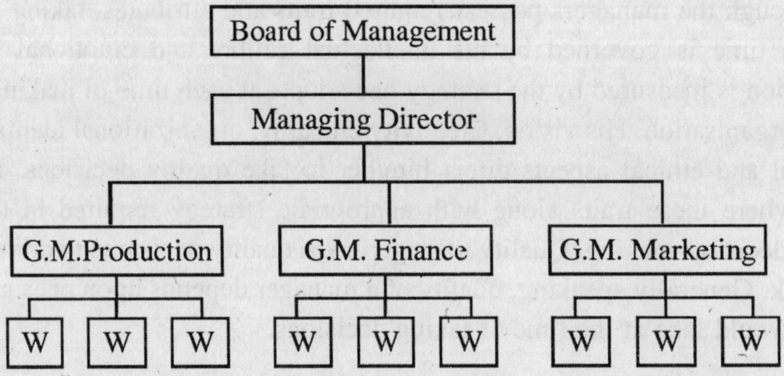

FIG. 2.4. Horizontal Distribution of Management Process

The complexity of work has necessitated the 'horizontal' expansion of the management process. In this system, the work is distributed according to functions like, production, finance, marketing, human resources development, accounting etc. The following chart shows the horizontal functioning of an organisation.

In this system, the work is distributed according to functions and functional manager is answerable to the top management.

Due to the increased complexity in business operations, today we notice the mix of both horizontal and vertical systems and a blended system is in operation in many of the complex organisations. The following chart exhibits this blended system:

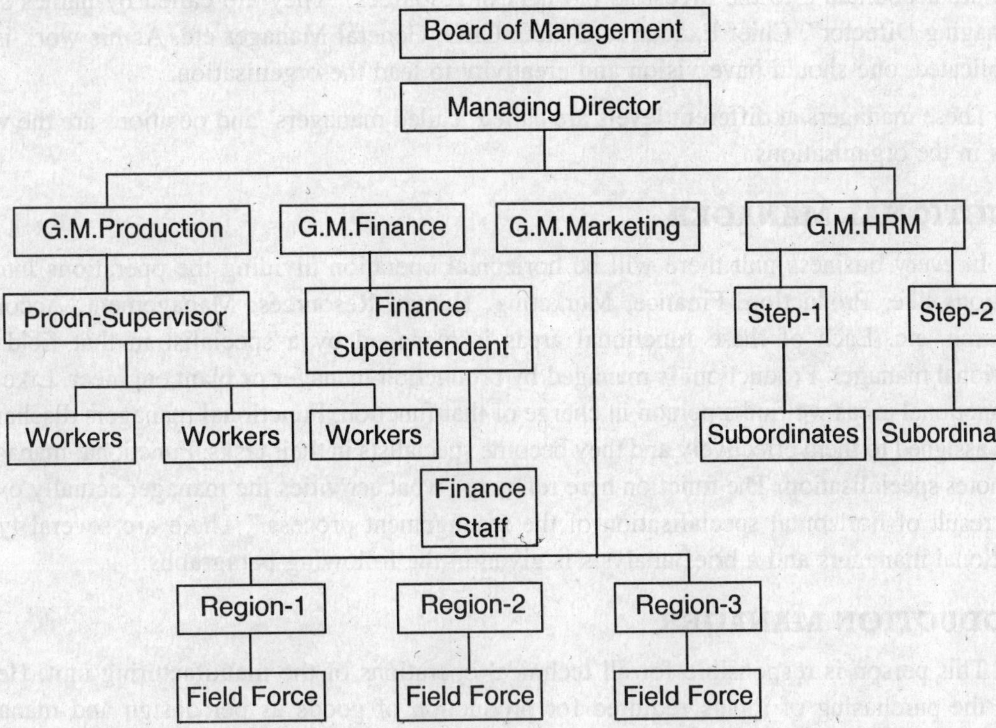

FIG. 2.5. Horizontal-Vertical System

Thus, at the outset managers are classified as (i) First-line managers (i i) Middle managers and (iii) Top managers.

(i) First-line Managers: These persons manage at the bottom line and co-ordinate the work of subordinates. They are only the executors and not the policy makers. They are called "Foremen" in production line and "supervisors' in other functional areas. They are responsible for the basic work to be carried out as prescribed by the top brass. They will be very close to the work force and guiding the subordinates. and are accountable to the production activities.

(ii) Middle Managers: These managers are called by the names, Plant Manager, Departmental Manager, Director of operations etc. The operations of these managers arc mixed with the functions of top managers and bottom line managers. They plan, lead, organise and control the activities of the organisation to help the top management in taking up these functions and also work like first line workers. He co-ordinates the activities of his unit. Before the emergence of information science in a big way, middle managers were functioning in large numbers in complex organisations. The introduction of new technologies in production process and the development of information science in the last quarter of twentieth century, have actually reduced the personnel in this level.

(iii) Top Managers: They are the front-line persons who emerge in the management hierarchy. They are not actually executors and are only decision-makers. They are also planners and design strategies for successful management. They look at the organisation as a whole. They design policies and programmes and ask the second and bottom line managers to execute them effectively. They are accountab'e to the investors (owners of resources). They are called by names such as "Managing Director", Chief Executive Officer-CEO, General Manager etc. As his work is more complicated, one should have vision and creativity to lead the organisation.

These managers at different levels are called 'called managers' and positions are the vertical ranks in the organisations.

FUNCTIONAL MANAGER

In every business unit there will be horizontal operation dividing the operations into main functions like, Production, Finance, Marketing, Human Resources, Management, Accounting, Research, etc. Each of these functional areas is managed by a specialist in that field called functional manager. Production, is managed by production manager or plant engineer. Like this in all functional areas we find a person in charge of that function. Functional managers discharge the tasks assigned to them effectively and they become specialists in their tasks. Functional management promotes specialisation. The function here refers to "what activities the manager actually oversees as a result of horizontal specialisation of the management process." There arc several types of functional managers and a brief analysis is given in the following paragraphs.

PRODUCTION MANAGER

This person is responsible for all technical operations of the manufacturing unit. He looks after the purchasing of inputs required for production of goods as per design and manage the production process. He is called by different names like "Production Engineer," "Plant Engineer,[1] "Operations Manager," "Manager-Production' etc. They are solely responsible for plant layout, inventory management, production control and quality control. They have to manage "input-output operations" qualitatively and effectively.

FINANCE MANAGER

This manager takes up the responsibility of preparing financial plan. He visualises the financial needs of the organisation and accordingly prepares a viable plan. He suggests the sources through which the finance can be availed for both fixed and working capital. Cost of finance will also be studied by him and he suggests the least cost source to raise the required finance. He should be an expert in the field of finance and should know the tools and techniques like ratio analysis, funds flow, cash flow analysis, capital budgeting, costing techniques etc., to prepare a sound financial policy. He will also act as guide to the management on all financial matters. Management is assisted by the finance manager in taking sound financial decisions.

MARKETING MANAGER

In every manufacturing organisation, marketing function plays a vital role. It is the marketing department that decides the fate of the organisation. If the marketing department functions well, the organisation will earn good profit. The marketing wing of the business unit will always be aiming to increase the turnover, market share and profitability of the organisation. Hence, the person in charge of this wing is "Marketing Manager". Strengths and weaknesses of firm's product should be assessed by the marketing manager and design and implement strategies to maintain and increase the market share of his firm. The marketing concepts like product mix, price mix, promotion mix, distribution mix etc. are to be properly understood. He will also be aware of the requirement of the consumers and will have the knowledge of close substitutes available in the market and the type of competition, they pose to the product of his organisation. The marketing manager has the responsibility of securing maximum turnover to the firms product or service.

HUMAN RESOURCES DEVELOPMENT MANAGER

Another function that has assumed importance these days in the business world is development of human resources. Every business or non-business unit is giving importance for the quality work culture. The main element involved in the process is human element. The person in charge of HRD in an organisation is mainly responsible for the recruitment and development of human resources required for the organisation. HRD manager is involved in manpower planning selection, training and maintenance of human resources of the organisation.

OTHER TYPES

There are several sub-functional areas in business units. Each sub-functional area is headed by a person known for that skill or sub-function. For example, a corporate enterprise may have a "Research and Development" (R & D) wing. This wing mainly conducts research on the product development or to innovate a new product. Similarly, the functions like accounting, costing, correspondence, records maintenance, etc. are also looked after by the respective specialist managers. They may be of a lower cadre.

There are also managers who will be in charge of overall administration or the business unit called "General Managers." All functional managers are accountable to G.M. and this person should have the knowledge of each operations of his business unit. There are also called "Administrative Managers" who look after overall administration of the organisations like educational institutions, hospitals, welfare organisations, transport houses, hospitality organisations (Hotels). These managers are called by different names. As all these positions exist in the line of organisational hierarch and the managers who hold the positions are called "Line managers".

STAFF MANAGERS

He is a person attached to a line executive to assist the line in discharging its duties efficiently. "Staff function draws a clear line of demarcation between two aspects of administration, viz., planning and execution. The staff manager discharges the function of planning and he is only an advisory body. He does not execute anything. He only advises the general manager or functional manager regarding various matters or on specific matters. Today a separate branch has developed in the corporate world called "consultancy services." The consultants are the staff managers who give suggestions to improve the work conditions in a business unit. But they cannot enforce it. They act like a **think tank**.

See the following diagram to understand the line and staff difference

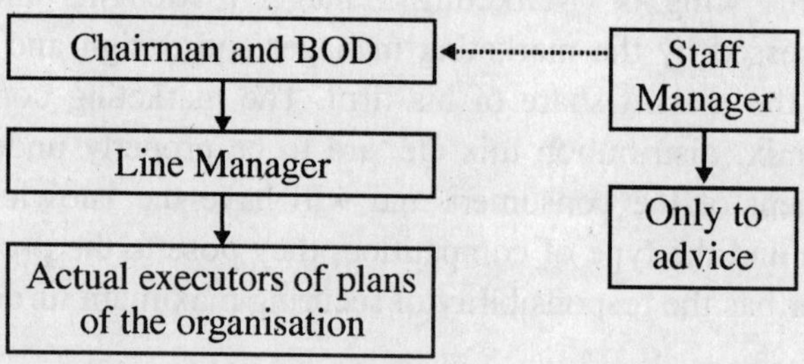

FIG. 2.6. Distinction between Line and Staff executives

The concept of "Management level" discussed in the last chapter is discussed here in association with the skills required in each level. The different types of skills are addressed in terms of its degree that each level demands. As already discussed, there is no specific number of levels that an organisation has. Although three levels, viz top, middle and bottom line are identified, the number of levels that an organisation should possess depends upon the size, the nature and classification of the organisation. There may be more levels than the identified ones in complex organisations. In our discussion we have considered only three levels as they are common in most of the organisations.

MANAGERIAL SKILLS

What are the skills associated with the managers of these levels? Or what are the skills required for these managers and in what degree? Or what is the degree of involvement of levels in the aspects of management process, viz., planning, organising, staffing and controlling?

The answers to these questions will tell us the type of skills required to be possessed by the managers at different levels. A skill is an ability or proficiency in performing a particular task." The skills like (i) Technical skill (ii) Human Relations skill (iii) Analytical skill (iv) Conceptual skill (v) Decision-making skill (vi) Computer skill, and (vii) Communication skill are to be possessed by the managers to effectively manage the organisation. These skills are briefly analysed in the following paragraphs:

(i) Technical skill: This skill is required for first line managers. These managers will be in charge of direct production and hence should know the technical aspects of production and should be in a position to technically guide the subordinates. The "particular" knowledge has to be possessed by the operations manager. He should possess the ability to adopt techniques to have efficiency in production. Similarly, the bottom line managers should possess skill in their area of work. Accounting supervisor should have accounting knowledge to maintain accounts in order. Every manager of specific function at each level should have knowledge about his area of operation and bottom line managers like supervisors or foremen or superintendents should have more knowledge, techniques and resources to perform well. The manager who works as production manager should possess specialised knowledge and expertise to execute work-related planning, programming and accounting.

(ii) Human Relations skill: Every manager has to work with human beings. Human resources form a vital part in the organisation. Unless the managers understand the people working with them (top and lower cadres), they cannot become effective managers. As things have to be got done by other people, the managers should be able to understand, communicate and work with them. The quality of leadership is determined by the types of human relations the managers maintain with their workers. "Human relation skill is a reflection of manager's leadership abilities." The success of an organisation depends upon considerable human relations skill. Managements believe that employees have a basic desire to work with zeal and as members of a company they contribute their mite to society. They reward employees for good performance. They are honest in understanding their employees to the core. We can see alive human relations oriented philosophy in many companies and "TATA Group" practices this philosophy. This skill is their main stay, for success. Thus, Human skills are the ones that develop cooperation within the team lead by the manager. This is more concerned with attitudes, perceptions, communication power of the individual, human resource management etc. These skills are more concerned with people and working with them.

(iii) Analytical skill: This skill is concerned with the analysis of a situation to take sound managerial decision. Every manager is posed with several problems. He should be quick in his action to solve these problems. Here is the need for analytical skill. The manager should locate the real problem, identify the disturbing elements and then adopt suitable solution to solve that problem. Without understanding the situation, an action plan to solve the problem cannot be prepared. The vision, creativity and intelligence of the manager will take the organisation in a successful path.

(iv) Conceptual skill: Every manager should have an integrated approach to run the organisation successfully. Conceptual skill demands that every manager should have an approach to look at the organisation as a whole. The manager should understand as to how the various segments of the organisation go together. "Integrated Systems Approach" is the core of conceptual skill that manager should possess. How the systems and sub-systems are interrelated and work for the common cause of the organisation is well explained by conceptual skill. This skill "consist of the ability of a manager to see a big picture." Many managers blend conceptual and analytical skill to develop a long range plan for their organisations. It is said that Chairman of matxushita, japan has developed a 250 year plan for his company by combining conceptual and analytical skills. He picks-up a solution which he feels better for solving the problem.

Thus, **Conceptual Skills,** involve the ability to undertand the organisation as a whole. Policy making body should possess these skills to a greater extent to know how various functions of the organisation support one another how the organisation responds to the external environment and how changes in one operational function will affect the other, operational function.

Every manager should possess every type of skill. It is a challenging task. That is why managerial positions are occupied by challenging personalities who possess required skills to perform their tasks effectively.

(v) Decision-making skill: Selection of solution determines the managerial skill of the manager. The decision he takes determines the quality of his thinking and ability. A good decision-maker is a good analyst too. Every manager should be able to take sound decisions. They can develop this skill only when they are capable of analysing the situations well. Both analytical and conceptual skills of a manager help him in taking successful decisions. Take for example the Reliance Industries. "Although dogged by controversies, the company continues to maintain its lead in the Indian Corporate world. In spite of huge profits it has remained zero tax payer and has now entered into the new sectors like power, tclecom and infrastructure in a big way and the corporate ladder is gelling too short for this giant." (ET 500 special issue). This is an example of good decision-making at a lop level.

(vi) Computer skill: Today's manager should have a first hand knowledge about computers which provide fast information at finger tips. One should have the knowledge of computer terminologies like hardware, software, and should be able to adopt appropriate software for carrying out the tasks in the organisation. The manager, if need be, should develop a software fitting to his organisation activities. Today there is explosion of information technology and computers are widely used in all offices and industrial and service sectors. This acts as a sound decision-making tool, It increases the manager's productivity.

(vii) Communication skill: This skill requires the ability of person (Manager) to tell, what he wants, to tell in an effective way. This enables the receivers of the message to carry it promptly. The manager who has to get things done by others should be proficient in oral and written communication. "The communication skill is critical to success in every field, but it is crucial to managers who must achieve results through the efforts of others." Frequent communication is the only way to build employee trust and co-operation which is essential for the success of the organisation. Therefore every manager should possess sound communication skill to find out whether his fellow workers have understood his thinking and decisions. This can be made out by getting a feedback from the employees.

SKILL DIFFERENCE AT DIFFERENT LEVELS

The different types ot skills analysed in previous paragraphs vary from one managerial level to another. If technological skill is 'required more at the bottom line, the top managers need more conceptual and analytical skill. Every level manager needs communication skill at a reasonable degree.

The following fig gives an idea about the degree of different types of skills required at each level of management. They vary from one level to another. Top managers concentrate on decision-making skills which are assisted by conceptual, analytical and computer skills. They being the policy makers should be able to see the organisation as a whole. "Seeing the Big Picture" capacity should be possessed by them. The middle managers act as liaison officers and are a vital link between first level and bottom line. This managerial position is found in complex organisation. They need more of analytical and human skills and have more computer and communication, skills too Bottom line managers are more concerned with production and should know of skills concerning production. Therefore they have more of computer and technical skills. Observe the following picture :

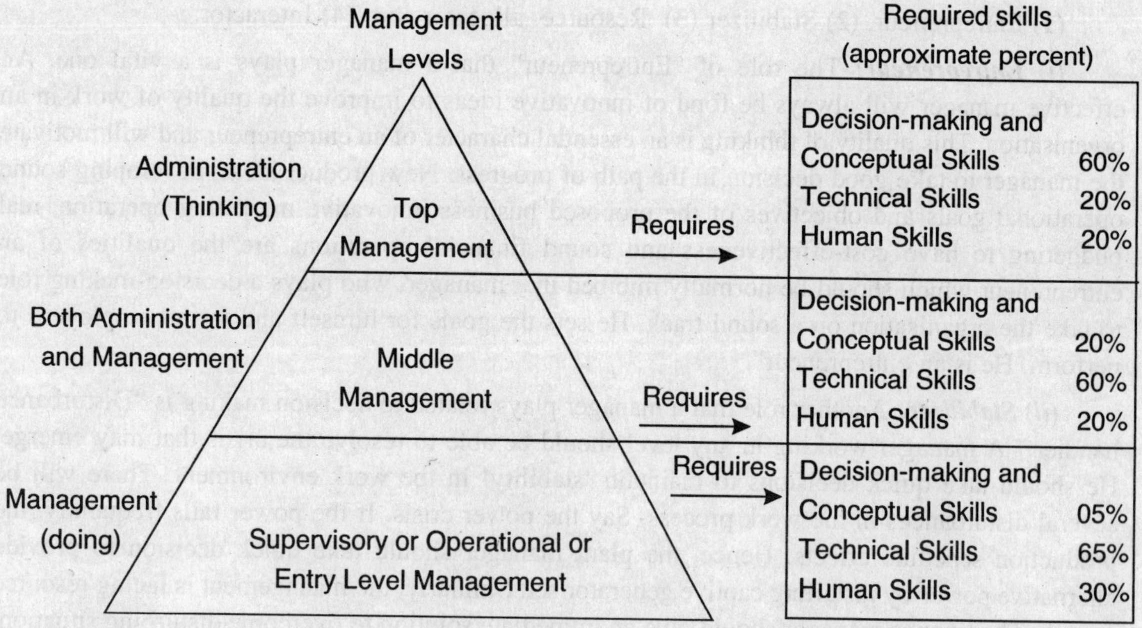

FIG. 2.7. Distinction Between Administrative and Management positions and Different Types of Skills Required at Different Levels.

This figure, when closely observed, explains the following aspects :

When a manager moves upwards from one level to another, technical skills become less important and conceptual skills become more important. This means as manager advances in his position, he or she will be involving more and more in guiding the organisation and less attention will be given to operational aspects.

MANAGERIAL ROLES AND CHARACTERISTICS OF MANAGERS FOR MANAGERIAL SUCCESS

The discussion on managerial skills so far in previous paragraphs reveal that every manager should possess skills to perform their jobs effectively. But what actually they do at their work place has to be examined. A vital study was made by *Henry Minzberg* regarding the work culture of managers. By observing five chief executives for two weeks, he concluded "That managers perform ten different but closely related roles." *(Henry Mintzberg: The Nature of Managerial Work P. H. 1980).* He has categorised three main roles in which all the ten roles arc performed. They are:(l) Decision Roles (2) Inter-Personal Roles and (3) Informational Roles.

(1) Decision Roles: As already discussed, decision-making is one of the vital functions of a manager. He is a good decision master. To take appropriate decisions, managers should gather correct information relating to the issue.

They should also develop interpersonal relationship. These act as vital tools in good decision-making. The decision roles that a manager plays are:

(1) Entrepreneur, (2) Stabilizer (3) Resource allocator and (4) Interactor.

(i) Entrepreneur: The role of "Entrepreneur" that a manager plays is a vital one. An effective manager will always be fond of innovative ideas to improve the quality of work in an organisation. This quality of thinking is an essential character of an entrepreneur and will motivate the manager to take good decision in the path of progress. New product ideas, developing sound operational goals and objectives of the proposed business innovative marketing operation, real budgeting to have cost-effectiveness and sound financial operations are the qualities of an entrepreneur which should be normally imbibed in a manager, who plays a decision-making role to take the organisation on a sound track. He sets the goals for himself and for all employees to perform. He is an entrepreneur".

(ii) Stabilizer: Another role that a manager plays related to decision making is "Disturbance handler." A manager working in any level should be able to resolve the crisis that may emerge. He should take quick decisions to maintain 'stability' in the work environment. There will be several disturbances in the work process. Say the power crisis. If the power fails frequently, the production schedule affects. Hence, the plant manager should take quick decision to provide alternative power by installing captive generator set. Similarly, the management is facing resource crunch. The finance manager should give an immediate solution to overcome disturbing situation. He is a link between top brass and workforce and acts as a liaison between them in times of conflict, providing necessary information. Thus, a manager at any level should be capable of handling any type of disturbance that may affect the work at his level. Thus, he plays the role of disturbance handler.

(iii) Resource Allocator: Proper allocation of resources is another crucial task before the manager. Resources here refer to monetary, technical and human resources. The organisations are not fully endowed with all the resources. The scarce resources are to be judiciously allocated to get the full advantage of production and sales. "Resource allocation, therefore, is one of the most critical of the manager's decisions roles." A finance manager should decide whether debentures are to be raised to get required working capital. Similarly, a marketing manager should decide whether a product has to be introduced to improve the market share of the firm, with the available resources. Thus, a manager, in a decision-making process, should also know about the real resources of the firm available to his tasks and allocate it judiciously between various tasks. Thus he is a good financial analyst, acts as a good guide in all concerned metters.

Management (means the people involved in the operations of the organisation) should be aware of the situations and should know as to how the organisational resources have to be utilized. The resources comprise of (i) human (ii) monetary (iii) raw materials and (iv) finance. All these resources have to be judiciously applied for the 'sucess of the organisation. Following diagram depicts the use of organisational resources, which is the key factor for the success of managers.

In Judicious application of organisational resources the management has to consider two vital aspects, (i) Managerial effectiveness and (ii) Managerial efficiency.

Effectiveness and Efficiency are required to maximise organisational success.

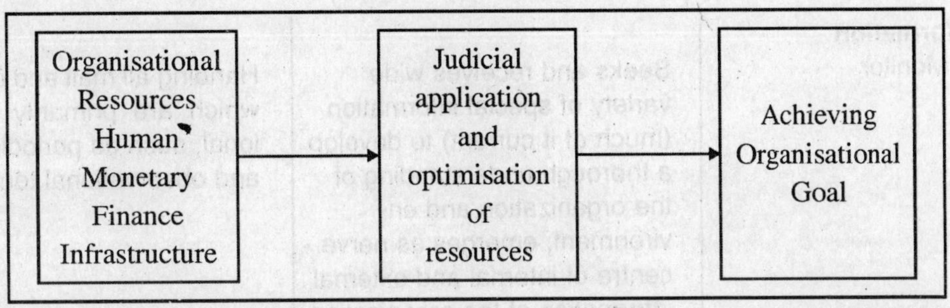

FIG. 2.8. Transormation of Organisational Resources to Achieve Organisational Goals

(*i*) ***Managerial Effectivenss:*** This aspect is examined in terms of resource utilization to achieve organisational goal. The concept explains the degree to which management achieves organisational objectives. This entails promptly achieving a stated objective. **It is doing things right.**

(*ii*) ***Managerial Efficiency:*** This depecits as how a management manager deploys organisational resources for the success of the organisation. It shows the degree to which organisational resources contribute to productivity of operational process of the organisation. This can be measured by the extent of resources used in the operational process in the organisation. Efficiency is assessed by weighing the resources against what is accomplished. If cost-benefit ratio is favourable, it is more efficient. It is to do right things.

The following box information explains the managerial roles performed by manager. This is explained by Henry Mintzberg in his famous book. "The nature of Managerial work:

Mintzberg's Management Roles

Roles	***Description***	***Identifiable Activities***
A. Interpersonal		
1. Figurehead	Symbolic head; obliged to perform a number of routine duties of a legal or social nature.	Ceremony, status, requests, solicitations
2. Leader	Responsible for the motivation and activation of subordinates; responsible for staffing, training, training, and associated duties.	Virtually all managerial activities involving subordinates
3. Liaison	Maintains self-developed network of outside contacts and informers who provide favours and information.	Acknowledgements of mail external board work, other activities involving outsiders.
4. Interactor	Interacts with other depart-mental heads and with co-workers to achieve the goals	Acts as good communicator and negotiates with works on production.

B. Information		
1. Monitor	Seeks and receives wide variety of special information (much of it current) to develop a thorough understanding of the organization and environment; emerges as nerve centre of internal and external information of the organisation.	Handing all mail and contracts, which are primarily informational, such as periodical news and observational tours
2. Disseminator	Transmits information received from outsiders or from subordinates to members of the organization; some information factual, some involving enterpretation and integration.	Forwarding mail into the organization for informational purposes, verbal contacts involving information flow to subordinates including review sessions and spontaneous communication
3. Spokes-person	Transmits information to outsiders on the organization's plans, policies, actions and results; serves as expert on the organization's industry.	Board meeting handling mail and contracts involving transmission of information to outsiders
C. Decisional		
1. Entrepreneur	Searches the organization and its environment for opportunities and initiates "improvement projects" to bring about change; supervises design of certain projects as well.	Strategy and review sessions involving initiation or design of improvement projects
2. Disturbance Handler	Responsible for corrective action when the organization faces important, unexpected disturbances.	Strategy and review involving disturbances and crises.
3. Resource	Responsible for the Allocator allocation of organizational resources of all kinds - in effect the making or approving of all significant organizational decisions.	Scheduling, requests for authorization, any activity involving budgeting and the programming of subordinates' work
4. Negotiator	Responsible for representing the organization at major negotiations.	Negotiation

(***Source:*** H. Mintzberg. *The Nature of Managerial Work,* Englewood Cliffs, N.J. Prentice Hall, 1980, pp. 91-22.)

MANAGER - TODAY

The concept of "Global village" has made the business world a complex one. The managers of today, be in manufacturing or in service sector, are working under stress and strain. They have to adjust to internal and external environment of the business. Internal aspects are discussed in detail so far in this chapter. The external environment — a set of outside forces are difficult to control. But still the managers have to cope with external forces like government policies, competition, consumer behaviour, technological changes etc. A "turbulent environment" is created by technological changes. The competition between two major manufacturers of a product may create turbulent environment. The small firms suffer in the process. The managers of these units will be confronted with many problems which are beyond their control.

A hostile environment is also experienced by many managers. If an organisation faces "intense competition for customers or resources" it is said to be under hostile environment. Today automobile industry, particularly car industry, is in hostile environment. Besides Maruti range, Opel Astra, Escort Ford, Ceilo, Peugeot Uno, Tata range of cars, are engaged in fierce competition. This has affected the management policies regarding pricing, warranty stipulations, production conditions, labour activities etc.

Another external environment which is affecting management process and managers is "Diverse Environment." Because of major entry of multinational corporations (MNCs) the business units are facing diversity in work culture, consumers, languages, governments and food habits. These organisations are influenced by diverse environment and managers in these units have difficult time to manage. Multiproduct companies also face a diverse environment. The managers of multiproduct companies are posed with unique problems. They are real threats to the organisation's existence. Therefore each product is handed over to one segment by establishing subsidiaries. Decentralisation and specialisation are the only solutions to effective management of diverse environment.

Explosion in information technology has made the electronics, computers and telecommunication industries to stand on their toes. Technically complex environment has made the products of these industries obsolete at a faster rate. In the process, some of the giants in Computer industry can lose ground and vanish gradually. For example, IBM's profit comes mainly from big computers (main frame). Now small table computers and even notebooks type have emerged in a big way and IBM is incuring loss in main frame division. The managers in these industries should gradually shift over to products widely acceptable in the market and maintain their market share.

Therefore, the manager of today should be prepared for the threats emerging from his external environment. He should prepare for disaster and develop crisis management team. Very few organisations have crisis management teams. Majority of the small and middle sized companies are developing "Just-in-case" strategies to manage crisis. According to this, they identify potential disasters and develop action plans. Some companies prepare crisis management manuals and conduct simulation exercises for their managers to make them mentally strong to face crisis.

Management responses like (i) Strong organisation structure in which two elements, viz., 'Core' and 'Buffer' work together. 'Core' is the main line operators like production team and

'Buffer' is the team which supports the core, viz., marketing division, finance division etc. (ii) Strategic planning (determination of basic long-term objectives of the organisation and adoption of specific action plans for attaining these objectives), (iii) Fire fighting ('sitting back and allow things to happen and then deal with the result), and (iv) Linking two or more organisations to get market feedback and adopt rectifying measures (Boundary spanning job). With these supporting factors and regular in-built performance appraisal methods of managers, today's manager becomes strong and works for achieving the organisation goals.

EXECUTIVES - 21ST CENTURY

As stated earlier, manager of today is facing several problems. He is passing through a transitional period. The work style is changing over from traditional systems to new proficient systems. Information technology is playing a major role in every sphere of business activity and has emerged as a powerful tool in solving various business problems and adopting appropriate business strategy. Adopting to a new system itself is a real task before him. He is adjusting to this environment, understands the changing scenario, and is designing and developing a structure in which the managers of tomorrow have to work.

21st century executives have to work in a new environment. Their behaviour will be recognised well in a new organisation structure through their specialised operations. Organisations in the 21st century become terse and will have only one-third of the human resources they have today. Particularly at the managerial level, the levels will be reduced and organisations become flatter. This increases the responsibilities of the managers. As the human resources will be thinner in organisations, the manager of tomorrow has to work close with the human elements who work in the organisations. He has to understand them and work with a team spirit. The future organisation recognises values and wholism. The managers will be specialists in a specific area. They must be capable of identifying the disturbing elements, analyse them and take sound decisions to solve the business problems. The only supporting factor to solve business problem is that he has to adopt information tools. External agencies will be hired to solve major business problems. Thus manager of tomorrow will have to work in a sophisticated environment where "change is considered as an ongoing process to locate additional problems and develop best solutions and implement them through team work and team spirit." Organisations in future become "Learning Organisations." "Reengineering" or "Restructuring" will be a continuous activity in future organisations.

Today's Manager—Some data Day-to-Day Managerial Activity

1. No break in the pace of activity during office hours.
2. Attends on an average (per day): (i) 36 papers, (ii) Five telephone calls (iii) Eight meetings.
3. A real break never occurs. Coffee during meetings and lunch during formal or informal meetings.
4. No free time. Always engaged in some work.
5. Free only on observation tour or on leave.
6. Manager can never be free to forget the job. He is a perpetual preoccupant.
7. No matter what kind of managerial job, managers carry the nagging suspicion that they might be able to contribute just a little bit more.
8. They assume an unreleveting pace in their work.

Source: H. Mintzberg: *The nature of management-work-1973.*

SOCIAL RESPONSIBILITY OF MANAGERS

The social responsibility of manager refers to such decision and activities of a manager which provide for the welfare of the society as a whole along with the earning of profit for the firm. The business firm functions and acts in such a way that it will accomplish social gains (social output) along with the traditional economic gains (economic output) in which the business firm is interested. Manager has to function to discharge social responsibility.

Social Responsibility–The Concept

We give here some of the definitions of social responsibility.

Adolfe Berle has defined "social responsibility" as the managerment's responsiveness to public consensus." According to Prof. Andrews, "by social responsibility, we mean the intelligent and objective concern for the welfare of society that restrains individual and corporate behaviour from ultimately destructive activities, no matter how immediately profitable and leads in the direction of positive contribution to human betterment variously as the latter may be defined." According to keith Davis, "social responsibility" refers to "the businessman's decisions and actions taken for reasons at least partially beyond the firm's direct economic or technical interest."

Howard Bowen is of the view that "the social responsibilities are obligations to pursue those policies to make those decision or to follow those lines of action which are desirable in terms of the objectives and values of our society."

An analysis of the above definitions of social responsibilities reveals the following. Social responsibility refers to "*the objective concern of business firm for the welfare of the society and it involves following by the management of such policies, making of such decisions or following of such lines of action which are desirable in terms of objectives and values of our society.*" Further, decisions are taken by the business for reasons at least partially beyond the firm's direct economic or technical interest.

The theme of social responsibility is that;

(i) A business firm should not ignore the welfare of the society,
(ii) Policies and decisions of the business enterprise, should focus on values of society,
(iii) Earning profit by honouring values of society and finally assist the promotions of welfare of the society.

Traditional Economic Gains and Social Responsibilities

The difference between traditional business-making and social responsibility is that while the traditional decision-makers are concerned primarily with economic and technical values, social responsibility extends thinking to social values as well. Further, the traditional decision-maker thinks in terms of the narrow interest of a single enterprise or a person, whereas social responsibility envisages thinking in terms of the entire society. The traditional business decision are confined primarily to narrow economic and technical business decisions are confined primarily to narrow economic and technical gains while decision based on considerations of social responsibilities go beyond them. Keith Davis has stated that decision relating to social responsibilities are taken for reasons at least partially beyond the firm's direct economic or technical interest. Thus, we find that the objectives of business and social responsibilities, are not contrary to each other. It is not objectives of business vs. social responsibilities but "objectives of business and social responsibilities."

Social Responsibility Model of Keith Davis
1. Social responsibility arises from Social Power
This proposition says that business has a significant influence or power over such critical issues as minority employment environmental pollution. The means that total business of the country decides the degree or proportion of minorities employed and prevailing condition of environment in the country. Accordingly, business has this power over society and as business enjoys such power, society should hold business responsible for social conditions that result from exercising this power.
2. Business shall operate as a two-way open system, with open receipt of inputs from society and open disclosure of its operation to the public.
This proposition suggests that business must be willing to listen to the representatives of the society to sustain or improve societal welfare.
3. The social costs and benefits of an activity, product or service shall be thoroughly calculated and considered in deciding whether to proceed with it.
This proposition states that besides achieving technical excellence and profitable position, business should also consider both short-term and long-term societal consequences.
4. Social costs and benefits of an activity, product or service shall be passed on to the consumer.
This proposition indicates that the cost of activities taken up to serve society by the business need not be fully borned by the business. A portion can be covered by charging higher price to the customer.
5. Business institutions, as citizens, have the responsibility to become involved in certain social problems that are outside their normal areas of operation.
As per this proposition, if a business possesses the expertise to solve a social problem with which it may not be directily associated, it should be held responsible for helping society to solve that problem.

FIG. 2.9. Keith Davis Model of Social Responsibility.

Thus, the social responsibility of a business covers the issues such as welfare of the society, values of the society, profit making by fims following ethical aspects. The interests of stakeholders of business should also be protected. In this back drop, the managers have to discharge the responsibilities to the following stock-holders so that they have the satisfaction of discharfing their social responsibility. The stakeholders are (i) Owners (ii) Workers (iii) Consumers (iv) Society (v) Government (vi) Weaker Sections of the society and (vii) Economic policies of the State. Observe the following picture :

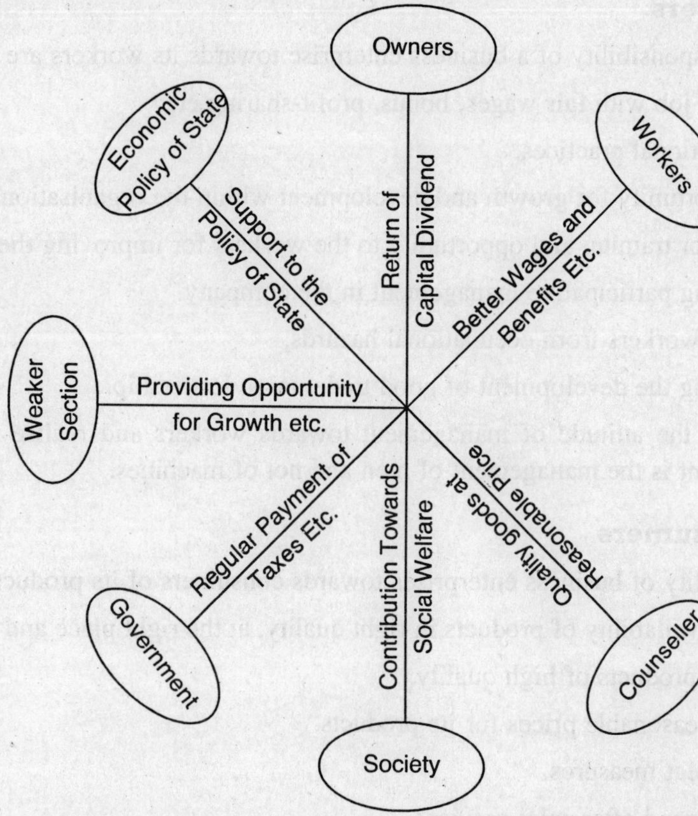

FIG. 2.10. Business Manager and his Social Responsibility

The picture depicts the various types of social responsibility to be discharged by the business and its managers to different segments who are concerned with business. A brief analysis is made in the following paragraphs:

1. Towards Owners of Enterprise

The responsibility of business enterprises towards their owners are :

(a) Payment of a fair rate of dividend regularly.

(b) Maximisation of the net present value of the business through effective management.

(c) Ensuring full participation of owners in the management of the affairs of the enterprise.

(d) Arresting the tendency towards the growth of "Oligarchic management."

(e) Supplying of accurate and comprehensive reports giving full information on the working of the company.

(f) Disclosing of financial information and clarifying information and clarifying doubts, if any.

(g) Accessibility of chairman and directors to the owners for getting information relating to the company.

2. Towards Workers

Some of the responsibility of a business enterprise towards its workers are :

(a) Security of job with fair wages, bonus, profit-sharing etc.

(b) Fair promotional practices.

(c) Equal opportunity for growth and development within the organisation.

(d) Facilities for training and opportunity to the workers for improving their skill.

(e) Encouraging participative management in the company.

(f) Protecting workers from occupational hazards.

(g) Encouraging the development of good trade union leadership.

(h) Change in the attitude of management towards workers and realise the fact that the management is the management of men and not of machines.

3. Towards Consumers

The responsibility of business enterprises towards consumers of its products are :

(a) Ensuring availability of products in right quality, at the right place and at the right time.

(b) Supplying products of high quality.

(c) Charging reasonable prices for its products.

(d) Using correct measures.

(e) Providing good after-sales services.

(f) Avoiding restrictive trade practices and other understand methods to exploit the consumer.

(g) Encouraging the formation of associations of consumers satisfaction and welfare.

4. Towards the Government

The obligations of business enterprise to the govenment are:

(a) Strictly observing of the various laws and enactments.

(b) Extending full support to the govenment in its efforts to solve national problems such as unemployment, food, inflation, regional imbalance in economic development, etc.

5. Towards the Society

The obligations of a business to the society are:

(a) Optimising the use of resources.

(b) Producing goods are services efficiently and contributing to the economic well-being of the society.

(c) Providing public amenities and avoiding the conditions of slums and congestion.

(d) Maintaining environmental econlogy and adopting anti-pollution measures.

(e) Participating in social welfare programmes, such as adopting villages for their all-round development, providing for medical facilities, sanctioning educational scholarships to deserving students, constructing shelter at bus stops contributing to funds meant for the benefit of society, undertaking social forestry, etc.

(f) Ensuring that the gains of improved production of the enterprises are shared by all the constituents of the society, viz., management, shareholders workers and consumers.

6. Towards Weakers Sections

(a) Helping the weaker sections by providing to them an opportunity for growth.

(b) Encouraging voluntary organisations and agencies engaged in improvement of the weaker sections.

7. Towards the Economic Policy of State

The obligations of a business enterprise towards the economic policy of state are:

(a) Encouraging development of small business, import substitution and self-reliance and dispersal of economic activity.

(b) Producing goods to meet the needs of the various sections of society.

(c) Helping the government in its efforts to hold the price line.

(d) Taking measures to subserve the national policy to establish an egalitarian social order in the country.

An analysis of the components of social responsibility of a business enterprise reveals that the business enterprise owes social obligations to consumers, workers, owners, society, government, weaker sections of society, and to the economic policy of the state. The manager is the key factor in coordinating these activities.

BALANCING OF VARIOUS INTERESTS

We have seen that there are different interests of public affected by the business. In view of this, it is necessary for a manager to manage its affairs in a manager such a way that it is able to strike an equitable and proper balance between the interests of the people affected by its activities. To quote *Ernest Dale,* the manager of an enterprise "sees himself as an arbiter among the many interests of public affected by the business: the stockholders, the employees, the suppliers, the local community and the customers. It is his duty to distribute the returns from the business equitably by providing a 'fair' return to the shareholders, fair working conditions and pay for the employees, 'fair' price to the suppliers and customers and to make the business in general an asset to the local community and the nation."

GLOBAL AWARENESS/GLOBAL MANAGERS.

As the business of a country has been extended to the global arena. The managers of such global companies besides possessing the goals and skills to manage, they have to possess certain other skills to effectively carry on their business in the global market. They have to move from country to country (whenever they have business operations) to manage the business and facing international competition. The global business emerged considerably in fourteenth century. Asian countries developed business with western countries such as Europe and America. Sea transport was the only major transport system that was available then. With the development of Air transport and information technology, the global business became the order of the day and world became too small. The managers managing global business (Global Managers) should possess additional skills to stimulate cultural and global awareness, to explore comparative management and develop cross-cultural training programmes to the upcoming global managers.

Global business of any company in any country involves the following business practices and procedure:

- A global company of a country, first should possess license from both the country of origin and importing country to deal with their product or service.
- Export procedure has to be understood of the country of origin and import rules and regulations of the country of import has to be well-known.
- The products to be exported may be finished ones or semi-finished or raw material like iron ore or any specialised services. The company should be aware of **packaging** and **transporting** mode to the destiny.
- In case of joint ventures where the business operations are shared between the country of origin and importing country (ex: A joint venture between a company in the USA and a company in India – IBM – India) the practices should be demarcated (i.e. who has to pool the resources, Who has to produce, stores, transport and market the product or service etc. have to be distinctly show in the agreement).
- Strategic alliances have to be properly defined.
- Warehousing and selling procedures are to be clearly laid down.
- Financial aspects viz. providing capital for the business, The ratio in which it has to be shared, managing the financial income and expenditure, sharing profits, international money transfer etc. have to be dealt without giving room for confusion, dissatisfaction or any sort of financial disturbance.
- Other social and ethnic aspects involved in a global business viz., the local history, culture, customs, language, knowledge religion, politics, social structure, moral standards, educational level, food habits, business ethics humour values, negotiation techniques etc of the host country are to be fully understood by global corporations.

The awareness of international business practices or otherwise called 'global awareness' is essential for managers/leaders of global corporations. The managers in global business will be discharing different functions. Specialists in functions like, finance, marketing production, HRD etc will be functioning in global business also. These functional managers in global business should possess the traits and attitude required for that specific function they discharge.

As far as attitude is concerned, it may be (i) Ethnocentric (ii) Polycentric or (iii) Geocentric (as suggested by Howard V. Perlmutter in an article in "Columbia Journal of World Business" – Jan-Feb. 1969).

1. Ethnocentric attitude may be understood as the attitude possessed by the managers of country of origin who assume and believe that their country's beliefs, practices, technology and their decisions are superior and trust worthyness compared to host country's business practices. This attitude is rigid, conservative and greatly disturb the international business. Therefore such managers should change their attitude and be flexible in thinking and practicing to have a successful global business.

Ethnocentric managers are highly home-oriented. Authority and decision making is more in head office situated in home country. Evaluation and control will take place in home office as per the standards of home country. Communication and information will be commanding and advicing in nature. These managers will recruit people for key positions from their own country.

These practices of ethnocentric managers will create problems in ethnically diversified countries. Indian business people and society are much apposed to business practices of foreign countries which act against its culture, ethics and social practices.

2. Polycentric attitude focuses on the behaviour of host country managers. These managers know very well the business practicess of their country, based on local social habits, culture, ethics, values, language etc. They are tuned to their country's business environmen and they know how to conduct business in such environment.

Polycentric managers are host country-based and will have less authority and decision-making power. They will have less communication and information flow compared to the country of origin of business. These managers encourage local people to take up jobs in their organisations, particularly for key positions. The organisation structure, is not as integrated as ethnocentric and will be a sort of loose federation consisting independent subsidiaries. This structure may be positive in nature, providing scope for greater use of local markets and increased sales with the assistance of local government and managers possessing high morale.

3. Geocentric attitude will have a wide angle focusing on the whole world. The managers possessing such attitude are truly international in character and understanding. But they donot forget to identify with their country's interests. They try to collaborate business interests of both home and host countries. They establish business evaluation and control systems which are standardised and applicable comfortably in global business. Two-way communication and information flow will be developed. Second-line managers will also be a part of management team and participate in decision-making. The key positions will be filled with best people selected from the global talent. The managers are real global managers honouring cross-culture multi-language and multi-religion. They design business practices according to host country's needs.

Considering the traits and attitudes of these types, managers having geocentric attitude and behaviour ore best suited to global business. Today global market is very competitive in nature. Many countries are in the growing list. These countries have to stabilize their export business for sustained growth. Managers with geocentric attitude can truly develop international business as their outlook will be very broad and global in character. They will have positive global awareness.

Volumes can be written about Global Awareness and Global Manager. The key factors that are considered for global management are religion, culture, language, political situation, the type of government and their policies towards business of the country in which business is to be conducted. The global manager should avoid cultural-shocks, manoeuvere language barriers, adopt to local needs, appease local consumers satisfying their real needs to have a successful business and become a true global manager.

Manager Tomorrow – Peter F. Drucker's View

— Manager of tomorrow must re-learn how to manage by giving up old ideas which may be not relevant to current business.

— Learn to manage glued situation, where manager is neither superior nor subordinate.

— Information is replacing authority. Corporation is not a stable pyramid but more like atent. It is transitory in character or atheist. It will be changing. Manager should be visionary and is responsible for his carrer. "Step ladder" is gone. Titles don't mean what they used to.

— Manager will have series of assignments.

— Mere management education is not enough for him Manager should understand himself for career success.

— He should understand his competencies – as also that of his boss and peers.

— As future organisation will be flatter, perception of manager is more important than analysis. He must define his own contribution to the organisation.

— Managers must be specialists and synthesizers of different areas of knowledge.

— Structure of rank and power will be replaced by sponsor and mentor relations based on mutual understanding and responsibility.

— The key to the productivity of knowledge workers is to make them concentrate on the real assignment.

— Power to executives comes from transmitting information to make it productive and not from hiding it.

Source : Harvard Business Review, May-June 1993, Volume-71, Number-3.

SUMMARY

1. Management functions such as planning, organising, staffing, directing and controlling are to be coordinated for the success of the organisation.
2. Manager is a person who coordinates the functions and gets the tasks done by his fellow workers at each level of management. He/she is a person who is responsible to discharge certain tasks assigned to him/her.
3. The mix of management functions which are to be performed by a manager would depend upon the level (Top, middle and First lime) at which he/she functions.
4. In organisational hierarchy three levels of management normally exist and each level is headed by a manager.
5. Functional managers also exist in each functional area of management such as production, finance, marketing, HRD etc.
6. Each functional manager is a specialist in his area of management.
7. Non-managers are those who discharge the functions of managers without having any authority. In real terms they are not managers. But some experienced sectional supervisors in vorious

departments of the organisation are delegated with certain authority to take decisions and implement without seeking permission from their higher-ups.

8. Manager should have the qualities of creativity vision, empathy and ethics.
9. Other qualities possessed by good manager are; (i) a good goal setter honest worker, good guide recognise good work of fellow-workers, capable assigner, person of integrity, visionary, quick decision-maker, good financial analysit, good controller and a good communicator.
10. A line manager is one who is an executive in the line of heirarchy such as Top manager or CEO, middle manager and front line manager. These managers in the hierarchy are the executors of the tasks as per the set policies and programmes.
11. A staff manager is only an adviser to the manager at the top level or middle level. However his advice may or may not be followed by the line manager.
12. A manager should possess certain managerial skills. They are (i) Technical skills (ii) Human relation skill, (iii) Analytical skill, (iv) Conceptual skill (v) Decision-making skill (vi) Computer skill and (vii) Communication skill.
13. Manager performs the roles as (i) Decision-maker (ii) Entrepreneur (iii) Stabilizer (iv) Resource allocator, etc. other roles such as Inter-personal roles and Information provider, are also discharged.
14. Managers of today have to efficiently handle internal and external threats concerning to their tasks.
15. Global managers should be aware of global business practices. They have to function in multi-cultural, multi-religion environment. Therefore they should possess trait's and skills suitable to global business.

STUDY QUESTIONS

1. Give the meaning of "Manager".
2. Give the meaning of functional manager.
3. Who is a "Non-manager" ?
4. Analyze the characteristics of a good manager.
5. Give a note on different roles played by a manager.
6. Explain in detail the various types of skills required for a manager.
7. Analyze the functions of a marketing manager.
8. Give a note on functions of each of the following:
   (i) Production Manager (ii) Finance Manager (iii) Human Resources Development Manager. (iv) Office Manager (v) Global Manager.
9. What do you mean by Line Manager ?
10. What is Staff Manager ?
11. Briefly explain the role of Executives in Twenty First Century.
12. Explain the concept of "Social Responsibility" and the role of managers in discharging social responsibility.
13. Give a note on Peter Drucker's view on the managers of tomorrow.
14. Give the meaning of each of the following :
    (i) Ethnocentric attitude, (ii) Polycentric attitude, (iii) Geocentric attitude
15. Give a note on quality and performance awareness of managers.
16. Write an explanatory note on Global Manager.
17. Explain the functions of different levels of managers found in an organisation.

3

EVOLUTION OF MANAGEMENT THOUGHT

LEARNING OBJECTIVES

After reading this chapter, you should be able to know;

- To understand the growth path of Management Thought
- Understanding contributions to Management Thought from various thinkers from time to time.
- To know about Indian contributors to Management Thought

The current thoughts of management or management theory in the current situation can be understood in a better way if we have some idea about its evolution. In this chapter, we shall first discuss the evolution of management theory and then take up the study of current thoughts on management. The evolution of management thought can be studied under the following headings:

1. Pre-scientific management period.
2. Classical Approach: Early management approaches represented by scientific management, process management theory and human relations movement.
3. Modern management approaches represented by behavioural scientific movement, quantitative approach, systems approach, contingency approach, etc.

Following figure gives a descriptive idea of the evolution of management thought.

EVOLUTION OF MANAGEMENT THOUGHT

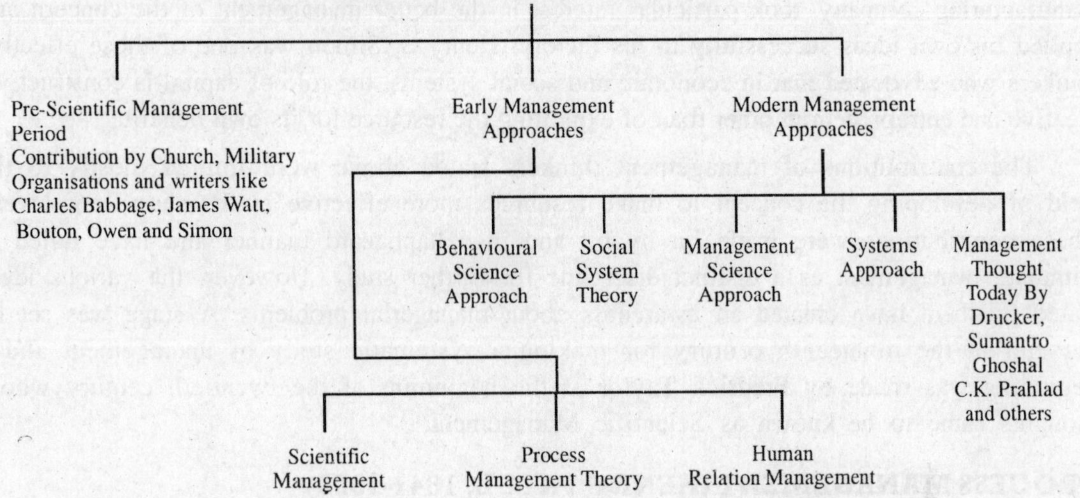

CHART : Management Thought – Growth Path

PRE-SCIENTIFIC MANAGEMENT PERIOD

The real development of management thought began with the scientific management approach stated by Taylor, though some of the concepts have been developed by thinkers earlier to Taylor. For example, early management thoughts have come from the Roman Catholic Church, military organisations, the Cameralists, a group of German and Austrian public administrators and intellectuals from the sixteenth to the eighteenth centuries. Their concepts of management were mostly related to the principles of specialisation, selection of subordinates and their training and simplification of administrative procedures.

Pre-scientific Management

Prior to Industrial Revolution, many organizations like churches, military administrator, German and Austrian administrators worked in their domains adapting certain systematic work practices. In the later stages, in seventeenth century, Charles Babbage and other thinkers practiced the concept of "Management" on the shop floors. However the practices and ideas suggested by them gave way for the development of management concept bit-by-bit.

In the later period, contributions were made by Charles Babbage, James Watt and Robinson Boulton, Robert Owen, Towne and Simon.

Charles Babbage was a Professor of Mathematics at the Cambridge University and suggested the use of accurate data obtained through rigid investigation in the management of an undertaking. James Watt Junior (1796-1848) and Robinson Boulton (1770 to 1842) used the management techniques such as market research and forecasting, production planning, planned machine layout, standardisation of components and parts, elaborate statistical records, maintenance of control report, cost accounting data, provision of welfare of personnel etc. Robert Owen (1771-1858) managed a group of textile mills in Scotland and is well-known as the promoter of co-operative and trade union movements in England. Henry R. Towne, president of the famous lock manufacturing company, took particular interest in the better management of the concern and applied his own ideas successfully to his factory. Henry S. Simon was one of those effective thinkers who advocated that in economic and social systems, the role of capital is constructive, creative and entrepreneurial other than of exploiting the resource for its own benefit.

The contributions of management thinkers stated above were limited mostly to the field of developing the concept to make resources more effective at the shop-floor levels. These contributions were made bit by bit and in a haphazard manner and have failed to stimulate management as a distinct discipline for further study. However, the various ideas stated by them have created an awareness about managerial problems. A stage was set by the end of the nineteenth century for making a systematic study of management and a beginning was made by Fredrick Taylor at the beginning of the twentieth century whose thoughts came to be known as Scientific Management.

PROCESS MANAGEMENT (HENRY FAYOL, 1841-1925)

Around 1910, H. Fayol, a French engineer, initiated the administrative theory of management (process management) in Europe. Sheldon, Mooney and Reiley, L.F. Urwick and L. Gulick also contributed a lot to the administrative theory of management. This theory is called process (functional) management and the advocates of this theory belong to the process school of management. In 1916, Fayol published his book "General and Industrial Management" in French, of which later an English edition was brought out. Fayol identified management as a separate set of skills or functions performed by a supervisor in an organisation. He clearly distinguished the difference between technical and managerial skills and emphasised that a supervisor must be efficient in both. He stated that technical ability is more dominant at the lower level of management, whereas managerial ability is more important at the higher level of management.

Fayol, in his famous book, stated fourteen management principles that can capture the entire flavour of the process management theory. They are subordination of individual interests to general interests, authority and responsibility, discipline, division of work, remuneration of personnel, centralisation, scalar chain, equity, initiative, stability of tenure of personal, unity of command, unity of direction and esprit de crops.

Fayol also stated that all operation in business organisation can be classified under six heads, *viz.*, (1) technical (production and manufacturing), (2) commercial (purchase and sales), (3) financial (financing and controlling of capital for its optimum use), (4) security (protection of property and persons), (5) accounting (stock-taking, balance sheet, costing and statistics), and (6) managerial (planning, organising, communicating, co-ordinating and controlling).

Foyol's Fourteen Principles of Management

1. **Division of Work:** This leads to specialisation of work and organisational success.
2. **Authority:** The right to order should go with responsibility.
3. **Discipline:** Mutual respect and obedience facilitates smooth running of operations.
4. **Unity of Command:** Each employee should receive one order having only one boss.

5. **Unity of Direction:** Every employee's effort should be channelised in one direction.
6. **Subordination of individual interest to the general interest:** Manager should strive hard to divert personal interest towards organizational interests.
7. **Remuneration:** Employee should be paid fair wage.
8. **Centralisation:** There should be a balance between centralization and decentralization.
9. **Scalar Chain:** Employees should follow formal chain of command unless otherwise expressed.
10. **Order:** Both people and materials should be in their places.
11. **Equity:** All should be treated equally with kind and justice.
12. **Stability and Tenure:** Allow people to stabilize in their jobs.
13. **Initiative:** Allow and motivate people to take initiative to design and implement plans.
14. **Espirit de corps:** Harmonious relationship has to be developed amongst workers.

Other Contributors: The other contributors to the process management theory include Mooney and Reiley, Mary Follet, L. Urwick and Gulick.

Mooney and Reiley categorised certain principles of management that were considered to be fundamental. They are: (1) the coordination principle, (2) the scalar principle, (3) the functional principle, and (4) the staff phase of functionalism.

Mary Follet educated at Harvard and Cambridge was of the view that her principles were common to all spheres of administration. Follet stated four fundamental principles of organisation, *viz.,* (1) coordination by direct contract, (2) coordination in the early stages, (3) coordination as the reciprocal relating of all factors in a situation, and (4) coordination as a continuing process.

L. Urwick and L. Gulick also made some contributions to the process management theory. They emphasised the functional or process approach to management. They synthesized the ideas of various writers on the process management theory and indicated the probability of the science of management.

Evaluation of Process Management Theory

Approaches to Management Thought: There is no confirmation theory of management. It has changed from time to time. Important ones are as follows.

- Process approach
- Operational approach
- Behavioural approach
- Systems approach
- Contingency approach
- Attributes of excellence approach

The process management theory was mainly concerned with the conceptualisation of principles and functions of management in large organisations. This theory provided guidance on how to design an organisation. Gulick called the management functions as POSDCRBO, *i.e.*, Planning, Organisation, Staffing, Directing, Co-ordinating, Reporting and Budgeting. A study of organisation through an analysis of management function has become important because of the influence of process theory, and now many textbooks on management have been centred on management functions. This theory is considered by many social scientists as ideal bureaucracy and it enjoys all the advantages of a bureaucracy such as order, stability, certainty, etc. But this theory also suffers from certain disadvantages such as rigidity, excessive categorisation, impersonality and less scope for individualism. Some critics have stated that the principles professed by the process theory of management are only proverbs because they were based on observation and not on research.

Some of the principles stated by Fayol contradict with each other. For example, principle of unity of command and principle of specialisation cannot be followed simultaneously. If an accountant (specialist) in a marketing department is subordinate to the marketing manager, and if unity of command is observed, then the finance department cannot issue direct orders to him regarding the technical and accounting aspects of his work.

Some authors have criticised these principles on the ground that the principles are often stated as unconditional statements of what ought to be done in all circumstances when what is needed are conditional principles of management. For example, it is not correct to say that the authority and responsibility of an employee should be explicitly described in all types of environments. Because as shown by Burns and Stalker, in a technologically turbulent environment, an employee's job should be as little defined as possible, so that it can shape itself according to the changing needs of the situation.

Further, some principles (*viz.*, the principle of specialisation, chain of command, unity of direction and span of control) result into the formation of mechanistic organisation structures which are insensitive to employee's social and psychological needs. Some writers feel, that the principles stated by Fayol are based on the assumption that the organisations are closed systems. But this is not so. Organisations are open systems. Hence, the rigid structure which these principles tend to create, do not work well under unstable conditions. Further, the concept of universality of management has also been criticised. Inspite of these limitations, many of the principles of process theory of management have been applied with great success even today in all types of settings, though with some modifications.

Inspite of several criticisms leveled against Fayol's principles of management, they are relevant even today. His principles provide the learning managers an useful framework for understanding the management process.

Although it is said that Fayol's functions are more rigid, they provide a base to develop managerial process on rational lines covering concepts, techniques, situational refinements adapting modern approaches. His thinking provides as to what managers should do. "What" concept of management is addressed by Fayol's functional principles.

SCIENTIFIC MANAGEMENT

F.W. Taylor, F. Gilbreth, Lillian Gilbreth, Gantt and others have made tremendous contributions to the concept of scientific management. Of all these persons, Taylor's contribution is the most significant and because of this, he is considered as father of scientific management. We shall give here the contributions of Taylor and some others.

Scientific Management

An early management thought which tells about developing performance standards on scientific lines through systematic study and observation.

Frederick Winslow Taylor (1856-1915): Taylor worked as a chief engineer in the Midvale Steel Works where he joined as a worker. Afterwards, he worked in the Bethlehem Steel Works and after retirement from his concern, he worked as a consultant.

Taylor, the founder of scientific management movement, states that the object of management should be to secure the maximum prosperity for each employer, coupled with the maximum prosperity of each employee. According to Taylor, scientific management, in its essence, consists of a certain philosophy which results in the combination of four great principles of management, *viz.*, the development of true science, the scientific selection of workers, their development, and intimate and friendly co-operation between the management and their workmen. When management of a business unit is based on a systematic study and analysis of various aspects of work involved with a view to finding out the best way of doing things, we call it scientific management of business. Broadly speaking, scientific management is the art of knowing exactly what is to be done and the best way of doing it.

Elements of Scientific Management

1. Determination of the task.
2. Planning of industrial operations.
3. Proper selection of training of workers.
4. Improvement in methods of work.
5. Modification of organisation.
6. Mental Revolution.

Taylor observed that inefficiency prevails in the organisation because of three causes, *viz.,* (a) workers feel that any increase in output would lead to unemployment, (b) defective systems of management and because of these, each worker restricts his output in order to safeguard his interests, and (c) inefficient rule of thumb efforts and wasting methods of work.

A brief explanation of these elements are as follows:

1. Determination of the task

This invoices determination of day's work for an average worker after making a thorough scientific investigation. The task is set on the basis of following studies:

(a) Method study, (b) Routing, (c) Motion study, (d) Time study, (e) Fatigue study, (f) Rate setting.

Method study: A preliminary survey of condition of production process to familiarise with the tools, methods and operations, collecting data on plant profile, *viz.*, speed etc., to avoid adverse production conditions and avoiding unnecessary operations.

Routing: Preparation of a sheet showing exact route for each task, the shop floor in which it is to be performed and also showing the sequence of operations.

Motion study is the study of movement of men and machine with the purpose of eliminating useless motions and arranging useful motions in sequence of operations.

Time study is a study of time in relation to task which involves, observation of time taken to finish a task, determining standard time for completing a task avoiding indefiniteness and creating a base for settling piece-rate.

Fatigue study is a study of exhaustiveness of workers to fix rest time and at what intervals rest should be given.

Rate setting is a study to fix differential wage plan to workers to motivate them to work to their full capacity and complete the task as per standard.

2. Planning of industrial operation

This involves the planning of production so that the work goes on systemically. This requires the taking of decisions such as —

(1) What work shall be done?, (2) How the work shall be done?, (3) Where the work shall be done? and (4) When the work shall be done?

3. Proper selection and training of workers

This step involves proper selection of workers by the central personnel department (instead of by the foreman) with the help of specialists like psychologists, engineers, etc. Proper selection of workers would lead to increase in efficiency. Further, on the basis of the aptitude and skill of workers, correct placements are given to them. In addition, management has to undertake the training of workers before allotting them to certain tasks.

4. Improvements in methods of work

In order to make the workers complete the job, as per the conditions set by the management, there is a need for improvement in the methods of work. Improvement in methods of work includes the standardisation of tools and equipments, speed, condition of work, materials and symbols. Taylor stated that output by man and machine can be increased easily by improving methods of work rather than by simply goading workmen at each stage.

5. Modification of organisation

Under old type of organisation, usually one foreman was in charge of a number of workers and workers were directly under his control. Under scientific management, Taylor suggested functional foremanship which involves appointment of eight functional foremen. They are:

1. *Route clerk:* His job is to prepare the sequence of operations and the route,
2. *Instruction card clerk:* His work is to give instructions to workers as to how work is to be done,

3. *Time and cost clerk:* His work is to give necessary information to workmen regarding time and rate for each job,
4. *Gang boss:* His job is to look to the preparatory part of the work,
5. *Speed boss:* His work is to maintain proper speed of both machines and men,
6. *Repair boss:* His job is to make immediate necessary repairs if there is any breakdown,
7. *Inspector:* His work is to maintain the quality of work, and
8. *Shop disciplinarian:* His work is to maintain discipline among the workers.

6. Mental revolution

Taylor has suggested that for the success of scientific management, there should be a thorough change in the mental outlook of both the employees and the employer and their mutual hostility and suspicion should give place to co-operation and goodwill. Further, the workers must change their attitude towards their work as well as their employers.

The other contributions to the scientific management movement were F. Gilbreth, H.L. Gantt and Emerson.

F. Gilbreth and Lillian Gilbreth: F. Gilbreth and his wife Lillian Gilbreth, made pioneering efforts in the field of motion study and laid the entire foundation of our modern application of job simplification, incentive wage plans, work standards and better work methods, F. Gilbreth is regarded as the father of motion study. Lillian Gilbreth emphasised the human factor in industry and stressed psychological effects of fatigue.

H.L. Gantt (1816-1919): H.L. Gantt's contribution to scientific management includes task and bonus approach for remunerating workers, indicating more humanitarian approach, management responsibility to teach and train workers and emphasis on service rather than on profit. Gantt by his contributions made scientific management more humane.

H. Emerson (1853-1931): He was one of America's management consultant. He has advocated twelve principles of efficiency. He also suggested line and staff organisation and also different levels of efficiency plus a guaranteed minimum wage.

An Evaluation of Scientific Management

Scientific management emphasised faster and better methods of production and also increased output and efficiency. Great advances were made in the scientific management era for more efficient forms of organisation and management. Primary emphasis was on the analysis, planning and control functions related to the performance of basic tasks. It emphasis was for achieving efficiency, standardisation, specialisation and simplification.

The greatest limitation of scientific management is that it ignores human aspect of management.

Scientific management was criticised on the grounds:

1. Worker's emotions were not considered and he was measured in monetary term (more work - more wage). Stress on workers was more.

2. Taylor failed to understand complexes of human behaviour and ignored human aspect of work in an organisation.

THE HUMAN RELATIONS MOVEMENT (NEO-CLASSICAL THEORY)

Taylor's scientific management and Fayol's administrative management did not achieve complete production efficiency and workplace harmony. Managers in charge of the departments observed that the employees did not always follow predicted pattern of behaviour. There was also a feeling that the manager should take little more interest in the employees of the organisation. All these have led to the emergence of human relation movement, the real inspiration for the movement conducted from the Hawthorne Experiments which were conducted by Prof. Elton Mayo and his colleagues at the Western Electric Company's plant in Cicero, Illinois from 1927 to 1932. The plant employed 29,000 workers to manufacture telephone parts and equipments. We briefly describe these experiments in the following four parts:

1. Illumination Experiments.
2. Relay Assembly Test Room.
3. Interviewing Programme.
4. Bank Wiring Test Room.

Theme of HR Movement

- A business unit is both techno-economic and social system.
- Besides monetary aspects, non-monetary aspects like mutual trust and mutual help play a major role in developing both organisation and workers.
- Replaces task-centered leadership by employee-centered, participative and democratic style of leadership.
- Informal groups along with formal authority, play major role in organisational success.
- Production norms set by workers group are to be followed by each members of the group. Otherwise defaulting employee is penalised by isolation.

Recognised Experiments Relating to Human Relations Movement

1. Illumination Experiment
2. Relay Assembly Test Room Experiment
3. Interviewing Programme
4. Banking Wiring Observation Room Experiment.

1. Illumination Experiments: This was the first phase of the study. In this phase, the impact of illumination on productivity was tested. Experiments were done on a group of workers. Their productivity was measured at various levels of illumination. But the results were erratic. The researchers who were puzzled with this result improved their methodology of experiment. This time, they formed two groups of workers in different buildings. One group called the Control Group worked under constant level of illumination and the other group called Test Group worked under changing level of illumination. The productivity of the two groups was compared and it was found that illumination affected production only marginally.

(Finding: No correlation between productivity and working conditions).

2. Relay Assembly Test Room: This phase aimed at knowing not only the impact of illumination on production but also of such other factors as length of the working day, rest hours, their frequency and duration and other physical conditions. A group of six women workers was selected for this experiment. These women workers who were friendly to each other were informed about the experiment and were asked to work in very informal atmosphere under the supervision of a researcher who acted as their friend, philosopher and guide. During the study, several variations were made in the working conditions to find which combination of conditions was most ideal for production. Researchers found that there was no relationship between the production of the group and the working conditions. Productivity went on increasing and stabilised at a high level when all the improvements were taken away and the poor pre-test conditions were reintroduced. The researchers attributed this phenomenon to the following:

(i) Feeling of importance among the girls because of their selection for the experiment.

(ii) Friendly and tension free atmosphere as a result of the relative freedom from strict supervision and rules.

(iii) High group cohesion among the workers.

(Finding: No relationship between production and rigid working conditions).

3. Interviewing Programme: In this phase, the researchers wanted to know as to what were the basic factors responsible for human behaviour at work. For this purpose, more than 2,000 workers were interviewed. First direct questions were asked relating to the type of supervision, working conditions, living conditions and so on. But the researchers observed, that the replies of the workers were guarded and hence, they changed to non-directive type of interviewing. In this type, the workers were free to talk about their favourite topics related to their work environment. This study revealed that worker's social relations inside the organisation had influence on their attitudes and behaviours.

(Findings: Workers social relationship improves productivity).

4. Banking Wiring Observation Room: This phase of research aimed at making observation of 14 men making terminal banks of telephone wiring assemblies, to determine the effect of informal group norms and formal economic incentives on productivity. It was observed that the group evolved its own production norms for each individual workers, which were made lower than those set by the management. Because of this, workers would produce only that much, thereby defeating the incentives system. This policy, saved the workers from a possible cut in their piece rates or an upward revision of their standard by the management and protected the weaker and slower workers from being criticised or removed from the job. Those workers who tried to produce more than the group norms were isolated, harassed or punished by the group.

(Finding: Human relationship through informal group play a vital role in an organisation.)

This study revealed that the informal groups play an important role in the working of an organisation. This result made the researchers to concentrate more on the human aspect of management.

Contribution and Limitations of Human Relations Movement

Contribution : The contributions of this movements are :

(1) A business organisation is not merely a techno-economic system but is also a social system. Hence, the management has to provide social satisfaction to the workers to make them to improve their productivity.

(2) There is no correlation between improved working conditions and high production.

(3) Production norms for workers are set by their group and not by the time and motion study done by any specialist.

(4) Those workers who deviate from the production norms set by the group are isolated, harassed and penalised by their co-workers.

(5) A worker does not work for money only. Non-financial factors such as affection and respect of his co-workers play a significant role in influencing his behaviour.

(6) Employee centred, democratic and participative style of supervisory leadership is more effective than task-centred leadership.

(7) As informal groups play an important role in influencing workers' behaviour, the informal group and not the individual is the dominant unit of analysis in the organisation.

Threat of HR Movement:

- The threat of this movement for all time is unionisation and agitation to improve productivity.
- Cost of HR factor is high in improving the organizational efficiency and still cannot be achieved on many occasions.

Limitations: The limitations of human relation's movement are as follows:

(1) While Taylor and Fayol ignored the human variable in their approach, the human relations writers saw only the human variable as critical and ignored other variables.

(2) This approach over-emphasises the importance of symbolic rewards and underplays the role of material rewards. But in practice generally symbolic rewards fail to achieve their objective of higher production.

(3) This approach has emphasised the importance of informal groups by describing them as a major source of satisfaction for industrial workers. But many research studies have revealed, informal groups wherever they exist, can only make the worker's day more pleasant and not his task which continuous to remain repetitive, monotonous and uncreative.

(4) This approach claims that it is employee-oriented. But actually this approach is production-oriented and not employee-oriented. Many of its techniques such as running subsidised canteens, arranging picnics for the employees, socialising with workers, trick workers into a false sense of happiness but their is no improvement in their well-being.

(5) In emergencies, where quick decisions are to be taken, human relations approach cannot work.

(6) This approach is based on wrong assumption that satisfied workers are more productive workers. Attempts to increase output by improving working conditions and the human relation skills of a manager generally do not lead to expected increased productivity.

Evaluation of Human Relations Movement

"Human Relations Approach" or otherwise called Neo-classical approach emphasises that "human factor" is the key to productivity. This is very true in today's and future organisations. Advocates of human relations approaches firmly stick to the view that technology, work rules and standards do not assure good performance at work stations. On the other hand, desired results can be obtained by motivating human factor and returning performers who are committed to organisational objectives.

Managers or executives, as they are called today, can achieve, if they care for individuals in the organisation.

This approach was criticised as "simple and vague". Critics are of the opinion that supportive supervision and good human relations will not automatically increase the morale of employees and lead to better job performance. To support this view, the results of Hawthorne studies on" behavioural approach were not fully accepted. Study revealed that "productivity was much less effected by changes in work conditions than by the attitude of the workers themselves". Experiments and theories evolved from this study are criticised today for its unacceptable methodology and inaccuracies in compiling data. But still, the study gave a clear direction that human element in the organisation is a key factor for success of the organisation.

The modern concept — "Organisation Behaviour" (OB) is a scientific extension of human relations. It attempts to "determine the cause of human work behaviour and translate the results into effective management technique". OB has become our interdisciplinary field and human psychology is in the forefront. It has created heavy impact on modern management thought which focuses on 'human' element at work.

Behavioural Science Movement

The behavioural science approach through its research studies of individual behaviour and motivation indicated the relation between morale and productivity. Behavioural science experts made a further refinement of human relations movement and also covered a much wider scope in interpersonal roles and relationships. This is also recognised as Neo-classical Theory.

The behavioural science movement which started after 1940 emphasised the importance of individuals and their interpersonal relations psychology of the individual as related to personal needs and motivation and motivational potential in people. The important contributors to the behavioural science movement are A. Maslow, F. Herzberg, V. Vroom and D.McGregor. While Maslow developed a need hierarchy to explain human behaviour within an organisation, Herzberg and Vroom developed motivational models which explained the causes of human behaviour and motivation in business. Behavioural science movement has drawn heavily on the work of Maslow to explain human behaviour and the dynamics of the motivation process. McGregor developed his two theories, *viz.*, Theory X and Y and also explained certain basic assumptions about the human element. The classical theory reflected almost all the aspects of Theory X while the behavioural approach theory of management reflected almost all the aspects of Theory Y.

Some important features of behavioural approach are :

(1) This approach attaches great weightage to participation and group decision-making.

(2) It stressed the importance of humanising the administration of the control process and encouraged the process of self-direction and control instead of imposed control.

(3) It advocated steps such as participation of employees in the management, measurement and evaluation of standards of performance, prompt information feedback to those whose performance is not satisfactory and the need for positive and reformative measures instead of punitive measures.

(4) Behaviouralists felt that while in general, the democratic participative style is desirable, the autocratic, task-oriented style may also be appropriate in certain situations.

(5) They observed that different people react differently to the same situation or react the same way to different situations. No two people are exactly alike and the manager should tailor his attempts to influence people according to their individual needs.

(6) Researchers of this approach have stated that every organisational change involves technological and social aspects and generally people resist social aspect of a change.

Elements of Neo-Classical Theories

It may be noted here that the theories stated by Taylor and Fayol are called by writers as classical theories while the theories stated by the human relations movement and the behavioural science movement are called neo-classical theories.

Issues involved in Comparative Analysis of Classical and Neo-classical Thinking:

- Individual at work
- Work groups in organisation
- Participative management
- Orientation
- Leadership
- Employee development
- Motivation

1. Individual: Neo-classical theory recognised the individual differences which were ignored by the classical theory. Every individual has emotions, feelings, attitudes, hopes, aspirations and expectations. Interpersonal relations at work, physical and economic conditions and ease at work determine productivity. The neo-classical theory advocated a package deal of motivation, including financial and non-financial incentive, to make the workers feel at ease at work and increase their productivity.

2. Work groups: An individual in a group develops social wants. As he is a social being, he develops a desire to belong and to be accepted by his work group. Informal organisation develops and management must recognise its importance and integrate it with the formal organisation. Classical theory ignored the importance of formal organisation.

3. Participative Management: Neo-classical theory suggested workers' participation in management for improving their productivity (Taylor opposed workers' participation in management). A concept which expresses the joint participation of employers and workers in building the organisation and empowering workers to assume greater control of the workplace.

4. Orientation: Classical theory was job-oriented while neo-classical theory is employee-oriented. There is a shift in managerial style from product-oriented approach to employee and group-centred approach. Classical theory was concerned with the basic needs of organisation and society whereas neo-classical approach tried to satisfy the personal security and social needs of workers. Neo-classical writers emphasised satisfaction of workers whereas the classical theory emphasised productivity.

5. Motivation: Neo-classical writers considered business organisation as a social system, and not just a techno-economic system. The employees could be motivated by social and psychological wants and not solely by economic incentives.

6. Leadership: Democratic style of leadership is essential to develop co-operative attitude of employees towards management.

7. Employee development: As there is a close connection between moral and production, neo-classical writers emphasised that management must take greater interest in employee development and workers' satisfaction.

MODERN MANAGEMENT APPROACH

In recent times, many contributions were made for the development of management science. Among them following contributions are visible:

1. Chester Bernard's Social Systems Theory
2. Quantitative or Management Science Approach
3. Systems Approach
4. Contingency Approach
5. Other Contributions

1. Social Systems Theory

This theory speaks of sociological aspects of managerial process and emphasizes the importance of leadership and communication for the executives.

Chester Bernard's book, "The Functions of an Executive" is regarded as the most influential book on management during the modern management era. It is considered as a pace-setter in management theory. His approach to management is a social systems approach. His important contributions to the management thought are:

1. Management is a social system, a system of cultural relationships. Co-operation and team spirit among the group members are necessary for the achievement of organisational objectives.
2. Bernard feels that the explanation of the concept of organisation given by the Classical school of thought does not state the features of an organisation.
3. Formal organisation represents cultural relationship of the groups working within the organisation. He has suggested that the management should encourage the development of informal organisation to serve as a means of communication to protect the individuals from the dominance and onslaught of the organisation and bring cohesion in the organisation. Both formal and informal organisation depend on each other and hence managers in managing an organisation should take into account both types of organisation.
4. He has given a new concept of authority which is termed, "Acceptance Theory of Authority." In his opinion, a person accepts authority only when four conditions are met simultaneously, *viz.,* (1) he can understand communication, (2) communication is not inconsistent with the organisational purpose, (3) it is compatible with his personal interest as a whole, and (4) he is able to comply with it.
5. According to him, an executive performs three types of functions in an organisation, *viz.,* (i) maintenance of organisational communication through formal interaction, (ii) achieving organisational purpose by securing essential service from individuals in the organisation, and (iii) formulation and definition of organisational purpose.
6. Bernard has suggested that there should be both financial and non-financial incentives to motivate people.
7. An executive, in order to become effective, should possess the qualities of a responsible leadership such as high caliber, technological competence, technical and social skills etc.

Social systems approach is very much valuable to the practicing managers. All the managers operate in a social system and the organisation can prosper if the social demands of the society in which it operates are fully recognised.

QUANTITATIVE APPROACH

> This approach focuses on the use of scientific method and quantitative techniques such as mathematical models to increase organisational success.

This is also known as Management Science approach. During World War II, Defense Department in the USA was experiencing several operational problems. In order to overcome the situation, the scientists were requested to conduct research and provide solutions for these operational problems. The scientists accepting this challenge, observed the problems, developed operational general frameworks or models, used the models and made necessary corrections and finally tested before servicing the models.

This whole process of scientific study gave way for the development of a new branch of management called "Quantitative Approach."

Quantitative approach to management is also known as Operations Research in management science. This approach which is developed after 1950 offers a systematic analysis and solution to many complex problems faced by management. For decision-making on complex issues, mathematical and stastical tools are applied by the management. Operations research is the most widely accepted branch of management science. Churchman has defined operations research "as an application of scientific method to problems arising in the operations of a system which may be represented by means of a mathematical model and the solving of these problems by resolving the equations representing the system." Operations research techniques and computers are being used to solve many complex problems concerned with strategic planning, long-range planning, production scheduling, replacement of capital equipment, inventory control, plant location, transportation and warehousing problems, etc.

Eventhough quantitative approaches to management have become very popular in modern days, their usefulness is limited. Operations research or electronic data can merely suggest the best alternative based on quantitative or mathematical data but cannot make final decisions. It is left to the manager whether or not to accept the solution suggested by quantitative approaches. It means that managerial decision involves human judgement, eventhough quantitative approaches are used. Quantitative analysis can only be a valuable supplement rather than a substitute for management.

3. Systems Approach to Management

Systems approach is based on General System Theory of Ludwing Von Bertalanffy which contains tow basic types, *viz.*, open and closed system. System means to bring together or to combine. A system is a set of interconnected and interrelated elements or component parts to achieve certain objectives. The systems approach has made a significant contribution to management discipline and practices.

Fred Luthans in his book, "Organisation Behaviour" has stated that "a system viewpoint may provide the impetus to unify management theory." By definition, it considers the various approaches, such as the process quantitative and behaviour ones as sub-systems in an overall theory of management. Thus, systems approach may succeed where the process approach has failed to lead management out of the theory jungle.

System: A system is a set of parts or components interrelated or interconnected to achieve and objective.

Open System: This system is a system which is influenced by and is constantly interacting with its environment.

Closed System: This system is not influenced by and does not interact with environment.

Management System: This is an open system whose major components are organisational input (OI), organisational process (OP) and organisational output (OO).

Some important characteristics of systems are:

(i) A system has a number of sub-systems. For example, human body which is a system has a number of sub-systems such as circulatory system, reproductive system and so on.

(ii) A system has a number of parts and sub-parts and they are mutually related to each other. A system is an interdependent framework in which parts are fitted and a change in one part will affect changes in others.

(iii) A system may be classified into two, *viz.,* (a) Closed system, and (b) Open system. A closed system has no environment and no outside system impinges on it. An open system has environment and in interacts with it. All living systems are open systems, while non-living systems are closed systems.

As management has all the characteristics of a system, it can be identified as a system. Management is a social system and it has sub-systems which are integrated to unify it as a whole. Management is an open system and it interacts with the environment and takes resources from the environment. Management adjusts to the changing environment and hence it is dynamic and adaptive. Management as a system is also multi-disciplinary and it draws and integrates knowledge from various disciplines such as economics, mathematics, statistics, operations, research, psychology, sociology, etc.

The modern management system is based on the three approaches to the management, *viz.,* (i) Classical, (ii) Neo-classical, and, (iii) Management science approach. These three approaches are integrated to arrive at an open adaptive management system. This is also called Triangular Management.

In management analysis, both closed and open system approaches are taken. The closed system which is concerned mainly with internal relationships and consistency which are represented by principles such as span of control, unity of command, etc. ignores the effects of environment and its input but does not functionally relate it to management concepts and techniques. The contingency approach to management concepts and techniques attempts to fill this gap.

CONTINGENCY APPROACH

> Contingency Approach is a management theory that lays emphasis on what managers do in practice depends upon the situation or circumstance in which they function.

Neither behavioural approach nor quantitative approach could claim universal application in real world situations. It was found that these two approaches worked only in certain situations. It is believed by many management experts that only a system-based theory could remove the deficiency of the above mentioned theories.

A business organisation is now regarded as an open and adaptive system. which is called **"contingency"** or **"situational"** approach. It can be adjusted to the demands of changing environmental situations. Situational approach recognises that all the sub-systems of an organisation and the supra-systems of environment are interconnected and interrelated, and by analysing their interrelationships, it helps the management in finding solution to specific situations. Different situations or circumstances demand different solutions.

There cannot be universal principles of organisation and management appropriate to all situations. In other words, there is one way to manage. Democratic or participative managerial style may work under certain situations and we may have to adopt an autocratic managerial style under specific circumstances. Financial incentives may be effective in one situation while non-financial incentives can work wonders under certain other situations. If the condition is X, action A may be effective and if the condition is Y, action B may be needed.

Thus, we find that the contingency theory states that the pattern of management is influenced by a number of interrelated internal and external factors, and there is no 'one best theory' of management or organisation. The situation decides the pattern of organisation and management. For example, the pattern of organisation and management that may suit a country like USA. which has a mature economy may not suit a developing country like India, where a different set of circumstances prevail.

Challenges of Contingency Approach:

- Perceiving organisational situations as they really exist.
- Adapting the best strategy suiting to the situation.
- Effective implementation of the chosen strategy.

As decisions are taken according to situations that prevails in a specific time, the theory is also called " Situational Theory of Management". This is relatively a new theory and has become popular amongst the contributors on management thought. The contributors feel and suggest that principles of management and management techniques have to be adapted considering the real-time situations in the organisation.

OTHER CONTRIBUTORS

In the recent past, a number of persons have contributed to the development of management science. We give here the contributions of some of these writers.

Oliver Sheldon: Oliver Sheldon tried to develop a complete theory of management and enunciated the principles governing its practice. His important publication was "Philosophy of Management." Management was viewed by him with these perspectives – administration, management and organisation. He has stated that 'administration' is concerned with the determination of policy, 'management' is concerned with the execution of policy and 'organisation' is concerned with combining the work of individuals of groups with faculties necessary, for its execution.

Mooney and Reiley: Mooney and Reiley have published one important book 'Principles of Organisation'. They worked mainly on the theory of organisation and put forth nine principles of organisation which occupy an important place in the modern theory of organisation and management.

Lyndall Urwick: Among the many books written by Urwick, his book, "The Elements of Administration" is an outstanding one. In fact, the real explosion in the number of principles of management came with the publication of this book. He is not an innovator in the field of management. His work actually crystallised similar concepts that have been independently developed by the other writers like Taylor, Fayol, Mooney, Reiley and other early management theorists, thereby giving them more credence and serving to mould them into a system of management thought. Some of the several principles he advocated are:

(1) There must be clear line of authority from the top management to the lowest employee.

(2) The authority and responsibility of each employee should be communicated to him in writing.

(3) Each individual should perform one function only.

(4) Authority can be delegated but not responsibility.

(5) The span of control of a manager should never exceed.

Harold Koontz and Cyril O'Donnell: These two management experts are the champions of Management Process school. They are of the opinion that management is a dynamic process of performing the functions of planning, organising, staffing, directing and controlling. They are also of the view that the management functions and principles have general or universal applicability. Managers, whether they are managing directors or supervisors, perform the same functions of planning and control although the degree of complexity may differ. Similarly, management functions are not confined to business enterprises alone but are applicable to all organisations wherever group effort is involved.

Peter Drucker

Peter F. Drucker was a management consultant and Professor of Management in the New York University. Drucker outshone all other contemporary management thinkers. He was considered as the father of modern management thought. He has written number of books on managerial topics. The more important ones are:

1. The Effective Executive (1967)
2. The Age of Discontinuity (1969)
3. Management: Tasks, Responsibilities and Practices (1974).

Peter F. Drucker – Profile

Born – November 1909 – Vienna, Australia.

Died – November 2005.

Educated in Austria and England.

Ph.D. in Public and International Law – Frankfurt University – Germany.

Career: A social ecologist, writer, consultant and retired Professor from New York University. Wrote regular columns in The Wall Street Journal, for 20 years. Wrote and published innumerable number of articles in professional journals and publications including, The Economist, Harvard Business Review, The Atlantic Monthly, Financial Times, Foreign Affairs, Fortune Inc. and Harpers.

As a consultant, Dr. Drucker specialised in strategy and policy for governments, businesses, and non-profit organisations.

Special focus was on the organisation and work of top management. Part of his life, he worked extensively with non-profit organisations.

A top consultant for US, Canada and Japnese governments of the world.

Academic Career

- Served as Professor of Philosophy-Bennington College Bennington, Vermont, 1942-1949.
- Professor at Graduate School of Management at New York University, 1949-1971.
- Clarke Professor of Social Science and Management at Clarament Graduate University in Clarament-California, 1971-2002.

In 1987, CGU named its graduate school of management after him.

Now it is Peter F. Drucker and Mastoship Ito Graduate School of Management.

Established, Peter Drucker Research Library and Archive at CGU.

Received highest civilian honour "Presidential Medal of Freedom" from US Government in 2002. He holds 25 honorary doctorates from American, Belgian, Czech, English, Spanish and Swiss Universities. From 1955 to 1960, served as the President of Society for the History of Technology.

1. The Practice of Management (1954)
2. Managing by Results (1964)

In his early career, Drucker was an economist for an international bank in London. American economist for a group of British and European Banks.

Drucker's Thinking on Management: "Management is an art – a liberal art which includes History, Economics, Social Theory, Law and The Sciences".

It deals with "People, their values, their growth and development, social structure, the community and even spiritual concerns........ the nature of mankind good and evil".

He contributed "Knowledge Workers" concept.

Important Contributions of Drucker

1. Drucker is against bureaucratic management and he emphasises on management with creative and innovative characteristics.
2. He treats management as a discipline as well as a profession. He considers management more a practice rather than a science.
3. According to him, a manager has to perform several functions: setting of objectives, decision-making, organising and motivating. But he attaches great importance to the objective-setting function.
4. He advocates the replacement of bureaucratic structure because it has many dysfunctional effects.
5. He advocates centralised control and decentralised structure.
6. He also advocates the concept of Management by Objectives (MBO). The MBO includes the method of planning, setting standards, performance appraisal and motivation. According to Drucker, MBO is not only a technique of management but it is a philosophy of managing. MBO has become such popular way of managing that today it is regarded as the most modern management approach. In fact, it has revolutionised the management process.

Contemporary Thinkers

Peters and Waterman: Thomas J. Peters and Robert H. Waterman Jr., two management consultants released a book in 1982 titled **"In Search of Excellence".** This book tried to explain how best-run companies in America are following the success methods. Although the management experts did not fully agree with the viewpoints of Peters and Waterman, the book gave sufficient food to thinkers on management. The factors explained in the book were considered to be the remedy for productivity problems. The very fact that 5 million copies were sold in first five years of publication worldwide is the testimony for the guidelines given in the book for the success of business enterprises.

The approach to management theory in this book was unconventional. The writers said that the earlier thinking on management was "too conservative, unemotional, inflexible, negative and pre-occupied with bigness."

They also opined that terms in management like planning, control etc. were conventional and the Modern American Corporate World, instead used the terms like "Do it", "fix it", "try it" etc.

Successful managers were using stories to analyse their critical issues and to explain vital points.

Peters and Waterman, conducted a detailed survey of about sixty companies which were managed well for over twenty years with innovative ideas and making steady profit. After this survey, they identified about **eight key factors** which were mainly responsible for the success of these companies which included, IBM, McDonalds, Cater Pillar, Delta Airlines, 3M, Johnson and Johnson etc. These eight factors were not present in the same degree in all the successful companies subjected to survey. But they were clearly visible.

These eight vital factors were considered as the latest approach to the management. But they were also critised vehemently by many observers and subsequent researchers. However, the view points of Peters and Waterman are the guiding factors to the present executives to attain excellence in their operations. Therefore this was termed as **"Excellence Approach"** to management which may be a part of contingency approach.

The Eight Key Factors of Peters and Waterman

1. **Bias for Action:** Managers adopted small experiments to develop knowledge among workers. They involved in all areas of work personally and visibly. This was called "Management by wandering around (MBWA)".
2. **Customer Feedback:** Customers' opinions could be found in design/production/marketing cycle. This was practiced to delight customers.
3. **Autonomy and Entrepreneurship:** Employees were encouraged to take risk and the failure was tolerated. Innovative employees were encouraged to complete their innovations. Small team of zealous innovators called SKUNK WORKERS were allowed to work on special projects. Creativity of employees were motivated.
4. **People Prominance:** "Productivity through people" was the practice in all successful companies. HR practices were to the core. Individuals were treated with respect and

dignity. Mutual trust and family feeling were fostered. A relaxed atmosphere was always there with fun to achieve something big. Work units were small and humane.

5. **Hands-on, Value Driven:** The philosophy of the company was clearly disseminated and followed. Individual values were openly discussed and not ignored. The belief system of the organisation is strengthened by continuous sharing of legends, myths and stories. The leaders were positive in their approach. They were not "Do-as-I-say, not-as-do" authoritarians.
6. **Stick to the Knitting:** Management does not encourage mergers and strongly insist on internal growth. Organisation sticks to the business it knows best.
7. **Simple Structure Thin Staff:** Decentralisation of authority is to the maximum. Staff at head office is very thin and entire talent is pushed to the field.
8. **Operation of Loose-Tight Activities Simultaneously:** Organisations had tight control over financial and strategic activities. But it is counter balanced by decentralised authority, autonomy and opportunity for creativity.

Adapted: "Eight Attributes of Excellence" from "In Search of Excellence" by Thomas J. Peters and Robert H. Waterman.

Jack Welsh:

Born in the year 1935, Jack Welsh started his career in 1957 and joined GE in 1960. One of the top management Gurus of the day, Jack Welsh, during twenty year reign as chairman and CEO of General Electric (GE), one of America's largest and most well-known companies, developed many management skills, which become almost legendary. In the process of making GE "the world's most competitive enterprise." Jack Welsh knew that it was a tough job, as bureaucracy ruled the day when he took over its administration in 1981. But still he believed that it will be a sort of "Management Revolution" in GE, which will give many contributions to the management world. The effort of Jack Welsh made GE to possess an unique learning culture and become a **boundaryless organisation.** Practices introduced in GE by Jack Welsh have become recognised contributions to the management world. His main contribution to management thought was is on leadership which is called "Management by Leadership".

Contents of his contribution are as follows:

1. **Lead More:** (i) Lead, (ii) Manage, (iii) Articulate your vision, (iv) Simplicity, and (v) Get less formal.
2. **Manage Less:** (i) Energize others, (ii) Face Reality, (iii) See change as an opportunity- (iv) Get good ideas from every where and (v) Follow-up.
3. **Build a Winning Organisation:** (i) Get red of bureaucracy, (ii) Eliminate Boundaries, (iii) Put values first, (iv) Cultivate leaders and (v) Create learning culture
4. **Harness your people:** Involve every one, (ii) Make everybody a team player, (iii) Stretch targets, (iv) Instill confidence and (v) Make business fun.
5. **Build the market-leading company:** (i) Be number 1 or number 2, (ii) Live quality, (iii) Constantly focus on innovation, (iv) Live speed and (v) Behave like a small company.

His most admired book "WINNING" along with SUZY WELSH contains his thoughts on management .

Winning organisation is a comparatively low-cost efficient in method of operation to save customer time as well as money and adapting flexibility in operation to serve multilingual, multicultural, multichannel, and multicurrency environment.

Being strong advocate of "Learning organisation," Jack Welsh says, "Keep learning. Don't be arrogant by assuming that you know it all, that you have a monopoly in the truth. Always assume that you can learn something from someone else or from another GE business or from a competitor. Especially from a competitor."

Welsh transformed routing meetings into rousing debate sessions and launched initiatives such as the Six sigma quality process and the "workout approach" to tam problem-solving that reached particularly every employee (direct or indirect) around the world.

He is of the opinion that "Generation-Y" are driven, thoughtful and open-minded in a way that will be great for their careers and for the entire economy. One thing he has deduced from his meeting with "Gen Y" management students is that many want to win through becoming entrepreneurs, adapting **ethics and social responsibility** in their respective business entities. Jack feels that the future management of business would be lying in the hands of "Gen Y"ers of every economy will emerge as great economies. To put in his words "Gen Y, besides winning themselves, boost the economy in the years to come".

"Generation Y" (Gen Y) is the generation born after baby boomer and baby bust.

Baby boomer is some body born during baby boom generation, *i.e.,* born in UK and USA in the late 1940s and early 1950s.

Baby bust is the generation after 1950s.

Contributors on Quality

> **Quality**
>
> The intrinsic worth of a product or service, measured in terms of user's expectations, *i.e.*, how closely and reliably it satisfies the specifications to which it is produced or the degree of excellence on which products or service can be ranked.

As business activities are stretching to global domain, "Quality" has become the main mantra in business processes. In last decades of twentieth century, quality concept occupied the front line in business operations. In this century, it is the order. When Japan started sweeping the US market in late 1980's business people of the US started thinking that "quality" is the factor for the success of business. The quality concept took its roots first in manufacturing and trade sectors and gradually started percolating to every activity of human life. Today, majority of the countries give top priority for quality operations. The thinkers who strongly advocated the introduction of quality concept in business operations are:

(i) Kaouru Ishiwaka, (ii) Walter A. Shewhart,
(iii) W. Edward Deming, (iv) Joseph. M. Juran,
(v) Philip B. Crosby, (vi) Armand V. Feigenbaum,
(vii) Stephen Covy, (viii) David Aller.

KAORU ISHIKAWA

Company-wide Quality – CWQ

CWQ is a concept which tells about the continuous process of involving all organisation members in ensuring that every activity related to the production of goods and services, has an appropriate role in establishing product quality.

A Tokyo University Professor, Kaoru Ishikawa founded the Union of Japanese Scientists and Engineers (JUSE) before World War II. This Union started working on quality concept and became a driving force for quality revolution in Japan. Ishikawa's customer concept comprised both internal and external customers and said that quality alone will bring success to business. He developed a diagram called "Fishbone Diagram" showing the routes for attaining quality. Company-wide Quality (CWQ) was the concept developed in the USA and widely accepted in Japan for quality development. JUSE propagated CWQ.

Fishbone Diagram

Which looks like a fish in shape is a picture which shows the cause and effect of an operation. The aspects involved in the diagram are environment, methods, materials, machine, and people.

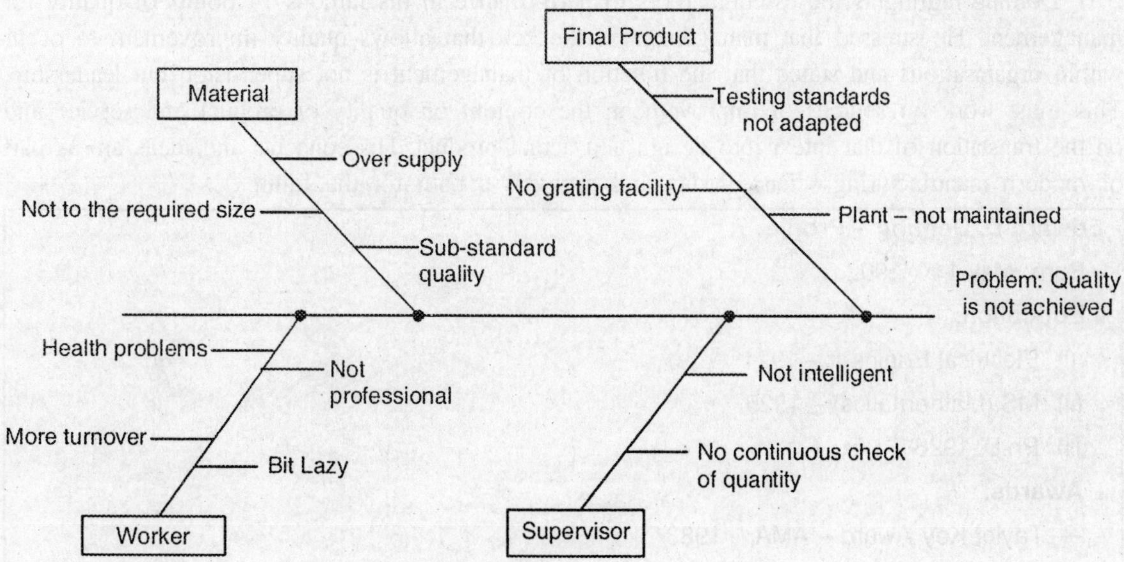

FIG. 3.1 Fishbone Diagram

How to Construct?

- Convert complex problem to distinct high priority problem.
- Develop fishbone for major causes.

- Show most recent causes nearest to the problem.
- Write specific causes.

WALTER A. SHEWHART

W.A. Shewhart was a statistician at Bell Laboratories. Working on quality control, he introduced "Economic Control of quality of Manufacturing Product" in 1931. It is popularly known as "Statistical Quality Control" (SQC). SQC helped workers to keep important quality measurements with in an acceptable range. A control chart was developed and used to observe actual operations with desired quality measurements. This control process chart paved way for controlling cost and improving quality in operations. Thus, Shewhart contributed for "quality control" — an effective management concept.

W. EDWARD DEMING (1900 – 1993)

Statistical Quality Control

Statistically measuring the quality of finished goods or service, what it was planned to be.

Dr. W. Edward Deming is known as the father of quality movement. His model focused on 14 points to achieve quality, productivity and competitive position. His overall philosophy focused on management's obligations and commitment to quality.

Deming highlights the essential roots to performance in his famous 14 points of quality for management. He stressed that management is the key that allows quality improvement to occur within organisations and stated that the function of management is not supervision but leadership. This must work on sources of improvement, the content on quality of product and service and on the translation of that intext into design and actual product. His concepts and ideas are as part of modern manufacturing science today and provides a path for the future.

Edward D. Deming – Profile

- Born: May 11th, 1902
- **Education:**
  - (i) Electrical Engineer – 1921
  - (ii) MS (Mathematics) – 1925
  - (iii) Ph.D.,1928
- **Awards:**
  - — Taylor Key Award – AMA – 1983
  - — Recipient of second order medal from Emperor of Japan
  - — Shewart Medal – 1985 of American Society for Quality Control
  - — Samuel, S. Wilks Award from American Statistical Association – 1983
  - — National Academy of Sciences – 1988
  - — National Medal of Technology from the President or the USA – 1987

- **Honours**
  - —American Society for Quality Control installed "Deming Medal" – an annual award for improvement and productivity
  - —Union of Japanese Scientists and Engineers (JUSE) instituted Deming Prize in three areas
  - —Deming Application Prize (for enhanced performance through TQM)
  - —Deming Prize for individual scholar for application of TQM
  - —Quality Control Award (for exceptional implantation of TQM)

Deming, in his book "Out of the Crisis," brings out his fourteen point model on quality. They are presented (only concepts), here.

14 Points of Deming on Quality

1. **Create constancy of purpose** towards product and service with the aim to become competitive and to provide jobs.
2. Adopt new philosophy for new economic age. Western management must awaken to the change, must learn their responsibilities and take on **leadership for change.**
3. **Cease dependence on inspection** to achieve quality. Eliminate the need for inspection on a mass basis by building quality into the product in the first place.
4. End the practice of awarding business on the basis of price tag, **minimise total cost,** move toward a single supplier for any one item, on a long-term relationship of loyalty and trust.
5. **Improve constantly** and forever the system of production and service, to improve quality and productivity, and thus constantly decrease costs.
6. **Institute training on the job.**
7. **Institute leadership.** The aim of supervision should be to help people and machines and gadgets to do a better job. Supervision of management is in need of overhaul as well as supervision of production workers.
8. **Drive out fear**, so that everyone may work out effectively for the company.
9. **Break down barriers** between departments, people in research, sales, and production must work as a team, to foresee problems of production and in use that may be encountered with the product or service.
10. Eliminate slogans, exhortations and target for the work force asking for zero defects and new levels of productivity. Such exhortations only create adversarial relationships, as the bulk of the causes of low quality and low productivity belong to the system and thus lie beyond the power of the workforce.
11. (a) **Eliminate work standards** (quotas) on the factory floor. Substitute leadership.
    (b) Eliminate management by objective. Eliminate management by numbers, numerical goals. Substitute leadership.
12. (a) Remove barriers that rob the hourly workers of his right to **joy of workmanship**. The responsibility of supervisors must be changed from sheer numbers to quality.

(b) Remove barriers that rob people in management and in engineering of their right to joy of workmanship. This means **abolishment of the annual merit rating** and management by objective.

13. Institute a vigorous programme of education and self-improvement.

14. Put everybody in the company to work to accomplish the transformation. The transformation is everybody's job.

***Source:** Original – Out of The Crisis – Edward B. Deming. Excerpts: Indian Management – May 2004.*

Deming's website (www.deming.org) reveals his philosophy in "The Best of W. Edward Deming's Philosophy". Excerpts are given here.

- The prevailing style of management must undergo transformation. A system cannot understand itself. The transformation requires a view from outside.
- The first step is transformation of individual which is discontinuous. It can be understood from profound knowledge. Transformed individual will perceive new meaning to his life, to events, to members, to interactions to people and it in his workplace.
- Profound knowledge to be acquired by the individual for transformation involves appreciation of knowledge about variation and knowledge of theory of psychology. These aspects have to be interacted with each other.
- The person who manages people should know at the outset all people under him are different. This is not ranking people. He needs to understand that the performance of any one is governed largely by the system that he works in, *i.e.,* the responsibility he has to discharge, fixed by the management.
- Information provided by manager to top management in the form of statistical and accounting figures should be genuine. Statistical and accounting calculations and predictions based on warped figures may lead to confusion, frustration and wrong decisions.
- A leader of transformation and managers involved should understand the psychology of individuals, of the group, of the society and the psychology of change.
- Some understanding of variation including appreciation of a stable system, and some understanding of special causes and common causes of variation are essential for a management of a system, including management of people.

Ever since, he started advising Japanese industries and war torn economy in 1950, Japan never looked back and gradually posed threat to American economy. Thus, Dr. Edward D. Deming contributed immensely to the world of management. He was a good musician and composer. His Gospel – Survival is optional.

Dr. Joseph M. Juran

Born: December 24, 1904, Romania, Emigrated to US,1912.

Education

- BS (Elect) – 1924.
- Law degree – Loyola University
- Hon. Doctorate in Engineering – 1988 from Stevens Institute of Technology
- 3 honorary Doctorate in 1992

Founder

- Juran Centre for leadership in Quality – 1979

Books

- Statistical Methods applied to manufacturing problems – 1928
- Conceptualized Pareto Theory – 1941
- Quality Control Handbook – 1951
- Management Breakthrough – 1964
- Quality Trilogy (Focus on Quality Planning) – 1986.
- 13 medals from various universities and Associations of USA
- 6 medals from foreign Associates

Joseph Moses Juran is an advocate of **quality.** There has been a similarity of thinking and operation with that of Deming. Juran is a Romanian born US citizen. From the day he entered to workstation, Juran has created a richly varied career as writer, educator and consultant. He contributed to the management thought on "Quality" aspects. He has been called **"Quality Guru"** and **"Father of Quality".** After completing his long service at Western Electric and other place, he started visiting Japan to deliver lecturers on quality development and taught "quality" to the Japanese. He is recognised as the person added the human dimension to quality, broadening it from its statistical origins to what now called "Total Quality Management." He worked as a business consultant in 40 countries besides his teaching career in New York University.

Although Juran has received less exposure, his impact on managers, business, nations and the products has been profound. He is a great contributor to quality movement and says "that quality has two aspects. The first relates to features. Higher quality means a greater number of features that meet customers' needs. The second aspect relates to 'freedom from trouble.' Higher quality consists of fewer defects. But is simple to know that achieving higher quality is no simple task."

In 1941, Juran conceptualised the "Pareto Principle", named after the Italian economist Vilfredo Pareto, which provided a technique for separating major problems from minor problems. It analyzes **that 20 per cent of possible causes lead to 80 per cent of all problems.** This principle made managers rely on to help separate the 'vital few' from 'vital many' in their activities. His book on quality control handbook published in 1951 analysed various dimensions of quality control through general theories on quality control. His book "Managerial Breakthrough" presented a more general theory of quality management comprising quality control and quality improvement. Thousands of managers who have learnt from Juran speak of his ideas with respect, that transcends appreciating his capabilities in quality development asserts that "whatever advances American manufacturing has made in the last thirty to forty years, we owe to Joe Juran and to his Untiring, steady, patient self-effacing work." In Japan, his lectures on quality management were delivered soon after Edward Deming delivered lectures on statistical quality methods.

Pareto Principle

A principle named after Italian economist **Vilfredo Pareto,** which provides a technique to separate major problems from minor problems.

Thus, Joseph Juran's thinking and the scope of his influence on business leaders, legions of managers and his fellow theorists worldwide recognise him as one of "The vital few" figures in the development of management theory. But he says that "it would not bother me if I am not remembered at all."

Philip. B. Crosby (1926-2001)

Born: June 18,1976.

Left this world : 18 Aug. 2001

Career:

A businessman. Started his managing consulting firm after serving at ITT, in 1979.

Works:

One book titled " Quality is Free" 14 research articles on various dimensions of quality from 1967 to 1999.

During the late 1970s and into the 1980s, American manufactures had to compete with Japanese quality products. American products were virtually losing their markets. At this point of time, Philip B. Crosby, released his book came as "Silver line in the dark cloud." Crosby said that the solution to quality crisis is "doing it right the first time – (DIRFT)."

The title provided the following four principles to improve quality.

1. The definition of quality is conformance to requirements.
2. The system of quality is prevention.
3. The performance standard is zero defects.
4. The measurement of quality is the price of nonconformance.

His thinking was that a company that adopts quality programmes and activities will see savings more that pay off the cost of quality programme.

His concept of quality was that a product or service should meet and satisfy the expectations of the customers. If the customers are satisfied, the product is considered to be qualitative one.

He explained "14 step quality improvement process." "Zero Defects" is the 7th step in that process. Although applicable to any type of enterprise, it was mainly adopted in supply chains wherever large volumes of components are being purchased.

Zero Defect

A concept developed by P.B. Crosby to explain the huge cost involved redoing a work or a process and said that if a process managed without defect or doing every activity right, the cost can be saved. Zero defect reduces the process cost.

Being a promoter of 'quality' concept in manufacturing, his "Zero Defect" idea caught the minds of many manufactures.

Armand. V. Feigenbaum

Born: 1922

Education: Ph.D. – MIT

Career: Engineer and Quality Control Expert

President and CEO: General System Company – Pittsfield MAS

President: American Society for Quality – 1961-1963

Message for Management

TQC – Total Quality Control "Quality is everybody's job and, it may become nobody's job"

Awards and Honours:

— ASQ's Lancaster Award.

— ASQ's Edwards Medal – 1965

— National Security Industrial Award of Merit – for leadership in defense of the nation

— Member - Advisory Group – US Army

— Founders Medal – Union College

— Fellow American Association for the Advancement of Science Books

— Quality Control: Principles Practice and Administration (McGraw-Hill)

— Power of Management Capital (McGraw-Hill)

— Total Quality Control (McGraw-Hill Professional)

Armand V. Feigenbaum's name is synonymous to "Total Quality Control." In his long career in quality field, the percepts of total quality control were carefully laid out and it was practiced in the US and other countries of the world.

Feigenbaum's quality ideas are portrayed in his need book "Total Quality Control." This was first published in 1951, under the title "Quality Control: Principles, Practice and Administration." This book is translated into many languages of the world including Japanese, Chinese, French and Spanish.

Working as CEO of General Systems Co. which designs and installs operational systems in the US, Europe, the Far East and Latin America, he has spent more time on quality control. He has been a leading voice on the international view, in the field of quality control and quality management.

Feigenbaum is recognised as an "Innovator" in the area of quality cost management. He is the first person to characterise quality costs as the costs of prevention, appraisal and internal as well as external failure.

Having contributed to quality management concept, Feigenbaum is recognised as "The originator of basic foundations for modern quality control."

He says that "total approach to quality requires the involvement of all functions of the quality process, not only manufacturing." He stresses that "build quality in the early stage rather than inspecting and controlling after the processes have been completed."

Stephen Covy

Born: October 24, 1932

Education:

— BS in Business Administration

— MBA – Harvard University

— DRE – Mormon Church History and Doctrine from Brigham Young University

Career

— Taught in Brigham Young University

— Established the Covy Leadership Centre – 1997

— Later Merged with Franklin Covy – A global professional service which provides training and productivity tools to individuals and organisations.

Books:

— Spiritual Roots of Human Relations – 1970

— The Divine Centre – 1982

— The Seven Habits of Highly Effective People – 1989

— Principle Centered Leadership – 1992

— First Things First – 1994 (Coauthored with Roger and Rebecca)

— Living The Seven Habits – 2000

— 6 Events: The restoration model for solving life problems – 2004

— The 8th Habit: From Effectiveness to Greatness – 2004

7 Habits

- **Habit-1. Be Proactive:** Principles of Personal Vision
- **Habit-2. Begin with the End in Mind:** Principle of Personal Leadership
- **Habit-3. Put Fist Things First:** Principle of Personal Management
- **Habit-4. Thinking Win-Win:** Principle of Interpersonal Leadership
- **Habit-5. Seek First to Understand then to be Understood:** Principle of empathic communication
- **Habit-6. Synergize:** Principle of creative communication
- **Habit-7. Shapen the Saw:** Principle of balanced staff renewal

Stephen Covy is a noted contributor to the management thoughts. Covy in his works emphasise that leadership qualities of managers in business place have taken roots in the family life of leaders/managers. He exhibits a central philosophical ideal which some would consider it as conservative. He is a theoligist.

His book "The Seven Habits of Highly Effective People" focuses on corporate executives. He opposes "quick-fix" methods to solve business problems. Changes in mindset of executives to align with natural principles is required to get real solutions for their problems. "Quick-fix" solutions are of short in nature and they cannot lead business to produce results for the long-term productive capabilities.

The book "Seven Habits of Highly Effective People" has sold more than 15 million copies world wide since its publication in 1989. the book more or less conveys the ideas of Peter Drucker stated in "The Effective Executive." Covy says that "Effectiveness is a habit." He argues against "The Personality Ethic" which aligns one's values with "Universal and time less principles." He bifurcates principles and values. Whereas principle is an external natural law, value is internal and subjective. Value governs people behaviour but principles ultimately determine the consequences. Covy presents his opinion in a series of habits, manifesting as a progression from dependence, to independence to interdependence. His book "The 8th Habit: From Effectiveness to Greatness" (2004) is sequel to "Seven Habits". Covy opines that in a "Knowledge Society," being effective is not enough. The challenges and complexity faced today are of a different magnitude. Therefore, "Find your voice and inspire others ot find theirs."

Thus, his contribution to management thought is that leaders have to develop the concept of empathy and lead the team on value based principles for the success of the organisations.

David Allen

Born: Dec. 28,1945

Education: At New College of Florida

Career:

Served many organisation of carried type and understood the concept of management –Getting Things Done

Founder

David Allen Company which trains people on "Productivity"

Books:

— Getting Things Done — The art of Stress-free productivity

— Ready For Anything — 52 productivity principles for work and life

David Allen is a contributor on productivity. A productivity consultant David Allen is the creater of the "Getting Things Done." He claims to have had 35 professions before the age of 35. He is recognised as "Productivity Guru." Having understood the varied dimensions of several professions he focuses in his book on "Productivity" of worker and time management.

Allen says that he wrote the book to encapsulate the system he had developed in working with various organisations. Speaking an productivity in various seminars and workshops presented his system for "Mastering Workflow."

INDIAN CONTRIBUTORS

Many Indians have contributed for the development of management process. Even Indian Epics such as Mahabaratha, Ramayana and Bhagavathgeetha have greatly contributed for the development of management thought. Four Vedas throw light on management thought. Lord Krishna has been recognised as a great strategic manager. Bhagavathgeetha (Divine Songs) is more secular in preaching and is relevant for all times to manage. Historically speaking, "Artha Shastra" of Chanakya gives an insight into many management issues. Besides throwing light on managing a kingdom (an economy) including man management, Chanakya sutras deal with the principles of management. They cover the management aspects such as Rajaniti, good behaviour in a civilised society, establishing a governing hierarchy, recruiting people for different occupations and specific jobs, framing tax-laws, ethical aspects of business, alliances, enforcement, resources, working methods, work accomplishment and role of manager, human relations, managerial actions, wealth and desires, character, mistakes, enthusiasm, our own people engaged in our business. (We strongly recommend to read the work of Ashok R. Garde on "Chanakya on Management" published by Jaico Publishing House to understand the Artha Shastra of Koutilya another name for Chanakya).

Sutra is a short, pithy statement or an aphorism about a concept

Many advanced countries in the world have developed their management principles according to their environment and work culture. But Koutilya's Artha Shastra is the oldest literature on management in the world (330 BC). The management practices developed in other countries have taken roots from Koutilya's work.

Other recognized works such as "Analects" of Confucious (China – 430 BC) "Politics" of Aristotle (Greece – 350 BC) are later ones which throw light on management thought.

"Panchatantra" taught to three princes by Vishnu Sharma in 200 BC also throws certain light on management thought. But Chanakya is considered as "First Management Guru" of the world. He taught these management principles to some youths, including Chandra Gupta, who over threw Nanda dynasty of Paataliputra who were very oppressive and established, Mourya dynasty. This conversion bears testimony to power of management sutras taught by Chanakya and are more relevant (because of their secular approach) even today in the management world.

Many rulers who ruled Bhaarat have given sufficient inputs for the development of management thought. After Industrial Revolution, business houses such as Tata and Birla through their innovative business practices have contributed for the development of "Management" as a science who are living legends focusing on India. We too have prominent contemporary "Management Gurus." In recent times, following are recognised as prominent management Gurus. These personalities, before being called contemporary management trend-setters, have studied, travelled, worked, operated, managed and made their presence felt in many parts of the globe.

1. Sumantro Ghoshal
2. C.K. Prahalad
3. Ram Charan
4. Gita Piramal
5. Promod Batra
6. Shiv Khera
7. Arindam Chauduri
8. Debashish Chatterjee

1. Sumantro Ghoshal (1948 -2004)

Sumantro Goshal — A Profile

Born: 1948

Education: Graduate, Delhi University and Indian Institute of Social Welfare and Business Management

Career:

Before moving to USA worked for Indian Oil Corporation.

Achievements

— Fulbright Scholar – 1981

— Achieved two Ph.Ds.: (i) MIT Sloan School of Management, (ii) Harvard Business School

— Joined INSE AD – France – 1985

— London School of Business in 1994 as Professor of Strategic and International Management

— Fellow of Advanced Institute of Research and Management UK

— Served as a member of the Committee of Oversees of Harvard Business School

Books and Publication:

Produced seven books Published over forty-five articles

Award

Management Book of the year Award for his book "Managing Radical Change" Economist – A leading international magazine described him as EUROGURU"

Left for Permanent abode - March, 3, 2004

His Works

1. ***A Bias for Action***: How effective managers harness their will power, achieve results and stop wasting time (7-1-2004)
2. ***Managing Across Borders:*** The Transnational Solution (1988)
3. ***Transnational Management: (1990)***
4. ***Organisational Theory and Multinational Corporation (1993)***
5. ***The Individual Corporation (1997)***
6. ***World Class in India:*** A case book of Companies in Transformation
7. ***Managing Radical Change***

(*Book 2, 3, 4 and 5 are coauthored with Christopher A. Bartlet and Book 7 is co-authored with Gita Piramal*)

"Theory that managers cannot be relied upon by shareholders can make managers less reliable."

– Sumantro Ghoshal

Sumantro Ghoshal, born in India, educated in the USA and lived in Europe in his last days. He was a great teacher, author and consultant in the field of international management. He was also founding Dean of the Indian School of Business, Hyderabad.

He was a close associate of many leading management thinkers of the world. In association with and independently contributed many gospels to the management thought. His early demise denied management thinking of one of its most innovative and influential thinkers.

He was a rare combination of idealist, contrarians and intellectual and it was the interplay between these attributes that allowed him to make such an influential mark on the practice of management. He visualised the Universe as it could be, rather than as it were.

His thinking domains were strategy, organisations and management. Through intensive research, he deduced his opinions to reveal a defining view of management. Drawing thoughts from economics, sociology, psychology and philosophy, explained the role of the organisation in shaping human activity and modern corporate behaviour. Particularly he focused on the behaviour of managers to fully use their energy to fulfil the objective of the organisation with responsibility.

He felt that business units are creative and versatile amplifiers of human will and effort across natural and cultural boundaries. He desired these managers should be responsible and reflective leaders. He was of the opinion that better management theory learnt at business schools will be the genuine root of positive practices adopted in organisations.

His treatment of management issues at the level of individual led him to conclude that management theory that focuses on the economic aspects of man to the exclusion of all others is incorrect at best. He was of the opinion that a theory which assumes that managers cannot be relied upon by shareholders, can make managers less reliable. He said that such theory would become self-fulfilling prophecy. This opinion made him a controversial person. He was a contrarian. But to his last breath, he fought against the narrow idea that led to today's management a parody of the human condition more appropriate to a prison or mad house than an institution which should be a "force for good."

He along with Christopher Bartlett, on the basis of strategic competences categorized international enterprises as: (i) Multinational, (ii) Global, and (iii) International. But said that fast changing environment forces the organisations to combine the strategic competencies of multinational, global and international enterprises to become *"Transnational Enterprise."*

The world in general and India in particular, lost a great management thinker.

2. C.K. Prahalad

C. K. Prahalad — A Profile

Education

— B.Sc. – 1960, Madras University

— MBA – IIM Ahmedabad

— Ph.D. – Harvard University

Career:

— Manager — Union Carbide — 4 years — Faculty – IIMA

— Professor at Stephen M. Ross School of Business. University of Michigan

Area of Recognition:

— Corporate Strategy

Honours and Awards:

— Management Guru (Suntop Media, 2007 – UK)

— Harvard Business Review Awarded him the 'McKinsey Prize" three times for his articles on different topics.

— 2009 Awards: (i) Padma Bhushan – GOI (ii) Pravasi Bharatiya Samman Award.

CKP's Books:

— Competing for the Future – 2006 (coauthored with Gary Hamel)

— The Fortune At the Bottom of the Pyramid (coauthored with Gary Hamel)

— The Future of Competition: Co-creating Unique Value with Customers – 2004 (coauthored with Venkat Ramaswamy)

— In Search of Excellence

— Multinational Mission: Balancing Local Demands and Global Vision – 1987

Award Winning Articles

— The end of corporate imperialism – 1998 (with Kenneth Lieberthol)

— The core competence of the corporation – 1990 (with Gary Hamel)

These three articles won HBR – McKinsey Prize Strategic Intent – 1989 (with Gary Hamel)

— The New Frontier of Experience Innovation – 2003 (Won SMR-PWC Award published in Sloan Management Review)

— Weak Signals vs. Strong Paradigms – 1995

(Won award in 1997 – ANBAR Electronic Citation of Excellence)

C.K. Prahalad was one of the greatest business thinkers of the world. He was recognised as a great Indian contributor to the management thought. He was well-known for his management perceptions, works and management strategies. He was a luminary in management world. He had several crowns on his head for his contributions to the management thought. He was a professor, researcher, author and globally recognised management consultant.

Born in India and living in the USA, Coimbatore, Krishna Rao Prahalad, besides his contributions to strategic management, had made two great contributions to the management literature.

1. Core Competency
2. Bottom of the Pyramid.

"Core Competency" is a concept which tells about synergisation of individual capabilities of human resources at work in an organisation, to provide customer benefit, which is hard for competitors to imitate and widely leveraging it to many products and markets. Core competency can be in the form of technology, subject matter know how, a reliable process, close relationship with customers and suppliers, product development or in the form of organisational culture focusing on employee dedication.

Prahalad puts "Core competency" as an area of specialised exercise that is the result of harmonizing complex streams of technology and work activity." This concept was first published in 1990, in an article of Harvard Business Review, written along with Gary Hamel. The concept was further illuminated and highlighted by many researchers in 1990s. The improvement was that "capabilities are considered core, if they differentiate a company strategically." "Core competency differentiates not only between firms but also inside a firm it differentiates among several competencies." This means, a core competency guides a firm recombining its competencies in response to the demand from environment.

Prahalad cited the example of Honda company which moved from product to product in automobiles which become quality auto products to improve the image and profitability of Honda company. He also expressed that "VOLVO" company considered "safety" as its core competency in producing passenger coaches.

Prahalad also highlighted the difference between individual competencies of workers in the organisation and aggregated (integrated) competencies projected in the form of "Core competencies of an organisation." He said that core competencies of an organisation are harmonized. International constructions to build the brand for products of a firm, cannot be achieved by the capabilities of the individuals which stand isolated.

Tests of Core competencies are:

(i) potential access to wide variety of markets;

(ii) whether it can make significant contribution to the perceived benefits of end products;

(iii) whether they can make it difficult to intimate, and

(iv) can it have a sustainable competitive advantage in the market.

Not many management thinkers actually follow up important early ideas with genuinely ground breaking future ideas. This is what Prahalad has done. His book of the 1990s with Gary Hamel set the strategic agenda. The book of 2004 written along with Gary Hamel, ***"The fortune at the bottom of the pyramid"*** has established the social, entrepreneurial and economic agenda of our times. In this book, he identifies the world's poor as a potential untapped market. This means the future of business lies in the economically weaker and weakest people who are real consumers of the world in future and they are to be tapped. They are at the bottom of the pyramid who can contribute to business anything worth $13 trillion (Rs. 52 trillion) a year.

Prahalad has placed all consumers in the world in four tiers. Tier one are considered rich and affluent who represent a small percentage to the total population. Tiers 2 and 3 cover poor customers in developed nations, raising middle class in developing countries. Tier 4 covers the poor of the developing countries which constitute over 4000 million. He is of the opinion that tier 4 population which is at the bottom of the pyramid will be the potential market in future.

His book on **"Competing For The Future"** with Gary Hamel puts a question whether "Strategy" of "Execution" is important to a company's future. The immediate answer would be "Execution." But CK and GH say that it is reengineering the strategies to reshape the business that brings success.

Considering his ability and contribution to the management thought, Suntop Media an UK based leading media firm, awarded him "Management Guru 2007." This award was instituted in 2000 by Suntop Media. Under the name "Thinkers – 50." In 2006, this title was awarded to Microsoft's Bill Gates and C.K. Prahalad was number 3 amongst 50 thinkers. In 2007, C.K. Prahalad occupied first place, pushing Bill Gates to third place.

C.K. Prahalad's last book **"The New Age of Innovation: Driving Cocreated Value through Global Networks,"** published by Ross School of Business along with M.S. Krishnan throws light on new strategic path for companies in the 21st century.

Year 2009 was perhaps the best year in his life as he was showered with following awards.

1. *"Padma Bhushan"* third highest civilian award of Government of India.
2. Named "the World's most Influential Business thinker" by thinkers50.com published by "The Times".
3. "Pravasi Bhartiya Samman" Award.

He was a member of the **"Blue Ribbon Commission"** of the **United Nations** on Private Sector and Development.

CKP was the first recipient of the **"Lal Bahadur Shastry"** Award in the year 2000 for contributions to Management and Public Administration.

Almighty was jealous of his achievements and with drew him from this world on April 16, 2010. A great loss to the Management World.

3. Ram Charan

Ram Charan – A Profile

Born in a city of UP near Delhi, Ram Charan lived with his parents, a family of seventeen members engaged in milk vending, in a house without electricity.

Enrolled as engineering student at the elite Benaras University in Varanasi and graduated with third rank.

Left for Australia on an exchange programme, with extreme difficulty, worked as a draftsman at a utility company. He studied financial statement during his spare time after joining a course in the evening.

His talent in financial analysis learnt in four years at Sydney, made Charan to leave for US to join MBA course at Harvard Business School. Graduated as top 3 of his class, became a Banker Scholar with high distinction. He stayed to earn a doctoral degree (Ph.D.).

Joined as Faculty member at North Western University, got "Best Teacher" award.

Has been consultant over 35 years for leading companies of India, Middle East, and other countries and rests always in hotels or in aircraft.

He got Economic Times Award (India) in 2009 – Global Indian.

Quotes:

— "CEOs are failing and it has become a common feature. Cause and Effect — Cause of what is wrong with management and effect of that wrong on organisation — has to be identified."

— ***Ram Charan***

— "Today's management do not develop leadership qualities which are potential in their CEOs and unit managers."

— ***Ram Charan***

— "Managers being underdeveloped and their execution being weak, the problems in their organisations aggravate." — ***Ram Charan***

— "Good Leadership is the core competence of any organisation. It is a hands on integral business function that has to be implemented at all levels." — ***Ram Charan***

Born in 1940, educated in India and the USA, Ram Charan is a highly acclaimed business advisor, speaker and author. He has trained and is training innumerable CEOs in the world including CEOs of GE, DuPont, Novaritis KLM, and such other gaint companies of the world.

"What Peter Drucker's *The Practice of Management* and *Effective Executive* were to the 20th century industrial age, Ram Charan's "Know-How" is to the 21st century global digital knowledge worker age. Brilliant, immensely practical and comprehensive – with almost self-evident prophetic wisdom" says Stephen R. Covy, a contemporary management thinker and the author of famous "7 habits of Highly Effective People and the 8th Habit."

Always on wheels and air and spending his nights in hotels or in aeroplane, Ram Charan is a globally known "Management Guru" and is a top consultant of the world's foremost companies. His contribution to the management thought is about "leadership." As a management consultant and recognised author on management subjects, Ram Charan has taught at Harvard and Kellogg Business schools.

His contribution to management thought – **"CEOs and unit managers are failing."** It has become a common feature. Working with the tool of "cause and effect" which is his core competence, he analyses as to what is wrong with the management or leaders decisions and the impact of such wrong decisions on management. He says that managers and CEOs are underdeveloped and because of this, their execution has become weak. The problems in the organisations aggravate. Diagnosing the basic cause of weak leadership trait in managers and CEOs, he advocates the development of "Leadership" in leaders of the organisations. He observes that "Good Leadership" is the core competence of any successful organisation. It is a hands-on, integral business function that has to be implemented at all levels." His method is no method. He is wary of abstraction and belongs to no school of management theory.

"Thinkers – 50" instituted by UK based Suntop Media, in association with Skill Soft, it is definitive biannual guide to which thinkers and ideas are in, Ram Charan is awarded as one of the top 50 "Management Gurus" of the world, in 2007.

4. Gita Piramal

Gita Piramal – A Profile

Education: Ph.D. in Business History

Career

— A prolific writer in leading and international publications such as Financial Times and Economic Times

— Consulting editor of World Executive Digest

— Producer of TV Programmes on Indian Business for the BBC and Plus channel

Books

— Business Legends – 1999

— World Class in India — A case book of companies in transformation – 2002

— Business Mantras

— Business Maharajas

Dr. Gita Piramal, as a journalist, has contributed her significant thought to management. A Ph.D. in business history and as an author four books, Gita Piramal, describes the Indian corporate sector having Indian historical and political references as the base.

Being one of India's foremost business writers and as managing editor of "The Smart Manager", (India's first world-class "Management" magazine). Dr. Gita describes as to how earlier systems have an influence on contemporary operations and radical changes that are taking place in today's management world.

She opines that "Old Business Mantras look like changing radically to keep abreast in this dynamic world. But they have strong roots in traditional business rules and procedures."

5. Promod Batra

Promod Batra – A Profile

Education:

— Doctor of Letters (Rani Durgavati Viswavidyalaya) Early education in India:

— MBA from Minnesota USA

Professional Training:

(i) General Mills Inc., Minnesota

(ii) Soyabean Counsel of America

Career:

1. Serveol Escorts Ltd. from 1963-1996 – Retired as Chief General Manager
2. Full time writer on management aspects

Books:

— Management Thoughts (Best seller)

— Born to be Happy

— Born to Win

— Cows do not Give Milk

— The Family

— Management Articles

— Management Ideas in Action

— Management Think Tank

— Management Wisdom

— Pulse of Wisdom for Managers

— Pulse of Wisdom for Happy Living
— Selling is Nobel Profession
— Simple Ways to Manage
— Simple Ways to Manage Stress
— When the customer has a problem
— Simple ways to make your boss succeed
— Management thought Starters
— Profitable passion discovers the spy

"Management Thoughts" written by Promod Batra in 1991 considered as a Think Tank which provides distilled wisdom on business and management processes. Being a collection of simple management thoughts supported by full page illustrations by reputed cartoonist Mickey Patel, the book is a hot seller for its great contribution to management world.

He has produced over forty five titles on different aspects of management. Through these books, seminars, workshops and lectures, his contribution to the management thought is to have "an integrated approach for management". His experience at Escorts Heart Institute as chief Administrator provided the base to understand the aspects of Crisis Management and Stress Management.

Conducting 150 one day workshop on an average per year since 1996, human aspects of management in India and abroad, Promod Batra is considered as a great contributor of India on management thought.

6. Shiva Khera

Shiva Khera – A Profile

Career

— After nationalisation of his family business of coal-mining, Shiva Khera left for the USA
— Early life in the USA was very humble – car washing and selling insurance
— Influenced by the talk of Norman Vincent Peale, he changed the direction of his life
— Founded, "Qualified Learning System Inc., – an organisation to conduct programmes on "Motivation and Attitude."

Books

He has written 9 books. All his works are best sellers and are translated into many languages.

— "You can Win" – 1998. The reatise tells about motivation as toll to craft thoughts which can ignite human spirit.
— "Living with humour" – throws light on the fact that it is better to be humoured.
— "Freedom is not Free" – the theme is that a progressive society is the basis for individual progress of its people.
— Attitude determines altitude.
— Attitude the key to success.

— Discipline your way to freedom

— Ethics of values

— Winner's Edge

— Winning Strategies

Honours and Awards

— Louis Machesi Fellow – By Round Table Foundation

— Life time Achievement Award – Lions Club International

— Centennial Vocational Award for Excellence

Management Mantra is "Total Quality People."

Shiva Khera, who was selling cars when entered the USA, has built his multi-million dollar empire from scratch using his signature-line **"winners do not do different things, they do things differently."** As a motivational Guru, Shiva Khera speaks of his struggle to find a footing in Canada and USA before he met Norman Vincent Peale whose motivational teaching changed his life forever.

Considered as "Motivational Guru", Shiva Khera says that "In order to get the winning edge, we need to strive for excellence, not perfection. Striving for perfection is neurotic, and striving for excellence is progress."

His contnribution to management thoughts is on "Motivation and Attitude." In his book **"You can Win"** (an international best seller) Shiva Khera emphasizes that "It is high time that people took a stand. Those who are indifferent to injustice are as much to blame as the preparators. We have to become responsible. We cannot ignore, we cannot ignore our neighbour's plight, we must get involved."

He opines that people must make a clear distinction between detached action and indifferent involvement. He firmly believes that everyone has to note ones social responsibility along with ones personal duties. "self-development, self-esteem and a winner's attitude are high" in his agenda. He supports this saying by his quotes – **"winners see the potential; losers see the past." "Winners see the gain; losers see the pain." The winner is always part of the answer; the loser is always a part of the problem."**

7. Arindam Chaudhuri

Arindam Chaudari – A Profile

Born: 1982

Education

— B.A. with honours in Economics Diploma in Industrial Engineering PGDBM (MBA) Fellowship – IIPM

Career:

— Honorary Dean – IIPM, New Delhi

Books

— Count your Chicken Before they Hatch

— The great Indian Dream

Awards and Honours

— Recipient of Academic Gold Medial while completing PGDBM

— "Management Guru" Award – 2000 (at the age of 28) by OM Venkatesa Society Channai

— Selected amongst 50 leading thinkers under the age of 40 to represent South Asia in 2001 (age 29 years)

— "Personality of the Decade Award" by KG Foundation Coimbatore

— "Example to the Youth Award"-2004, Rotract Counsel, Chennai

— Adviser to the consultative committee of Planning Commission of India – 2005

— Centinnal Service Award for professional excellence in the field of education and management 2005 – Rotary International

— Priyadarshini Academy's Biennial Global Award – 2006, along with NR Narayana Murthy

— Life Positive Leaders Award for change agent – 2007

— J.J. Irani Award – 2007 – PN Singh Foundation – Mumbai

Arindam Chaudhuri has been recognized as one of the great thinkers of management in the world. As a management consultant and thinker, Arindam has been contributing to the management areas such as strategic vision, leadership, social sector consulting, competitive management techniques and global opportunities and threat analysis.

He is an eminent author, a transformational leader, an authoritative speaker, a celebriety, a film maker and a "Management Guru." His contribution to management thought at his young age is "Par Excellence." He has produced innumerable articles on various issues of management and has developed a "Think Tank" of his own to conduct research on contemporary issues of management.

His best seller "Count Your Chickens Before They Hatch" created a benchmark in India by selling more than 1,00,000 copies in record time. This work gives an insight into various management practices.

"Theory of Management" developed by him is India-centric management ideas with global applicability.

His another commendable work "The Great Indian Dream" analyses the weakness of "Survival of the Fittest" and strongly portrays that "Survival of the weakest" as the guiding principle for future India and describes it as "Human way of Thinking." His achievements in his young age is commendable.

"Management Guru – 2000" award at the age of 28 bears testimony to his profound knowledge and contribution to management thought.

Undoubtedly he stands on par with giant management Gurus of the world in the days to come. We are proud of Arindam Chaudhuri to be an Indian.

8. Debashish Chatterjee

Debashish Chatterjee – A Profile

Debashish Chatterjee was a Fulbright scholar at the Sloan School of Management, MIT, USA and taught MBA programmes at the University of St. Thomas Minnesota and the Harvard Graduate School of Business.

He heads his Global Leadership Centre.

His works include:

— Leading Consciously and

— Managing Transitions

He has taught Leadership Courses through the world. His students include managers of fortune 100 corporations.

Harvard Business School chose him as one of the 15 thought leaders of the world A.

He is identified as a "motivational leader." He has contributed on "Leadership and Motivation" to the management thought.

Chatterjee speaking on motivation states "that more often than not, the presidency election in the USA, is won by the best performance on television! This leaves young minds with a great sense of image consciousness."

Talking about understanding self, Chatterjee says that – "I see the self as the central organising principle of personality. By "Self" I mean the How of injtelligence that shapes our identity from moment to moment. The self is the experience behind all our experiences. What I am experiencing today, as "I" or "me" is not the end of the story about my personality. My personality is what I am + what I should be. So there is hope, if we pay simple attention to what I am, when I am jealous and then what I am when I am generous. Before we attempt to win friends and influence people let us influence ourselves bit by bit. How do I do this? By being attentive to my thoughts, movements and behaviour from time to time. Just to have a date with oneself everyday is the most enchanting way to develop personality that I know of."

"Appearances may be deceptive but they are powerful". "We may take failure as fate or feedback. The blow of a hammer may break a glass but will forge iron. We have to develop both resilience of a rock and the fluidity of water, if we want to develop" opines Chatterjee, speaking on 'self-understanding' as a first step in leadership development.

Upcoming Gurus

India also presents other management thinkers who have made substantial impact on business minds and operations.

1. Vijay Govindarajan of Tuck Business School is considered as "Innovation Guru" and is awarded "Management Gurus-2007" and ranked 23 amongst 50 Gurus recognised by Suntop Media, UK.

2. Rakesh Khurana serving at Harvard Business School is given the 45th rank of 50 Gurus of Suntop Media recognition in 2007, for his contribution to management thought.

3. Venkat Ramaswamy has contributed his thought on management in the book "Co-opting Customer Competence" co-authored with C.K. Prahalad. Faculty at ROSS School of Management.

4. Vijay Vishwanath, through his book on the "Art of Developing Leaders at Kroft" and conducting workshops, has contributed to the development of "leadership".

5. Partha Bose has contributed to the management thought on strategy in his work "Alexander — The Great's Art of Strategy."

6. Rita Bhimani in her work on "Corporate Peacock," tells about business behaviour, which is significant contribution to management thought.

7. Jagadish Seth serving at GOLZUETA school of Business is a contributor on Management thought.

8. Nirmal Kumar of London Business School is a thinker on management.

9. Bala Balachandran is another great thinker on management. He is a professor at Kellog school US and a consultant for many leading companies. Has his Business School at Chennai-India.

STUDY QUESTIONS

1. State and briefly explain various approaches to management.
2. Briefly analyse the following approaches: (a) Taylorism, (b) Behavioural approach, (c) Human relations approach, (d) Systems approach, (e) Contingency approach.
3. What is an Open system? Analyse.
4. What is closed system? Analyse.
5. Compare and contrast the classical approach, contributions made by F.W. Taylor, Frank and Lillian Gilbert and H.L. Gnatt.
6. How does Henry Fayol's approach differs from F.W. Taylor? Briefly analyse.
7. Give an analytical note on scientific management.
8. What do you mean by; (i) Time study; (ii) Motion study, (iii) Fatigue study?
9. Briefly explain the general principles of management as said by Henry Fayol on process management.
10. What are the limitations of classical approach to management?
11. Briefly analyse the management science approach or quantitative approach to management.
12. Explain the contingency approach to management.
13. Explain the central theme of Human relations movement.
14. Analyse Chester Bernard's social system theory.
15. Give a note on each of the contributions of (i) Oliver Sheldon, (ii) Moon and Reiley, (iii) Lindall Urwick, and (iv) Harold Koontz.
16. Write an explanatory note on the contributions of Peter F. Drucker on management.
17. Give a note on each of the following contributors and their perceptions about management. (a) Peter F. Drucker, (b) Joseph M. Juran, (c) W. Edward Deming, (d) Stephen Covy, (e) David Allen, (f) Henry Mintzberg, (g) Armand V. Feignbaum, (h) Philip B. Crosby, (i) Kaoru Ishikawa.
18. Briefly write on the contributions to management thought by Indian management thinkers. (a) Sumantro Ghoshal, (b) C.K. Prahalad, (c) Gita Piramal, (d) Promod Batra, (e) Ram Charan, (f) Shiva Khera, (g) Debashish Chatterjee, and (h) Arindam Chaudhuri.

4

LEARNING ORGANISATION

LEARNING OBJECTIVES

After reading this chapter, you should be able to know:

- Learning organisation - The Concept.
- Meaning and Definitions.
- Reason for Developing Learning Organisations.
- Features of Learning Organisation.
- Problems that emerge in Learning Organisations.
- Disturbing factors that come in the way of Learning.

"Learning Organisation" concept is used as a tool to implement the themes of knowledge management and change management in an organisation. In a knowledge society (the term which came to limelight only recently) people are thinking-oriented and are always looking for a change in the organisations to improve the quality of operation. **"Learning Organisation"** concept has been used as a tool to the changes required to improve the quality of operations. When the concept emerged in a big way, after the publication of Peter Senge's book "The Fifth Discipline" in 1990, people began to understood the concept of "Learning Organisation". Many consultants and organisations understood the commercial importance of Learning Organisation. It was realised that organisational learning is quite essential to improve productivity of workers, to have Organisation Learning better organisational structure, better work atmosphere in the organisation etc. But still the arguments are going on the issue of effective implementation of Learning Organisation concept in organisations. Many believe still it is an ideal and abstract concept which cannot be fully understood by the people at work and cannot be practiced with full vigour. However, it should be accepted that Peter Senge's book has given a new dimension to organisational effectiveness. With the adaptation of modules suggested by him, organisations can have a new look.

With all its limitations, risks involved in implementation, and difficult to practice, Learning Organisation philosophy gives an insight into operational aspects of the organisation which are governed and monitored by human factor. Learning Organisation concept mainly focuses on behavioural aspects of workers and suggest to change their behaviour, if need be, to improve the productivity of the organisation. It is said that the perfect Learning Organisation cannot be achieved and it is only a desirable concept. It is a tool to achieve a business objective. *i.e.* improving productivity and profit of the organisation through behavior modification of the employees. How long this concept will be practised in workplace is a matter to be decided by the time. But, introducing new knowledge to the work practices in organisations to compete in a global market, continuous change—the main theme of Learning Organisation—is the only way out. In this background, let us examine the concept of Learning Organisation.

LEARNING ORGANISATION—THE MEANING

Number of interpretations have been given about Learning Organisation, after the introduction of the concept in 1990 by Peter Senge. Without going into the various meanings, definitions and interpretations, only some definitions are given here to understand the main theme of the concept.

1. "Learning Organisations are organisations where people continually expand their capacity to create the results they truly desire, where new and expansive patterns of thinking are nurtured, where collective aspiration is set free, and where people are continually learning to see the whole together." ***— Peter Senge (1990-Fifth Discipline)***
2. "The learning company is a vision what might be possible. It is not brought about simply by training individuals, it can happen as a result of learning at the whole organisational level. A Learning Company is an organisation that facilitates the learning of all members and continuously transforms itself." ***— Pedler et al., 1991***
3. "Learning organisations are characterised by total employee involvement in process of collaboratively conducted, collectively unaccountable change directed towards shared values or principles". ***— Watkins and Marsick, 1992***

These three definitions of Peter Senge and others explain the various dimensions of Learning Organisation. Peter Senge explains the five disciplines, *viz.*, (i) Personal mastery, (ii) Mental models, (iii) Shared Vision, (iv) Team learning and (v) Systems thinking. His two important aspects, *viz.,* (i) Systematic thinking and (ii) Dialogue are considered more important in increasing the productivity of the organisation. Particularly, "dialogue" element exhibits its virtues.

The Fifth discipline of Peter Senge, integrates other four disciplines. It acts as a corner stone in developing interrelationship between others. This also provides both the incentive and the means to integrate the disciplines.

Systems theory, the fifth aspect of Peter Senge, attracts three vital aspects.

(i) Systems thinking (theory) tries to analyse the links which connect to the whole organisation and make the people involved to look at the organisation as a whole and beyond. It tells about the people to look beyond the immediate context and to appreciate the impact of their actions upon others. This may happen in reverse process also. This provides a base to understand the organisation as a whole (integrated approach). Every employee can have a holistic view and understanding, rather than just work only on his task.

(ii) The sub-systems or building blocks of the system theory are easy to understand and to develop them. But organisations, using this model can develop more sophisticated Sub-systems. When sophisticated or complete sub-systems are developed and adopted, the people involved can see the whole and appreciate the organisation as a dynamic one. If people at work understand the organisation in a better manner, they complete their tasks in an appropriate manner.

(iii) Systems thinking, as he puts, helps the people involved in the organisations to understand the feedback mechanisms in organisation. These are essential to adopt corrective actions, if the feedback suggests.

He says "that the systems view point generally oriented toward the long-term view. That is why delays and feedback loops are so important. In short-term, you can often ignore them; they are inconsequential. They only come back to haunt you in the long-run." (Fifth Discipline, p. 22, Published in 1990).

The other two definitions are also developed on the lines of Peter Senges opinion. Infact they have only stressed the models of Peter Senge. The second definition of singe says that—Learning Organisation is one which expects that every individual worker must look at the organisation as a whole and have an integrated approach. Continuously learning the happenings of the organisation will facilitate the worker to improve his performance and make him to grow without his knowledge.

The third definition of Watkins focuses on collabarative action of all workers to have a continuous change in work processes through shared values and principles.

Considering these opinions, "Learning Organisation" may be defined as follows:

> **"An organisation that learns and encourages learning among its people. It promotes exchange of information between emloyees hence creating a more knowledgeable workforce. This produces a very flexible organisation where people will accept and adapt vision."**

The spirit behind Learning Organisation is that, people at work in an organisation, at all levels continuously and collectively increase their productivity which is inherent in them to produce the results as per the goals set by the Organisations.

HISTORY OF LEARNING ORGANISATION

Learning Organisation is not a new concept. It gained momentum in 1990 when Peter Senge produced his monumental work. "Fifth Discipline." The history reveals that Chinese philosopher, Confucious said in 479 BC that — "everyone, without learning, wise become foolish and the foolish become wise." Further he said that "Learn as if you could never have enough of learning, as if you might miss some thing."

These two statements of Confucious stress on the concept of continuous learning of an individual. Now it is extended to organisations. In the corporate world, those corporate enterprises which have considered "continuous learning" as an important aspect of growth, adapt learning process quickly to attain innovations in work practices and change the work practices accordingly to perform better in the constantly changing environment.

Though there was little attempt to understand the concept of "learning", sincere attempt was made only after 1900. In 1950s, The "Systems approach" was developed as a part of learning process. But this approach was not fully recognised and implemented. Gould-Kreutzer Associates, defined systems thinking as "A framework for seeing interrelationships rather than things; as we see the forests and the trees inside system was like a forest and sub-systems were like trees."

In system approach, a framework to see interrelationship was developed. The framework made the companies to be aware of organisation as a whole and the workers within the company were viewed as sub-systems. Prior to the publication of 'Systems' concept, organisations did not recognise the needs of workers. But 'System' thinking though not fully implemented, made the corporates to change their managerial view to increase the productivity of workers, besides achieving the business goals.

One of the tools developed by systems approach was "Decision Support System – DSS". DSS helped corporate top brass in taking sound decisions in developing strategic plans and also to change the work culture continuously. Different working models were developed to define the system. These working models helped the organisations rather than the development of systems operation. The models so developed were the ones suiting to the organisational needs and for the future development of the business. DSS tool made "implicit knowledge an explicit one." It facilitated the availability of extra knowledge to the organisations. The DSS enhanced the communication system of the organisation. However, the system tool did not develop fast.

In nineteen seventies (1970s), the DSS tool was called with a new name "Organisational Learning". Chris Arygris, a Harvard Professor, published a book depicting the various dimensions of organisational learning in 1978. Even then the concept of Learning Organisation did not attract the corporate world in a big way.

In nineteen eighties (1980s), "TIME" concept was considered as a "Competitive Advantage". This means that the organisations, if they complete their work schedules as per the stipulated time or ahead of prescribed time, they would be greatly benefitted and compete effectively in the business. This "Time" concept indirectly motivate the firms to be learning organisation, completing the tasks or projects on schedule. It was thought that "time" would develop the capabilities of the organisation. The competition will be "capability-based" one and capability includes "Learning" as one of the components.

The major breakthrough took place in introducing Learning Organisation concept, after the research publication of Peter Singe in 1990 in the form of a book called "Fifth Discipline". After the publication of this research work, the corporate world is opening it's eyes in a big way. Many companies have accepted the concept of Learning Organisation" and are trying to adopt effectively.

The adoption of Learning Organisation concept, although it is dynamic and flexible, is a big task to the top management. Workers may agitate to accept the new work culture. They have to unlearn the old practices and learn new practices. This takes time to implement and the process is gradual. Companies which are capable of striking a balance between stability and change can implement Learning Organisation in an effective way. However, the business environment is changing at a faster rate after the introduction of the concepts "global market" and "global village". This has forced the business units, irrespective of the size, to adapt themselves to the changing business environment for their survival.

Benefits of Learning Organisation

1. **To Workers:**
   * Motivates workers to work more.
   * Workers will be more flexible.
   * They become more creative and innovative.
   * Improvement in social interaction.
   * Knowledge sharing between the groups and teams produces new work practices to improve the productivity.
   * Interdependency increases for better operations.
2. **Organisational Benefits:**
   * Ingrained traditional practices are broken to better the organisation.
   * Improvement in customer relations.
   * Over a time period, organisation pools up expertise and knowledge within Learning Organisation, which will be larger than average and can be used for solving problems at a faster rate.
   * Workers being innovative and creative Learning Organisations can adapt to changes quickly and effectively in terms of new technology adoption, market improvement and facing competitions.

FACTORS LEAD TO LEARNING ORGANISATION

The Learning Organisation emerges due to various disturbing factors prevailing in the organisations. The disturbing factors generally observed are as follows:

* Employees are demotivated or not interested in their work.
* Employees lack the skill and knowledge to adjust to the new work culture introduced to improve overall productivity of the organisation.
* Only few employees have innovative ideas and ready to experiment them which is apposed by co-workers.
* Employees implicitly follow orders without understanding the implications.
* Many employees simply beat about the old things and lack real productive skills.
* Workers in the organisation may be isolated and do not have communication between themselves.

* If the sectional manager is absent, the employees may not work as per stipulations.
* Whenever the problems crop up employees may not try to solve themselves and push it to the manager to solve.
* People at work may not address the customer complaints.

When such issues disturb the organisational work, the importance of Learning Organisation emerges. Learning Organisation addresses all these disturbing factors.

Important aspects of Learning Organisation are:

* It increases communication process in the organisation and creates openness so that employees can work freely. It encourages employees to be honest with oneself to a given situation (self-reflection) and pushes the group to clarity and evaluate the assumptions underlying how work gets done with in the organisation. (Participatory reflection). It encourages two-way communication.
* Learning Organisation has its importance in allowing the workers to become adept at questioning things as a normal course of their work. This facilitates the employees to take risks in improving their work. Positive feedback helps them to learn from their enquiries. This enhances their knowledge and thinking power. They become proactive rather than reactive or have defensive thinking.
* In the learning process, TIME plays a major role in communicating, reflecting, feedback, adopting flexibility and making enquiries with immediate top officer to get information to discharge the task properly.
* Mutual respect and support is one of the important aspects of Learning Organisation. Irrespective of the positioning of persons in the hierarchy, every person in hierarchy should respect and support the others in the same level or in any other level. Treating others (co-workers, supervisors, etc.) equally and constantly with one's ability to constitute positively to the organisation, is an important aspect.

Thus, the importance of learning organisation is recognised in the form of solving the various problems that are encountered and disturb the performance of the tasks. The solutions found out in, normal course to solve these problems will be only short-term in nature (single loop learning) and re-emerge in the future. Learning Organisation as a tool of solving the problems on a long-term basis, looks at the restructuring the organisation making it flatter or a workable one. This provides strength to the organisation to be more competitive and develop a customer responsive culture.

Argyris says that "The objective and purpose of Learning Organisation is to maintain knowledge about new products and processes, understanding what is happening in the outside environment and produce creative solutions using knowledge and skills of all employed within the organisation. The co-operation and trust between individuals and groups is required to do this. Free and reliable communication is also needed. All these needs can be met by the tenets of Learning Organisation".

ADVANTAGES OF LEARNING ORGANISATION

The main advantages of Learning Organisation are as follows:

1. Learning Organisation makes the organisation an exclusive and powerful one to respond to the external pressures.
2. The knowledge acquired by workers and the resources of the organisation are better used to respond to the needs of customers.
3. The new skills acquired make the workers to produce quality output at all levels. This will be a continuous activity.
4. Organisation becomes people-oriented and this enhances the image of the company.
5. Innovation becomes the order of the organisation and this facilitates the organisation to be competitive.
6. As the change is a continuous activity within the organisation, The pace of change increases and organisation becomes active.

FEATURES OF LEARNING ORGANISATION

As Learning Organisation concept is slowly emerging on the business scene, its features have yet to be crystalised. However Peter Senge provides five components of Learning Organisation, which can now be considered as features. They are: (i) Systems Thinking; (ii) Personal Mastery; (iii) Mental Models; (iv) Shared vision and (v) Team Learning.

These five aspects are briefly analysed in the following paragraphs:

1. Systems Thinking

Peter Senge says that "Systems Thinking" is the 'corner stone' of his approach. He considers this as "Fifth Discipline which integrates others, fusing them into a coherent body of theory and practice." Systems theory as enunciated by Peter Senge is an elaborate one. However, the focal points of the theory are briefly given.

System is an integrated whole. When the tasks are to be performed or problems to be addressed, the managers or people concerned look at the problem not in an isolation, but considering the system as a whole. This provides long-term solutions to the problem.

Systems thinking is a conceptual framework. That permits workers to study the tasks or problems as bounded objects. Learning Organisation adopts this method of thinking when assessing their company.

In the process, it also becomes essential to develop information systems that measure the performance of the organisation as a whole and its various systems and sub-systems.

Learning Organisation concept strictly expects that all the characteristics listed must be apparent at once in an organisation. Any of these Characteristic is missing, the organisation cannot be constructed as Learning Organisation. But it is said that characteristics of Learning Organisation are gradually acquired rather than developing them simultaneously.

Regarding systems, Peter Senge says that "We learn best from our experience. but we never directly experience the consequences of many of our most important decisions". This statement is with reference to organisational behavior and decisions we take regarding the problems to be solved. The short-term decisions may solve the problem temporarily. But these problems crop up again and again. For example; as a measure of cost-cutting we may reduce the advertising budget. temporarily. But considering the system as a whole it is not a wise decision as the people may forget the product in the long-run. Continuous advertising involves more budget. But it is essential for a long-term benefit. An appreciation of systems will lead to recognition of the use of and problems with, such reinforcing feed back and also understanding the place of balancing feedback.

2. Personal Mastery

How do an individual will commit to the process of learning is explained by the term "Personal Mastery". If the workers in the organisation are fast in learning, the organisation will have the competitive advantage over other organisations, whose workers are slow in learning. Although the organisations frequently conduct innovative training methods in the respective functional areas to make their employees learn new things and to make learning process faster, the researches reveal that in organisations' learning is incidental.

Learning through training process contributes less compared to incidental learning. Personal mastery in learning regularly in workplaces has to be practised on continuous basis to improve the overall productivity of the organisation. This continuous learning culture has to be developed in firms. As Learning Organisation is described as the sum of individual learning, the mechanisms have to be evolved to transform individual learning into organisational learning. Through these mechanisms, personal mastery is transferred to the organisation mastery to make an effective Learning Organisation. Thus personal mastery is the attainment by individual workers of efficiency and effectiveness of learning of new things which will be used for the overall benefit of the organisation.

3. Mental Models

Some deep rooted assumptions and organisational theories play a dominant role in the work place and are disturbing factors for change management. They never allow the organisations to become Learning Organisations. Although new theories are evolved to have innovative work practices, some memories of the organisations which preserve certain behaviors, norms and values donot allow the new theories to be practiced. To become a good Learning Organisation, these unwanted values, behaviors and norms are to be discarded. The new work models which are essential to make the Organisation a bearing one, are to be implemented in the place of ingrained theories and assumptions. Old mental models should not be an abstruction to Learning Organisation.

4. Shared Vision

Traditional Organisational structures impose their own vision to be followed by workers. But to make the organisation a decentralised and flatter one, the most successful new visions have to be built-up, based on the individual visions of employees of all levels. This new "shared vision" are transistory goals which facilitate change. Besides these there should also be long-term goals that are intrinsic within the company. Shared vision is required to succeed against competitor.

5. Team Learning

Every individual in the organisation will be learning new things and cultures in a Learning Organisation. Team learning here refers to the sum total aspect of individual learning. If individuals share their learning with each other, all are bound to grow at a faster rate. This helps in improving the problem solving process of the organisation. Because every individual, in the process of learning new things, will have access to better knowledge and expertise. Learning Organisations have structures that facilitate team learning with features such as boundary crossing and openness. Team learning also demands the workers to engage in "Dialogue and Discussion". This results in open communication, shared meaning and understanding in the organisation. Learning Organisation develops through team learning, excellent knowledge management centres, which allow creation, acquisition, dissemination and implementation of knowledge throughout the organisation.

In a learning organisation,these five aspects are to be practiced. This means that organisations should recognise the commercial significance of organisational learning. The concept of Learning Organisation has been a central orienting point in this. However, there should be a permanent dictum of Learning Organisation which can be emulated by organisations. But this is not possible as the economies and business practices are exposed to global environment which is flexible in nature. Therefore,organisational learning to become Learning Organisation is inevitable.

The issues related to organisational learning have concentrated on the detached collection and analysis of the process involved in individual and collective learning inside the organisation. Whereas Learning Organisation is an action-oriented and is geared towards adopting specific tools which can help to identify, promote, and evaluate the quality of learning process inside the organisations. Thus organisational learning is the "activity" and "process" through which a Learning Organisation could be reached.

The "Dialogue" Factor

'Dialogue' simply means "a process of two people understanding each other through conversation" However dialogue is a risky process as it questions our beliefs and assumptions.

Gadmer, a thinker on Learning Organisation writes in 1979 as follows. "It is a characteristic of every conversation that each opens himself to the other person, truly accepts his point of view as worthy of consideration and gets inside the other to such an extent that he understands, not a particular individual, but what he says. The thing that has to be grasped is the objective rightness or otherwise of his opinion, so that they can agree with each other on subject".

This statement clearly indicates that dialogue improves the communication system. In organisations, to become a successful Learning Organisation, developing good communication system is very essential. The dialogue will not takeplace to win the argument on an issue, but to advance understanding. The decisions in an organisational hierarchy is not imposed, but implemented after a better understanding the decision through sound communication system and a meaningful dialogue. Dialogue develops good social relationship which entails certain virtues and emotions.

Peter Singe is also of the opinion that dialogue facilitates team learning through genuine thinking of the parties involved in a dialogue. He further opines that "dialogue is also necessary to necessary to other disciplines, e.g., building a shared vision and developing mental models. All the dialogues may not be fruitful. Many may go waste and be irrelevant to the organisational issues. But when had with good intention, it provides a base for the development of good communication system.

The brief discussion had so far brought out distinctly the features of Learning Organisation.

* Learning Organisation provides continuous learning opportunities.
* Learning acts as a tool to reach the goals.
* Individual performance is linked to organisational performance to have good growth.
* Motivates people in workplaces to share openly and to take risks. This happens through meaningful dialogue.
* Make people to understand about environment and interact with it.

LIMITATIONS OF LEARNING ORGANISATION

Within the Learning Organisation, several issues crop up which bring the learning process to a halt. These issues may not necessarily be connected with the aspects involved in learning process. When problems and issues are properly identified, finding solutions to address the issues may be easy and make the organisation a continuous learning one. But it is really very difficult to find real life examples of Learning Organisations to identify the issues that thawrt Learning Organisation. However, certain drawbacks can be identified in an organisation which are not conducive for the growth of Learning Organisations. The limitations listed below may be the genuine factors or limitation of Learning Organisations, which are to be addressed.

1. Transforming Bureaucratic Organisation to a Learning Organisation is a tough Job

In bureaucratic organisations, the policies and programmes flow downwards as per strict dictums of bureaucrats. Bureaucrats by themselves are rigid in their thinking and operations, will not allow any new practice, out of the accepted ingrained norms, to be implemented. Learning Organisation always demands flexibility in operations. Because of these conflicting features, bureaucratic organisations cannot that easily be converted into learning organisation. But the concept of Learning Organisation can make bureaucratic organisation less threatening and more acceptable to participants. However, individual and collective learning which has undoubtedly taken place has not really been connected to organisational change and transformation. Bureaucrats suggest to do with the concept of Learning Organisation. But it is not an acceptable aspect as the entire world is hoping to have a new working environment with flexibility and aspiring for change management.

2. Focus mainly on the cultural aspect

Learning Organisation's another issue that is subjected to discussion is that Learning Organisation considers mainly the change in organisational culture and gives less importance to other aspects of the organisation. But the argument is that in order to have a full-fledged Learning Organisation, besides the cultural change, the organisation should also consider the change in structure as and when it is required. But it is not so as per the norms of

Learning Organisation. Training is the only considered tool for learning, which is made Learning Organisation purely cultural biased. This shortcoming has to be addressed.

3. Individual and collective learning processes at all levels of the organisation are not properly connected to the organisation's strategic objectives

Acceptable models have to developed and made popular for organisational learning at all levels so that these models not only link individual and collective learning processes, but also connect to strategic objectives. The organisation learning models should help to understand whether the organisations have become a real learning organisation. It also becomes possible to access the extent to which such learning contributes or not towards strategic objectives.

4. Necessity to develop "a true management system" having capacity to evolve learning capacity

The 'true management system' here refers to committed management which can implement all changed learning concepts. The individual and collective indicators of learning have to be developed which can be used as standard indicators to assess the performance of learning organisation.

Besides these noticeable limitations, there are several problems which go unnoticed and really disturb the adoption of Learning Organisation concept in an organisation. One real aspect which greatly contribute for the development of Learning Organisation is "Zeal and initiative" of employees *vis-a-vis* management to make the organisation a learning one.

Eversince the concept of Learning Organisation was conceived in 1990, much water has flown in this direction to find out and add various dimensions. The concept of Learning Organisation, today, provides managers and others with a picture of how things could be within an organisation. Peter Singe's work is an elaborate one on this subject and exhibits many dimensions of Learning Organisation which enhance the organisational effectiveness, especially where the enterprise is firmly rooted in the "knowledge economy." But limitations are also existing. Some of the dimensions may not suit to the globalised capitalist economy.

Many other writers since 1990, also have said that there are other issues, if addressed or implemented can make the organisations very strong. These writers think beyond Learning Organisation "The Developing Organisation" (Gilley and Maybunich, 2000), "The ever-changing organisation" (Peters and Young, 1999) and the workbooks produced by Peter Senge in 1994, 1999 and 2000 have all given new concepts of Learning Organisation. The latest concept being the "Social Capital" which focuses much on "mutual trust" in the organisation to achieve organisational effectiveness.

"Social Capital" is understood as "The stock of active connections among people; the trust, mutual understanding, shared values and behaviours that bind the members of human networks and communities and make co-operative action possible" (Cohen and Prusak, 2001).

Thus, "Learning Organisation" concept though focuses on organisational effectiveness has barriers to learning both organisational and individual. These barriers have to be overcome to make the organisation a learning organisation. The concept simply says "Unlearn the unwanted practices which hinder the growth of the organisation and learn new practices which make the organisation effective one".

HOW TO DEVELOP A LEARNING ORGANISATION?

In order to develop a Learning Organisation, a strong foundation has to be laid by considering the following issues:

(i) Creating awareness about Learning Organisation.
(ii) Creating a flatter and flexible structure.
(iii) Providing required resources by the management.
(iv) Employee empowerment.
(v) Learning through real-time labs.

(i) Creating Awareness: The first step in developing Learning Organisation is to make the workers in the organisation understanding the usefulness of Learning Organisation. The concept of Learning Organisation should become an accepted thing in each and every employee. Everyone in the organisation should feel the necessity of restructure and change. This will facilitate the top management to adopt changes and create a new environment for development.

(ii) Creation of Flatter Structure: The organisation which wishes to change itself into Learning Organisation should be a decentralised, flexible and flatter. Centralised and vertical structures will have many hindering factors to develop the organisation. This leads to organisational politics and disturbs learning process. Flatter and flexible structures promote strong information systems, wherein, the worker gets the information uninterruptedly. This facilitates learning process much easier. This also encourages innovations amongst workers. Meaningful dialogues between employees take place for better understanding the need for change and work in new direction.

The flatter and flexible structures develop an open organisation, infuses a new philosophy of questioning and discussing the new work practices before they are accepted for adaptation. The discussions at the initial stages will avoid major mistakes that may creep in at a later stage. The concept of anonymity may be introduced to avoid the fear of identification. Only the matter for discussion will come up and who has raised the issue will not be known. Thus, flatter and flexible organisation can be created to develop a learning organisation.

(iii) Resource Mobilisation: Resource crunch will be a permanent problem of every business or non-business organisation. To convert the organisation, the management may feel that it requires huge resources. But when we look at the changing process of an organisation towards Learning Organisation, we observe that it is not the resource that becomes a big problem, but the "Dynamic Leadership" that takes the organisation to new heights.

The good leadership can lead the organisation in critical times. Dynamic leaders besides providing required resources, encourage the workers to understand the concept of Learning Organisation. Leaders should develop "Systems Thinking" (Holistic approach) in the organisation. The resources are to be provided on a long-term basis. The money, people and time they provide will determine the quality and quantity of learning. This goes without saying that the leadership or the management should be prepared to develop a learning organisation at any cost for their success.

(*iv*) ***Employee Empowerment:*** In a Learning Organisation, both employers and employees work together. The employer, besides creating a learning atmosphere, should involve workers to become responsible for their actions. They should be encouraged to learn and ignore minor mistakes of workers when they occur. This gives a feel of safety in workers and they develop organisational identify. This helps in bringing out more work from each empolyee and increases overall productivity of the organisation. Therefore, employers should learn as to how to learn together through simultation games and empower employees through equal participation at all levels.

(*v*) ***Learning Through Laboratories:*** The learning process can be implemented through specially designed learning laboratories. Small-sized, real-time models have to be evolved and implemented. During learning, failures can be experienced and corrective measures can be adopted immediately to overcome further failures. The implementation of these modules requires open and flexible atmosphere and therefore a congenial learning atmosphere has to be created. Continuous learning labs will make the organisation a Learning Organisation.

After developing firm base through these five issues, the strategies to develop a Learning Organisation have to be evolved.

STRATEGIES

There are no time-honoured and tested strategies that are considered as "Standard" ones to implement a Learning Organisation. However, certain strategies or approaches that are general in nature can be considered.

The first approach may be quite "Accidental." This means that an organisation might be in the process of implementing Learning Organisation concept without its knowledge. It might have taken it as a reorganising and restructuring process, which in hindsight fit the framework of Learning Organisation. This is an accidental strategy or approach.

The second approach may be that the organisation may not openly declare that they are implementing Learning Organisation concept, but they know that they are into the process of implementing Learning Organisation. This is what is called "Subversive" approach.

The third approach is to openly declare that the organisation is into Learning Organisation process.

Another aspect to be considered in developing a Learning Organisation is as to how people at work places react to the Learning Organisation proposal. People behaviour or reaction is fully explained by the five features, *viz.*, (i) Systems Thinking, (ii) Team Learning, (iii) Shared Visions, (iv) Mental Models, and (v) Personal Mastery. These five features, particularly the "Systems Thinking" which Peter Singe called **"Fifth Discipline"** tell us that an organisation should be looked as a system and their should not be isolated approach for development. Every worker should examine and implement an issue considering the impact on the whole organisation. This worker behaviour will solve many problems at the initial stages itself.

LIMITATIONS OF LEARNING ORGANISATION

The concept of Learning Organisation has emerged to cover up the drawbacks in the existing business practices, *viz.*, traditional approach of organisational development, to meet. The demands of economic shifts to globalisation, and to adopt information based business practices. Although many benefits are derived from Learning Organisation, problems in implementing the aspects of Learning Organisation are very many. Top management has to respond positively to a drastic change in organisational business practices. Huge money is involved in implementing the new and innovative practices. But still the results are indefinite. People at work may not be active always. Sharing of knowledge may not take place as expected. Every worker may not have positive approach towards various activities. These aspects hinder the growth of Learning Organisation.

THE FUTURE

The concept of Learning Organisation looks like an ideal concept. The features of Learning Organisation such as flexibility, team learning, continuity, creativity of workforce, etc., should take place simultaneously in organisational learning. It may be difficult for any organisation to continuously adopt training processes to improve the quality of workers (making it an integral part of work process).

Besides this, adaptation of technology to make it more cross-functional and transparent, considering knowledge as the key factor, access to information by all workers (hitherto restricted only to top management) to improve their work culture, developing learning culture in employees at all levels, establishing good relationship between the stakeholders of the organisation, etc., will make an organisation a learning one. Whether these activities take place in an organisation is a big question mark?

But it may be said that a changing business environment at the global level, organisations cannot keep silent. They have to change themselves and adapt to new practices for survival. Whether the organisations like it or not, the years ahead will be an era of change and competition. Every one has to adapt to change.

SUMMARY

1. Learning organisation is one which continuously encourages, teamwork, flexibility in operation, develops knowledge workers, access to information by all at all levels, making training an integral part of firm's work culture, adaptation of new technology and make the workers creative, for the success of the organisation.
2. The concept of learning organisation is not a new one. The Chinese philosopher said way back in 479 BC about Learning Organisation. Even after industrial and commercial revolutions of eighteenth century, the elements of Learning Organisation were in practice in business and manufacturing organisations.
3. The concept Learning Organisation was recognised by Peter Singe in 1990, when he published his book "Fifth Discipline". "Systems Thinking", what Peter Singe describes as "Fifth Discipline", was developed in 1950s. But no one either seriously discussed it or implemented. However, the systems approach made the companies to view the organisational practices with a different tool called "Decision Support System – DSS." This tool in 1970s got a new name called "Organisational Learning."

4. Peter Singe's "Fifth Discipline" gave a new turn to the concept Learning Organisation, explaining the various dimensions such as Personal Mastery, Mental Models, Team Learning, Shared Vision and Systems Thinking and said that these are to be practiced to make an organisation a Learning Organisation.
5. The Learning Organisation converts an inactive organisation into an active organisation. The importance of Learning Organisation lies in the advantages or benefits derived by both the workers and the company, when it is implemented.
6. For the Workers: They are motivated to work with new work practices; make them to be more flexible in operations and thinking; allows them to develop innovative work culture; improves their social interaction increasing interdependency and developing good communication process.
7. For the Organisation: Age old, deep-rooted, traditional practice's will be replaced by new, innovative, ones which make the organisation a productive one; improves customer relationship; facilitates the organisation to create a pool of experts and expertise to taken quick decisions; the workers being converted as "Knowledge workers" make them to adapt quickly to changing work culture; facilitate the company to adapt new technology, implementing strategic marketing and financial plans and make the organisation to face any type of competition.
8. Very important aspect to be considered in Learning Organisation, is dialogue between the workers. This develops very meaningful and powerful communication system.
9. Learning Organisation provides continuous learning opportunities at the levels to achieve the organisational goals. It facilitates the calculated risk-taking to improve productivity of the individuals and the organisation as a whole. Holistic and integrated approach will be visible in Learning Organisation.
10. The Learning Organisation concept focuses on organisational effectiveness but it may be bit difficult to develop a learning organisation. Learning Organisation can be developed by: (i) creating awareness in workers, (ii) making an organisation a flatter one with minimum management levels, (iii) providing good leadership and resources on a long-term basis, (iv) making the employees empowered through quality work culture and (v) providing learning laboratories.
11. The future of Learning Organisation is certain in the sense that every organisation, to survive in their business, have to adopt Learning Organisation dimensions. World-over, in future, organisations become thin (Flatter), more flexible in operations and technology-driven. Knowledge workers will be in the front line. If the organisations do not become Learning Organisations, they cannot survive. Continuous or periodical change in work practices should be the order.

STUDY QUESTIONS

1. Give the meaning of Learning Organisation. Narrate the historical development of the concept of Learning Organisation.
2. Briefly explain the importance of Learning Organisation.
3. Explain five features of Learning Organisation.
4. Explain the importance of "Dialogue" factor in Learning Organisation process.
5. Briefly explain the limitations of Learning Organisation.
6. Give a detailed note on how to develop learning organisation.

5

PLANNING

LEARNING OBJECTIVES

After reading this chapter, you should be able to know:

Planning—I

- Meaning and Nature of Planning
- Objectives of Planning - MBO
- Planning Steps
- Planning Premises
- Planning Types

Planning—II

- Types of Plans
- Planning Methods

PLANNING I

Regardless of the size of the business or non-business unit, planning emerges as a critical management activity. Modern managers are facing the challenge of designing a sound action plan for their organisations to achieve their organisational goals. Planning gives a scientific direction to managers as to where the firm has to move to attain its objectives. A good organisational plan minimizes risk, reduces uncertainties surrounding business conditions and it classifies the consequences of related action. Planning increases the degree of success and establishes co-ordinated effort in the organisation. It makes the managers future-oriented and their decisions co-ordinated. Good planning make the organisations reach their objectives. In this backdrop, various issues of planning are narrated in the following paragraphs.

Planning is a particular type of decision-making that addresses the specific future that managers desire for their organisations. It is the process of fixing goals of the business and finding the ways to attain these goals. Plan will help the managers to organise people and resources effectively. Plans develop confidence in managers.

Planning is the first managerial function to be performed in the process of management. It is concerned with deciding in advance what is to be done, when, where, how and by whom it is to be done. Thus, it is a predetermined course of action to achieve a specified aim or goal.

The definitions of planning given by the different writers are listed here.

In the words of Alfred and Batty, "Planning is a thinking process, the organised foresight, the vision based on facts and experience that is required for intelligent action."

According to Koontz and O'Donnell, "Planning is essentially decision-making since it involves choosing from among alternatives." According to George Terry, "Planning is the selecting and relating of facts and making and using of assumptions regarding the future in the visualisation and formulation of proposed activities believed necessary to achieve the desired results."

A careful analysis of the above definitions of planning reveals that:

— Planning is concerned with future and its essence is looking ahead;

— it involves thinking and analysis of information;

— it involves a predetermined course of action;

— it is concerned with the establishment of objectives to be attained in the future;

— it is fundamentally a problem of choosing after a careful study of alternative courses;

— it involves decision-making;

— its objectives is to achieve better results;

— it is a continuous and integrated process.

In every human activity, there is an element of planning. For instance, we find that the head of the family plans his expenditure, the housewife plans her daily chores, the teacher plans his teaching work, the student plans his studies and the farmer plans his agricultural activities. In the business field, the need for planning is all the more because of various factors such as fluctuations in demand, growing competition, introduction of new products, scarcity of resources, changing technology, change in prices, government policy, etc. Organisational activity without a plan is likely to be ineffective and will drift without achieving success. Hence, planning is a must for business organisations.

NATURE OR CHARACTERISTICS OF PLANNING

The following are the important characteristics of planning:

1. Focus on objectives. A plan starts with the setting of objectives and then makes efforts to realise them by developing policies, procedures, strategies, etc.

2. It is an intellectual process. According to Koontz and O'Donnell, planning is an intellectual process involving mental exercise, foreseeing future developments, making forecasts and the determination of the best course of action.

3. Planning is a selective process. It involves the selection of the best one after making a careful analysis of various alternative courses of action. It is concerned with decision-making relating to (a) what is to be done, (b) how it is to be done, (c) when it is to be done, and (d) by whom it is to be done.

4. Planning is pervasive. Planning is a pervasive activity covering all the levels of enterprise. While top management is concerned with strategic planning, the middle management and the lower management are concerned with administrative planning and operational planning respectively.

5. Planning is an integrated process. Planning involves not only the determination of objectives but also the formulation of sound policies, programmes, procedures and strategies for the accomplishment of these objectives. It is the first of the managerial functions and facilitates other managerial functions like organising, staffing, directing and controlling.

6. Planning is directed towards efficiency. To increase the efficiency of the enterprise is the main purpose of planning. The guiding principles of a good plan is the maximum output and profit at the minimum cost. Terry has aptly stated that "planning is the foundation of the most successful action of an enterprise."

7. Planning is flexible. The process of planning should be adaptable to the changes take place in the environment. Koontz and O'Donnell emphasise that "effective planning requires continual checking on events and forecasts and the redrawing of plans to maintain a course towards a designed goal."

8. First function in the process of management. Planning is the beginning of the process of management. A manager must plan before he can possibly organise, staff, direct or control. Because planning sets all other functions into action, it can be seen as the most basic function of the management. Without planning, other functions become meaningless activity, producing nothing, but chaos.

9. It is a decision-making process. Decision-making is an integral part of planning. It is defined as the process of choosing among alternatives. Obviously, decision-making will occur at many points in the planning process. For example, in planning for their organisation, the managers first decide the goals to pursue. Such as without all companents have to be produced internally or a partion of it has to be outsourced etc.

10. It is a continuous process. Planning is a continuous process. Koontz and O'Donnell rightly observe that like a navigator constantly checking where his ship is going in the vast ocean, a manager should constantly watch the progress of his plans. He must constantly monitor the conditions, both within and outside the organisation, to determine if changes are required in his plans.

ESSENTIALS OF GOOD PLAN

According to I.F. Urwick, essentials of a good plan are as follows:

1. It should be based on a clearly defined objective.
2. It must be simple.

3. It should be rationale and appropriate.
4. It should be comprehensive.
5. It should provide for a proper analysis and classification of actions.
6. It must be flexible.
7. It must be balanced.
8. It must use all available resources and opportunities to the utmost before creating new authorities and new resources.
9. It should be free from social and psychological biases of the planners as well as of subordinates.
10. There should be proper co-ordination among short-term and long-term plans.

Advantages of Planning

The following points emphasise the importance and benefits of planning:

1. Planning offsets future uncertainty and change. A business concern has to work in an environment which is uncertain and ever-changing. Planning helps the manager carving out the future course of action and this brings a higher degree of certainty and order into the organisation than would be present without planning.

2. It tackles increasing complexity in modern business. To run a modern business undertaking, there is need for a large number of people with different specialisation and complex machines. This makes it necessary for the management to depend on planning to get a clear idea of what is to be done, when it is to be done, where it is to be done and how it is to be done.

3. It helps co-ordination. Planning, through its defined objectives, well-publicised policies, programmes and procedures, helps the management in the co-ordination process. According to Koontz and O'Donnell, "plans are selected courses along which the management desires to co-ordinate group action."

4. It helps in exercising effective control. Planning involves the determination in advance of the work to be done, the person responsible to do it, the time to be taken to do that work and the costs to be incurred. This makes it easy to compare the actual performance with the planned one. In the case of deviations, steps may be taken to find out the reasons for such deviations. Thus, planning helps in exercising effective control. H.G. Hicks has rightly said that "planning is clearly a prerequisite for effective controlling. It is utterly foolish to think that controlling could be accomplished without planning. Without planning, there is no pre-determined understanding of the desired performance."

5. It helps in the proper utilisation of the company's resources: As planning involves deciding in advance of what is to be done, when, where, and by whom it is to be done, etc., there is a possibility for the proper utilisation of company's resources and for the achievement of company's objectives at the cheapest and the best manner.

6. It facilitates unity of action. Under planning, policies, procedures and programmes are predetermined and every decision and action should be within the framework of predetermined policies and procedures and programmes. This facilitates unity of action and also avoids confusion or misunderstanding at any level.

7. It helps in avoiding business failures. As planning involves the selection of best objectives, unity of action, co-ordination of activities, economy in operation and offsetting of future uncertainty and change, there is a great possibility of avoiding business failures.

8. Focuses attention on organisation's goals. Planning helps the manager to focus attention on the organisational goals and activities. This makes it easier to apply and coordinate the resources of the organisation more efficiently. The whole organisation is made free to embrace identical goals and collaborate in achieving them.

9. Improves competitive strength. The enterprises which adopt planning will have a competitive edge over other enterprises which do not have planning. This is because, planning enables the enterprises to discover new opportunities and thereby shape its own future. According to Earnest Dale, the enterprises which have planning continually monitor the environment for new ideas and developments.

10. Improves adaptability. Planning helps the organisation in coping with the changing environment. Planning is looking ahead and is anticipatory in nature. It means planning precedes action. The anticipation of future events and changing conditions prepares the organisation to meet them and adapt them for managing the operations effectively.

11. Guides decision-making. The success of an organisation depends to a great extent on the type of decisions that are made at the various levels of an organisation. Decision-making involves making a choice from the various available alternatives after evaluating each of these. Planning targets, objectives and course of action provide managers with guidelines and criteria against which to evaluate alternatives and choose those which are the most suitable. Thus,planning guides decision-making.

12. Secures economy in operation. As planning involves the selection of the most profitable course of action after evaluating the various alternatives, the enterprise can achieve the best results at a minimum cost.

Limitations or Disadvantages of Planning

Though planning is a primary function of management and facilitates various other management functions and brings orderliness, stability and continuity in operation, it suffers from certain limitations. They are:

1. Limitation of forecasts. Planning is based on forecasts and if realiable information data are not available for making forecasts, planning is sure to lose much of its value.

2. Rigidity. Planning implies strict adherence to predetermined policies, procedures and programmes. This restricts individual's freedom, initiative and desire for creativity.

3. Time-consuming. Planning is time-consuming and may delay action in certain cases. But to make plans realistic, it is necessary that sufficient time should be given to the planning process.

4. Costly. Planning is an expensive exercise as a lot of money has to be spent for preparing estimates, collecting information and facts for analysis, etc.

5. Influence of external factors. Sometimes, because of the influence of external factors like government control, natural calamities, break-out of war, changes in political and economic situations, etc., which are beyond the control of the planners, the effectiveness of planning becomes limited.

6. Limited scope. The scope of planning is said to be limited in the case of organisations with rapidly changing situations. It is claimed that for industries producing fashionable articles or for those engaged in the publication of textbooks, working on a day-to-day oasis is more economical than on a planned basis.

7. People's resistance. Planning may sometimes generate people's resistance to it. In old established organisations, managers are often frustrated in instituting a new plan simply by the unwillingness or inability of people to accept it.

8. Failure of people in planning. Sometimes, the persons involved in the planning process fail to formulate correct plans. Some of the reasons for failure are lack of commitment to planning, failure to formulate sound strategies, lack of clearly-defined objectives, tendencies to overlook planning premises, not having a clear idea of the scope of plans, lack of support from top management, lack of effective control technique, lack of delegation of authority etc.

Some of the above limitations can be overcome by taking measures such as proper organisation of the management's system for collecting relevant facts and figures for making forecasts, making of flexible plans, etc.

Objectives — A Type of Planning

Objectives are the ends towards which the activities of an organisation are directed. According to Robert C. Appleby, "Objectives are goals. They are aims which management wish organisations to achieve." They lay down guidelines for the various .activities of the enterprise and decide the direction, nature and quantum of efforts needed for these activities.

For effective planning in any business organisation, objectives are essential and in fact, planning has no meaning if it is not related to objectives. Objectives are not only useful for effective planning but also for other managerial functions like organising, directing and controlling. This may be constructed as a method of planning.

Organisational objectives are the basis for Developing a plan. Planning dimensions include the relationship between management and organisational objectives, individual versus organisational objectives, operational objectives and management by objectives. This also throws light on strategic planning, decision-making process, various types of plans and planning tools, available to managers.

Specifically, planning offers the following:

— Definition of planning.

— Steps in planning process.

— Strategies to be developed to fit into organisational process.

— Environmental analysis establishing organisational direction.

— Strategy implementation and control.

— Failure of plans.

Organisational objectives are the ones which provide strong base to design and develop a workable plan. In an open management system, organisational objectives act as the basis to design and develop operational procedures which is called "Plan." The objectives give a specific direction to formulate an operational system which reflects the purpose of the organisation.

Organisational purpose is what organisation wants to do and for which it exists to serve target group of customers and their needs.

As organisations exist for different purposes, the objectives also differ. The chart given here provides the basis to understand the organisational objectives which provide the input to draft an organisational plan.

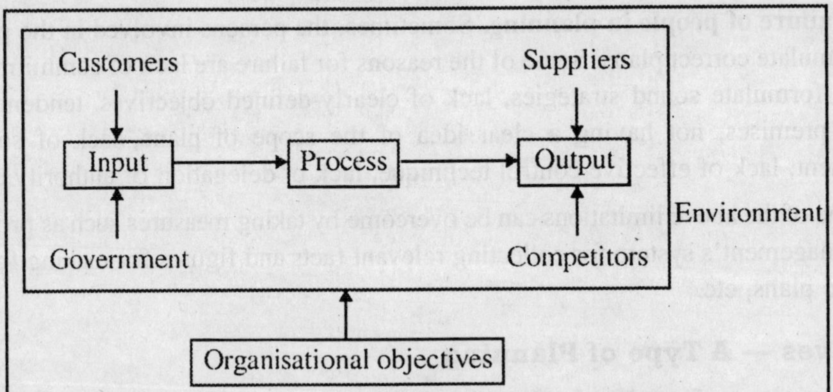

Fig. 5.1. Open Management System and Organisational Objectives to Design a Plan

Organisational objectives focus on three common aspects:

(i) Earning profit for the organisation.

(ii) Servicing the customers effectively to survive in the society

(iii) Undertaking social responsibility task as per ethical and moral codes of the society.

Objectives should be neither demanding nor sub-standard as to incapable of maximising potential of employees. If objectives are non-workable, plans designed and adapted prove abortive. "Fixing your objective is like identifying the North Star – you right your compass on it and then use it as the means of getting back on track when you tend to stray" (Marshall E. Demock). Therefore, proper objectives have to be formulated to give good guidlines to draft organisational plans which will be consistent and performance-oriented.

While formulating objectives following aspects are to be considered:

— Productivity

— Physical and financial resources

— Profitability

— Marketing

— Managerial performance and development

— Innovation

— Worker performance and attitude.

— Public responsibility, *i.e.,* Accountability to society, ethical and moral aspects.

The important characteristics of business objectives are as follows:

(1) Multiple in nature: Objectives are needed in all areas of business on which its survival depends and hence there must be multiple objectives rather than a single one. According to Peter F. Drucker, the objectives of the business may relate to market standing, innovation, productivity, physical and financial resources, profitability, worker's performance and development and social responsibilities.

(2) Objectives have hierarchy: The objectives which are based on a mission or purpose of the company from a hierarchy from the top level to the lowest position in the organisation structure. The organisation's objectives, for instance, may be to earn a certain rate or return on the investment. This objectives in turn may generate objectives to other departments, then to sections and individuals. This process of creating objectives from the top level to the lowest position creates a hierarchy of of objectives. See Fig. 5.2 for the hierarchy of objectives.

(3) Objectives may be long-range or short-range: The objectives may be of two types: long-range objectives such as survival and growth and short-range objectives like market standing, maximisation cf sales, product development, productivity, effective utilisation of resources, etc.

(4) Objectives are interdependent: Objectives are interdependent and must support one another so that they may be realised simultaneously.

(5) Objectives are either tangible or intangible: For some of the objectives such as in the areas of productivity, market standing, physical and financial standing, there are quantifiable values available. Other areas of objectives such as manager's performance, workers' morale etc., are not readily quantifiable and are completely intangible.

(6) Objectives have a priority: This implies that at a given point of time, the accomplishment of one objective is relatively more important than that of others. For example, for a firm which is facing difficulty in meeting pay rolls and due dates on accounts, the goal of maintaining a minimum cash balance may be critically important.

(7) Objectives sometimes may clash with each other: In an enterprise, each department is given the responsibility for attaining a specified objective. This creates the problem of potential goal conflict and sub-optimisation, because achieving the goal of one department may jeopardise the achieving of goal of another department. For example, the production goal of low unit costs achieved through mass production of low quality products may conflict with the sales goal of selling high-quality products.

The following diagram depicts the hierarchy of objectives.

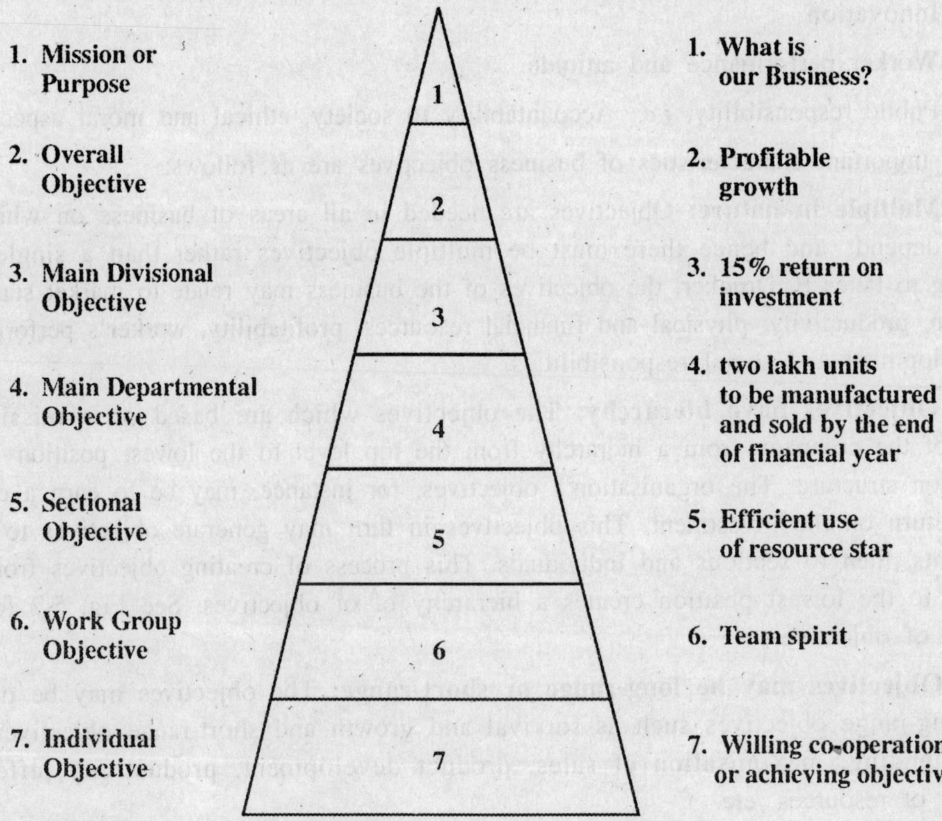

Fig. 5.2. Hierarchy of Objectives

Requirements of Sound Objectives

While laying down objectives, there are certain requirements that the managers should always keep in mind. They are:

1. Objectives must be clear.
2. Objectives must support one another.
3. Objectives must be precise and measurable.
4. Objectives should always remain valid.
5. Objectives should be result-centered.
6. Objectives should encourage higher performance, yet be realistic.
7. Objectives must be balanced.

Advantages of Objectives

The following are the important advantages accruing from the sound and carefully chosen objectives:

(a) Unified planning: In the process of objective-setting, the various plans prepared by several people are adjusted to a common objective and this encourages unified planning.

(b) Individual motivation. The objective setting process involve specifying the purpose of each job and fit the individual purposes and goals into the overall company's goals. This results in individuals accepting organisational objectives as being desirable and fulfilling them becomes a source of satisfaction to him.

(c) Co-ordination. As there is a common agreement on a set of objectives, there is a possibility for co-ordination of work and efforts.

(d) Standards for control. Objectives provide the yardstick to measure the performance at various levels and by this, they facilitate the control of human effort in an organisation.

(e) Basis for decentralisation. As the objectives indicate the contributions to be made by each unit towards the realisation of a common objective, there is a need for the managers concerned to exercise their individual skills and initiative. This means, assigning of decision-making power to subordinates to enable them to perform their work effectively. Thus, objectives from the basis for decentralisation.

(f) Basis for planning. Objectives provide a basis for planning and for developing other types of plans such as budgets, policies and procedure.

(g) Eliminate haphazard action. Objectives eliminate haphazard actions which may result in undesirable consequences.

(h) Better management. They facilitate better management of the enterprise by providing a basis for leading, guiding, directing and controlling the activities of people of various departments.

(i) Reduce misunderstanding and conflict. They reduce misunderstanding and conflict and facilitate communication among people by minimising jurisdictional disputes.

OBJECTIVE SETTING

The process of setting objectives is not simple but quite complicated. The objectives must be realistic and attainable and at the same time, they should represent a high level of efficiency. The objectives should neither be too high nor too low. If they are too high, they cannot be achieved and the managers and workers would become frustrated and if they are too low, they serve no purpose. Further, the objectives must be defined clearly so that the concerned persons can understand them correctly. According to L. Gulick, "a clear statement of purpose universally understood is the outstanding guarantee of effective communication."

The process of setting objectives involves the following:

(a) Classifying of objectives into major and derivative goals and long-range and short-range objectives.

(b) The objectives that are set must be reasonable, realistic and they should have consistency. In other words, the objectives must be attainable with reasonable ease and they should be set in realistic terms and not in idealistic terms. Only when they attainable, they can provide incentive and job satisfaction for high performance. In addition, they must be consistent.

(c) Most enterprises have multiple goals and objectives at a time, covering different areas. As has already been stated, according to Peter F. Drucker, there are eight areas for which objectives have to be set. The areas consist of market standing, innovation, productivity, physical and financial resources, profitability, manager performance and development, worker performance and attitude and public responsibilities.

The management should consider the various areas for setting the objective and also specific objectives for different areas and they must be deduced from the broader and overall objectives of enterprise.

(d) Adequate thought should also be given for balancing of the various objectives and for removing their conflicts. Short-range objectives and minor objectives should not conflict with the long-range and major objectives of the concern and they should be recognised as a distinct step in the realisation of long-term and major objectives. Further, although objectives are more stable than other plans, the management has to recognise the fact that business is functioning in a dynamic business environment which necessitates the company to make periodic adjustments of objectives to keep pace with the progress of time and changes in environment.

Approaches to Objective Setting (or Goal Setting)

Two approaches of objective setting can be identified. They are:(a) Traditional approach and (b) Management by objectives. The important features of these two approaches are as follows:

(a) Traditional Approach: In this approach, the objectives are set by the people at the top of the organisation for those at the lower levels. This approach is essentially one-way and it is called an **authoritarian** approach. This approach is likely to reduce their motivation, sense of commitment and responsibility.

(b) Management by Objectives — MBO : MBO is a technique and philosophy of management based on converting an organisational objective into a personal objective on the presumption that establishing personal objectives makes an employee committed, which leads to a better performance. The objective setting in MBO creates an integrated hierarchy of objectives throughout the entire organisation. In the process of objective setting in MBO, superiors and subordinates jointly identify common objectives, set the result that should be achieved by the subordinates, assess the contribution of each individual and integrate individuals with the organisation so that the resources of the organisation are put to their best use. Thus, we find, in MBO, the process of objective setting involves participation and collaboration among the various levels of organisation with the intention of achieving organisational objectives.

Koontz and others have defined MBO thus: "MBO is a comprehensive managerial system that integrates many key managerial activities in a systematic manner, consciously directed towards the effective and efficient achievement of organisational objectives."

According to Prof. S.K. Chakravarthi, "MBO is a result-centered, non-specialist, operational managerial process for the effective utilisation of material, physical and human resources of the organisation by integrating the individual with the organisation and organisation with the environment."

Based on the definitions given above, we can state some important features of MBO. They are:

1. MBO is a technique and philosophy of management.
2. In the process of objective setting in MBO, superiors and subordinates jointly identify common objectives and set the result that should be achieved.
3. Objectives are established for all levels of the organisation, including the corporate level, all the units or departments and individual managers.
4. It is directed towards the effective and efficient achievement of organisational objectives.
5. It is concerned with converting an organisation objectives into a personal objective on the pesumption that establishing personal objectives makes an employee committed which leads to better performance.
6. As an approach to management, with the objective orientation is its essence, MBO is bound to have some relationship with every management technique.
7. The basic emphasis of MBO is on objectives. MBO tries to match objectives with resources.
8. Periodic review of performance is an important feature of MBO.
9. MBO provides the means for integrating the organisation with its environment, its sub-systems and people.
10. Employees are provided with feedback on actual performance as compared to planned performance.

The concept "MBO is a management approach that uses organisational objective as primary means to manage organisations." MBO concept was popularized by the writting of Peter Drucker. It is a tool adopted by managers of both profit and non-profit organisations. MBO will have three vital components:

1. Every worker is asked to complete a specialized set of objectives, which were mutually agreed upon by both manager and employee during normal working period.
2. Whether set objectives to each employee is attained or not will be measured periodically through standard review process.
3. Based upon their achievements of set objectives, each employee is rewarded.

The following diagram reveals the MBO process.

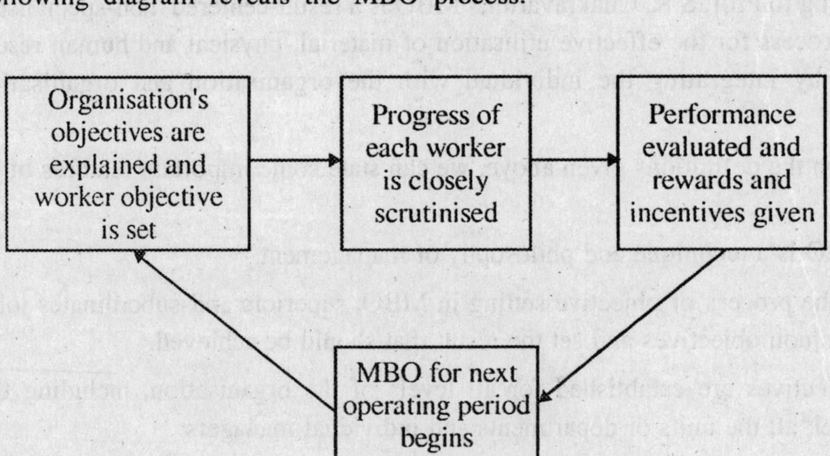

Fig. 5.3. The MBO Process

As depected in the figure, MBO process involves the following steps.

1. Manager has to understand and review organisational objectives to have clear knowledge of them.
2. Manager has to discuss with every member/worker of his team about the objectives to be set for the worker well within the framework of the organisational objectives.
3. Periodical review of the performance of each worker has to be evaluated with the set objectives for him/her besides continuous monitoring.
4. Rewards to be given based on performance and MBO for new operating period has to be given.

To make MBO successful, following aspects are to be considered.

(i) MBO goals for each worker should be set within the framework of organisational objective and it should be appropriate. Inappropriate objectives tend to produce unwanted results and will be unproductive.

(ii) The objectives to be attained by each worker have to be discussed in detail before they are implemented. Each employee should feel that the task assigned to his/her is just and attainable.

(iii) Continuous evaluation system of each employee's work should be adopted. This facilitates the correction of mistakes in the initial stage itself and avoids much of loss. This also helps in adopting meaningful procedures to attain the objectives.

(iv) Rewards and incentives should be the part of MBO which motivates employees to work hard and attain the set goals and objectives.

(v) Managers must be shrewed enough to precisely evaluate the performance. Otherwise imbalance in setting the objectives for workers will creep in.

Benefits of MBO

- MBO gives specific direction to all employees as to what is to be achieved by every one to attain the organisational objectives.
- It commits employees to perform their tasks effectively as the tasks to be performed are mutually agreed upon.

An effective MBO system results in several benefits of the organisation. They are:

1. As the managers at all levels are involved in setting their objectives, they are more committed to the goals fixed and generally they work hard to achieve them.
2. Mangers at all levels become more aware of the overall objectives and this helps them in understanding their role in the total organisation.
3. MBO implies that the objectives of each department are consistent with the overall objectives of the organisation. This ensures that people and the departments do not work at cross purposes.
4. MBO also helps in making a more systematic evaluation of performance. This is made possible, as MBO not only states what one is expected to achieve but also measures criteria to judge the performance. This also helps the organisation in taking corrective action if required.
5. We find in the MBO technique clarity of objectives, role clarity, periodic feedback of performance and participation by managers in the management process. Because of these, resources and activities are put to use in such a way that they result in better performance.
6. MBO provides greater opportunity to managers for personal satisfaction. This is possible, because of the two important features of MBO, *viz.,* (i) participation in objective setting and (ii) rational performance appraisal. Participation in objective setting makes them feel that they are important to the organisation. Further, as their performance is measured in terms of their actual performance without any managerial" prejudices or biases, the managers feel that their interests are protected.
7. MBO is the basis for organisational change. If the MBO is applied, there is a constant process of interaction between superiors and subordinates for objective setting and performance review in this system of objective setting and performance evaluation by the superior without associating subordinates.

Limitations of MBO

- It increases paperwork and number of meetings to be conducted as each employee's task is to be defined and agreed upon by both manager and each employee. Managers may not find time to conduct meetings.
- The time for performing the tasks may be less, as objectives for all workers have to be set simultaneously.
- Sometimes, it is difficult to set verifiable goals to workers and research department.

- Differences in the states of subordinates may not create an open atmosphere which is necessary for appropriate goal setting.
- Managers fail to understand and appreciate MBO philosophy. They have number of doubts about MBO. They do not understand. The purpose served by MBO or how the performance to be appraised. They consider MBO as another tool of control. Because of this way of thinking, it is difficult to introduce MBO sucessfully.
- Environment in which an organisation operates is dynamic and because of this, a particular objective may not be valid for everyone. But may members often hesitate to change the objectives during a period of time. This inflexibility may cause harm to the organisation.

Inspite of these limitations, MBO is considered to be one of the important techniques of managing the business and more and more organisations are adopting this technique. Full benefits of the MBO programme can be derived if certain basic requirements are taken care of. They are:

1. Top management should support the MBO programme.
2. Defining the purpose of MBO clearly.
3. Setting individual's objectives jointly by the superior and subordinates.
4. Evaluating individuals periodically and providing them with feedback concerning their performance.
5. Rewarding individuals on the basis of objective evaluation of their attainment.
6. Implementing MBO at lower levels also, *i.e.*, it must be carried all the way down to the first line of organisation.

MANAGEMENT BY EXCEPTION

This means that a manager should devote his time and attention only to exceptional matters, which are of crucial significance and cannot be taken care of by the subordinates. All routine matters should be handed down for disposal to the subordinates.

PLANNING PROCESS

The various steps involved in the planning process are as follows:

1. Awareness of opportunities and problems. The first step in planning is the awareness of the unexploited business opportunities or the problems to be provided for in future. The following types of question will help in ascertaining clearly the opportunities and problems:

(a) What business opportunities or problems are likely to arise in future?

(b) What is the plan to be formed to exploit such opportunities or such problem?

(c) Whether it is necessary to devise a new plan or will it be sufficient to modify the existing plan?

(d) By effectuating the plan, what benefit the organisation will get?

2. Collecting and analysing information. The next step is to gather adequate information and data relating to the planning to be made and to analyse it to find out the cause-effect relationship between the various factors.

3. Determination of objectives. Analysis and interpretation of data facilitate in determining the enterprise objectives. Objectives must be specific and clear and should indicate the end result of planning activity. The objectives should be for the enterprise as a whole and then they must be broken down into departmental and sectional objectives.

4. Determining planning premises and constraints. Premises are planning assumptions on the basis of which planning takes place. Thus, it is a forecast of conditions like trends in population, political and economic environment, production costs, advertising policy, availability of labour, material, power, etc. Some of the premises like population growth and political environment are uncontrollable while some degree of control can be exercised on the technology to be used, availability of raw materials, etc. Further, there will be constraints like government control which affect the plans. Plans should be formulated by the management in the backdrop of such premises and constraints.

5. Finding out the alternative courses of action. The next step is to find out the various alternative courses of action. For every plan, there are a number of alternatives and hence, all possible alternatives to work out a plan for achieving the desired objectives, should be found out for their evaluation.

6. Evaluation of alternatives and selection. The next step is to evaluate all possible alternatives with reference to cost, speed, quality, etc., and select the best course of action.

7. Determining secondary plans. After selecting the best course of action, the management has to formulate the secondary plans to support the basic plan. Without the secondary plans, the basic plan which is prepared for the whole enterprise cannot be effectively implemented. For example, for effective operation of the basic production plan, a number of secondary plans for purchasing of raw materials, acquisition of plant and machinery, training of workers, arranging for adequate finance, etc., have to be prepared for the successful operation of the basic plan.

Steps In Planning

Step-1 | Stating organisational objectives

↓

Step-2 | List the alternative channels of reaching the objectives

↓

Step-3 | Develop premises on which each alternative is listed

↓

Step-4 | Select the best alternative which fits into organisational objectives

↓

Step-5 | Prepare a sound plan out of selected alternative. This will be a master plan which contains various functional plans

↓

Step-6 | Implement the designed plan

Fig. 5.4. Planning Process

8. Securing participation of employees. The successful execution of plan depends to a large extent on the wholehearted co-operation of the employees. In view of this, the management should involve employees in planning through communication, consultation and participation.

9. Providing for follow-up and future evaluation. In order to see that the plans are proceeding along right lines, it is necessary for the management to devise a system for continuous evaluation and appraisal of the plan. By this, the management can notice shortcomings in time and can also take immediate suitable corrective action.

PLANNING PREMISES

We have observed that establishing premises is one of the steps in the planning process. Now let us give more details about this.

Planning premises are certain assumptions about the future on the basis of which the plan will be ultimately formulated. Planning premises are vital to the success of planning as they supply pertinent facts and information relating to the future such as population trends, the general economic conditions, production costs and prices, probable competitive behaviour, capital and material availability, governmental control and so on.

Classification of Planning Premises

Planning premises can be classified as under:

(a) Internal and external premises.

(b) Tangible and intangible premises.

(c) Controllable and non-controllable premises.

(a) Internal and external premises. Premises may exist within and without the company. Important internal premises include forecasts, policies and programmes of organisation, capital investment in plant and equipment, competence of management; skill of the labour force—other resources and abilities of the organisation in the form of machines, money and methods, and beliefs, behaviour and values of the owners and employees of the organisation. External premises may be classified into three groups: (a) business environment, (b) factors which influence the demand for the products of the enterprise and (c) factors which affect the resources available to the enterprise. These external premises may include the following:

(i) General business and economic environment.
(ii) Technological changes.
(iii) Government policies and regulations.
(iv) Population growth.
(v) Political stability.
(vi) Sociological factors.
(vii) Demand for industry's product.

(b) Tangible and intangible premises: Some of the planning premises may be tangible while some others may be intangible. Tangible premises are those which can be quantitatively measured while intangible premises are those which being qualitative in character cannot be so measured. Population growth, industry demand, capital and resources invested in the organisation are tangible premises whose quantitative measurement is possible.

On the other hand, political stability, sociological factors, business and economic environment, attitude, philosophies and behaviour of the owners of the organisation are all intangible premises whose quantitative measurement is not possible.

(c) Controllable and non-controllable premises: While some of the planning premises are controllable, some others are non-controllable. Because of the presence of uncontrollable factors, here is need for the organisation to revise the plans periodically in accordance with current developments. Some of the examples of uncontrollable factors are strikes, wars, natural calamities, emergency, legislation, etc. Controllable factors are those which can be controllable and normally cannot upset the well-thoughtout calculation of the organisation regarding the plan. Some of the examples of controllable factors are: the company's advertising policy, competence of management members, skill of the labour force, availability of resources in terms of capital and labour, attitude and behaviour of the owners of the organisation, etc.

Although these classifications can be made, at the operational level we observe the integrated approach and all these are merged at different levels of management. The following figures show the types of plans followed at each level:

Top Management Plan

Adopts long-term planning
It is a master plan, involving strategic plan for the entire firm.
Describes central concept, mission, purpose and creed.
Covers all departments and respective research and development.
Formulation of corporate objectives to be followed by all divisions.
Basic Corporate policies.
Total Budget including financial plan and capital budgeting.

Fig. 5.5. Planning at Top Level

Middle Management Plan

These are the segment plans involving:
— Objectives, strategies and policies to achieve one or some of the corporate obejctives (Functional Plans).
Divisional or departmental objectives are the local aspects
— Concentrate on medium term or tactical plans.

Fig. 5.6. Planning at Middle Management

Botton Line Management Plan

— These plans involve actual operations of the firm. The systems, methods and procedure adopted by the firm will be implemented at this level. It is only an operational plan.
— The focus on projects, schedules, operating goals, programmes and short-run budgets

Fig. 5.7. Bottom Line Planning

PLANNING SECTION-II

1. Types of Plans

There are many types of plans which are prepared for different purposes at different points of time. However, the ultimate obejctive is to minimise risk in business operations and to improve the level of success of business. Risk can be minimised by analyzing controllable and uncontrollable factors which hover round the business. Success level can be improved by coordinating various business operations at different levels of the organisation. Planning, therefore, increases the organisational effectiveness, if propertly designed and implemented. However, a single master plan can depict the whole organisational objectives. But it will comprise of various functional plans. Considering all these aspects plans are categorised and classfied.

Planning can be classified in different forms. Basically, it is classified on the basis of: **(i) Time, (ii) Managerial levels, (iii) Repetitiveness of the operations in the firm, and (iv) Scope.**

Based upon time, the plan is classified as (i) Long-range Planning, (ii) Medium-range Planning and (iii) Short-range Planning.

On the basis of managerial levels, the plans may be: (i) Strategic plans, (ii) Administrative plans and (iii) Operational plans.

In terms of repetitiveness of operations in the firm, planning may be: (i) Standing plan and (ii) Single use plans.

Planning is also classified on the basis of scope. They are: (i) Companywise or Master Plan and (ii) Functional or Departmental Plan for each department like production, finance, marketing, human resources, etc.

From the three charts shown previously, it may be observed that an integrated approach is taken for planning to achieve main goals of the organisation. Different types of planning activity are taken up at different levels. Standing plans (repeated use plans) and single-use plans are the **two basic types we observe in any organisation with different activities at different levels.** Therefore, these two types of plans are discussed in the following paragraphs.

2. Planning Methods

Planning as said earlier, can be classified according to different dimensions of business operations. However, there are two basic methods normally followed in every organisation. They are:

(i) Standing or repeated use plans

(ii) Single-use plans

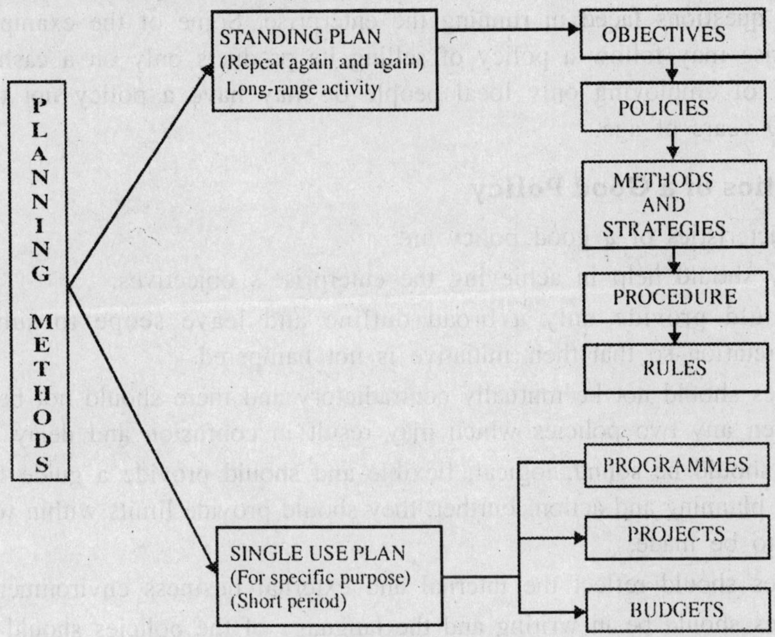

Fig. 5.8. Standing Plan and Single-use Plan

On the basis of stated objectives, an organisation develops standing plans and single-use plans. Standing plans which are to be used over and over again lead to the development of policies, procedures, methods, rules and strategies. Single-use plans which are to be used in specific situations only produce programmes and budgets. In the following pages, we have made a detailed explanation of these plans.

STANDING OR REPEATED USE PLANS

As stated earlier these plans are repetitive in nature (used again and again) and may change, not quite often, to suit the needs of the organisation. Objectives, policies, procedures, rules, methods, strategies form the part of standing plan. Every individual in the organisation has to follow the methods and procedures. Thus, every activity takes place in a disciplined and planned way and repetitive action will be there. The elements of standing plans are discussed in the following paragraphs.

Policy

Policies provide the framework within which the decision-makers are expected to operate while making decisions relating to the organisation. They are a guide to the thinking and action of subordinates for the purpose of achieving the objectives of the business successfully. According to George R. Terry, "Policy is a verbal, written or implied overall guide setting up boundaries that supply the general limits and directions in which managerial action will take place." Thus, the policies are a guide to thinking and action of those who have to make decisions.

They also lay down the limits within which decisions have to be made for accomplishing the enterprise's objectives. They are the basis for executive operation and provide ready answers to all questions faced in running the enterprise. Some of the examples of policies are: an enterprise may follow a policy of selling its products only on a cash basis or may adopt a policy of employing only local people or may have a policy not to employ any person over 60 years of age.

Characteristics of a Good Policy

The characteristies of a good policy are:

(a) Policy should help in achieving the enterprise's objectives.

(b) It should provide only a broad outline and leave scope to subordinates for interpretation so that their initiative is not hampered.

(c) Policies should not be mutually contradictory and there should not be inconsistency between any two policies which may result in confusion and delay in action.

(d) They should be sound, logical, flexible and should provide a guide for thinking in future planning and action. Further, they should provide limits within which decisions have to be made.

(e) Policies should reflect the internal and external business environment.

(f) Policies should be in writing and the language of the policies should be intelligible to the persons who are supposed to implement them and to those who are to be affected by them.

Policies

On the basis of source
1. Original Policies
2. Appealed Policies
3. External or Imposed Policies

On the basis of functions
1. Production Policy
2. Marketing Policy
3. Financial Policy
4. Personal Policy

On the basis of level
1. Basic Policies
2. General Policies
3. Departmental Policies

Fig. 5.9. Kinds of Policies

Kinds of Policies

Policies may be of different types. They can be classified on the following basis:

Originated Policies. These policies are formulated by the managers. They tell subordinates how to act in a given situation and the subordinates are expected to follow them strictly. They are the basic policies and they have the support of organisational authorities.

Appealed Policy. If, on any matter, the subordinate is not clear and the doubt about his authority to handle a situation and if that subject matter is not already covered by the existing policies, he may refer the matter for his superior's verdict. Superior's verdict generates appealed policy and thus becomes a guide for the future action of the subordinates.

External or Imposed Policy. Sometimes, outside agencies like government, trade associations, trade unions etc. may also have instrumental in the formulation of a policy by the enterprise. For example, if the government imposes a condition on the enterprises to reserve a certain percentage of jobs for the backward sections of society or for persons within the state, it becomes an external or imposed policy.

Functional Policies. Policies which are formulated for various functional areas of management are known as functional policies. Some examples of functional policies are: financial policy, production policy, marketing policy and personnel policy.

Policies on the Basis of Levels. Policies formulated on this basis may be basic policies meant to be used by top managers, general policies meant to be used normally by middle managers and departmental policies meant to be used by the departmental managers.

Guidelines for Effective Policy-making

Guidelines for making effective policies are as follows:

1. Policies as far as possible should be in writing.
2. They should be clearly understood by those who are supposed to implement them.
3. They should reflect the objectives of the organisation.
4. To ensure successful implementation of policies, the top managers and the subordinates who are supposed to implement them must participate in their formulation.
5. Conditions change and policies must also change accordingly. Hence, a policy must strike reasonable balance between stability and flexibility.
6. Different policies in the organisation should not pull in different directions and should support one another.
7. Policies should not be detrimental to the interests of society.
8. Policies should be periodically reviewed in order to see whether they are to be modified, changed or completely abandoned.

Procedure

Objectives and policies do not state the ways and means through which objectives are to be accomplished and policies put into effect. Hence, there is a need for procedures. Procedures are clear-cut administrative specifications prescribing the time sequence for work to be done. They can be defined as plans "prescribing the exact chronological sequence of specific tasks required to perform designated work." Thus, procedures tell how a particular activity is to be carried out.

Features of Procedures

Some important features of procedures are:

(a) They are a guide to action.

(b) They are generally meant tor repetitive work so that some steps are followed every time that activity is accomplished. This is the reason why 'procedures' are also called 'repetitive use plans.'

(c) Procedures are established in keeping with the objectives, policies and resources position.

(d) They are concerned with establishing the time sequence for work to be done.

Procedures can be established for a wide variety of work such as purchase and issue of raw materials from store, recruitment of staff, termination of staff, wage payment, holding of meetings, etc.

Distinctions between Policies and Procedures

The main points of difference are:

(1) Policies are a guide to decision-making whereas procedures are a guide to action only.

(2) In the case of policies, there is some room for interpretation and discretion but in the case of procedures, as they are more rigid and specific, there is no scope for discretion.

(3) While policies are a part of strategies of the business concern, procedures are only operational tools and a guide to action only.

(4) While policies are basic things and are formulated by the top management, procedures are generally based on policies and are decided generally at a somewhat lower level of management.

Methods

Method specifies the way in which a particular step is to be performed. Procedure tells the various steps to be taken to perform a particular task, but method tells how a particular step in the procedure is to be performed. Thus, the method, as it explains the steps, is more detailed than procedure.

Rules

A rule specifies what is to be done and what may not be done in given situation. Rules do not leave any scope for decision-making or judgement. They are to be enforced rigidly and also a fine or penalty may be imposed for ignoring them. 'No smoking' is an example of a rule. Fig. 5.10 indicates the freedom that management has to act in the case of policies, procedures and rules.

Strategy

Strategy is a term which is normally used in the Lattlefields for planning a military movement, handling of troops, etc.

In modern times, the word 'strategy' has found its way into the management field. In the context of a business concern, strategy indicates a specific programme of action for achieving the organisation objectives by employing the firm's resources efficiently and economically. It involves preparing oneself for meeting unforeseen factors. It is also concerned with meeting the challenges posed by the policies and actions of other competitors in the market.

Definition and Characteristics of Strategy

A.D. Chandler defines strategy as "the determination of the basic long-term goals and objectives of an enterprise and the adoption of courses of action and the allocation of resources to carry out these goals."

According to the R.N. Anthony, strategy is "the process of defining the objectives of the organisation, on changes in their objectives, on the resources used to attain these objectives, and on the policies that are to govern the acquisition, use and disposition of these resources."

The above definitions reveal the following important characteristics of strategy:

(1) It provides guidelines to the enterprise for thinking and action.

(2) It involves in finding out a judicious combination of human and other resources to achieve the objectives of the organisation.

(3) Its formulation involves taking into consideration external environment (opportunities and challenges) and internal environment (organisation's resources and capabilities).

(4) As strategy depends on both external and internal factors which are not static, it has to be adjusted to the changed circumstances. Hence, strategy is not static but dynamic.

(5) Because of the importance of strategy to the business concern, it is formulated by the top management and not delegated downward in the organisation.

Types of Strategies

According to Steiner and Miner, strategies can be classified into the following types:

(1) Master strategies. They refer to the entire pattern of a company's objectives and involve unified direction to the entire organisation. They may be formulated for the areas of marketing, finance, production etc. For example, a master strategy for the field of marketing may be to enter a new market with the objective of capturing 15% of the market demand within a year.

(2) Programme strategies. These strategies are more specific and refer to the specific deployment of resources to achieve organisational purposes. They support the master strategies. For example, if the master strategy is formulated to capture 15% of the market demand, a programme strategy for extensive advertising and intensive personal selling campaign may be decided to enable the organisation to achieve its master strategy.

Sub-strategies (or Minor Strategies)

These strategies are oriented towards deployment of resources for achieving specific objectives but they are not of overall importance to an organisation. However, they provide guidance to decision-making and action. For example, for capturing 15% of market demand within a period of one year, an organisation may formulate a sub-strategy to make use of the services of a particular advertising company to take care of its advertising compaign.

Uses of Standing Plans

The organisation derives the following advantages from standing plan which involves objectives, policies, methods, procedure rules and strategies.

(i) Efficiency. Standing plan minimises time and brings out efficiency in managerial effort. Instead of giving instruction every time regarding the operations, policy and procedure will be followed which are pre-determined by top management. They act as guidelines. They are the recommended practices to be followed in the organisation. Flexibility in methods and procedure helps the organisation to change them according to the needs and this brings about efficiency in operation. Routine decisions are promptly taken with the help of these elements.

(ii) Delegation of Authority. Standing plan facilitates smooth delegation of authority, well laid down rules and procedure. Strategy or method helps the subordinates to quickly act on an issue as long as that issue fits into the standing plan.

(iii) Control. The operational elements of standing plan, *viz.*, methods, procedure etc., are designed in such a way that the operations in the organisation are automatically controlled/ Manager will have a smooth time in directing the operations.

(iv) Co-ordination. Standing plan brings about co-ordination in the activities of the organisation. The effort of every individual in the organisation is synchronised by these elements (method, policy etc.) and introduces consistency in operation.

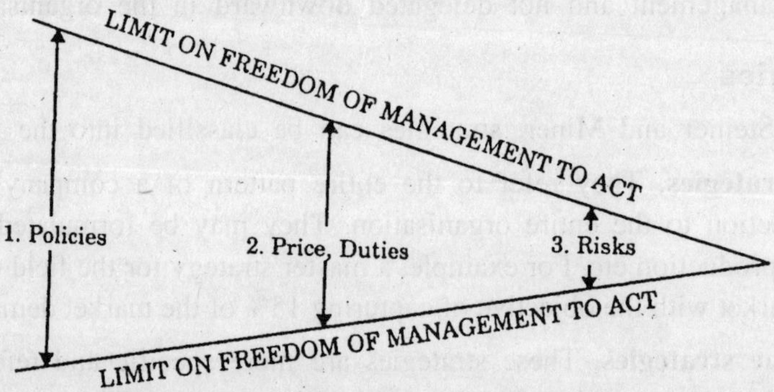

Fig. 5.10. Standing Plans and Management Freedom

Thus standing plan brings people together in the organisation and make them to work in a scientific and disciplined way. "Standard operating procedures and methods evolve considerable use of *'one best way'* under Scientific management." This plan makes even the ordinary and not well informed workers of perform better. People at work can be easily trained in the organisations with these procedures and methods. But standing plan prevents innovation and increases resistance to change.

Single-use Plans

Single-use plans are designed for a specific purpose and for a short-period. They are not respective in nature. As soon the purpose is served, they become redundant. Progammes, projects and the budgets from the part of single-use plan.

Programmes

A programme is a precise plan which lays down the operations to be carried out to accomplish a given work. It includes all activities necessary to achieve the given objectives and prescribes how the enterprise's resources should be used. A programme is drawn in conformity with the objectives and it consists of steps to be taken to achieve the tasks.

Production of 1,000 tonnes of cement in March or manufacturing of 1,000 scooters by the end of March or a programme for opening 10 branches in the next year or deputing its employees for training or introducing a new product in the market are some of the examples of programmes.

Programmes are result-oriented and provide practical guidelines to managerial activities. Further, when compared to policies or objectives, they provide greater motivation to the managers.

Project — The Single-use Plan

Project is a single-use plan developed to carryout a specific business activity. In order to formulate a project, people concerned take the ideas and intentions of a group of people who can visualise the need for the project and convert them into a formal, planned, resourced, funded and result-oriented activity called "Project". For example: Establishing a 500 MW Elctricity Production centre. This whole activity on a turn-key basis from conceiving the business activity to launching stage (concept coneiving to commissioning) is called "Project". This is a specific activity carried out for a specific purpose and hence is considered as a single-use plan.

Thus, project is an activity (business or non-business) which provides an integrate framework for project-organisation, planning and control which is designed:

- to ensure timely and cost-effective production of all the end products,
- maintain acceptable standards of quality, and
- achieve for the enterprise, the benefit for which the investment in the project has been made.

Preparation of project report and implementation involves three main stages.

1. Project Initiation: This stage involves: (i) Project start-off, (ii) Determination of project objective and scope, (iii) Project schedule and budgeting, (iv) Stage scheduling and budgeting, (v) Project organisation, (vi) Project control procedure, and (vii) Business Analysis.

2. Project Control: This considers different types of control to be adopted in a project which include: (i) quality control, (ii) progress control, (iii) change control, (iv) problem management, (v) exceptional situation analysis, and (vi) closing stage administration.

3. Project closure: In this stage: (i) Final product evaluation, (ii) Project completion, and (iii) Process improvement are involved.

Project Report — Contents and Process

The project report for any business enterprises is prepared considering several aspects connected with the project. Every project considers same main features.

— Investment Pattern

— Time Limit

— Performance Parameters

— Project Cost

— Benefits Expected

A project report, gives a detailed pictures of the project and also tells whether it is feasible to take up the project. The following stages are followed in project formulation.

— Search for Business Idea

— Project Concepts

— Project Identification

— Project Formulation

— Project Analysis

— Project Risks

— Project Planning

— Project Design and Network Analysis

— Project Report

— Project Appraisal

1. Conceiving the Business Idea

This can be obtained from different sources:

1. Innovable features and creative ability of entrepreneur can bring a good product idea.
2. Hiring the potents and product ideas from others who have potented on franchise or hire basis.
3. Purchasing the patents.

2. Project Concepts

— A project is a "scheme of something to be done, a proposal for undertaking".

— Innovation and vision form an integral aspect of a project programme.

— A project is a productive activity which can be analysed, appraisal and monitered independently. It has a geographic location, specific starting and closing points.

— Projects may be national or sectoral or individual or techno-economic.

— Project classfication facilitates the graphical expression of essential features of the project in quantifiable or qualitative terms.

— It gives the size of the project in terms of investment — small, medium or large scale.

— Project concept involves all activities concerning investment to create develop and expand certain facilities to produce or increase the capacity of goods and services, in a certain period of time.

Project Identification

— Project identification involves, collection compilation and analysis of economic data for the eventual purpose of locating possible opportunities for investment and with the development of such opportunities. "Opportunities may be additive, complementary or break through".

— Opportunities can be innovative or can be availed by searching magazines, trade bulletins, research amagazines, government publications.

— After awaiting the product idea, a project can be accepted or dropped after examining investment size, location, technology, equipment and marketing.

— Project identification is the first step in successful implementation of the project.

4. Project Formulation

— Means, "taking a firm look carefully and critically at a project idea by an entrepreneur to build up an all-round beneficial to project after carefully weighing its various components".

— It is an analytical management aid.

— It is an objective and independent analysis of various aspects of an investment proposition of the idea conceived.

— Project formulation involves:

1. Feasibility analysis
2. Techno-economic analysis.
3. Project design and network analysis.
4. Input analysis.
5. Financial analysis.
6. Social cost-benefit analysis.

— All these aspects are examined before a project is approved for implementation.

— Other vital aspects to be examined are, organisational aspects, commercial aspects, legal aspect, project constraints, effluent disposal energy conservation, utilisation by products, choice of technical process, environmental analysis.

— Thus, project formulation involves a detailed study of the environment weighting objectively the internal and external constraints and development of the project idea, stage by stage into an investment proposition.

5. Project Analysis

— Various dimensions of the project work are to be examined, both separately and in relation to each other in varying degrees this is called project analysis.

— Project analysis involves dimensions like technical analysis economic analysis (Resource allocation and benefits derived), financial analysis, social analysis (how society is served by the project?), institutional anaysis (quality of institution implementing the project), environmental analysis and the role of consultants.

6. Project Risks

— Economic viability of project is appraised by IRR (Internal Rate of Return), computation of IRR requires a set of assumptions regarding the condition faced by the project. These conditions may change for various reasons.

— Risks facing a project could be large and all the risks cannot be identified.

— Only risks which have majro economic impact on the project are analysed. These risks have to be identified through sensitivity analysis.

— However, greater care should be exrcised in identifying risks which substantially reduce the projects IRR and render the project uneconomic.

7. Project Planning

— It is a process involving joint effort of a team of entrepreneurs, technicians and skilled workers. In this, micro and macro aspects are blended.

— While preparing the project plan or a business plan (I use the term business plan as the discussion is mainly concerned with business), we have to know the business destination, strategies to be adopted to get there, where we would like to be at specific times. The burden come in the way and the approaches to be considered for overcoming the obstecles.

— The business plan outline will be as follows:

A. Facing Sheet:

(i) Name of business
(ii) Name and address of owners telephone number, etc.

B. Purpose of the Plan:

(i) Description of business product or service
(ii) Business structure
(iii) Objectives

C. Marketing Plan:

(i) The profile of the product
(ii) Competition for the product
(iii) Market size and opportunity
(iv) Market segments served
(v) Marketing mix
(vi) Key factors to success in market

D. Financial Plan:

(i) Capital requirement
(ii) Sources of funds

(iii) Application of funds
(iv) Balance sheet analysis
(v) Break-even anaysis
(vi) Income statement analysis
(vii) Proforma cash flow statement

E. Organisational Plan:

(i) Location of business
(ii) Organisational structure
(iii) Management
(iv) Non-management personnel

F. Incentives and Subsidies:

Details of the incentives are to be projected.

G. Summary:

Application and effect of loan on business. Detailed findings should be given.

Documents to be owned:

(i) Personal resumes
(ii) Job descriptions
(iii) Credit reports
(iv) Letters of reference
(v) Copies of contracts
(vi) Copies of leases
(vii) Copies of letter of intent
(viii) Legal documents
(ix) Production requirements

— Planning for a small enterprises

Phases are:

(i) Project selection
(ii) Information collection
(iii) Creative phase
(iv) Evaluation phase
(v) Recommendation
(vi) Implementation
(vii) Follow-up and feedback
(viii) Replanning

8. Project Design and Network Analysis

— Project design is the heart of project entity. It defines the indivudal activities which go into the corpus of the project and their interrelationship with each other. It enables to identify the flow of event which must take place for the successful implementation of the project.

— Network analysis help the management of an organisation in performing these functions efficiently and effectively.

— A network comprises a set of exponents connected with each other in a sequential relationship with each step till the completion of the project.

— PERT and CPM are the examples of Network analysis.

— NW facilitates analysis of project activities, splitting project activities into simple activities which are then arranged in logical sequence. This also decides as to which activity will be performed simultaneously and which other sequencially.

— The NW analysis will be as follows.

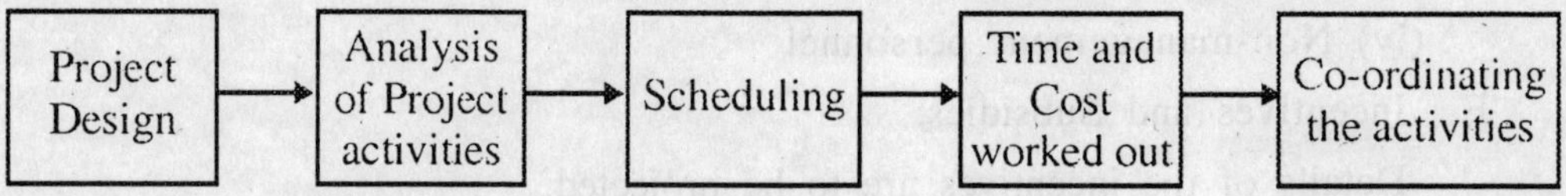

9. Project Report

— Serves as a guide to managmeent.

— This contains the analysis of inputs and outputs of the project.

Budgets

A budget is a proposed plan of action prepared in advance. It is an estimate of future needs covering some or all of the activities of an enterprise for a definite period of time. It may be expressed in numerical terms, *i.e.,* rupees, man-hours, product units and so forth. The important budgets prepared in a business enterprise are cash budget, production budget, sales budget, capital budget and master budget. This is a control tool.

Benefits

Budgets are very useful to the enterprise. Some of the important benefits of budgeting are:

(1) It lays down enterprise goals and provides a basis for the future course of action by the management.

(2) It is time-bound and helps in introducing definiteness in planning.

(3) By laying down attainable targets and prescribing means to achieve them, it provides the right motivation to employees.

(4) Budgets, by laying down objectives and plans in numerical terms, facilitate the verifiability of planning.

Business Plan — The Concept

When an entrepreneur conceives the idea of starting a business, has to convert this idea of starting a business, has to convert this idea into action. This prompts him to prepare a plan, as to how to go about it. This may be called "Business plan". Business plan is one of the essential tools that an entrepreneur can possess. If the entrepreneur masters it, he can become a successful businessman. But it is challenging to master.

"Business Plan is a summary of how a business owner intends to organise an entrepreneurial venture and emplement activities necessary and sufficient for the venture to succeed."

Business plan is prepared to explain as to how the concept of business conceived by an entrepreneur can be commissioned. It tells about: (i) What is the concept/idea/business?, (ii) Where to go? and (iii) How to go about it? Millions of dollars are paid through out the world to consultants to answer these three questions. Because, the business plan will tell the entrepreneur to make a successful business.

The business plan gives a direction to present the entrepreneur's business concept and tell the concerned people to understand quickly as to what the entrepreneur has in mind and what he wants to achieve by implementing the proposed business.

The contents

The business plan should contain the information required by the cencerned to whom it is presented and it should indicate, with clarity, the expectation of the entrepreneur from them. Considering these aspects, a business plan comprises of the following:

1. Mission statement: The statement defines the business objectives on a long-term basis and tells how the business is exclusive and what it aspires to achieve.

2. Main objectives: It tells about the financial objectives such as turnover and profits for the plan period, the growth expectd over the years. It also depicts strategic objectives such as marketing product positioning, HRD, etc.

3. Business Environment: This tells about the current scenario of the proposed business in terms of market background, competitors to the proposed business, competitive conditions in the market, competitive advantage of the venture, product offerings, target markets, government policies, political environment, risks ahead, etc.

4. Strategy: This depicts the various types of tactics to be followed in marketing. The strategies such as product strategy, price strategy distribution strategy, promotional strategy, networking, etc., are given.

5. Project: This reveals the business to be executed in detail.

6. Financial Forecasts: This is the crucial part of the business plan. In this, cost-benefit analysis of the business is done. This shows the propored capital and revenue expenditure, income, cash-flow, funds flow and forecasting for three to four years. This will be prepared with all care considering the existing business environment.

7. Human Resources: The hierarchy of proposed business will be explained. The positions and the people tasks will be defined. This also identifies the bankers, investors, venture capitalists and other experts concerned with the business.

8. Conclusing Remarks: This tells about general matters such as gestation period, probable commissioning time, trial production, commercial production, etc.

Business plan, thus, is a powerful tool and an asset to the entrepreneur. It may encourage the outside investors to invest in the proposed business. "Entrepreneur's concept is only a seed and Business Plan is everything that nurtures and develops that seed". Business plan is similar to the project plan discussed earlier. But this is a general plan and the project plan is a specific plan.

PLANNING FOR GLOBAL BUSINESS

In the context of globalisation of business, entrepreneur of any country who wishes to start a business in any other country should prepare a business plan catering to global business scenario.

Global business plan contains the following vital aspects:

(i) General aspects, (ii) Description of major elements, (iii) Strategies and (iv) Employee participation.

(i) General Aspects: An international business plan include, (a) company's history and background, (b) the products of the company to be dealt in global business, (c) available resources (human, financial and material), (d) current channels of distribution, (e) risk elements involved in global business and (f) how to overcome such risks.

(ii) Major elements: This comprises of people involved in business and their capabilities, marketing and sales strategy, production process and the financial plan for promoting and maintenance of business.

(iii) Strategies: The business plan for an international business has to be based on strategies to demonstrate how the company achieves its business goals in the global scenario. Even for mobilising finance, a more professional plan has to be prepared.

(iv) Employee participation in decision-making has to be properly incorporated. This means the employee involved in decision-making at different level should agree for business strategies and obejctives to be implemented. It is upon these people that the company will ultimately rely for the success of the plan.

SUMMARY

1. Planning is the first managerial function and it is concerned with deciding in advance what is to be done, when, where, how and by whom it is to be done. It is a predetermined course of action to achieve a specified aim or goal.
2. The characteristics of planning are: it focuses on objectives, it is an identical process, it is a selective process, it is pervasive, it is an integrated process, it is directed towards efficiency, it is flexible, it is a decision-making process, continuous process etc.
3. Plan should be based on clearly-defined objectives. It must be simple, rational, comprehensive, flexible, balanced. It must use all the available resources and opportunities, and it must be free from biases.
4. The benefits of planning are: it offsets future uncertainty, tackles increasing complexity in modern business, helps in co-ordination, helps in exercising effective control, helps in the proper utilisation of company resources, facilitates unity of action and helps in avoiding business failure, improves competitive strength of the organisation, guides decision-making and improved adaptability.
5. Planning suffers from certain limitations such as a rigidity, time-consuming and lack of accurate forecast. It is also costly. Further, because of the influence of external factors, the effectiveness of planning is limited. Its scope is limited and may generate resistance from the people.

6. Planning involves a number of steps such as: awareness of opportunities and problems, collecting and analysing of information, determination of objectives, visualising planning premises and constraints, finding out the alternative course of action, evaluation of alternatives and optimal selection, determining secondary plans, securing participation of employees and providing for follow-up and future course of action.
7. Planning premises are certain assumptions about the future on the basis of the plans will be ultimately formulated. They are vital to the success of planning. Classification of planning premises are: internal and external, tangible and intangible and controllable and non-controllable premises.
8. Planning consists of several individual plans. Depending on their nature and scope, plans can be classified into: (a) Standing or repeated-use plans and (b) Single-use plans. Standing plans are used over and over again and they include objectives, policies, procedures, methods, rules and strategies. Single-use plans are used in specific situations and they include programmes and budgets.
9. Objectives are goals or aims which management wish the organisation to achieve. Characteristics of objectives are multiple in nature; they have a hierarchy they may be long-range or short-range, they are interdependent and verifiable They facilitate unified planning, control, co-ordination, decentralisation, etc.
10. For objectie setting, two approaches are followed, *viz.*, (a) traditional approach and (b) management by objectives. In the traditional approach, objectives are set by the people at the top of the organisation for those at the lower levels. This approach is called authoritarian approach and it may be resented by the employees.
11. In the MBO, the process of objective-setting involves participation and collaboration among this various level of organisation with the intention of achieving organisational objectives. Steps in the process of MBO are: preliminary objective setting, setting subordinates' objectives, matching goals with resources, recycling objectives and periodic performance review. MBO results in several benefits to the organisation.
12 Policies provide the framework within which the decision-makers are expected to operate while making decisions relating to an organisation. They are a guide to thinking and action of the subordinates. Procedures tell how a particular activity is to be carried out. It prescribes the chronological sequence of specific tasks required to perform a designed job. While a procedure tells the various steps to be taken to perform a job, method tells how a particular step in the procedure is to be taken. Rule specifies what is to be done and what may not be done in a given situation. Strategy is the determination of the long-term goals and objectives of the enterprise and the adoption of a course of action and allocation of resource to carry out these goals.
13. A programme is a precise plan which lays down the operations to be carried out to accomplish a given work. It is drawn in conformity with the objectives and it consists of definite steps to be taken to achieve the task. A budget is an estimate of future needs covering some or all the activities of an enterprise for a definite period of time. It may be expressed in numerical terms. Types of budgets are cash budget, sales budget, capital budget and master budget.
14. A project is also a single-use plan which is designed to complete a major task on time with cost-effectiveness and to provide specific benefit.

STUDY QUESTIONS

1. Give the meaning of planning.
2. What is planning premise?
3. What is single-use plan?
4. What do you mean by 'Policy'?
5. What is 'Procedure'?
6. What do you mean by strategy?
7. What is standing plan?
8. What do you mean by budget?
9. What is 'Method'?
10. What is project?
11. Name the types of plans.
12. Name the planning steps.
13. What do you mean by MBO?
14. What is appealed policy?
15. What is functional policy?
16. Give the meaning of imposed policy.
17. What is programme strategy?
18. Give a note on "Planning Process."
19. Analyse the essentials of a good plan.
20. Give an analytical note on importance of planning.
21. Give a note on types of planning.
22. Give a note on Standing plan.
23. What are the objectives of planning?
24. Give a note on Policy and Procedure.
25. Analyze the characteristics of planning.
26. Distinguish between policy and procedure
27. Analyze the dimensions of a strategy.
28. Give a note on project management.
29. Explain the different steps in planning.
30. Explain the advantages and limitations of planning.
31. Briefly explain the various types of planning.
32. Give an explanatory note on policy and procedure
33. Briefly explain the aspects of project as a form of single-use plan.

Practicals

1. You wish to start a small business (assume any product or service) to grow yourself as an entrepreneur. Keeping in view the various aspects of planning discussed in this chapter, prepare a plan for producing product-X.

CASE STUDIES

1. Case Study

A leading consumer product manufacturing company has decided to restructure its operational aspects based on the report of the functional managers. It has five functional divisions — production, finance, sales, human resources, and general operation.

Production manager reports that there was a fall in production by 20% of the target due to power cut. This, has a major concern for him and wishes to have continuous power supply.

Finance manager reports that cash flow operations are imbalanced due to liberal credit policy followed by the company. This has caused unpredictable receipts from debtors. He strongly feels that reliance on short-term debt to meet current obligations be minimised.

Sales manager is of the opinion that prices of the products sold by the company are high compared to the prices of rival products. He identifies that transport and distribution costs are the main causes for the high price of the product. He reports that a reasonable policy regarding prices has to be adopted considering the problem area — transport and distribution cost.

Human resources department has two major problems: (i) High turnover of technical staff due to attractive remuneration offered by other companies and (ii) First-line supervisors are not effectively managing their subordinates.

The general operations department reports that it is facing a severe threat, from Pollution Control Board, of taking stern steps against the non-provision of effluent treatment plant.

The report of each functional department is alarming and hence replanning is required to bring stability.

You conduct a group discussion on these problem areas and suggest:

1. The order of priority according to which replanning has to be made.
2. Should these problems be solved with independent plans or integrated approach has to be taken with common policies and procedures?
3. Identify Common planning principles and steps. List them and discuss with your teacher.
4. Prepare a restructured plan.

2. Case Study

You want to take up self-employment in sales line. You have identifed products X, Y, Z which are used by students of engineering for selling. Prepare a plan incorporating all stages of planning to make your proposal a successful venture.

6

ORGANISING

LEARNING OBJECTIVES

After reading this chapter, you should be able to know;

- Organisation and Organising—The Concepts.
- Organisation Structure
  (i) Functional, (ii) Divisional, (iii) Matrix, (iv) Formal and Informal Organisations.
- General Benefits
- Directions in Structure
  (i) Team Structure, (ii) Network Structure, (iii) Boundaryless Structure.

"Organisational structures are becoming increasingly short-lived and unstable."—said Peter. F. Drucker, the modern management Guru. This statement clearly indicates the direction in which the modern organisations are moving. He is of the opnion that organisations and their structures are having short span of time and they are not consistently functioning. They are always subjected to change, as they grow or if they face any problem in their operations. Thou is why the modern organisations are fairly flatter one or horizontal ones with the marvellous support of technology. They are highly dynamic and are becoming "Learning organisations". In this changing scenario of organisations, we will examine the various aspects of organising our organisation.

ORGANISING AND ORGANISATION — THE CONCEPTS

Organising means "To Organise." What to Organise? Organise any activity, *i.e.*, business or non-business. In this chapter, our focus is on organising a business enterprise. Business enterprise is one compact unit called "Organisation." It is to be systematically organised considering the various business activities to be carried out. This should be an effective unit which should bring in the desired results. That is why it is said that "It should be organised." Today, most of the business enterprises are structured very well in a formal way. Even informal organisations which are not properly structured also exist. Whether it is formal or informal, in all organisations we observe that people are put together and kept together to achieve some common goal and thereby get some benefits.

The goal or purpose may vary from organisation to organisation. The organisations set the goals (in the form of planning) and try to achieve these goals by acquiring and allocating the resources. Organisational activity is a team work of people involved in designing, manufacturing, marketing, etc. Each of these activities can become an organisation. Thus, the two terms "Organisation" and "Organising" give different meaning. "Organisation" is an unit showing relationship between various functions of a business carried out by a person or body corporate and between the people work in this unit in different levels in a hierarchical form.

The term "organisation" has been viewed from two angles, *viz.*, (i) Organisation as a "***structure of relationships***" and (ii) a "***process of management.***" These aspects are discussed in greater detail in the following paragraph.

"Organising" is a managerial activity. This function tells about the way in which the activities of an organisation are put in a systematic manner to achieve the goals and objectives of an organisation. The outcome of organising is organisation.

ORGANISING — A MANAGERIAL FUNCTION

Organising is an ongoing managerial function. The structure may be newly created. The policies, programmes, strategies, organisational environment, etc., can change. But, the managers cannot get uniform efficiency (to do things right) and effectiveness (to do right things). However, every organisation is built-up with four vital elements: (i) Division of work, (ii) Departmentalisation, (iii) Hierarchy and (iv) Coordination. These four elements are observed whether it is a new company or an ongoing concern or an organisation which is subjected to radical change.

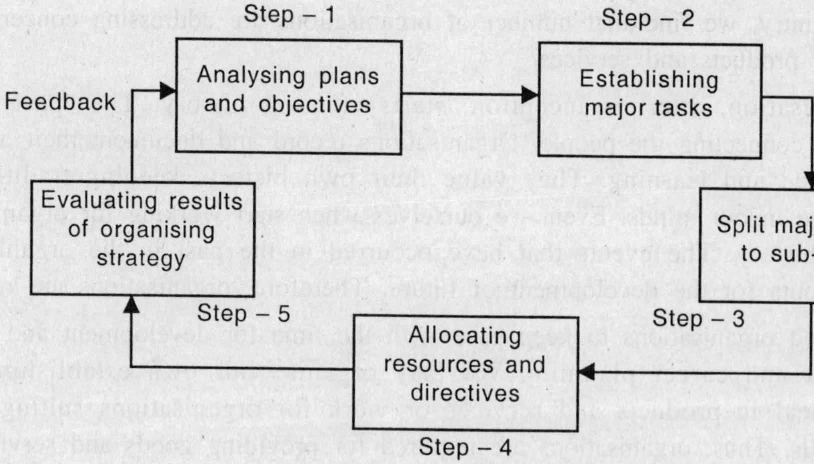

Fig. 6.1. Organising Process

"Organising" is different of "organisation." Organising is the process of establishing orderly uses for all resources in the organisation. Organising function is the primary mechanism with which managers activate plans. A sound organising mechanism minimises cost, optimises organisational resources and avoids duplication of effort. A good organising mechanism creates and maintains relationship between all organisational resources. This mechanism identifies the resources to be applied for specific activities. When, where and how the resources are to be used will be effectively told by this mechanism. Chart 6.1 will explain the organising process.

Thus organising is a managerial function. It describes the way in which the matter is arranged, how the people work together, effectively organising comprises of functions such as the improvement of teamwork, particularly in large organisations where many experts have to work together in teams.

It contains the role and responsibilities of managers and discussed relationships between people working at different levels and also between people and groups.

Organisation — Need and Purpose

Every individual comes across with many organisations (both formal and informal) every day. We interact with them without our knowledge. But when we start studying them, three compelling reasons strike to our mind. We study them to understand the past, present and future of organisations under the guidance of managers. It will tell us, how effective an organisation is.

We need the organisations to provide our daily requirements like food, shelter, clothing, entertainment, transport, education, and host of other requirements. This is the present need of organisation.

We also need organisations to build a desirable future. The dynamic economy needs continuous growth and innovations. When people work together in organisations, create new products and innovative services. These innovative activities are continuous practices and have impact (positive or negative) on future status of the economy. If we look at the growth of our country, we find that number of organisations are addressing concern about the future in their products and services.

Every organisation, after its inception, starts creating history. The 'past' of the organisation helps connecting the people. Organisations record and document their activities for future reference and learning. They value their own history, keeping tradition and organization culture in our minds. Even, we ourselves when start working for organisations, add to our own history. The events that have occurred in the past in the organisations, provide us the inputs for the development of future. Therefore, organisations are required.

Thus, we need organisations to keep pace with the time for development and for our own development and career planning. We may organise our own establishments to manufacture or deal in products and services or work for organisations suiting to our education and skills. Thus, organisations are required for providing goods and services that are demanded by the society.

Viewing the Organisation

The term organisation is viewed from different angles. The term 'organisation' is used as ***"a process of management"*** and as ***"a structure of relationships"***. We give below the explanation of the term 'organisation' in these two senses.

ORGANISATION AS A PROCESS

In this sense, organisation is interpreted as a process of welding together a framework of positions which can be used by the management for the purpose of accomplishing the enterprise goals. It involves co-ordination of the employees' activities in an efficient manner for accomplishing the objectives of the enterprise. This is a dynamic concept of the term. Experts like Allen, Koontz, O'Donnell, Oliver Sheldon and others have defined the term 'organisation' in the dynamic sense. Some of the definitions are:

1. Louis A. Allen. "Organisation is the process of identifying and grouping the work to be performed, defining and delegating responsibility and authority and establishing relationships for the purpose of enabling people to work most effectively in accomplishing objectives."

2. Koontz and O'Donnell. "Organisation involves the grouping of activities necessary to accomplish goals and plans, the assignment of these activities to appropriate departments and the provision for authority delegation and co-ordination."

Organisations as a Framework of Relationship

In this sense, organisation is interpreted as a structure of relationships among positions and jobs for the purpose of achieving enterprise objectives. This is a static or classical concept of organisation. Experts like Mooney and Reily, Chester Bernard, etc., have defined the term 'organisation' in a static sense. Some of the definition are:

Mooney and Railey. "Organisation is the form of every human association for the attainment of a common purpose."

Chester Bernard. "Organisation is a system of co-operative activities of two or more persons."

Thus, it is clear from the above definitions that while in the first sense, the act or process or organisation is highlighted, in the second sense it is the structure of the organisation.

The definition given by different writers reveal the nature of the organisation:

1. Organisation, as a process of management is concerned with identifying and grouping of activities to be performed.

2. It defines and delegates responsibility and authority to appropriate departments.

3. It establishes relationships for the purpose of enabling the people to work most effectively in accomplishing the objectives of the enterprise.

4. Organisation is also interpreted by some writers as a structure of relationships among positions and jobs for the purpose of achieving enterprise objectives.

5. It is a system of co-operative activities of two or more persons for the attainment of a common purpose.

6. Organising process involves taking a number of steps, such as determination of objectives, grouping of activities, assignment of duties to persons, delegation of authority

authority relationships. Further, the organising process leads to the creation of the organisation structure.

PRINCIPLES OF ORGANISATION

There is a need to follow certain principles in order to formulate and develop a sound and efficient organisation structure. Some of the important principles of organisation are as follows:

1. Principle of objectives: The formulation of organisation structure is very much influenced by the objectives of the business concern. In view of this, first, the objectives of the business concern should be clearly stated. This helps the management in formulating the organisation structure and also in achieving the enterprise objectives with minimum cost and effort.

2. Principle of specialisation: The organisation structure should be formulated in such a way that the activities of the enterprise are divided according to the different functions and the same are assigned to person according to their specialisation. This means that effective organisation must include specialisation.

3. Principle of span of control: The span of control should be minimum because there is a limit to the number of persons that can be effectively supervised by one boss.

4. Principle of exception: Only exceptionally complex matters should be referred to the executives for their decision and matters of routine nature should be decided by the subordinates themselves. This is necessary, because the executives at a higher level instead of spending their time for deciding routine matters can concentrate on more important matters.

5. The Scalar Principle: For making management effective, there should be clear line of authority. The line of authority from the chief executive at the top of the enterprise to the first line supervisors at the bottom must be clearly stated.

6. The Principle of authority: Authority that is given to the manager enables him to accomplish the objectives of the enterprise. Hence, the authority of each manager should be clearly defined and also it should be equal to the responsibility entrusted to him.

7. Principle of unit of command: According to this principle, each subordinate should have only one superior and dual subordination should be avoided. Dual subordination may result in indiscipline in subordinates, undermining of authority, disorder, delay and confusion.

8. Principle of delegation: The organisation structure should provide for the delegation of authority at every level. The authority delegated should be equal to responsibility so as to enable the concerned person to accomplish the task assigned to him by his superior.

9. Principle of responsibility: The superior should not be allowed to avoid responsibility by delegating authority to his subordinates. It means that the superior should be held responsible for the acts of his subordinates to whom he has delegated authority.

10. Principle of flexibility: The organisation structure should be such which should be adaptable to the changing circumstances. There should be a possibility, if circumstances warrant, for expansion and replacement without disrupting the basic design of the structure.

11. Principle of simplicity: The organisation structure should be simple with a minimum number of levels. If the organisation structure has a large number of levels, the problem of effective co-ordination and communication may arise.

12. Principle of continuity: The organisation structure should be serviceable for a long time. This is possible if it is dynamic and capable of adapting itself to the needs of changing circumstances.

13. Principle of unit of direction: It means, for a group of activities having the same objective, there should be one plan and one objective. This facilitates verification and co-ordination of activities and also completion of task as per the schedule.

14. Principle of efficiency: The structure that is formulated should enable the business concern to function efficiently and achieve its objectives with the minimum cost and effort.

Thus, we find that to develop a sound and efficient organisation structure, certain principles are necessary. Every manager should have a knowledge of these principles and apply them efficiently. Mooney and Reiley have aptly remarked, "This does not mean that a knowledge of these principles will make everyone who knows them an efficient organiser. To know the principles is one thing and to apply them efficiently is another. Nevertheless, it stands to reason that a knowledge of these principles must be the first step in the acquisition of a sound organising technique."

ORGANISATION STRUCTURE—THE NEED

Structure of an organisation which results from the organising process is the basic framework within which the decision-making behaviour of an executive takes place. It is an established pattern of relationships among the components of the organisation. March and Simon have stated that "organisation structure consists simply of those aspects of pattern of behaviour in the organisation that are relatively stable and change only slowly." It is the system of relationship that governs the activities of people who are dependent upon each other for achieving the common objectives. In a large concern, the structure is planned initially by the design of the major components and then by the establishment of relationship among these components.

Four Vital Aspects of Organisational Structure
1. **Division of work.** Divide the work of an organisation into workable tasks effectively and efficiently.
2. **Departmentation**. Combine the tasks in a logical order and group right employees accordingly.
3. **Hierarchy**. Show the levels in terms of who reports to whom.
4. **Coordination**.Integrate departments into a coherent whole for effective monitoring.

FIG. 6.2. Four corner stones of organisational structure.

FACTORS INFLUENCING ORGANISATION STRUCTURE

The organisation function is the immediate logical function after planning. To achieve the objectives set in the plan, somebody should work and should do the right work. The organising function makes the people to work. The function "involves managers in decisions which result in which result in a system of specialised coordinated jobs." In an organisation structure, so many aspects are involved. Human and non-human elements will be working. Organisational structure is an integrated whole. Job of each worker is specified, control measures are adopted for performing those jobs effectively. An organisational chart depicts tangibly the reporting relationships and channels of communication. Work flow and accountability are also shown. The structure varies according to mission purpose and strategy of the firm. What factors actually determine the organisation structure? It is grouping activity of men, machine and material for attaining a specific objective. Hence, the following factors determine the organisation structure. (This is based on four aspects given in the box.)

1. Size of the unit
   (a) Capital employed
   (b) Development of Science and Technology
   (c) Men employed
   (d) Nature of activity
2. Job design
3. Grouping of activities
4. Span of control
5. Delegation of authority
6. Work Force
7. Technology
8. Change in business environmental factors.

1. Size of the Unit. Size indicates the scale of operation. Normally, there are three scales of operation, *viz.,* small, medium and large. Size is an important factor governing cost, efficiency and profitability of a business enterprise. Before any business or non-business enterprise is started, the organisers will have to decide the most profitable and viable size of the unit. Optimum or the best size is a dynamic concept and it changes with the development of science and technology. Therefore, technology is one factor which determines the size and the organisation structure. To introduce new technology, in business enterprise, the activity has to be expanded and hence the structure changes.

The size of the organisation is also determined by the capital employed in the unit. There may be heavy capital outlay but it may be less labour-intensive. In such cases, the size will be small as authority relation will be less. However, capital outlay is one factor which determines the size of the organisation.

Another important factor which determines the size of the organisation is "**men employed**." If more men are employed there will be more level of management and more authority relationships. If men employed are less, the size of the organisation will be less and less levels of management and authority relationships.

The **nature** of business unit also determines the size and organisation structure. If it is capital goods industry with huge capital outlay, the organisation structure will be complex in nature. Consumer goods industries will have more authority relationships in marketing division and less in production and finance line. Thus, the nature of activity also determines the organisational structure.

2. Job Design. The bricks that develop an organisation structure are jobs. What are the jobs to be done in an organisation has to be decided by the top brass. Job design is the first managerial decision of the organisation structure. Jobs in a task have to be specified as one person cannot perform a task. It is a teamwork. Job in each task is to be specified and assigned. What an individual has to do to contribute to the overall tasks and objectives has to be decided. Therefore the fundamental factor, which determines the organisation structure is "**Job designing**" and "**numbering**" them. These numbers decide the size of the organisation.

3. Grouping of Activities. The designed jobs have to be formed into groups according to the nature of activity. Grouping of activities are essential to achieve co-ordination. Each group is termed as "DEPARTMENT." Departmentation is another factor which determines the organisational structure. Thus, in each business organisation, we observe departments like Marketing Department, Production Department, Finance Department etc which discharge their functions. In each department, we find authority relationships like Finance Manager, Assistant Finance Section Officer, Finance Supervisor, etc., each assigned with specific job and responsibility to perform. There will be accountability to higher ups also. Like this in every business or non-business activity, there will be grouping of similar jobs in the form of departments which are responsible to perform the specific task. There will be sub-departments in each basic department like Production Department in which we find: (i) Purchase Department, (ii) Stores Department, (iii) Technical Design Department, etc. These sub-departments constitute Production Department. All the functional departments put together forms an organisation. **Grouping of the designed jobs according to their nature and activity** is another factor which determines the organisational structure.

4. Span of Control. Another factor that decibles the pattern of organisational structure is **"Span of management"**. Span of management refers to the number of people that a manager can comfortably control or manage. The span aspects are discussed in detail elsewhere in this chapter.

5. Delegation of Authority. Delegation refers to the distribution of authority, right and responsibilities to the next step in the hierarchy of the organisational system or sub-system. This aspect is also dealt in detail elsewhere in this chapter.

6. Work Force. Work force here refers to the human element that works in the organisation. Different people hold different positions in the organisation. The work force is divided according to their capabilities and talent. In identifying the talent skill and core capabilities, the concept of "Division of Labour" plays a major role and this decides the pattern of organisational structure. Division of labour refers to the distribution of organisational activities and tasks to the people in the organisation according to their skills and behaviour. The division of labour leads to specialisation of tasks by the individual workers. When the structure of the organisation is to be decided, the skills and competencies of the workforce will be taken as one of the factors. This may prove well as workers specialise in the job and time taken to perform the task assigned will be less due to specialisation. The work for them will be easy and will be more effective. Although monotony for them will be a disturbing factor, advantages are more.

7. Technology. With the introduction of information technology, many changes have to take place in all functional areas. Similary in manufacturing units, change in technology introduces innovative plants and equipment. These changes influence the structure of the organisation.

8. Environmental Factors. Enviornmental factors such as, competition, government policies, consumer behaviour etc. also determine the organisation structure.

These seven factors are the basic ones to decide the structure of the organisation. But research and experience have shown that performance, attitudes, satisfaction and other factors also influence the structure.

An organization is a system of relationships which are interwoven. People working in this framework pursue their goals, which are normally common in nature, under the able guidance of their managers. The goals may be bit ambitious, open-ended and far-reaching. Therefore organizations are designed to ensure stability in operation and endure for a long time. The structure should be understandable by the people at work. The work flow should be smooth and should not have disturbing factors. Thus organizational design involves the determination of the organizational structure that is most appropriate for the strategy, people, technology and tasks of the organization.

Organisational Design

Organisational design is a concept which narrates the operational aspects of the organisation. It synergises the whole activities and issues such as tasks of the organisation to be performed within the set objectives, people involved in performing tasks, technology adapted in the organisation, strategies to be considered etc.

Organisations may be departmentalised on the basis of function, product, place, or some combination of the three. An organisation's authority structure may range from the highly centralised to the decentralised. There may be small or large spans of management. Broadly, however, there are two types of structure: classical and behavioural. They are also called "Tall" and "Flat" organisations respectively.

A classical organisation structure is usually pyramid-shaped. This implies centralisation of authority at the top, departmentalisation of jobs, hierarchy of command, narrow span of supervision and intense division of labour. This is shown in Fig. 6.3.

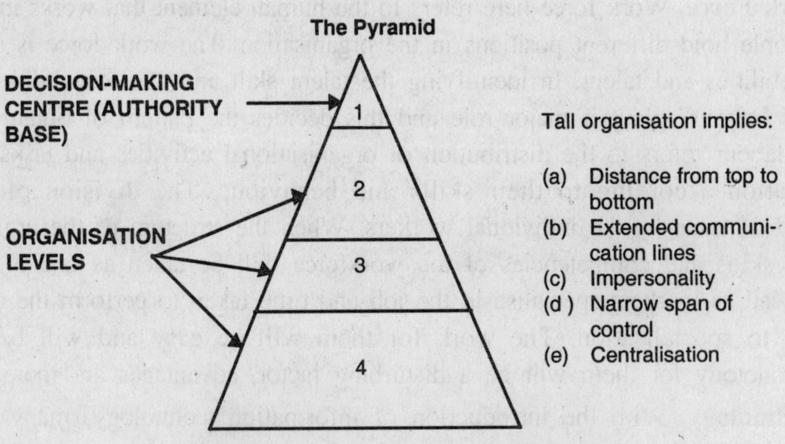

FIG. 6.3. Tall Organisation

The behaviourists generally advocate wider span of control which foster a flatter organisation structure, more general supervision, and more decentralisation. An example of a behavioural structure is presented in Fig. 6.4.

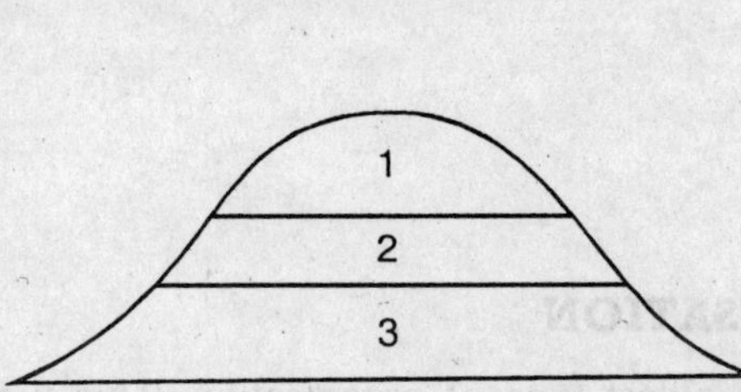

Flat organisation implies:
(a) High levels of decentralisation.
(b) Extremely wide spans of control.
(c) Less extended communication lines.

Fig. 6.4. Flat Organisation

ORGANISATION STRUCTURE—TRADITIONAL

Organisations are formed with a specific purpose. It may be business organisation established with the purpose of earning profit for owners. It can even be established for serving the society like universities, hospitals or welfare organisations. These are called non-profit organisations. Some organisations are formed to serve and satisfy the needs of their members, which are called mutual benefit organisations like clubs, unions, political parties, etc. These are also organisations which provide standardised service to large groups of people, *i.e.,* people at large. These are called "Commonwealth" organisations (non-profit organisation serving all members of given population) which are in the form of Indian services, Fire stations, Police department, Government educational institutions, Public utility services, etc.

These organisations are functioning with some standard structure. Our discussion here is focused on business enterprises. Keeping in view the business concept, the activities of the organisation have to be divided, grouped, and establish relationship between managers and employees, between managers and between employees. Each major activity becomes department with specific function. These departments have to be formally structured. There are three general structures standardised over the period. There are three common types. One of them is selected by an organisation according to its objective. The three types are: (i) Functional, (ii) Product or market and (iii) Matrix form. In business enterprises, we can observe all those three types which are time-honoured, time-tested and traditional ones. These organisations will have formal structure. But informal structure (invisible relationship between members) also exists. These are briefly analysed in the following paragraphs.

TYPES OF ORGANISATION

Organisation is a structural relationship between the factors in an enterprise. It involves the determination of duties and their assignment among the various personnel according to enterprise objectives. Grouping of activities and establishment of authority relationships among the various people working within the enterprise to achieve the desired results will be shown in the form of chart. This necessitates chalking out the line of authority and introduces the well-recognised principles which are suited for a specific business unit.

For the purpose of administration, four patterns have been well recognised. They are:

1. Line, Military or Scalar Organisation.
2. Functional Organisation.
3. Line and Staff Organisation.
4. Matrix Structure.

LINE OR MILITARY TYPE OF ORGANISATION

Line or military type of organisation is the oldest type of organisation. This type is also known as scalar organisation. In line organisation, each department is generally a complete self-sustaining unit. Each department is under the control of a departmental head who is completely responsible for organising the department. Above all the departmental heads, there is a general manager to whom all the department heads are responsible. The general manager in turn is responsible to the board of directors elected by the shareholders of the business concern (Fig. 6.5 shows the line authority.)

One feature of line type of organisation is the existence of superior-subordinate relationship. A superior delegates authority to a subordinate who in turn delegates authority to his subordinates and so on. Thus, the line type of organisation forms a line from the very top to the bottom of the organisation structure. Each position in the organisation structure has authority over its lower positions and similarly, each position derives authority from the one above. At each level, the superior makes decisions within the scope of authority derived by him from his own boss.

The following chart exhibits the time-tested and which is still practiced in almost all business enterprises, irrespective of the size of the unit.

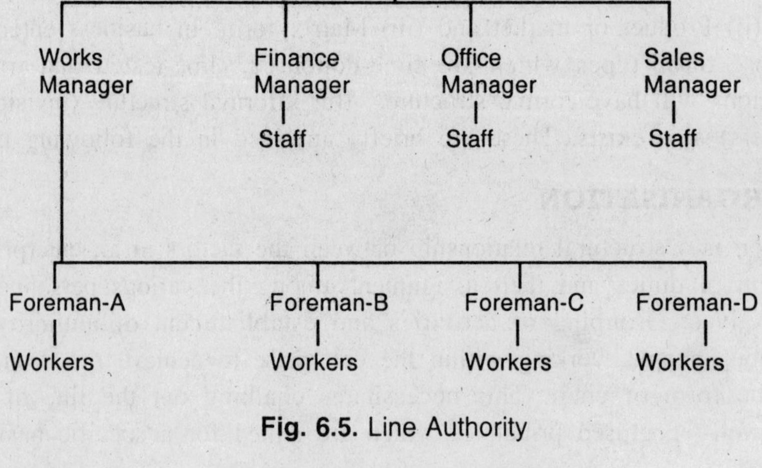

Fig. 6.5. Line Authority

Characteristics of Line Organisation

1. It consists of direct vertical relationships.
2. Departmental head is given full freedom to manage his department.
3. It does not make provision for staff specialists.
4. Operation of this system is simple.
5. Existence of superior-subordinate relationship.
6. Instruction is given by the boss directly to his subordinates.
7. Superior at each level makes decisions within the scope of his authority.

Type of Line Organisation

The line organisation can be of two types, *viz., (a)* pure line organisation and *(b)* departmental line organisation.

(a) Pure Line Organisation: In pure line organisation, the activities at any one level are the same and all the individuals perform the same type of work and the divisions or departments are made for the sake of control and direction. For example, at the lowest level of an organisation, workers may be performing a similar type of work, but for the sake of control and supervision, they may be divided into different groups and each group is placed under the control of a foreman. Fig. 6.6 shows a pure line organisation.

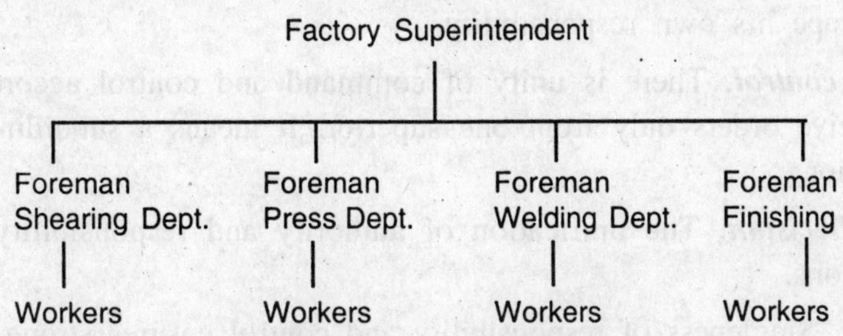

Fig. 6.6. Pure Line Organisation

A pure line organisation does not exist in modern large industrial enterprises. This is suitable only for businesses which are run on a small-scale producing only one item and in which the workers are divided into departments according to the type of work performed by each one of them.

(b) Departmental Line Organisation: In this type of organisation, the whole unit is divided into different departments that are convenient for control purposes. Each department is under the control of a departmental manager who is responsible to the superior over him. All the departmental managers enjoy equal status and work independently. Again, even within a department, there may be several sub-departments. For example, in the production department, there may be a number of foremen each in charge of a sub-department and controlling a certain number of workers (Fig. 6.7). Each foreman works independently, without any formal line of authority or responsibility with other foremen and takes orders from his superior or superintendent to whom he is directly responsible. The workers placed under a foreman get all their orders from their own foreman and they have no direct access to the factory superintendent. Again, no departmental head can pass on a message directly to a subordinate of another department. The message can be passed on only through the manager who has the authority over both the departments.

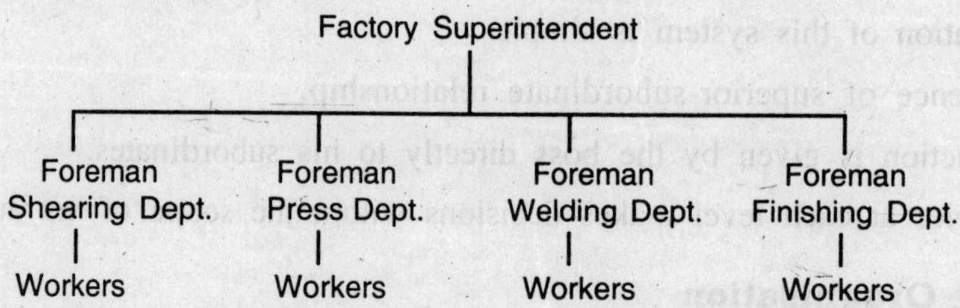

Fig. 6.7. Departmental Line Organisation

Advantages of Line Organisation

Some of the advantages of line organisation are as follows:

(a) Simplicity. It is easy to establish and operate. It is also easy to explain to the workers.

(b) Fixed Responsibility. Every member of the organisation knows his exact function, to whom he is responsible and who are responsible to him. Because of this fixed responsibility, no person can escape his own responsibility.

(c) Unity of control. There is unity of command and control according to which an employee can receive orders only from one superior. It means a subordinate is responsible to only one superior.

(d) Prompt Decision. The unification of authority and responsibility facilitates quick and prompt decisions.

(e) Discipline. Singleness of responsibility and control ensures strong discipline among the employees.

(f) Flexibility. This type of organisation is elastic. The adjustments in the organisation can be easily made to suit the changing conditions.

(g) Co-ordination. As all activities relating to one department are managed by one individual, there is a possibility for effective co-ordination.

(h) Definition of Authority. As the powers and authorities of various person are defined, the conflict in their powers and authorities is avoided.

(i) Less Expensive. It is less expensive as no expenditure on staff personnel is involved.

Disadvantages of Line Organisation

(a) Lack of Specialisation. As one person looks after all the work relating to his department, there is no scope for specialisation.

(b) Overloading. In this type, an executive is overloaded with work and hence he may not be in a position to direct and control the efforts of his subordinates properly. This leads to the losing of economies to scale.

(c) Scope for Favouritism. Since only one executive controls all the activities relating to his department, there is much scope for favouritism and nepotism.

(d) Limited Communication. In this type, there is no communication from subordinates upwards and the workers should follow the orders of superiors, without expressing any opinion about the orders communicated to them. This affects their creativity and capacity for independent thinking. Further, if superiors were to make a wrong decision, it would still be carried out, because the subordinates are afraid of pointing out that the decision is wrong.

(e) Unitary Administration. All decisions relating to a department are taken only by one executive and hence, the successful functioning of that department depends on his abilities.

(f) Lack of Co-operation. One executive controls the various activities of a department and gets undue importance while the importance of other people in the department is not recognised. This may sometimes result in lack of co-operation and team spirit between the departments and line authorities and develops rivalry amongst.

Suitability of Line Organisation

Inspite of many limitations, the importance of line organisation cannot be minimised. It is suitable for concerns.

(i) which are run on a small scale;

(ii) which do not have many subordinates and operatives;

(iii) which have straight and simple methods of operations; and

(iv) which are engaged in the work which is largely of a routine nature.

FUNCTIONAL ORGANISATION

Under the line type of organisation, one person is in charge of all the activities relating to a department or section but there is a difficulty of getting men with sufficient capacity and training who can look after all the activities efficiently. Taylor, recognising this limitation, proposed a functional type of organisation. Under this type of organisation, men with special abilities or training in a specialised function may be employed. The specialists will be performing the functions which are common to different departments under one organisation. Thus, under the functional type of organisation, identical functions of various departments in an organisation are performed by a specialist, while in a departmental line organisation, one person looks after all the activities of the department of which he is the head. The workers under functional type of organisation receive instructions from a specialist in each of several supervisory functions which are assigned to the different specialists.

F.W. Taylor recommended a functional organisation of activities at the shop floor level. He was of the view that the foreman should not be burdened with too many activities and instead, he should be assisted by a number of specialists in solving the problems of a technical nature (See Fig. 6.8). F.W. Taylor has recommended the following specialists.

In the Planning Department

(1) Route Clerk: His function is to lay down the exact route through which each and every piece of work should travel in the various stages of manufacture.

(2) Instruction Card Clerk: His function is to issue the necessary instructions to workers with regard to the manner in which they have to handle the job assigned to them.

(3) Time and Cost Clerk: He prepares the standard time for the completion of work and compiles the cost of that piece of work.

In the Factory

(4) Gang Boss: His work is to see that the various machines and materials are kept ready for workers to perform their operations.

(5) Speed Boss: His is concerned with prescribing of proper speeds for the machines.

(6) Inspector: His work is to check the quality of work done by the workers.

(7) Repair Boss: His function is to look after the maintenance of machines for the entire job.

(8) Disciplinarian: He enforces the rules and regulations of the organisation so that each job is performed in a systematic and perfect manner.

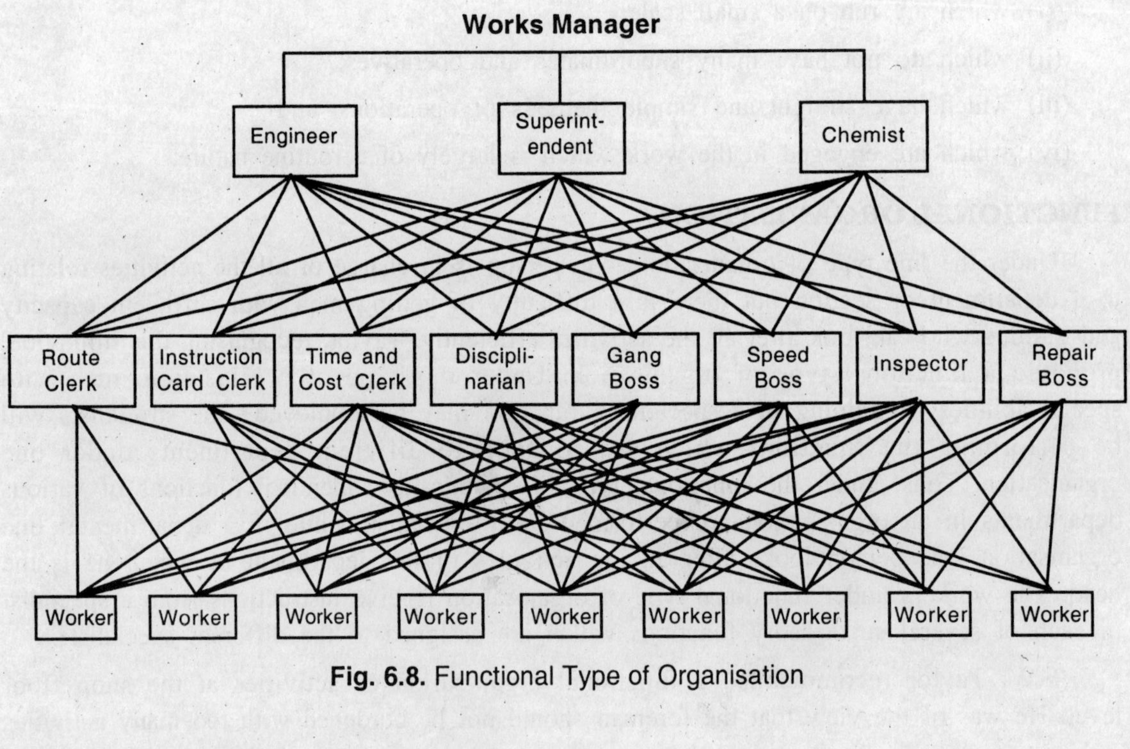

Fig. 6.8. Functional Type of Organisation

Functional Foremanship

Taylor called functional type of organisation "Functional Foremanship." The eight persons mentioned above are specialists in their jobs. The workers under this type of organisation are required to take orders from all the eight specialists. Taylor introduced this functional foremanship, because otherwise a single foreman has to look after all the functions. But no single person does have the capacity to perform all the functions.

Functional Organisation at the Top

At the higher levels, Taylor's functional system involves the grouping of all functions into major functional departments and entrusting each department to one executive. For instance, the personnel manager may be entrusted with personnel matters relating to all the departments, the marketing manager with the responsibility for marketing of all the products of all the plants and so on. Another feature of this type of organisation is that the line executive receives orders not only from his line boss but also from one or more specialists (See Fig. 6.9).

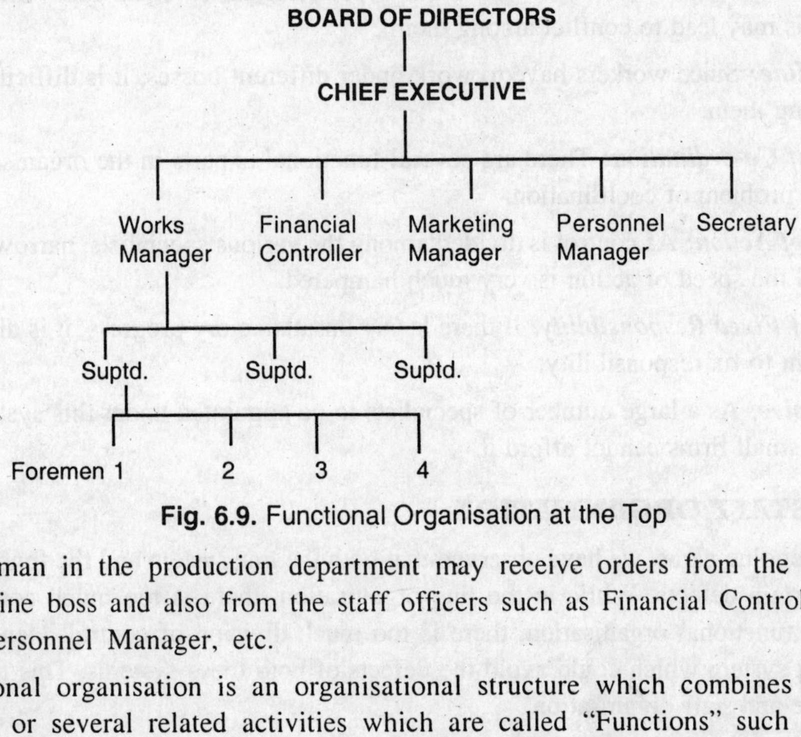

Fig. 6.9. Functional Organisation at the Top

A foreman in the production department may receive orders from the superintendent who is his line boss and also from the staff officers such as Financial Controller, Marketing Manager, Personnel Manager, etc.

Functional organisation is an organisational structure which combines all aspects of one activity or several related activities which are called "Functions" such as production, finance, marketing, HRD etc. It is structured according to products dealt or service rendered in the organisation. It is the most logical and basic form of departmentation. Functional organisation leads to specialise in business skills. It also makes it easier to mobilise specialised skills to needy areas of the business.

Advantages of Functional Organisation

1. Specialisation: It ensures maximum use of the principle of specialisation at every work point.

2. Efficiency: Since the workers have to perform a limited number of function, their efficiency would be very high.

3. Mass Production: Due to specialisation and standardisation, large-scale production can be undertaken without much inconvenience.

4. Co-operation: As there is no scope for one-man control in the organisation, there is the possibility of promoting cooperation.

5. Relief to the Executives: Since instructions from specialists flow directly to the lower levels, the line executives are free from worries about the technical problems faced by the workers.

6. Flexibility: Any change in the organisation can be introduced without disturbing the whole organisation and hence there is an element of flexibility in this type of organisation.

Disadvantages of Functional Organisation

1. Conflict amongst Foremen: Under this type, foreman of equal rank will be many in number and this may lead to conflict among them.

2. Discipline: Since workers have to work under different bosses, it is difficult to maintain discipline among them.

3. Lack of Co-ordination: There are several functional experts in the organisation and this may create the problem of coordination.

4. Speed of Action: As control is divided among the various specialists, narrow perspectives are created and the speed of action is very much hampered.

5. Lack of Fixed Responsibility: If there is any unsatisfactory progress, it is difficult for the top management to fix responsibility.

6. Expensive: As a large number of specialists to be appointed under this system, it is very expensive and small firms cannot afford it.

LINE AND STAFF ORGANISATION

In the foregoing paras, we have observed that both the line system and the functional system suffer from certain defects. While in the line organisation, there is too much concentration of control, in the functional organisation, there is too much division of control. Hence, there was need for a new system which could avoid the defects of both these systems. This need has been fulfilled by line and staff organisation.

In a line and staff organisation, the work of administration of business units is divided into two broad divisions, *viz.*, the staff which is responsible for planning and the line for the actual execution of the work. The staff is attached to the line to assist the line in discharging its duties efficiently. This method clearly distinguishes the difference between the two aspects of administration, *viz.*, planning and execution. The staff personnel only give advice to the line officials but do not enforce it. The staff officials prepare plans and recommend to the line officials who implement them with the help of their departmental personnel. Thus, the staff members are thinkers while the line officials are doers. A typical line and staff organisation is given in Fig. 6.10.

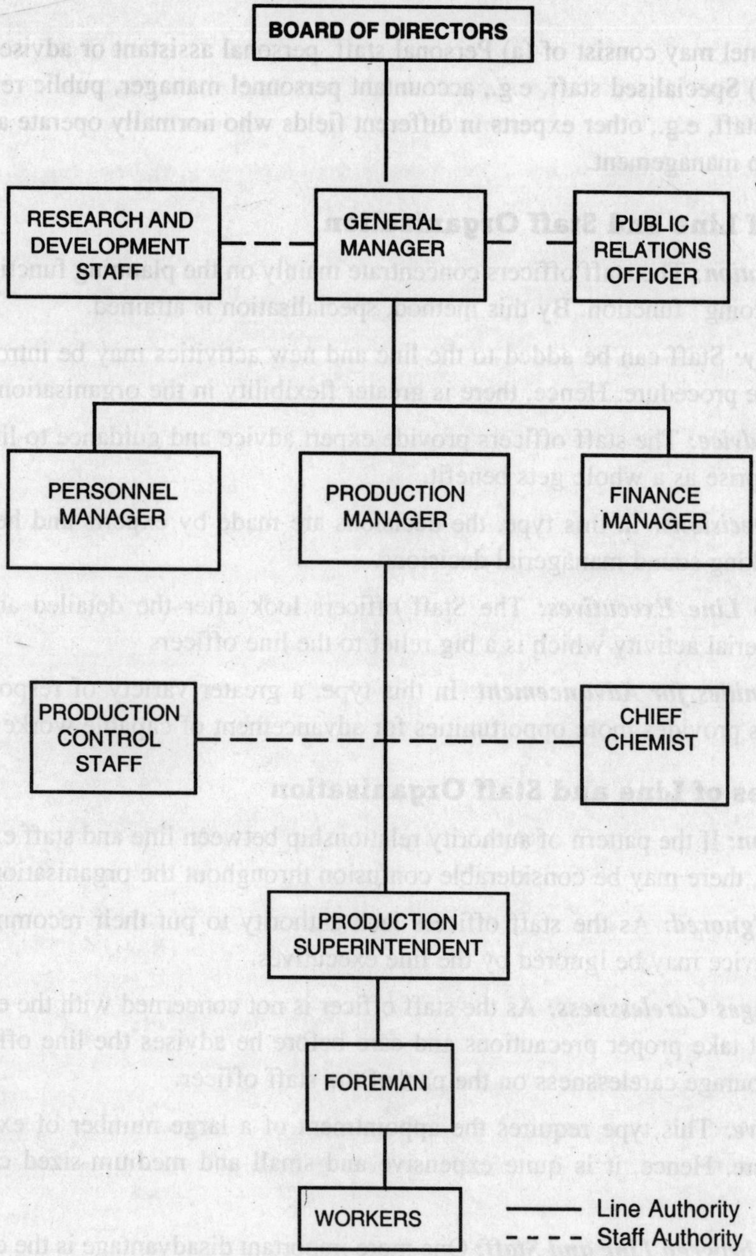

FIG. 6.10. Line and Staff Organisation

The line and staff organisation is based on the principle of specialisation. In the line organisation, as executives look after the entire work relating to their departments, there is no scope for specialisation. Whereas in the line and staff organisation, the staff officer is concerned with only one aspect of the total assignment of line officer and hence, attains specialisation in his job.

Type of Staff

Staff personnel may consist of (a) Personal staff, personal assistant or adviser attached to a line executive, (b) Specialised staff, e.g., accountant personnel manager, public relations officer, etc., (c) General staff, e.g., other experts in different fields who normally operate at higher levels and advise the top management.

Advantages of Line and Staff Organisation

1. Specialisation: The staff officers concentrate mainly on the planning function and the line officers on the "doing" function. By this method, specialisation is attained.

2. Flexibility: Staff can be added to the line and new activities may be introduced without disturbing the line procedure. Hence, there is greater flexibility in the organisation.

3. Expert Advice: The staff officers provide expert advice and guidance to line officers and by this, the enterprise as a whole gets benefit.

4. Sound Decisions: In this type, the decisions are made by experts and hence, there is a possibility of making sound managerial decisions.

5. Relief to Line Executives: The Staff officers look after the detailed analysis of each important managerial activity which is a big relief to the line officers.

6. Opportunities for Advancement. In this type, a greater variety of responsible jobs are available and this provides more opportunities for advancement of capable workers.

Disadvantages of Line and Staff Organisation

1. Confusion: If the pattern of authority relationship between line and staff executives is not clearly indicated, there may be considerable confusion throughout the organisation.

2. Advice Ignored: As the staff officers lack authority to put their recommendations into practice, their advice may be ignored by the line executives.

3. Encourages Carelessness: As the staff officer is not concerned with the execution of the plan, he may not take proper precautions and care before he advises the line officer. Thus, this system may encourage carelessness on the part of the staff officer.

4. Expensive: This type requires the appointment of a large number of experts involving heavy expenditure. Hence, it is quite expensive and small and medium-sized concerns cannot afford it.

5. Conflict between Line and Staff: One more important disadvantage is the conflict between the line and staff officers. The viewpoints of both line and staff of this conflict are given below:

A. The Line Viewpoint. The line managers have the following to say about the staff people:

(i) Staff authority undermines line authority and interferes in the work of line managers.

(ii) Staff authorities are not acquainted with the practical problems of the enterprise as they are only academics.

(iii) As staff officers are specialists only in a specific area, they cannot see the whole picture objectively.

(iv) Advice given by the staff is not always sound. Advice is only theoretical and unrealistic.

(v) Staff take credit if the programme (as per the advice of the staff) is successful and blame the line if it is not successful.

B. The Staff Viewpoint. Staff authorities have the following complaints against line officers:

(i) Line officers do not make proper use of advice given by staff.

(ii) Line officers reject the advice without giving reasons.

(iii) Line officers are slow to accept new ideas and they resist change.

(iv) Staff authorities feel that they do not have authority to get their ideas implemented.

Improving Line and Staff Relationship

For improving the relationships between the two and to resolve their conflict, the following steps may be taken:

1. The limits of authority of both line and staff should be prescribed clearly.
2. Staff authority should be restricted to a purely advisory role.
3. Line officers should give due consideration to staff advice. They should state reasons in case they cannot accept the advice.
4. Line should value the special skills of staff and similarly the staff should try to appreciate the difficulties in implementing new ideas.
5. The advice of staff should be realistic and practicable.
6. Both line and staff should try to understand each other's responsibilities and difficulties and try to co-operate with each other for the achievement of enterprise objectives.

MATRIX STRUCTURE

This is an organisational structure in which each employee reports to both functional manager and group manager. This is a "Multiple Command System." Workers will have two bosses. They work in two chains of command. In matrix organisation, two types of structure operate simultaneously. One is vertical structure and the other is horizontal. In vertical structure, the command moves vertically and in horizontal, the command moves horizontally. As the business activity is becoming more and more global, matrix organisations, which are complex in nature, are emerging.

An Incident — Matrix Organisation

A leading IT Company of India is exporting its products to three countries say: (i) Bangladesh, (ii) Nepal and (iii) Sri Lanka. The basic product being same, there is slight change in product features exported to three countries. Product being X, it is XB for Bangladesh, XN for Nepal and XS for Sri Lanka. The workers working to produce these products report to two authorities: (i) The Departmental Head in India where the product is produced and (ii) The Country Manager (Second Process) to which country the product is exported. This reduces several problems of production and product acceptance in the country to which it is exported. See the diagram.

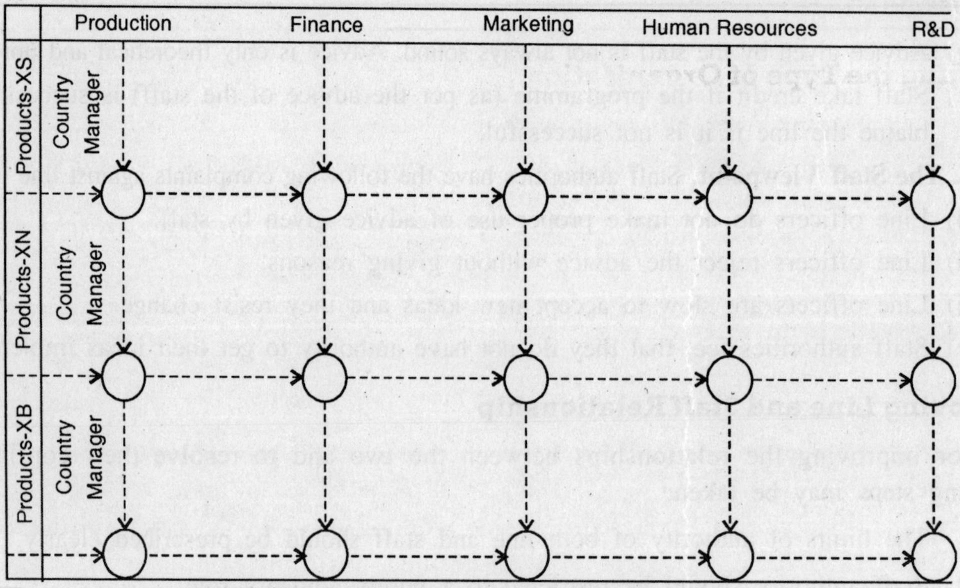

FIG. 6.11. Structure of Matrix Organisation

In this diagram, it may be observed that functional managers and their workers interact with each country manager regarding individual products are concerned. Workers look at functional managers for general policy solutions and country managers for individual product policy.

Advantages of Matrix Structures

1. It is an efficient means of bringing together the diversified specialized skills required to solve a complex problem. Authority and responsibility are shared. Stress is distributed.

2. There will be many problems in functional designs. In matrix organization, it is minimized as people work together on various diversified issues. Workers of both teams acquire realistic attitude about the work as they work together. For example, if hardware people and software people work together, they can produce better systems. Many problems will be solved in the process. The structure balances the time, cost and performance. Information is shared.

3. Matrix structure provides a great deal of cost-saving flexibility. Duplication of work is avoided. Resources are shared.

4. Conflicts are less in this structure.

Limitations

1. Workers do not easily adapt to a matrix system as members may not possess interpersonal skills and may be conservative in their attitude. This increases stress and confusion in workers.

2. If hierarchies are not firmly fixed, there will be the danger of conflicting directives and ill-defined responsibility. This increases conflict between managers and between managers and workers.

3. They are suitable only to large organisation and projects.

4. Decision-making will be slow.

Selecting the Type of Organisation

In the foregoing pages, an analysis of the features, merits and demerits of the different types of organisation has been made. It may be stated here that there is no hard and fast rule for the type of organisation suited to a particular business unit. However, while selecting a suitable type of organisation for a business unit, the management should consider such factors as the nature of industry, size of the business unit, scope for expansion in future, etc.

Formal and Informal Organisation

According to Chester Bernard, "an organisation is formal when the activities of two or more persons are consciously co-ordinated towards a common objective." In a formal organisation, the position, authority, responsibility and accountability of each level are clearly defined. By means of rules, policies and other regulations of the organisation, it prescribes the relationships amongst the people working in the organisation. In this way, all enterprises which have a system of well-defined positions, authority, responsibility, relationships, rules, policies, etc., are considered formal organisations.

An informal organisation arises from the personal and social relations of the people, not established by any formal authority.

The people cut across formal channels (as established by the formal organisation) and communicate amongst each other. It arises spontaneously and not based on rules, regulations and procedures. It is influenced by the personal attitudes, whims, likes and dislikes etc. For example, an assistant sales manager may take advice from the production manager instead of the sales manager. He may prefer to approach the production manager for advice,

Distinctions Between Formal and Informal Organisation

Formal Organisation	*Informal Organisation*
1. It is a prescribed structure of roles and relationships consciously co-ordinated towards a common objective.	1. It is a natural and spontaneous structure arising out of the social tendency of people to associate and interact.
2. Its goals and tasks are oriented towards productivity, profitability, growth and so on.	2. Its goals and tasks predominantly centre around individual and group satisfaction, affiliation, friendship, etc.
3. It is hierarchical, pyramid-shaped and bureaucratic in structure.	3. It is shapeless and uncharitable.
4. Emphasis is on status differentials and based on superior-subordinate relationships..	4. It is based on friendship, common values, and interests.
5. There is a prescribed system of behaviour. People are rewarded for their "desired behaviour" and punished for their "undesirable behaviour." Rewards can be both monetary and non-monetary.	5. There are unwritten norms of behaviour enforced by common consent by all the members. Rewards for obeying the norms can take the form of continuous membership, social esteem, group leadership, etc. Punishments are isolation, censure, etc.

personal friendship with him or due to his regard for the production manager's job knowledge, skill, personality, age, seniority, leadership qualities, etc. This type of inter-relationships which are found in an informal organisation, cannot be shown in the organisation chart while the inter-relations of formal organisation can be shown.

An informal organisation exists in every enterprise and at all levels of managerial hierarchy. However, there cannot be a completely formal or a completely informal organisation. The formal managers should not try to abolish informal relationships of employees because they are very important and useful for managing the concern efficiently and for achieving the objectives of an enterprise. In the words of C.I. Barnard, "Informal organisation brings cohesiveness to a formal organisation. It brings to the members of a formal organisation, a feeling of belonging, of status, of self-respect and of gregarious satisfaction." According to Keith Davis, an "informal organisation is a powerful influence upon productivity and job satisfaction." Both formal and informal systems are necessary for group activity, just as two blades are essential to make a pair of scissors workable."

Benefits of Informal Organisation to its Members

Employees by becoming members of the informal group, derive certain benefits. They are:

1. Sense of belonging. In a formal organisation, the worker is one among the thousands of workers and to the management, he is just a worker without any attachment. Under these circumstances, the workers will not have a sense of belonging. Informal organisation fills this void by constantly emphasising and re-inforcing each member's individual personality. It gives to each member that human consideration which boosts his self-image and personality.

2. Safety valve for emotional problems. In the daily work routine of a worker, there are many opportunities for tension and frustration. For example, his supervisor might have reprimanded him or an overbearing customer might have harassed him. In all such situations, he seeks a sympathetic ear of a friend in the informal organisation. His friend is mostly the person who has had similar experiences and can thus share and understand his trouble.

3. Aid on the job. In the case of accidents or illness, members of an informal organisation may help one another. If a member breaks a company rule, they may cover up for him. They may protect one another from authoritarian action. They may increase the group's efficiency by changing work assignments or by increasing the specialisation of their tasks beyond what is prescribed in the job description.

4. Breeding ground for innovation and originality. By enabling members to modify the job situation more to their liking, the informal group creates the necessary environment for individual innovation and originality. Protected by his group, the individual can experiment with his novel ideas without having to persuade the boss before trying them out.

5. Important channel of communication. News travels quickly via informal organisations. It is the clandestine transmitter and receiver of information before it is officially released. After the news is released, the informal organisations amend, amplify and interpret it. Thus each person gets a larger, more detailed and meaningful but possibly distorted and erroneous picture of what is going on the organisation.

6. Social control. The informal organisation provides all its members a set of norms — "guides to correct behaviour." These guides serve as dividing lines between good and bad behaviour, between moral and immoral acts, between legitimate and illegitimate activities. Members are expected to conform to these norms. A deviant may be ostracised, condemned or censured.

7. Check on authority. Informal organisation forces the manager to plan and act more carefully than he would otherwise. Every manager knows that it is a check and balance on his unlimited use of authority.

Benefits of Informal Organisation to Management

The following are the advantages of informal organisation co-operating with the management:

1. Self-policing: This relieves management of much of the burden of supervision. When the manager knows that the group is cooperatively-oriented, he feels less compelled to check on them frequently and is encouraged to delegate and decentralise his authority.

2. Fills in gaps in a manager's abilities: If a manager is weak in some ability, one of the members of the informal group may help him without letting others know about the manager's weakness.

3. Gives the manager feedback about employees and their work experiences: This increases the understanding of the manager as to what he needs to do to be a supportive manager. It also helps interpret management to the workers so that they may be more supportive. It makes up for any management failures in communication. Management, in fact, often depends on it to convey certain types of information which the formal system does not wish to carry and purposely leaves unsaid. For example, a manager cannot announce his bad mood officially to his subordinates. The best way to do this would be to put this information on the grapevine so that it reaches the subordinates informally.

Disadvantages of Informal Organisation

Informal organisation is not an unmixed blessing. If it does not co-operate with the management, it may create serious problems. These are as under:

1. Resistance to change. Although there are no charts or blueprints to bind an informal organisation, there are customs, conventions and culture which bind it. Therefore, the group resists those management demands which are perceived by it as detracting from its culture or threatening the existing relationships among the members.

2. Organisation objectives may be affected. Members of the informal group are likely to put their own group need satisfaction ahead of organisation's objectives. By this, the group's objectives are likely to conflict with or take precedence over the organisation's goals. The result is, the organisation suffers.

3. Rumour. One undesirable characteristic of informal communication called the 'grapevine' is its function as a carrier of rumours. Research shows that the story given at the origin of a rumour is filtered, elaborated or amended in the informal communication channel. This leads to undesirable consequences.

4. Group-think philosophy. Some members begin to worship the group. They come to believe that what they seek must be "good" because the group has decided so. Thus, there develops a delusion of righteousness. Conformity is induced in which an individual loses his identity.

Harmonising Informal and Formal Organisation

Since management can neither order the informal organisation out of existence nor circumvent it by the logical course is to harmonise it with the formal organisation. A number of steps can lead towards this result. These are as under:

1. Where informal rules are acceptable, they should be institutionalised. Similarly, that informal pattern of relationships which serves the company well should be incorporated into formal structure.
2. If normal lines of communication exist, they should be used by management.
3. When informal leaders develop, they should be appointed to positions of formal authority.
4. Employees should be made to know that management not merely tolerates but willingly accepts the existence of an informal group.
5. All major cliques comprising the informal organisation should be catalogued and informal collected about their reactions to one another and to the company.

Organisation Charts

Organisation charts are the important tools for providing information on organisation relationships and activities. An organisation chart is a diagrammatic representation of the framework or structure of an organisation. The organisation chart portrays managerial positions and relationships in a company or department. Organisation data are graphically presented. They show only the formal organisation and depicts it for only a given moment in time." Organisation charts have the following contents:

(1) Ranks, names, titles and the lines of command, various authorities from top to bottom of the organisation.

(2) Authority and responsibility of various authorities.

(3) Relationships between different authorities.

(4) Kinds of relationships prevailing in the organisation.

Three types of charts are commonly followed by the business concern. They are:

(a) from top to down,
(b) from left to right, and
(c) circular.

In the top-to-down method at the top level, the highest person or position is placed and after that the next highest and this process is continued to the lowest level.

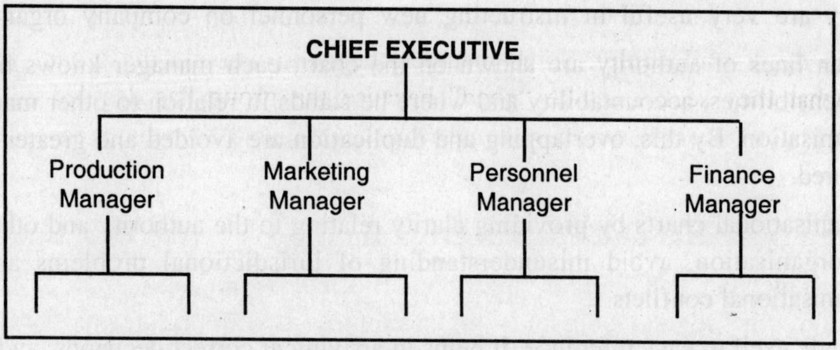

FIG. 6.12. From 'top-to-down' type Organisation Chart

In the left-to-right type the highest position is shown at the extreme left and those with lesser authority move towards the right.

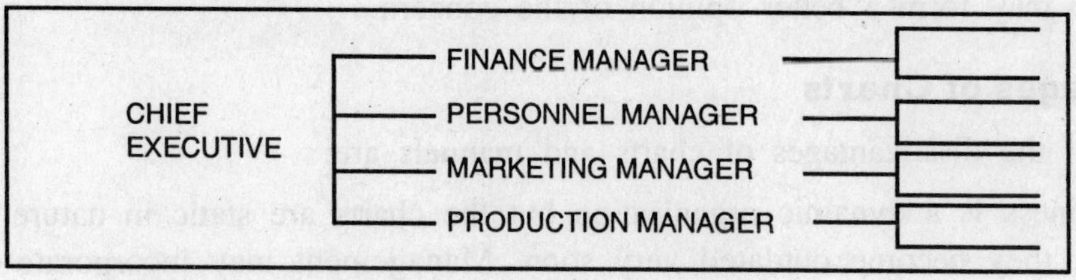

FIG. 6.13. From 'left to right' type of Organisation Chart

In the circular form the highest position is shown in the centre and the lowest position at the outermost circle.

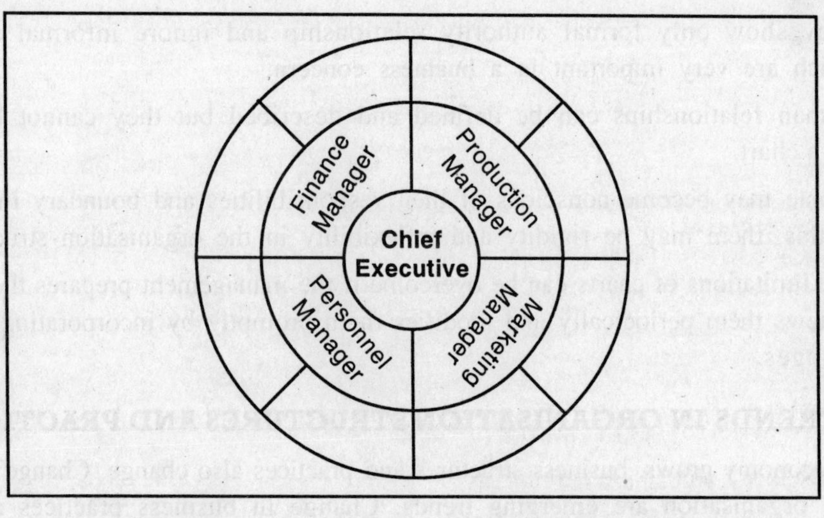

FIG. 6.14. Circular type Organisation Chart

Advantages of Organisational Charts and Manuals

1. They define the organisational relationships and draw a picture of the structure which is useful for understanding the organisation as a whole.

2. They are very useful in instructing new personnel on company organisation.
3. When lines of authority are shown on the chart, each manager knows his functions, responsibilities, accountability and where he stands in relation to other managers in the organisation. By this, overlapping and duplication are avoided and greater efficiency is secured.
4. Organisational charts by providing clarity relating to the authority and other aspects of an organisation, avoid misunderstanding of jurisdictional problems and minimise organisational conflicts.
5. It lends itself to easy reference. It helps in arriving at correct decisions, and can be used as a basis for making any modifications in the organisation structure.
6. With the help of an organisation chart, outsiders can easily know the person they have to approach in connection with their work. By this, they save their time and also they may form a better opinion of the concern.

Disadvantages of Charts

Some of the disadvantages of charts and manuals are:

1. Business is a dynamic organisation but the charts are static in nature. Because of this, they become outdated very soon. Management may incorporate the relevant changes in charts and manuals. But this can be done long after the change has taken place.
2. They tend to make people overconscious of being superiors and inferiors. This may destroy team spirit and encourage red-tapism.
3. They show only formal authority relationship and ignore informal relationships which are very important in a business concern.
4. Human relationships can be defined and described but they cannot be portrayed on a chart.
5. People may become conscious of their responsibilities and boundary lines. Because of this, there may be rigidity and inflexibility in the organisation structure.
6. The limitations of charts can be overcome if the management prepares them carefully, reviews them periodically and modifies them promptly by incorporating the relevant changes.

RECENT TRENDS IN ORGANISATION STRUCTURES AND PRACTICES

As the economy grows, business structures and practices also change. Change management and learning organisation are emerging trends. Change in business practices according to changing business and general economic environment, the structures and practices in individual business houses should also change. Otherwise the organisation will be in deep trouble. The change of practices and structures in business houses is termed as "change management". In order to introduce change, old practices are to be eliminated and new ones are to be incorporated. This process of giving up of old ones is called "Unlearning" and understanding and implementing new practices is called "Learning". Unlearning the old pratices learning the newly required practices is called "Learning Organisation" — LO. LO is the order of the day. In this backdrop, the trends in organisation structures and practices are analysed.

Development in Structure

Besides the basic organisational structures discussed earlier, the following structures are found in recent times.

(i) Team structure

(ii) Network structure

(iii) Boundaryless structure

(iv) Virtual organisations.

These new structures are briefly explained in the following paragraphs:

(i) Team structure. As the name itself suggests, this structure is designed in such a manner that all concerned (experts and workers) work in a team to finish a task. This structure is found in specific project surveys and project executions. Even in other business houses, to solve functional problems such as marketing, financial, HRD production, etc., special teams can be formed in hierarchical pattern. The competencies of team members will be fully utilised to solve the specific problem or in preparing the project reports for expansion of business or in establishing new projects. These teams have litte or no underlying functional hierarchy and rely almost exclusively on project type team. Thus, team structure organises separate functions into a group based one. These cross-functional teams comprise of members from different departments. They work in a team to solve problems and explore opportunities. The purpose of team structure is to cut functional boundaries among departments and create a more effective relationship for solving problems as and when they crop up.

Supposing, company wants to develop a new product. The services of different functional teams are to be drafted for this purpose. The team structure, then will be as follows:

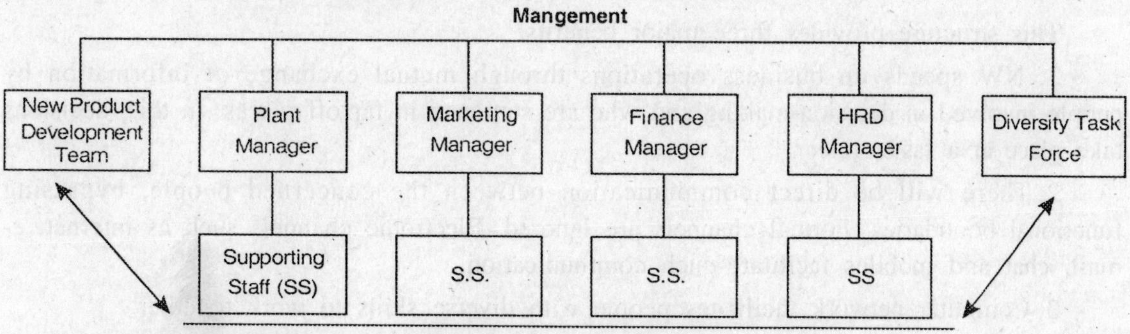

Fig. 6.15. Team structure

This structure is advantageous: (i) to break inter-departmental barriers to solve problem, (ii) to speed up decision-making process, (iii) to motivate employees, (iv) to reduce management levels and (v) to reduce administrative costs.

But, it has the limitation of: (i) conflicting loyalties among team members, (ii) time management issues and (iii) more time consumption in meetings. But these limitations can be overcome by group managers who have quality interpersonal relations, and their team management abilities.

(ii) Network Structure. Organisational structure is dynamic in nature. Restructuring will be taking place due to change in environment, to have control over resources, to boost the moral of employees, etc., one of the structures—Network structure—exhibits a big degree of flexibility, covering three aspects, *viz.,* (i) technological aspects, (ii) economic aspects and (iii) social aspects. As and when business operations developed complexity, network structure becomes popular.

Network structure is one which is developed in electronic form to control and coordinate internal and external relations with more flexibility in operation and focusing on low-cost strategy. This type of structure will be developed to operate any type of business function such as production, finance, marketing, HRD, R&D, to innovate new product design and development. But it is very appropriate for projects. It is a structure linked together in electronic form, particularly through computers to conduct business operations simultaneously. The structure is a set of interconnected terminals or computers with different business functions, which are co-ordinated and controlled by central office. Network structure does not rely on strait forward management and the chain of command. It works on checks and balances. Identical ideas are collaborated to take best decision. Each decision is arrived at after consulting the employees concerned and who are in network.

Very many examples can be given for network structure consider banking operations — the core banking system that is in practice. As per this business operation, a bank head office installs a central server system and all of its branches are linked to the main server through a network. Cash withdrawals or obtaining information from their accounts can be made through personal computers maintained in their residence or can got from nearby ATM. State Bank of India managers over 18,000 branches in the central office through network.

Similarly, a transnational company producing of products in one country, selling in other country and having a head office in another country, can be conducted through network structure.

Benefits—Network Structure

This structure provides three major benefits.

1. NW speeds up business operations through mutual exchange of information by people involved in decision-making and who are stationed in far off places. In this, decisions take place at a faster rate.

2. There will be direct communication between the concerned people, bypassing functional boundaries. Formal channels are ignored. Electronic channels such as internet, e-mail, chat and mobiles facilitate such communication.

3. Computer network facilitates people with diverse skills to work together.

The following example willgive an idea of network structure. In a project organisation assume that seven divisions are functioning to complete the project on time. All divisions are interlinked with a network technology. Of them, five divisions have direct interactions to serve three activites or objectives and the other two are independent divisions. However, they are connected to other divisions to access data in times of necessity with a central control system. Of the two independent divisions one serves three objectives and the other only one objective. Observe the following diagrams. Divisions are shown in the form of squares and objectives are shown in the form of circles. Funds are separately provided to each division. The structure will appear in the following format.

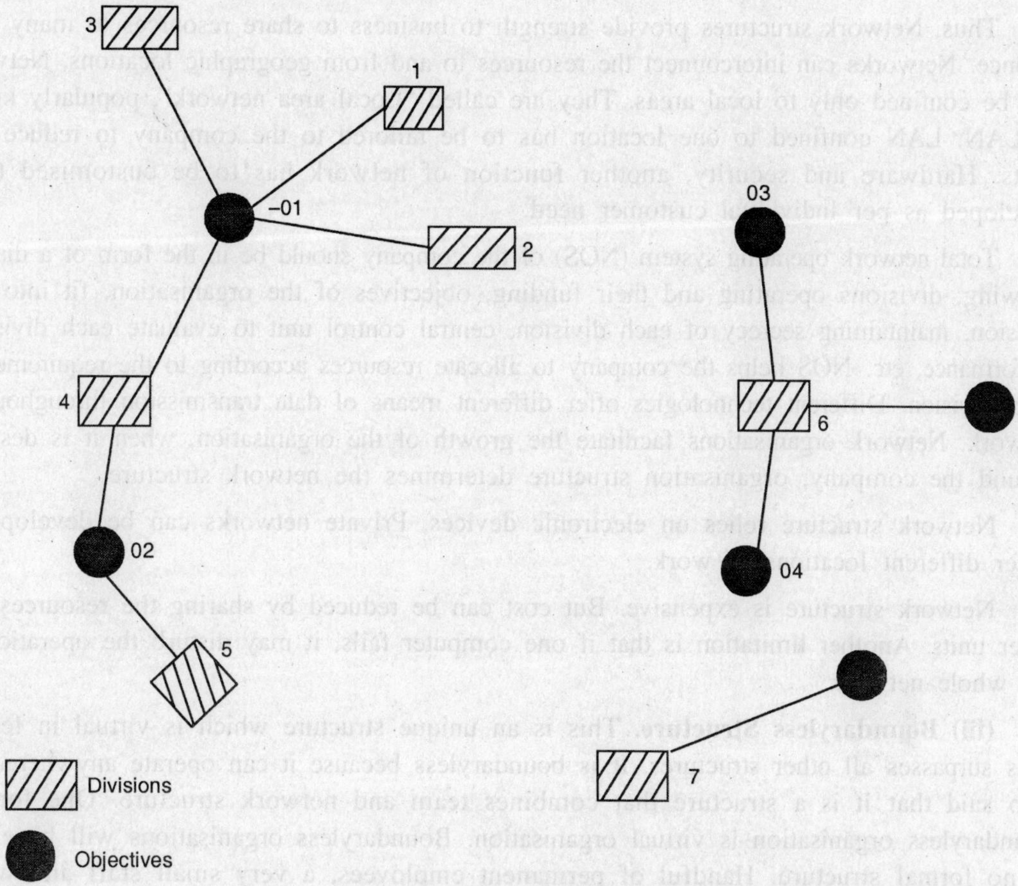

FIG. 6.16. Network Diagram

Network structures are defined by structure, process and purpose. They are designed after conducting research, analyzing empirical studies on identical business, microworlds and experiments, survey research, brain storming sessions and include disciplines such as economics, management, political science, organisational behaviour, computer science, artificial intelligence etc.

As stated earlier, network structure comprises of three disciplines *viz.* (i) Technology—computers, (ii) Economics and (iii) social aspects.

Computer network takes care of communications, errors, protocols and control architecture. All these are related to objectives and strategies of the organisation.

Economics network related to coalations and externalities. They are mainly concerned with vertical integration, efficiency of scale, firm boundaries, decentralised incentives and non-cooperative aspects of agents. This mainly considers cost-benefit aspects.

Social aspect of network considers human element, *viz.*, equality of workers, alienation, in group bias, peer pressure, desire, loyalty, status and rymotism. It is mainly concerned with behavioural aspects.

Thus, Network structures provide strength to business to share resources to many users at once. Networks can interconnect the resources to and from geographic locations. Networks can be confined only to local areas. They are called "Local area network", popularly known as LAN. LAN confined to one location has to be tailored to the company to reduce total costs. Hardware and security, another function of network has to be customised to be developed as per individual customer need.

Total network operating system (NOS) of the company should be in the form of a diagram showing, divisions operating and their funding, objectives of the organisation, fit into each division, maintaining secrecy of each division, central control unit to evaluate each division's performance, etc. NOS helps the company to allocate resources according to the requirement of each division. Different technologies offer different means of data transmission throughout the network. Network organisations facilitate the growth of the organisation, when it is designed around the company, organisation structure determines the network structure.

Network structure relies on electronic devices. Private networks can be developed to cover different locations of work.

Network structure is expensive. But cost can be reduced by sharing the resources with other units. Another limitation is that if one computer fails, it may disturb the operations in the whole network.

(iii) Boundaryless Structure. This is an unique structure which is virtual in feature. This surpasses all other structures. It is boundaryless because it can operate anywhere. It is also said that it is a structure that combines team and network structure. One form of boundaryless organisation is virtual organisation. Boundaryless organisations will have little or no formal structure. Handful of permanent employees, a very small staff and with a modest administration facility, boundaryless organisation functions. The typical structure can be seen in the following figure:

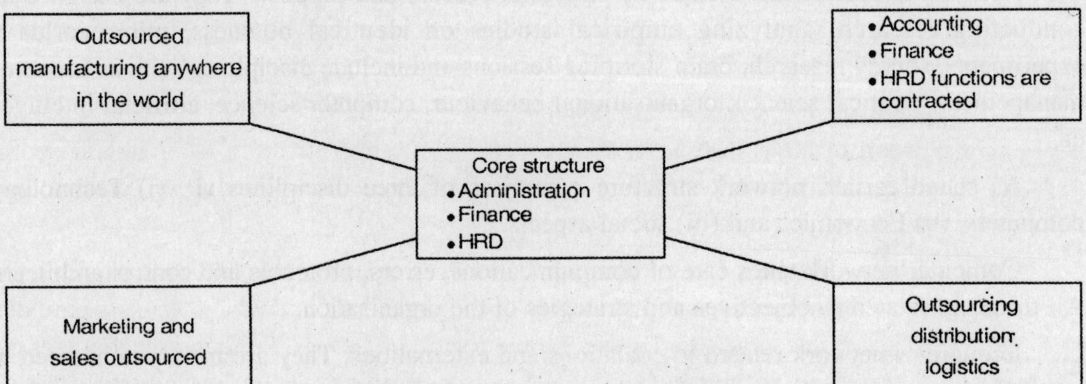

Fig. 6.17. Boundaryless organisation

ORGANISATION — GENERAL BENEFITS

A sound organisation is a must for every enterprise not only for its continuity but also for its success. It is the backbone of management and without it, no management can manage the various operations of an enterprise. It lays down the basis for other managerial functions such as planning, direction, co-ordination and control. It is the means by which the problems of an enterprise relating to policies, procedures, operations and administration can efficiently be solved. As Lounsbury Fish points out, "organisation is more than a chart. It is the mechanism through which management directly co-ordinates and controls the business. It is indeed the foundation of management." Another management expert Kenneth C. Towe states that "a sound form of organisation is the answer to every business problem, that a poor organisation could run a good product into the ground and that good organisation with a poor product could run a good product out of the market." With these general remarks, now we state here the important advantages of organisation.

1. Aid to Management: Organisation aids management in accomplishing enterprise objectives. It helps management in performing other management functions such as planning, direction, delegation control, etc. It increases management's efficiency and promptness, avoids delay and duplication of work and motivates the employees to perform their job efficiently. It lays solid groundwork for focusing the attention and action of management on the accomplishment of the objectives of an enterprise.

2. Facilitates Growth of Enterprise: An organisation is concerned with activities such as recruitment of staff, delegation of authority, assignment of responsibility, co-ordination and control of activities at different work centres, etc. With these activities, the organisation provides a framework within which the company grows. Thus, organisation facilitates growth of enterprise.

3. Ensures Optimum Use of Human Resources: Organisation affects human resources in a number of ways such as recruitment, training, placement of workers, bringing harmony in their efforts, improving the communication network and motivating them to improve their efficiency. All these ensure an optimum use of human resources of enterprise.

4. Stimulates Creativity: Sound organisation stimulates creative thinking and initiative on the part of employees. Delegation of authority provides sufficient freedom to supervisors and this encourages initiative, creative thinking, resourcefulness, independent thinking, spirit of innovation and enterprise among them.

5. Adoption of New Technology: A sound organisation structure facilitates the optimum use of technological improvements such as automatic techniques of production, control devices, computer system, etc.

6. Encourage Human Use of Human Resources. A sound organisation provides for job rotation and job enlargement and makes jobs meaningful and interesting. It also provides for efficient methods of selection, training and promotion of employees. Further, it encourages people to work in a team and as human beings and not as machines. Thus, it facilitates human use of human beings.

7. Facilitates Stability of Enterprises. A sound organisation has flexibility to adjust to the changes in the conditions, promotes effective leadership, promotes employee morale, provides for delegation of authority and develops co-ordination, co-operation and communication. All these factors assure stability to the enterprise.

8. Executive Development. A sound organisation by providing for training of staff at different levels and by proper delegation and decentralisation, helps development of managers.

In short, a properly-conceived organisation structure facilitate effective communication, precise delegation, smooth management, proper co-ordination and control, closer co-operation, effective leadership, higher employee morale, managerial efficiency, steady growth and diversification, optimum use of human and other resources, optimum use of technological improvements, development of managers, creativity among the staff and accomplishment of enterprise objectives.

Virtual Organisation

"Virtual organisation" concept is slowly emerging on the corporate scene. This is a sort of "network of independent companies (including suppliers, customers, old competitors) connected by information technology to share skills, costs, and access to one another's markets". There will be no central office for VO. It does not possess organisational chart. VO is neither having integration nor hierarchy. In the context of globalisation of business, VO helps in exploiting quickly, the fast-changing opportunities. Strategic alliances (SA) and joint ventures (JV) are the first expressions of the future of corporate world.

In a VO, a temporary network is created amongst partners of JVs and SAs, to share "Technology" at global level in the form of electronic contracts to avoid legal hurdles, to share specific market opportunity which is of short-term nature and depart after availing the opportunity, to have the best of every activity as each partner brings its core competence and having no boundary for such structure.

Organisation Structure — Tomorrow

— There is a rethinking of work culture in every business enterprise today. It is having a major impact on organisational structure.

— Job and work pattern are changing.

— The workers are now moving from one job to another. The concepts of job security and steady income are losing ground.

— Part-time, contract and self-employed workers are increasing as a per cent of total employees.

— Organisational structure is down-sized and is becoming thinner and flatter. Levels will be reduced.

— Organisations linked to global competition have to overhaul their organisation structure.

— Boosting productivity and cost cuts have become major "mantras."

— Emphasis is on changing technology and developing entrepreneurship.

— Products and services are becoming smart and hence the employers and employees should be smart and be in the learning process as products lose ground at a faster rate.

— Therefore,tomorrow's organisation will be "virtual" which means, the personnel need not be in office. They need not see each other every day. They communicate with each other with some communication system. Office will be small and will have few furniture not occupied all the time. Much of the work will be done outside the office. "Mutual Trust" becomes a vital factor.

— Intelligence, information and ideas are the key factors of tomorrow's organisation.

— Organising an organisation is not an ordinary task. Several aspects are to be considered while formulating an organisational structure. Size of the business, authority flow, interpersonal relationships, functions of the firm etc decide the pattern of structure.

SUMMARY

1. The term 'organisation' is used as a process of management and as a structure of relationship. In the first sense, organisation is interpreted as a process of welding together a framework of positions which can be used by the management for the purpose of accomplishing the enterprise goals. In the second sense, organisation is interpreted as a structure of relationships among positions and jobs for the purpose of achieving enterprise objectives.
2. Organisation structure which results from the organising process is the basic framework within which the decision-making behaviour of executives takes place.
3. The important steps involved in the process of organisation are, the determination of objectives, the grouping of activities, assignment of duties to person, delegation of authority and creating authority relationships.
4. There is a need to follow certain principles in order to formulate and develop a sound and efficient organisation structure. The principles are: principle of objective, principle of specialisation, principle of span of control, principle of exception, scalar principle of delegation, principle of responsibility, principle of flexibility, principle of simplicity, principle of unity of direction and principle of efficiency.
5. An organisation is formal when the activities of two or more persons are consciously co-ordinated towards a common objective. Informal organisation arises from the personal and social relations of the people not established by any formal authority. Both formal and informal systems are necessary for group activity.
6. Sound organisation aids management in accomplishing enterprise objectives, facilitates growth of enterprise, ensures optimum use of human resources, stimulates creativity, facilitates optimum use of technological resources, ensures stability of enterprise and facilitates executive development.
7. Organisation chart portrays managerial positions and relationships in a company or departmental unit. The organisation manual contains information such as details of various positions, their authority and responsibilities, job description, salaries, relationships, activities, duties and functions of each position and organisation procedure and methods.
8. For the purpose of internal organistion, there are three principles which have been well recognised. They are: (i) the line organisation; (ii) functional organisation; and (iii) line and staff organisation.
9. In line organisation, each department is a complete self-sustaining unit and departmental head is given complete freedom to manage his department and there is no provision for staff specialists. Line organisation is suitable for concerns run on a small scale.

10. Under functional type of organisation, specialists will be performing the functions which are common to different departments under the organisation and the workers receive instructions from a specialist in each of several supervisory functions which are assigned to different specialists. Specialists include route clerk, time and cost clerk, gang boss, instruction card clerk, speed boss, inspector, repair boss, and disciplinarian.
11. In line and staff organisation, the work of business unit is divided into two broad divisions, *viz.*, staff responsible for planning and line for the execution of work. The staff is attached to the line to assist the line in discharging its duties efficiently. Conflicts between line and staff may take place, but they can be overcome by taking such steps as specifying the limits of authority of both line and staff, making them understand each other's responsibilities and difficulties, making staff to give advice which is realistic and practicable, etc.
12. Matrix structure is becoming popular as the business goes global. In matrix structure, multiple command system exists. Workers will have two bosses. But the problems in the organisation will be minimised.
13. Team structure involves the drawing of expert functional managers and employees across the organisation and forming a team recognising the individual authority and responsibility to complete a project.
14. Network structure is a technology-based one, in which different functional departments will be functioning in different places or in the same place, connected with computer and other electronic forms to conduct business operation. A network is created as per requirement and this network will be used for completing business transactions.
15. Boundaryless organisation structure has no boundary to conduct business. This means it will not have little or no formal structure. It is a virtual organisation.

STUDY QUESTIONS

1. What is an organisation? Give the meaning of organisation structure.
2. Give the meaning of: (i) Line organisation, (ii) Staff organisation, (iii) Line and staff organisation, (iv) Functional organisation, (v) Matrix organisation, (vi) Network structure, (vii) Boundaryless or virtual organisation, (viii) Formal organisation, (ix) Informal organisation, (x) Flat organisation and (xi) Tall organisation.
3. Distinguish between Dynamic and Static concepts of Organisation.
4. Give a note on Principles of Organisation.
5. Distinguish between Formal and Informal Organisation.
6. Distinguish between Organisation as a Structure and Organization as a Process.
7. Write a note on Line Organisation.
8. Analyse the concept of Functional Organisation.
9. Narrate the reasons for conflict between line and staff officials. How can they be developed into an integrated team?
10. Give a note on committee type of organisation.
11. Write a note on Matrix organisation. Explain how network structure resembles matrix structure.
12. What an organisation chart exhibits? Explain.
13. Give an explanatory note on boundaryless organisation.
14. Write an essay on various organisation structure.
15. Briefly explain the various principles of organisation.

Practical Exercise

1. Form a group of five to six. You be the observer. Ask the group to discuss about the following aspects:
   (*i*) Organisation as a process and as a structure. (*ii*) Formal, informal and line organisations. Based on this discussion develop one organisation structure for a manufacturing firm which produces three popular consumer products.
2. What form of organizational structure is best suited to a custom-made product produced in a stable environment and a mass-produced product in an unstable environment?

7

ORGANISING–TRENDS AND PRACTICES

LEARNING OBJECTIVES

After reading this chapter, you should be able to know:

- Chain of Command
- Span of Control
- Decentralisation
- Organisational Configuration
- Committees
- Departmentation.
- Unity of Command
- Delegation and Empowerment
- Organisational Design
- Organisational Manuals
- Direction

Organisations are not static but are dynamic. Many business organisation have lived for long crossing century mark. GE, The Hindu and many such organisations who are still functioning with force and recognition bear testimony to this. The concepts like "change management" and "learning organisation" pervade all organisations and organisations established long back live today with totally a different structure. Organisational activities expand and restructuring the design and configuring authority relationships as per changed requirement will take place. This is a continuous activity in every organisation.

Effective and efficient management of the organisations are expected through out their life. Practices such as decentralisation, considering the span of management, chain of command, unity of command, delegation and empowerment, designing the structure and configuring it, establishing departments as per directions, formulating committees, preparing manuals have been the order in every enterprise. These trends and practices are briefly analysed in the following paragraphs:

1. CHAIN OF COMMAND

This concept exhibits flow of authority. It is a system whereby authority flows down from the top through a series of executive positions in which each functional manager is accountable to the immediate superior. This is a structure concerning decision-making which shows. The flow of responsibilities from the higher levels of authority to the lower levels. This concept was originated from defence operations. In military hierarchy, the succession of commanding officers from a superior to a subordinate, commands are exercised. It is a continuous chain of authority that links the most junior worker to the top brass. The concept of the chain of command was first introduced to management theory by Henry Fayol under one of the fourteen principles, he propounded, *viz.*, "Scalar Chain". According to this principle, people at the top of the organisation have all authority and other individual's authority scales down as per their relative position in the hierarchy.

Thus, chain of command, which is practiced in military structure is extended to organisations. In the organisational context, it means that the commands or orders flow from the top down the line to last worker of the organisation. Persons or line managers who receive the command from their immediate superior are accountable to them only and they do not normally have direct link with the top management. The following diagram shows the flow of authority or chain of command.

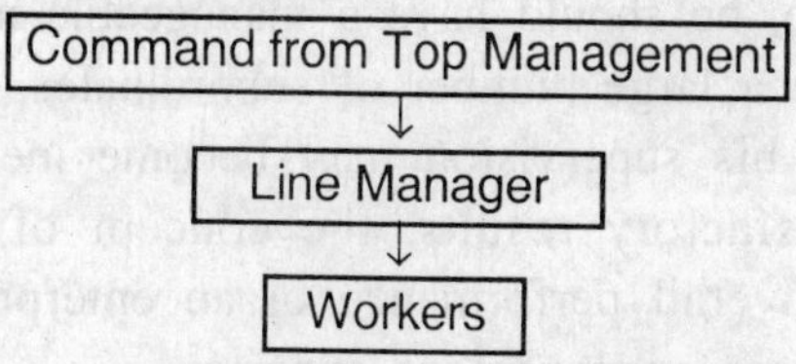

Fig. 7.1. Chain of Command.

Supposing, two or more units are functioning and the command is to be given to both units from one unit officer. The authority flow from the executive of one unit cannot directly take place. It should pass through the unit head of another unit except under permitted circumstances. See the following figure:

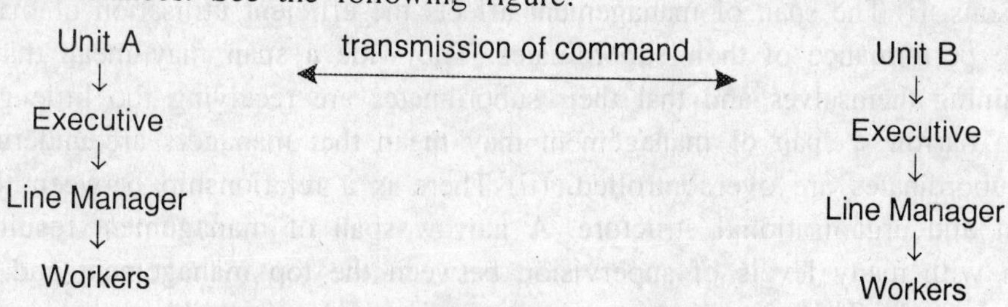

Fig. 7.2. Flow of Command to Other Unit.

The flow of command takes place only in the concerned line and not in lines which are adopted for special purposes such as health cares, sports, etc., activities of the organisation. If any order is to be executed in these units, it should be sent to the unit head in the form of request to implement it or it has to be transmitted through top class.

Thus, chain of command is the flow of authority from top to bottom in written form. The concept which was originated in military operations, is extended to organisations. This indicates the set of relationships as to who gives direction to whom and who reports to whom.

2. UNITY OF COMMAND

This concept focuses on "one command" to one issue and not multi-commands. In hierarchical organisation, which is pyrimidical in feature. Person in charge of a function (production, finance, etc.) receives command from the top and has to follow it implicity. The central point in unity of command is that **"no subordinate should report to more than one boss"**. Receiving two commands from two bosses for one activity will hamper the implementation of that activity. This is one of the principles propounded by Henry Fayol.

If many bosses give order to one individual, the situation leads to confusion and chaos. Because the orders may be conflicting and may contradict each other. Therefore, a subordinate should report to only one boss. Two bosses are not better than one.

3. SPAN OF CONTROL

The term 'span of management' is also referred to as span of control, span of supervision, span of authority or span of responsibility. It indicates the number of persons that a manager can manage effectively. A manager's ability to manage a large number of subordinates is limited by his time and energy. In order to enable him to give personal attention to work performance, he should have a manageable number of subordinates. If the manager is made to supervise a large number of subordinates, not only will he have mental and physical strain; but also his supervision may become ineffective. This means, he will not be able to produce satisfactory results, the concept of span of management has a significant influence on the overall performance of an enterprise and hence its importance has been recognised by modern management experts.

Importance of Span of Management

Ernest Dale, in his study of 100 large companies, has found that the median number of executives reporting to the Company President was 8 and in some cases, there were as many as 20 or more. Thus, determination of an appropriate span of management is important for two reasons. (i) The span of management affects the efficient utilisation of managers and the effective performance of their subordinates. Too wide a span may mean that managers are overstraining themselves and that their subordinates are receiving too little guidance or control. Too narrow a span of management may mean that managers are underutilised and that their subordinates are overcontrolled. (ii) There is a relationship between the span of management and organisational structure. A narrow span of management results in a tall organisation with many levels of supervision between the top management and the lowest organisational levels. This creates more communication and cost problems. There is also the problem of finding trained managerial personnel.

On the other hand, a wide span, for the same number of employees, means a tall organisation with fewer management levels between the top and bottom. This can be understood with the help of an example. Suppose a sales manager has 16 salesmen reporting directly to him. His span of management is 16. Let us assume that he feels that he is not able to work closely enough with each salesman. He decides, therefore, to reduce his span each salesman. He decides, therefore, to reduce his span by adding four assistant sales managers each to supervise four salesmen. His span of management is now 4. But as shown in Fig. 7.3, he has added a level of management through which communication between him and the salesmen must pass and at the same time, he has added the cost of four additional managers.

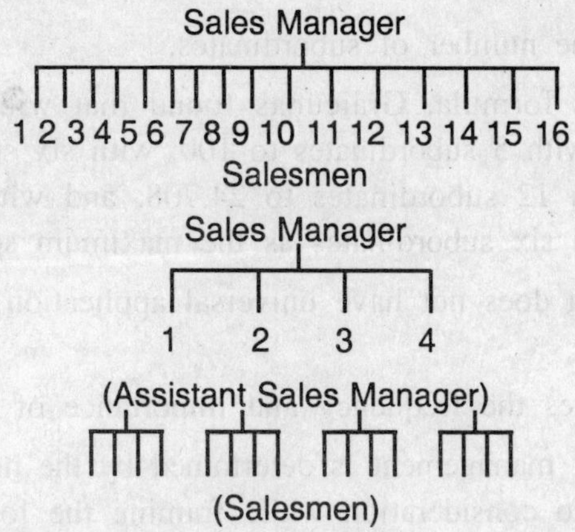

FIG. 7.3. Decreasing the span of management increases the number of levels.

V.A.Graicunas, a management consultant of Paris, has made a significant contribution to the span of management theory. His theory identifies three subordinate-superior relationships. They are:

1. Direct single relationship.
2. Direct group relationships.
3. Cross relationships.

(1) Direct Single Relationships: For example, if a supervisor supervises two persons, he can speak to them individually and this is called a single relationship. Thus, if A supervises two subordinates, B and C, there will be direct single relationships, *viz.,*A to B and A to C.

(2) Direct Group Relationships: If an executive speaks to each possible combination of subordinates under him, it is called direct group relationship. If we take the above example, A, B and C will have following direct groups:

A to B with C; and

A to C with B.

In other words, depending on the need of a situation. A might consult B, while C is in attendance or he might consult C while B is in attendance.

(3) Cross Relationships: If the subordinates consult with one another, it will result in cross relationship. In the example given above, two cross relationships can take place between B and C, *viz.,*B with C and C with B.

From the above, it is clear that when A has to supervise B and C, he has to manage not only his single relationship but also his relationship with B and C as a group keeping themselves in view. This number of direct and cross relationships keep on increasing in a geometrical progression as the number of subordinates assigned to A increases.

The Formula

The formula prescribed by Graicunas to ascertain the number of subordinate-superior relationship is given below:

$$\text{Number of relationships} = n\left(\frac{2n}{2}+n-1\right)$$

where, n stands for the number of subordinates.

With the help of this formula, Graicunas found that with 4 subordinates, the total relationships go up to 44, with 5 subordinates to 100, with six subordinates to 222, with 10 subordinates to 5,210; with 12 subordinates to 24,708; and with 20 subordinates to more than a crore. He prescribed six subordinates as the maximum span of management.

The Graicunas formula does not have universal application and has been criticised on the following grounds:

(a) The formula ignores the frequency and importance of relationships;

(b) The actual span of management is determined by the number of factors which has not been taken into consideration while framing the formula.

Factors Determining the Span

• Quality leadership • Competence of Subordinates • Repetitive work • Delection of well defined Authority • Well structured plan • Higher degree of decentralisation • Objective standards of work • Method of Communication (written communication) is better than oral communication • Geographic location • Economic consideration.

The number of managerial levels in an organisation is determined by span of management. If the span is less managerial level will be more and *vice versa*. If more levels prevail due to narrow span it is called **"Tall organisation".** If the span is wide, the structure is called **"Flat".** To avoid problems of planning, control, communication of skilled workers and to reduce cost of operation, flat organisation are becoming popular. Finally, empirical studies reveal that one manager can manage six members effectively.

Problems of Narrow Span (Tall Organisation)

— Over supervision
— Long times of communication
— Slow, multi level decision-making
— Limited initiative due to minimal delegation of authority
— Restricted development of managers as they have to spend on over-supervision.
— Expensive operation

Problems of Wide Span (Flat Organisation)

— Efficiency erodes
— Inflate costs due to lack of training for workers
— Behavioural problem with less trained and less supervised workers
— Lack of co-ordination

Problems of Different Structures

Different Concepts of Reasonable Span

Different management experts have suggested different number of subordinates for effective supervision by the managers. For example, L. Urwick found that the ideal number of subordinates is four at the higher level and from eight to twelve at the operating level. According to Hamilton, the ideal number of subordinates for all superiors appear to be four. Some writers from the traditional school of management are of the opinion that the best number of subordinates for a manager can be between three and seven. Another management expert, J.C. Worthy, optimistically believes that the manager can effectively manage as many as twenty subordinates. Thus, the management experts are not unanimous on the question of span of control. However, many experts feel that a manager can effectively supervise up to six subordinates.

4. DELEGATION AND EMPOWERMENT

(i) Delegation

This is a concept concerned with the division of labour and organisational effectiveness. When the organisational grows, irrespective of size, the activities cannot be managed by one boss. Particularly in medium and large-sized business houses many levels of management prevail. The leaders or managers of these levels should bave authority responsibility and accountability to carry out the tasks assigned to them. "Delegation" refers to this.

Delegation is a process of giving power or assigning task to some one or to the immediate lower authority so that persons who receive the authority are responsible for part of what they normally do.

When the authority is delegated to any person to do certain tasks, that person has to strictly follow the set of rules or protocol to perform the tasks. Those persons cannot take any independent decision, except that such decisions are well within the approved and delegated framework of authority. Personal innovations which deviate from the set rules, cannot be implemented without the approval of higher ups.

Delegation comprises of the following aspects.

- Assignment of rights and duties to the right people.
- Give authority to perform the tasks.
- Time should be set to complete the task.
- Critical tasks should be discussed and should not be delegated to do in a routine way.

The process. Before delegation of a task, the person who performs the task has to be properly informed as to what they have to do. Show them as to what they have to do. Make them to perform the tasks to be assigned and observe as to what they do. If they are going in the right direction appreciate their performance. Make them to be competent enough to perform and till such time train continuously. Then transfer the responsibility and monitor their work continuously.

Thus, delegation needs, well defined expectations, proper communication, training the performer, monitoring, feedback and mutual trust.

Supposing, you work as a superviser in finance department of an organisation. Assessing your capabilities, the management elevates you to the position of manager to manage one sub-function of finance department. You will be trained as a manager before you assume charge as manager you are given the authority to perform as manager. Certain rights are also given. You are accountable for all your decisions. When you function as manager, you have to work within the frame work of delegated rules and regulations and achieve the targets given to you. This is the process of delegation.

(ii) Empowerment

Today, revolution is taking place regarding organisational effectiveness. Organisations are realising that tighter controls, greater pressures more clearly defined jobs and tighter supervisions as found in delegation may not work fully to achieve goals. Attention is shifting to the need for employees to take personal responsibilities for the success of business and hence the empowerment.

Empowerment may be defined as "according official authority or legal power to a person to perform a task independently with strength and confidence on his/her own intivitive". Empowerment instills a sense of power in performer as he/she gets decision-making authority. It creates opportunities to those who have competencies to take independent decisions. This is more concerned with giving someone more control over their own life or situation. Empowerment makes employees full partners in decision-making process and gives them the necessary tools and rewards.

Employment requires shared values, analysing identical or typical situation, identifying commonsense solutions and defining common sense as value. Empowering is a **"Mentor-Mentee"** process. As a mentor, leader assigns task to competent worker to work independently and monitor the progress. However, certain critical activities cannot be empowered and can only be delegated. Empowerment allows the performer to assume leadership position but he works under the mentor. Through Empowerment, individual's potential is converted into productivity. Empowerment is a building block of progressive management. In this process, "Power" is an unlimited resource which authoritarian managers do not give.

A leader who empowers his people not building a great work, but builds great is people. When people are empowered, they will be able to take ownership of the task that they have to perform. The leader need not be present during the course of performing the task as in case of delegation.

Decision to empower the employee depends upon the nature of the task to be assigned. If the competent people are not available, the task has to be delegated.

Empowerment realises and reconceptualises the relationship among tasks, achievements and connectedness. It can serve to re-energise recollective spirit and focuses on out performing our competitors while looking for better to live together. Empowernment has become a building block of progressive management. In this process "power" is identified as an unlimited resource. "The more power you give, the more power you have" has become the dictum. Authoritarian managers do not like to give more power to their employees. Because of this, empowerment has become slow. But empowered employees who get power in a previously powerless situation have the feeling of control and self-efficacy.

As empowerment is emerging as the order of the day, managements should provide more tools and techniques to their employees to make them empowered.

Benefits:

- Employees can develop confidence, courage, conviction and commitment.
- Dishonesty, unworthiness, selfishness are minimised.
- Individual skills are developed, which can be utilised for to achieve organisational goals and objectives.
- Helps employees to develop organisational identity.

The process. Empowerment is a job enrichment process. Therefore the process of empowering includes the following:

– Give more autonomy, *i.e.,* freedom over their activities.

– Allow them to decide work methods.

– Employees themselves have to check quality of the work and formulate work designs.

– They have to be allowed to take decisions on various problems so that they are solved without much difficulty.

– Assign only high significance tasks to them who are capable of performing themselves and allow a small degree of flexibility.

– Provide necessary information to perform tasks and to develop their own control techniques suitable to the task.

Thus, "Delegation" and "Empowerment" are two different concepts related to the discharging of tasks while delegation focuses on control of employees in performing the task within the frame-work of rules and regulations empowerment allows the employees to perform the task independently by adopting their own tools and techniques which may be innovative and provides an opportunity to them to bring out their hidden talents.

Delegation requires	**Empowerment requires**
• Defined expectations • Communication • Coaching • Monitoring • Feedback • Trust	• Shared values • Shared power • Defined boundaries • Communication • Recognition • Feedback • Trust
Principles	**Principles**
• Assign duties to the right people • Grant authority to do the job • Make due date specific • Do not delegate critical things • Tell subordinates as to what to do and show them how to do • Let them try-observe • Praise their progress • Repeat untill they get compitancy • Transfer the responsibility and monitor	• Share the values • Brainstorm typical situation • Identify your commonsense solutions • Define common sense as values

5. DECENTRALISATION

As organisations grow, many problems crop up regarding administration. Authority cannot be centralised when the organisation is expanding authority should disperse to the lower levels for smooth functioning of the organisational activities. Decision-making becomes easy at all levels, if authority flows downwards. The process of dispersing the authority to the lower levels of administration is called "Decentralisation".

"Decentralisation" means the transfer of authority and responsibility for smooth functioning of organisational activities. It may be applied to any type of organisation including the government. It is a complex multifaceted concept. Different types of decentralisation should be distinguished. Because each type has its own features, policy implications and conditions for success. The types, include, political, administrative, fiscal and organisational. Our analyses is made in the context of organisations.

In decentralisation, decision-making process is dispersed or deregularised. But it is a matter of degree. In an organisational structure, if the managerial levels are more, decentralisation of authority will also be more. If the levels or subunits are more autonomous, then the decentralisation will be most effective. In such situations, cost-benefit analysis can be independently made.

Cost is governed by: (i) manager's perceptions to look at their division and relegating back the overall objectives of the organisation, (ii) costly duplication of services and (iii) increase in cost to obtain information required by the submits.

Benefits derived are as follows:

(i) People working at different levels will have the knowledge of their working environment and it facilitates decision-making easier.

(ii) Greater managerial input in decision-making leads to desirable motivational effect. This means that it encourages motivation and creativity by allowing many minds to work simultaneously on the same problem.

(iii) Provides greater control to manager on results.

It is said that organisations in future will be highly decentralised to provide more opportunities to participating people to make decision on issues that matter to them. Experience in organisations which have decentralised their activities reveals that productivity of people and organisations increase and quality of life will be better. Particularly in professional organisations such as Accounting, Law, Engineering, Medicine, Performing Arts, Information technology, etc., where creativity and innovation are essential, decentralisation of authority pays to the maximum. Because, these are knowledge-based activities and require many intellectual brains to take sound decisions. Decentralisation is not only a pure objective one, but also a matter of strategic choice.

Strategic choice, whether the organisation should have centralised control or decentralisation depends, upon the nature of business and mental make-up of the top brass. Some organisations systemise their structure and have central control of decision-making. Only very insignificant decisions are taken at the lower level. But majority of the organisations decentralise their authority to encourage line managers and workers by providing autonomy in decision-making.

When decentralisation considers cost factors, many organisations, although they have strong desire for decentralisation will have to be satisfied with rigid hierarchies. Fragmentation of activities may provide greater benefits. But organisations may be incapable of doing it, because of the cost factor. Resource crunch will disturb decentralisation. Particularly in recession period of the enterprise or of economy, consolidation process takes place to minimise decision-making centres and will have flat structure. Always, decentralisation takes place considering the economies of scale in operations. Ability to resolve conflicts may be at a medium level.

Staff Utilisation

The use of staff knowledge in decision-making process will be high in decentralisation. Decentralisation provides a democratic structure, wherein knowledge people involved will be simultaneously used for decision-making. In this structure, innovative practices can be developed. Autonomy to managers and workers provide opportunity for them to exhibit their talent for the good of the organisation. It minimise conflicts.

Thus, decentralisation or centralisation depends upon several factors. Important ones are: (i) cost, (ii) availability of more knowledge workers, (iii) the nature and size of business, (iv) business environment, (v) mindset of top management, (vi) opportunity to expand business, (vii) consumer behaviour, (viii) market structure, (ix) government policies, etc.

Decentralisation can take place: (i) by creating subsidiary units which will be independent in nature or (ii) by developing tall structure within the organisation with more hierarchical levels, each having autonomy to work with a control control to convert then organisation into rigid hierarchical structure.

6. ORGANISATIONAL DESIGN AND CONFIGURATION

We have discussed so far the various types of organisation structures and their benefits and limitations. But to design various types of structures, certain influencing factors have to be considered. It is really challenging to design an effective and workable organisation structure. The designer has to bear in mind the attributes such as: (i) cultural alignment, (ii) transparancy and (iii) communication to have well laid structure. Besides these three basic attributes, (i) talent retention and (ii) well-defined goals of the organisation and vision have to be considered in designing. Challenges and constraints are also identified in drafting the structure. These aspects are widely discussed with stakeholders to understand the intensity of each attribute across the proposed set-up. This will facilitate the designer to come up with best structure.

The Process

The designer will have to undergo the following phases of designing on organisation structure:

(i) To start with, the designer has to understand the organisational objectives and the environment in which it exists. Besides studying deeply the concerned decuments (Memorandum, Articles, Partnership Deeds, etc.), he has to have consultations with all concerned to come out with a draft design.

(ii) Vital aspects of business activities such as business processes, interface between the company and ouside stakeholders like vendors, volume of business activities and the quantum of resources that the organisation has at its command are to be fully understood by the designer.

(iii) Preparing two to three alternative models adopting required processes and interfaces, roles and relationships for offshore activities and for internal operations.

(iv) Have brainstorming sessions with all concerned to discuss these draft structures and note down all relevant opinions that are not found in the alternative drafts.

(v) Prepare the final draft structure exhibiting key challenges to be faced, opportunities to be explored and benchmarking the structure with industry best practices.

(vi) Discuss with the top management regarding the defined roles and responsibilities shown in the final structure, make necessary corrections in the final draft and finally prepare the structure to be adopted. Make provision for flexible operations.

Main Challenges in Designing

While designing the organisation structure, designer should consider certain following challenges that organisation may face.

(i) Infrastructure, (ii) Attrition, (iii) Lack of clear vision and goals, (iv) Lack of proper communication, (v) Lack of certain budgets.

These challenges have to be addressed in the structure to be designed. This facilitates the organisation to tackle all these challenges.

The concept of "Global Meltdown" has assumed serious dimension in all business activities. While designing the structure, this issue also has to be addressed by establishing environment department. This department has to work on the the following issues.

- Cost-benefit of analysis of various green initiatives
- Extensive qualitative and quantitative research around green workforce, infrastructure and data centre initiatives.
- Multiple scenario comparisions to help view results and make business decision.
- Developing flexible and intelligent green initiative programmes combining industry research results with successfully run programmes.

The whole programme should focus on reducing carbon emissions and fuel consumption. The structure should have practices to be followed which are organisation specific and flexible to change as and when required.

7. DESIGNING OTHER ASPECTS

Although fundamental and traditional structures act as base for exhibiting roles, responsibilities and authority relationships to develop an organisation structure today very many softwares have emerged to design a customised structure. Varieties of templates showing different structures have been designed. Any structure shown in the templates can be adopted suiting to the be adopted suiting to the organisational needs. One such template is shown here to understand the possible structures that can be drawn.

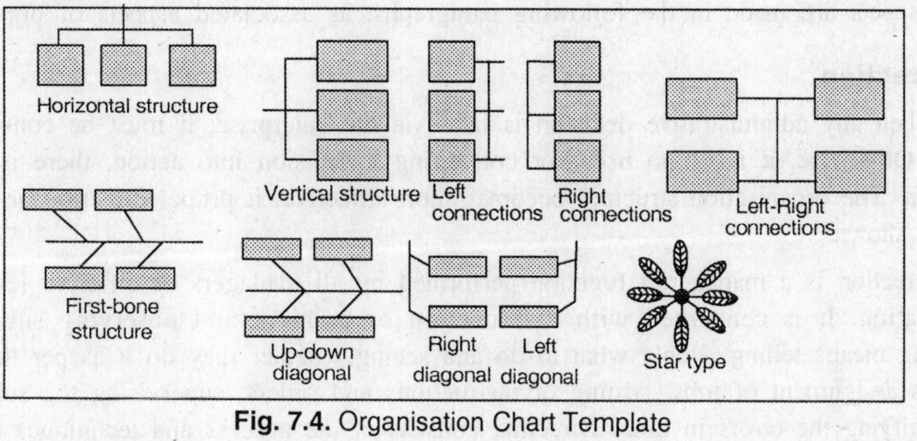

Fig. 7.4. Organisation Chart Template

Any structure shown in the above template can be picked up suiting to the organisational needs.

Configuration

The term "configuration" is normally used in computer operations showing the programmes incorporated in it. The programme includes the capacity, volume of things that can be stored etc. This concept is also extended to designing an organisational structure keeping any one of the types of structure shown in the template. Customised structures are designed. Thus, preparing a chart altering the basic structure as per the need may be called "configuration" of organisation structure.

The basic structures, *viz.,* line staff and matrix can be configured according to the purpose, goals and objectives of the organisation. Any number of configured charts can be prepared for any activity of an enterprise. The examples of configured charts are: (i) Business organisation chart, (ii) Photo organisation charts fixing photos of every individual working at different levels of organisational hierarchy, (iii) company organisation chart, (iv) city organisation chart showing different parts of a city with different hierarchical structure in each branch, (v) city organisation chart showing different branches of an enterprise functioning in different parts of a city with different hierarchical structure in each branch, (vi) Marketing organisation chart showing different sub-functions of marketing plan of a firm, (vii) Human Resources Development Chart, (viii) Financial operations chart, (ix) Team organisational chart, (x) Organisation charts for different activities with hierarchy like, police, school, Hospital, Hotel, IT company, consumer marts, etc.

These are customized charts and are configured as per the needs of the organisation. While designing the structure, certain other issues are considered. These aspects are operational ones and have greater impact one organisational flow and cost of operations. They have to be considered for organisational effectiveness. Aspects are:

(i) Direction and (ii) Departmentation. Besides, these aspects, tools such as organisation manuals and committees act as a part of desingning. The designer has to fix up the flow of direction, the size of departments, the type and quantum of information to be incorporated in the manual and at what level the committees are required and their size. Brief analysis of these aspects are made in the following paragraphs, as associated aspects of organising.

(A) Direction

When any administrative decision is taken in the enterprise, it must be converted into action. Otherwise, it is of no use. For converting a decision into action, there is need for direction. The organisation structure becomes more effective, it proper direction or command flow is shown.

Direction is a managerial function performed by all managers of different levels of an organisation. It is concerned with the function of building and observing subordinates. Directing means telling people what to do and seeing whether they do it as per the plan. It includes assignment of jobs, issuing of instructions and orders, supervising the subordinates and rectifying the errors in time. Directing consists of the process and techniques utilised in issuing instructions and making certain that operations are carried on as originally planned." According to Koontz and O'Donnell, "direction is the interpersonal aspect of managing by which subordinates are led to understand and contribute effectively to the attainment of enterprise objectives. Directing is the guidance, the inspiration, the leadership of those men and women that constitute the real core of the responsibilities of management."

From the above definitions, we observe see that directing has the following components.

(a) issuing of instructions and orders to the subordinates for getting the work done;

(b) guiding subordinates in the proper methods of work;
Without the issuance of directives and without guiding subordinates, nothing or at best very little, would be accomplished;

(c) supervising subordinates to ensure that their performance conforms to the plans and contributes effectively to the attainment of enterprise objectives.

Success of management is largely a matter of effective direction. Direction deals exclusively with people. It is concerned with directing the human effort towards enterprise objectives. This means, the manager in order to be successful in direction, should also be well-versed in other functions like communication, supervision and motivation which also deal exclusively with the people. Further, the manager should have qualities of leadership. Thus, the scope of direction is very wide and it embraces, supervision, motivation, communication and leadership.

Features and Importance

Direction has the following features:

(1) Direction is one of the important functions of management and it is also considered as the essence of management.

(2) It is concerned with the direction of human efforts towards enterprise objectives. Hence, direction deals exclusively with people.

(3) It helps in achieving co-ordination among the various operations of the enterprise. Co-ordination is a necessary by-product of good directing.

(4) The purpose of planning, organising and staffing is achieved only after the performance of directing function.

(5) It exists at every level, location and operation throughout the enterprise. It must be performed by every manager at different levels of the enterprise. Hence, direction is a pervasive function of management.

(6) Direction is a continuing activity. A manager never ceases to direct his subordinates and he must continuously supervise the execution of his orders or instructions by the subordinates.

(7) Direction stimulates the organisation and its staff to execute the plans for achieving the desired actions and results. Hence, it is called management-in-action. Earnest Dale has stated that direction constitutes the life spark of the enterprise which like electric power sets it into motion.

(8) It motivates, commands, communicates, supervises the staff and controls the organisation.

(9) It also provides the necessary leadership to the business.

(10) It facilitates in securing co-operation of the employees for attaining the objective of the organisation.

Principles of Direction

Following principles are to be followed in directing the employees.

Harmony of objective – Integrating organisational objectives and employee perceptions.

Maximum individual contribution – Inspire the employees to contribute their maximum by the organisation.

Unity of command – Only one direction to employee.

Direct supervision – Personal touch with employees ensure successful direction.

Flow of information – Distorted information should not be disseminated.

Appropriate of direction – Proper directive technique has to adopted.

Comprehension – How much directive is understood by employees has to be known through feedback.

Effective leadership – Person who gives direction should be a good leaders and motivate the employees to work.

Monitoring – Besides giving direction to workers, they should be closely observed whether they are working in the desired way.

Orders or Instructions

An order is a fundamental tool used by the management for directing its subordinates. It may be stated that the terms 'order', 'instruction', 'directive' and 'command' are used interchangeably in management literature. An order can be issued by a superior only and he has the right to enforce the order to be followed by his subordinates. According to Koontz and O'Donnell, "As a directional technique, an instruction is understood to be a charge by a superior requiring a subordinate to act or refrain from acting in a given circumstance". Order may be in oral or written form.

Characteristics of a Good Order

The characteristics of a good order are as follows:

(a) an order should be reasonable and enforceable;

(b) it should be clear and easily understandable;

(c) is should be compatible with the purpose and objectives of the enterprise;

(d) it should be complete;

(e) it should stimulate willing, enthusiastic acceptance by the subordinates;

(f) preferably, the order should be in writing;

(g) the tone of the order should be appropriate; and

(h) it should specify the time within which the order should be carried out and completed.

Forms of Direction

The techniques of direction that are used by the managers are as follows:

(a) ***Consultative direction:*** Under this method, the executive takes a decision and issues a direction only after consulting his subordinates regarding the feasibility and workability of the problem. One advantage of this method is that as the subordinate also has been consulted about the feasibility and workability of the problem, his best co-operation and enthusiasm can be secured in carrying out the direction.

(b) ***Free-rein direction:*** Under this method, the subordinate is encouraged and enabled to show his own initiative and give independent thought to the solution of the problem. The manager assigns the task in general terms and not in a specific way. The subordinates must take the initiative and find a solution to the task assigned and carry it out.

(c) ***Autocratic direction:*** Under this method, the subordinates are not allowed to take any initiative in solving the problem. The executive himself solves the problem and gives orders to his subordinates with instructions as to how and what is to be done by them.

(B) Departmentation

One of the aspects that designer of structure has to consider is department in the grouping of similar activities of a business concern into small units for the purpose of facilitating administration is called departmentation. According to Koontz and O'Donnell, "Departmentation is a process of dividing the large monolithic functional organisation into small and flexible administrative units". Thus, departmentation may be defined as the process of grouping of activities into units and sub-units for purposes of administration. The administrative units and sub-units so created may be designated as divisions, units, branches, sections, or jobs.

The process of departmentation takes place at all levels in the organisation. The chief executive groups activities into major divisions such as production, marketing, personnel, etc. These divisions are administered by senior executives who report directly to the chief executive. The senior executives also may further divide these activities. For instance, the senior executive in charge of marketing may further divide his activities in relation to market research, customer service and so on.

Importance

Departmentation contributes to the success of an organisation in number of ways. The importance is understood by knowing the following aspects:

(a) As departmentation involves the grouping of activities and employees into various departments, it increases the operating skill and efficiency of organisation.

(b) Departmentation involves division of functions and fixation of responsibilities to different executives. The fixation of responsibilities makes the executives alert and efficient.

(c) The managers in charge of different departments are given certain powers and are allowed to take their own decisions within the powers given to them. This increases their prestige and skill.

(d) The activities of various departments can be evaluated by the management and pinpoint the departments which are not managed properly. This makes the departmental manager efficient.

(e) As departmentation involves division of functions and responsibilities among different executives, there is scope for expanding the organisation to an indefinite degree.

(f) Departmentation also provides some other advantages such as facilitating budget preparation, effective control of expenditure, attaining specialisation, better co-ordination among the managerial personnel, etc.

Types

There are certain basic methods of dividing responsibilities within an organisation structure. They are (a) by functions, (b) by product or service, (c) by regions, (d) by customers, (e) by process, (f) by time, (g) by numbers, and (h) by marketing channel.

(a) Functional Basis

This is a very popular method of departmentation. This method of departmentation refers to grouping of activities of the enterprise into major functional departments like production, sales, purchases, accounts, personnel, etc. (see Fig. 7.5).

Each department is headed by an executive who is directly responsible to the top executive. According to George R.Terry, "the functions or activities are the pivot around which effective executives develop effective and efficient organisation". Observe the following chart:

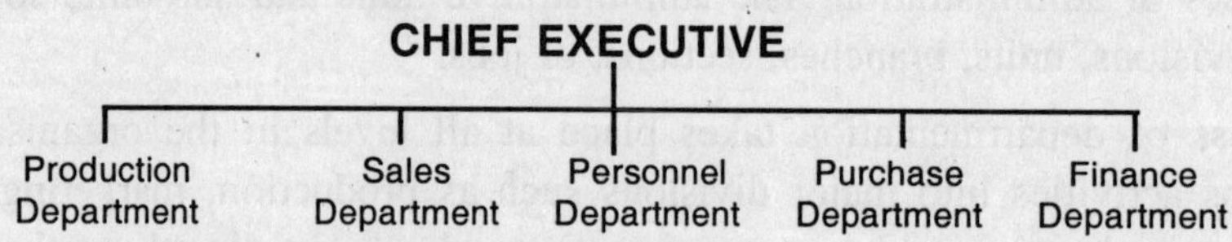

FIG. 7.5. Functional Organisation Plan of a Company

(b) Departmentation by Product or Services

This type suits to organisation which manufacture multi-products. Under this, for each major product manufactured, a separate department is created and each department is put in charge of a manager. For example, an electric company may have different departments dealing with light bulbs, fluorescent tubes, household electric appliances, etc. Each product department may be responsible for production and sales as also finance, personnel, accounting, public relations, etc. The departmentation by product is also known as multifunctional product departmentation because each department handles all the functions concerning it. Fig. 7.6 is a typical organisation chart of product departmentation:

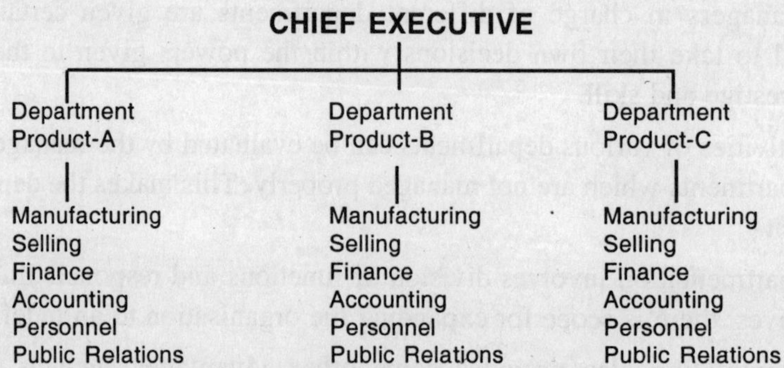

FIG. 7.6. Product Departmentation

Combined Type: Some business concerns, in order to secure advantages of both the functional and product departmentation, have adopted a composite pattern of departmentation, *i.e.,* a combination of functional and product departmentation. Under this method, some functions such as finance, personnel, public relations relating to all departments may be placed in separate departments and the remaining functions may be performed under the respective product departments. The chart of combined type departmentation is given below:

By adopting the combined type of departmentation, the business concern can enjoy the advantages of both functional and product departmentation. However, there is the need for making a clear distinction between line and functional authority. For instance, we find from the observe the fig. 7.6 that the managers concerned with finance, personnel and public relations will report to

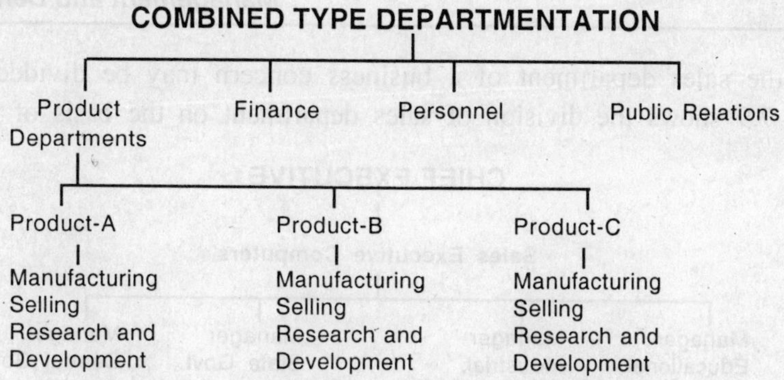

Fig. 7.7. Combined Type of Departmentation

public relations will report to the Chief Executive directly. They have only functional authority but no line authority. The executive resembles matrix types.

(c) Departmentation by Regions or Territories

Departmentation by regions may also be called departmentation by territories or areas. This method may be suitable for enterprises whose activities are widely dispersed. Activities may be grouped area-wise and assigned to the executives in charge of the respective areas. For instance, sales activities of an enterprise can be organised area-wise. This is because adaptation to local situations and customer needs, peculiar to a given area, is easier under this type of departmentation. The sales manager can appoint local people as salesmen. These salesmen will be naturally familiar with the local language and the preference of the consumers. Further, there will be no communication barrier. Fig. 7.8 shows departmentation by territory.

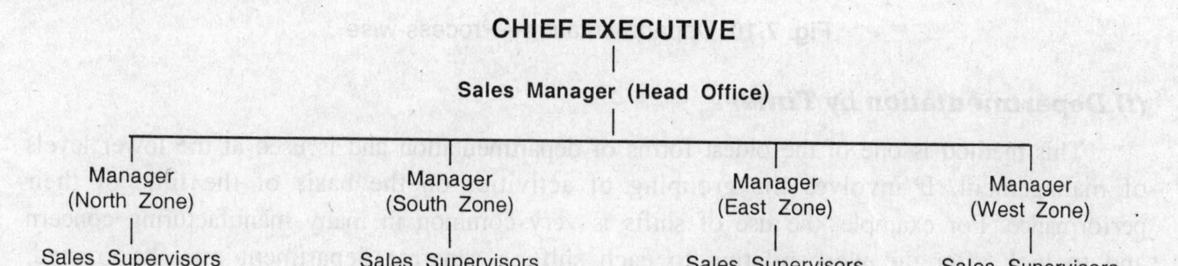

Fig. 7.8. Departmentation by Regions or Territories

(d) Departmentation by Customers

An enterprise may be divided into a number of departments on the basis of the customers that it serves. For example, a commercial bank may divide its loan section into a number of departments, each specialising in loans to traders, industrialists, professionals, agriculturists, etc. Similarly, the sales department of a business concern may be divided on the basis of customers. Fig. 7.9 shows the division of sales department on the basis of customers.

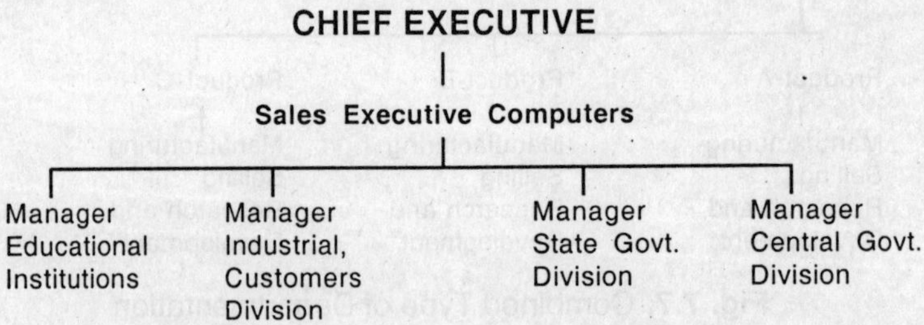

Fig. 7.9. Departmentation by Customers

(e) Process-wise Departmentation

In this method of departmentation, the enterprise is organised on the basis of processes involved in the manufacture of the product. For example, a concern engaged in the production of oil may have separate departments for crushing, refining and finishing. Similarly, a cotton textile mill may have separate departments for ginning, spinning, weaving, dyeing and printing and packing and sales. Fig. 7.10 showing the division of a cotton mill on the basis of processes is given below:

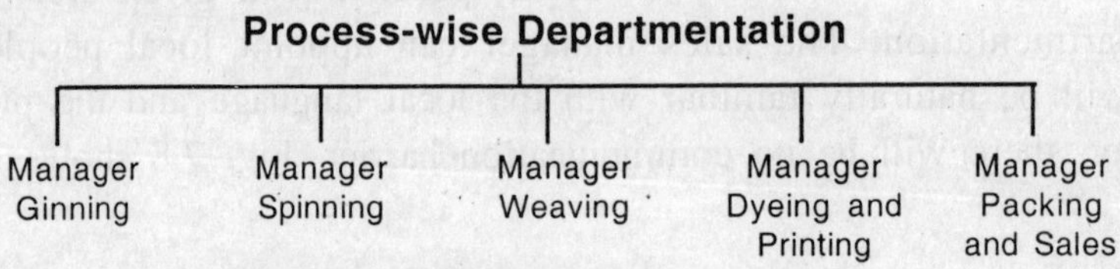

Fig. 7.10. Departmentation—Process-wise

(f) Departmentation by Time

This method is one of the oldest forms of departmentation and is used at the lower levels of management. It involves the grouping of activities on the basis of the time of their performance. For example, the use of shifts is very common in many manufacturing concern and to look after the work relating to each shift, a separate department may be created. Generally, this type of the departmentation is found in the production function of the enterprise.

This basis of departmentation can be advantageously applied by firms which cannot cope with the volume of work within the normal working hours. But the disadvantage of this system is that there is the problem of co-ordination among the workers of different shifts.

(g) Departmentation by Numbers

In the case of departmentation by numbers, the persons who are to perform the same duties are divided into small groups and then each group is placed under the control of a supervisor or officer. For example, in the army, troops are grouped into squads, battalions, brigades and regiments on the basis of the number of men prescribed for each unit. In the industrial world, this method of departmentation is not used.

(h) Departmentation by Marketing Channels

Under this system, departmentation takes place on the basis of channels of marketing used by the enterprise. It is one of the new forms of departmentation. This form is similar to the customer-wise departmentation but its basis is the marketing channels. This method of departmentation has grown in importance as businesses have become increasingly market-oriented.

Thus, we see, there are a large number of alternative methods of departmentation. All the methods possess certain merits and demerits. For selecting any method, the management must consider factors such as the nature of the enterprise, the nature of product technology employed, the people involved etc., and must balance the advantages of having one method of departmentation as against the disadvantages of another. According to Koontz and O'Donnell, "the process of selection involves a consideration of the relative advantages of each type at each level in the organisation structure. In all cases, the central question concerns the type of environment that the manager wishes to design and the situation being faced".

FUNDAMENTALS OF DEPARTMENTATION

The important considerations which should be kept in mind by the management at the time of drafting departmentalised organisation plans are as follows:

1. Specialisation: The method of departmentation used should be such as to yield the benefit of specialisation. The benefit of specialisation can be secured if the total effort required to be undertaken by the enterprise is divided into functions and sub-functions.

2. Coordination: Under departmentation, the work is being carried on in a number of departments. There must be a proper mechanism for coordinating the activities of different departments so as to enable the enterprise to achieve its objectives successfully.

3. Control: The purpose of departmentation is to enable the enterprise to function efficiently and economically and hence, departmentation should provide for effective control of activities performed in different departments.

4. Economy: The expenditure involved in introducing departmentalised organisation is also another point to be considered. Whatever the type of departmentation used, it should not result in an excessive financial burden to the enterprise.

5. Groundwork: Before the management decides on any scheme of departmentation, it should make certain preparations and prepare the ground, for instance, for decentralisation of authority, for enforcing adequate controls, for providing facilities for management development, for introducing effective communication network, etc.

ORGANISATIONAL MANUALS

It is a small book containing information such as the details of various positions, their authority and responsibilities, job description, salaries, relationship, activities, duties and functions of each position and organisation procedure and methods. Organisational manual is an authentic guide to the company's overall organisation and its sub-parts.

COMMITTEES IN ORGANISATION

In modern business houses, there is a widespread use of committees for performing certain administrative tasks. According to Hicks, "A committee is a group of people who meet by plan to discuss or make a decision for a particular subject." Thus, a committee consists of a group of persons specifically designed to perform some administrative acts. Committees are widely used in the modern concerns for the purpose of discharging advisory functions of management relating to personnel, finance, industrial relations, production, etc. A committee's duties, responsibilities and authority are well-defined and are accountable to the authority that appoints it.

Kinds of Committees

Committees are of two types, *viz.,* (i) Advisory committe and (ii) Executive committe. Advisory committee is vested with staff authority and its functions are to advise and recommend but has no power to enforce its advice or recommendations. Some examples of an advisory committee are sales committee, finance committee etc. Those committees are not constituted on a permanent basis and they may be dissolved at any time.

In the case of executive committees, they are vested with line authority. These committees take decisions but also have the power to enforce their decisions. The Board of Directors of a company is an example of an executive committee. Executive committees are more or less of a permanent nature and are not likely to be dissolved.

Advantages of Committees

1. A committee may consist of all the departmental heads as members. In the committee meetings, the members are enabled to understand the various problems faced by the other departments in the organisation and this promotes better understanding among the departmental heads.

2. In committee meetings, decisions are taken after taking into consideration the different views of its members and thus the committee provides a forum for the pooling of knowledge and experience of many persons.

3. The committee encourages team spirit and co-operation of various departments in the execution of the plans.

4. The committee's work develops awareness of the problem of other departments among the members and this promotes co-ordination of the various activities of an enterprise.

5. In committee meetings, members discuss the various organisational problems and hence it can be said that the committee is an excellent means of transmitting information and ideas to the interested organisational members.

7. Members of the committee take part in the decision-making process and because of this, they will not resist the implementation of the decisions.

Disadvantages of Committees

1. Members with different background and ideals may express different views on the same subject and this may cause delay in taking a decision.

2. Committee is an expensive form of organisation because of the huge amount to be spent for convening committee meetings.

3. In case there is no mutual confidence among the members, not only will they fail to appreciate each other's views but also misrepresent each other's statements.

4. Because of the large number of members in a committee, it is difficult to maintain secrecy regarding the committee's decisions.

5. No member can be individually held responsible in case the committee takes incorrect decisions. Because of this, members may not actively participate in the deliberations of the meeting.

6. Decision may be arrived at on the basis of compromise among the members or the decisions may reflect accommodation of various viewpoints of the members and because of this, the quality of decision is watered down and not the best from anyone's viewpoint.

Suggestions for Making Committees Effective

Even though a committee may suffer from certain disadvantages, an enterprise, by a careful concern for the weaknesses of the committee, can use it effectively for accomplishing its objectives. Herbert has rightly said that "the problems with committees are not so much as how to eliminate them as it is how to use them properly." For effective functioning of committees, certain conditions need to be adhered to. They are:

1. The functions and authority of the committee should be clearly stated.
2. The committee members should be selected carefully and they should be in a position to take part in the meetings actively.
3. To avoid lengthy discussion and delay in decisions, the number of members on a committee should not be large.
4. Frank discussion must be encouraged in committee meeting and every member must have the freedom to express his views without any fear.
5. Committees must be worth the cost. The benefits that are secured from the functioning of the committee should be more than the cost involved.
6. There should be team spirit among the members and they should co-operate with the chairman of the committee in conducting the meetings properly.
7. The committee meetings should be organised and regulated in such a way that all the departments must get equal importance.

SUMMARY

1. Flow of authority from top to bottom in an organisation is called chain of command. These commands or orders or directions have to be obeyed by the subordinates. As the authority flows from one level to another covering many levels, each level becomes a link and all links put together is called chain.
2. Unity of command is a management principle which says that an employee should answer only to one boss. Two or more bosses means the destruction of productivity of the individual.

3. The term 'span of management' indicates the number of persons that a manager can manage effectively. Different management experts have suggested a different number of subordinates for effective supervision by the managers. However, many experts feel that a manager can effectively supervise up to six subordinates.
4. Graicunas has stated a formula to ascertain the number of subordinate-superior relationships and he has prescribed six subordinates as the maximum span of management. However, the Graicunas formula does not have universal application and has been criticised by some writers.
5. Span of management depends on factors such as quality of leadership, competence of subordinates, nature of work, delegation of authority, clarity of plans, degree of decentralisation, methods of communication used in the concern and geographic location of employees and economic considerations.
6. The process of dividing authority and responsibility among the various executives is called creation of levels of management. The number of levels of management prescribed for a particular organisation depends on such factors as nature of organisation, size of enterprise, span of management, etc. If the span is narrow, there will be a large number of levels and if the span is wide, there will be a less number of levels.
7. Delegation is a process of giving power or assigning task to someone or to the immediate lower authority so that persons who receive the authority are responsible for part of what they normally do.
8. Assigning a task to an employee to complete the task independently with strength and confidence on his own intuitive is called "Empowerment".
9. Decentralisation refers to the transfer authority to the new level created to have organisational effectiveness. This normally happens when span of control is unmanagable or when business is expanded.
10. Developing a workable organisational framework showing authority relationships is called designing the structure. While designing the structure, designer should bear in mind the aspects such as cultural alignment, transparancy, free flow of communication well-defined goals of the organisation and vision. Other challenges and constraints are to be identified.
11. Organisational configuration refers to the configuring the organisation structure according to the needs of the individual firm. Selecting the suitable structure (Line, staff of matrix) and altering it into customer's needs is called organisational configuration.
12. The grouping of similar activities of a business concern into small units for the purpose of facilitating administration is called departmentation. Departmentation contributes to the success of an enterprise in a number of ways such as increase in the operating skill and efficiency of organisation, making the executives alert, increase in the prestige, skill and efficiency of managers, facilitating budgetary preparation, effective control of expenditure, attaining specialisation, better coordination, etc.
13. Departmentation can take place on the basis of functions, products or service, regions, customers, process, time, numbers and marketing channel.
14. All methods of departmentation have certain merits and demerits. For selecting of any method, the management must consider the factors such as the nature of enterprise, the nature of product, technology employed, the people involved, etc. and must balance the advantages of having one method of departmentation as against the disadvantages of another.

15. Important considerations which should be kept in mind while drafting departmentalised organisation plans are specialisation, co-ordination, control, economy and adequate groundwork.
16. Direction is a vital managerial function and also is the essence of management. Directing consists of the process and techniques utilised in issuing instructions and making certain that operations are carried on as planned.
17. Nature and characteristics of direction. It is the essence of management, helps in achieving coordination, exists at every level, a continuous activity, stimulates organisation and its staff, motivates, commands, communicates, supervises the staff and controls the organisation. It provides leadership and secures co-operation of the employees.
18. Principles to be observed by management in the direction of its subordinates are: harmony of objectives, maximum individual contribution, unity of direction, direct supervision, flow of information, appropriateness of direction technique, efficiency of direction, comprehension, leadership, motivation and follow through.
19. An order is a tool used by the management for directing its subordinates. It may be oral or written. It is issued by a superior only and he has the right to enforce the order to be followed by his subordinates. An order should be in writing, should be reasonable, understandable, appropriate, clear, complete and enforceable.
20. Techniques of direction adopted are: consultative direction, free-rein direction and autocratic direction.
21. A committee consists of a group of persons specifically designed to perform some administrative acts. It can be an advisory committee or an executive committee. In order to make committees effective, there is need to state its functions clearly, members must be carefully selected and there should be team spirit among the members.

STUDY QUESTIONS

1. Give the meaning of the following:
(i) Chain of command, (ii) Unity of comand, (iii) Span of control, (iv) Delegation of authority, (v) Employee empowerment, (vi) Decentralisation, (vii) Organisational design, (viii) Organisational configuration, (ix) Manual, (x) Direction, (xi) Departmentation, (xii) Committees.

2. Distinguish between Chain of Command and Unity of Command. Analyse the problems that are confronted when unity of command is not followed.

3. Examine in detail the pros and cons of delegation of authority.

4. "Decentralisation is a positive solution for attaining organisational effectiveness." Examine this statement considering all aspects of decentralisation.

5. Explain the factors that have to be considered in designing our organisation structure.

6. Explain briefly the various factors that determine the span of management.

7. Give an analytical note on "Graicunas' Theory on span of management.

8. Distinguish between wide span and narrow span structures.

9. Briefly explain the different types of direction.

10. Explain the principles and characteristic features of direction.

11. Explain the importance of direction in an organisation.

12. Briefly analyse the various bases on which departmentation takes place.

13. State the advantages and limitations of each category of departmentation. (i) Functional departmentation, (ii) Customer-based departmentation, (iii) Product based departmentation,

(iv) Time-based departmentation, (v) Process-based departmentation, (vi) Marketing channel-based departmentation, (vii) Territorial departmentation.

14. A company is producing two products (i) Tooth paste and (ii) Bathing soap. Products are selling in all the regions of the country. Based on the text you have studied in this chapter, prepare the following departmentation formats charts for: (i) Functional department, (ii) Product service department, (iii) Geographic location department and (iv) Customer classification department.

8

DECISION-MAKING

LEARNING OBJECTIVES

After reading this chapter, you should be able to know:

- Decision-making — The Concept
- Decision-making Process (Steps)
- Approaches to Decision-making
- Types of Decisions
- Techniques Adopted for Decision-making

Decision Making—The Concept

A manager's duties mostly involve making decisions of one kind or the other. Everyday hundreds of decisions are made in a company consciously and unconsciously. According to Peter F. Drucker, "Whatever a manager does, he does through making decisions." Decision-making is connected with formulating plans, establishing objectives, laying down policies and so on. According to Rustom S. Davar, "Decision-making can be defined as the selection based on some criteria of one's behaviour alternative from two or more possible alternatives. To decide means to cut-off or in practical context to come to a conclusion."

According to Manley H. Jones, "the decision is a solution selected after examining several alternatives chosen because the decider foresees that the course of action he selects will do more than the other to further his goals and will be accompanied by the fewest possible objections and consequences". Thus, a decision essentially involves choosing a particular course of action, after considering the possible alternatives. It may be expressed in words or it may be implied from behaviour.

IMPORTANCE OF DECISION-MAKING

Decision-making permeates through all managerial functions. Management and decision-making are inseparable activities. Managers use the tool of decision-making for discharging their duties. Whatever a manager does, he can do it by taking some decision—the selection of suitable course of action from a number of alternatives.

According to Melvin T. Copeland, "Administration essentially is a decision-making process and authority is responsible for making decisions and for ascertaining that the decisions made are carried out." In business, whether the enterprise is large or small, changes in condition occur, shifts in personnel take place and unforeseen contingencies arise. Moreover, just to get the wheels started and to keep them turning, decisions must be made. "The business executive", observed John McDonald, "is by profession a decision-maker. Uncertainty is his opponent, overcoming it is his mission. Whether the outcome is a consequence of luck or of wisdom, the moment of decision is without doubt the most creative event in the life of the executive".

All management functions such as planning, organisation, direction and control are settled by managers with the tool of decision-making. Decision-making is important in planning, for in planning, the manager has to decide many things such as what to produce, what to sell, where, when, how and so on. In an organisation, decision-making relates to the structure, nature of organisation, division of work and so on.

Decision-making is also an important tool in the management functions of direction and control. In direction, decisions relate to determining the course of action, deciding the type of motivation, deciding the orders and instructions to be given etc. whereas in control, the decisions relate to deciding of standards, control points, procedures etc.

Decision-making is necessary in a business concern because there are many alternative courses of action to most business situations. For instance, for establishing a business. The entrepreneur may select one of the forms of organisation such as a sole trading concern or a partnership or a joint-stock company. For raising money, he may issue shares or debentures or borrow from financial institutions. Similarly, for selling his finished products, he may sell through a retailer or through middlemen or through his own retail shops. Thus, decision-making is vital to all management activities.

DECISION-MAKING PROCESS (STEPS)

Decision-making consists of the following steps in the order of their sequence. (See Fig. 8.1)

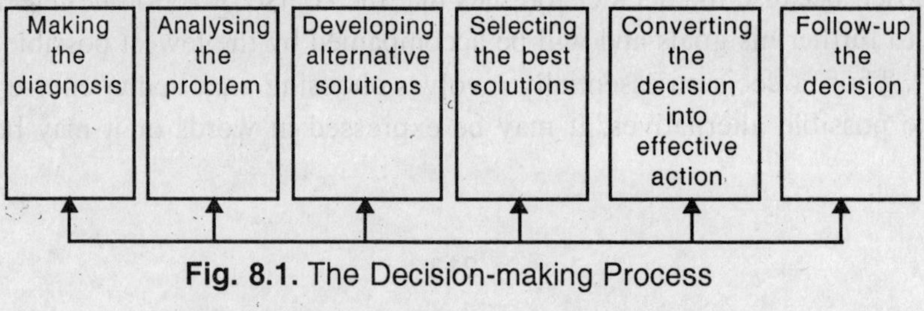

Fig. 8.1. The Decision-making Process

1. Making the Diagnosis: The first step in decision-making is finding out what really is the problem. If the problem is not correctly diagnosed, efforts made to solve it will be of no use. For example, if the sales decline, the management may think that the problem is one of increasing cost. But the real problem may be inadequate sales planning or decrease in quality or inadequate publicity. Hence, the efforts made by the management to reduce cost may not help in increasing sales. Joseph L. Massie has rightly said that "a good decision is dependent upon the recognition of the right problem". A correct diagnosis of the problem is of utmost importance because a disease can be cured only if it is properly diagnosed.

2. Analysing the Problem: After ascertaining the correct problem, it should be thoroughly analysed and information and data relating to it should be collected. This will help the management to get a clear idea of the problem. There may be innumerable factors involved in any problem, but to minimise the expense of time and effort, analysis should be directed towards pertinent and closely connected factors for the purpose of collecting information and data. Further, out of the data and information collected, the management should separate facts from beliefs and opinions and it should depend mainly on facts for making decisions.

3. Developing alternative solutions or courses of action: The next step is to develop alternative solutions or courses of action. The management after evaluating the various alternatives can make the decision and the evaluation of alternatives help the management in taking the best decision. For instance, if the management wants to fill up a vacancy, it should consider various alternatives such as whether to promote from within, or recruit from outside or to appoint a relative of the previous employee. Similarly, the methods of selling its products may involve various alternatives such as whether to sell directly, or through middlemen or a combination of both, *viz.*, direct selling and through middlemen. Thus, for every problem there are alternatives and they should be evaluated before taking a final decision.

4. Selecting the best solution: The next step is to select the best solution out of the several alternatives developed. For this purpose, the management has to consider the merits and demerits of each alternative solution and costs and sacrifices involved in each. Some criteria for selecting the best solution are the economy of effort, degree of risk, time required for implementation, practicability of the solution, availability of resources, consonance with the goals of the enterprise, etc. Generally, sound knowledge and practical experience of the executive will help him to select the best solution.

5. Converting the decision into effective action: After selecting the best solution or decision, the management takes steps to translate the decision into action with the co-operation of the employees. In order to avoid opposition from the employees in implementing the decision, it is desirable that the employees should be associated with the decision-making process.

6. Follow up the decision: Sometimes, it is possible that a decision taken by a manager may not be a correct one. Hence, the manager, while translating the decision into action, should introduce a system of follow up. This helps in safeguarding against incorrect decision and also in modifying or altering the decision without loss of time.

Thus, decision-making process can be divided into sequential operations as shown in figure 8.1. In a narrow sense it can amount to simply choosing among two or more alternatives.

alternatives. The chosen alternative will be the "Decision". Whether the decision is routine or unique one, the systematic, step-by-step approach will be effective.

APPROACHES TO DECISION-MAKING

Decision-makers normally will have different decision-making situations and many a time it will be very difficult for them to take a sound decision. In order to adopt a sound decision, they resort to one suitable approach of the number of approaches available to them. The approaches available to them are as follows:

(i) ***Quantitative approach*** involving mathematical and statistical models.
(ii) ***Environment approach*** comprising risks, uncertainties involved in business practices.
(iii) ***Systems approach*** considering decision a holistic one.
(iv) ***Intuitive approach*** involving intuition, creativity and judgement.
(v) ***Ethical approach*** considering moral aspects.
(vi) ***Case study approach*** involving the analysis of identical cases.

There are many more models or approaches in decision-making. Some of them are analysed under the heading "Decision Techniques." Only basic approaches are listed and a brief analysis is given in the following paragraphs:

(i) Quantitative approach: This approach considers numerical aspects involving mathematics and statistics to make decision. No decision can be taken without the help of mathematics and statistics. In a mathematical approach equations, and symbolic notations are used to relate many decision making variables. These variables are expressed in numericals.

Similarly, statistical models in the form of graphs, diagrams, frequency tables, averages of first and second order, correlation coefficients, regression equations, time-series analysis, etc.

Mathematical and statistical approaches wholly called quantitative approach scientifically analyses the decision-making alternatives and provide a strong base to take sound decision.

(ii) Environmental Approach: Under this approach, issues such as uncertainties, risks involved and even certainties are considered for decision-making.

In an **Uncertainty** situation, decision-maker will have only meager information which may or may not be reliable. It is also not definite whether the information will be changed. For example, a company having its business in Bengaluru would like to expand business to neighbouring states. The company will have insufficient data about the market behaviour consumption pattern of the concerned product cultural change etc. However, decision has to taken by analysing the available data.

Under **risk** situation, calculated risk will be analysed adopting quantitative techniques (mathematical and statistical models). The result so obtained will be used as a base for decision-making. Objective and subjective (based on personal experience of the manager and judgement) probabilities which are risky ones, will be adopted for decision-making.

Certainty situations will provide, reliable information and it will be easy to make decisions. In this case, cause-and-effect relationship is known and decisions made under such situation will prove sound.

(iii) Systems Approach: While arriving at decisions, the manager should openly consider the activities of various departments that are related to the proposed decision. This means that the decision-makers should consider the organisation as a system in which the departments (sub-systems) work in a co-ordinated manner. There should be a holistic approach in decision-making and consider various elements in the system environment. Managers have to provide opportunities to all concerned in the system to express their views about the proposed decision and finally arrive at the decision. This approach is democratic in character and how best it can be adopted depends upon managers.

(iv) Ethical Approach: Decision-makers can consider one more approachs, *viz.*, Ethical approach. No decision-maker is barred from adopting ethical aspect. While taking decisions, ethical and moral considerations in decision-making have to be viewed from the angles of: (i) justice which demands distribution of cost and benefit equally, (ii) the aim of decision should bring greatest happiness to the greatest number and (iii) decisions should protect fundamental rights. Ethical approach has to be taken by decision-makers to reflect the social responsibility of the organisation in terms of the three objectives cited above.

(v) Intuitive Approach: This is based on intuition of the decision-maker. Intuition is the power of attaining direct knowledge without evident rational thought or the drawing of conclusions from evidence available. It is a Hunch (a strong intuitive feeling) which comes to the mind abruptly from unconscious mind. A thought that emerges instantaneously will be considered for decision-making.

(vi) Case Study Approach: According to this approach, a decision that has to be taken on an issue will be arrived at, after studying an identical case occured elsewhere. This approach is taken when the uncertainty prevails regarding an issue fully or partially. The underlying principle in case study approach is that an identical situation as that of the situation arised in the organisation has occured, certain decision is already taken, the effect is experienced and the same decision can be taken with certain modification, if need be, as per the organisational requirement. A careful analysis exhibits various dimensions of the decisions and decision makes can arrive at possible decision which will be beneficial to the organisation.

For example, a company which is doing well with product "X" in all markets would suddenly faces stiff competition with arrival of a new product "Y". The market share for "X" is likely to fall by 30 per cent or more as the rival has adopted an aggressive sales policy. Therefore, the marketing executive of the company selling "X" product has to analyse an identical case and find out the extent of fall of market share and take a decision to adopt corrective measure.

Case study approach can throw light on the problem and many a time provide good base to take sound decisions.

TYPE OF DECISIONS

Decisions are of several types. Classification of these types is as follows:

1. Programmed and non-programmed decisions: Decisions are classified into programmed and non-programmed decisions. While the former deals with the routine and repetitive type of problems, the latter deals with problems which are not routine and non-repetitive. For example, an enterprise has a set of procedures to handle normal orders from the buyers and this matter need not be referred to the Board of Directors or any other higher authorities for decision. As this problem is repetitive, a standard procedure should be used for handling such problems. This is a case of programmed decision.

On the other hand, if the enterprise receives unusually very large orders for its products in any particular year, it would constitute a problem involving non-programmed decision. For handling such large orders, the sales department may take the guidance of board of directors, since it has to deal with the problem which is non-repetitive and for which no definite procedure has been laid down.

2. Major and minor decisions: Decisions may be classified as major and minor. For example, a decision to purchase a machine worth lakhs of rupees or deciding to open some branches is a major decision. On the other hand, purchase of some pencils or paper for office use is a minor decision which can be taken by the office superintendent.

3. Routine and strategic decisions: One more method of classification of decisions is routine and strategic decisions. Usually, routine decisions do not require lengthy deliberations and such decisions are taken in a routine way. Some of the examples of routine decisions are: deciding to send samples to government test house, deciding to place an order with the supplier who has given a favourable quotation, deputing an employee to annual conferences, etc.

Strategic decisions generally involve lengthy deliberations and also may have much impact on the functioning of the business concern. Some examples of strategic decisions are: decisions relating to product diversification or product line, entering a new market, pricing strategy, advertising strategy, etc.

4. Policy and operating decisions: Decisions can be policy decisions and operating decisions. While policy decisions are taken at a high level after lengthy deliberations, operating decisions are taken at a much lower level. For example, deciding to grant leave encashment benefit to employees is a policy decision whereas calculating the amount due to each employee because of the leave encashment benefit is an operating decision.

5. Organisational and personal decision: If any decision is taken by an executive in his official capacity, that decision is called organisational decision. For example, decisions relating to appointment, promotion or transfer of employees are organisational decisions. In the case of personal decisions, an executive takes decisions as an individual and not in his official capacity. For example, to opt for voluntary retirement from the business concern is the personal decision of the executive.

6. Individual and group decisions: Another method of classification of decisions is individual and group decisions. Individual decisions are taken by any individual and generally, they relate to routine matteres. For example, sanctioning of leave to a worker is an individual decision.

In the case of group decisions, the superior managers take decisions in collaboration with their subordinates. For example, taking a decision by the production manager in consultation with his subordinates to change the design of the product slightly is a group decision.

7. Departmental, inter-departmental and enterprise decisions: Decisions can be departmental, inter-departmental or enterprise decisions. Departmental decisions relate to the concerned department and they are taken by the departmental heads. For example, allotting work to the employees of a department is a departmental decision.

Inter-departmental decisions are made by the managers of the concerned or affected departments with the help of the controlling manager. For example, a decision relating to change the product design slightly is an inter-departmental decision.

Enterprise decisions are those which are taken at a higher level, *i.e.,* Managing Director or Board of Directors. These decisions are concerned with the entire enterprise. For example, decisions relating to opening of branches, entering a new market, pricing decisions or decisions relating to giving of bonus to employees are enterprise decisions.

These are the basic types of decision taken in an organisation. Adopting a specific type, depends upon the situation that prevails in the organisation. Good decision or bad decision is better than indecision. Managers should not postpone decision on an issue. Postponing any type of decision will make the problem more complex and put the organisation into trouble.

DECISION-MAKING TECHNIQUES

Whatever may be the type of decision taken by the managers, it will have some method which may be 'scientific' or 'unscientific'. The methodology adopted is called "technique". If it has a professional approach, it can be called scientific and if it is taken without considering the systematic process or otherwise called trial and error method, it is 'unscientific'. The writers and thinkers on management have termed these two basic approaches as "traditional techniques" and "modern techniques".

1. Traditional Techniques

Traditionally, the decision-making at organisational level was taking place in the following forms and even today some of them are adopted in unstructured organisations.

(i) Adoption of standard operating procedure.

(ii) Incorporation and imbibing well-defined information channels in the organisational structure.

(iii) Taking decisions by habit.

(iv) Deciding through ituition, creativity and judgement.

(v) Training the selected executives in decision-making.

(vi) Adopting Rules of thumb method.

These techniques are briefly analysed in the following paragraphs.

(i) Standard procedure: This is the most accepted and traditional technique of decision-making. For every type of general or functional problem, certain standards for decision-making are fixed based on past experience. This may be subjected to change whenever need arises. However, managers, without much botheration adopt the standard operating practices in a routine manner. The decision in such cases is automatic. If any disturbance is caused in carrying out the operations as per standards, the managers can discuss with higher ups and implement the modified decision. Standard operating practices are routine in nature and manager will not be liable for penalty or any other positive action, if anything goes wrong.

(*ii*) ***Incorporating well-defined information system:*** For taking any good decision, correct information related to the issue should be made available to managers. Well-defined information on every activity of the organisation, facilitates managers to take appropriate decisions. Each and every worker in every functional department should be told about the norms and procedures by respective managers. This ensures the managers to avail necessary information from subordinates to take sound decisions when issues arise.

(*iii*) ***Decision by habit:*** Decisions are also taken by habit. Habit may be described as settled tendency or usual manner of behaviour. It is an acquired pattern or mode of behaviour of a person. This is concerned with behaviour of a person. Decision-making may be **archaic — a** mental make-up. The decision-making is habitual to managers and as and when the problem crops up, decision is taken as a habit.

(*iv*) ***Decision-making by creativity, intuition and judgement:*** Some instant decisions are taken at time. This will be a decision of creativity of the manager. Creativity is something that comes out of mind. This emerges from subconsciousness and will be vague. This vague idea will be connected to consciousness by intuition. As the managers have to take quick decisions for want of time, the creative decisions may be pre-matured. Still, many a time, they workout wonders. The creative process can be observed in the following map.

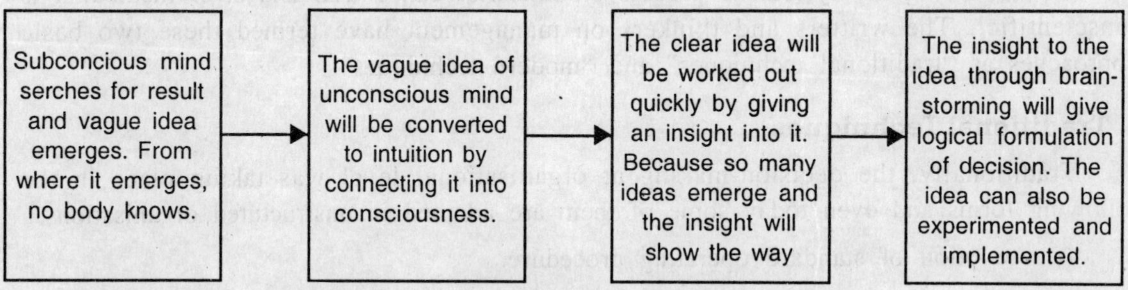

Fig. 8.2. Emerging Decision by Creativity

The decision will also be taken by innovation. The decision emerges from various types of experiments on process and practices. Of these processes or practices, certain process may prove cost-effective and very palatable to adopt. This may be adopted by managers for better results. Innovative decisions are relevant to any size of business and any type of activity.

Decision by value judgement is another way of taking decisions. Managers just decide that certain ethical value bring image to the organisation. Considering these values they may take certain decisions that may do good for the organisation. Sometimes personal values of decision- makers also influence decision-making. The judgement based on personal and ethical values, shared beliefs and behaviour pattern of decision-makers will emerge as decision.

(*v*) ***Training the selected executives:*** The organisation may select some top executives and form a core committee to take certain decisions. These executives who form the core committee for decision-making, will be trained in decision-making process, considering all techniques of decision-making. Whenever the curcial decisions are to be taken, the committee will meet and discuss the problem threadbare, come out with a viable decision which may be approved by top management and implemented.

(vi) Adopting Rule of Thumb Method: This will have no logical thinking. This will be only trail decision taken by the manager which may or may not work in proper direction. However series of corrections are made to the original decision and gradually a workable decision emerges which may be standardised. As the 'Change' is the dictum for growth, these decisions also go an changing.

Some or all these traditional decision-making tools still prevail in many business enterprises. Particularly in small enterprises, this is the order of the day. Even medium and large enterprises who adopt modern techniques, they finally resort to these methods as a cross-practice.

2. Modern Techniques

Many modern methods have been evolved to take decisions. Following are the ones which are in practice.

(i) Operations Research.
(ii) Electronic Data Processing
(iii) Training decision-makers in heuristic (allowing people to learn for themselves) problem-solving techniques.
(iv) Developing heuristic computer programmes.
(v) Adopting "Decision Tree" technique.

(i) Operations Research: This is a scientific approach developed after World War II. Originally, during World War II, the group of scientists called "Operations Research", the group were asked to give solutions to solve complex military operational problems. The group, consisting mainly physicists used problem-solving method and very successful solutions to solve complex military problems.

The OR concept was introduced in 1955 to develop production process models, which also showed amazing results. Cost-saving was the main benefit derived from OR.

The same process came handy to managers to take sound decisions on complex issues. The technique will have the following phases:

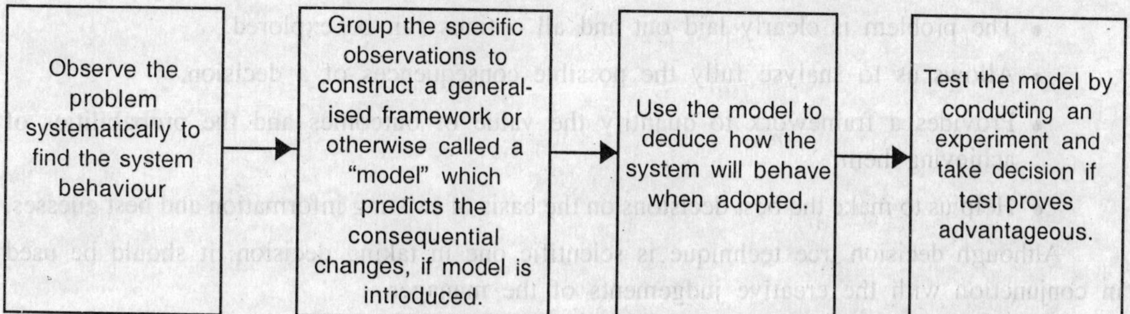

Fig.8.3. Decision-making process under operations research.

This is a scientific technique, which may give near-precision result, provided other associated factors remaining same. Today, many managers take a scientific approach to decision-making. OR technique is extensively used in large, complex organisations to take decisions and this happens to be a programmed decision-making process.

(ii) Electronic Data Processing – EDP: This technique is adopted to analyse the information in electronic form, *i.e.,* through computers. If enormous data are to be analysed to take decision, this technique is very useful. Analysis will be precise and this facilitates effective decision-making. The consequences of the decision can also be understood when precious analysis takes place through EDP. But the information fed for processing should be correct to arrive at sound decision.

(iii) Training Decision-makers in Heuristic Problem-solving Techniques: Another modern technique of decision-making is to train the managers to take decision through self-learning. Heuristic (allowing people to learn for themselves) problem-solving techniques can be adopted by intelligent managers, as the decision is self-made based on their own analysis of the problem requiring decision. EDP will analyse the problem and gives the result which may be adopted. This technique is useful in non-programmed decision.

(iv) Developing Heuristic Computer Programmes: Several self-learning decision models can be developed and made available to decision makers to adopt it implicitly or modifying it as per the need of the situation in the organisation. This can be applied to non-programmed decisions.

DECISION TREE TECHNIQUE

This is a tree type of diagram used in decision-making. This can determine the best or of the greatest value, (sometimes under certain parameters or restrictions) or a course of action to be taken for solving an existing problem, when several possible alternatives depicted in a tree form. The decision tree chart, which looks like a cluster of tree branches exhibits the structure of a particular decision. This also shows interrelationships and interplay between different alternatives, decisions and possible outcomes.

Decision trees are useful tools in selecting a decision between several courses of action. They help to form a balanced pictures of the risks and rewards associated with each possible course of action. Decision trees provide an effective method of decision-making, because of the following benefits:

- The problem is clearly laid out and all options can be explored.
- Allows us to analyse fully the possible consequences of a decision.
- Provides a framework to quantify the value of outcomes and the probabilities of achieving them.
- Help us to make the best decisions on the basis of existing information and best guesses.

Although decision tree technique is scientific one in taking decision, it should be used in conjunction with the creative judgements of the manager.

Developing a Decision Tree

A decision tree will have four components, *viz.*, (i) Nodes, (ii) branches, (iii) probability estimates and (iv) Pay-offs.

Nodes are indicated in the form of squares (❑). Square nodes represent the points where the manager has to take decision or to analyse the chance factors.

Branches represent the alternative course of action which is to be explored and is shown in the form of circle (O).

Probability estimates show the quantitative analysis of good, moderate or poor outcome of a particular alternative with attached values say. Good outcome – 0.8 value. Moderate outcome 0.6 value poor outcome 0.2 value.

Pay-off shows the quantitative outcome of each alternative Example: Good 25% profit. Moderate 10% value. Poor 10% Loss or it can be in absolute figures. Pay-offs are shown at the terminal points of each node.

Construction of a decision tree will have the different phases depending upon the nature of a problem. Problems may relate to production, finance, marketing or HRD. For every problem, which has alternative solutions, a decision tree can be developed.

The decision tree is so called as the decision options will be analysed and end result in each option is presented in the form of a graph. This graphic presentation looks like a tree and hence, it is called decision tree.

DECISION TREE – HOW TO CONSTRUCT?

The construction of decision tree starts with a decision that one has to make.

(i) The decision you have to make will be represented by a square (o) on the left hand side in the middle of the large piece of paper.

(ii) From this square, draw lines towards the right for each possible solutions.

(iii) Write a short description of the solution along the line.

(iv) Keep the lines apart as far as possible so that you can expand your thoughts.

(v) Show the probable result at the end of each line.

(vi) If the result shows uncertainty about decision, draw a small circle (O) (circles represent uncertain outcome and the squares represent possible decisions).

(vii) If the result is another decision that you have to make draw another square.

(viii) Write the decision or factor above the square or circle.

(ix) If the result is complete at the end of the line, do not write anything further.

Thus, go on writing new decision squares in the picture for each option as much as possible. Draw out lines for each option you select. Show the possible result after drawing the circle. Again make a brief note on the line saying what it means. This entire diagram, commencing from the square which represents the decision you have to make to the alternative decisions you arrive at, looks like a tree. This is how the decision-tree is constructed.

The following illustration will help us to understand the practical aspect of the consrtruction of a decision tree.

Illustration

Ramesh, an investor in stocks, has two independent investment options, *i.e.,* (i) investing in stocks and (ii) investing in Fixed Deposits. But he can invest only in one channel due to certain constraints. First, he can invest in stocks and if he is successful, then he can invest in "Fixed Deposits" and *vice versa*. The probability value of stock investment is 0.6 and for Fixed Deposit is 0.4. An initial capital outlay of Rs. 20,000 is required for both the investments. If the investments are not successful, returns will be nothing. [Here, the Fixed Deposit is assumed to be done in a private finance company which is vulnerable]. If successful, stock investment will yield a return of Rs. 40,000 above the cost and Fixed Deposit will yield Rs. 48,000 above the cost. From this information, construct a decision tree.

(First value for each type is to be calculated)

Calculation of Values

Calculation Table

Decision points	*Result*	*Probability*	*Conditional Value Rs.*	*Expected Value Rs*
D_3 (i) Accept Stock	Success	0.6	40,000	24,000
Investment	Failure	0.4	(–) 20,000	(–) 8,000
				16,000
(ii) Stop	–	–	–	0
D_2 (i) Accept FD	Success	0.4	48,000	19,200
investment	Failure	0.6	(–) 20,000	(–) 12,000
				7,200
D_1 (i)Accept Stock	Success	0.6	40,000 + 7,200	28,320
Investment	Failure	0.4	(–) 20,000	(–) 8,000
				20,320
(ii) Accept FD	Success	0.4	48,000 + 16,000	25,600
investment	Failure	0.6	(–) 20,000	(–) 12,000
				13,600
(iii) Do not invest in any option	–	–	–	0

From the calculation of values and presenting them in a tree form as shown in the figure, the investment decision can be taken as follows.

Decision: The EMU (Estimated Mean/Marginal/Value) in D_1 is highest, *i.e.,* 20320, it is better to adopt stock investment at the first instance and if it is successful, investment in Fixed Deposit may be made afterwards.

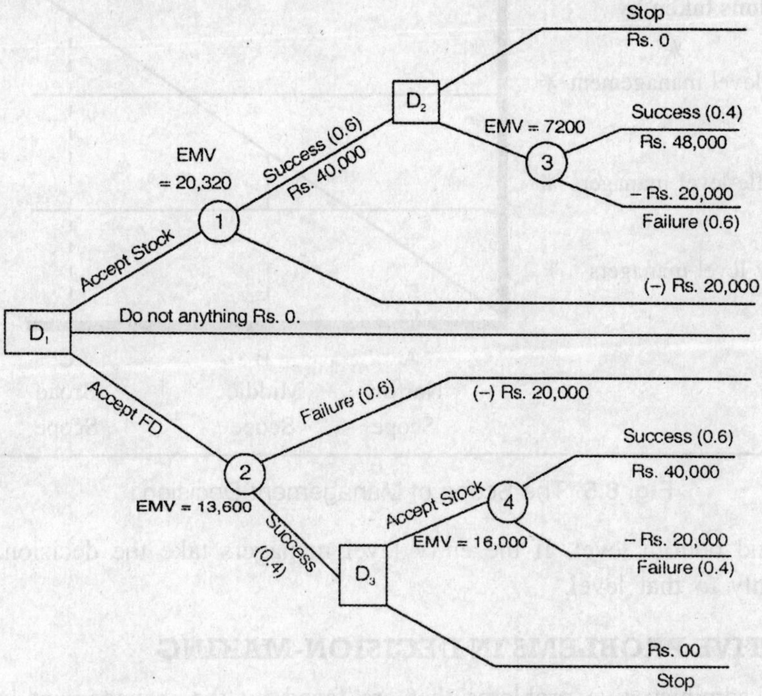

Fig. 8.4. Decision Tree

Thus, decision trees developed for various managerial decisions on different functional aspects, proved to be effective decision tools. Because (i) problems are clearly laid out to examine all options, (ii) possible consequences are fully analysed, (iii) values of outcomes are quantified and probabilities of achieving them are stated and (iv) best possible assumptions. Further, decision tree analysis has to be adopted in conjunction with normal thinking of the decision-maker.

WHO TAKES THE DECISION?

In every organisation, very many decisions have to be taken. It may relate to finance, marketing, HRD, quality assurance of product, consumer relationship, etc. When such wide variety of decisions have to be taken, decision-makers at different levels have to be identified. Some sort of rationale has to be developed to authorise the persons to take decisions. The rationale will have the following two aspects to be considered: (i) The scope of the decision and (ii) Management level.

The scope of management decision refers to the span of decision applicable in an organisation. This means, upto what level the decision can be applied.

Whereas "Management level" refers to different levels of management that exist in an organisation. The following picture indicates the decision taken and its span of applicability.

This diagram explains the span of applicability of decisions and who will take the decision. If top management takes the decision, it will be normally policy decisions and are applicable to bottom level. Whereas the decision taken by middle management, it is applicable

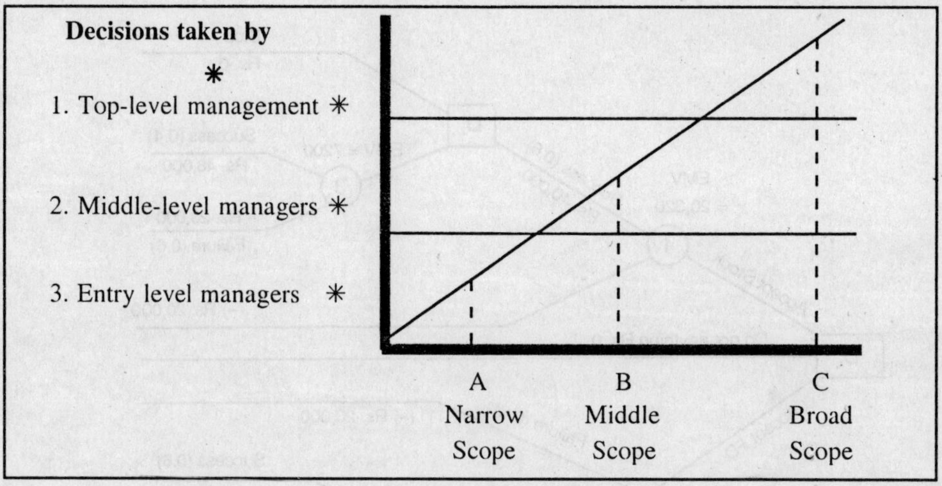

Fig. 8.5 The Scope of Management Decision

to both middle and bottom level. If the entry level managers take the decision, the span of applicability is only to that level.

ADMINISTRATIVE PROBLEMS IN DECISION-MAKING

The various administrative problems that are faced by the management in the process of decision-making are as follows:

1. Correctness of decision: Correctness of decision is a very important problem of management. Correctness depends on several factors such as sophistication of the decision-maker, accuracy of information and ability of the decision-maker to visualise all possible alternative courses of action available in a given situation.

2. The decision environment: The environment, organisational as well as physical that is prevailing in the enterprise, influences the nature of the decision taken. If the general environment is satisfactory, there will be mutual confidence among managers, and also wholehearted co-operation by the subordinates for implementing the decision effectively. Further, there will be great scope for conducting research and analysis of the factors that have a bearing on the decision. Again, a good environment encourages managers to take decisions with confidence instead of avoiding them.

3. Timing of decisions: In decision-making, timing is an important factor. The problem is not merely taking a decision, but when to take it. If the decisions are not taken at the right time, they will not serve any purpose. For example, if the management has to decide the time of introducing a new product in the market, and if the decision taken in this respect is not correct, it may lose the market to its competitors. Thus, timing of decision plays an important role.

4. Effective communication of decision: Another important administrative problem is the effective communication of decisions to those for whom they are meant. The decision should be communicated in a simple language and without any ambiguity. If the decisions are properly communicated, the implementation would not be difficult.

5. Participation in decision-making: Employees who are likely to be affected by a decision should be encouraged to take part in arriving at the final decision so that their wholehearted co-operation will be available for the effective implementation of decision. However, the extent of participation depends on the nature of organisation. If it is an authoritarian organisation in which the executives feel that decision-making is their monopoly, the extent of participation is at a minimum and if it is a "democratic organisation", the extent of participation is great.

6. Implementation of decision: After taking a decision, the problem that has to be faced is its effective implementation. For implementation, not merely effective communication but also good incentives and motivation of subordinates are essential. The management should create such an environment that would help the subordinates perform their jobs better and more easily.

SUMMARY

1. Decision-making involves choosing a particular course of action after considering the possible alternatives. Most managerial duties involve decisions of one kind or another. Whatever the manager does, he does through making decisions. Decision-making permeates through all managerial functions, and management and decision-making are inseparable.
2. Decisions are of several types. They are: (a) programmed and non-programmed decisions, (b) major and minor decisions, (c) routine and strategic decisions, (d) policy and operating decisions, (e) organisational and personal decisions, (f) individual and group decisions and (g) departmental, interdepartmental and enterprise decisions.
3. Decision-making involves a number of steps such as making the diagnosis, analysing the problem, developing an alternative solution or course of action, selecting the best solution, converting the decision into effective action and following up of the decision.
4. An organisation adopts several techniques, depending upon the nature of problem, to take decisions. The traditional methods include, (i) taking decision by habit (ii) Adapting standard procedure (iii) Imbibing the decision-making process in the structure itself, (iv) judgement, intuition and creativity, (v) rules of thumb and (vi) selection and training of executives.

   Modern techniques are; (i) operations research involving the development of mathematical models, computer simulation etc. and (ii) Electronic data processing – EDP.
5. The Decision Tree technique is an useful tool to select a decision between number of courses of action. Decision trees provide a highly effective structure with in which you can explore options and examine the possible outcomes of those options. DT also presents situations which help the decision-maker to choose between different strategies, projects or investment opportunities, particularly when the organisation is facing resource crunch. It also presents a balanced picture of the risks and rewards associated with each possible cource of a action.
6. The various administrative problems that are faced by the management in the process of decision-making are: the correctness of decision, the decision environment, timing of decision, effective communication of decision, participation in decision-making and implementation of decision.

STUDY QUESTIONS

1. What is Decision-making?
2. Name the types of decision.
3. What is programmed decision?
4. What is non-programmed decision?
5. What is strategic decision?
6. What is policy decision?
7. What is organisational decision?
8. What is operating decision?
9. What is group decision?
10. What is decision environment?
11. What do you mean by Decision Tree? State the method of constructing it.
12. What is Operations Research? Briefly analyse the concept.
13. Give the meaning of EDP.
14. What is Heuristic problem-solving technique? In what way it will have positive effect on decision-making?
15. Name the different forms of traditional decison techniques.
16. Give an explanatory note on various approaches to decision-making.
17. Briefly explain the decision-making process.
18. Examine the importance of decision-making.
19. Give an analytical note on different types of decisions taken in an organisation.
20. Explain the administrative problems of decision-making.
21. Briefly explain the method of constructing a decision-tree.
22. "Good decision or bad decision is better than indicision". Substantiate this statement.
23. Give the meaning of: (i) Node, (ii) Pay-off, (iii) Probability value and (iv) Branch contained in a decision tree.

Practical Exercise

You are CEO of an organisation which is dealing in all electronic consumer durable like TV, Computer etc., of a single popular brand.

The market is volatile for electronic goods. The company is facing stiff competition from another brand in two segments, *viz.,* Washing Machines and DVD players. The sales of other products is likely to be affected, because of the slow movement of these two products. There are three alternatives before you to solve the problem.

1. To withdraw the two products from the market.
2. To adopt aggressive sales promotion for these products.
3. To reduce the price of these two products.

What decision you take to avoid fall in sales of other products? Analyse.

9

LEADERSHIP

LEARNING OBJECTIVES

After reading this chapter,you should be able to know:

- Leadership – The Concept
- Leader and Vision
- Leadership Traits
- Classic Leadership Styles
- Leader Behaviour
- Managerial Grid

Business enterprises will be growing with the introduction of innovative business practices. Change and growth are inseparable activities. In the process of growth, human factor plays a vital role and technology supports the thinking of human factor. One individual normally takes the decision and it will be implemented through his team and acheive success. It can be observed that a company which will be in the verge of closure will be making huge profit after an innovative individual is appointed as a manager. In fact he will be a turn-around leader. Therefore, any enterprise needs a leader. Various activities of the enterprise are directed and co-ordinated by a leader to accomplish the objectives of that enterprise.

LEADERSHIP – THE CONCEPT

Every enterprise expects that the people at work should strictly follow a certain course of work which comprises of policies, procedures and job description. It can be achieved only through proper direction. The person who gets things done through others effectively is called manager and this person should have leading qualities. Following definitions highlight the leadership qualities.

Definitions

1. "The relationship in which one person, or leader, influences others to work together willingly of related tasks to attain that which the leader desires." **— *George R. Terry***
2. "It is an interpersonal influence, exercised in situations and directed, through the communication process, towards the attainment of a specified goal or goals." **— *Tannenbaum and Others***
3. "It is the name for that combination of qualities by the possession of which a person is able to get something done by others chiefly because through his influence they become willing to do it." **— *Tead Ordway***
4. "It is the ability to shape the attitudes and behaviour of others, whether formal or informal situations." **— *Hodge & Jhonson***
5. "It is influencing people to follow you and to work willingly for the advancement of a common goal." **— *Koontz & O'Donnell***
6. "It is the knack of getting other people to follow you and to do willingly the things you want them to do." **— *Bittel L.R.***
7. "It is the quality of the behaviour of the individuals whereby they guide people or their activities in an organised effort." **— *Chester Bernard***
8. "Leadership can be defined as the ability to cause others to follow willingly, usually in initiating change. The ability to cause others to follow for a common goal is one sure way of recognising leadership. Leaders initiate change either by making decisions or by encouraging others to make them." **— *Robert Dulbin***
9. "Leadership is one form of dominance, in which the followers more or less willingly accept direction and control by another person." **— *Max Richard***
10. "Leadership is an influence process of inducing a subordinate to behave in a desired manner." **— *Warren Bennis***

These definitions tell about various aspects of leadership. The central theme is that a leader, through his personal skills, takes his team together, make his team to work willingly to achieve organisational goals.

LEADER AND VISION

"The very essence of leadership is that you have to have a vision. It's got to be a vision you articulate clearly and forcefully on every occassion." – ***Theodore Hesburgh***

"Vision" is a statement prepared by business units which tells about the ultimate objective to be achieved and how they go about to achieve it. Vision is expressed to foresee the growth of the business. The process of growth is exhibited in the form of vision which has to be achieved. It is more a group-oriented. But not necessarily democratic one. Individual opinion of team members are heard and acceptable ones are incorporated into vision. Vision is an image and idea of the future.

But leader will have his vision which will be made to work in the organisation. Leader shares his dream and direction with his team members and make them to follow. It is beyond organisational mission statement. The vision of a leader permeaters the workplace through manifestation of his actions, beliefs, values and goals of the organisation. Vision is a fundamental source of power leader has the final responsibilities and the final word in finalising it.

Leader understands that business is a process in which competition plays a vital role. He has to prepare his vision statement or a roadmap of attainment to compete. His vision implies an understanding of the past and present. Then develop a growth path to the future and suggest, guidelines to them as to how to act and interact to attain what they regard as desirable. Thus, vision statement of the business and leader's vision are different.

A leader's is vision may be highly intuitive or structured. But it is very essential for success. Suppliers of business house being global in scope, markets and customers are widely distributed, they are to be respected for the success of the business. Therefore, the vision of a leader should look into the fundamentals of ethics, values, aspirations and expectations of consumer distributed across the globe. He must indicate a clear understanding of where the corporation is today, and offer following a roadmap for the future where will it be. Therefore, the leader to lead, should create vision to be shared with his people and make them to follow. The leader should be forward looking honest persons who can envision possibilities of genuine course of action and enlist others in a shared view of the future. This is what the vision of a leader should be. The vision and shared view of the future make a leader's team enjoying the worth, to achieve the organisational goals which are meaningful and one that provides an opportunity for them workers to contribute to a large purpose.

A true vision of a leader inspires him to contribute for great work, putting a meaningful dent in the organisation and make him feel that he is contributing something significant for the success of the enterprise. Vision particularly shared vision is not a miracle moment. It is a daily journey which requires constant spending of time on modelling the right behaviours, developing good communication and managing people's expectations. Leaders without vision will destroy the organisation.

A leader's vision is targetted to mobilise his energy and resources to achieve organisational success. It adds life to the enterprise. Leader's vision is discussed with fellow workers, perfected and directs them (workers) to follow the decided path for the success of the firm. The vision of leader which is full of meaningful information and logical will enthuse the workers to contribute their full mite to achieve the goals of the organisation and make them active and creative.

Fundamentals of a Leader's Vision

The following essential aspects of a leader's vision motivate his people to follow him.

- Well-defined purpose and direction of the firm.
- Care for your fellow workers by involving all of them in organisational tasks and develop loyalty in them.
- Inspire enthusiasm, belief, commitment and excitment in company member.
- Display and reflect the unique strengths, culture, values, beliefs and direction of the organisation.
- Make workers believe that they are part of something bigger than themselves and their daily work.
- Communicate and share views regularly with workers.
- Challenge people to out do themselves to stretch and reach.

Thus, the vision of leader is essential to develop the organisational vision. His vision is shared with his fellow workers, their opinions if they are sound are accepted and final vision statement is prepared. This framework contains the leader's vision on the way in which the organisation should work for its success.

TRAITS OF A LEADER

The exclusive qualities or traits of a leader are as follows:

1. The leader in an organisation is viewed differently by different employees. Some may feel that the leader exercises more bossism and some others may feel that he is not too bossy.
2. The nature of a leader is to induce and develop responsibility and initiative among his subordinates. He has to motivate the employees.
3. Decision-making is another important trait of a leader. His nature should prompt him to take good decisions and implement them effectively.
4. The leaders are bestowed with authority and such authority should be continuously exercised for the benefit of the organisation.
5. In every organisation, the group of workers will be strong and even in that group few persons will be dominating and have a saying. The nature of the leader in such situations should be that he should be capable of handling this strong group for the better of the organisation.
6. The leader should be aggressive and ambitious, and tell pleasantly his subordinates the task to be performed. He should not exhibit his weakness.
7. The nature of a leader is identified through certain traits:

   (a) From the personal qualities of the leader;

   (b) The situation in which the leader operates; and

   (c) The tasks he has to discharge. Therefore, the nature can also be viewed from these angles.

   (i) As per the *personal quality,* the leader should be courageous, should have willpower, should be flexible, knowledgeable, should possess physical and nervous energy, have enthusiasm, technical mastery, should be a person of intelligence, integrity and faith, and possess stability in behaviour, decisiveness, persuasiveness, self-confidence, fairness and moral qualities.

   (ii) From the *situation angle,* the leader should understand his duties and responsibilities, the time frame in which he has to complete his tasks, understand his subordinates, co-ordinate his work and be capable of managing the crises and conflicts. He should be capable of providing a congenial work atmosphere.

   (iii) As far as *tasks* are concerned, the leader should have the nature of understanding each task he has to direct, analyse coolly the tasks and decide, the plan of action in an effective routine way, watch the operations, take corrective measures then and there to complete the tasks successfully.

(iv) All the definitions stated earlier throw light on one common nature of leader that "Leadership is a process whereby one individual exerts influence over others." *As French and Raven* puts, influence is acquired through five different types of powers, *viz.*, "Coercive power, reward power, legitimate power, expert power, and referent power." One more power "incremental influential factor" (which means the act of influencing others depends on objectives and operations of the firm and the way in which the employees view their leaders) adds to the power line.

Thus the qualities of a leader gives a guideline for successful running of an organisation.

Skills

As a part of personal traits, the leader should possess the following skills:

Leadership is closely associated with human skill. The other factors which influence leadership are, team building and interpersonal interaction. But human skills greatly influence, the style of functioning of leader. "Human skill is the ability to interact effectively with people and to build team work. No leader, at an organisational level, escapes the requirement for effective human skills. It is a major part of the role behaviour. Conceptual skill becomes increasingly important in higher managerial jobs because these leaders are dealing more with long range plans, broad relationship and other abstractions. Conceptual skills deal with ideals, while human skill concerns people and technical skill is with things." *(Keith Davis — Human Behaviour at Work).*

From this statement we make out that leaders mainly should have three types of skills: (i) Human skills, (ii) Conceptual skills and (iii) Technical skills. These three types of skills are analysed in the following paragraphs:

(i) Human Skills: These skills are mainly concerned with human resources working in the organisation. These skills of the leader tell as to how a leader should handle the available human resources for the benefit of the organisation. The human force working in the organisation will be of varied type and the leader has to generally understand the mood of the workers in order to have healthy relations with them. The real leader should be a visionary. He must have the clear vision of the workforce under him, and manage them tactfully. He must have concern for people. Concern for the people includes "Concern for the degree of personal commitment to completing a job one is responsible for, accountability based on trust rather than on obedience, self-esteem or the personal worth of an individual; establishing and maintaining good working conditions, maintaining an equitable salary structure and fringe benefits; desire for security in work; Social relations or friendship with associates; and so on" *(Robert R. Blake and Jane S. Mouton).* This statement indicates as to how the leader should establish healthy relationship with workers to attain organisation objectives.

Human skills include the "Influence" that the leader has to exert on his workforce. There are three aspects of influence: (a) The person who is exerting the influence (leader), (b) The method of exerting influence (influencing process) and (c) The person subjected to influence.

The three aspects of influence are co-ordinated to make it work for the better of the organisation. Influence is a skill in the sense that it makes the fellow workers of a leader to act according to designs of a leader. Influence is exerted through power.

Human skill also involves the role the leader has to play with his fellow workers. These roles include: (i) Group task which is concerned with defining human problem and finding out solutions for them, (ii) Group building and maintenance which includes encouraging, harmonising, compromising, standard setting, observing the group and commenting on performance and (iii) Individual roles like aggressor, blocker, recognition seeker, self-confessor, playboy, dominator, help seeker, etc.

Thus, human skills are the personal traits of a leader to motivate his fellow workers to work for the organisation.

(ii) Conceptual Skills: These skills are concerned with creative activity of the leader. Every leader should know his organisation. It is his responsibility to see that organisation grows on sound lines. Similarly, the segment leaders like production manager or finance manager should have complete perception of their work. Every leader, while leading the organisation knows as to what are the problems that confront in the operational process. He should find out solutions to solve such problems. Being a visionary, should visualise the rate of growth of the firm and also plan for good growth.

Conceptual skills include: (a) The understanding the organisation behaviour, (b) Understanding the competitors of the firm and (c) Knowing the financial status of the firm and work for the smooth running of the firm. He should think of expansional programmes and work for product diversification, etc. He should have the skill to run the firm in such a way that overall performance of the firm in the long run will be sound. This skill mainly is concerned with the development of the firm. It is non-technical and non-human skill concerned with comprehensive growth of the firm. It involves every task and functional aspect of the organisation. Being the head of the organisation unit, the leader should be capable of running the firm on firm footing.

(iii) Technical Skills: This refers to the technical knowledge, the leader possesses. Every leader should have the technical background relating to the business he runs or the output he produces. Without possessing the technical knowledge, the leader cannot perform well in his organisation. He is actually supported by the technical expert for possessing the technical knowledge. "Technical" means not only the engineering aspects relating to plant and machinery but also other operational aspects which involve some sensitive thinking in implementing a programme or a plan of action. For example, promotion of an employee. The leader is interested in promoting a good worker to next higher position, but he will not have seniority. If that person is promoted surpassing the eligible persons, it tantamounts to "technical snag."

Thus, technical skill involves the study and understanding the technology used in business operations of the respective firms and also the other skills which are sensitive in nature. The leader should possess them.

Besides these three types of skills discussed so far, the leader should possess skills like (i) Marketing skills, (ii) Financial skills, (iii) Production skills, (iv) Vision and creativity, (v) Integrating skills, (vi) Adaptation skills and (vii) Restructuring or re-engineering skills. One becomes a perfect leader, if one posseses all these skills.

IMPORTANCE OF LEADERSHIP

An organisation comes into existence with certain specified objectives and hence there is need to direct the activities of its members towards the achievement of the objectives. Direction of activities in the organisation is effected by the leader. This emphasises the importance of leadership in achieving the organisational goals. According to Peter F. Drucker, good leadership is a must for the success of a business. But business leaders are the scarcest resources of any enterprise. John G. Gloves, in his book, *Fundamentals of Professional Management,* states that "more failures of business concerns are attributable to poor leadership than to any other cause." This observation also indicates the importance of good leadership for the success of a business. Apart from this, the following points highlight the importance of leadership:

1. Performance of workers very much depends on their motivation. Higher the motivation, the better would be the performance. A good leader influences the behaviour of his subordinates in such a way that they are motivated to high performance.
2. A good leader creates confidence in his subordinates by giving them sound advice and by directing them for good performance. A good leader also sustains the enthusiasm of his subordinates and secures their involvement in the organisation goals.
3. Good leadership increases employee morale which in turn ensures high productivity and stability in the organisation.
4. A manager, in spite of his authority, may or may not have the ability to influence the behaviour of others. Further, the use of authority may not always ensure high performance. Whereas a good leadership by the use of influence can secure high performance. Hence, leadership helps in the use of formal authority effectively.
5. Leadership directs and unifies efforts of the individuals of a group towards the attainment of enterprise goals. In other words, in the absence of good leadership, the organisational goals of the enterprise would remain unfulfilled.

FUNCTIONS OF A LEADER

Krech and Grutchfield give a list of 14 functions performed by leaders in general. A brief explanation of them is given here.

1. Goal Setter: A leader either establishes organisational goals and objectives himself or he may participate with his superiors or subordinates in establishing them.

2. Planner: This function is intermediate between the determination of goals and their execution. In this connection, the leader makes decisions concerning the ways and means with which the organisational goals can be achieved.

3. Executive: In his role as executive, a leader is responsible for seeing that the appropriate activities of the organisation are carried out.

4. Expert: The technical information and skills the supervisors possess are useful in aiding and instructing their subordinates in effective work procedure.

6. Surrogate for individual responsibility: The leader relieves other members of the group of certain responsibilities and they in turn place their trust in his decisions. For example, in an informal group of workers, one individual may be given the responsibility of passing on of complaints to the superior.

7. Controller of internal relationship within the organisation: It is the responsibility of a leader to see the various departments in his purview to coordinate their activities.

8. Administrator of rewards and punishments: As leaders, the supervisors encourage, upgrade and promote workers who deserve, and remove, transfer or dismiss workers who violate rules or regulations of the organisation.

9. Arbitrator and Mediator: The leader tries to maintain harmony among the members of the organisation. For example, the president of an organisation makes efforts to maintain harmony among competitive and ambitious Vice-Presidents.

10. Exemplar: Leader serves as an exemplar, a model for others to emulate. For example, the office manager who is invariably 15 minutes early at his desk in the morning is seeking to influence the members of his group by being a good example.

11. Symbol of the group: In this role, the leader provides a kind of continuity and stability to the group, standing for it despite changes in circumstances and membership.

12. Ideologist: The leader functions as an ideologist. By presenting his ideas concerning the group, he is a source of moral strength to them.

13. Father Figure: The leader, by functioning as a father figure, fulfils an emotional role for the members of the group. By identifying themselves with their leader, the members of a group draw strength and feeling of security.

14. Scapegoat: The leader functions as a scapegoat. He provides a ready target for the aggressions of the members of the group. Failure can be projected upon him. For example, the foreman in a production section may be blamed for any shortfall in production in his department and for insufficient co-operation on the part of the departmental manager.

FORMAL AND INFORMAL LEADERS

Though a successful manager is also a good leader, in actual practice, every manager is not able to provide the kind of leadership needed by his subordinates. Because of this, informal leaders who do not occupy any post in the organisation come into the picture. While a formal leader in an organisation who holds the post fixed by the management, possesses the organisational authority to direct and control the activities of his subordinates. An informal leader chosen by the workers themselves and not appointed by the management does not possess organisational authority to control the activities of the workers.

Informal leaders do not exist outside the organisation but are part of the formal organisation. There can be several informal leaders each functioning for different groups. Sometimes, informal leaders become more acceptable to the workers than formal leaders. Hence, it is necessary for the formal leaders not to antagonise the informal leader. As informal leaders have a lot of influence on the workers, they can make an action of formal leaders ineffective. In view of this, it is

In view of this, it is desirable for the formal leaders to recognise the importance of informal leaders and to associate them in the decision-making process of the organisation so that there would not be any resistance by the workers at the time of implementation of decisions.

THEORIES OF LEADERSHIP

The researches carried out by many behavioural scientists to find out what makes a leader effective have resulted in various theories of leadership. In this section, however, we shall discuss only three categories of theories of leadership:

1. Trait theory.
2. Behavioural theory.
3. Situational theory.
   (a) Fidler's contingency theory
   (b) Hersey-Blanchard's Situational Leadership
   (c) Path Goal Leadership Theory.

1. Trait Theory

The trait theory seeks to determine the personal characteristics or traits of a successful leader. A successful leader is supposed to have the following traits: good personality, intellectual ability, initiative, imagination, emotional stability, desire to accept responsibility, flexibility, honesty, sincerity, integrity, ability to make quick decisions, courage, reliability, persuasive power, etc. To determine the personality traits of a successful leader, studies were conducted by selecting successful leaders and find out their traits. It was presumed that persons possessing these traits could become successful leaders.

But this theory suffers from many limitations. They are:

1. It emphasises mainly personal traits and does not consider the environment or situation in which they have to be applied.
2. It assumes that leadership is an in-born quality and cannot be acquired.
3. There is no common list of traits found in all successful leaders.
4. There is no objective criteria to measure individual traits of leaders.

Inspite of the limitations, the trait theory of leadership is not completely invalid. Their theory indicates that a leader should have certain personal traits. This helps the management to develop such qualities in a leader through its various programmes of training and development. The traits stated above can be consolidated into the following broad categories:

- Intelligence including judgement and ability.
- Previous attainments in meritorious activities and sports.
- Initiative, drive to persist and achieve and reliance.
- Adaptability to social actions and participate in group events.
- Emotionally matured and having consistancy in thinking.
- Having exceptions about social recognition and stable economic position.

Traits theory considers only one dimension of leadership quality. But only traits cannot make a leader. Other aspects should be looked into.

2. Behavioural Theory of Leadership

In this approach, the emphasis is on the actual behaviour and action of the leaders and not on their traits or characteristics. In other words, this approach emphasises that strong leadership is the result of effective role behaviour.

This approach states that the leader uses three skills to lead his followers. These skills are: technical (refers to a person's knowledge of the process of technique), human (refers to ability to interact with people) and conceptual (refers to manager's ideas which enable a manager to set up models and design plans).

This approach assumes that a particular behaviour of a manager will make him a good leader while its opposite would discard him as a leader. Determining goals, motivating employees for achieving the goals, effective communication ability to interact effectively, building team spirit, etc. are the functional behaviour of a successful leader.

This theory emphasises the point that the favourable behaviour of a leader provides greater satisfaction to the followers and they recognise him as their leader. However, one limitations of this approach is that a particular behaviour and action of a leader may be relevant and effective at a particular point of time while at another, it may be irrelevant and ineffective. Thus, in this approach, the 'time' factor which is a vital element has not been considered.

Another characteristic that we may find, is the leader that surges from certain situations. These may be known as situational leaders, and there are many examples to illustrate this.

Let us assume that an aircraft crashes in an isolated forest. While still flying, the captain was the leader, holdiang the power of decision. From there on everything will depend on the situation. If there are many wounded passengers and a doctor is present, he will become the leader. After all the people are attended, leadership will then pass automatically to anyone who has the knowledge of surviving and a sense of orientation in that type of vegetation. He will be the only hope left and everyone will follow him.

This goes to show the importance of know-how in relation to the situation, and many times without anyone noticing, leadership flows from one place to the other. Great leaders know how to get people to share their knowledge.

We must not forget that although technical and professional skills are important in authority, it is not everything. To become a leader, you need to have leadership abilities, the power of decision and the facility to communicate with people. A person must be flexible and have the good sence to transfer certain decisions, when the mater gets out of your own knowledge sphere.

The true leader is a person who can adapt himself to many different situations, and never stops learning. He is always interacting with people, and getting everyone to work together with a common vision, so as to produce fantastic results. People will follow him without even recognising they have taken on the role of follower...this is what makes the leader different from the others.

3. Situational Theory

According to this theory, leadership is affected by a situation from which a leader emerges and in which he works. In other words, the situation — the group, the problem and its environment — will affect the type of leadership. An important aspect of this theory is the interaction between the group and its leader and the people tend to follow the person who is capable of fulfilling their desires.

The leader recognises his followers' desires and follows such methods (depending on the situation) which satisfy them. The main thrust of the situational theory is that the leadership style may be effective under one situation and ineffective under the other. In other words, situational theory emphasises that there is no one best style of leadership universally applicable to all situations and that the leader has to change his style of leadership from situation to situation. If the leader adopts the same style under all situations, he may not be successful. For example, Winston Churchill was the most effective and successful Prime Minister of Britain during the period of the Second World War, but he was a flop afterwards when the situation changed.

Though this theory states leadership ability of an individual in a given situation and measures his leadership potentialities, it is silent on the point whether this individual will fit in another situation.

There are many situational or contingency theories out of which (a) Fiedler's Contingency Theory, (b) Hersey and Blanchard's situational leadership and (c) Path-Goal theory are considered as vital theories.

(a) Fiedler's Contingency Theory

The Austrian psychologist Fred Edward Fiedler proposed this theory. The contingency model emphasizes the importance of both the leader's personality and the situation in which that leader operates. A leader is the individual who is given the task of directing and coordinating task-relevant activities, or the one who carries the responsibility for performing these functions when there is no appointed leader.

Fiedler relates the effectiveness of the leader to aspects of the group situation. Fred Fiedler's Contingency Model also predicts that the effectiveness of the leader will depend on both the characteristics of the leader and the favourableness of the situation.

(b) Situational Leadership or Hersey – Blanchard's Theory

Situational Leadership Theory (SLT) takes the Distributed Functions Model of leadership one step further by stating that there is a most effective style of leadership in any particular situation. SLT states that Task Behaviour is the extent to which a leader engages in one-way communication by explaining what participants are supposed to do as well as when, where, and how tasks are to be accomplished. Relationship Behaviour is the extent to which a leader engages in two-way communication by providing emotional support, "strokes" and facilitating behaviours.

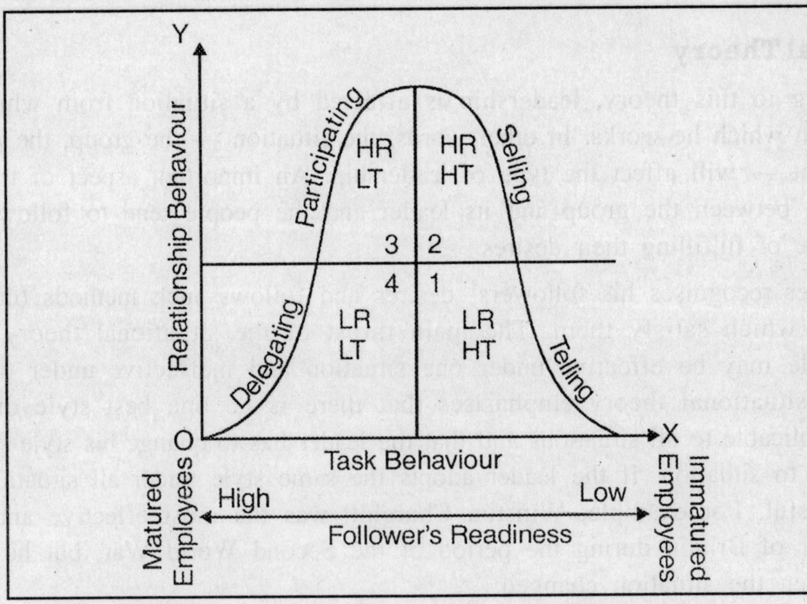

Fig. 9.1. Hersey and Blanchard's Situational Leadership Model

SLT is based on an interplay between:

- The amount of direction (task behaviour) the leaders give,
- the amount of emotional support the leaders provide, and
- the "maturity" level that participants exhibit on a specific task, function, or objective.

Participant Maturity is defined as the capacity to set high but attainable goals (achievement motivation), willingness and ability to take responsibility, and education and/ or experience of and individual or group. These variables should be considered only in relation to a specific task to be performed.

Example: On the first day of a canoeing trip, the participants have a low maturity. Most have never done it before. They don't know the strokes, the terminology, or how to canoe with a partner. Also the group is new to the area and not known each other. On the fourth day of the trip, the group probably has a high degree of maturity in canoeing. They have learned how to successfully maneuver the canoe and how to work together with a partner. They may be able to handle easily the water that you would not have taken them down the first day.

SLT defines four general styles of leadership based on the degree of Task Behaviour and the degree of Relationship Behaviour. See the figure 9.1.

To the 'X' axis, we take the task behaviour and to the 'Y' the relationship behaviour. We do take a continum of immatured employees to matured employees, from right to left. Refer diagram 9.1 for a clear understanding.

High Task/Low Relationship Behaviour: is referred to as "telling" because this style is characterised by one-way communication in which the leader defines the roles of participant(s) and tells them what, how, when, and where to do various tasks.

High Task/High Relationship Behaviour: is referred to as "selling" because with this style most of the direction is still provided by the leader. She also attempts through two-way communication and emotional support to get the participant(s) to buy into decisions that have to be made.

High Relationship/Low Task Behaviour: This is called "participating". Because with this style the leader and the participant(s) now share in decision-making through two-way communication and much facilitating behaviour from the leader since the participant(s) have the ability and knowledge to do the task.

Low Relationship/Low Task Behaviour: is labelled "delegating" because the style involves letting participant(s) "run their own show." The leader delegates since the participant(s) are high in maturity, being both willing and able to take responsibility for directing their own behaviour.

SLT connects the style of leadership with the maturity level of the group. That is, to determine the most effective style of leadership, first determine the maturity level of the group in relation to the specific task. Then draw a line from the maturity level axis to the bell-shaped curve in the drawing. The intersection of the line and the bell curve indicates the most effective leadership style for that situation. As the group matures, the most effective style of leadership changes along the bell curve.

Example: Supposing, you are going on a trip to a place in a group. On the first day of a trip,the participants have a low maturity when it comes to setting up a camp. The most effective leadership style is High Task/Low Relationship (Telling) since participants need to be taught how and where to set things up. On the fourth day of the trip, the group probably has a high degree of maturity in relation to setting up camp. In this case the most effective leadership style is Low Task/Low Relationship (Delegating) since the participants can handle it on their own.

The important point to remember regarding SLT is that *there is no one "best" way to be a leader*. Rather, from one situation to the next there is a *most effective style*. As situations change, the tasks change and so do the maturity levels of the individual or group in relation to the task. Thus, throughout the trip,you will be changing your style in order to provide the most effective leadership. This also does not mean that using another style of the bell curve is "wrong" but it probably will be less effective or appropriate. On the fourth day of the trip, the participants know what to do about setting up camp and are good at doing it themselves. If the leader(s) use a High Task/Low Relationship style the participants are likely to wonder why they are being "told" what to do and may get frustrated or angry with the leader(s).

As the group matures they take on more responsibility for running the group both in terms of tasks and relationships. The Distributed Functions Model comes in here because the participants have begun to take on many of the leadership roles originally provided by the leaders. As much as possible it is a goal to move to a Delegating style (as long as the participants are ready for it) since this helps to facilitate growth through the Cycle of Change.

Use of different leadership styles may vary with:

- Age of group
- Motivation of participants
- Trip situations/activities
- Safety issues

Example: Assume that you are teaching skills to the group. When teaching an important skill, you would be more task-oriented. Also in any emergency situation you need to take quick charge of things via the task-oriented style. Remember to use your "leader's radar" to assess not only the state of maturity of the group but also the maturity of each individual. You may need to use one style with the entire group and different styles with individuals within the group.

Thus, the situational theory, says that a successful leader will act according to the prevailing situation and mood of followers (workers) at that point of time. The theory denotes that it is a function of leader, workers and situations.

(c) Path Goal Leadership Theory

The American psychologist, Robert House proposed this theory. **The Path Goal Theory** contends that the leader must motivate subordinates by: **(1) emphasising the relationship between the subordinates' own needs and the organizational goals; (2) clarifying and facilitating the path subordinates must take to fulfill their own needs as well as the organisation's needs.**

House's theory also attempts to predict the effect that structuring behavior will have under different conditions. Based on assumptions from Vroom's Expectancy Theory, this model explains how behavior of the leader causes expectancies/motivations in the subordinate that create effort and satisfaction. The rationale is that followers will perform better if they think they are capable, and if they perceive the work will get results and be worth the effort.

In choosing which of the leadership behaviours to use, two variables influence the choice: the subordinate's characteristics, and the characteristics of the task. The leader behaviour is contingent on these characteristics, making this a situational leadership theory. No one leadership behaviour works for motivating every person and the leader supplies what is missing to motivate the follower. After this initial assessment of the follower and the task, the leader then helps the follower define goals and then reach them in the most efficient way. Leaders may even adapt their styles with an individual during the completion of a task, if one part of the job needs a different motivation from another.

Although it is a complex and sometimes confusing theory, it reminds leaders to continually think of their central purposes as a leader: to help define goals, clarifies paths to get there, remove obstacles that may exist, and provide support and encouragement for achievement of goals. Most of the responsibility is on the leader however, and there is little emphasis identified for the follower. Some argue this kind of leadership may be counterproductive over time, resulting in learned helplessness.

Path Goal theory is one of the most respected approaches of understanding leadership. It is a direct extension of **expectancy theory** of motivation. It proposes that the leader is a key individual in bringing about improved **subordinate motivation, satisfaction** and **performance.** According to this theory, the leader's job is to assist his or her followers in attaining their goals and provide the direction or support needed to ensure that their goals are compatible with the overall objectives of the group or organisation.

The **Path goal theory** of leadership suggests that the primary functions of a leader are to make valued or desired awards available in the workplace and to clarify for the subordinate, the kinds of behaviour that will lead to goal accomplishment and valued rewards — that is **the leader should clarify the path to goal attainment.**

According to this theory, the leader's behaviour is acceptable to group members to the degree that they view it as an immediate source of satisfaction or as a means of future satisfaction.

According to House, there are four types of leadership styles depending on the situation. Four Styles of Leading Subordinates are:

1. **Directive:** The leader directs and there is no subordinate participation in decision-making. The directive leader lets subordinates know what is expected, or gives specific guidance on how to accomplish tasks.
2. **Supportive:** The leader is friendly and shows concern for the needs of followers (subordinates).
3. **Participative:** The leader consults with group members and uses suggestions from subordinates (group members) before making decisions.
4. **Achievement-oriented:** The leader sets challenging goals and expects followers to perform at their highest level.

In **Directive Leadership,** the leader gives specific guidance of performance to subordinates. In **Supportive Leadership,** the leader is friendly and shows concern for the subordinates. In **Participative Leadership,** the leader consults with subordinates and considers their suggestions and in **Achievement-oriented Leadership,** the leader sets high goals and expects subordinates to have high-level performance.

The information given in the following box is an example of a great individual who overcome his disability with positive attitude and became a popular leader.

> Jerry White is the co-founder of Survivor Corps (formerly Landmine Survivors New Work). In 1984, he lost his leg in a landmine explosion while visiting Israel. After this experience he has championed the cause of survivorship and became a leader in the International Campaign to ban Landmines. In 1997 he shared the Nobel Peace Prize with Jody Williams for his efforts. He recently published a book called *I Will Not Be Broken: Five Steps to Overcoming a Life Crisis.*

The path goal theory, unlike Fiedler's theory, suggests that these four styles are used by the same leader in different situations.

In this theory, the most important factor is the way the leader affects the path between subordinate's behaviour and goals. The leader can affect the path by performing the following:

1. Recognising and stimulating subordinate's need for rewards over which the leader has some control.
2. Rewarding goal achievement.
3. Supporting subordinates' efforts to achieve the goals.
4. Helping to reduce frustrating barriers to achieving goals.
5. Increasing the opportunities for personal satisfaction for subordinates. Basically, the leader attempts to help the subordinate to find the best path, to set challenging goals and to remove stressful barriers along the path or way.

Modifying Levels of Maturity

Developmental Approach: Maturity can be increased by the leaders using a little less task behaviour (direction) allowing the participant(s) to take on more responsibility. If this responsibility is well handled, the leader should encourage the participant(s) with a slight increase in relationship behaviour (encouragement). *Keep in mind that the movement towards changing leadership styles must be gradual.* As the participant(s) reach moderate levels of maturity, the leaders can begin to reduce both task behaviour and relationship behaviour. The reduction in relationship behaviour means that the participant(s) have reached a point where they are confident enough and sharing enough among themselves that the leaders do not need to provide so much.

Regressive Approach: It is possible that as the situation changes the groups maturity can decrease. If this occurs, the leader(s) must modify their style in the opposite direction on the bell curve by increasing task and relationship behaviour.

Example: On the fourth day of the trip it is pouring rain. When the group gets into camp, everyone just stands around and somewhat mopey. Even though they know what to do, the weather reduced their zeal and their maturity level has decreased. The leaders need to become more directive in terms of task behaviour to get camp set up and to increase relationship behaviour to help lift people's spirits.

Leader's Behaviour and Styles

All leaders are not alike. Situational theory reveals that they cannot stick on to one behavioural pattern to lead the organisation or his team. His behaviour should be versatile and be adaptable to any type of situation that occurs. Versatility here refers to changing behaviour according to the changing organisational scenario or changing attitude of his team members. Leader's behaviour, thus, will change according to the circumstances that he confronts.

The behavioural pattern which a leader adopts to direct the behaviour of members in an enterprise for achieving the organisation goals is known as the style of leadership. Different leadership styles may be adopted by the leaders at different times and in different circumstances. Among the different leadership styles, the four important leadership styles are: *(i) autocratic or authoritarian, (ii) democratic, (iii) laissez-faire,* and *(iv) Transformational.* A brief explanation of these three styles is as follows:

1. Autocratic or Authoritarian Leader: The autocratic leader is one who centralises the decision-making power in himself and gives orders to his employees and also insists also insists that they should be obeyed. He decides policies for the group without consulting the group and also asks the group to take steps as per policies determined by him. He does not delegate authority and runs the whole show by himself. He does not inform the employees the purpose of the orders given to them and does not inform them about the future plans. He expects his employees to obey him blindly and without question and has no regard for them and does not like to seek their suggestions or advice. Such leadership is negative because the followers are uninformed, insecure and afraid of leader's authority. Autocratic leadership can be of two types. They are:

(a) Strict autocrat: A strict autocrat is one who relies on negative influences and gives order which must be obeyed by the subordinates without question. His method of influencing subordinate behaviour is through negative motivation, that is, by imposing penalty, criticising subordinates, etc.

(b) Benevolent autocrat: A benevolent autocrat is one who uses a positive motivation style. He disperses rewards to his group. This type is effective in getting higher productivity and in developing good human relationships.

The main advantages of autocratic leadership style are:

(a) Some employees get satisfaction by working under centralised authority sitaution and strict discipline.

(b) As the decisions are taken by a single person, it permits quick decision-making.

The disadvantages of this style are:

(a) Because of the strictness and negative motivational style, the employees dislike it.

(b) Lack of motivation, low morale, frustration and insecurity affect organisational efficiency.

(c) There is no scope for individuality and initiative.

(d) Future leaders in the organisation do not develop.

This style of leadership is unpopular and it is resented and resisted by the employees.

2. Participative or Democratic Leader: A democratic leader is one who takes decisions in consultation with his subordinates. He emphasises consultation with and participation of his subordinates and encourages initiative from them. He also seeks their advice and opinions on matters which affect them and their jobs.

He does not take a unilateral decision and decentralises his decision-making process and also authority. Participative leaders have a high concern for people and work.

The various advantages of participative leadership are:

(a) It increases the acceptance of management's ideas and reduces resistance to change.

(b) As the ideas and suggestions of employees are considered for decision-making, they are highly motivated and their morale also is high.

(c) The decisions are implemented wholeheartedly and the employees productivity is increased.

(d) It reduces the number of grievances of employees.

(e) It seeks to evolve a self-regulating and self-disciplining mechanism.

(f) As the subordinates are involved in the decision-making process, there is a possibility of making better decisions.

(g) Good relationship between the leader and the followers can take place.

Some of the limitations of this style of leadership are:

(a) Lower level of employees may not understand the complex nature of organisation and hence their participation cannot be effective.

(b) This style of leadership can at times be dilatory and subject to pulls and pressures from different groups.

As the advantages are more than the disadvantages, most employees prefer this style of leadership.

3. Laissez-faire or free-rein style: Under this style of leadership, the leader entrusts the decision-making authority to his subordinates. He does not direct and hardly makes any contribution to the overall effort. He avoids using power and leaves it to his subordinates to establish the goals and work out the plan to attain the goals. While the group members provide their own motivation, the manager usually contacts the outside sources and brings information and material which the members of the group require to perform their job.

This style of leadership can be adopted only if the subordinates have a sincere desire to discharge their responsibilities, and are highly competent and duty conscious and motivated to do the job even without any direction by the manager. Such instances, of course, either do not exist or are found to be rare. Hence, this style is used very rarely in business concerns.

4. Transformational Style: Because of change in organisational structure, (*i.e.*, organisations becoming flat or tall). The leaders should change their's as well as their follower's behaviour to "transform" the organisation as per the need. Converting the existing structure to the new desired structure to run the organisation successfully, is a challenging task for the leader. Besides changing his behaviour to adopt to new environment, he should also transform the followers to work as per changed plan. Transforming the mindset of fellow workers and make them adopt to new work norms and work effectively and efficiently is the main theme of transformational leadership style.

In the process of conversion or tansformation, the leader has to instill new organisational values and integrity in the minds of fellow workers and make them understanding their duties to be performed in new environment. This style, develops relationship have an open communication system and considers team building. The new vision of the changed organisation structure have to be understood by team members. They should work according to the priorities enshrined in the vision statement and they have to know as to what happens it they donot work as per the listed priorities.

The leader, after preparing the vision statement with in the framework of new objectives set, he/she has to formulate the policies and work methods and procedures to be followed by the workers as per the vision statement one the whole, the leader has to transform the whole organisational activities as per new structure and objectives.

This is called "Transormational leadership" style. Because of changes that are taking place in global business practices, "Transformational Leadership" style is being adopted in many organisations and has become an attractive style.

CONTINUUM OF LEADERSHIP STYLES

In actual practice, we hardly find leadership styles which can be classified under the categories stated above and what we find is a blend of different leasership styles or overlapping of the various leadership styles. Way back in 1957, Harvard Business Review published an article on "How to choose a leadership pattern" authored by Tannenbaum and Schmidt who have depicted a broad range of styles on a continuum. moving from authoritarian leadership behaviour, at one end, to free-rein on the other. In this broad range they show the types of behaviour in which a leader can adopt any one behaviour that is suitable to a situation. This is considered to be highly recognised article on leadership behaviour. The degree if freedom enjoyed by a leader and his followers in decision-making is shown in continuum. This continuum shows seven types of behaviours, which are shown in the following diagram:

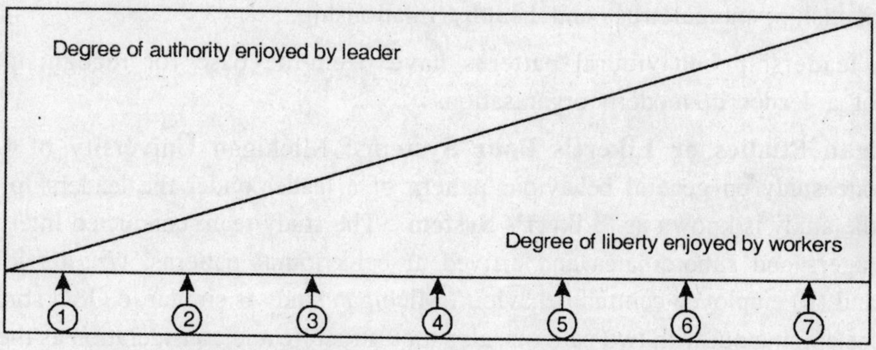

Fig. 9.2. Continuum of Leader-workers Behaviour.

1. The leader takes the decision : He identifies and analyses the problem. Leader asks the workers to implement it. Workers do not have any opinion in the decision.

2. The manager "sells" the decisions : This means that after taking decision by himself, he/she persudes the workers to implement it.

3. Leader presents ideas and invites question : In this behaviour type, leader presents his decision to fellow workers and allows them to put questions on decision. However, he persuades to accept his decision. Some element of participation is provided to workers.

4. Presents tentative decision that is subject to change : Leader analyses the problem, takes a temporary decision and place it before workers for discussion and finalise the decision afterwards.

5. Presents the problem, gets suggestion and then makes the decision : In this style of leader behaviour, decision-making is participatory one in which workers also analyse the problem and offer solutions. Then the leader takes the final decision considering workers opinion.

6. The leader defines the limits and asks the group to make a decision: This style allows the leader to have group decision on the identified problem. The group decision should be within the limits set by the leader. Such decisions are accepted with or without modification.

7. The leader permits the group to make decision within prescribed limits: In this, the group completely, makes the decision. The leader will also be acting as group member.

General Behaviour

General behaviour of leaders are found out by two empirical studies made by Ohio State University popularly known as OSU studies and another by Michigan University, known as Michigan Studies.

Structural aspects, besides formulating the relationship between the leader and fellow workers, state the well-defined work procedures that are to be strictly followed by workers in discharging their duties.

Consideration depicts that a leader should exhibit in his behaviour, respect for co-workers, friendship, mutual trust and healthy relationship.

These leadership behavioural patterns have been the base for recognising general behaviour of a leader in modern organisations.

Michigan Studies or Likert's Four Systems: Michigan University of USA, also conducted one study on general behaviour pattern of a leader under the leadership of Rennis Likert and the study is known as "**Likert's System**". The study team conducted interviews with leaders/managers and subordinates and arrived at behavioural patterns, *viz.*, (i) job-centered behaviour, and (ii) employee-centred behaviour. Michigan study is similar to OSU study and this study, besides coming out with two patterns, also took structure and consideration as their premise for study.

Job-centred behaviour focuses primarily on the work of a subordinate. The attention of a leader will be on the efficiency of work of a worker.

Employee-centred behaviour considers the personal needs of the workers. In this leadership behaviour pattern, harmoneous relations will have to be developed between workers and leader to achieve organisational objectives. For this, healthy and co-operative work teams have to be developed by the leaders. Considerations and structural aspects are revealed by OSU studies also play wital role in designing these patterns. Accordingly following four patterns prevail showing the effectiveness of each pattern.

Four Styles of Leadership

(a) Low structure and high consideration.
(b) High structure and high consideration.
(c) High structure and low consideration.
(d) Low structure and low consideration.

Managerial Grid

"Managerial Grid" is an Organisational Development" (OD) concept. However this has close relationship with leadership. A leader, in the process of developing the organisation considers managerial grid as one of the tools for development. In this grid, different managerial or leadership styles are described. As in case of OSU and Likert's Studies, grid is developed on the attitudes of a leader. Two attitudinal variables which act as premise for managerial grid are: (i) concern for people and (ii) concern for production. These two variables are projected on 1 to 9 point scale horizontally and vertically. Five leadership/managerial styles are identified in this grid, *viz.*, 1-1, 1-9, 5-5, 9-1 and 9-9. Following diagram clearly shows these styles.

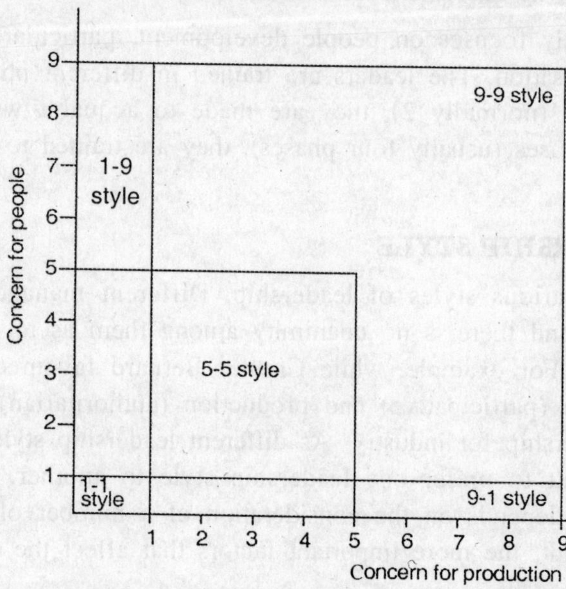

Fig. 9.3. Managerial Grid Showing Five Managerial Styles

In this diagram, five leadership styles are shown.

(i) 1-1 style (one point for concern for people and one point for production) states that minimum equal effort (for both concern for people and production) is put to achieve the organisation goal.

(ii) 1-9 style says that a leader should give maximum attention to people and less effort for production to have healthy and friendly organisation which can achieve its goals. This also means that production process is sound enough in that situation to have a sustainable growth. Leader focuses more on people.

(iii) 5-5 style depicts that both people and production are balanced. Morale of people will be at a satisfactory level and production process is normal. In this style, leader's attention is equal to both variables.

(iv) 9-1 style, production process needs maximum attention. The leader has to organise the production process in such a manner that workers' work efficiently and have minimum degree of interference in the work process. There is more reliability of workers.

(v) 9-9 style, people are fully committed to the assigned task and production is achieved without disturbance. This means that a leader/manager motivates people for full commitment, develops healthy interpersonal relationship through mutual trust and respect to attain maximum production.

Managerial Grid is a People-Production Combination to be followed by a leader. Different situations prevail in different organisations. Hence, the grid shows different combinations of people and production, of which any suitable combinations can be adopted by a leader according to the situation he/she faces at a given point of time. As per the grid shown above, 9-9 style can be the best style that a leader can follow. Because, maximum effort is put by him/her to manage people and production to achieve the organisational goal. But in situations where variables are varying, he has to choose a suitable style which falls with in the grid.

Managerial Grid firmly focuses on people development, particularly the development on teamwork in the organisation. The leaders are trained in different phases to achieve 9-9 style. In the initial phases (normally 2), they are made to acquaint with managerial grid concept and in the later phases (usually four phases), they are trained to achieve 9-9 pattern of leader behaviour.

CHOOSING A LEADERSHIP STYLE

We have observed various styles of leadership. Different management experts have suggested different styles and there is no unanimity among them as to which are the most suitable for an enterprise. For example, while Chester Bernard favoured a leadership style having concern for people (participative) and production (authoritarian) Mr. Rensis Likert suggested democratic leadership for industry. As different leadership styles have their merits and demerits, it is difficult to prefer one leadership style to another. The selection of a particular leadership style depends on the consideration of a number of factors. According to Tannenbaum and Schmidt, the more important factors that affect the choice of a suitable style of leadership are:

1. Forces in the Manager: These include manager's confidence in his subordinates, own leadership inclination, feeling of security in an uncertain situation, etc.

2. Forces in the Subordinates: These include readiness of subordinates to assume responsibility for making decisions, need of subordinates for independence, interest in the problem at hand, knowledge to deal with the problem, etc.

3. Forces in the Situation: These include group objectiveness, complexities of the problem itself, type of organisation, etc.

Today, many managers believe that adopting a particular leadership style is difficult because of their complexity and are represented by unique traits or behaviours. Now they feel that effective leadership behaviour depends on the situation. Here also some feel that the managers (leaders) should change themselves to the situation and some others feel that it is difficult to alter the leaders and hence situation itself must adjust to the leader. This situational theory makes one point very clear, that effective leadership cannot be defined by one factor. Leader's personal traits are not undermined. But this theory states that every factor must be considered in the context of situation.

LEADER-MANAGER DISTINCTION

Are leaders and managers are different? Or are there any overlapping functions similar to each other? These questions arise many a time and hence a brief analysis about these two roles are made.

Some writers treat managership and leadership as synonymous. But there are distinct differences between these two terms. They are as follows:

1. While management (manager) is responsible for various management functions such as planning, organising, staffing, directing and controlling which relate to the total organisation; leadership (leader), is one of the aspects of directing that influences the group in achieving the goals set by the management.
2. Management formulates broad policies to guide the operations of the enterprise, whereas leadership initiates activity for the accomplishment of its goals.
3. There can be leadership (leader) for completely unorganised groups, but generally, management (manager) is associated with the organised structure.
4. Leadership is the process of influencing the behaviour of others regardless of reasons. It may be for one's own goals and may or may not be congruent with the goals of the organisation, whereas management is concerned with the organisational goals.
5. While management is concerned with the promotion of the welfare of the entire organisation without given scope to vested interests, leadership influences the performance of individuals which will contribute to the attainment of group goals.

From the above, we can conclude that leadership is a part of management but not all of it. A strong leader can be a weak manager (if he is weak in planning or in any managerial duty) and similarly, a strong manager can be a weak leader.

Characteristics of Managers and Leaders

Leader	*Manager*
1. Innovates the task	Administers the task
2. Has original thinking	A True-copy performer
3. Designer and developer	A monitor and maintainer
4. Focuses on systems and structure	Focuses on people
5. Inspires trust	Relies on control
6. Long-range perspective	Short-range view
7. Asks what and why	Asks how and when
8. Eye on the horizon	Eye on the bottom line
9. Originates	Initiates
10. Challenges the status quo	Accepts the status quo
11. Own person	Classic good soldier
12. Does the right thing	Does things right

(**Source**: "Managing the Dream: Leadership in 21st Century," Warren G. Bennis, Journal of Organisational Change Management, Vol. 2. No. 1, 1989.)

Leader-Boss Distinction	
Leader	*Boss*
1. Leader is always affectionate towards his team members. He treats them with "LOVE AND AFFECTION."	Boss creates FEAR in his fellow workers. This leads to develop animosity and ranover in his fellow workers against him.
2. Leader develops good feeling about his co-workers which increases productivity of workers. He works on the concept of "GOODWILL."	Boss always works on "AUTHORITY." This makes him to forget human aspect which results in fall in productivity of his team mates.
3. Leader is one who "INSPIRES" his fellow workers to achieve the goals for which they are working together	Boss will not allow his team to express and adapt their opinion in their assigned task. He "DICTATES AND DRIVE" them.
4. Leader works with humility and address a group with "WE."	Boss, on the other hand, is egoistic and address the group "I Worked," "I Did" etc.
5. Leader focuses on a work and tells "WHAT IS RIGHT OR WRONG."	Boss focusses on human beings and tells "WHO IS RIGHT OR WRONG"
6. Leader knows his task and how to accomplish it.	Boss knows as how the task is accomplished
7. Leader commands respect.	Boss demands respect and sometimes is beyond respect.

(**Source:** Effective Executive—The ICFAI University Press, Jan. 2006, p.24.)

SUMMARY

1. A leader is a person who guides the organisation on sound lines and helps it attain its objectives.
2. The nature of a leader is to induce and develop responsibility and initiative among his subordinates. He has to motivate the employees. He should be capable of handling employees.
3. The nature of the leader is identified from his personal characters, the situation in which he works and the tasks he performs.
4. Leader will have different types of skills: (i) Human skills, (ii) Conceptual skills and (iii) Technical skills. Besides these three major skills, he possesses, marketing skills, financial skills, production skills, and integrating skills.
5. A good leadership is a must for the success of business. A good leader motivates his subordinates, creates confidence in them, sustains their enthusiasm, increases their morale, ensures high productivity and stability in the organisation, help in the use of formal authority effectively and in achieving organisational goals.
6. A formal leader holds a post in the organisation and is appointed by the management while an informal leader does not occupy any post in the organisation and is chosen by the workers themselves. It is desirable for the management to recognise a formal leader because of his influence on the workers.
7. Functions of a leader are: goal-setter, planner, executive, expert, external group representative, surrogate for individual responsibility, controller of internal relationship within the organisation, administration of rewards and punishments, arbitrator and mediator, exemplor, symbol of the group, father figure and scapegoat.

8. Number of leadership theories have been developed by many thinkers on management. Of these theories, important ones are: (i) trait theory, (ii) behavioural theory, and (iii) situational theory which includes: (a) Fiedler's contingency theory, (b) Hersey-Blanchard's situational leadership and (c) Path goal leadership theory.
9. Researches carried out by many behavioural scientists have resulted in various theories of leadership. Some of them are: (a) The Trait Theory, (b) The Behavioural Theory, (c) Situation Theory, (d) Transformation style, (e) Likert system and (f) Continuum of leadership style.
10. The behavioural pattern which a leader adopts to direct the behaviour of organisation members achieving the goals of the organisation is known as "Leadership Style." Three important leadership styles are: (a) Autocratic or Authoritarian, (b) Democratic and (c) *Laissez faire*. The styles of leadership are: forces in the manager,forces in the subordinates and forces in the situation.
11. Skill of a leader consists of an instinct to lead and take initiative, quick grasp of the situation, power of judgement, sense of responsibility, moral quality, flexibility, intellectual capacity, technical competence, ability to inspire, well-versed in human relations, will power, integrity, enthusiasm, physical fitness, friendliness, etc.

STUDY QUESTIONS

1. What do you mean by leadership?
2. State four skills required by a leader.
3. Give the meaning of formal leader.
4. Give the meaning of informal leader.
5. State the central point of trait theory of leadership.
6. Mention the theme of behavioural theory.
7. What is the essence of Situational theory of leadership.
8. Name the different styles of leadership.
9. Give the meaning of autocratic leader.
10. Who is a benevolent autocrat?
11. Analyse the features of a leader.
12. Give an analytical note on various types of skills that a leader should possess.
13. Write a note on the following:
    (i) Human skills, (ii) Conceptual skills, (iii) Technical skills, (iv) Managerial Grid.
14. Distinguish between leadership and manager
15. Write a note on importance of leadership.
16. Distinguish between formal and informal leaders.
17. State the functions of a leader.
18. Analyse: (i) Trait theory, (ii) Behavioural theory, (iii) Situational theory, (iv) Continuum of Leadership style and (v) Likert's system.
19. Give an analytical note on leadership styles.
20. Briefly explain the types of skills a leader should possess.
21. Give an explanatory note on various leadership theories.
22. Explain: (i) Formal and Informal leaders and (ii) Various styles of leadership.

Leadership Skills – Self Assessment Exercises

Indicate whether the following statements are "True" or "False"

1. Leading and Managing are one and the same. ☐

2. The VYJ model suggests that a leader should match one of the five, decision-making styles to the particular situation faced by the leader. ☐
3. According to the path goal theory of leadership, a leader should carefully inform followers about the rewards that are made available to them by the organisation and then permit them to choose their own methods of earning the rewards. ☐
4. The myths that "leaders are born, not made and that there is one best leadership style" has been proved to be true by Fiedler's studies. ☐
5. Transformational leaders modify organisation by precisely carrying out strategic plans and emphasising only the follower's values to a small extent. ☐
6. Eventhough a leader may have little or no impact on the outcome in some situations, the leader is nevertheless an important part of management. ☐
7. Leaders in modern organisations have been confronting many many situations which were rarely encountered by organisational leaders of the past. ☐
8. Behavioural approach to leadership emphasises the assumption that a good leader is born, not made. ☐
9. A leadership style is the behaviour a leader exhibits while guiding his followers in appropriate directions. ☐
10. The life cycle theory of leadership model does not consider the Maturity level of the followers. ☐

Answer key: 1. F, 2. T, 3. F, 4. F, 5. F, 6. F, 7. F, 8. F, 9. T, 10. F

Practical Exercise-1

1. "Transformational leaders are the visionaries who challenge people to achieve exceptionally high levels of morality, motivation and performance" ***- James McGregor on "Leadership"***
2. "The Servant Leaders: Leaders are servants first. They articulate goals. They inspire trust. They know how to listen. They are masters of positive feedback. They relay on foresight. They emphasise on personal development."

   Rober K. Greenleaf, Management Research, Writing on the concept of "The servant as a leader". (1970)
3. "Leadership is not a basket of tricks or skills. It is the quality and character and courage of the person who is the leader. It is a matter of ethics and moral compass, the willingness to remain highly vulnerable".

   - Francis Hasselbein (Lady responsible for revitalising the girl scouts in USA).

Questions

(i) State how transformational leadership matches with Hasselbein's description of leadership quality.

(ii) Does she mean servant leader? Analyse with an imaginary situation.

Practical Exercise-2

Visit a successful business venture and analyse the leadership quantities of Chairman/President/CEO/Functional managers or even first time supervisors, as the case may be and assess how their leadership quality has an impact on the growth of the enterprise.

10

COMMUNICATION

LEARNING OBJECTIVES

After reading this chapter, you should be able to know:

- Communication – The Concept
- Directions of Communication.
- Barriers to Communication.
- Organisation and Communication
- Channels of Communication.
- Informal Communication or Grapevine.

COMMUNICATION — THE CONCEPT

Every business concern has certain specified objectives. For achieving these objectives, there is a need for co-ordination among the employees who are engaged in the different activities of the concern. This co-ordination is possible only through communication which provides for exchange of information, ideas, facts and opinions.

Communication has been defined by a number of writers and here we give some of the definitions:

"Communication is an intercourse by words, letters, symbols or messages; and is a way that one organisation member shares meaning and understanding with another."

— **Koontz and O'Donnell**

"Communication is an exchange of facts, ideas, opinions or emotions by two or more persons."

— **Newmann and Summer**

"Communication is a sum of all the things one person does when he wants to create understanding in the minds of another. It involves a systematic and continuous process of telling, listening and understanding."

— **Allen Louis A.**

Thus, communication involves interchange of thought or information among persons in an organisation and is a systematic and continuous process of telling, listening and understanding.

The proper understanding of a message is an important aspect of communication. If it is not understood by the receiver in the same way in which the sender of the message wants him to understand, there may be confusion, chaos, and organisational inefficiency, leading to non-fulfillment of goals which are set by the business concern. In view of this, communication is not merely the transmission of message from one to another but also the correct interpretation and understanding of the message. In the words of Theo Haimann, "Communication is the process of passing information and understanding from one person to another .... It is the process of imparting ideas and making oneself understood by others."

ORGANISATION AND COMMUNICATION

Communication is a process which transmits information to the target person or group. Without communication, no activity in the organisation or elsewhere will take place. Business organisations have recognised the importance of communication and it is increasing considerably.

The Hawthorne experiments made people realise that communication among persons working at different levels in a business concern is essential for achieving the objectives of a business. It is said that the world of modern management is the world of communication and the success of a manager in performing his duties depends on his ability to communicate. According to Paul Pigors and Myers, about 70% of an executive's time is spent on communication. Today, communication has become one of the important aspects of management and it helps the management in attaining the following:

1. Helps in achieving co-ordination: Modern business firms which are organised on a large scale consist of a large number of workers working on the basis of division of labour and specialisation. To attain the goals of the business unit, there is need for co-ordination among workers and this can be achieved only through communication. According to Mary Curling Niles, "Good communications are essential to co-ordination. They are necessary upward, downward and sideways, through all the levels of authority and advice for the transmission, interpretation and adoption of policies, for the sharing of knowledge and information and for the more subtle needs of good morale and mutual understanding."

2. Helps in smooth working: Communication helps in the smooth running of an enterprise. To achieve the goals of an enterprise, co-operative action of the persons working in its different activities is necessary. Co-operative action in turn depends on the communication process prevailing in the organisation. Herbert G. Hicks has pointed out that "communication is basic to an organisation's existence — from the birth of the organisation on through its continuing life. When communication stops, organised action comes to an end." According to G.R. Terry, "communication serves as a lubricant fostering the smooth operations of the management."

3. Increased managerial efficiency: It is said that about 75% of the manager's time is spent on communication to others of business targets, rules, policies, etc. Communication helps the manager in performing his duties quickly and systematically and also facilitates in increasing his effectiveness.

4. Helps in decision-making: For taking decision by the management, and also for its effective implementation, a good communication system in the enterprise is a primary requirement.

requirement. Information from different levels which helps the process of decision-making is received through the system of communication. Again, these decisions are passed on through communication to those who are involved in executing them. Chester Bernard has rightly stated that "the first executive function is to develop and maintain a system of communication."

5. Helps in maintaining industrial peace: Very often, lack of communication or improper communication may result in industrial disputes between management and workers. Communication helps both management and workers in putting forth their views to each other and thus it facilitates in maintaining industrial peace.

6. Helps in recruitment process: Communication is needed in the recruitment process to acquaint potential employees with the merits of working for the enterprise. The recruits are told about the company organisation structure, its policies and practices. After selecting the candidates for the jobs, communication is needed at the time of orientation to make candidates acquaint themselves with peers, superiors and with company rules and regulations.

7. Helps employees to perform effectively: It is needed to enable the employees to perform their functions effectively. Employees are required to know their job relationship and importance to the overall operation. This knowledge makes it easy for them to identify themselves with the organisation's mission. If a nurse in a hospital knows why she has to follow certain procedures with a patient and how this relates to the total therapy programme for him, it is much easier for her to develop an ideological commitment to the hospital.

8. Helps to acquaint subordinates with their evaluation: Communication is needed to acquaint the subordinates with the evaluation of their contribution to enterprise activity. It is a matter of some motivational importance for the subordinates to know from their superior how they stand and what the future may hold for them. This appraisal if intelligently carried out will boost the morale of the subordinates.

9. Helps in teaching employees about personal safety: Communication is needed to teach employees about their personal safety on the job. This is essential to reduce accidents, to lower compensation, to minimise legal costs and to reduce recruitment and training costs for replacement.

10. Helps in projecting the image of the enterprise: It is of vital importance in projecting the image of an enterprise in the community. The amount of support which the enterprise receives from its social environment is affected by the information which elite groups and the wider public have acquired about its goals, activities and accomplishments.

11. Helps manager in performing his functions: Communication helps the manager in performing his managerial functions such as planning, organising, staffing, directing and controlling. Planning requires detailed communication among the managerial and other personnel.

Effective communication in important in executing a planned programme and also in controlling the activities with the help of feedback information. Information relating to subordinates' performance is necessary to know whether planned objectives are being realised. Again, in the process of organising, communication plays an important role. It is also an important aid in directing and in motivating the employees. Thus, communication is an indispensable part of the management process.

From the above, we can state that a proper system of communication is essential for the existence and smooth running of an organisation. It may be noted here that in recent years, the importance of communication has been increasing due to certain factors such as increase in the size of organisations, growth of trade unions, technical improvements, emphasis on human relations in industry and increasing importance of social responsibilities of business. Alvin Dodd has rightly remarked that "the number one management problem today is communication."

Communication Process

A communication process involves the following elements:

(a) **Communicator**, *i.e.*, the person who intends to communicate the message to other persons.

(b) **Message**, *i.e.*, the subject matter of communication. This may be opinion, order, appeal, views, suggestions, etc.

(c) **Transmission**, *i.e.*, the act of conveying the message.

(d) **Channel**, *i.e.*, the medium used to transmit the message.

(e) **Receiver**, *i.e.*, the person for whom the message is meant.

(f) **Response**, *i.e.*, replying or reaction of the receiver.

The process of communication is illustrated in Fig. 10.1.

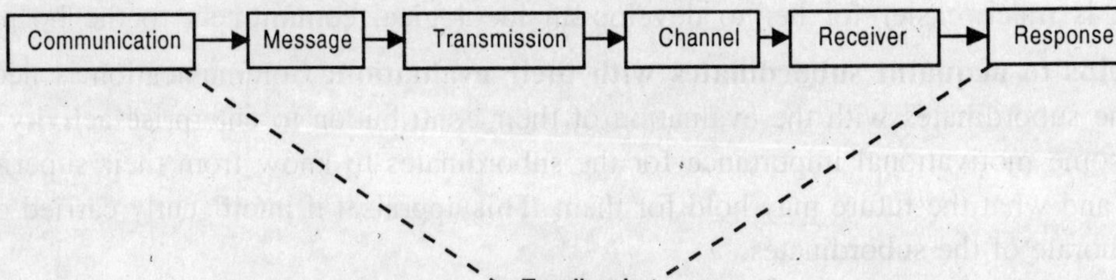

Fig. 10.1. Communication Process.

In this diagram, communication flow is exhibited. It is a general form in which the information flows. Information flow in organisations will be between the managers, between the managers and subordinates, and between the subordinates. All these three types of flow of information will have a standard channel as shown in the figure 10.2. All these three types are recognised as "Interpersonel communication," which comprises of three main elements, *viz.*, (*i*) Originator of information called "Encoder," (*ii*) The information sent called message or "signal" and (*iii*) Receiver of message called "Decoder" who implements the message. Figure 10.2 can be redesigned as follows.

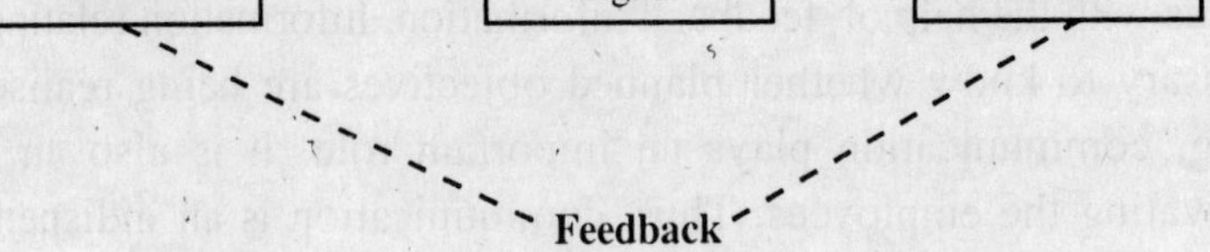

Fig.10.2. Redesigned Communication Process.

In this figure, interpersonal communication starts from Encoder who creates and sends the message/signal and Decoder receives the messages for implementation or can send a feedback to encoder if signal is detrimental to the growth of organisation so that a corrected message as required can be sent.

Encoder is the originator of message who creates at the source and sends it in the form of signal to the destination which is received by Decoder.

Message or signal is the information which Encoder wants to share with his team members to implement it.

Decoder is the person who has to receive the information and implement it or sends it back for correction as per requirement.

In this communication process, communication will be successful when decoder implements and gets the benefit from transmitted message.

Communication will be unsuccessful when signal sent by Encoder will not be beneficial to Decoder and transmitted message is different of the one that is required by Decoder or in ultimate destination. Hence, the feedback.

In the process of communication, "Listening" plays a vital role.

Listening in Communication

One vital aspect of communication is "listening." Without proper listening or simply hearing will be a disturbing aspect of good communication system. We all feel better when we feel listened to. It is more important for us to feel heard than to actually get what we said we wanted. By developing our own listening skills, we can model them to others. Then we will feel heard, understood and respected.

In the organisational context, when an oral message is sent, the receiver, first, should properly listen it, understand it and then retransmit it properly or have dialogue to clearly perceive the message. Listening in this context refers to understanding the message in its full form in order to take correct action as per the message. If the receiver does not understand the message and properly perceive it, the communication is distorted and will have a negative consequence. Therefore, it is stressed that 'listening' should be an essential component of good communication system.

Active Listening

Active listening is a way of listening and responding to another person in such a way that the person feels that he has been really heard. It takes conversation one step further into the feelings of the speaker active listening is not only a learnable skill, it is also an attitude. If you truly want to listen to the people, you need to accept them for who and what they are, not you want them to be. Active listening builds trust and respect between people. It prevents misunderstandings that can lead to conflict, frustration or hurt feelings. Active listening facilitates learning of new things and it will be fascinating.

Active listening needs, rapt attention to perceive clear message, evaluation of your listening with questions and without jumping into conclusions and respond with speaker to make him understand that you have heard him.

Types of Listening

There are three types of listening.

(i) Passive Listening: Listener does not verbally respond to the speaker as he may be engaged otherwise (watching TV, listening to a joke, etc.) while hearing the speaker.

(ii) Active/Reflective Listening: Listener provides verbal and non-verbal feedback in the way of questioning, gestures and paraphrasing. Listener also uses whole body (eyes, relaxed body, etc.) to listen to the speaker.

(iii) Empathetic Listening: Listener projects oneself into the personality of the speaker in order to better understand that person's emotions or feelings.

Empathetic Listening Tips

- Be willing to let the other person dominate the discussion.
- Be attentive to what is being said.
- Be careful not to interrupt the flow of thought.
- Be sensitive to the emotions being expressed.
- Be able to reflect back to the speaker the substance and feelings they have expressed.

Benefits of Empathetic Listening

- It forces people to listen to other and not at each other.
- It avoids misunderstanding between the speaker and listener.
- It builds trust, teamwork, cooperation and trust.
- It enables people to release their emotions in a safe environment.
- It reduces tension and stress.
- It creates a safe environment that is conducive to collaborate problem solving.

Empathetic listening is essential in resolving conflicts. It is a powerful communication system in settling the disputes.

Listening Techniques

Following are the basic techniques used in listening.

(i) Attending/Focusing: Keep your focus on the speaker to better understand him. Do not talk-listen-overlook distructions Do not interrupt — Do not jump into conversion while the other is speaking.

(ii) Responding: Make the speaker know that you are listening. Convey the warmth and caring to encourage the speaker to talk further.

(iii) Controling the emotions: Control your emotional "hot buttons". Certain words, issues, situations can trigger emotions. Messages can be distorted. So, control emotions.

(iv) Restating: Restate the key points of the speaker in your own words. Let it be very short. This makes the speaker that he is heard and provides an opportunity to him to correct the understanding of speakers message by the receiver.

(v) Corrections/Clarifications: As a listener, ask questions on the aspects that you have not understood properly. This makes the speaker confident that you really understand what the speaker is saying. Speaker feels that you are listening and not judging. Questions that are asked should not be threatening, should not be based on assumptions and should encourage elaboration of message by the speaker.

(vi) Feedback: Feedback should be immediate, honest and supportive of the speaker's need. Feedback involves sharing your feelings/reactions to the speaker. Do not advice. It should be only suggestive and speaker should understand that his words are respected.

Barriers to Listening

In communication process, listening will have many disturbances both from outside and from inside. These barriers are to be overcome.

External barriers include noices (distortions) clutter and other interruptions. These are to be avoided while listening.

Internal barriers within listener include past experiences that occur to mind while listening, prejudices, assumptions made, certain attitudes personality traits, sparring (attacking the speaker while talking) perceptual errors etc.

Barriers within the speaker, such as, expectations from the receiver, risk taking, avoidance of certain disclosures speaking in code etc., also distort the good communication system.

These barriers of listering have to be overcome to have sound communication systems.

Good Listening Traits

- Keep an open mind. Set aside your prejudices and opinions.
- If the speaker becomes quiet, allow them the time to gather their thoughts and process information before you jump into the conversation. Periods of silence can be very cathartic.
- Active listening does not mean you agree with, but rather understand, what the other person is saying. Acceptance is different from agreement.
- Acknowledge any personal emotional state. Try to suspend your emotions or just passively listen. All feelings are acceptable, but not all behaviours. A person might express feelings of anger, which is fine. However, it is not okay for a person to physically attack in anger.

Many have not understood the implication of listening in communication process. As understood so far it plays a vital role in communication process and more so in organisational communication system.

COMMUNICATION CHANNEL

Different types of communication channels can be experienced in our activities. Following chart exhibits various forms of communication.

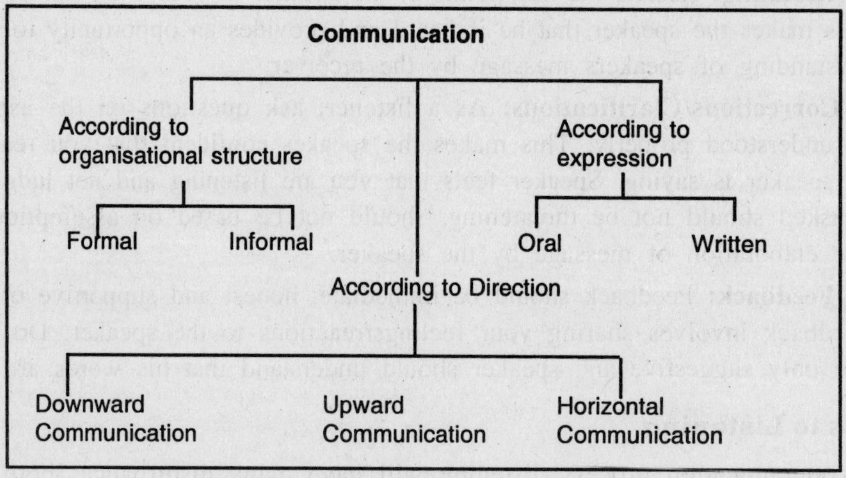

Fig. 10.3. Forms of Communication

1. On the Basis of Organisational Structure

(a) Formal Communication. Communications which are associated with a formal organisation structure and which are to be sent through the formal or officially recognised channels are called formal communications. Generally, orders, instructions, decisions, of the superior officer, etc. are communicated through this channel.

(b) Informal Communication. Informal communications are also known as 'grapevine' communications. In the case of informal communication, the formal channels of communication are not used. In this channel, very often, a person can obtain information which would take a few days for him to receive through the officially recognised organisational channel. Informal communication may be conveyed by a gesture, nod, smile etc.

(c) Non-verbal Communication. This is a type of communication according to which the message will be communicated to the concerned without words. Encoding of thoughts used in this type are facial expressions, vocal tones, gestures, etc. Non-verbal communication method is adopted naturally in all communication systems. Perhaps this is more powerful communication system. Research studies bear testimony to this.

Many decades passed since Albert Meherabian developed a formula which exhibits a relative usage of verbal and non-verbal communication methods. According to this, 0.55 facial expressions, 0.38 vocal tones and 0.07 words are used in a communication process. From this, it can be observed that 0.93 (0.55+0.38) are non-verbal elements of communication system. This clearly indicates that in every communication system, non-verbal factor of communication plays a vital role. But, the communicators should take care of the fact that both verbal and non-verbal communication methods are properly synchronised in communication process. Both elements (verbal and non-verbal) should give the same message and should not contradict each other. If the verbal message communicates the acceptance of an issue to be communicated, non-verbal system should also give acceptance. Not the non-acceptance.

2. On the Basis of Direction of Communication

(a) Downward Communication. In the case of downward communication, the communication flows from the superiors to the subordinates. Communications sent through this channel are generally directives requiring actions to be initiated by the subordinates. These communications include orders, policy directives, instructions, etc.

(b) Upward Communication. In the case of upward communication, communication flows from the subordinates to the superiors. It includes reports, suggestions, reactions of workers, proposals, etc. Upward communication enables the management to evaluate the effectiveness with which its orders have been carried out and also to know the grievances or suggestions of the subordinates.

(c) Horizontal or Lateral Communication. It means communication among the subordinates who are working at the same level of organisation. For example, communication among foremen or superintendents, or functional managers or supervisors is horizontal communication.

(d) Diagonal Communication. It means communication between people who are neither in the same department nor at the same level of organisational hierarchy. In this type, communication cuts across departmental lines (See Fig. 10.4).

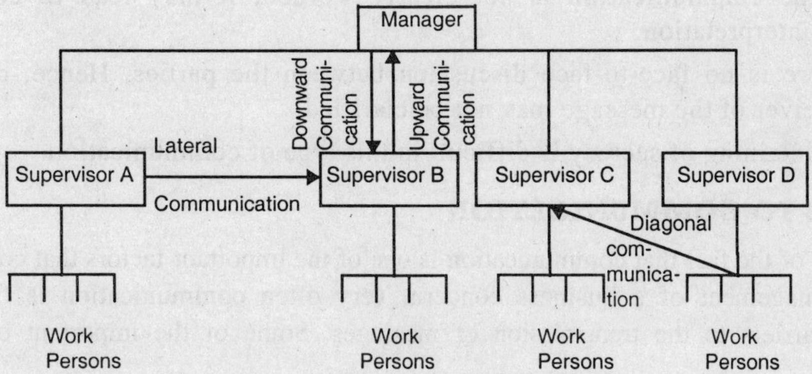

Fig. 10.4. Communication Flow

3. On the Basis of Way of Expression

(i) Oral or Verbal Communication. In the case of oral or verbal communication, communication is made direct face-to-face or through telephone or intercom system. Oral communication has some merits. They are:

(a) It saves time and money.

(b) On-the-spot clarification of any doubt is possible.

(c) Because of personal touch between the communicator and listener, communication is more effective.

(d) While communicating, important points can be emphasised by the communicator.

Some of the disadvantages of oral communication are:

(a) There is no permanent record of communication passing through this device.

(b) Oral communication is not suitable for a subject that has to be kept as a record.

(c) There is greater possibility of communication being misunderstood or misinterpreted, if the communicator is poor in vocal expression.

(d) It is suitable only for communications which are not lengthy.

(ii) Written Communication. Written communications include statements, circulars, letters, reports, memos, manuals etc. Some of the advantages of written communication are:

(a) Written communications can be kept as a permanent record and it can be referred to by the management whenever it wants.

(b) This method is suitable for communications which are lengthy.

(c) As communication is in writing, there is a lesser chance of missing any points in the communication.

(d) This method is suitable for passing of messages to far-off places.

Written communication, however, suffers from certain limitations. They are:

(a) Generally, written communications are more time-consuming,

(b) If the communication is not clearly worded, it may lead to confusion and misinterpretation.

(c) There is no face-to-face discussion between the parties. Hence, doubts of the receiver of the message may not be clarified.

(d) Maintaining of secrecy is difficult in this type of communication.

BARRIERS TO COMMUNICATION

In spite of the fact that communication is one of the important factors that contribute to the efficient management of a business concern, very often communication is faulty because of certain barriers to the transmission of messages. Some of the important barriers are as follows:

1. Badly expressed messages: If the objectives of the message are vague, imprecise, or fail to clarify implications or if the message omits essential information or contains ideas which lack coherence or lack of clarity, the communication will be poor and ineffective.

2. Faulty organisation: The effectiveness of communication largely depends on the nature of organisation prevailing in the concern. If the chain of command is too long, and the span of control is poor and defective, communication will be ineffective. Again, communication is affected because of the rigid application of the medium of formal channel of communication.

3. Use of technical language: There are large numbers of specialist fields such as systems analysis, computers, operations research, etc., in which technical jargon or vocabulary are used to communicate messages. This factor also contributes to poor communication.

4. Filtering: Distance between the sender and the receiver of the message may also affect the effectiveness of communication. As a message has to pass through several persons and several points in the communication channel, there are bound to be alternations or filtration of messages. Koontz and O' Donnel have rightly remarked that "the successive transmissions of the same message are decreasingly accurate."

5. Unclarified assumptions: Uncommunicated assumptions underlie practically all messages. Because of this, the receiver of the message may have some assumptions (regarding the message) which are different from the assumptions of the communicator. This may lead to incorrect action or lack of action on the part of the receiver of the message.

6. Distrust of communicator: It is common with some executives to make a number of changes or reverse the messages that are already communicated. The executives may resort to this, if the decision regarding the original communication is not correct. The subordinates who work under such type of superiors may not take such communication seriously and may not act immediately because of their distrust of the superior. Koontz and O'Donell have rightly stated that the "Distrust of a superior for any reason necessarily restricts communication effectiveness."

7. Distortion: The superior officer or manager who communicates the message which he has received from his superior may withhold some part of the information which in his opinion need not be conveyed to his subordinates. Similarly, in the case of upward communication, the officer or manager omits unpleasant information which he has received from his subordinates and conveys to his superior only that part of information which is palatable to his superior (see Fig. 10.5). Thus, his communication will be distorted and the distortion of the message is a barrier to effective communication.

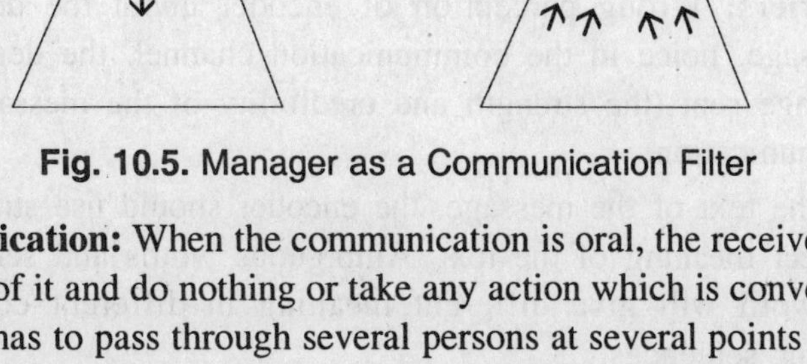

Fig. 10.5. Manager as a Communication Filter

8. Oral communication: When the communication is oral, the receiver of the message may take undue advantage of it and do nothing or take any action which is convenient to him. Further, if the communication has to pass through several persons at several points in the communication channel, some part of information is lost in each transmission, resulting in some loss of meaning in the message.

9. Poor retention: It is said that, normally, employees retain only 50% of the information communicated. Hence, another serious bottleneck of effective communication is the poor retention of information by the employees.

10. Different backgrounds: Different individuals often interpret the same communication differently because of their different backgrounds. Thus when people with different knowledge and experience try to communicate, they often have trouble in getting their meaning across.

11. Inattention: Another common barrier is that many receivers do not pay attention to the messages they receive. One reason for this is selective listening. Selective listening results from the common tendency to block out information that conflicts with what we believe. When we listen to a speech or read a newspaper, we generally pay attention only to those things that conform to our beliefs. Sometimes, people do not pay attention to communication, because of the communication overload or information is unsolicited.

12. Overloaded Information: As the business expands, communication tracks are overloaded with information which will distart the information. This is one of the barriers to communication system. Therefore, managers should supply only essential information to subordinates which is enough to perform the task. This gives some relief to information track and distortion will be minimised.

13. Advanced Technology: Advanced technology is adapted to supply information to the employees. But employees are not well versed with the technology and it will be a hinderance to the good communication system. Therefore, employees are to be trained in the technology adopted. This facilitates workers to adopt themselves to the new technology and communication is well perceived.

14. Multi-language System: In a gloabal market, operators will be coming from different culture and language. English can only facilitate to certain extent the barier created by multi-language adoptation. A person from Germany knows only German language. A dealer from France knows only French. A person from India knows only Hindi. Within India, people coming from Tamil Nadu, use Tamil and a person from Karnataka uses only Kannada. A person from Andhra Pradesh uses only Telegu. Thus, so many languages are used in national and international markets. This is a major barrier to communicate. In a multi-language system, a common language like English has to be adopted for smooth flow of communication. More time is consumed in training different languages to people and managers will have less time to interact with their people. Hence, a common language has to be adopted to have a sound communication system.

15. Other Barriers: Wrong perception of encoder about the decoder while creating and sending the message, noice in the communication channel, the degree of efficiency and meaning of the message sent (the strength and credibility of the message), etc., will also be barriers to the communication.

While creating the text of the message, the encoder should use straightforward language which gives the correct meaning of the text. Ambiguous words and sentences lead to wrong interpretation. One word will give different meaning in different contexts. For example, examine the following sentences.

1. I **function** as a Managing Director in my company.
2. I attend the marriage **function** today.
3. I take class in **functional** english.
4. I have to discharge seveal **functions** in my office.

It we observe the term "Function" in each of the above sentences. It gives different meaning in each sentence. One of the studies an Article "Do you know how to listen?" by Lydia Strong in "Effective communication on the job", in the year 1956 reveal that 500 most common words in English have 4,070 dictionary meanings. Therefore, the sender of the message should create a message considering its efficiency and effectiveness in transmitting the message.

Remedial measures

Many types of barriers to communication analysed so far, need some solutions to make the communication effective. Following remedial measures may help the managers to make their communication more effective.

1. Feedback

Several communication problems occur due to misunderstanding and inaccuracies. This can be avoided by adapting a sound feedback system in the communication process. The feedback may be verbal or non-verbal. Feedback system should include **more** than "Yes" and "No" answers to the questions whether the receiever has understood as to what manager has said. "More" here means that manager in order to determine whether or not the message was received as intended, he can ask the receiver to repeat the message as said by him. If the receiver has not understood the message, the accuracy and understanding of the message has to be enhanced. Feedback covers subtler methods than asking direct questions. General comments by the receivers to a message can give a better feedback. Important methods of feedback are, performance appraisals, salary reviews, promotions, etc. Feedback need not be conveyed in words. Actions are more effective than words. For example: you ask your team members to submit a sales report within certain time period. If it *is* not submitted by some member within the stipulated time, you have to understand that it is a feedback to you to clarify further the intitial initiative.

2. Language

Language may be one of the key barriers to the communication. The messages sent to the subordinates should be clear and understandable. Therefore, the manager or anybody who communicates should prepare the message in a catchy, crisp and understandable language. Understanding the communication is vital in communication process. Therefore, common, easily understandable terms have to be used in the message, simple language removes the barrier of understanding.

3. Careful Listening

In oral communication process, the receiver of the message not only hears the message, but also should properly listen. Hearing is passive and listening is active. It the message is properly listened it will not give scope for the pre-mature judgement or interpretation. Active listening demands total concentration and it improves communication even when emotions are strong. The purpose of active listening is to improve one's ability to receive the full meaning of a communication without any distortion of the message.

4. Control Emotions

Managers cannot be rational all the time in communicating the messages to their teams. When a manager is emotionally upset, he cannot express his message clearly and accurately. Therefore, he has to control his emotions to send proper message. When he is emotionally upset, he should not send the message until he gains composure.

5. Non-Verbal Cues

If manager's action is more louder than verbal draft, then his actions have to be watched. His action should align and reinforce the words that go along with action. Non-verbal messages carry very heavy weights. Therefore, the manager should watch his non-verbal cues and then send the messages which will be heard and listened by the receiver. This enables the manager to convey the desired message.

INFORMAL COMMUNICATION

As the name itself suggests that the communication does not take place or flow in formal communication channel. It will not follow the hierarchy. The information will be spread through friends through out the organisation. It is a powerful mechanism which coordinates activities through sharing information by the concerned people in the organisation. Mental models will be framed by like minded people in the organisation which will be a mental map for all persons performing interdependent tasks to obtain information. This is highly flexible in nature and integrates work activities. The speed in this channel will be very fast compared to hierarchical flow of information. This channel carries voluminous information through face-to-face communication.

Although informal communication is not recognised by organisations, this channel is more powerful in transmitting information. Information flows through friends and personal relationship modes among organisational members. In small units, this spreads the information at a very fast rate and co-ordination becomes easy. Barriers for communication are less.

Even in large organisation, electronice communication system is playing a vital role in developing good communication system. Organisations having activities across the globe, encourage informal communication system by developing temporary cross-functional teams and placing them in common physical places to perform the tasks as fast as possible. Employes themselves co-ordinate the tasks of different units through informal communication system to share information. Heads of these cross-functional teams are the "**Integrators**" who play the liaison role to encourage the workers of different units. This will take place through mutual trust. As employees have the tendency of believing informal communication more than the formal information system which flows through hierarchy, companies release the information through these integrators, besides sending it through formal channel.

Informal communication system is so strong for the reason that people in the organisation do not get information in the formal channel. Many a time, necessary information does not reach the concerned people at the appropriate time or before time. Informal communication system is also called "Grapevine".

Grapevine is a network which always carries information in an informal way. It automatically emerges and adopted irregularly in the organisation. Top management and executives in the hierarchy are unable to control it. Although Grapevine is entertained in some situations by the management to perform the tasks, many a time it is used to serve the self-interests of the people in the organisation. Sometimes, Grapevine will be dangerous to the organisational development as it spreads rumours which are detrimental to the growth of the organisation.

The information in informal way will flow in the form in (*i*) Gossip, (*ii*) Cluster, (*iii*) Probability grapevine and (*iv*) Single-stranded grapevine. This model was evolved by Keith Davis in an article in Harvard Business Review.

In gossip grapevine, a member will inform all other member about a specific information. For example Ananth, an informal group member informs Balu, Christopher, Dharam, Eusuph, etc., who are the members of the team. See this diagram.

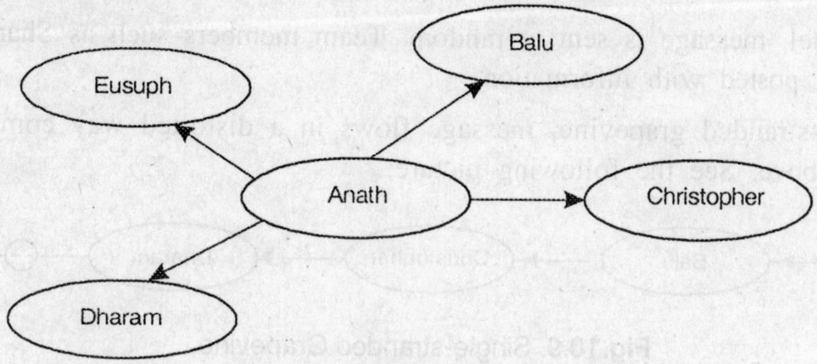

Fig. 10.6. Gossip Grapevine.

In this diagram, Ananth, a team member informs all other team members about a message. This is construced as Gossip Grapevine.

In Cluster Grapevine, one member selects two-three team members and conveys the message and one of these three members, conveys the message to others. Grapevine will be in the form of cluster and information will reach only to selected members. See the following picture.

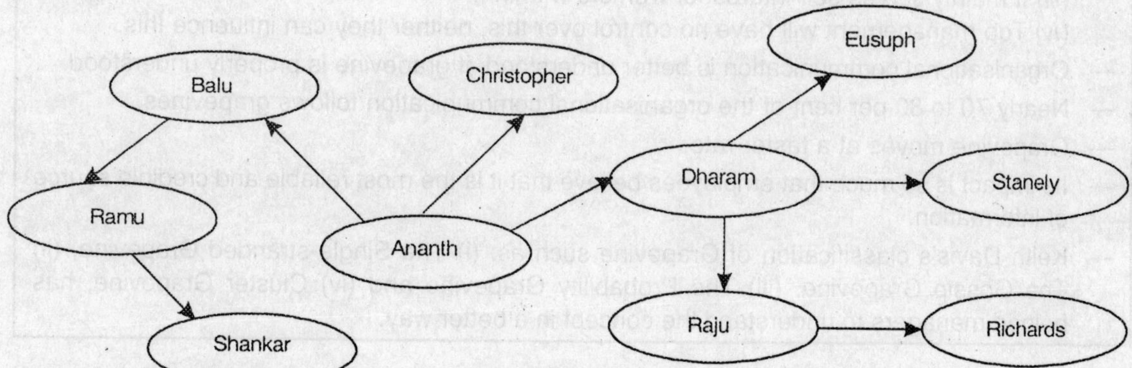

Fig. 10.7. Cluster Grapevine.

In this diagram, information reaches only to selected members.

In probability grapevine, information flows at random. See the following picture.

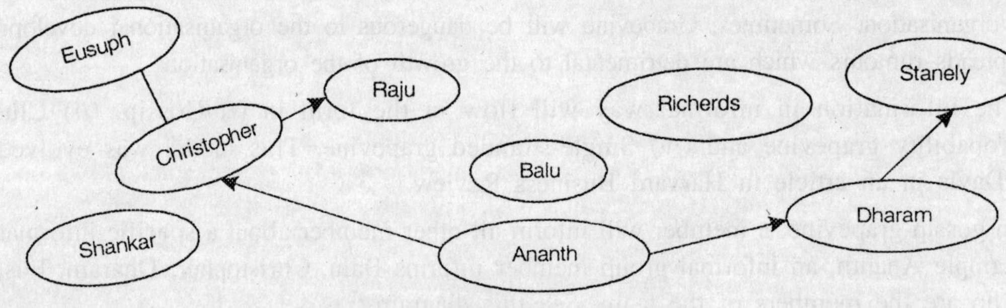

Fig. 10.8. Probability Grapevine.

In this model, message is sent at random. Team members such as Shankar, Balu and Richards are not posted with information.

In a single-stranded grapevine, message flows in a distorted way compared to other patterns stated above. See the following picture:

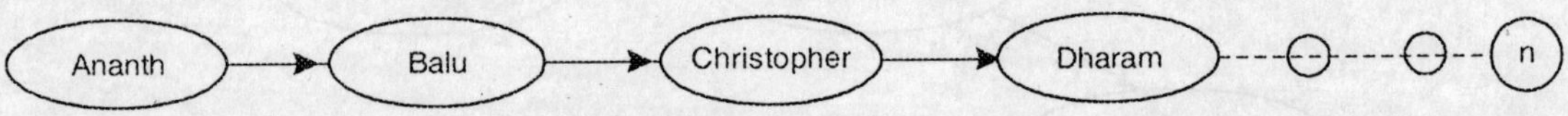

Fig.10.9. Single-stranded Grapevine.

The information about "Grapevine" analysed so far is given in the following box at glance.

> **Grapevine — Some Facts**
>
> — The alternative name for informal communication is "GRAPEVINE".
>
> — This has certain characters:
>
> (*i*) It comes to the fore instantaneously.
>
> (*ii*) Not regularly used in the organisation.
>
> (*iii*) It mainly serves self-interest of workers with in it.
>
> (*iv*) Top management will have no control over this, neither they can influence this.
>
> — Organisational communication is better understood, if grapevine is properly understood.
>
> — Nearly 70 to 80 per cent of the organisational communication follows grapevines.
>
> — Grapevine moves at a faster rate.
>
> — Its impact is so much that employees believe that it is the most reliable and credible source of information.
>
> — Keith Davis's classification of Grapevine such as: (i) The Single-stranded Grapevine, (ii) The Gossip Grapevine, (iii) The Probability Grapevine and (iv) Cluster Grapevine, has helped managers to understand the concept in a better way.

Experience in organisations reveal that informal communication system will be strong enough in every organisation. Hence, the managements cannot ignore the grapevine. Organisations can encourage this channel with an element of control. Harmful rumours ruin the organisations. Although they cannot avoid informal communication system, should control it by developing strong formal systems and watching informal channel.

Information Technology and Communication

Information is the primary source of power of any organisation and communication process controls the happenings in the organisation. Central Information system (CIS) which is in practice in all leading enterprises provide business information to all functional areas. While providing such stored information, there may be distortion in the message or the information provided may not be relevant for current business practices.

With the introduction of information technology, personal computers are playing a major role in the communication channel. This is "a device of radical democratisation." PCs broke the firm grip of organisation's central control system. Computer networking in organisations revolutionised communication system. Routine as well as important information was made easily accessable. Distortion in communication is made almost zero. Message is transmitted with cent per cent accuracy, E-mail is playing a vital role in external communication. CHAT transmits information instantaneously to any part of world. An array of softwares popularly known as GROUPWARE have made it possible. Electronic messages have cleansed the communication system.

Principles of Effective Communication

In all types of communication, the communicator must keep in view the following principles in order to have an effective communication:

1. Simple language: The language used in communication should be simple and easily understandable.

2. No ambiguity: The communicator should be clear in his mind about the objective of his communication and there should not be any ambiguity.

3. Proper medium of communication: There are different media for passing of communication. The communicator should select the proper medium by considering such factors as the nature of matter to be communicated, urgency of communication, distance between the communicator and the recipient of communication, etc.

4. Adequacy of information: In order to make communication effective, one more condition to be fulfilled is that it should be adequate and complete in all respects.

5. Right climate in the organisation: There should not be any communication barriers in the business concern. The organisation structure of the unit consisting of physical setting and human setting must facilitate the process of communication.

6. Follow-up action: There should be follow-up action to know whether the recipient of the message has understood it correctly and the action he has taken is on the basis of that message.

7. Training to the communicators: Proper training should be given to the communicators in the communication skills. This helps in increasing the effectiveness of communication considerably.

8. Co-operation of personnel: Co-operation of the organisation personnel is essential in order to make communication effective. Hence, the communication should aim at strengthening the business concern through the co-operation of the organisational personnel.

9. Messages should not be mutually conflicting: Messages should not be mutually conflicting and should be in line with the overall objectives and policies of the concern. This will avoid chaos and confusion in the organisation.

10. Action should be in line with the Message: The communicator should not act in any way which contradicts his message. A communicator is judged not only by what he says but also by what he does. Actions speak louder than words. Hence, the action of the communicator should be in line with the message conveyed.

SUMMARY

1. Communication involves interchange of thought or information among persons in an organisation and it is systematic and continuous process of telling, listening and understanding. A communication process consists of 6 elements, *viz.*, (a) communicator, (b) message, (c) transmission, (d) channel, (e) receiver and (f) response.
2. Communication helps in achieving co-ordination, in smooth running of the enterprise, in increasing managerial efficiency, in decision-making, in maintaining industrial peace, in the recruitment process. It also helps employers to perform effectively, to acquaint themselves with evaluation and personal safety. In addition, it helps in projecting the image of the company and helps the manager in performing his functions.
3. Communication can be classified on the basis of: (a) organisation structure, (b) on the basis of direction of communication and (c) on the basis of way of expression. On the basis of organisation structure, there can be formal communication, on the basis of direction of communication, there can be downward communication, upward communication, horizontal communication and diagonal communication and on the basis of way of expression, there can be oral or verbal communication and written communication.
4. Important barriers to communication are: badly expressed messages, faulty organisation, use of technical language, filtration of message, unclarified assumptions, distrust of communicator by the receiver of message, distortion of message, loss of information in the transmission of message, poor retention of information communicated, different backgrounds of communicator and receiver and inattention.
5. In order to have an effective communication, certain principles are to be observed. They are: simple language, no ambiguity in the message, proper medium of communication, adequacy of information, right climate in the organisation, follow-up action, training to the communicators, and co-operation of personnel, messages should not be mutually conflicting and action should be in line with the message.
6. Informal communication system otherwise called "Grapevine" is strong in every organisation. It may be in the form of Gossip, cluster, probability or single-stranded. Informal channel has to be controlled.

STUDY QUESTIONS

1. Give the meaning of communication.
2. Name the types of communication.
3. What is formal communication?
4. What is informal communication?

5. Give the meaning of: (i) Downward communication, (ii) Upward communication and (iii) Lateral communication.
6. What is Grapevine?
7. Analyse the elements of communication.
8. Give a note on importance of communication.
9. Give an analytical note on types of communication.
10. Briefly analyse the barriers to communication.
11. State the principles of communication.
12. Give a brief note on Informal Communication System.
13. Briefly explain the various elements of communication.
14. Explain the importance and advantages of communication as a tool of success in an organisation.
15. Explain the various types of communication.
16. Explain the various principles of communication.
17. Explain the principal barriers to communication and suggest measures to overcome the barriers.
18. Give an explanatory note on Informal Communication System.

Practical Exercise

1. Form a group of five and sit side by side. You be the originator of the message. Develop one piece of information on salary increase to staff and whisper the same to the person sitting in your side and ask him to pass on the message upto last person by whispering only. Ask the last one to speak loudly the message he has received. Then you read your original message loudly and give a report to your teachers on the following:

   (i) Whether the message was distorted or the original message reached to the last person.
   (ii) If distorted, at what stage it is distorted and why?

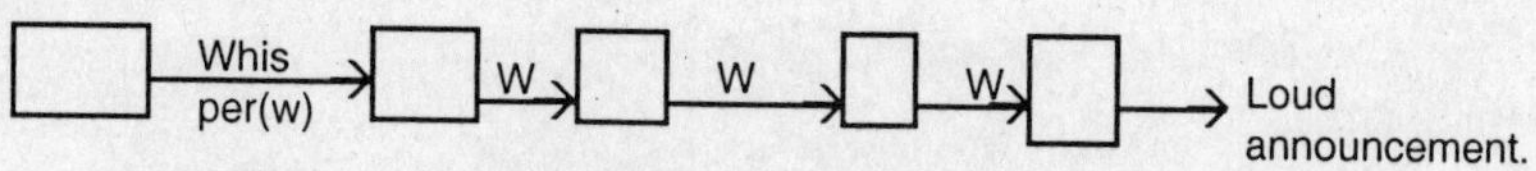

2. Today in organisations, communication system has radically changed. Messages are electronically communicated. Paper is less used. In this backdrop of change over to electronic system of communication, as a communicator, (i) Prepare a business message to be flashed electronically, considering the type of receivers, crisp and catchy words; (ii) What barriers you visualise in electronic transmission of message to your workforce?

CASE STUDY

A Television manufacturing company issues series of circulars about the various policies of production marketing and finance to its employees. The head of production who issues orders about policy decisions, shares his production information with his fellow workers in those circulars which are complex in nature. Besides formal circulars production executive (PE) has the habit of sending messages informally also. The PE is expected to know the intricacies of organisational communication, as communication system adopted in the company is the key factor for the success of the company. Formal communication is sent through the line chart of this company. Downward communication was sent to follow the production activities and upward communication was sent by the employees about the tasks performed by them. Sometimes, the tasks were not performed as per the circular messages. As PE did not have lateral communication system, he was getting feedback about the performance privately to correct the actions or redesigning the production plants. With this brief information,answer the following questions:

1. Whether the complexity of the message would distort the message? Substantiate.
2. Whether the Grapevine is prevailing in the organisation?
3. Is production executive a part of grapevine? Analyze.
4. What is the best system of communication you would suggest to this company?
5. What Communication concepts you learn from this case? Analyze.

11

MOTIVATION

LEARNING OBJECTIVES

After reading this chapter, you should be able to know:

- Motivation—The Concept
- Characteristics of Motivation
- Benefits of Motivation
- Motivation Theories
  (i) Maslow's Hierarchy of Needs Theory, (ii) X and Y Theory of McGregor
  (iii) Expectancy Theory of Victor Vroom, (iv) Equity Theory of J. Stacy Adams.
- Integrated Model of Motivation
- Sound Motivation System
- Motivation and Rewards/Recognition

'Motivation' means to provide someone with a motive. It is a complex force inspiring a person to work, to use his capacities willingly for achieving certain objectives. According to Dalton E. McFarland, "Motivation refers to the way in which urges, drives, desires, aspirations, striving or needs direct, control or explain the behaviour of human beings." In the words of Koontz and O'Donnell, "Motivation is a general term applying to the entire class of drives, needs, wishes and similar forces." According to Mr. Brech, "Motivation is a general inspiration process which gets the members of the team to pull their weight effectively, to give their loyalty to the group, to carry out properly the tasks they have accepted and generally to play an effective part in the job that the group has undertaken."

Motivation is something that motivates a person into action and continues him in the course of action willingly to get the results expected of him. It refers to the way in which desires and aspirations direct, control or explain the behaviour of human beings. It also refers to the carrying out the task properly and with loyalty to the group that has accepted the task.

Motivation is a driving force that initiates and directs behaviour. It is a kind of internal energy which drives a person to do something in order to achieve something. It is not concerned with personality but with temper and dynamic state within a person.

Motivation of a person is essential to achieve something personally or in workplaces, to identity oneself with some work or to affiliate to something, to develop ones own competence, power and attitude.

Motivation is governed by three vital and specific aspects. They are: (i) Arousal of behaviour (what activates behaviour), (ii) Direction or behaviour (what directs behaviour towards a goal) and (iii) persistence of behaviour (how the behaviour is sustained).

Many studies reveal that motivation is driven by motives such as: (i) homeostatic motives, (ii) non-homeostatic motives and (iii) learned or social motives.

Homeostatic motive includes thirst, hunger, respiration and excretion. Homeostatic concept relates to personal or internal needs as stated above.

Non-homeostatic motives are external in nature and includes seeking shelter, having curiosity about one's own environment and happenings concerned with the individuals.

Social motives are construed as learned motives which includes desire for novelty, power, achievement, social affiliation and social recognition.

Thus, motivation is an inner push of an individual driven by motives, which is essential to succeed in any endeavour one undertakes. It may be positive or negative, subtle or obvious, tangible or intangible. In the context of business organisation, motivation is very important as it plays a vital role in the effective performance of employees. Managers in business enterprises focus on motivating employees to achieve the organisational success. They adopt different employee motivation techniques to increase the productivity.

NATURE AND CHARACTERISTICS OF MOTIVATION

A manager gets work done through others and this requires motivation. Motivation is the process of channelling a person's inner drives so that he wants to accomplish the goals of the organisation. Motivation is a behavioural concept by which we try to understand why people behave as they do. The nature and characteristics of motivation can be explained as follows.

1. Whereas in the past, 'money' was regarded as the only cause of human behaviour, today in industry, there is a great concern with multi-motivational determinants of behaviour. The earlier monistic approach to motivation under which man was supposed to act only to increase his monetary rewards has now given place to a more complete pluralistic explanation which recognises that man works to fulfil a variety of needs.

2. Motivation is not an easily observed phenomenon. We observe an individual's action and then interpret his observed behaviour in terms of underlying motivations. This leaves a wide margin of error. Our interpretation does not necessarily reveal the individual's true motivation.

3. Motivation is highly situational in character. A football player may play for one team but much better for another. Little has changed in the player but the context in which he plays is different. The job-connected experience of worker plays an important role in determining motivation. Organisation structure, physical facilities, type of machines, nature of work etc. affect motivation.

4. Culture, customs, images and attributes conferred by the society on particular job play a strong motivational role. An individual, for example, may find that his work has a substantial degree of respect and social acceptance accorded by society, quite apart from holding a position in a particular organisation.

5. Individuals may differ in their motivation, even though all of them are performing the same type of job. For example, if two men are engaged in cutting stones for constructing a temple, one may be motivated by the amount of wages he gets by performing his job, *i.e.*, job satisfaction.

6. Motivations of each individual change from time-to-time, even though he may continue to behave in the same way. For example, a temporary worker may produce more in the beginning to become permanent. When made permanent, he may continue to produce more, this time to get promotion and so on.

7. Motivations are varied. The viewpoint that there is only one, 'economic drive' which determines behaviour is untenable. The goals to which an individual aspires are many and so are his motivations.

8. Motivation is complex. It is difficult to explain and predict the behaviour of workers. The introduction of an apparently favourable motivational device may not necessarily achieve the desired ends if it brings the opposing motives into play. In a factory where blue-green lighting was introduced to reduce eyestrain, the output of men workers increased but that of women workers decreased. On investigation, it was found that the latter disliked change in lighting because they felt the new type of lighting made them look "simply ghastly." In this case, while men workers were motivated, the women workers were demotivated.

IMPORTANCE AND BENEFITS OF MOTIVATION

In the directing process, motivation is one of the important elements. By motivating people, the manager guides people's actions in the desired direction so as to enable him to achieve the organisational objectives. For performing any job, two important things are necessary, *viz.,* will to work and ability to work. The importance of motivation lies in converting this ability to work into the will to work. For performing any job, there is a need for both, *viz.,* the ability and willingness to work. Without willingness, ability to work is of no use. Hence, there is a need for motivating a person to do his job. Performance depends on ability and willingness and in turn, willingness depends on motivation. It can be expressed in a formula: Performance = Ability × Motivation.

The following points highlight the importance of motivation:

(1) Maximum utilisation of factors of production: Motivation makes workers work sincerely for completing the task assigned to them. By this, there is a possibility of utilising the enterprise resources, *viz.*, human, physical and financial, to the maximum.

(2) Reduced employee turnover and absenteeism: Attractive motivational schemes bring about satisfaction to employees and by this, their commitment to organisation increases and they are not easily tempted by offers from competitors. This means reduced employee turnover. Further, because of their satisfaction, they will be attending to their work regularly.

(3) Increase in efficiency and output: As motivation brings about satisfaction to employees, they work wholeheartedly. Because of this, there will be an increase in their efficiency and output.

(4) Sense of belonging: A proper system of motivational schemes promotes closer identification between enterprise and workers. The workers begin to feel that the enterprise belongs to them and the interests of the enterprise are their interests and there is no difference between them. This result in better relations between management and workers.

(5) Easy availability of right personnel: Because of the proper motivational schemes, the enterprise is in a position to attract highly talented and competent persons from external sources to serve in its organisation. This helps the company in increasing its efficiency.

(6) Helps in realising organisational goals: Motivated employees develop a feeling of total involvement in the task of organisation and put forth their efforts wholeheartedly for the relations of organisational goals.

THEORIES OF MOTIVATION

A large number of theories exist on motivation but among them two theories evolved by Abraham Maslow and Frederick Herzberg are considered outstanding. It can also be stated that McGregor also has contributed a lot by his two theories, *viz.*, Theory X and Theory Y, in which he has explained the various approaches to motivation. In the following paras, the contributions of Maslow, Herzberg and McGregor are discussed.

1. Maslow's Hierarchy of Needs Theory

Maslow's theory which is based on the needs of the people states that an individual is motivated to satisfy certain unsatisfied needs. His theory is based on certain assumptions. They are:

1. An individual's behaviour is influenced by his needs. Needs that are not satisfied motivate or influence his behaviour. In other words, behaviour is not influenced by the satisfied needs.

2. Needs have priority and they are arranged according to a hierarchy of importance. They start from physiological needs.

3. An individual's needs at any level on the hierarchy emerge only when he is reasonably well-satisfied with the lower level needs.

Maslow's theory has proposed a hierarchy of five needs which are discussed below (see Fig. 11.1).

1. Physiological: According to Maslow, the most fundamental of the needs are physiological. They are food, clothing, shelter, etc. These are basic needs and anyone would give the first perference to these needs. Once an individual is satisfied reasonably with these basic needs, he thinks in terms of higher level needs.

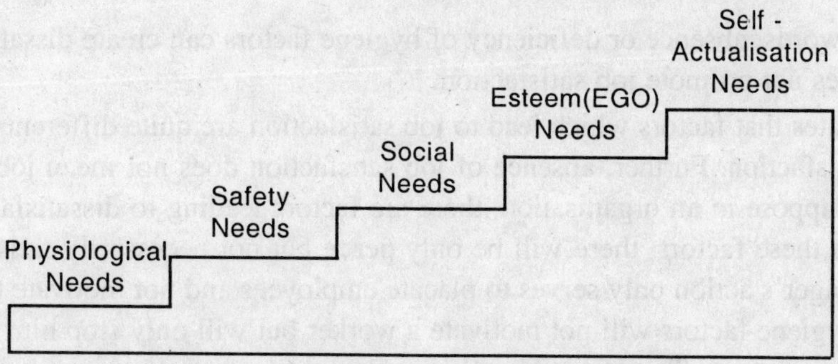

Fig. 11.1. Maslow's Hierarchy of Needs

2. Safety needs: These are the needs for protection against danger, threat, deprivation and the need for job security. These needs will arise for an individual only when he is reasonably well satisfied with his physiological needs.

3. Social needs: These needs include those of belonging, association, acceptance, friendship and love. Social needs become important to an individual only when he is basically satisfied with physiological and safety needs.

4. Esteem (or ego) needs: These needs include those of self-confidence, independence, achievement, status and recognition. These needs dominate only when an individual is reasonably satisfied with the first three needs.

5. Self-Actualisation (Self-Fulfilment) needs: These needs are concerned with the need to realise one's capacities and potentialities by achieving specific goals. He accepts such work which is challenging and creative and also provides opportunities for self-development. These needs become important to an individual once he is reasonably satisfied with the esteem needs.

An Appraisal of Maslow's Theory

This theory states the hierarchy of needs with some reasonable assumptions. It points out that the people are motivated by unfulfilled needs. It also states that once a particular need is satisfied, it ceases to be a motivating factor. Maslow has pointed out that as lower level needs are satisfied, upper level needs replace them and become important.

However, this theory has been criticised by some writers. It is said that the need hierarchy may not follow the sequence stated by Maslow. In some cases, the egoistic need may become important even before the safety needs are satisfied. Man's behaviour at any time is mostly guided by the multiplicity of motives and hence, the proposition that one need is satisfied at one time may not hold good.

Herzberg's Motivation Hygiene Theory

According to Frederick Herzberg, motivation factors (also called intrinsic factors) such as feeling of achievement, job itself, responsibility, recognition, opportunity for advancement motivated the workers, whereas hygiene factors (also called extrinsic factors) such as salary, status, job security, company policy and administration, supervision, working conditions etc., only maintain or placate him and do not motivate him. They simply provide a working environment to the worker. In other words, absence or deficiency of hygiene factors can create dissatisfaction, while their presence does not promote job satisfaction.

Herzberg states that factors which lead to job satisfaction are quite different from those that lead to job dissatisfaction. Further, absence of job satisfaction does not mean job dissatisfaction and *vice versa.* Suppose in an organisation, there are factors leading to dissatisfaction and if the manager removes these factors, there will be only peace but not necessarily satisfaction. This is because, the manager's action only serves to placate employees and not motivate them. It may be noted here that hygiene factors will not motivate a worker but will only stop him from becoming dissatisfied or unmotivated. Therefore, Herzberg advocates intrinsic factors (motivating factors) to motivate the worker. Intrinsic factors lead a worker from the stage of no job satisfaction to 'job-satisfaction', whereas hygiene factors lead from the stage of dissatisfaction to no dissatisfaction only.

Thus, Herzberg made managers to give their mind to analyse as to what actually makes employees motivated. He says that opposite of job satisfaction is not job dissatisfaction, but rather 'No' job dissatisfaction. At the midpoint of "Dissatisfaction-Satisfaction", exists a silent zone or zero point and the employee is caught at this point. Although he is dissatisfied with pay and facilities he is getting, he is actually not motivated to work, as the job may not be challenging. Therefore, besides money and other incentives, real motivating factor is "Meaningful, interesting and challenging work". This means "Job Enrichment".

"Job Enrichment" involves the process of redesigning job to enhance the motivational potential of employees. It "infuses more complexity and depth into jobs by introducing planning and decision-making responsibility normally carried out at higher levels".

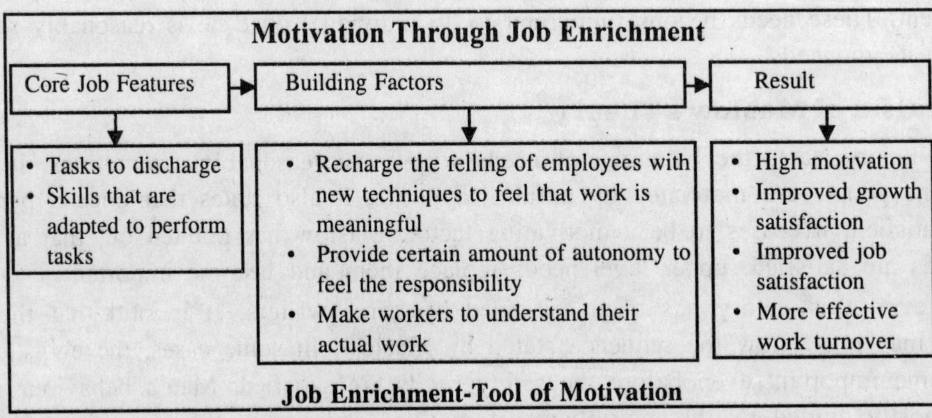

2. McGregor's X and Y Theories

Prof. Douglas McGregor in his book "The Human Side of Enterprise" has introduced two theories, *viz.,* Theory X and Theory Y on the basis of two sets of assumptions. The first set of assumptions is contained in Theory X and the second in Theory Y.

Theory X

Theory X is based on the following assumptions:

1. Workers have an instinctive aversion to work. They are lazy and desire to work as little as possible and find every pretext to avoid or do it half-heartedly.
2. Only 'fear' can force workers into action. A worker will work only when he knows the harmful consequences of not working.
3. He avoids to accept any responsibility. There is need to make him aware of the dreadful consequences of his inaction.
4. He is not interested in achievement. He believes in maintaining the *status quo* and hates to improve his lot. He prefers to be directed by others.
5. He is concerned mainly with the retaining of his job and he feels that if he does not perform well or takes more time to perform the job, he may lose that job.
6. As the worker has no instinctive liking for work, there is a need for monetary incentive to make him work harder.
7. Worker is only one of the factors of production and does not deserve any special treatment simply because he is a human being.
8. He lacks integrity.
9. He avoids making decisions whenever possible.

McGregor has described Theory X as a traditional theory and states what managers must do to manage the workers. He points out the need for autocratic leadership to manage such workers. He also states that most people must be coerced, controlled, directed, threatened with punishment to make them put forth adequate efforts towards the achievement of organisational objectives.

Theory Y

McGregor has called Theory Y a modern theory. It is exactly opposite to the traditional Theory X. In Theory X, the worker's role is minimum in the process of management whereas in Theory Y, the worker is given a pride of place and active co-operation between workers and management is emphasised to enable the organisation to accomplish its goals. According to this theory, a worker by nature has integrity; he works hard towards the objectives of enterprise, wants his organisation to succeed, is not passive, is willing to make decisions and shows a sense of creativity and imagination in his work performance and willingly accepts responsibility. In this sense, Theory Y can be said to be positive and optimistic whereas Theory X is negative and pessimistic.

Assumptions of Theory Y

Theory Y is based on the following assumptions:

1. The average human being does not inherently dislike work. Work is as natural as play or rest. Once he understands the purpose of work, he exerts himself to perform it regardless of the kind of remuneration.
2. For making the worker put forth his best efforts towards organisational objective external control and threat of punishment are not the only means. The worker exercise self-direction and self-control for achieving the objectives to which committed.

3. If the right motivational schemes are available, every worker will take delight in shouldering responsibility and discharging successfully. If a worker is unwilling to accept responsibility, it may be due to the fact that he is afraid of the consequences of non-performance on his part.
4. It is not correct to think that the worker is incompetent for the job and cannot make the right decisions.
5. A worker wants that his achievement to be noticed by others and expects recognition for the successful accomplishment of responsibility.
6. For a worker, financial reward is not the only a inspiration. He works efficiently even for non-financial rewards like recognition, greater participation in decision-making, increased responsibility, etc.
7. In the present-day industrial life, the intellectual potentialities of an average human being are not utilised fully.

Thus, Theory Y is democratic in practice. It advocates an active participation and involvement on the part of workers in the various activities of the enterprise.

3. Victor Vroom's Expectancy Theory

This theory tells us that simply making motivation factors available to people is not enough. People must believe that by working, they will receive rewards that are important to them. People's actions are based on their expectations as well as their needs. Unless there is a positive expectation of a reward that will satisfy a need, an individual will not take action. To illustrate, consider a person who is thirsty. There may be need for water, but the action of going to the faucet and getting a drink occurs only if he expects that efforts will result in obtaining water.

The experience of one manufacturing company indicates the importance of expectations. The management had decided to expand the company, and it knew that a number of supervisors would be needed. To prepare for the expansion, the company decided to run a training programme for its employees (non-supervisors) to prepare them to become supervisors. The programme was open to all employees at no cost. When the programme started, only three people attended the programme. Management interviewed the employees who did not participate to find out the reasons for their poor participation. Many employees stated that they would like to be promoted but did not feel that attending the programme would help. "Promotion is based on whom you know, not what you know", was the commonly expressed opinion. In other words, although promotion was a motivating factor to employees, they did not participate in the training programme because they did not believe it would help them in getting promotion.

...imilarly, how hard people work is affected by their needs and whether or not they expect a ...rformance to resulting rewards that will satisfy their needs. To be motivated, people ...working hard, they will fulfil the needs that are important to them. In short, ...er wants to motivate his employees, he should do the following:

...f the employees.

...ards (motivation factors) that are important to his employees.

...e expectations.

4. McClelland's Need for Achievement Theory

According to McClelland, the three important needs are:

(a) The need for achievement,

(b) The need for affiliation, and

(c) The need for power.

A person who has a high need for achievement has the following characteristics:

(1) He wants for setting moderately difficult but potentially achievable goals.

(2) He prefers to do most of things himself rather than getting them done by others.

(3) He wishes to take personal responsibility for his success or failure and does not want to hold others responsible for it.

A person who has a need for affiliation, reflects a desire to interact socially with people and is concerned about the quality of an important personal relationship. Thus, social relationships take precedence over task accomplishment for such a person.

A person who has a high need for power concentrates on obtaining and exercising power and authority. One important characteristic we find in him is that he is concerned with influencing others and winning arguments.

The implications to managers of the McClelland theory are significant. If the needs of employees can be accurately measured, organisations can improve the selection and placement processes. For example, an employee or recruit with a high need for achievement could be placed in a position that would enable him to achieve. This could result in improved performance because of the mutual fit of need intensities and job characteristics. Thus, it is important to identify the behaviours required to perform a set of tasks effectively and then to determine what individual characteristics are most associated with their behaviours.

5. Equity Theory

Besides the theories analysed so far, another theory which throws light on inner feelings of a worker is "Equity Theory." The central point of the theory developed by J. Stacy Adams is that "employees perceive what they get from a job situation (outcome) in relation to what they put into it (inputs) and then compare input-outcomes ratio of theirs with the input-outcomes ratio of fellow workers". If this comparison result is positive, they are highly motivated to work. If the ratio is negative they are demotivated. The theory focuses on "Equity" aspect. If the ratio is enough to exhibit equity in input-outcome aspect, employees work with zeal. If inequity exists, employees may resort to any one of the following five options:

(i) Distortion of inputs of their own or of fellow workers.

(ii) Try to change their own inputs or outcomes.

(iii) Try to change the inputs or outcomes of other workers.

(iv) Try to select another person for comparison and lastly.

(v) Get out of the job.

The theory has clearly exhibited (supported by consistent research studies) that workers are motivated significantly be relative rewards as well as absolute rewards. The productivity of the worker is related to equity of rewards and incentives that motivate. Whenever inequity exists the affected workers are demotivated and productivity of such workers fall proportionately.

In Equity theory "Referents" play a vital role in varying the motivation of workers. Referents are the people, systems, or selves against which a person compares himself to assess equity.

6. Other Theories

Besides the theories analysed so far, there are other contemporary theories which throw light on motivation. They are:

(i) Reinforcement theory propounded by B.F.Skinner. (This theory states that "a person is motivated when he or she responds to stimuli in consistent patterns of behaviour over time.") This theory exhibits how the consequences of part behaviour affect future actions in a cyclical learning process.

(ii) "Goal-setting theory" developed by a psychologist called Edwin Lacke. The theory states that "Individuals are motivated when they behave in ways that move them to certain clear goals that they accept and can reasonably expect to attain." The theme is that when goals are specific and challenging they work effectively as motivating factors in individuals and in group performance. Here,the goals are motivators.

Integration of Models (Theories)

The theories of motivation discussed so far cannot be viewed independently as these theories are complementary to each other. The central point of every theory has to be put in a pool and should be integrated to maximise motivation and thereby achieve the best possible productivity. Maximisation of production in terms of fixed targets can be attained by linking workers' efforts and performance to motivating factors such as, attractive rewards and incentives.

The attractiveness of a reward or incentive depends upon the perception, attitudes, personality and needs of the employee. The degree of attractiveness decides the motivation levels such as positive, negative or neutral. This is a behavioural aspect. To improve or change their behaviour, employees must know as to how to go about,i.e., the type of adaptation to change over has to be properly recognised. Employees should also know whether they have the type of skills and ability to change themselves to get better rewards or incentives which are the motivating factors.

All these issues have been properly answered by different motivational theories which have to be studied with an integrated approach. The sum and substance of these theories, when integrated, bring out the following:

— "Jobs that score high in motivating potential are likely to lead higher actual job performance". Effort and performance are linked here.

— "Jobs that score high in motivating potential also increase an employee's control over key elements in his work".

Thus, the Integrated Model is the one which takes in its fold the following:

- Employees are motivated when their needs as explained in Maslow's theory are satisfied.
- Motivational factors such as feeling of achievement, recognition, opportunity for advancement etc. influence the workers to work with zeal and initiative. Therefore these zealous factors are to be provided by the employer.
- Hygienic factors such as salary, status, job security, working conditions etc. make the workers to stay on the job. These factors also are to be continuously monitored.
- Positive aspects of motivation are to be implemented and negative people are to be avoided as far as possible in work places (Theory X and Y of McGregor). Autocratic Leaders can direct such situations.
- Rewards and recognitions should be given at the appropriate time to develop sense of belongingness in employees.
- Motivational practices of the organisation should be made to well understand by employees and employees should feel that they are treated equally adopting standard performance prictices and unbiassed evaluations.

As said earlier, integrated motivational approach is the best to achieve organisational effectiveness.

Other Current Issues

Today's work force is diverse. Full time employee needs, part-time employee needs and retired and re-joined employee needs are different. Similarly the needs of female employees will be different of that of male employees. These different types of needs of different type of employees influence the behavioural pattern of each type and give scope for the formulation of different type of motivational factors.

"Flexibility" is one key factor which motivates and satisfy the needs of employees. Solutions such as flexibility in time, flexibility in operation etc. have emerged today to motivate the workers. "Virtual office" the modern concept provides opportunity to employees to work from their house itself. But the quality of technology has to be adapted for this purpose.

Besides flex time operation and compressed work week (reducing working days by increasing working hours on the working days in a week, i.e., instead of working for six days a week, only five days in a week can be fixed by increasing working hours on all these working days, "Job sharing", "Telecommunicating", "Pay-for-performance", "Employee Stock options (ESOP)", "Motivating minimum wage employees", "Matching people to jobs", "Fixing attainable goals", "Individualisation of rewards", "Linking rewards to performance", "Adaptation of Equity concept" are some of the contemporary issues of motivating the work force in an organisation. These issues are considered as motivating tools and are implemented according to the situation that prevails in the organisation.

Motivation — Rewards/Recognition

Motivation of employees is a HRD concept. Employees are fully motivated and become positive, when they are properly recognised through incentives, awards and retention programmes.

Rewards in the form of annual cash awards, providing congenial working environment, small surprises and tokens of your appreciation can spread throughout the year. Giving employees recognition cards or gifts for birth days, wedding anniversaries, the anniversary of their start dates in your office etc, according compulsory leave for a day to one week depending upon the job features with pay and some money for spending and various such other rewards will go a long way in motivating the employees. Priortizing recognition for employees will ensure a positive and productive organisation. Many employers believe that employee recognition brings positive results and understand that employees are to be motivated.

There are organisations in which employee recognition is limited or no recognition at all. In such organisations employees are demotivated. The thinking of employer/manager such as "why should I recognise or thank the employee ? Employee does his job" etc. make the workstations a miserable one. Employees are frustrated in such situations. Mysterious selection of employees who are unworthy for rewards, dampen the morale of many worthy employees who are not recognised for awards. Not recognising them or prejudised and biassed treatment etc. will make employees to lose identity with the organisation and their moral is put down.

Employee recognition through reward and performance is not just a nice thing. It is a communication tool that reinforces and rewards the most important results that employees bring to the organisation. When employees are effectively recognised through chosen means of recognition, they are motivated and continuously repeat their positive actions and gradually develop positive behaviour which is required for the maximisation of organisational productivity. Employee recognition should be simple, immediate and powerfully recinforcing. It ensures a positive, productive organisational climate.

Every employee has his own reason to work. They work to obtain something that they need from work. Thus, something obtained from work impacts their morale, motivation and their quality of life. To create positive employee motivation, treat employees as if, they matter-because employees matter. This will help the organisation to fulfil what the employees want from work and to create employee motivation.

It should be noted that some people work for personal fulfillment. Others work for love of what they do. Some also work to accomplish goals and feel as if they are contributing to something larger than themselves. The bottomline is that every one works for money and for reasons too individual to assign similarities to all workers. In this context, monetory and non-monetory rewards and incentives to workers given at the appropriate time will help the organisation to keep the morale of the organisation on top.

Employee reward and recognition process to motivate them should be benefitial to both the organisation and employees. Following aspects are to be considered while recognising the employees.

- Consider that all employees are eligible for the recognition.
- The recognition must provide the employer and employee, the specific information about what behaviours or actions are being rewarded and recognised.
- List all those who perform to the levels or standards fixed by the organisation to receive the rewards and to be recognised.

- Reward those who match to the fixed standards as close as possible, so that the employer will be happy to know that the behaviour of selected employees will be re- inforced to positive development of the organisation.
- The designed process of recognition should not encourage bias or favouritism.
- It is better to avoid frequent recognition programmes such as "Employee of the month" etc. which is ineffective and demotivates the employees to certain extent.

Essentials of Employee Motivation

- Praise the employee for his/her admirable work. Identify the work that needs admiration.
- Appreciate the hardwork of employees by saying "Thank you". To have a polite and gracious workplace, always prefix "Please" when you speak to your co-worker. Because it is a social nicety that is expected at workplaces.
- Exhibit your genuine concern to your co-workers by asking questions about their family, daily living etc. This makes the employees feel that they are cared about and they are valued.
- In hectic period, you cannot allow your employees to be at leasure. This has to be managed by giving flexible work schedules.This facilitates workers to work hard in such situation as well as enjoy some free time. Critical time and enjoyment of workers are to be balanced.
- Give small gifts occasionally to co-workers. This will boost the morale of workers and light up their day.
- Give annual bonus in kind or in money form. Any periodical bonus [Qly/hly/yrly] given saying "Thanks" will motivate them to develop "Organisational Identity".
- Greet employees on their birthdays over a cup of tea or simply presenting a flower or with a small gift.
- Take your employees on an excursion for a day or two at the end of year. Make them relaxed at the cost of organisation.
- Meet employees on a luncheon/Dinner meeting and give scope to express their grievances, sort-out them and extend facilities within your policy framework.
- Provide opportunity for training and cross-training to employees. Put them on special committees where their talents can be exhibitted. Allow them to attend outside professional association meetings. These procedees motivative employees to be honest to their work.

Requirements of Sound Motivation System

While adopting a motivational system, the management should take into account certain essential points. They are:

1. The motivational system should reflect not only the requirements of the employees but also the objectives and philosophy of the organisation. Motivational system should be a fine blend of the two.
2. As the motivational system is designed for the members of the organisation, it should be well understood by them. If the employees understand the system clearly, they get motivated to work.
3. The motivational system should be adequate and cover the entire work force in an enterprise. Further, it should cover all activities of the employees.

4. In the motivational system, there should be positive interconnection between efforts and rewards. In other words, motivation should be directly related to efforts.
5. It should be flexible and not rigid. There should be scope for incorporating change in the motivational system.
6. Analysis of factors which motivate the employees of an enterprise, the various needs of the employees, degree of intensity and the prospective consequences of satisfying or not satisfying them should be made and duly incorporated in the motivational system.

Every organisation trys to get best out of their workers to maximise organisational productivity workers have different styles of working. Approach to work will be a composition of positive and negative nature. The group will be heterogenous in character. Although they are supposed to work in a common framework of policies and programmes, the contribution towards productivity of each worker will be varying. The organisation sets the goal to achieve. But with this varying contribution, goal cannot be achieved. The workers work with different intentions and many do not contribute their full mite to achieve the set goals.

Motivation is one of the positive tools to pull up the workers and put them on the right task to achieve the organisational objective. Motivation makes the working teams to be more effective. It gives proper direction to the workers and empowers them to succeed by doing right things as desired by the company. Leader of each team of workers has to coach each individual worker to excel in his work through motivation. Although rewards and recognition are the tools of motivation, the leader has to play the role of mentor to adopt these tools and motivate the employees to excel.

Thus, to motivate employees, the top management of the organisation has to adopt the following practices:

- Prepare and provide a budget for excellence of wrokers and not to develop mediocres.
- Set achievable goals and put right people at work.
- Be a mentor and direct the team.
- Motivate every one, by giving the opportunity to recognise and reward excellence as it happens.
- Set up an environment where employees are best motivated and empower themselves. Leader cannot motivate workers any more than he empowers them.
- Money is not only the motivating factor. Different people are motivated by different factors. Some want to save time in office work to spend more time with the family. Some will be motivated by recognition of a job well done. Hence, the main factor of motivation is to understand what motivates each of the employees and address such needs as far as possible.
- Align the goals of the organisation with the goals of the workers to make them to work effectively towards the objectives of the organisation.
- Support employee motivation by using organisational systems (*i.e.*, policies and procedures). Do not just count on good intentions.

SUMMARY

1. Motivation is something that motivates a person into action and continues him in the course of action willingly to get the results expected of him. It refers to the way in which desires and aspirations direct, control and explain the behaviour of human beings.
2. Motivation converts one's ability to work into will to work. Motivation helps in the maximum utilisation of factors of production, reduces employee turnover and absenteeism, increases his efficiency and output, creates better relations between management and workers, helps the company in increasing its efficiency and in realising organisational goals.
3. Among the theories of motivation, the theories of Abraham Maslow, Frederick Herzberg and McGregor are outstanding. Maslow's theory propagates a hierarchy of five needs, *viz.,* physiological needs, safety needs, social needs, esteem needs and self-actualisation needs.
4. Herzberg's theory states that motivational factors such as feeling of achievement, recognition, opportunity for advancement, etc. motivate the worker whereas hygiene factors such as salary, status, job security, working conditions etc. only maintain or placate the worker but do not motivate him.
5. McGregor's X and Y Theories are based on certain assumptions. Theory X is based on certain assumptions such as workers by nature are lazy, not interested in achievement, have no liking for work, etc. Hence, McGregor advocates autocratic leadership to manage such workers. Theory Y is based on assumptions such as the worker does not dislike work, that he is willing to work, and take responsibility, etc.
6. McClelland's need for achievement theory states that needs of employees are to be properly assessed to motivate them accordingly.
7. Equity theory suggests that the input-output of each employee has to be compared and if the result is positive, it means that employees are motivated. The productivity of worker is related to equity of rewards.
8. Integrated model expresses that the all theories are complement to each other and hence all the opinions are to be pooled and has to be used to maximise motivation.
9. Rewards and recognition should be in proportion to the efforts put in by employees and be given as it happens.
10. Requirement of a sound motivational system is that it should reflect the requirements of employees and the organisation. It should be well understood by the employees and should be adequate to cover the entire work force. It should be related to efforts and should be flexible.

STUDY QUESTIONS

1. Give the meaning of motivation.
2. Name the theories of motivation.
3. State the features of motivation.
4. Analyse the benefits of motivation.
5. Give a note on Maslow's theory of motivation.
6. Write a note on McGregor's theory of motivation.
7. Analyse expectancy theory of motivation.

8. Analyse the requirements of sound motivation system.
9. Give an analytical note on Herzberg's theory of motivation.
10. Briefly analyse equity theory of motivation.
11. Briefly explain the importance and benefits of motivation.
12. Breifly explain the theories of motivation.
13. Explain the basic assumptions of motivation processes in organisations.
14. Identify any three contemporary motivation theories and explain the main theme of these theories.
15. Briefly explain the integrated model of motivation.
16. Give an explanatory note on type of rewards and recognitions that motivate employees.

12

CONTROLLING

LEARNING OBJECTIVES

After reading this chapter, you should be able to know:

- Controlling – The Concept
- Control Process
- Essentials of Effective Control Systems.
- Control Techniques
- Scope of Control
- Control Stages
- Control Problems
- Factors Determining Effective Control System.

Controlling is the last, but not the least function of management process. In the following process, objectives are set for achieving them, policies methods, and procedures are designed to implement the plan. Along with this, techniques are also developed to assess whether the plan is implemented as per accepted design. This assessment and corrective actions are called "controlling" in management. Planning and control are the two sides of the same coin. There cannot be planning without control. Control facilitates to understand whether actions are being taken as planned and the type of corrective actions taken to make them conform to plan and then to take necessary steps to prevent the accurance of variations in future.

IMPORTANCE OF CONTROL

Control is an important function of management. It is an essential feature of scientific management. It is a force which guides the management to a predetermined objective by means of predetermined policies and decisions. It helps the management in verifying whether everything occurs in conformity with the standards set. By bringing to light, the variations from the standards stipulated in the plans, control points out the weakness and errors in order to rectify them and prevent recurrence. It helps the management in realising adequate progress and satisfactory performance.

Control is the basis of planning and the essence of control is the adherence to plans. Control keeps a check on other functions of management so as to facilitate the management in achieving its objectives. As the control system covers almost all management activities, there is a possibility for the overall improvement in the organisational efficiency. Further, proper control smoothens the working of an organisation. As the control system strengthens the functioning of the company, the morale of the employees will be high. Again the existence of an efficient control system creates an atmosphere of order and discipline in the enterprise.

Approaches to Design Controls

William G. Ouchi suggests the following three approaches to design control system.

Market Control: This type throws light on a mechanism to be developed for controlling external market operations which involve standards to be fixed for achieving market share, price competition, etc.

Bureaucratic Control: This approach stresses on organisational authority and relies on administrative and hierarchical mechanisms such as rules, regulations, procedures, policies, standardisation of activities, budgets, etc., to see that employees adapt themselves to these programmes and policies of the organisation to achieve goals. This throws light on monitoring employee behaviour towards organisational policies and programmes.

Clan Control: This provides inputs to design control systems through which employee behaviour is controlled by the shared values, norms, traditions, rituals, beliefs, and other aspects of organisation culture. This control system focuses on the behaviour of individuals or groups (clan) to monitor performance measures.

(**Source**: William G. Ouchi, "A Conceptual Framework for the Design of Organisational Control Mechanism." Management Science, 1970.)

Definitions

1. "Control is checking current performance against predetermined standards contained in the plans with a view to ensuring adequate progress and satisfactory performance."
   — ***E.F.L. Breck***
2. "Management control seeks to compel events to conform to plans." — ***Billy E. Goetz***
3. "In an undertaking, control consists in verifying whether everything occurs in conformity with the plans adopted, the instructions issued and the principles established. Its object is to point out the weakness and error in order to rectify them and prevent occurrence. It operates on everything, *i.e.*, things, people and actions." — ***Henry Fayol***
4. "Controlling is determining what is being accomplished, that is, evaluating the performance and, if necessary, applying corrective so that the performance takes place according to plans."
   — ***George R. Terry***
5. "Without watchfulness and feedback of an efficient control system, there is little likelihood that even the best plan will ever workout as expected". — ***J. Batty.***

These definitions provide the meaning of control, a vital element of management. Control is concerned with checking whether everything occurs in conformity with the standards stipulated in the plan. It measures and evaluates performance and brings to light the variations, if any, for purpose of necessary action by the management and to prevent the recurrence of such variations in future. The important features of control can be summed up as follows:

(a) It is an important managerial function.

(b) It is concerned with setting standards.

(c) It involves the measurement of actual performance.

(d) It brings to light the variations, if any, from the standards set.

(e) Its object in checking the variations is to rectify them and prevent their recurrence.

Thus, "control is a systematic effort by business management to compare performance to predetermined standards, plans or objectives to determine whether performance is in line with these standards and presumably to take any remedial action required to see that human and other corporate resources are being used in the most effective and efficient way possible in achieving corporate objectives". (Robert Mockler – Readings in Management Control).

SCOPE OR AREAS OF CONTROL

1. Control over policies of an enterprise.
2. Control over organisation.
3. Control over personnel employed in a concern.
4. Control over wages and salaries paid to the employees.
5. Control over costs of material, labour, overheads etc.
6. Control over capital expenditure.
7. Control over production.
8. Overall control.

NEED FOR CONTROL

A control system is needed for three purposes:

1. To measure progress.
2. To uncover deviation.
3. To indicate corrective action.

1. To Measure Progress

There is a close link between planning and controlling the organisation's operations. We have discussed in Planning chapter how in the planning process, the fundamental goals and objectives of the organisation and the methods for attaining them are established. The control process measures progress towards those goals. As Fayol so clearly recognised decades ago, "In an undertaking, control consists in verifying whether everything occurs in conformity with the plan adopted, the instructions issued and principles established." As the navigator continually takes readings to ascertain where he is relative to a planned course, so does the manager take readings to see whether his enterprise or department is on the charted and predetermined course.

2. To Uncover Deviations

Once a business organisation is set into motion towards its specific objectives, events occur that tend to pull it "off the target." A successful control process is one that effects corrections to the organisation before the deviations become serious. Major events which tend to pull an organisation "off the target" are as follows:

Change: Change is an integral part of almost any organisation's environment. Markets shift, new products emerge, new materials are discovered and new regulations are passed. The control function enables manager to detect changes that are affecting their organisation's products or service. They can then move to cope with the threats or opportunities that these changes represent.

Complexity: Today's vast and complex organisations, with geographically separated plants and decentralised operations, make control a necessity. Diversified product lines need to be watched closely to ensure that quality and profitability are being maintained; sales organisation's various markets — foreign and domestic — require close monitoring.

Mistakes: Managers and their subordinates very often commit mistakes. For example, wrong parts are ordered, wrong pricing decisions are made, problems are diagnosed incorrectly, and so on. A control system enables managers defect these mistakes before they become serious.

Delegation: When managers delegate authority to subordinates, their responsibility to their own superiors is not reduced. The only way managers can determine if their subordinates are accomplishing the tasks that have been delegated to them is by implementing a system of control. Without such a system, managers will not be able to check on subordinates' progress, and so will not be able to take corrective action until after a failure has occurred.

3. To Indicate Corrective Action

Controls are needed to indicate corrective actions. They may reveal, for example, that plans need to be redrawn or goals need to be modified or there is need for reassignment or clarification of duties or for additional staffing. When the corrective action indicated by the control system is implemented, the loop in the system closes on the operating principle of a thermostat as shown in Fig. 12.1.

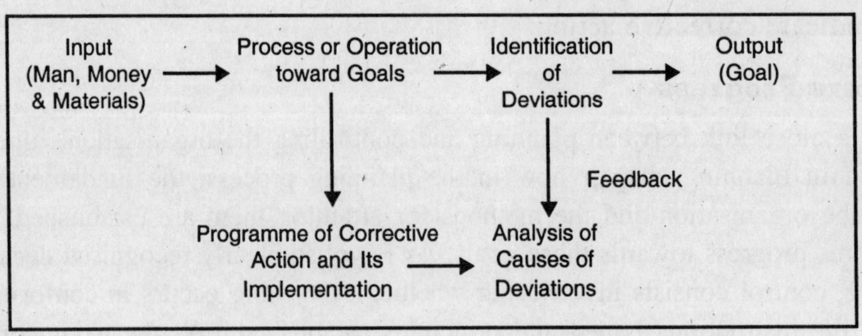

Fig. 12.1. Control as a closed loop system

Control Process

Prof. Newmann identifies the following essential steps of control process.

(a) establishment of standards for measuring performance;

(b) checking and reporting on performance; and

(c) taking of corrective action.

***(a) Establishment of standards*:** Standards are set to constitute criteria against which results can be measured. The standards which can be fixed for measuring performance are:

(i) Physical standards like quantities in units, man-hours, etc.

(ii) Cost standards such as cost per unit produced, material cost per unit, selling cost per unit of sale, etc.

(iii) Revenue standards such as annual sales for a department, etc.

(iv) Capital standards as the rate of return on capital invested, ratio of current assets to current liabilities, etc.

(v) Intangible standards such as competence of managers and employees, success of a public relations programme, morale of employees, etc.

(b) Checking and reporting on performance: To check performance against the pre-determined standards is the process of control. In other words, actual performance is compared with the standards fixed. For getting a correct idea of the variation from the standards fixed, it is necessary that standards are developed adequately and actual performance is measured accurately. Performance can be found out by a study of various summaries of figures, reports and statements. Similarly, the appraisal of performance of subordinates can be done by personal observation when they are at work. A quick comparison of actual performance with the standards fixed is possible if the control system is well organised. The manager, while comparing the performance with the standards fixed, has to find out not only the extent of variation but also the causes of variation. Some of the variations may be unimportant while some others may turn out to be important which need immediate corrective action. Managers may use techniques such as ratios, indexes, averages, control charts, etc. for appraising performance.

(c) Taking corrective action: The manager, after finding out the deviations from the prescribed standards, has to take steps to correct the deviations. There is need for the manager to take corrective action immediately so that the normal position can be restored without any delay. Further, the manager has to find out the causes of deviations. The causes of deviations may be due to inadequate communication, defective system of remuneration, defective system of selection of personnel, inadequate training of personnel, lack of motivation of subordinates, inadequate or outdated machinery, ineffective supervision, etc. Depending on the nature of causes, the manager has to take remedial action.

PLANNING AND CONTROL

Planning is a first step in management process which prepares a consistent, integrated and tactical programme. It consists of sequential operations to be conducted in future to attain the organisational objectives. Whereas the control system watches these sequential operations and stresses the events to conform to plan. Control and planning are two sides of the same coin. There cannot be planning without control. Control system uses certain standards to measure the planned operations. Control reveals the limitations of planning and suggests for revision. Revision may include setting of new goals, restructuring the organisation, correcting the staff position, change in directing and communication system. Therefore, planning and control go hand in hand.

Planning process will be designed in such a way that they are automatically controlled. Systems, methods and procedure are designed to conduct the planning operations as per the objectives of planning. Systems themselves are the control tools. Control by nature is restrictive and regulative. Current day planning adopts a system which is relative in nature. Current planners do not like restrictions in their operations but they want to regulate. "The authority to control vests with the higher level of management. Because it is the superior who has delegated authority to the subordinate to carry out certain activity." But this higher level control regarding plan activity is not appreciated by management thinkers. They feel that it is restrictive in the sense that the workers involved in planned activity are controlled from the top. Peter F. Drucker is of the opinion "that there should be self-control rather than control from higher level." Therefore, control system should be regulative and "it should be a method of measuring progress through self-discipline of the workers." "Self-control here is a system of control wherein each level of management ensures for itself that it follows the planned course and attains the targets assigned to it. Self-control is a self-regulatory process." Thus, planning sets the system for operation and control performs the duty of watchman to implement the plan successfully and if the plan does not get the desired result, control suggests the successful measures which can be adopted in replanning.

RELEVANCE OF CONTROL

The relevance of control in the management process is already discussed in terms of the need for control. However, it should be noted that scarce resources of the firm can be effectively utilised if control systems are fully adopted. The men at work allowed themselves to work without control. There will be deviation from the plan and the work will be casual. Therefore, it is relevant to have control systems in the management process. It enhances the work efficiency and boosts the morale of the organisation and ultimately brings efficiency in production. Less or no control results in inefficiency and conflicts among workers. Controls keep the workers under check. It introduces discipline amongst workers. It ensures effective utilisation of resources. "Control consists of verifying whether everything occurs in conformity with the plans adopted, the instructions issued and principles established. It has to point out weaknesses and operating procedural errors in order to rectify them and prevent recurrence. It operates on everything — things, people and action." (McFarland).

FACTORS INFLUENCING OF EFFECTIVE CONTROL SYSTEM

Some of the influencing factors of effective control system are as follows:

(1) Reflecting Organisational Needs: The control system adopted should suit the needs of a concern. Control system used in the finance department will be different from that used in the sales department or the production department. Similarly, the control system for a capital-intensive or machine-based method of production is different from the control system that is needed in the labour-intensive methods of production. Hence, the manager should choose such control system which is appropriate to the nature and needs of a concern.

(2) Promptness in Reporting Deviations: The control system should enable subordinates to inform their superiors in time about their performance. This would help the managers in detecting the deviations and also in taking prompt corrective actions.

(3) Forward-looking Controls: A good control system is one that detects deviations early enough so as to enable the manager to take quick corrective action. For example, cash control forecasts cash needs well in advance and the manager is enabled to take corrective action immediately in case there is any deviations from the forecasts.

(4) Objective Control Controls should be objective. Objective controls clarify the expected results in clear and definite term and they also provide the control standards by which actual performance can be measured.

(5) Flexible Control: Plans and other predetermined standards or criteria need to be altered from time to time. Hence, the control system should be flexible so that it can be adjusted to suit the needs of any modification or alteration in the plans or other predetermined criteria.

(6) Economical Controls: The control system should be economical. The benefit derived by the business concern from a control system should be more than the cost involved in its maintenance.

(7) Simple Controls: To be effective, controls must be simple and easily understandable by the manager as well as the subordinates. A control system which is complicated and not intelligible cannot be practised by the manager.

(8) Corrective Action: The control system should not only detect deviations from the predetermined standards but also should provide solution to the problems that are responsible for deviations. In fact, this can be said to be an important factor on which the effectiveness of control system depends. In the words of Koontz and O'Donnell, "An adequate system should disclose where failures are occurring, who are responsible for them and what should be done about them."

(9) Acceptable to Organisation Members: The system should be acceptable to organisation members. When standards are set unilaterally by upper level managers, there is a danger that employees will regard those standards as unreasonable or unrealistic. They may then refuse to meet them. Status differences between individuals also have to be recognised. Individuals who have to report deviations to someone they preceive as a lower level staff member may stop taking the control system seriously.

(10) Reveal Exceptions at Strategic Points: A control system should be such as reveal exceptions at strategic points. Small exceptions in certain areas have greater significance than larger deviations in other areas. Five per cent deviations from the standards in office labour cost is more important than 20 per cent deviation from the standard in cost of postage stamps. That we can quantify something is no reason for measuring it. The question is "Is this what a manager's attention should be focused on?"

(11) Motivate People to High Performance: A control system is most effective when it motivates people to high performance. Since most people respond to a challenge, successfully meeting a tough standard may well provide a greater sense of accomplishment than meeting an easy standard. However, if a target is so tough that it seems impossible to meet, it will be more likely to discourage than to motivate effort. Standards that are too difficult to attain may, therefore, cause the performance of organisation members to decline.

(12) Other Requirements: Controls should be such that they should be positive, constructive, must be helpful and also provide guidance to the employees. Further, the manager should recognise the importance of human beings in the control system.

METHODS OF ESTABLISHING CONTROL (CONTROL STAGES)

Control methods are adopted in three stages.

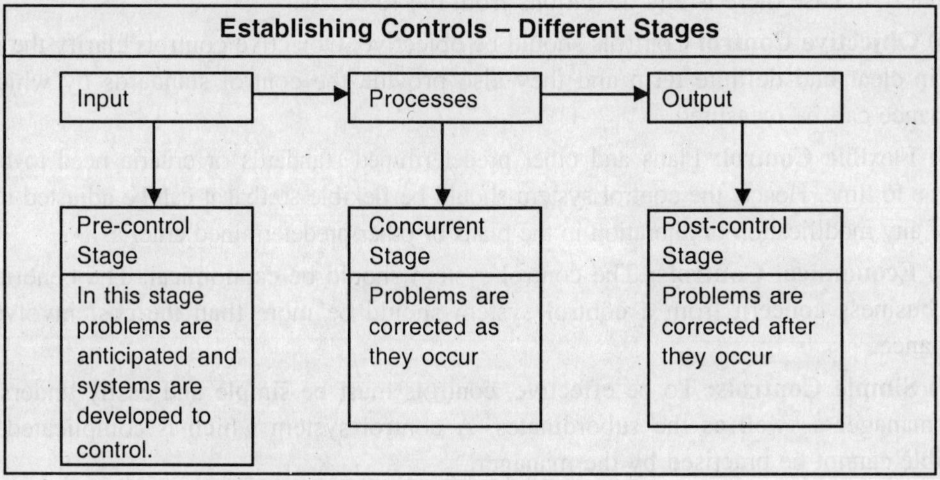

Fig.12.2. Designing Control Systems.

1. Pre-control or Feed Forward Control Stage

In the **first phase**, the controls are evolved even before the plans are implemented. These methods are termed as "**Pre-control**" **operation**. In this stage, the proposed operations are devised in such a way that actual results will compare favourably with planned results. Therefore, the important aspect to be considered is that the management policies are to be fully reflected in action plans. The policies actually give direction in which the objectives are to be achieved. The methods and procedure should be framed in accordance with policies.

As actual operation methods and procedure are prepared as per the objectives and policies, **Pre-control** becomes an effective control system and facilitate the attainment of desired results. Resources allocation is another aspect which gets importance in pre-control system. Both human and non-human (technical financial) resources are to be properly allocated and "monitoring" devices are to be developed for proper utilisation of these resources. Control devices should see that resources are utilised for the purpose for which they are appropriated. Control system should signal the top management about dangers of diversion of resources immediately.

Thus, precontrol devices, develop inbuilt control systems to be adopted in operational plans. The term "inbuilt" refers to the very operational procedure which gives the desired result. The purpose of control system is to achieve the desired objectives. For example, devising an "Internal check" system which controls a method operated by two or more persons without the knowledge of one another. In this system, there will be check of procedure at every point of operation without the knowledge of one another who are involved in that method. You just imagine the process of clearing a cheque in a bank counter. When you present your cheque to the ledger clerk, that person examines your ledger and passes cheque to the accountant who will be sitting in a different place. Accountant will examine the entries made by ledger clerk and pass the cheque for payment after making an entry, in his scroll. Then the cashier will make payment to the customer across the cash counter. In this procedure, you find that a transaction is checked by three persons — ledger clerk, accountant and cashier — without the knowledge of one another. This is a pre-control system evolved to monitor the operations. Similarly in every control, pre-control devices are designed and incorporated in the operational procedure. This facilitates the automatic control of operations. These pre-control devices are a must in every planning operation and are designed for human, financial and marketing operations. These control systems are evolved by the top management in accordance with objectives and policies of the organisation.

2. Concurrent Control Stage

In the **second phase of controlling**, the operation managers have to monitor the procedures in accordance with the plan already laid down. The manager should observe the operations and instruct subordinates in the proper methods and procedures. He/She is only a link between top management and workforce and directs the operations in accordance with the laid policies, methods and procedures. The relative importance of direction depends upon the nature of task to be performed by the workforce of that unit. This technique is called "***Concurrent control.***"

In this stage every operation is directed. The director (*i.e.*, manager) should possess "*interpersonal communication skill.*" The operational aspects are to be properly communicated to the workforce (Subordinates). If there is no clarity in communication, the subordinates, when they do not understand clearly the policies and procedures may deviate in their operations. Hence, the manager should have communication skills to regularly inform the subordinates about their operations. Many managers think that laid down methods and procedures are clear and there is no necessity for further clarification to be made to the workforce. But, many a time the workers had failed to understand their task and had deviated from the set task. Therefore proper communication of procedures is very essential.

The concurrent control depends upon "not only the manner in which the directives are communicated but the manner of the person who directs." The style and character of the manager also will have an impact on the direction and control technique. If the managers are intelligent, democratic and more humane in nature, they give proper direction and any deviation in operation from the set standard will be rectified immediately and the desired results are achieved. If he is autocratic or permissive, these will have different effect on control methods.

Besides these aspects, the fast changing technology, market forces compel managers to resort to decision-making approach. They cannot stick on to the formal chain of command. This deviation will help the organisation to complete the task in emergency situations. Thus, the concurrent control technique involves, proper communication of methods and procedure, clarity in communication and right decision-making technique in case of emergency.

3. Post-control or Feedback Control Stage

Besides Pre-control and concurrent control systems, **post-control measures** are to be adopted for successful completion of planning. Historical documents provide a base for post control operations. The financial statements, the production documents, marketing data, etc., available after the implementation of plan will provide data for corrective actions. The routine post-control methods used in several organisations are: (i) Standard costing techniques. (ii) Financial Statement analysis, (iii) Performance appraisal of employees and (iv) Quality control systems.

Standard costing system provides a mechanism which facilitates the comparison of actual cost of production with standard costs already set in each element of costing, *viz.*, raw material, labour and overheads. Standard costs are predetermined costs. Although standard costing and variance analysis technique have been used profusely in production, the adopting of this technique in sales and administrative expenses is increasing. **Variance analysis** shows the difference between actual expenditure and standard cost. This will help the management to take corrective action.

Every firm prepares annually financial statements like Income statement (P&LA/C), Balance sheet, Funds Flow statement, Cash Flow Statements, Management reports etc. These are all post operation documents and provide the real situation of the firm for a given period which includes assets, liabilities, equity, income and expenditure. They also show how the funds are obtained (sources) and spent (application). Cash movement is also disclosed. These are all the historical aspects and provide data to formulate a new strategy, if need be.

Periodical performance appraisal of human resources in a firm is essential and is a post control technique. Evaluating human resources is a very critical task. Their work cannot be weighed physically or cannot be easily quantified. Whether the assigned duties to the managers and their subordinates are properly performed or not, have to be examined periodically to see that there will not be deviation from the set task.

Another post-control device to be adopted is Quality Control. "Systems have to be developed and efforts have to be put in to control the quality of the product or service. The strategist should establish quality centres in each system to ensure quality in operation or production etc. It is not possible to ensure cent percent quality in operation or production. It is due to variation in raw material, imperfect operational aspects, monotony of workers at later stages of their daily routine, etc. Everywhere "*Quality*" has become buzzword. People are prepared to pay high price for quality product. Therefore, the planner should incorporate quality standards in operations and monitor the same throughout the implementation of operational plans. Quality control should be linked to organisational performance. There are several dimensions of quality that are percieved by consumers. They may be: (i) Performance (the product's primary operating character), (ii) Features, *i.e.*, exclusive characters of the product, (iii) Reliability (iv) Conforming to the standards, (v) Durability of the product, (vi) Serviceability, (vii) Aesthetics (taste, looks, smell, sound, etc., of a product or service) and (viii) Perceived quality.

All these quality dimensions of consumers cannot be imbibed in one product or service. One or two dimensions may be adopted in this. For example, purchase of TV set. One consumer may examine the functions and durability. Another may look into the appearance of the set. Third may look into the price. Fourth may consider the after sales service etc. Thus,the quality dimensions are different and the strategist should consider the quality concept and adopt it in his strategy.

Integrated control

Therefore, every control system involves **three** fundamental sub-control systems, *viz.*, **precontrol, concurrent control** and **post control systems**. Planner has to design an integrated control incorporating these control systems. The integrated control system should provide for "standards, information and corrective action at every point from inputs to process to output."

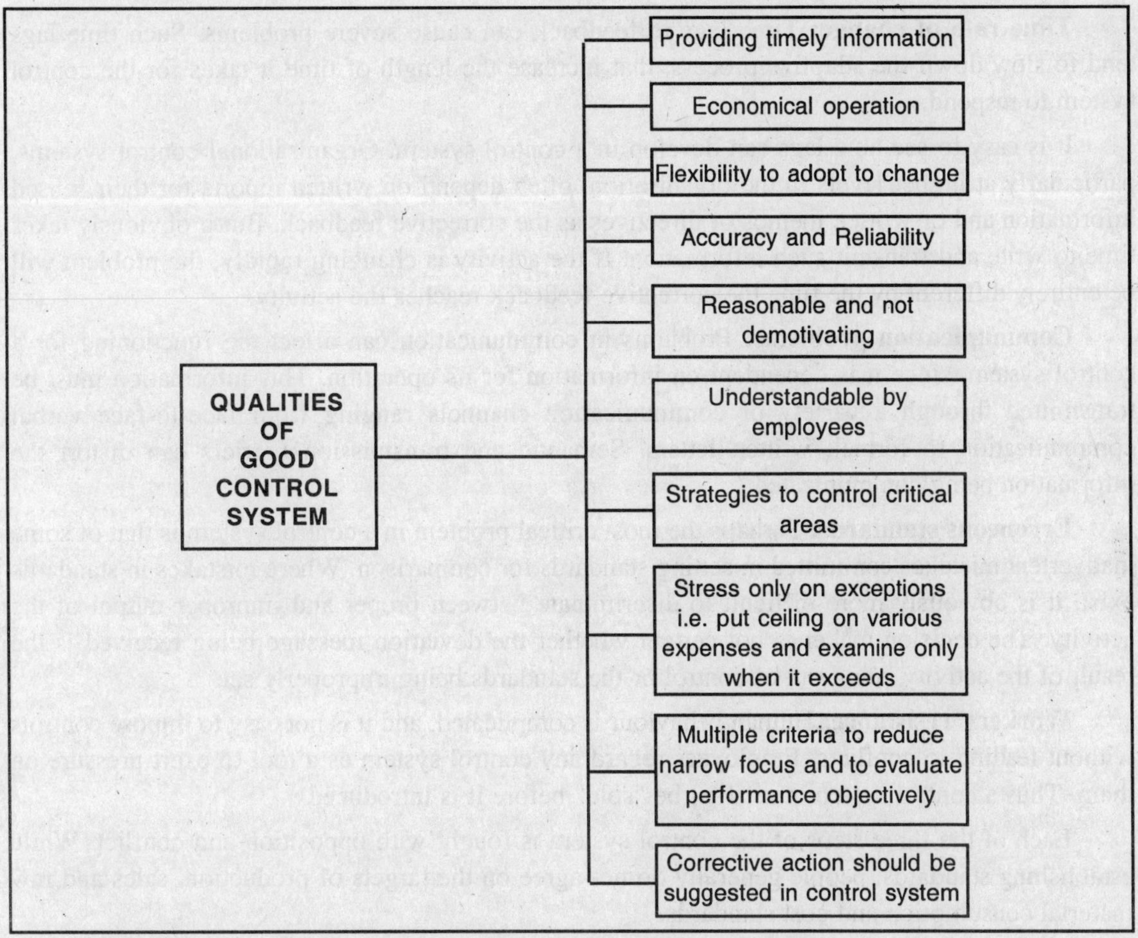

Fig.12.3. Features of Good Control System

PROBLEMS IN THE CONTROL PROCESS

Magnitude of change: Control system is mostly to cope with changes of certain magnitude. Certain decisions are made regarding which of the variables in the system can change, how much will they change, and what actions can be taken to correct changes. The system is designed around these variables. For example, management recognises that not all employees will show up each day on a production line and that production problems will occur because of equipment or material problems, or absence of workers in shop floor.

Therefore, it provides for alternative labour sources and for maintenance men or production engineers who can be called when technical problems occur. These corrective actions are programmed into the foreman's decision rules. But these corrective actions can work only when the assumptions are met, e.g., when only one or two employees do not show up or only one machine at a time breaks down. If 90 per cent of the workers go home after lunch because they had food poisoning after eating in the cafeteria, there is very little the foreman can do to correct the change. The variables have gone outside the range that the control system was designed to handle.

Time rate of change: Time lags in feedback can cause severe problems. Such time lags tend to slow down the adaptive process, that increase the length of time it takes for the control system to respond.

It is easy to see how lags can develop in a control system. Organisational control systems, particularly at higher levels in the organisation, often depend on written reports for their sensed information and or written memos or directives as the corrective feedback. But it obviously takes time to write and transmit such information. If the activity is changing rapidly, the problem will be entirely different by the time the corrective feedback reaches the activity.

Communication problems: Problems in communication can affect the functioning for a control system, since it is dependent on information for its operation. This information must be transmitted through a variety of communication channels ranging from face-to-face verbal communication to formal, written letters. Semantic and transmission barriers can distort the information being communicated.

Erroneous standards: Perhaps the most critical problem in a control system is that of some inadvertent mistakes committed in setting standards for comparison. Where mistakes in standards exist, it is obviously more difficult to discriminate between proper and improper output of the activity. The decision-maker is not certain whether the deviation message being received is the result of the activity being out of control or the standards being improperly set.

Workers' resistance: Human behaviour is complicated, and it is not easy to impose controls without leading to conflicts. Employees regard any control system as a tool to exert pressure on them. Thus a control system must first be "sold" before it is introduced.

Each of the three steps of the control system is fought with opposition and conflict. While establishing standards, people generally do not agree on the targets of production, sales and raw material consumption and cost standards.

The conflicts which originate during the first step come into sharp focus when the actual performance is being compared with the planned targets. People complain that the targets are unreal and non-feasible, control people lack objectivity, and the time span of appraisal is too short to enable a fair assessment or evaluation. People also resent the authority of the control department to sit in judgement and ask for explanations. In the final step when the corrective action is being taken, disagreement arises primarily over the location of the decision level regarding remedial action.

FACTORS DETERMINING GOOD CONTROL

A good control system has been influenced by certain vital factors. They are as follows:

1. Simplicity: The control system should be simple and should be easily understandable by those who operate it. If the operating system is not properly understood by the users (managers and workers) the control becomes ineffective. The control information supplied by the top should be assimilated at the operation level by the workers. The information relating to control should serve the purpose of that operation or method or procedure otherwise it becomes useless. Supposing finance manager sends some financial data to the lower level, like finance superintendent, in the form of statistical or mathematical formulae, the superintendent cannot understand that easily. Hence it will be of doubtful utility. Therefore, simple and easily understandable control system have to be evolved.

2. Adaptability: The control system should suit to the kind of operation it is intended to serve. Control systems vary from business to business, department to department in the business and one level to another in the same structure. Different control systems are adopted at the policy levels and different ones at the operation level. Even in functional areas like marketing, finance, production, human resource management or any other functional and sub-functional areas, the control systems differ. Techniques are different. The size of the business also determines the type of control systems to be adopted. Therefore whatever the control system devised should be adaptable to that particular activity for which it is designed.

3. Cost: There should be cost effectiveness in control systems. It should be economical in operation. Operations which do not require high degree of accuracy or quality which are expensive should not be designed for such operations. Control system should be based on the actual standard of accuracy. This brings down the cost of operation. Hence, control system should be economical and effective.

4. Versatile: The control system should be more dynamic in nature and versatile. It should be adjustable to changes. More flexibility is needed in control systems. There will be contingency in every plan of action irrespective of the fact that plan is thoroughly prepared. In such a contingency, if the existing control system fails, it should permit necessary changes that are required to meet the contingency. Control system should also identify the deviation in operation from the original plan. As Goetz puts "It is possible that some aspects of plan might fail. The control system should report such failures and deviations and should contain sufficient elements of flexibility to maintain managerial control of operations." Therefore one of the essentials of control systems is that it should be versatile and should be adjustable to any change required at the activity level. An element of flexibility should be there.

5. Quick Action: The control system should provide for quick action on the part of the concerned to correct the deviations in planned activity. "Day after the feast" policy should not be there in the control system. Deviations bound to take in planned programmes as plans are for costs of future activity. Therefore control system should facilitate to take quick corrective measures by the men at work. Late action will not serve the objectives of the plan. Therefore the control system should provide for quick corrective measures, whenever deviations are noticed in planned activity.

6. Progressive Feature: Control system should possess progressive feature and should foresee the possible deviations in the planned activity. This facilitates the corrective action to be taken even before the deviation takes place. The control system should be positive, progressive and forward looking. For example, raw material control in production activity. If the firm foresees the variation in production or anticipates the supply variation it can adopt a corrective measure even before the problem could arise and see that the production takes plase as per the plan.

7. Need Based System: The control system should be in accordance with the needs of the organisation. It should conform to the organisation pattern. It must be capable of fixing responsibility on the deviators. If concept of "Accountability" is not found in the control system, it loses its ground. Organisation and control are interdependent of each other and control system should match to the organisation needs.

8. Identify the Sensitive Areas: Plans contain certain sensitive or critical areas in their operations. Management principle of exception should be followed to operate such sensitive activities. The control system should also identify such sensitive operations to have effective control.

9. Purposeful: Human element is more involved in planned activity. The control system to be adopted should consider the human instinct and adopt control measures which are objective and purposeful. As far as possible human element should not be disturbed in the operational procedure. Control measures should be objective and make human element to react positively to the control measures.

10. Scope for Corrective Action: The control system, besides identifying the deviations, should also contain a system which can suggest corrective measures. Supposing the production cost has increased and has resulted in fall in profit. The deviation — excess cost of production over the predetermined cost should be identified and in what area it has occurred. Is it in raw material or labour or other overheads should be identified and accordingly corrective measures can also be suggested. If the control system only identifies the deviation and does not suggest the corrective action, the system fails in operation.

Control Tools and Techniques

Business enterprises adopt several control techniques. But all these techniques can be basically classified as (i) budgetary control devices and (ii) non-budgetary devices. Various control devices adopted in different functional departments have to be integrated or co-ordinated for the success of the organisation. Therefore, integration of activities of an enterprise and monitoring the activities itself is the essential technique of control. Considering "Cordination" of activities as the vital tool of control, some aspects of co-ordination are analyzed in the following paragraphs:

Co-ordination – A Control Measure

Principles of specialisation is one of the features on which the management of a modern enterprise is based. The workers and specialists either working in the same department or in different departments of the enterprise are entrusted with various activities. But merely applying the principles of specialisation will not ensure the desired results for the company. The management has to take responsibility for the harmonious blending of the activities of the different specialists so that the entire undertaking progresses as a viable, well-knit unit.

Moreover, a modern enterprise consists of a number of departments such as production, purchase, sales, finance, personnel, etc., and there is need for the management to see that all the departments function in such a way that they move harmoneously towards the realisation of the stated objectives of the enterprise. This function of management, i.e., harmoneous blending of the activities of the different specialists and also of the different departments for the achievement of desired ends, is called co-ordination. This is the best way of controlling.

Planning and execution in spite of the best efforts by the management cannot be effective if there is no co-ordination of activities of different specialists and also different departments of the concern. Because of this, co-ordination is regarded as a culmination of the managerial process. Koontz and O'Donnell have considered co-ordination as the very essence of management.

According to J. Lundy, "Co-ordination involves the development of unity of purpose and the harmoneous implementation of plans for the achievement of desired ends." Mooney and Reiley have defined co-ordination as the "orderly arrangement of group efforts to provide unity of action in pursuit of a common purpose." George R. Terry also has defined co-ordination as the "orderly synchronisation of efforts to provide the proper amount, timing and directing of execution resulting in harmonious and unified actions to a stated objective." Thus, co-ordination aims at an orderly arrangement of group efforts for the achievement of the desired ends. It includes all such efforts on the part of managers which are aimed at putting together the various parts of the organisation in such a way that they move harmoneously towards the realisation of the stated objectives of the enterprise.

To co-ordinate is to keep expenditure proportionate to financial resources, equipment and tools to production needs, stocks to the rate of consumption, sales to production and so on. Co-ordination is the management of interdependent activities, in work situations. It is the orderly synchronisation of fitting together of the interdependent efforts of individuals in order to attain a common goal. For example, in a hospital, the activities of doctors, nurses, ward attendants and lab technicians must be synchronised if the patient is to receive good care. Similarly, in a modern enterprise which consists of a number of departments such as production, purchase, sales, finance, personnel, etc., there is a need for all of them to properly time their interdependent activities and to efficiently reunite the sub-divided work. Thus, co-ordination of organisational activities will be the best general tool of controlling.

Co-ordination might best be considered as a control tool to integrate managerial functions. If a manager performs managerial functions efficiently and expertly, co-ordination is generated automatically and there remains no need for special co-ordination as such. This facilitates automatic and smooth controlling of activities.

Features or Characteristics of Co-ordination

An analysis of the above definitions indicates that co-ordination has certain characteristics. They are:

1. Co-ordination is the orderly arrangement of group efforts and is the best concurrent control tool.
2. It provides unity of action in pursuit of a common purpose. Unity of action is considered to be the heart of the co-ordination process.
3. It aims at achieving the common purpose of the enterprise through the orderly synchronisation of the efforts of the subordinates.

4. It is a process whereby an executive develops an orderly pattern of group efforts for accomplishing the common objectives of the enterprise.
5. The task of co-ordination is a managerial responsibility; co-ordination can be made effective only if an executive makes conscious efforts.
6. It is a continuous process to have continuous control over various activities of the organisation.

Aims of Co-ordination

Some of the important aims of co-ordination are as follows:

(a) To ensure a smooth interplay of the functions and forces of all the different component parts of the organisation.

(b) Operation of business activities in a systematic sequence.

(c) To complete the various activities of the enterprise as per planned schedule.

(d) To avoid inconsistencies in priorities, objectives and policies which may adversely affect the realisation of overall objectives of the company.

(e) To avoid interruptions in operations due to reasons such as delay in the supply of materials, tools or vague directions or omissions or wrong allocation of duties etc.

(f) Elimination of overlapping or duplication of work.

(g) To ensure proper synchronisation of the activities of the enterprise, *i.e.*, the actions of different departments are properly scheduled or timed, so that the various operations and processes are completed in a planned way. For example, if an engineering concern opens a new branch, its personnel department must be ready with personnel to run it.

(h) To remove the possible causes of difference of views and conflict of interests among the personnel of the concern.

(i) To develop team spirit among the staff and to canalise their efforts in the direction of reaching the chosen goals of business.

Types of Co-ordination

1. Co-ordination may be **internal or external** to the enterprise. Co-ordination among the employees of the same department or section, among workers and managers at different levels, among branch offices, plants, departments, sections is called **internal co-ordination,** whereas co-ordination with customers, suppliers, government and other outsiders with whom the enterprise has business connections is called **external co-ordination.**

2. Another classification of co-ordination is **vertical or horizontal**. Co-ordination of the activities of manager, deputy manager, superintendent and others below him is called vertical co-ordination. This means co-ordination from top down or bottom up. On the other hand, horizontal co-ordination takes place sideways, for example, co-ordination among different departments of the enterprise such as production, sales, purchasing, finance, personnel, etc., is called horizontal co-ordination.

Co-ordination Techniques

1. Co-ordination of Command: The manager or superior directs or commands his workers to control their efforts by balancing accountability and operating time.

2. Group Meetings: The managers and other officials meet to discuss common problems of organisation and the top management will provide solutions for smooth working.

3. Co-ordination Through Leadership and Delegation

4. Hierarchy: One boss will co-ordinate the activities down the line as a measure of control.

5. Liaison: A PRO or Liaison officer will co-ordinate the activate the functions of various departments and facilitate control of activities.

6. Incentives: This is a positive control measure and co-ordination process by which the incentives are given as and when the achievements happen.

7. Other Techniques: Co-ordinations, as measure of control, will be achieved voluntarily by informal contacts among people, by providing for interpersonal and inter-department contacts, making provision for unforeseen happenings, conducting frequent committee meeting to solve problems, creating a climate of mutual trust and collaboration and indoctrinating organisational members with goals and mission of the organisation.

Effective Co-ordination Principles

Co-ordination will be effective, when the following principles are followed:

1. **Early Start:** Co-ordinating activity should commerce from the planning stage itself. Before finalising the plan, mutual consultation among he concerned people will facilitate the smooth implementation of the plan. This will avoid resistance from the workers.

2. **Direct Contact:** Co-ordination is easier by direct personal contact among the people concerned. This avoids misunderstanding or misrepresentation and the tasks are successfully implemented. This is a self-control technique.

3. **Other Principles:** Continuity of activities from the stage of planning through the life span of the organisation, dynamism of leaders and workers to adopt themselves to change in internal and external environment, flexible operations, simple organisational structure to rearrange the tasks and activities which are similar or dissimilar, clear-cut objectives that are to be properly understood by managers and employees as well, defining clearly the authority and responsibility to minimise conflicts, violations etc, effective communication system through out the organisation to develop harmoneous relationship amongst workers and effective leadership and supervision are the other principles of effective co-ordination.

Effective co-ordination of programmes tasks and functions of various departments of an organisation will be an inbuilt control technique, which takes care of effective implementation of plans.

Co-ordinating Techniques (Tools)

Co-ordinating Techniques (Tools)

Oral Techniques (Tools)
— Regular staff meetings
— Problem review meetings
— General organisational meetings and information meetings
— Technical meetings
— Task-force meetings
— Routine meetings of manager-workers
— The Grapevine
— Special co-ordination activities

Written Techniques (Tools)
— Written objectives and management philosophy
— Organisation charts
— Documented plans
— Operating and policy manuals
— Programme instructions, work packages, work orders
— Memos, reports, letters, bulletins
— Minutes of meetings
— Designs and Drawings
— Specifications

Co-ordination, as a tool of control technique, monitors the tasks and operations without the knowledge of employees. Continuous supervision of work through co-ordination itself is a strong control measure.

Besides co-ordination of activities which serves as a general control measure, "Budgetary control" devices including budgets such as production budget, cash budget, capital budget, sales budget etc., play a major role in controlling the plan activities. Non-budgetary control devices such as managerial statistics, break-even analysis, internal audit, cost accounting etc. also act as effective tools of control system. Brief explanation of these devices is given in the following paragraphs:

Budgeting or Budgetary Control

A budget is a financial or quantitative statement prepared for a definite period of time. It states the policy to be pursued during that period for the purpose of attaining a given objective. It provides standards for comparison with the results actually achieved. According to George R. Terry, "Budget is an estimate of future needs, arranged to an orderly basis, covering some or all of the activities of an enterprise for a definite period of time". In the words of Professor Larders, "the essence of a budget is a detailed plan of preparations for some specified future period, followed by a system of records which will serve as a check upon the plan."

Budgeting is the process of preparing budgets whereas budgetory control is a device or technique of managerial control through budgets. According to J. Batty, "Budgetary control is a system which uses budgets as a means of planning and controlling all aspects of producing and/or selling commodities or services". Thus, budgetary control is planning in advance of the various aspects of business can be controlled. The important characteristics of budgetary control are: planning of activities of each department, co-ordination among various departmental plans, recording of actual performance, comparison between budgets standards and actual performance, determining the deviations, if any, finding out the reasons for deviations and taking of follow-up action.

ESSENTIALS OF EFFECTIVE BUDGETARY CONTROL

(1) **Effective Organisation:** The concern should be effectively organised and the responsibilities of each departmental managers are clearly defined and the line of authority sharply drawn.

(2) **Quick reporting:** The subordinates must send reports on performance without any delay. The managers on their part must analyse the report and take necessary action immediately.

(3) **Support of top management:** The top management must have a clear idea of the objectives of budgetary control and should implement the budgetary control programme seriously in order to infuse a sense of seriousness among the subordinates.

(4) **Reward and Punishment:** The employees whose performance is according to the budget plans should be suitably rewarded and the employees whose performance is not as per budget should not go unpunished.

(5) **Appropriate Authority:** The employees who are entrusted with the responsibilities of implementation of budgetary control should also be given appropriate authority to do so. If a person lacks authority to enforce his decision, it is difficult for him to fulfil his responsibilities

(6) **Flexibility:** If the circumstances warrant, the management should not hesitate to alter the budget figures. But at the same time, care must be taken to see that the budget figures are not altered too much or too often.

CLASSIFICATION OF BUDGETS

Budgets may be classified on the basis of purposes for which they are prepared. On this basis, we have the following types of budgets:

(1) **Cash budget:** Cash budget gives the estimated receipts and payments for the budget period and indicates the position of cash arising from it. It shows the cash requirements at various times of the budget period and helps the management in planning and arranging cash for the business concern. Thus, it ensures that a business concern never suffers from a shortage of funds. In additions, the cash budget helps the management in controlling and coordinating the activities concerned with receipts and payments.

(2) **Capital Budget:** Capital budget gives the estimates in respect of the capital resources of the business concern. It also states the plans with the estimated cost for investment, expansion, replacement, etc. Thus the budget serves as a device for planning capital expenditure.

(3) **Sales Budget:** Sales budget gives a comprehensive sales programme and plans for a specific period. It states the sales potential in terms of quantity, values, period,

types of budgets. Generally, the sales manager prepares the sales budget with the assistance of sales supervisor, salesman, market research officers and other connected with sales. For preparing the sales budget, factors such as the price trend of the product, population trend, customer's purchasing power, extent of advertising, past sales, nature of competition, economic situation in the country etc. are considered.

(4) **Selling and Distribution Cost Budget:** This budget gives the cost of selling and distribution of the products during the budget period. It includes costs of selling and distribution such as cost of insurance, packing, storing, transport, advertisement, sales commission, market research etc. Generally, the sales manager, advertising manager and distribution manager take responsibility to prepare the budget.

(5) **Production Budget:** This budget is also known as output budget and is based on sales budget. It indicates the quantity of units to be produced during the budget period. This budget helps in maintaining optimum balance between production, sales and inventory position of the firm. This budget is prepared by the production manager.

(6) **Production Cost Budget:** Production cost budget which is based on the production budget, lays down the estimated cost of carrying out the plans relating to production. Production cost budget is subdivided in to various sub-budgets like labour budgets, raw material budget, production overhead budget, etc.

(7) **Labour Budget:** Labour budget gives the estimated requirements of labour for carrying out the estimated production during the budget period. It may state both direct and indirect labour requirements. Generally, the personnel department prepares the labour budget in co-ordination with other concerned departments.

(8) **Raw Material Budget:** This budget which is prepared by the production department gives the estimated requirements of raw materials of different types for carrying out production during the budget period.

(9) **Production Overhead Budget:** This budget lays down the estimates of all production overheads to be incurred for carrying out the estimated production during the budget period. It breaks up the production overheads into fixed overheads, variable overheads and semi-variable overheads.

(10) **Master Budget:** Master budget is summary of all functional budgets and indicates how they affect the business as a whole. A master budget generally includes particulars regarding sales, production, cash position, fixed assets, labour, factory overhead, administration overhead, and selling and distribution overhead, major financial ratios and profit.

Advantages of Budgetary Control

Some of the important advantage of budgetary control are as follows:

(1) The various functional budgets state clearly the limits for expenses and also the results expected in a given period. By this, the uncertainties that may have to be faced by the enterprise are eliminated. Further, it should be possible for the enterprise to adopt a planned approach to various activities of the enterprise.

(2) As limits and authority of each manager are laid down in the budget, the management should delegate authority and responsibilities without sacrificing the overall control of the enterprise.

(3) Generally, the budgets are prepared by committee consisting of important executives of the enterprise and this provides to the enterprise the fruits of combined wisdom.

(4) Budgetary control tries to keep the expenditure within control and also to achieve the targets laid down. This keeps everybody always alert and encourages the optimum use of the enterprise resources.

(5) Budgetary control helps in finding out the deviations from the predetermined standards and by this, the management is enable to take suitable corrective action promptly. It means wastages and losses of the business concern are reduced to the minimum.

(6) Budgetary control is concerned with the activities of various departments which are interrelated or interconnected. This may help in promoting co-operation and team spirit among the employees of the different departments.

(7) Budgetary control involves the communication of management's policy and objectives to all the managers. Again, the reports of actual performance against the budget, how each manager has fared, what actions are necessary etc., are communicated to the managers. Thus, Budgetary control ensures proper communication in the enterprise.

(8) Budgetary control involves two function, *viz.*, (a) planning for its own future performance and (b) control to ensure adherence to the plans laid down. Thus, budgetary control ensures proper performance of the above two managerial functions.

Limitations of Budgetary Control

Budgetary control is not a foolproof tool and it has some limitations. They are:

(1) Since an effective budgetary programme reveals the performance of employees, there may not be wholehearted co-operation from inefficient employees for budgetary programmes.

(2) Budgets are based on estimates and hence the effectiveness of budgetary control depends on the accuracy with which the estimates are made about the future.

(3) Conditions and circumstances under which an enterprise functions are not static and hence, budgetary control to be effective must be so flexible as to suit the requirements of any change in the circumstances. But it is very difficult to attain flexibility in budget making.

(4) Budgetary control will not be effective if no arrangements are made for proper supervision and administration.

(5) Budgeting is only one of the tools of management. But often budgeting is taken as a substitute for management rather than as a tool of management. This may result in harmful consequences for the business.

(6) Budgetary control programme is very cumbersome and time- consuming process.

(7) The manager is discouraged from undertaking activities for which provision was not been made in the budget, but which are otherwise useful for the enterprise. Thus, the managers are discouraged from taking initiative.

We may conclude that inspite of these limitations, budgetary control confers many benefits on modern management. The benefits are such that the management cannot afford to disregard budgetary programme and control. Moreover, by planning and operating budgetary programmes carefully and wisely, some of the limitations can be overcome. Prof. C.T. Horngreen has rightly said that "if budgets are administered wisely, they compel management planning, provide definite expectations for judging subsequent performance and promote communication and co-ordination among the various segments of the business."

NON BUDGETARY CONTROL DEVICES

1. Cost Control

Cost control includes techniques such as (a) Cost Accounting, (b) Standard Costing and (c) Break-even point analysis.

(a) Cost Accounting: Profits of a business enterprise depend very much on the cost of production. Because of this, cost accounting and cost control are given the much importance by the business concerns. Costs are incurred by an enterprise for different types of activities. Management uses a number of systems for determining the cost of products and services. The management by keeping in view the nature of each industry, designs the cost accounting procedures, methods and records for effective cost control and cost reduction.

Advantages: The costing system provides a number of benefits to the management. They are:

(1) By avoiding all types of wastes and by more effective utilisation of labour and machine, it helps in reducing real cost of production.

(2) It helps in ascertaining the reasons for variation in the rate of profit.

(3) By highlighting the costs incurred and the profit earned by different departments, it provides a basis for future production policies.

(4) It helps in discovering which activities of the enterprises are profitable and which are unprofitable. The management may eliminate unprofitable activities in order to reduce losses.

(5) It helps the management in making decisions. For example,a decision relating to whether to make or buy a product can be taken with the help of cost accounts.

(b) Standard Costing: Standards costing is one of the important techniques of cost control used buy the business concerns. The steps involved to standard costing are as follows:

(1) Deciding cost standards for various components of costs such as labour overheads, raw materials,etc.

(2) Management of actual performance.

(3) Comparison of actual cost with the standard cost and finding out the variances.

(4) Finding out the causes of variances and taking measures to prevent the occurrences of variances in future.

(c)Break- even Point Analysis: Break-even analysis is a useful tool of management control over business profits. It is mainly concerned with the cost-volume-profits analysis. "Break-even analysis indicates at which level costs and revenue are in equilibrium". It is the point at which total revenue is equal to total cost, *i.e.*, the point of no profit and no loss. It helps in finding out the probable profit at any level of production and the relationship of different volumes, costs sales prices and sales mix to profits.

The break-even analysis is used by the manager for a number of purposes. Some noteworthy uses of break-analysis are:

(1) For calculation of profit for different sales volume;

(2) For calculation of sales volume to produce desired profits;

(3) For calculation of the sales required to offset reduction in price;

(4) For finding out the most profitable alternatives;

(5) For finding out the selling price per unit for a particular break-even point;

(6) For taking decision relating to the expansion of productive capacity;

(7) For determining the most profitable prices for the products of an enterprise;

(8) For maximum utilisation of resources; and

(9) For optimisation of profit.

Thus, the break-even analysis helps the management in number of ways.

2. Managerial Statistics

According to Kermit O. Hauson, "Managerial statistics deals with data and methods which are useful to management executives in planning and controlling organisation activities." By using such data, an analysis of past performance is made for control purposes. Managerial statistics also enable the manager to make a comparison between the past and present results with a view to ascertaining the causes of changes that have taken place and for making projection for future. They are also helpful to the management in planning and decision-making.

3. Internal Audit

In the case of internal audit, the internal auditor who is an employee of the organisation makes an independent appraisal of financial and other operations. In addition, he appraises the company's policies and plans and performance of management. Further, the internal auditor not only pinpoints defects in the management policies or plans but also gives suggestions for eliminating them.

4. Production Control

Production control which is one of the tools of control in the hands of management involves planning of production, routing, scheduling, stock control and manufacturing control. According to Spreiget, "production control is the process of planning in advance of operations, establishing the exact route of each individual item, part or assembly, setting starting and finishing dates for each important item, assembly and the finished product, and realising the necessary orders as well as initiating the required follow-up to effectuate the smooth functioning of the enterprise." Thus, production control covers every aspect of production so as to effectuate smooth functioning of the enterprise.

5. Personal Observation

The manager by observing their subordinates while they are engaged in work can exert more fruitful control. By personal observation, the manager will be in a position to know workers attitude towards their work and also correct worker's mistakes, if any. Further, the worker will not be wasting his time as he knows that he is being observed by his superior. Thus, the personal observation is also a valuable tool of control in the hands of managers.

6. External Audit Control

External audit is compulsory for all joint-stock companies. External audit ensures that the interests of shareholders and other parties connected with the company are safeguarded against the undesirable practices adopted by the management. The external auditor certifies the annual statements of the company after examining the relevant books of accounts and documents. The external audit is conducted by a qualifies Chartered Accountant.

7. Standing Orders, Limitations, etc.

Management also uses standing orders, limitations etc., as tools of control. The manager who delegates some of his powers to his subordinates lays down the limits for them. In business concerns, standing orders are issued by the management and they are to be observed by the subordinates. Standing orders may relate to rules, discipline, procedure etc. For Example, a standing order may say that no worker should absent himself from work without prior sanctions of leave.

8. Inventory Control

Inventory control or material management involves the controlling of inventory used by the enterprise. The enterprise might be using the inventory of different kinds and in different quantities. The controlling of inventory involves the maintaining of stock of the right kind of inventory in the right place and in right quantity and quality. It also refers to the controlling of the movement and timings Inventory. The process of inventory control consists of the following elements:

(a) Ascertaining the material requirements of the enterprise;

(b) Placing order with suppliers for necessary materials;

(c) Storing the materials in safe and good condition;

(d) Issue of materials only against the orders of the proper authority; and

(e) Deciding the reordering level for each kind of material.

9. Reports

A major part of control consists of preparing reports to provide information to the management for purposes of control and planning. The following are certain types of reports which are prepared and submitted tot he management regularly:

1. Top Management

(i) Profit and Loss statement, (ii) Balance sheet, (iii) Position of stock, (iv) Cash-flow statement, (v) Position of working capital, (vi) Capital expenditure and forwards commitments together with progress of projects in hand, (vii) Sales, production and other appropriate statistics

2. Sales Management

(i) Actual sales compared with budgeted sales to measure performances by (a) Products; (b) Territories; (c) Individual salesman; and (d) Customers

(ii) Standard profit and loss by products (a) For fixing selling prices; and (b) To concentrate sales on most profitable products.

(iii) Selling expenses in relation to budget and sales value analysed by (a) Products; (b) Territories; (c) Individual salesman; and (d) Customers

(iv) Bad debts and accounts which are slow and difficult in collection.

(v) Status reports on new or doubtful customers

3. Production Management

To buyer: price variations on purchase analysed by commodities.

To foreman (a) Operational efficiency for individual operators duly summarised as departmental averages. (b) Labour utilisation report and causes of lost time and controllable time. (c) Indirect shop expenses against the standard allowed. (d) Scrap report.

10. Special Reports

These reports may be prepared at the request of the management accountant or manager. The necessity for them may arise on account of the need for a more detailed information on matters of interest first revealed by the routine reports. Some of the matters in respect of which such reports may be prepared are: (a) Taxation, legislation and its effect on profits. (b) Estimate about the earning capacity of a new project. (c) Brerak-even analysis. (d) Replacement of capital equipment. (e) Special pricing analysis. (f) Make of buy decisions.

11. PERT and CPM

Both PERT (Programme Evaluation Review Techniques) and CPM (Critical Path Method) used the same basic concept and are being used for a wide range of planning and control problems. These two techniques are new management tools used in project management. They are useful to the management for the purpose of planning, scheduling and controlling the activities of various business projects. Business projects, particularly in modern days, are large and take a number of years for their completion and PERT and CPM techniques help the management in co-ordinating the activities of the different jobs in the project, in minimising the interruption in work and in completing the project as per schedule.

Steps for using PERT and CPM

Steps involved are as follows:

(1) First step is to break down the entire project into a number of independent jobs or activities and to list them.

(2) After preparing the list of various activities or jobs, the order of precedence for doing these jobs should be determined. This involves considering which activity must be completed first, before a particular activity can start (precedence), which activity can be undertaken while a particular activity is in progress (concurrence) and which activity cannot start until after a particular activity is completed (sub-sequence).

(3) The next step involves the drawing of a diagram indicating the precedence, concurrence and subsequence of all activities. The diagram also tells the time required for the completion of each activty or job.

(4) Another step involves the determination of the critical path, indicating the network in terms of the amount of time the entire project will take and them time needed for the completion of each activity. PERT and CPM techniques are applied in order to shorten the time spent on activities along the critical path so that the total time spent on the project will be shortened. For example, a project consists of three activities, *viz.*, X Y and Z and these three activities require for their completion 12 days, 6 days and 4 days respectively. Activities X and Y should be carried out simultaneously but activity Z can be commenced only after the completion of X and Y activities. In this case, the critical path would be along the paths of X and Y (fig. 12.4).

If X activity takes 12 days, Y activity takes 6 days and if these two activities are to be carried out simultaneously and Z activity can start only after the completion of these two activities, there is no use of spending money and making efforts for reducing the time of Y activity, but there may be good reason for spending money and making efforts to reduce the time of X activity for shortening the total time of project.

Advantages of PERT and CPM

(1) It involves identifying of critical elements and paying more attention to those activities.

(2) It helps in securing co-operation from all the departments.

(3) It helps in shortening the total time of the project.

(4) It helps in the best possible use of resources of the enterprise.

(5) It ensures attention and vigilance at all levels of management.

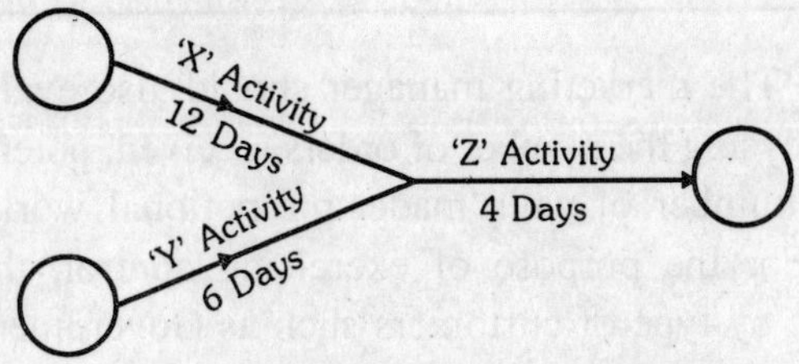

Fig. 12.4. Critical Path

Limitations of PERT and CPM

(1) it can be used mainly on cases where time is the essence of a programme.

(2) It is not suitable for continuous production and processing activities.

12. Marketing Control

Marketing is one of the most important functions of business enterprise. Marketing managers have to evaluate current marketing performance in order to take corrective action if necessary, so that the actual and desired results would become closer. The marketing manager has to identify the customer needs and should try to satisfy them. This helps the enterprise in earning profit. There is a needs to enforce certain control in the areas of sales and marketing costs so that the marketing division of the enterprise functions well.

The sales control includes control over products, sales personnel, customers, areas and market penetration.

Sales turnover indicates the consumer acceptance of a product. This requires the marketing manager to access on a regular periodical basis the performance of sales areas in terms of units sold and total rupee sales. The sales areas may be identified geographically by product or by customers and the marketing manager should get information on the performance of different areas and compare the results. For example, if a company sells in four areas, *viz.*, A,B,C and D, sales in areas C and D may be higher while in areas A and B may be below the targets. The marketing manager should find out the reasons for not achieving the target in A and B areas. The reasons for not achieving the targets in A and B areas may be competition from other firms, ineffective advertisement and promotional efforts etc. The marketing manager should take appropriate steps to achieve the target that is decided. He should also try to find out whether these targets are realistic.

Market penetration which is usually expressed as percentage of company sales to total potential sales for a given area is one of the important techniques for marketing control. The market penetration of company in an area may be affected due to poor performance of the total marketing programme of the company or due to some unforeseen events. It is here the company can exercise control. The marketing manager should find out the difference between the actual and contemplated market penetration and take corrective actions.

For exercising control over marketing, the marketing manager should get data about the sales performance of specific products, so that on the basis of trends in data, he would be in a position to decide to concentrate either on only the highest profit-earning products or to continue with the existing product mix. The marketing manager should also evaluate the performance of individual salesmen budget analysing the number of orders received, potential customers contacted by them, sales area covered, number of calls made, promotional work undertaken, marketing costs incurred by them etc. For the purpose of exercising control, the manager should also analyse the percentage of sales by type of customers such as Government and non-Government, institutional and non institutional, wholesaler and retailer, home and foreign buyers etc.

13. Quality Control

Quality of an item refers to the ability of a product to satisfy its intended purpose in relationship to the price. The function of quality control is an integral part of management control. Quality control, if it is effectively done, results in many benefits. They are: (a) it minimises waste, (b) reduces cost, (c) builds up goodwill of the product in the market, (d) facilitates advertising and (e) increases sales.

The techniques of quality control are:

(1) **Inspection:** Inspection involves checking the product so that it conforms to established standards in terms of appearance, packaging, performance etc. the inspection department of the company will have to take decisions relating to what to inspect, where to inspect, how much to inspect, how to inspect and when to inspect. Inspection of products may be done by testing the products or measuring them or by looking at them. Inspection helps in identifying the products which do not conform to established standards and in removing them from the inventory and also in stopping further production of imperfect products.

(2) **Statistical Quality Control (SQC):** SQC technique is used for the control of quality of the products by the application of theory of probability to the results of examination of samples. It is concerned with the problem how many items of larger number should be inspected to determine a probability that the quality of the total number conforms to the quality standards determined. This technique is used because in many instances, it is not possible to test each item of a total group. For example, in the case of manufacture of electric tubes, only a random sample can be tested to find out the quality of the whole lot. There is no certainty, however, that a random sample is representative of an entire lot. But a manager by means of SQC can determine the probability of the sample's reliability.

Advantages of SQC are (a) it is economical and saves cost, (b) it reduces waste of time, (c) it helps in determining whether the quality of manufacture is satisfactory and (d) it ensures uniformity in the quality of products manufactured.

14. Financial Controls

Business concerns exercise financial control for several purposes. It has to determine the need for retaining the earning for company growth. For this, it should consider the pros and cons of retaining the earnings. The company also has to take a decision with regard to the utilisation of retained earning for various purposes. Further, there is a need to take a decision as to how the additional funds required by the company will be made available, that is, whether by the issue of shares raising of loans or by retaining profits. For the purpose of exercising financial control, many control techniques are available. Some of them are:

(a) Comparative financial statements.

(b) Financial ratios

(a) Comparative Financial Statements: Analysis of the financial statements helps in judging the (1) profitability and (2) financial soundness of the company. For exercising the overall financial control of the company, balance sheet and income statement of the company are very helpful.

***Balance Sheet*:** For control purposes, a comparative balance sheet is prepared in such a way as to show; (a) balance of accounts on different dates and (b) the extent of increase or decrease in the balance of accounts over a period of time. From the balance sheet, one can know the increase or decrease in the various assets liabilities and shareholder's equity or capital over a period of time due to operation of business. The changes in increase or decrease in various items may be shown, both in absolute figures and percentages. The managers, with the help of comparative figures for different periods, can identify those aspects of the company which are contributing to or detracting from, overall financial stability.

***Income Statement*:** The income statement helps the manager in finding out the net income generated and losses suffered by the company from its operating activities over a period of time. The operating results may be shown in absolute terms as well as in percentages.

The comparative income statement contains particulars relating to sales (revenue), expenditure and net income. The statement can be analysed in its entirety with each item being judged in relation to all other items in the statement. If the manager finds that the deviations are significant and unfavourable, he can identify the reasons for the deviations and take corrective action.

(b) Financial Ratio Analysis: For analysing financial data, ratio analysis is used. From the figures in balance sheet and income statement, financial ratios are computed. Financial ratios are relationships stated in mathematical terms between figures which have a cause and effect relationship or which are connected with each other in some other manner. For example, a ratio of gross profit to sales may indicate the relationship between turnover and profit of the company.

Financial ratios provide a measure of financial condition of organisation and hence they are useful in control. As financial ratios help managers in understanding the current financial state of an organisation. It would be possible for him to plan for future financial requirements more accurately. Understanding of the current financial position also helps him to take corrective action to improve positions. However, for a thorough investigation of the financial position of an organisation, the manager should not depend on any single ratio but on a number of ratios. The different ratios should be analysed over a period of time and compared with the ratios of other firms in industry. This helps the manager to determine the firm's relative position in the industry. Many financial ratios are in use. Some of them are:

(*i*) ***The net profit ratio:*** It expresses the profit as a percentage of sales.

(*ii*) ***The operating ratio:*** This ratio states the ratio of total operating expenses to sales.

(*iii*) ***Return on networth:*** This ratio gives the rate of return on the shareholder's money.

(iv) *Liquidity ratios:* These ratios show the capacity of the organisation to meet its short-term liabilities.

(v) *Acid test ratio or quick ratio:* This ratio also indicates the ability of an organisation to pay current liabilities without relying on the sale of inventories and supplies.

(vi) *Leverage ratio:* These ratios measure the extent to which an organisation has been capitalised by debt. They indicate the extent of borrowings and scope for future borrowings.

(vii) *Debt-equity ratio:* This ratio indicates the soundness of financial position of the organisation.

(viii) *Inventory turnover:* This shows how often inventory turns over or is replenished each year.

(ix) *Fixed asset turnover:* It measures the turnover of fixed assets to net sales and shows the efficiency achieved in the use of fixed assets.

15. Information Control

Organisation gets information from its internal sources and also from outside sources such as customers, trade agencies, market research, consultants, and Government agencies. Within an organisation, information moves upward from lower levels. The information that is received by the manager from different sources, helps him in taking decisions relating to his business. Large organisations take the help of computers and other transmission equipments for getting quick information and also for processing and analysing them. In modern days, the Management Information System (MIS) is playing an important role in organisations in supplying the data for the purpose of taking decisions. MIS is a data bank, in which facts are stored and are made available readily to the individual decision-maker or a decision-making committee. The computers which are installed in organisations perform functions such as (a) storing the data in 'memories,' (b) performs mathematical computations, (c) combining new data with what are stored, and (d) prints answers at a great speed.

Information control is needed so that there would be a flow of right information, from right sources to right purposes and at right time. Manager should get only that information which is essential for the purpose of decision-making and should not be burdened with non-essential information. He should get not lengthy reports but 'essence' through the management reporting system. For managers, as they are concerned with creative thinking, quantitative aspect of information is not so important as the qualitative once. At the lower level, the quantitative aspect of information is important.

The manager should get information at the right time, so that they can take corrective actions without any delay. Further, upwards communication from subordinates must be encouraged and also the management should see that the downward communication is not blocked or filtered and reaches subordinates in time, so that they can perform their duties and responsibilities effectively. Downward communication flows generally through notices, circulars, house magazines, office orders, etc. and they should be drafted in such a way that they are understood by those for whom they are meant without any difficulty.

16. Responsibility Accounting

Responsibility accounting can be defined as a system of accounting under which each departmental head is made responsible for the performance of his department.

Under this system, each department is made a semi-autonomous profit centre, *i.e.*, a centre responsible for the generation of profit. A department earns profit by selling its output to other departments or profit centers in the same organisations. The prices at which one department or profit centre sells its output or services to other departments or profit centers are called transfer prices. The transfer prices may be fixed in any one of the following ways.

1. Markup on Actual Cost: Under this method, companies just add some percent as margin of profit on sales to the process cost as the transfer cost. For example, a steel company has three plants, *viz.*, Pig-iron plant, Steel plant and Finishing plant and the Pig-iron plant supplies steel to the finishing plant. If the performance of all the three plants is to be judged by the profits they earn, the pig-iron plant will supply iron to steel plant at a price arrived at by adding 15% profits to its process cost. This will be the purchase cost of the steel plant. Similarly, the steel plant will add 15% on its production cost and that would become purchase price of the finishing plant. Thus, each centre will show separate profit.

This method of fixing transfer price is not good method. This is because it passes on the inefficiency of one department to the other.

2. Markup on Standard Cost: Under this method, the markup on standard cost is allowed. If any department is working at, less than the standard efficiency, it will have a lower profit since its cost could be higher than the standard costs. This method has the advantage of revealing the inefficiency of each department. However, one disadvantage of this method is that the ultimate sale price of product becomes very high since it includes the markups on standard costs for each department.

3. Market price: Under this method, the transfer price is fixed at a price equivalent to the one prevailing in the market at the time when transfer is made. The receiving department thus pays the selling department the same price which it would have pay to an outside seller. One advantage of this method is that it reveals true profitability of the each department. The only limitation of this method is that very often the market prices for the semi-finished output which is transferred from one department to another department are not available.

4. Negotiated price: Under this method, the transfer prices may be fixed on the basis of negotiations between the heads of departments.

Advantages of Control

Much has already been said about various dimensions of control. Theses dimensions cover one or the other advantage of controls. However, they may be summarised as follows:

1. It prevents faulty operations and creates a good base for future faultless operations and help in taking sound decisions.
2. Control systems help taking corrective measures in case the plan activity is deviated from original designs and also assist in adopting follow-up actions.

3. Control systems provide a good opportunity for decentralisation of authority.
4. Control brings about co-ordination in planned activity.
5. Workforce in the organisation will be disciplined by adopting good control system and brings about operational efficiency.

Limitations of Control

Control systems are not free from 'Limitations.' Control system, functions as a component of management process which is controllable by the organisation. But there are other factors which are not controllable by the organisation like, government policies, consumer behaviour, political unrest, market behaviour, change in technology, etc. These uncontrollable factors may hamper the organisational efficiency if proper strategies are not adopted from time to time.

Some of the control systems are expensive and cannot be implemented by small firms. Only common systems are adopted.

Quantification of some of the control operations is not possible. The behaviour or morale of employees etc. cannot be analysed in terms of quantity.

Mental agitation on the part of employees may also affect control systems.

SUMMARY

1. Controlling is checking current performance against the predetermined standards contained in the plans with a view to ensuring adequate progress and satisfactory performance.
2. Control is an important function of management. It is the basis of planning and helps the management in achieving adequate progress and satisfactory performance. It covers almost all management activities and keeps check on the other functions of the management. It creates an atmosphere of order and discipline in the enterprise.
3. Essential steps in the control procedure are: (a) Establishment of standards for measuring performance, (b) checking and reporting on performance and (c) taking corrective action.
4. Essentials of effective control system are: control system should suit the needs of the concern, promptness in reporting deviations and it should be forward-looking, flexible, economical, simple and constructive.
5. Control involves the comparison of actual results with desired results. Firm has to plan for specific results. Strategic control involves three phases of operation: (i) Pre-control (ii) Concurrent control and (iii) Post-control systems.
6. There are several control techniques co-ordination of organisational activities will be a general control system co-ordination continuously monitors the activities of the organisation.
7. All devices of control can be classified into: (a) budgetary control devices, and (b) non-budgetary control devices. Budgetary control devices include budgets such as budget for sales, capital, cash, selling cost, production, labour, raw materials and production overheads.
8. Non-budgetary control devices consist of cost accounting and cost control, standard costing, break-even analysis, internal audit, production control, personal observation, external audit control, standing orders, limitations, inventory control through budgets.
9. Some advantages of budgeting control are possibilities for having a planned approach towards various activities, elimination of uncertainties, optimum use of resources, keeping expenditure

with control, reduction in wastages and losses, promoting co-operation and team spirit among employees, and proper communication in the enterprise.

10. Some limitations of budgetary control are lack of wholehearted co-operation from inefficient employees, difficulties in estimating the future accurately and inflexibly in budget. Further, budgetary control involves a cumbersome and time-consuming process and also discourages managers from taking initiative.

STUDY QUESTIONS

1. Give the meaning of "control" as perceived in management. Analyse the need for control.
2. What is objective control? Analyse the steps involved in control process.
3. What is flexible control?
4. What do you mean by economic control?
5. What do you understand by quality control?
6. What is Pre-control or Feed Forward Control?
7. What do you mean by concurrent control?
8. Give the meaning of post-control or feedback control.
9. Name two types of control methods. Analyse the features of control.
10. What is PERT?
11. What is CPM?
12. Name two types of Control Systems.
13. What do you mean by budgetary control? State its limitations.
14. Give the meaning of Budget.
15. Name various types of budget.
16. Give the meaning of non-budgetary control.
17. What is cost control?
18. What is break-even point? Give an analytical note on BEP.
19. Expand PERT. Analyse PERT as a control technique.
20. Expand CPM. Briefly analyse this.
21. What is Responsibility Accounting?
22. State the advantages of standard cost.
23. Give a note on "Report" as a control tool.
24. Give a note on quality control.
25. Establish the relationship between planning and control.
26. Briefly explain the essentials of good control system.
27. Analyse the factors that influence a good control system.
28. State the advantages and limitations of control system.
29. Give the meaning of budgetary control. Give a note on classification of budget.
30. Briefly explain the various forms of budgetary control.
31. Explain the various forms of non-budgetary control.
32. Explain co-ordination as a control tool.

Practical Exercise-1

1. There are several control systems to be developed in an organisation. They may be sales control, purchase control, inventory control, investment decision, quality control, employee appraisal system *etc.* you may select one of these and develop a control system for the selected issue. While developing the control system, issues to be examined are: (i) objectives of the control system you have selected to develop, (ii) standards to be set, (iii) strengths and weaknesses of existing system and of system to be developed.

   Present a report to your teacher on the system developed and discuss.
2. Based on the knowledge you got from control methods draft the following charts.

   (i) Production control chart, (ii) Inventory management, (iii) Channels of distribution chart, (iv) Sources of Finance chart and (v) Production cost control chart.

Practical Exercise-2

1. You have been asked to prepare a break-even chart adopting imaginary figures.
2. An organisation adopt several control system. You may select any one of these systems and develop a control system for the one selected (points to be incorporated in control system are: (i) objectives of the control system, (ii) standard to be set and (iii) strength and weaknesses of the existing system and system to be developed). Present a report to your teacher on the control system you have developed.

SECTION II:

BEHAVIOURAL PROCESS

13

BEHAVIOURAL PROCESS—AN OVERVIEW

LEARNING OBJECTIVES

After reading this chapter, you should be able to know:

- Organisation – The Concept
- Behaviour – The Concept
- OB – Concept and Definitions
- OB – Objectives and Goals
- OB – Elements: People, Structure, Technology Environment – **Sub elements:** Knowledge Management Disciplines Associated with OB, levels of study and Decision-making.
- Historical Development of OB
- OB Models
- OB and Global Business Organisations
- Problems of OB
- Limitations of OB
- Future of OB

"Organisational Behaviour" – OB or behavioural process in an organisation is a field of study which has emerged on the business scene is of a recent addition to behavioural literature. Human behaviour is purely a psychological study of human being. But the adjective in OB, "Organisational" is mainly concerned with behavioural aspects of human force at work in business or non-business organisations. Hence the study of OB is a segment study of human behaviour in organisations. Without going into the detailed analysis of human behaviour – a pure psychological analysis of human being — we take cognitive aspects (Mental Process) of the individuals to understand how they behave in an organisational set up. "Cognitive" variable is one of the variables which contribute mainly for understanding human behaviour at work in organisations. In this backdrop, we analyse the term" Organisational Behaviour".

"Organisation" refers to an unit-business or non-business, which is engaged in carrying out certain activity utilising the services of human and non-human factors. It is a social institution. In OB context, we have considered "organisation" as a business unit having ultimate objective of earning profit by adopting ethical means. Therefore, business organisation, irrespective of size, can be defined as follows.

"A business organisation is a co-operative social system, involving the co-ordinated efforts of two or more people pursuing a business purpose, *i.e.*, earning profit in a socially acceptable manner".

"Behaviour" is a general term applicable to human and non-human elements. When it is applied to human factor, it will be termed as human behaviour. When applied to non-human factor like "organisation", it will be "Organisational behaviour". We are now concerned with organisational behaviour and let us understand the definition of OB to understand the span of its operation.

"Organsisational behaviour (OB) is a theoretical frame work of behavioural sciences that are focused to understand, predict and manage human behaviour in organisations to achieve organisational goals". – **Fred Luthans.**

This definition throws light on the theme of the OB. It also clearly indicates that is comprehensive field of study focusing on the success of the organisation, considering human behaviour as a main factor.

Thus, organisation, in the context of OB, is considered as a structure in which both human and non-human factors work for achieving the set objectives. But the concept of "Behaviour" is concerned with human factor. People at work in organisations feel that they should be comfortable to work. This is essential for the survival and growth of the organisation. This means that the organisation *vis-à-vis* people working in the organisation must, be properly nourished to grow. The behaviour of the people in the organisation is guided by programmes, policies, and procedures set to achieve the desired objectives. Socially they are guided by culture and externally by environment. Therefore, the theme of organisational behaviour is to co-ordinate the activities of the human beings working in different functional areas of the organisation. In this context, the behaviour of each individual is to be monitored at every stage of their action, reaction, interaction and counter action.

Importance of Human Factor

People, when they perform interacting with other men and testing material and methods, should be positive in their approach, so that organisations function smoothly to achieve the set goal. But it will be a wishful thinking that organisations work without any hinderance. There will be hurdles and disturbances at every stage of work, which has to be crossed over by all concerned strictly following the rules and regulations set by the firm and by adopting ones own intellectual power, knowledge and common sense. Therefore, human factor in organisations is the key factor to be reckoned with. The success of the company or any business mainly depends upon the successful management of this factor.

The various elements of non-human factor (technology, ethics, inventions, innovative practices) can be obtained from external sources and adopted in the organisations. These are also essential aspects of organisational behaviour. But success of the organisation depends more on the human factor. Each human being is independent and has his/her own perception attitude, emotion, culture, personality creativity etc., and these guide the individual behaviour. Technology and other non-human factors can be borrowed from the environment and adopted for smooth running of the organisation. But human element of the uniform nature/behaviour cannot be hired or is not possible. Human element is independent and will have assorted behaviour which needs modification as per organisational requirement. Thinking and behaviour between two individuals will be different, and cannot be changed quickly.

As human thinking will be stable and continues for a long time, behaviour cannot be modified quickly. Every individual, in formative stage, learns and acquires, skills through education and gradually becomes 'human capital' which will be used by the society. The inherent character which includes perception, creativity, attitude, environmental impact etc., can be modified and fine tuned through training and development.

Training is a time-consuming process. Psychological factors of individual cannot be quickly changed. Such incorrigible persons are the real headache and pose challenges to managements in organisations. They will be the real disturbing factors for the success of the organisation. Technology or ethical practices or a specific culture adopted in the organisations even opposed by society can be quickly changed. But when an individual who is continuously trained by the organisation as per the needs becomes casual at work, management has to do something quickly to change this behaviour. This is the real challenge for management.

Changing Scenario

In the last two decades of twentieth century, far reaching changes took place in the business world. Globalisation concept attracted many developing countries. Information technology started playing its role in a big way. International business assumed a new role to widen global market. The "global village" concept increased the activities of business world. Multinational and trans-national companies became very active. This development posed many new management problems.

At the micro-level, individual organisations faced many new problems. Downsizing the organisation by applying technology, extending the business to global market, adaptation of ethical practices to improve the quality of business, adjusting to new culture as business expanded, fixing organisations in a dilemma at times to take major business decisions etc., occupied the frontline in business activities. When a paradigm shift has to take place, these problems are bound to occur. Managements do take steps to change over to new system. But real challenge for managements to succeed is the "Human factor" in the organisation. Non-human factors can be dramatically changed. But it is the experience over the ages that human factor is relatively stable in organisations and do not change that fast as non-human factor changes. Because the human nature is such that it slowly understands the concepts of change and react slowly for changes. Therefore, the behaviour of people at work has to be adjusted to the organisational requirements and objectives. The adjustment process is the theme of "Oganisational Behaviour".

Change Process

What is the adjustment process? It is a change over to new practices from traditional practices. Following information gives a picture of required change in organisations:

- From instable blending of technology and human elements to make human factor more comfortable to work and non-human factors to be subservient to human factor.
- Traditional practice of improper definition of jobs has to be changed to defend them properly, giving specific boundary to work.
- From the age old practice of influencing people at work and standard practices by clients, to make the workforce to strictly adhere to methods and procedures of the organisation.
- Convert the practice of working independently by workers to work in team and thus develop team spirit.
- Converting the organisational structure which do not properly exhibit the authority relationships to effectively workable structure which exhibits the networks of relationships that projects the organisation in its serial form.
- Avoiding unskilled temporary workers and fill the positions with skilled and professional workers.

In this backdrop, an overview of organisational behaviour is given covering the various aspects of OB.

Definition

1. Organisational behaviour is the study of what people think, feel and do in and around organisations". — ***Steven L. Mcshane, Mary Ann Von Glinow.***
2. "Organisational behaviour is action, reaction, interaction and counteraction of people in the organisation". — ***M.N. Misra***
3. "Organisational Behaviour is the study and application of knowledge of how people act or behave within organsation". — ***Keith Davis and Newstrom.***
4. "Organisational Behaviour is a field of study that investigates the impact that individuals, groups, and structure have on behaviour within organisations for the purpose of applying such knowledge towards improving an organisation's effectiveness". — ***Stephen P. Robbins.***
5. "Organisational Behaviour is directly concerned with the understanding,, prediction and control of human behaviour". — ***Fred Luthans.***

In simple terms OB helps the employers to understand, predict and controls employee's behaviour. OB does this by taking a system approach. That is, it interprets people-organisation relationships in terms of the whole person, whole group, whole organisation, and as a whole social system. Its purpose is to build better relationships by achieving human objectives, organisational objectives, and social objectives.

Organisational behaviour provides an umbrella for research that focuses on individuals and groups within the workplace. Research in this area examines individual processes as well as broader organisational processes. It also asks how these processes impact on organisational outcomes such as **performance, stress, absenteeism** and **turnover.**

Goals of OB

As we have understood, organisations, for their success, give importance for the development of human factor. Researches reveal that human factor can do anything for the success or failure of an organisation. Consider our public sector undertakings (PSUs). Government of India established hundreds of business houses in manufacturing and service sectors. But after many years of operation majority of the undertakings turned sick. It is mainly due to mismanagement. Government provided funds to operate. But the human factor at work in these organisations did not manage the units as per set methods and procedure. Because of this, economy could not grow at the expected rate. Only units identified as "Navaratnas" are functioning well and are competing with many leading companies. In these PSUS, human factor is playing a positive role and has developed organisational identity". Red tapism" was the main reason for unsuccessful growth of many PSUs.

The experience derived out of the growth path of PSUs says that human factor is critical in organisations. Graduates rolled out from universities, will have specialised in their field of study. But, they learn very little during academic pursuits on interpersonal and intrapersonal skills which are very essential for their success in any walk of life and for the organisations they work. Practical aspects of human behaviour at work are not taught. Only the behavioural aspects observed and retained in formative stages of the individual plays a key role in workplaces in which the person works in future. Therefore, importance is given for behaviour modeling in workplaces. Human Resources Development (HRD) in organisations have occupied the prime place compared to finance and other functional departments.

In this backdrop, what should be the goals of "Organisational Behaviour"? The main goal is to coordinate human and non-human factors for the success of the organisation. As human factors operates and controls non-human factor, further objective is to tune and finetune the human behaviour to suit the requirements of the organisation. Hence, the following activities may be considered as the goals of OB:

- Changing the traditional slow organisational practices to modern technology based fast workplaces.
- Empowering employees through training and development to improve their productivity and quality of work.
- The existing practices (traditional) cannot make workers to be dynamic and adopt new practices. The goal of OB is to make employees to behave rationally through behaviour modeling and be dynamic and visionaries. They should be prompted to analyse the changes taking place in the organisation and draw logical inferences through reasoning.
- Traditional managers are "command and control" type of people. The goal of OB is to convert these type of people. The goal of OB is to convert these managers into stable leaders who work as team members along with their subordinates. Although hierarchy of positions exist, it should not be exhibited.
- Many decision-makers, many a time, work on their instructions. But instructions do not work always. Therefore, the goal of OB is to make these people to take decisions after studying the problems in a systematic way.

- As technology is ruling the business world today, it has made 24 × 7 global business environment more sophisticated. Hence, one of the OB goals is to design and develop fast work practices adopting technology to increase speed and efficiency of work. This leads to increased productivity of both the work force and the organisation. The digital divide (separation of tech-savvy and non tech-savvy people) has to be minimized or eradicated by investing on human capital.
- Today's workforce comprises of more knowledge workers. Hence the organisations have to work on emotional aspects of workers which develops the creativity, innovation and enterprising spirit of each individual workers leading to better behaviour.
- The most important goal of OB is to induce workers to be ethical in their operations and in discharging assigned tasks.

Thus, the overall objective of OB is to improve the skills of the people working in an organisations in terms of changing individual behaviour and group behaviour so that organisation becomes successful. The main goal is to make the organisation a learning organisation.

Elements of OB

Elements here refer to the vital and major aspects which encompass OB. OB's focal point is to modify the behaviour of people working in organisations to achieving the objectives of the organisation. In order to modify the behaviour, Management will identify the elements or components and tools and techniques which can change the behaviour of people in organisations. Both individual behaviour and group behaviour are to be modified and modeled (modification standardised) as per organisational needs that are exhibited in the objectives of the organisation.

Many aspects are covered in OB. But under 'elements' we tell about major aspects such as people, structure, environment and technology. But the elements such as knowledge management, using different disciplines (Psychology, Antropology, Economics, Sociology, Industrial engineering, Information systems, Communication, Women studies, etc.) to analyse OB concepts, systematic methods are to be adopted for uninterrupted work flow. Analysis of behaviour at different levels of organisation, decision-making under contingency, etc., are also focused as supplementary aspects. Let us analyse both basic and supplementary aspects.

(a) People: People are the main resources for any organisation. It is the individuals that constitute the organisation. OB is a field where the study of human beings and their behaviour is involved. In an organisation, people exist both as individuals and in groups. As there is an individual difference existing with respect to perception, personality, motivation and individual learning, etc., it is necessary to understand the individual's traits and characteristics. This helps each individual to understand about other individual and his/her behaviour.

(b) Structure: Organisation is a social system. Any social system has its own structure and could be either formal or informal. The company forms formal organisation. Informal organisation is formed by the individuals depending on various factors like teamwork that is required to do a particular task, or during the lunch breaks, they form informal groups. As there is a saying, men may come and go but the company goes on forever. The organisation's structure may change due to technology and environment. But fundamentals remain the same.

(c) Environment: There are two types of environment in which the organisations operate. They could be categorised as internal and external. The internal environment acting on an organisation are the working environment, individual attitudes, etc., and the external environment comprises of the government rules and procedures, customers of the company etc., thus both the internal and external environment affect the organisation.

(d) Technology: Technology means the materials, equipments and machines and systems with which the individuals work on it. The company purchases for the production and service purpose and thesis an important element of an Organisation behavioural system. Below is the diagram of the organisational behavioural system.

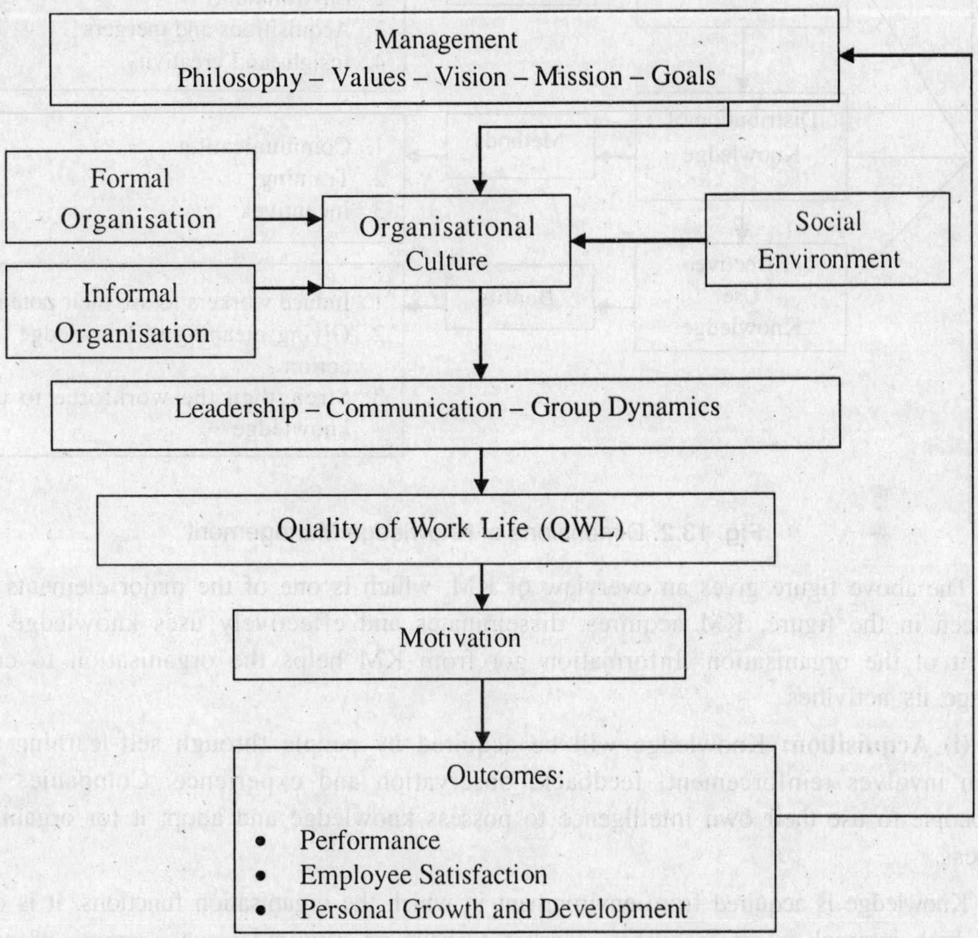

Fig. 13.1. An Organisational Behaviour System

Supplimentary Elements:

There are sub-elements which influence OB. They are: (i) Knowledge Management (ii) Associated disciplines, (iii) Systematic methods, (iv) Study at different levels and (v) Decision-making under contingency.

(I) Knowledge Management (KM): KM is one of the supplementary elements, but one of the key aspects of OB. Vital aspects of KM are (i) Availing knowledge from different sources, (ii) Using and distributing it amongst employer and employees of the organisation for the benefit of the organisation. (See the following figure.)

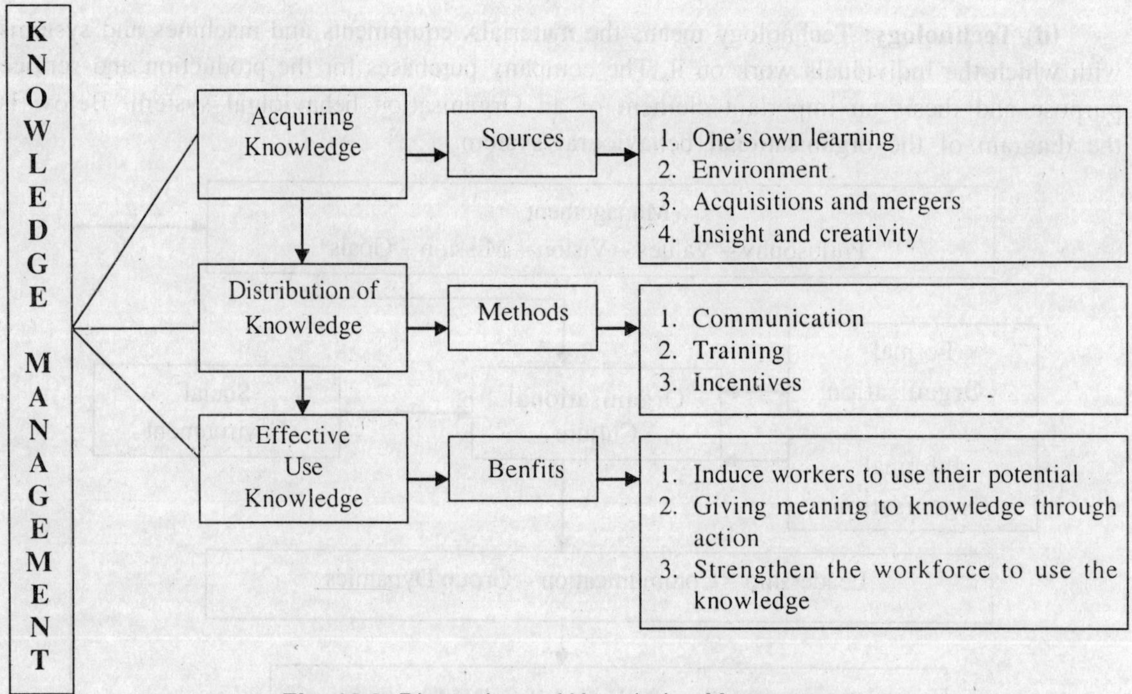

Fig. 13.2. Dimensions of Knowledge Management

The above figure gives an overview of KM, which is one of the major elements of OB. As seen in the figure, KM acquires, disseminates and effectively uses knowledge for the benefit of the organisation. Information got from KM helps the organisation to carefully manage its activities.

(i) Acquisition: Knowledge will be acquired by people through self-learning process which involves reinforcement, feedback, observation and experience. Companies support the people to use their own intelligence to possess knowledge and adopt it for organisational success.

Knowledge is acquired from environment in which the organisation functions. It is obtained from both internal external sources. Market surveys on required issues, reports prepared by others on required aspects, and media information are the external sources which help gathering information. As far as internal sources are concerned, employee meetings, discussion on problems faced by the organisation, internal reports prepared by various departments act as the source.

Another source of knowledge acquisition is "Acquisitions and mergers". When a company is acquired by another company, besides the assets, knowledge of good practices in that company is also acquired. The products, and services of good quality of the merged company will be possessed by merging company which is beneficial in terms of knowledge acquisition.

Knowledge is also acquired by research and experiments. Research in organisations is a continuous activity.

Individuals who work in the organisations give an insight into the problems confronted and through their creative ability acquire working knowledge of the tasks they have to perform.

(ii) Distribution: Knowledge availed from different sources are to be disseminated for the benefit of all concerned in the organisation. Sharing knowledge is essential. If the acquired knowledge does not reach the people who need it, it goes waste. The leaders/ managers should develop a system for knowledge acquisition and sharing.

Knowledge is distributed through oral or written communication (circulars) or by training the employees to update their`knowledge, or though holding seminars/panel discussions, group discussions etc., Electronic media is also extensively used these days to share knowledge. Appointment of experts to various top positions bring in knowledge which will be shared by existing employees.

If the people who possess knowledge are not willing to share must be induced to share it by adopting appropriate incentive systems for them.

(iii) Effective Use: The knowledge acquired and shared becomes useless, if it is not effectively used. Employees and employers must use the gathered knowledge without any reservation. Organisations, should design systematic structures to adopt acquired knowledge and implement it. People should be trained to adopt the information in an appropriate manner. Implementation of knowledge effectively provides confidence to employees, improves their quality of work and develops interpersonal relationships. People should freely use the acquired information. "Knowledge is power". Thus goes the saying and effective use of knowledge by workers empowers them. Thus, KM is VITAL element of OB.

(II) OB and associated disciplines: Various disciplines have associated with OB. The characteristics of psychology, Economics, Sociology, Anthropology, Industrial Engineering, Information systems, Communication are profusely found in Organisational Behaviour. But many principles of psychology and sociology are used extensively in explaining OB. The contribution of different disciplines can be observed from the following figure:

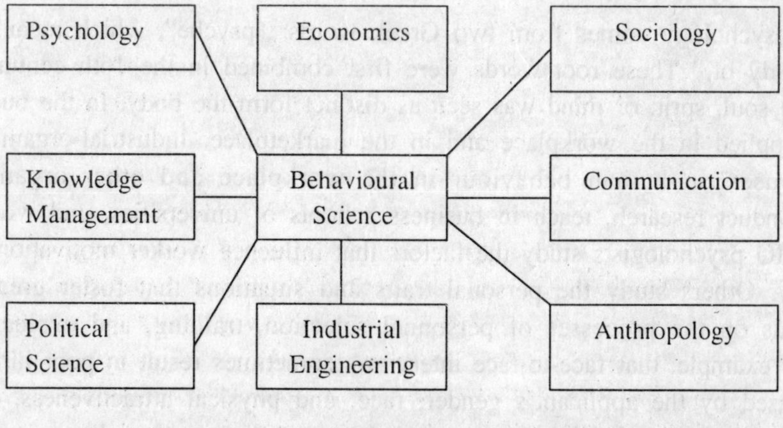

Fig. 13.3. Discipline Contributing to Organisational Behaviour

OB and Psychology:

Psychology is the scientific study of human behaviour and the mind. This meaning contains three elements. The first is that psychology is a scientific enterprise that obtains knowledge through systematic and objective methods of observation and experimentation. Second is that psychologists study human behaviour, which refers to any action or reaction that can be measured or observed — such as the blink of an eye, increase in heart rate, or the unruly violence that often erupts in a mob. Third is that psychologists study the mind, which relates to both conscious and unconscious mental states. These states cannot actually be seen, only inferred from observable behaviour. Many people think of psychologists as individuals who dispense advice, analyse personality and help those who are troubled or mentally ill. But psychology is far more than treatment of personal problems. Psychologists strive to understand the mysteries of human nature — why people think, feel and act as they do? Some psychologists also study animal behaviour, using their findings to determine laws of behaviour that apply to all organisms and to formulate theories about how humans behave and think.

With its broad scope, psychology investigates an enormous range of phenomena: learning and memory, sensation and perception, motivation and emotion, thinking and language, personality and social behaviour, intelligence, infancy and child development, mental illness and much more. Furthermore, psychologists examine these topics from a variety of complementary perspectives. Some conduct detailed biological studies of the brain. Others explore how we process information; others analyse the role of evolution, and still others study the influence of culture and society.

Psychologists seek to answer a wide range of important questions about human nature: are individuals genetically predisposed at birth to develop certain traits or abilities? How accurate are people at remembering faces, places or conversations from the past? What motivates us to seek out friends and sexual partners? Why do so many people become depressed and behave in ways that seem self-destructive? Do intelligence test scores predict success in school, or later in a career? What causes prejudice, and why is it so widespread? Can the mind be used to heal the body? Discoveries from psychology can help people understand themselves, relate better to others, and solve the problems that confront them.

The term psychology comes from two Greek words: "psyche", which means "soul" and "logos", "the study of." These root words were first combined in the 16th century, at a time when the human soul, sprit, or mind was seen as distinct form the body. In the business world, psychology is applied in the workplace and in the marketplace. Industrial-organisational (IO) psychology focuses on human behaviour in the workplace and other organisations. IO psychologists conduct research, teach in business schools of universities, and work in private industry. Many IO psychologists study the factors that influence worker motivation, satisfaction and productivity. Others study the personal traits and situations that foster great leadership. Still others focus on the processes of personnel selection, training, and evaluation. Studies have shown, for example, that face-to-face interviews sometimes result in poor hiring decisions and may be biased by the applicant's gender, race, and physical attractiveness. Studies have also shown that certain standardised tests can help to predict on-the-job performance. Thus, psychology is becoming and increasingly a discipline more relevance to OB.

OB and Sociology

Sociology and Anthropology explain about human societies and cultures and also intersect with psychology. Both psychology and sociology tell as to how people behave when they are in groups. Sociology focus on how behaviour is shaped by social forces and social institutions. Anthropologists investigate behaviour as well paying particular attention to the similarities and differences between human cultures around the world.

Sociology is the scientific study of how people think, feel and behave in social situations, Researchers in this field have tried to answer to the issues such as the persuation of people to change their attitudes or beliefs, the causes for people to conform in-group situations. Reasons for ignoring or helping a person in need by the people, under what circumstances do people obey or resist orders, etc.

By observing people in real-world social settings and by carefully devising experiments to test people's social behaviour, sociologists learn about the ways people influence, perceive and interact with one another. The study of social influnce includes topics such as conformity, obedience to authority, the formation of attitudes and the principles of persuation. Researchers interested in social perception study how people come to know and evaluate one another, How people form group stereotypes and the origins of prejudice. Other topics of particular interest to social psychologists include physical attraction, love and intimacy, aggression, attrition and group processes. Many social psychologists are also interested in cultural influences on interpersonal behaviour.

In Organisational behaviour, these issues play a job role. Business organisations in particular, focus on productivity of people working in their units. To improve and maintain productivity of people, the employers will have to look at the social behavioural aspects of their employees, which is one of the key factors in improving productivity. Here comes the role of sociological aspects of people. This contributes for the improvements of behaviour of people in work places, which will have its impact on productivity. Thus, sociology and its principles and functions influence the behaviour of people in workplaces.

OB and Political Science

Political science is a discipline, which speaks about the administration of the state. It tells as to how people are governed through a political system. Business and non-business organisations being a part of political administration, people at work in these organisations are directly or indirectly influenced by political decisions. One political party or the other controls particularly the unions industries and business house and these parties indirectly influence the work culture in the organisations.

The other disciplines contributing are Medicine from where the stress level of employees and the barriers to overcome stress are identified. The disciplines contributing to the behavioural sciences shown in Fig. 13.3 help us in acquiring knowledge about how to understand people, and to know how the individuals work in the organisations.

Influence of Individual Behaviour in Organisations

As organisations need and influence people, people also need and influence organisations. They are formed on the basis of mutual interest of the individuals. This will provide super ordinate goals for both the employees and organisation. The goals can be generally achieved through the integrated efforts of organisation and their employees. Organisational behaviour is also concerned with how individuals work, the way they perceive their physical and social environment and what meanings they derived from them.

The organisational behaviour philosophy arises from certain facts and values on how the individuals behave, *i.e.*, given in the descriptive way it is called as "facts". These facts are derived from both personal experiences and from behavioural science research. Facts are acquired through direct and indirect learning that takes place during an individual's life time. Their desirability of certain goals represents the values. Values are various beliefs that individuals hold and control.

Vision

Elements like vision, mission and goals should be framed into the organisational behaviour system, Vision represents a future portrait of where the company will be at certain point of time. 'What should be done' ultimately, is the vision of any business or NGO.

Mission

Mission on the other hand identified factors like, the business line of the company, the customers, the services to be rendered and other related issues. Goals are the ultimate formulation of achievement for which the organisations is focusing. For example, the goal of a company might be to increase productivity, reduce labour turnover, etc., Goals might be existed in an individual, group or organisational level. Goals provide a way to achieve the targets by achieving the mission. Therefore "Mission" is a concept which tell about our activities or objectives to be achieved in the long-run or ultimately through our actions and participation. Focus is on the line of activity to achieve our vision, *i.e.*, "How should we go about" to achieve our ultimate business or non-business objectives.

The disciplines such as Industrial Engineering (Productivity work measurement, job related aspects), communication (Transfering information in oral and written forms, body language and through electronic tools such as e-mail) information system (Knowledge Management, team building) and economics (Negotiation, Reward Systems, etc.,) also contribute to the discipline of OB.

Thus, OB is multi-disciplinary in approach and draws information and themes from the disciplines as shown in the chart. Woman studies also contribute for OB activities.

(iii) Systematic Methods: Today, all organisations are leaning towards the concept of **"Learning organisation".** Many researchers are conducted and will be conducted in future to develop and adopt systematic approach in organisational practices. Change in business environment and information technology compel organisations to change over to new practices that emerge. Professionalism through systematic methods and procedures has to be developed for organisational success. Another dimension that OB has to look into is systematic practices to be adopted for the success of the organisation.

(iv) Study of Behaviour at Different Levels: Basically, we observe three levels in organisations. (i) Individual level in which we examine intrapersonal behaviour and its contribution to organisational development, (ii) Group behaviour and its impact on the organisation and (iii) Organisation as a whole related to integrated issues. These are the three levels which are considered as a part of study of OB. Behaviour at different levels of organisation is one of the basic aspects to be considered in studying OB.

At the individual level features such as personality, perception, motivation, learning, ability, values, attitudes are the OB elements to be understood.

Group level considers the OB issues such as communication with group groups and individuals, decision-making, group structure, leadership, conflict, power and politics, work teams, etc.,

At the organisational level, aspects such as organisational structure and design, orgnisational culture, work design and technology, human resources development (HRD) policies and such other general matters concerned with behaviour are defined. The three levels of OB are shown in the following diagram:

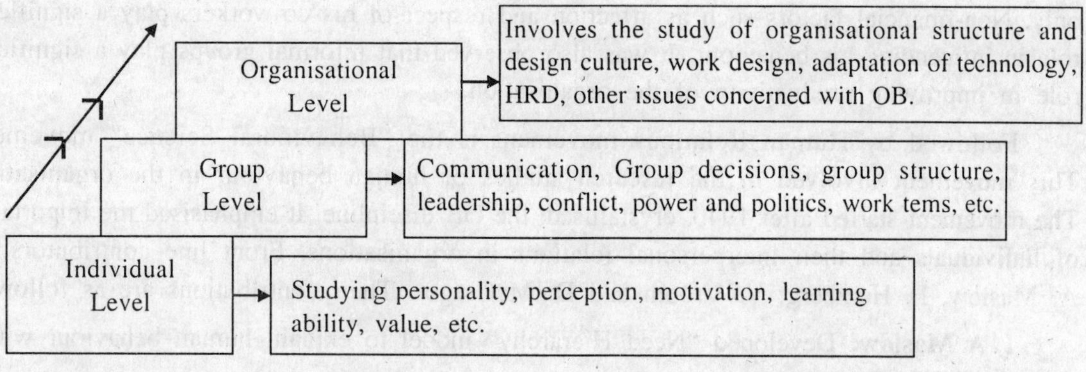

Fig. 13.4. Levels in Organisational Structure and Behavioural Aspects at Each Level.

This figure will be the basic structure to develop an OB model.

(v) Decision-making under "Contingency: Organisations follow established rules and procedures in their operations. But situations arise in which these rules and regulations cannot be applied to take decisions. People have to use their value judgments and take decisions during those contingency situations. OB modules explain how decions are to be taken in times of contingency. It is one of the vital elements of OB. Thus, organisations consider that these are the fundamental aspects which cover OB.

Historical Development

The concept and discipline OB is of a recent origin. When we study the development of management thought, the first work to come out on this topic was Henry Fayol's

"General and Industrial Management" in 1916. This period onwards many thinkers contributed to management thought focusing only on technical and managerial skills required for production of goods, — F.W. Taylor, who was considered as Father of Scientific management, also focused only on scientific selection of workers, their scientific development, harmonious relationship between workers and employers and scientific development of business. These thinkers never thought of **"Human"** aspect of management. Employees did not follow the predicted pattern of behaviour. Because they felt that they were totally ignored. This gave way for the emergence of **Human Relations Movement**. This is the starting point of "Organisational Behaviour" discipline.

Experiments conducted by Elton Mayo and others at the Western Electric Company's plant, between 1927 and 1932, popularly know as Hawthorne Experiments, gave birth to "Human Relations Movement". The four experiments conducted, *viz.*, (i) Illumination Experiments, (ii) Relay Assembly Test Room experiment, (iii) Interviewing programme and (iv) Bank Wiring Test Room, focused on human factor of management. The behavioural aspects of employees were studied in these experiments.

Studies revealed that a business organisation is not merely a techno-economic system but is also a social system. Therefore, management has to provide social satisfaction to workers to make them to improve their productivity. A worker does not work for money only. Non-financial factors such as affection and respect of his co-workers play a significant role in influencing his behaviour. It was also observed that informal groups play a significant role in improving productivity of the organisation.

Followed by Human Relations movement is the "Behavioural Science" movement. This movement involved in the research studies of human behaviour in the organisation. The movement started after 1940, crystallised, the OB discipline. It emphasised the importance of individuals and their interpersonal relations in organisations. Front line contributors are A. Maslow, F. Herzberg, V. Vroom and D. McGregor. Their contributions are as follows:

1. A Maslow: Developed "Need Hierarchy" model to explain human behaviour within the organisation.

2. Herzberg and Vector Vroom: Separately developed motivational models. These models explained the causes of human behaviour and motivation in business.

3. McGregor: Developed two theories, *viz.*, Theory "X" and Theory "Y" of these two theories, Theory "y" reflects the behavioural approach to management. Theory "X" projects that **work** and **productivity** are the main activities of management and ignores human element in the organisation.

Behavioural science movement stressed the importance of humanising the administration of the control process and encouraged the process of self-direction and control instead of imposed control. This movement focused on individual behaviour, work groups, participative management, employee-oriented approach to management, motivation, leadership empowerment of employees through training and development, etc.

Behavioural scientists stated that every organisational change involves technological and social aspects and generally people resist social aspect of change. They also observed that different people react differently to the situation or react the same way to different situations. No two people are alike and manager should make his attempts to influence people according to their individual needs.

Behavioural science movement added lot of literature to OB. It advocated steps such as participation employees in decision-making, measurement and evaluation of standards of performance, prompt information feedback to those whose performance is not satisfactory and the need for positive and reformative measures instead of punitive measures.

Later on many management Gurus including the father of modern management. Peter Drucker contributed for the development of OB discipline.

Psychologists and sociologists contributed several concepts of OB to make it more meaningful. While psychologists contributed on personality, attitude, emotions, learning, perceptions, etc., which are related to individual and group behaviour, sociologists said about social learning, communication systemsm, culture, organisational structure, etc.

These contributions of researchers and gurus of different disciplines have made OB discipline to take a shape for meaningful study. Still several researches are going on the various aspects OB to make it a comprehensive discipline of study. (For more details, study the chapter on "Development of management thought" of this book).

OB Model

A model is a replica of something that represents an idea for a pattern to be scientifically practiced to achieve something. OB has a set pattern to be followed in an organisation to make that entity a successful one. OB discipline tells about the behavioral pattern of individuals and groups, that work in an organisation. OB, being an inexact science, the pattern of behaviour may change due to diversity of workforce, globalisation, restructuring the organisation, outsourcing non-core activities, etc. Still the organisations have to have a basic structure which exhibits the behavioural pattern of people and the organisation as a whole. The OB model, exhibiting the behavioural aspects of people at work will be based on social and psychological aspects and environmental factors that iinfluence people and such other issues which will have impact on behavioural aspects in all the three levels of the organisation. Thus, the OB model explainins the dynamics and managerial pattern to attain high performance. OB model has to present a simplified structure of individual, group and organisation behavioural aspects that are practiced in real time situations. Following figure exhibits the general model of OB:

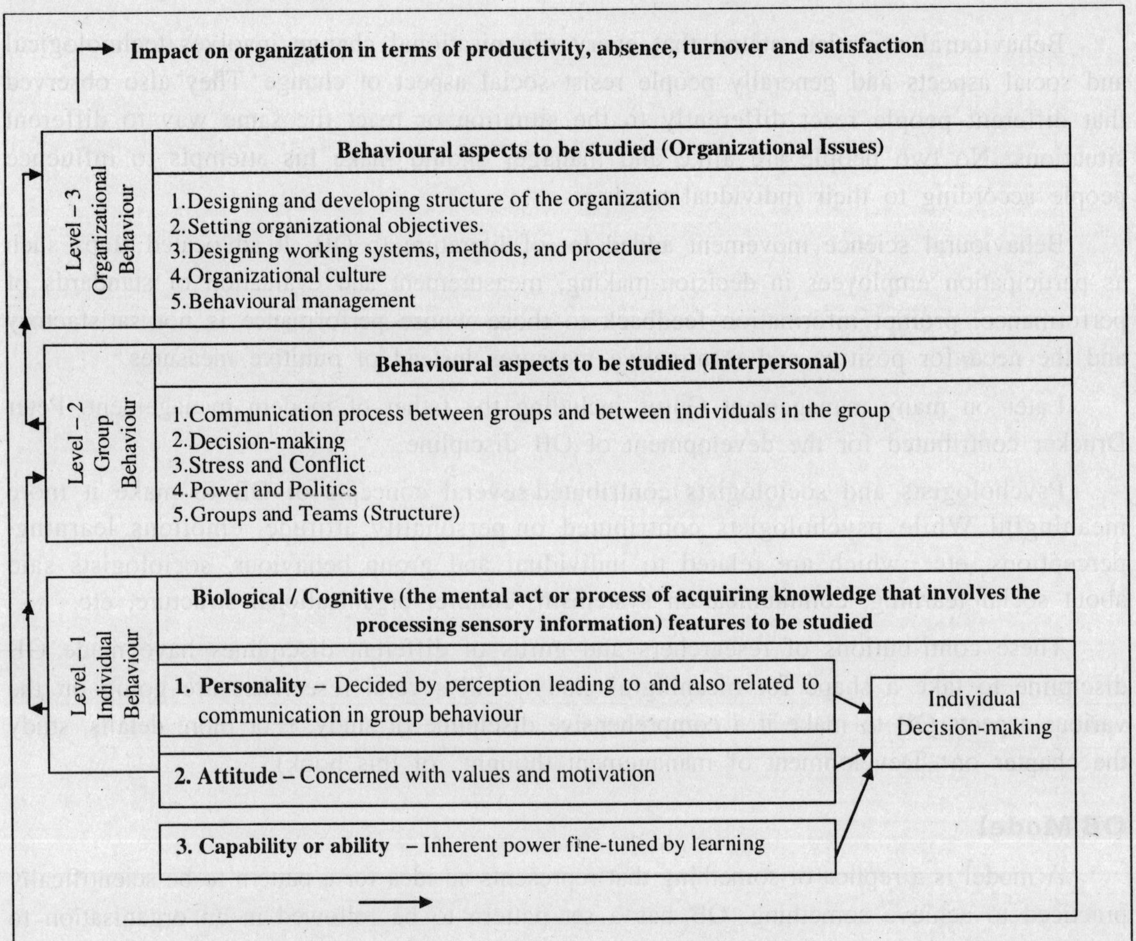

Fig. 13.5. General OB Model which shows the Behavioural Variables at Different Levels of Organisation and their Impact on Human Behaviour

This figure shows three levels of human behaviour in organisations. At each level of behaviour, the aspects to be discussed are shown. At the individual level, the cognitive (analysis of mental process) aspects are discussed which include personality, perception, values, attitude, motivation, ability, learning leading to individual decision-making.

At the second level, various aspects related to group and team structure, *viz.*, communication, stress and conflict, power and politics are discussed leading to decision-making.

At the third level, general issues such as organisational structure, job designing-system, methods and procedure, organisational culture, leadership and such other aspects required for overall management of the organisation are discussed.

This will be a general structure or model of OB, which integrates the aspects of all three levels to exhibit the human behaviour in terms of **"Productivity"**. **"Absence"**, **"Turnover"** and **"Satisfaction"**. How these four factors will have their impact on OB is briefly explained in the following paragraphs.

(a) Productivity

Productivity refers to the contribution of individuals or teams intellectual and physical energy at least possible cost for the success of the organisation. They should **do things right** and **do right things**. Productivity is concerned with the effectiveness of human factor which completes the task within the stipulated time in a given work place. Efficiency is recognised when the individual or a team completes the tasks, well within the accepted cost framework. Supposing teacher in a college has to discharge forty hours of work at a cost of Rs. 50,000. If he/she completes the task accordingly, it means that he/she has contributed fully and reached the maximum productivity. The productivity of human factor (individual or team) is measured in terms of output of labour per assigned unit of time, cost incurred, return on investment and Profit/Loss per rupee.

(b) Absenteeism

Absence of people at work, otherwise called "Absenteeism", affects the productivity of the organisation. Certain statutory leave provisions are included in the employment contracts. If an employee abstains from work beyond the allowed limit, the workflow is disrupted, and decreases productivity. Even within the allowed limits of leave, if an employee works under stress due to illness or fatigue, productivity of that worker decreases. In such situation, it is better that employee avails leave. However, the absenteeism should be at minimum level to have more productivity.

(c) Turnover

Turnover means leaving the work place by a worker voluntarily or compulsorily for a temporary period or on a permanent basis. If the turnover is on low key, productivity will be on a higher side and *vice versa.* The notable impact in case of turnover is that an intellectual and talented person leaves the organisation, it will be very difficult to find substitute of same caliber. This, at times, hampers productivity as the whole project (the left person was working upon) has to be restructured or abandoned. This affects the image of the organisation and cost of replacement will be very heavy.

Turnover of employees/executives is a common phenomenon in every organisation. When unwanted people leave, it will have insignificant impact and it may improve productivity of the organisation. It will also create more promotional opportunities for the existing employees. Management is also benefited, as new blood with innovative ideals is infused into organisation. One the whole, a high turnover rate in an organisation indicates that it is poorly managed. It also puts down the organisational effectiveness. Therefore, organisations should work for minimising employee turnover.

(d) Satisfaction

"Satisfaction" is related to the retention of employee in the organisation. This refers to the positive feeling of an employee about his job and the treatment given by the top management. The task that the employee performs should give him solace to his mind. It is possible only when certain things are satisfied. The worker should like the job he performs.

And then he has to be satisfied with working environment and the way in which the employee is treated by fellow workers and top management person should also be happy with monetary aspects, *i.e.*, the remuneration and other incentives he receives of the job he does.

It is experienced that the satisfied workers turnout more work than the one not satisfied. Non-satisfaction is not only measured by quantitative aspect via higher productivity and material acquisition, but also the quality of work life in organisations. This means that they should be provided with challenging jobs which go with additional rewards. Satisfaction is derived by attitude of the worker. This leads to behaviour, *i.e.,* putting more efforts to increase productivity.

Thus, this general model shows that the three levels of organisation contribution of human behaviour in terms of productivity absenteeism, turnover and job satisfaction of human factor in organisations. This will have impact on organisational efficiency and effectiveness.

This is the central theme of organisational behaviour and it is the subject matter of OB. It can be understood by observing the figure 13.5. Theories and principles related to various variables shown in different levels of organisation are considered totally as subject matter of OB at the individual organisational level (micro level).

Other Models

Every organisation has its own fundamental beliefs and values. The philosophy or model of organisational behaviour is based on certain assumptions and beliefs. The major models on behavioral philosophies are Autocratic, Custodian, Supportive and Collegial.

A model is one that constitutes the belief system. It has the management's thoughts, and it affects the internal management activities in an organisation. There were managerial modules, behavioural modes and general assumptions of human behaviour. Just as the organisations are different form one another, the Organisational Behaviour system is also different from organisation to organisation. Their practices also differ between departments of the same organisation. The sales department might be working on a custodial model while production might be working on autocractic mode. By identifying the model, one can distinguish the organisational pattern with which it works.

Autocratic Model

Autocratic model started during the period of Industrial Revolution. It generally focuses on power. There are certain verbal conversation like "always you do like this," never do this" and "you ought to do this work", etc., showing "I" dominant nature.

The environment of the autocratic model is very formal. It has the official authority that has been delegated by the 'right of command' over the individual towards others to whom it applies. In this model, the basic belief is that management knows what is best and the employees will have to listen to the orders and perform the task. The management is involved in the thinking process and the employees are involved in executing the process. The ultimate result, employees are dependent towards the management. The employees give minimum performance and in turn, they are paid minimum wage.

The limitation of this model is that it involves high human cost and hence is applicable under certain conditions.

The Custodial Model

Some management thinkers began to realize that they could not prolong with autocratic model. They comprehended that the employees did have some power and they wanted to tell many things. They also felt that the employees opposed every idea of management and reacted very badly to them. Employees were fully frustrated and there was no co-operation with the management. On the whole, the relationship between the management and the employees were not healthy one.

At this stage, number of welfare programmes were started to develop healthy relationship. These programmes were focused on the employees, unions and output. Manangements began to take care of the security need of the workers. Workers were often given rewards and the benefits for the work done. Management also started recognizing the employee's work. Due to this, most of the employees were contented and their contentment ultimately lead to strong motivation. It also produced positive cooperation. The **main focus** of the custodial model was on the **material rewards and security**. The entire model acts on a foundation for growth, leading the employees to give better performance. It also made the employees to depend on the organisation for all their needs. This particular model is useful because it focuses on the employee security.

Supportive Model

The supportive model of the Organisational Behaviour System emphasis on supportive relationships. The supportive model depends on leadership instead of focusing on the monetary rewards like the custodial model. By having an effective and efficient leader, the management helps the employees in accomplishing the interests of the organisations. The leaders take the responsibility and motivate the group members. The purpose of this model is to support the employees, job performance. The leader took the initiative and accountability for the teamwork. Since the management gives undue support to the employees in the form of leadership, the employee takes initiative to participate in management activities. There is high involvement of task and the employee's needs are met in a better way. This model is applicable for all the levels of management. The only drawback of this model is that it suffers from practical implementation.

Collegial Model

The extension of the supportive model is the "Collegial model". Collegial means a body of people who have a common purpose. The model emphasises on the team concepts and is widely applied in all industries. Basically this model is followed in assembly line, *i.e*, in production units where there is lot of rigidity in the work environment.

Collegial model focuses on management's feeling of having a partnership with the employees. In this model, the employees are highly recognised. Both the management and the employees work together in achieving the organisational goals. The managers accept the role of employees and in turn the employees feel that they are recognised. Teamwork is the key orientation. The employees give quality performance not because of fear, but because of the intrinsic motivation. They believe in providing high quality standards for the company.

Collegial model is based on two principles — self-actualisation and self-discipline. Self-actualisation is an environment where the employees feel that all their needs are fulfilled and they have contributed something worthwhile to the company.

Finally, all these above models are successful depending upon their usage. Number of new models have emerged recently. There is no any one best model. Any model can be applied depending upon the environment and situation that exist in the organisation. Ultimately these models built to accomplish certain things. The top managements' responsibility is not only to apply the model, but also make it flexible and update the model with respect to its use.

We have discussed different models of OB. All these models tell about the various dimensions of study of OB. Generally speaking, OB is a subject which mainly deals with cognitive social learning of the people working in organisations. Basically, it tells how people behave independently in groups and how they have to adapt themselves to organisational systems, methods and procedure. The general model given in fig. 13.4 of this chapter provides the information about the subject matter OB. The subsequent chapters explain the behavioural aspects of individuals, groups and organisation and how these three contribute for the success of the organisation.

OB and Global Dimensions

Gradually, organisations are sinking at a faster rate. Today, innumerable MNCs and Trans-national companies are functioning all over the world. Because of this, international business has increased at a faster rate. Business at global level (between all the countries of the world) and between the countries (international) demand certain very vital behaviours for their success. Very vital one is understanding the culture of the country/countries and organisations in which international business takes place. As organisations are becoming virtual, people have started working at home. This has become possible, because of fast adaptation of information technology.

Because of globalisation, management's perceptions have changed in terms of social, political, legal, economic and technological aspects. In a global business process, quality products and services are bought and sold. Business operates in a changed environment, Ethical practices will be on a higher side and people at work function in a cross-cultural atmosphere.

What has changed in global/international business ? Answer to this question is briefly explained in the following paragraphs:

1. As far as administration is considered, boss-follower concept is changing and moving towards team work, teaching-learning, sponsorship, coaching the business associates of other countries and so on.
2. Multicultural/multilingual aspects have occupied the place of monoculture and single language.
3. Product quality and ethics have changed from "After thought"/No thought", to "Fore thought". Every one involved in production has to identify and correct defects. Focus is on locating and eliminating causes of quality problems. Designing the product/service not only by producers themselves, but also involves in house workers as well as concerned customers. Continuous improvement of involved workers, processes and product is the order.

4. Co-operation is the key factor in interpersonal dealings.
5. Organisational unit is either virtual or is having collaborative (Domestic and parent organisations offers product. For example, Hindustan Lever Limited) unit or branch office. They together work, not the win-lose, but to achieve win-win situation. The success of both domestic and parent organisations is expected in international business.
6. As change becomes the order of the day, learning will be continuous, opportunities are provided for continuous improvement.
7. In international business, problems are anticipated and resistance should be avoided. In the place of reactions for occurrences of problems, organisations have to seek solutions. Instead of avoiding problems, they are sorted out channelised, and decision to solve the problems are taken.
8. Information has to be easily accessed and shared for the smooth running of the business.

All these trends in global business and increased air transport system and information technology, have resulted in strengthening global market. Comparative management styles have facilitated effective global business. More organisations are becoming global to reshape the world's economic landscape. Running a global company is a complicated aspect. "Global" here refers to viewing the whole world as a single market. MNCs also are considered as a part of global markets. But they are really not global. They may also carry the business in the similar way as global organisations. But it differs in scale of operation and quality.

A global company operates in world market in terms of production, research, raising capital, buying supplies wherever it is convenient and cost-effective. It keeps in touch with technology and market trends through out the world. ABB of Switzerland, Honda of Japan are some of the examples of global companies. Where as MNCs look like global companies. But they are not. They have strategic controls over production and markets in two or more countries. But the global companies have the operations such as product design, manufacturing and vendor management in many countries of the world. There is no boundry barrier as in case of MNCs.

OB Problems

People working in global or multinational companies will have certain difficulties, Culture differs in each country. People in such companies have to learn or adapt to cross-cultural aspects. Some workers of parent company go to other countries on a temporary basis and some will go on long tenure basis. Those who go on a temporary basis (for a week or two), cultural aspect will not be a problem, But those who visit on project work and has to stay for one or two years or till such time the project work is completed, cultural aspect poses a problem.

Those who visit for a short period will have limited knowledge of history, culture and customs of the visiting country. Language and skills vary. These people will be given some information about the task, and other operational aspects. But the executives and workers who go on a longer duration, will have to be trained in variety of challenges which are listed below:

- Pre-departure training to solve the problems posed to them on entry to other country.
- Language to be used in the contry of visit.

- Cultural differences and how to adapt to new societal culture as well as organisational culture in which, the worker has to work.
- Acclimatisation to new environment.
- Understanding the social system in terms of dress, daily routine, time management, etc.

Organisational Design: Besides these basic problems that are to be addressed, people who visit the foreign organisations should know the organisational design. Three basic designs are observed based on authority and decision-making, evaluation and control, communication system adapted for information flow and other routine matters such as recruiting, staffing, development, etc., The designs are (i) **Ethnocentric,** (ii) **Polycentric** and (iii) **Geocentric.**

Ethnocentric organisational behaviour is home country-oriented, identified by nationality of owner For example, Indian business house functioning in other countries), Decision is taken in head office which will be located in home country, evaluation and control applied are home standards, in all the countries that organisation has branches without modification, high volume information flows to subsidiaries and people for key positions are appointed from native country. Thus, this is a very rigid organisation. Such organisation does not allow workers to work freely and hence the settlers in such organisations will experience monotony, have no scope for introducing innovations and they cannot grow. Such organisations cannot easily operate in ethnically liberalised countries.

Polycentric organisation is identified by nationality of host country. For example, American company operating in India). Authority and decision-making is relatively low in head office. Evaluation and control takes place, locally, Communication and information flow is less from and to head office and on a low scale between subsidiaries. People recruited for various positions for host country branches are local ones. Intention is to to develop the people of the country in which the organisation opens its branch. This type of organisation practices a culture which is the integration of different cultures of people coming from other countries to this organisation. People of host country are given more opportunities to grow and in turn organisation is also benefited through intensive exploitation of local markets, availing more support and benefit from local governments. The structure is not highly integrated and subsidiaries or branches enjoy greater independence. This type also eases behavioural aspects of workforce, working in host country.

Geocentric Organisational structure is congenial for international business. It is truly an international organisation. However, it also identifies national interests of home country. It will have collaborative approach between Head Office and its branches. Operations and practices are an admixture of universal and local practices. These organizations have two way communication system between head office and branches and between branches. These organisations provide scope for development of best people to hold key positions, without considering the country, caste or creed. Only best intellectual people with adaptability and humility are picked up all over the globe.

Of these three types of organisations at global level, people will work with monotony and fatigue in ethnocentric organisation, bit liberally in polycentric organisations and work more comfortably in geocentric organisations.

Time Factor

Besides the problems posed to workers in behavioural aspects in the above said types of organisations, "Time" factor also influences behaviour of people working in global companies. "Time" is considered as a silent language of culture by Hall ("in Introduction to Monochronic and Polychronic Time" — Academy of Management Executive 1992 PP.17-26). Accordingly, two types of time are identified in global business operations which will have impact on worker's behaviour. They are **(i) Monochronic** and **(ii) Polychronic.**

Monochronic time is perceived as "unidimensional straight line divided into standard units, such as seconds, minutes, hours and days". In countries like the USA, Northern Europe, monochronic time is considered and people expect that everyone transacts with them will be on the same clock and time. As they consider time as money, they use time efficiently and work on time. They expect the same behaviour from others who transact with them.

Polychronic time is "a perception of time as flexible, elastic and multidimensional." People who work in polychronic culture do not consider "time" as very important. In such culture, operations are loosely scheduled and overlapping.

While transacting, people belonging to two different time culture, are exposed to behavioural conflict. Say an American from monochronic time culture visits or stays in India which is polychronic in nature. He feels that Indian worker is slow in work and has no time sense whereas the Indian worker feels that American, worker is impatient and self-centered. The reason for this behavioural conflict is perception of time between these two countries. Therefore, while transacting, people from different countries should understand and adopt time concept of transacting countries for smooth completion of the business.

Other Issues

There are other OB issues which cause distrurbance in handling global operations.

LANGUAGE SKILLS IN GLOBAL BUSINESS

International business experts say that learning foreign language is easier for some than others. But it is essential to learn for smooth business operations. The advantages are as follows.

- It enhances the traveler's sense of mastery, self-confidence and safety.
- Shows respect for foreign business hosts or guests.
- Help build rapport and trust with foreign hosts or business partners.
- Improves the odds of a successful foreign business venture.
- Builds a base of confidence for learning other languages.
- Promotes a deeper understanding of other cultures.
- Helps travelers to obtain the best possible medical care during emergencies.
- Minimises cultural shock and the frustrations of being an outsider.

Source: Adapted from "The Need for Linguistic Proficiency in Global Business," Business Horizons (May, June 1996), p. 39.

(i) Language

Each country will have its own language to speak and write. When two organisations of different countries have to transact on a business proposal, it is inevitable for them, to learn the languages of both the countries. It is not quickly possible. Although "English" is acting as an international language, many countries still communicate with their own language. Japanese, Chinese and most of the other countries transact with their own language. But at the global level, for better cross-cultural understanding, foreign language skills are essential.

(ii) Religion

Religious traditions of business colleagues of other countries should be understood for smooth running of business. In any country of the world, religion occupies the prime place and working style, behaviour and daily life is fully governed by religion. Any activity that affects, the religious practice will not accepted or will not be taken up by people. In order to develop lasting relationship and congenial behaviour, religious aspects of business partners are to be honoured. Supposing a company from India has established a business in Iran, and has appointed local people to run the business. These workers are to be given weekly off on Friday for prayer than on Sundays which is the practice in India. Friday is a precious day for that country and hence this religious concept has to be honoured in that country to elevate the mood of workers and to maintain their normal behavioural pattern. Thus, religious aspects play an important role behaviour of workers of different countries and they have to be properly addressed.

Comparative management styles depict how organisational behaviour and management practices differ across culture. The issues that have more impact on behavioural aspects across cultures are: (i) Adoption of accepted management practices of home country in host country, (ii) Management Theory- Z, (iii) Work goals of different culture and (iv) leadership in cross-cultural situations.

(i) Management theory adoption

Management theory and practices differ from country to country. A single theory cannot be applied to all countries. They are not universal in character. In order to assess the behavioural pattern in diversified management practices, one should examine issues such as: (i) acceptance of unequal distribution of power and positions in cross-country organisations (How people react for that?) (ii) How to avoid uncertain situations that may crop up in the course of managing the branches or subsidiaries or collaborative organisations? (iii) How the welfare of individuals have to be managed (*i.e.*, whether individuals look after themselves of their welfare or a group will look after the individuals)? and (iv) gender difference and its impact on behaviour in host country. This means, the management has to decide whether male or masculine attitude (assertiveness, money and possessions and performance) or feminine attitude (concern for people, the quality of life and good environment) is required.

After examining these issues, management has to design a management framework to be adopted in host country. The needs of workers and the organisation are to be given priority in designing the operational structure of a foreign branch. They needs that are basically considered are: (i) security, (ii) security and social needs, (iii) social needs and (iv) self-actualisation needs. Based on these needs, work methods and procedures are to be designed and implemented. There should be flexibility in operational procedure to correct the practices that are disturbing the operations.

(ii) Theory "Z"

This is a theory developed by management scholar, William Ouchi. This is based on success story of leading American companies and Japanese companies. Ouchi studied the contrasting features of American and Japanese companies, and found that successful companies of America exhibited a pattern of management that effectively blended the traits of typical American and Japanese companies,. This theory was called "Z" theory which exhibits the blending of American and Japanese style of management. Theory "Z" is not the imitation of Japanese practices. But some of them, were introduced in American management. practices to modify or improve the existing practices.

Theory Z owes its origin to America, but in practice, it resembles the blended style of both American and Japanese style. The theory gives an insight into the modification of behaviour as per organisational needs. The "Z" theory's equation = Japanese + American. The management aspects considered are, tenure of employment, evaluation of and employment, career paths, control policies, decision-making, responsibility and concern for organisation.

Regarding tenure, Japanese have long-term jobs, whereas Americans have short-term jobs. Theory Z says that long-term employment is good to retain people through good and bad times.

Other aspects are follows:

Japanese	+	**American**	=	**Theory Z**
Evaluation	→	Slow Rapid	=	Relatively slow evaluation and promotion.
Career Paths	→	Non-specialised Specialised	=	Cross-functional career path
Control Policy	→	Implicit Explicit	=	Balanced explicit and implicit control mechanism.
Decision-making	→	Collective Individual	=	Participative decision-making.

Regarding "Responsibility", Japanese adopt collective responsibility and Americans have individual responsibility and theory Z says that ultimate responsibility lies with relevant individuals.

As far as concern for organization, Japanese have holistic concern and Americans adopt segmented approach and theory Z says that holistic concern should be there for employees rather than fragmented approach.

Theory Z, although concerned with American and Japanese style of management, will influence behaviour of people working in organisations of different countries.

(i) Work Goals

Work goal will also influence behavioural aspect of workers working in global organisations. Work goals identified of employees in host countries such as interesting work, pay, job security, match between person and job, opportunity to learn, variety, inter personal relations, autonomy, convenient work hours, opportunity for promotion, working conditions, will have impact on behaviour. An empirical study conducted in international organisations in seven countries reveals that "Interesting work" can keep employees on a higher morale. It is an indication for employers to adopt motivational programmes according to local preferences of host country. Priority to various issues stated above differ from country to country. Hence, the managements have to take situational aspects into consideration to improve or maintain the behavioural tendency of workers.

(ii) Leadership

The leadership of any organisation will be one of the four categories identified, *viz.*, (i) Directive, (ii) Supportive, (iii) Participative and (iv) Achievement-oriented. Leadership also influences the behaviour of people in international or domestic organisations. As we are concerned here with international organisations. Leadership should cater to the needs of local culture of the country in which business operates. The four styles stated above are only the guidelines for managements operating in international arena. In most of the international companies **"Participative leadership style"** (empowering employees to assume greater control of the workplace) is practiced and 'directive style' is least operated.

Thus, global companies have to adapt contingency measures to improve and maintain the behaviour of their workforce. Cross-cultural training to understand the history culture, economics geography, institutions, etc., of the host country has to be given to employees. They should be exposed to inter cultural aspects though series of simulated incidents and typical problem situations. This helps those who have very short time to take up foreign assignments.

Comunicative language skills are to be taught in the language of host country. "To speak more than one language is no longer a luxury, it is a necessity" says a cross-cultural communication professor, Robert Moran.

Sensitivity training (impact of one's action on others) and field experience (exposure to ethnic sub-culture) also go a long way in developing behaviour of workers who work in global organisation.

Limitations of OB

As understood so far, OB is a subject or a behavioural discussion in organisations. The behavioural aspects are mainly concerned with, cognitive, behaviouristic and social cognitive frameworks. In the process of making people to adapt themselves to organisational situations and work as per the set rules and procedure, many problems crop up. Particularly cognitive aspects (mental processes is terms of perception attitude, emotion, values, etc.) put an individual in a dilemma while taking decision and performing the right task. Many a time, sound decisions are not taken resulting in low productivity.

Cognitive approach provides only conceptual aspects to study the human behaviour at work, Behaviouristic aspects direct the individual or the group to work according to observed behaviours. The experiments conducted by Pavlov, Watson and others provide a base to work on observations rather than cognitive approach which is based on elusive mental analysis. The experiments of Ivan Pavlov and Jhon. B. Watson provided the observed behaviour model, which is very prominent in behavioural analysis, *viz.*, "Stimulus-Response" model, popularly known as S-R model. Based on this basic modle, B. F. Skinner further analysed the S-R model through his "operant conditioning" experiments and said that "consequence" of a response will exhibit an improved behaviour over S-R approach and the model of Skinner is popularly called "R-S Model". According to this model, behaviour is influenced by its contingent environmental consequences.

In spite of these two approaches, *viz.*, cognitive and behavioural approaches, which are mechanistic and deterministic respectively, the recent thinkers and researchers such as Albert Bandura said these two approaches independently provide one dimension or the other of behaviour. They opined that an integrated approach has to be taken to understand behaviour. They projected "social learning" concept as a vital aspect of behaviour. According to this approach, a complex behaviour is acquired by directly observing and imitating others in the surrounding environment.

This theory popularised as "social cognitive theory" by Bandura and other modern researchers.

Social cognitive theory considers basic human capabilities such as **"symoblising'** (converting visual experiences of employees into cognitive models which act as guide for future actions), **"Forethought"** (employees plan their actions, anticipate the consequence and decide the level of performance), **"observational"** (employees learn by observing co-workers, their higher-ups, good performances of counterparts in other identical organisations and from their own previous experiences),**"Self-regulatory"** (adapting self-control measures) and **"Self reflective"** (making a self assessment of their actions and perceptually determine how strongly they believe that they can successfully accomplish the task in future in a given situation).

It is also called "Cognitive Social Learning Theory". Still many researches are going on, on behavioural aspects. The limitation of this subject is that in real time operations, no one model cannot be confidently applied to behavioural aspects of employees. All the theories can guide the people to take decisions on behavioural aspects. Behavioural aspect mainly being psychological and social phenomena, only contingency approach has to be taken in a given situation. Whether it is group or individual behaviour, they are mainly directed by mental process of the person and social system in which one works, in a given situation. Thus, the limitation of OB is that it cannot be standardised and is subjected to change as situation changes. It also changes as per the perceptions of the group or individual in a given situation.

Future of OB

Organisational behaviour exists as long as human factor works in organisations. Behavioural pattern may change in accordance with the needs of the organisations. If we observe the growth path of management thought since the days of Henry Fayol and F.W. Taylor to this day, we understand that human force at work has behaved according to the needs of the day and for the growth and success of the organisations.

Behavioural aspect is influenced by human psychology and the environment in which human factor lives and works. OB may be relatively a new field of study. But lived with organisations ever since the organisations started functioning for serving business objectives. Behaviour moves with any living object and more so with human factor. Only recently behavioural aspects in organisations are identified considering cognitive aspects and social systems in which organisations function. Today, OB has systems in which organisations function, and it has been considered as a strong factor for organisational success.

In the process of giving prime place for OB, "Human Resources Management" (HRM) is playing key role in organisational development (OD). Technology is replacing human force at work in organisations. Information technology and other highly advanced technology may be adopted in organisations. Rabots developed with faultless technology, may function lessening the burden for human factor at work. But brain behind this technology is human brain and only human factor should operate this technology. Thus, in future, human factor at work may be minimised, but behavioural aspect continues.

Behavioural aspects are unpredictable. Availing the assistance of various disciplines (such as psychology, sociology, anthropology, etc.), behavioural aspects are understood and accordingly methods and procedures are developed and adapted. The behavioural pattern changes. In non-technical organisations, human factor works more. As more and more technology is introduced, behavioural aspects of human factor also changes. But OB aspects are eternal.

SUMMARY

1. Organisational behaviour (OB) is of a recent origin. The behavioural aspects were there in organisations along with human factor. But the behavioural issues and patterns attained importance only after the "Human Behavioural Approach" movement took place.
2. OB focuses on what people think feel and do in and around organisations for their success and to achieve organisational objectives.
3. Organisational structure is changing. The intital structures of line, staff and matrix are now being converted into virtual and network structure through adaptation of information and other technologies.
4. OB is based on three vital components, *viz.*, cognitive biographical and social learning. Inter and intra-organisational aspects also direct the behaviour of human factor.
5. While the cognitive aspect analyses the mental process of human factor, biographical aspect throws light on mechanistic operations. Social learning facilities the modification of behaviour observing environment, co-workers, supervisors and ones own perception of individuals work in organisations.
6. The goal of OB is to study the behavioural pattern of workers and to model their behaviour according to the organisational needs providing required training and development facilities. So that they will be smart at work.
7. Elements of OB are people, technology, environment and structure. Other supplemental aspects which facilitate the study of OB are: (i) Knowledge Management, (ii) Relationship with other disciplines, (iii) Systematic or scientific methods and procedure, (iv) Levels in organisations and (v) Decision-making under critical situations.
8. OB general model states the activities at different levels. At individual level, cognitive and biographical aspects are analysed. At group level, interpersonal relationship aspects, such as communication, stress and conflict, power and politics, structure (groups and teams) are discussed. At organisation level, issues such as organisational structure, culture, work design, adaptation of technology, HRD, etc., are studied to understand the level of productivity, absenteeism employee turnover and satisfaction.

9. Other models of OB are: (I) Autocratic, (ii) Custodial, (iii) Supportive and (iv) Collegial.
10. OB in global operation differs from the domestic organisations. Management perceptions will be different. Companies have to work in cross-cultural situations. Strict ethical aspects in operations are to be followed. Quality goods and services only will have a place in business operations. Firms and people work in a changed environment. Cooperation is the key factor in interpersonal relationship. Organisational structure is virtual or collaborative or operate in the form of Head office and branch. There should be easy access for information. Problems have to be anticipated and quick solutions have to be given by sorting out the situation. OB in international business should consder the aforesaid aspects including the language barrier.
11. The limitation of OB is that management practices and decisions are not static and hence the behavioural aspects cannot immediately respond to the changes that take place from time-to-time.
12. The future of OB is bright as the behaviour is a part of change management. As and when any change regarding the functional aspects takes place in organisations, response will be positive. Organisations live long to support various business propositions and in the whole analysis behavioural aspect of people at work plays a key role.

STUDY QUESTIONS

1. Give the meaning of Organisational Behaviour.
2. Name the key variables that identify the nature of people.
3. What do you mean by organisational structure?
4. Give the meaning of "Individual Behaviour"
5. Name the elements of OB system.
6. Mention the models of OB.
7. Give an analytical note on OB concept
8. Analyse the scope and application of OB in management.
9. "Behaviour is generally predictable". Discuss.
10. State how psychology is more relevant to the filed of OB.
11. Give a note on the role of Sociology in OB.
12. Analyse the influence of Individual Behaviour in organisations.
13. Give a brief note on various elements of OB.
14. What is organisational behaviour? Enumerate the historical evolution of organisational behaviour.
15. Briefly explain the behavioural aspects of different levels of an organisation.
16. Discuss the nature of people in organisations.
17. What is organisational behaviour model? Explain the various models of OB.
18. What are the various disciplines contributing to organisational behaviour? Briefly explain their contribution to OB.
19. Explain the emerging trends in organisations.
20. Briefly explain the role of Knowledge Management as a sub-element of OB.
21. Briefly explain the future and limitations of OB.
22. Give the meaning of effectiveness and efficiency. State and explain the relationship of these two concepts with OB.
23. Briefly explain the OB issues in the context of global business.
24. Give a brief note on Autocratic model of OB.

25. Analyse the Custodial model of OB.
26. Briefly state about the supportive model of OB.
27. Analyse the collegial model of OB.
28. Give a note on OB as an interdisciplinary study.

CASE STUDY

ORGANISTIONAL BEHAVIOUR

Ranjani had completed her one-month of service at Lloyds company. Her previous employer, Pentamax, to reduce costs, downsized its staff. Ranjani was out. She was not depressed. She had tried hard to get though with references to her present company. Ranjani sitting in her new office recalls her memories towards Pentamax.

She enjoyed being with Pentamax. Things were working great for her. She was the team member from the very beginning. The company was decentralised and the communication between the employees was very easier. She loved her organisational culture. People shared every thing both personally and professionally.

The head of the unit was democratic in his leadership style. He was basically very supportive in nature. He listened to the views of the employees in the company's decisions. Ultimately, when the decision to close down many units came, it was hard to digest for Ranjani. She felt that nothing could replace Pentamax. She made a comparison always thinking about past and current company in which she was employed.

In Lloyds, to ponder over, the company was totally inflexible. The procedures and the plans made were highly bureaucratic. The decision-making process was left in the hands of top management. The decisions taken were also very slow. Many things were not implemented. It was only documented and went into files. These happenings, she thought would have merged from the management itself. The top management also was too busy to be seen around. They were indulged in their own work. The climate and the entire organisational behaviour were indifferent.

She was expected to do what was given to her. Her colleagues and co-workers treated her with a difference. She had also tried to be friendly with them. But unfortunately they had declined to accept her. One fine morning, she decided to go for a one day tour and she called her colleagues to join. They politely refused saying that they have some commitment with their families. But later that month end, through one of her co-workers, she came to know that her colleagues had planned for a tour for next month.

It was at this stage she decided to take a trip by her own to a small town nearby. She is bothered that her choice of entering with Lloyds is mistake. She regretted of accepting the offer from Lloyds.

Case Questions

1. Identify some basic concepts of organisational behaviour from this case.
2. As a consultant what advice you can give for Ranjani? Do you think all the organisations are an ideal place to work?

14

SOCIAL SYSTEM AND ORGANISATIONAL CULTURE

LEARNING OBJECTIVES

After reading this chapter, you should be able to know:

- Concepts – Social System and Organisational Culture
- Indicators of OC
- Common Features of OC
- Challenges of OC
- Forms of Culture and their Revelation
- Organisational Change and Culture
- Weak Aspects of OC

Organisation is a social unit or a system. Social system exhibits cultural relationship co-operation and team spirit among the members of the organisation, irrespective of the positions or levels. Chester Bernard, who recognised the features of an organisation, said that "A formal organisation represents cultural relationship of the groups working within the organisation." Therefore, two concepts, *viz.*, "Social System", and "Organisational culture" have to be properly defined and understood to practice an acceptable culture.

What is a Social System?

"Social" refers to a human society involving or promoting companionship or friendly interaction with others and contributing for the development of organised communities. Human society consists of institutions such as family, and other specialised groups or bodies which perform one function or the other related to the development and maintenance of society. These institutions are called in simple term "Organisation." It may be business or non-business entity. These institutions function with specific objectives and lay down rules and regulations to successfully run the programme. The institution is on integrated whole called "system".

The system comprises of many sub-systems designed according to functions to be discharged. Each system and sub-systems will have methods and procedures, which are systematically framed considering the cost factor. An organisation, business or non-business, thus, is considered as a "social system", at the micro-level. At macro-level, the whole society will be a social system.

What is Organisational Culture?

The concept of organisational culture (OC) within business has emerged from the application of culture to the organisational activities. Sociology and Anthropology have given much to the concept of culture.

"Culutre" as a concept is interpreted as a pattern of shared basic assumptions and beliefs that an individual or a group learns and practices them. These beliefs when applied to a problem would provide some decisive thoughts to solve the problem. Those beliefs and assumptions that worked well to solve problems, were passed on to new comers to have continuity of adapted culture. These are extended to an organisation to evolve an organisational culture over a period of time.

The two challenges thrown by sociology will also apply to business activities in different ways, giving scope for comparisons. The challenges are: (1) the one that occurs in external environment that affects the organisation to pass through different times and thrive though efforts and (ii) taking individuals from outside who are already in established organisational culture to work with existing individuals in the organisation to make them independent and cohesive whole that can benefit all in the organisation. Recruiting (fresh or experienced) people continuously into organisation to develop and maintain a culture in organisation is essential.

Definition

There are many definitions to OC which are similar and cover many of the same aspects. However, OC refers to **"the set of values beliefs and norms together with symbols like dramatised events and personalities that represent the unique character of an organisation".**

Norms describe tradition, structure of authority or routines of the organisation, shared values, beliefts, language, etc. and create a common identift and sense of community.

Thus, organisational culture is a group's general reaction to stimulus (information). This reaction of group is the outcome of training or learning by individuals on their own by observing others around them of how to act in any given situtation. Thus, organisational culture functions just as any social learning does.

Culture and Image

Another aspect to be understood about organisational culture is that it often deep rooted in people who work for an organisation for fairly a long period. It is just as we say about a person who works for considerable tenure in organisation such as TVS, BHEL, WIPRO, INFOSYS etc., we call them Infosyean or a TVS person. Because they will have imbibed the culture of that organisation. The culture of these reputed institutions speak about good value and ethical aspects of the organisation practiced by individuals.

Similarly, even a good person works for a bad company, will carry the image of that organisation. People in such organisation gradually learn bad habits of dysfunctional organisational culture. Organisations, in order to came out of this, they have to spend huge money, infuse new genes and additional resources with the help of outside professionals.

Thus, organisation as a social system practices certain beliefs and norms to meet the organisational objectives and practices. In the process, it may facilitate the success or destroy the organisation. However, leaders are to be watchful and closely observe the practices and correct quick the disturbing beliefs and norms. Ultimately, the culture develops an image (good or bad) to the organisation.

Quality of Culture

Organisational culture learned, relearned, passed on to new employees and continues as a part of a company's core identity. It is fully accepted that culture is an essential force that drives the performance of people in organisations. The cultural degree determines the quality of the organisation.

If the organisation is functioning well means that unit has adapted quality culture. The culture is invisible. It can be observed through the quality of work, that organisation performs and can be construed that employees are highly motivated by the quality of culture adapted in the organisation. They will be honest, sincere and value-oriented, if the quality of culture is on a higher side.

The quality of culture is measured by understanding the **values** that the organisation practices, **beliefs** that it has, **principles** that it follows, the quality and **characteristic features of the Personalities** who lead the organisation and **level of morale** of the employees. Thus, the quality and characteristic features of culture of our organisation can be measured through the following indicators:

Indicators of Organisational Culture

1. Value: This is revealed by sincerity, humanitarian approach, stead fastness (firmly needs of management and employees to achieve the goals of the organisation.

2. Selflessness: This exactly means that people who work for the organisation should identify themselves with the organisation. Self-centered people ruin the firm. This indicates the degree of dedication of people who work for the organisation and level of organisational consciousness they possess.

3. Faith: This refers to the extent of belief that employees have about practices in the organisation. Both top management and employees should believe each other to develop overall organisational culture. Good faith is indicated by win-win situation. For example: Tatas, Infosys, who give importance for human factor to achieve their goals.

4. Knowledge: People in organisation should have the knowledge of work and on other organisational aspects. This will help them to work with devotion and dedication to produce quality work. Knowledge worker can understand the situation and works. This leads to the development of good culture. This also tunes the behaviour of worker/manager/ top management in organisations.

5. Problem sharing: Every organisation at every stage is confronted with several problems. The good culture of the organisation in such problem situations is that management should share the problems with employees and together come out with a workable solvation. Hierarchy may prevail in the organisation. But good culture is that the top management should share the problem with employees to develop team spirit instead of bossing.

6. Risk Taking: Organisations have to take risk to achieve business goals. The culture of an organisation is also governed by the level of calculated risk taken by management and challenges faced by the workforce of that unit. The tasks to be performed by workers look like routine matter. But in each task, disturbing factors come on the way. Employees should face these challenges and drive the organisation to attain good result. To such an extent the employees should have confidence, courage, commitment and conviction. The cultural indicator is that the top management should train and develop their workforce to possess such spirit to manoeuver the risks that they have to face in performing the tasks. The employees who work for reducing risks in organisation should be suitably rewarded. It is a good culture. Most of the organisations adopt very attractive reward system for good work of their employees and adopt punitive measures for those who err in their work. A good culture is to weed out disturbing elements to encourage honest workers to work in full steam.

7. Management perspective: One of the cultural indicators is that the top management should have a healthy perception of keeping the morale of employees on a higher side by developing in them the feeling of security, safety, warmth, feelings of being superior, etc. The cultural aspect is to adapt the principles of equity and justice. This prompts the workers to be more productive.

8. Employee satisfaction: This aspect is much discussed in previous indicators of culture. It is an established plain truth that employees contribute more to productivity of organisation, if they are fully satisfied with working atmosphere and individual job satisfaction. The cultural indicator, "Employee Satisfaction" is the fundamental feature of organisational culture. Tolerance and patience, initiative to develop organisation, functional expertise, assisting fellow workers in times of need, focusing on one's own job are all the traits of workers which contribute for the development of healthy culture of the organisation. The managements make way for adapting these personal traits of employees of keeping them in good mood and satisfied.

9. Stability: Stability factor of culture says that whatever rules and regulations framed by the management should not hinder the progress of the organisation. This means operational rules should be positive and encourage the workers to stay on in the organisation to have stability in operations. It is a good culture.

OC – Not Ideal

OC is an invisible practice adopted in organisations to keep the people happy and work for the benefit of the whole unit. It is not an ideal thinking of management or experts imposed on workers. If practicable thinking is not implemented or practiced, the company plans can be toppled. OC may vary widely from one business unit to another. But certain variables are common in OC. These variables facilitate us to understand OC in a better manner. Variables identified by Harrison Matrices and Janice M. Beyer (in "Cultures of Work Organisations", PHI, 1993) are observed in all OCs and shown in the following box.

COMMON FEATURES OF OC

1. Organisation being a social unit, cultures brought by individuals and organisation's accepted culture are all blended and become "collective" agreement and become truly synergetic.
2. Without questioning the basic values of culture, people in organisations find OC as a security for their insecurity and uncertainty. They are **"EMOTIONALLY CHARGED"** and protect it by developing strong emotional attachment.
3. As a member of social unit, individual workers share experience with others and pass on good OC to incoming people. Thus, OC is **"Historically based".**
4. People working in organisations exhibit their emotions more in the form of work than they speak. OC in this context **is "Inherently symbolic".** This means that some statements are exhibited in work of the people than they speak. For example, OC statement of an organisation goes like **"Honesty is the Best policy".** Instead of every workers in the unit saying that "I am honest in my work" should exhibit. This in his/her performance. The vision and mission statements have a great symbolic meaning that encourage or induce workers to work sincerely and shapes the OC.
5. OC is not **static** but **Dynamic,** promoting **stability** in organisation after a certain period of time. In the long run, the benefit of good practice (culture) will be predictable and will be visible in actions and achievements. Thus, OC is **dynamic** in nature. Example: In a hierarchical situation, a front line manager or a seasoned worker does not call his chairman, by name. He simply addresses as "Boss". This is a culture developed to exhibit loyalty to the organisation.

   "Respecting others is respecting ourselves" is a time-honoured belief. Those who practice this will develop a positive thinking for themselves and in others and they become "dynamic" in their operations. Thus, OC has dynamic feature in the long-run.
6. OC does not exhibit only positive features. Many a time, negative aspects such as contradictions in operations exist leading to conflict. There will be ambiguity and dilemma to perform a task as instructions and rules are not clear. Thus, OC contains more of "FUZZY" aspects which is inherent in organisational practices. An intense and continuous observation is essential to understand good and bad aspects of organisational culture. Continuous corrective measures are required to develop a sound OC.

Information Source: "Cultures of Work Organisations", Harrison, M.Trice and Janice, M. Beyer, PHI, 1993.

Power of OC

Whether the OC is strong or not can be assessed by measuring the level of sharing the cultural forms and their consequences. There are many forms of OC. But vital forms by which OC can be properly understood are **Language, symbols, stories** and **practices.** Observe the following figure:

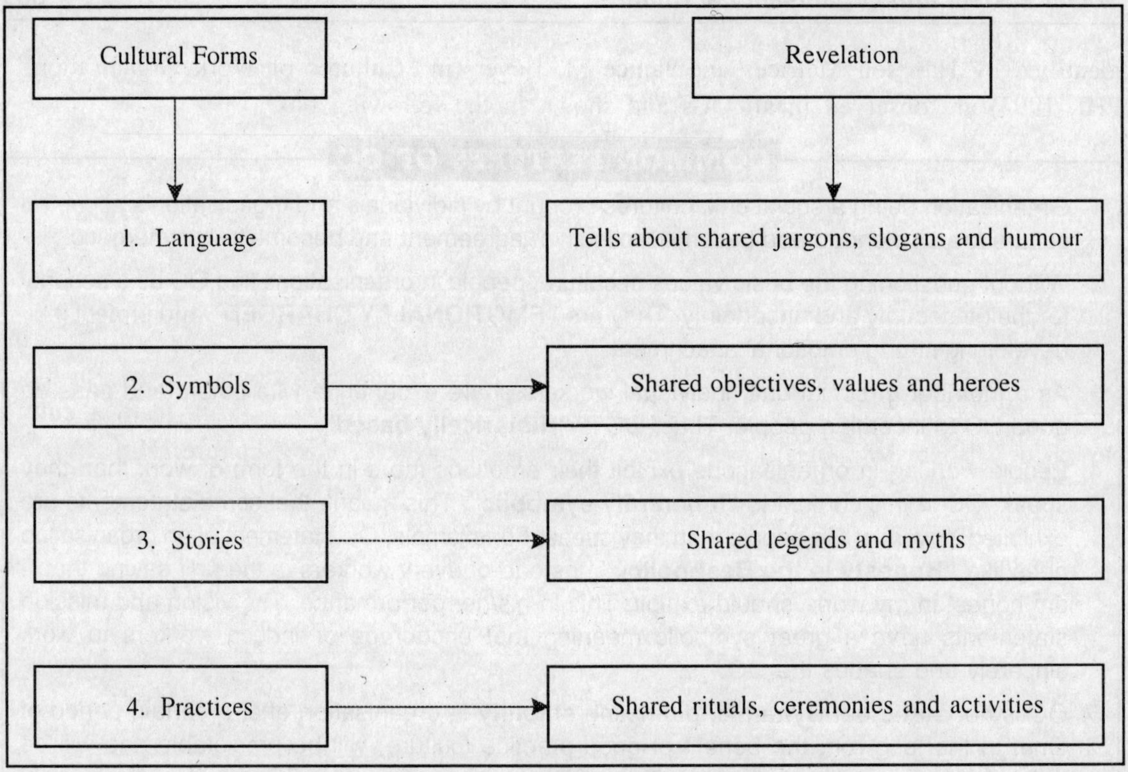

Fig. 14.1. Forms of Culture

This figure exhibits vital forms of OC and what each form reveals.

These forms tell that OC is a shared belief and what and why the organisation looks for. These forms and their consequences will reveal the culture of the organisations.

Consequences

The consequences of these cultural forms will identify the power of culture. It reveals the strength of culture — whether weak or strong. Following are some important consequences of forms of culture which measure the strength of an organisation.

- Individual commitment of people to organisation's vision and mission
- Contribution of each form to organisational stability
- Sense of identity for the individual
- Organisation should make sense to the individual.

These consequences/shared beliefs/values make an observer to understand the level of culture that the organisation possess. Very many instances can be quoted to testify this. Tata empire was established by JRD, TATA from scratch. The quality factors such as sincerety in service, caring for human factor, providing quality products and services to delight customers have made this group to live for long and still in the frontline of the industrial world. Like this, many industrial and service organisations have faced challenges through their strong cultural practices. Today people believe "TATA" as a symbol of quality — a form of culture. Thus, the founder is not alive, but his quality values and beliefs are embedded into Tata organisations' culture to make his thinking and contributions alive.

Similarly, previous notable events and happenings or otherwise called organisational stories or history also reveal the organisational culture. We hear about the personal achievements and stories of many successful organisations. The success has come to them as they faced challenges and walked through the thorny path. The leading companies such as Tata, Birlas, Singhania, Wipro, Infosys and Navarathnas of PSUs have all have their own stories about the culture they have adopted to succeed. Challenges faced by organisations, make them culturally dynamic. In a competitive environment, external factors influence the organisational activities and may affect the existing practices. Particularly, when fresh blood is introduced (experienced or freshers) into organisation people bring with them a culture imbibed in them which will not suit to the existing organisational culture. However, the modification needs to certain extent to make them adapt themselves to the practiced culture of the organisation. The process of making new entrants to adapt themselves into existing culture is called "Socialisation Process of OC."

Socialisation

Socialisation is not an easy process. For many entrants it will be a **"Cultural Shock".** This means that the culture the new entrants inherit or have acquired through previous

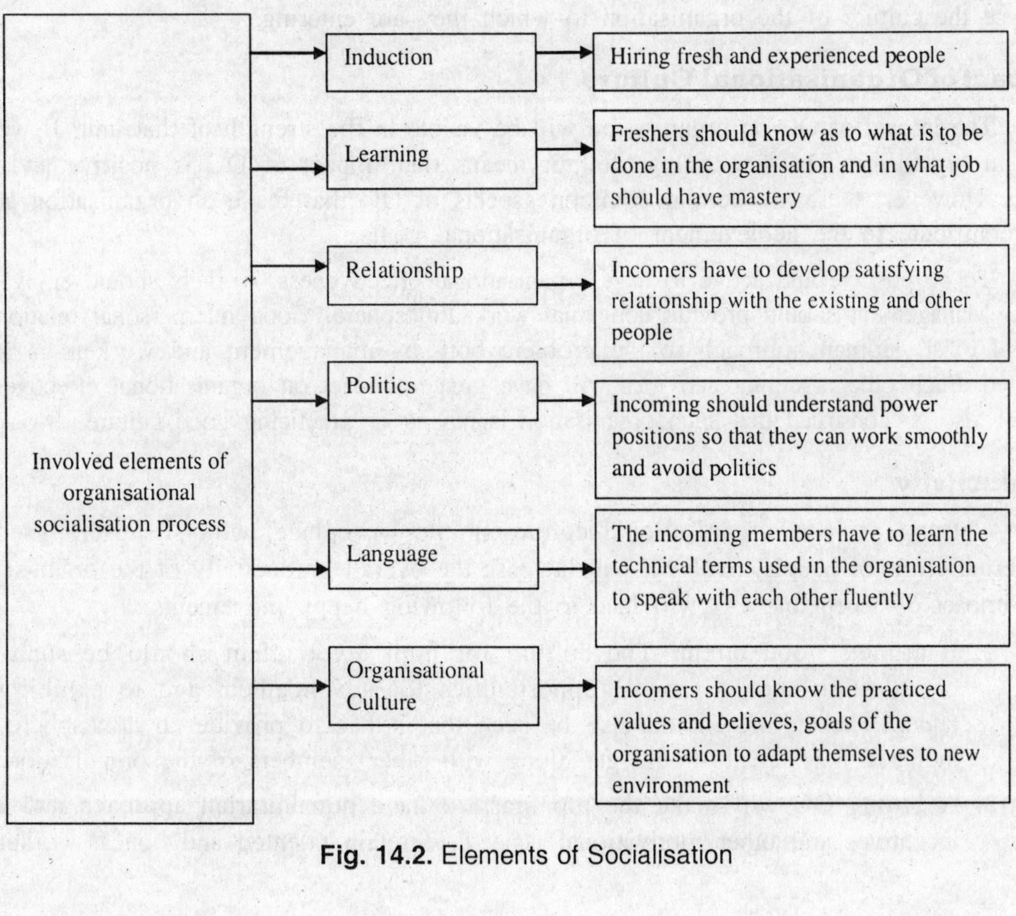

Fig. 14.2. Elements of Socialisation

experiences may develop a friction with the existing culture in the organisation. It is a psychological or social disorientation caused by confrontation with a new culture. This shock may not last long in many individuals. Because new entrants will be offered many training and mentoring programmes to adapt themselves to new culture. Another positive aspect for many entrants is that organisational practices and environment will be a priority over the salary and other benefits they receive. They need a clean and congenial atmosphere to give out their best. If the working environment gives them a mental solace, they are prepared to sacrifice the monetary benefits. They work comfortably.

Stability

In the process of socialisation of OC, many factors — dress code, ambience, minimum degree of autonomy in performing tasks etc. — have to be seriously considered and make new entrants comfortable in their workplaces. Stable and sustainable operations is one of the essential elements of OC and to practice, this element, entire workforce (new and existing ones) should honestly work in that direction. The managements have to provide a sustainable and clean environment in work places which include both economic and non-economic factors.

While socialising, new entrants should be stressed to understand the concept of "stability" in their operations and about the organisational stability. To be stable in their operations, new entrants have to adopt themselves to organisational culture. Therefore, it is not only the employers that should look into the behaviour of entrants, but also the new entrants should analyse the culture of the organisation to which they are entering.

Impact of Organisational Culture

The impact of OC on organisation will be visible in the strength of that unit. If we say that an organisation is functioning well, it means that impact of OC is positive and *vice versa.* However, there are certain common aspects of OC that make an organisation active and contribute to the achievement of organisational goals.

To be positive and active to have organisational effectiveness, workers should enjoy their work. Management should provide congenial work atmosphere. Good interpersonal relationship should exist. Human approach to the problem both by management and workers is to be adopted. Such other soothing activities will have greater impact on organisational effectiveness. It will also be construed that such organisation is having or practicing good culture.

Productivity

A strong positive organisational culture in the workplace, which is established by concerted effort of people involved, will increase the overall productivity of the organisation. The impact of acceptable OC will lead to the following happy movements.

1. It attracts good talent. The culture for high level talent should be such that organisation should provide opportunities for advancement and to exhibit their talent. The culture should also be such that it has to provide an atmosphere that inducted new talent should get along with other members of the organisation.
2. A Strong OC will make the top brass to have humanitarian approach and offer incentives and other motivational aspects to retain talented and honest workers.

3. A powerful OC will have its impact on energy and momentum of the organisation. A strong OC will gain a momentum of its own. It energises the organisation and make the employees to feel that they are valued. A sort of excitement will prevail in the entire organisation and a strong organisational identity in each member develops.
4. The identity of each worker with organisation that has developed due to strong OC, will motivate each worker to go to workplace happily. Absenteeism will be minimised. The impact is that each worker contributes his/her maximum to growth of the organisation. A social culture can make employees look forward to work, if they love coming to the work. They work hard and put extra effort to achieve the organisational goal. Job satisfaction they derive from their work will prompt them to love their tasks rather than hate them.
5. The impact of strong OC is that it makes every one in the organisation more work-oriented, happier and never shirk in critical times. It develops a strong "teamwork" concept and make people feel for one another in times of individual distress. Strong OC develops a highly positive emotional atmosphere. Emotions are positively charged.

Thus, the overall impact of strong OC is that it makes the organisation more healthier and the productivity increases.

How culture makes organisation healthier?

Many organisations practice healthy culture. The concept of "Healthy" can be measured only through the success of the organisations in terms of increasing profit, wealth and high morale of employees. As OC is invisible, exceptional or disastrous corporate culture can only be observed from the point of stability, sustainability and growth of the enterprise. Most of the business and other organisations fall somewhere in the middle between the two extremes (exceptional or disastrous). Healthy firms practice a high degree of good features. The elements that make an organisation healthier are as follows:

Elements		*Effects*
1. Organisational Pride	:	Employees of organisations which practice high degree of good features always defend their organisation against standard or any other Criticism. They take it as a pride to be in such organisations, on the other hand, people working helplessly in organisations, which are involved in scams, hesitate to say about their workplace. (An employee of Sathyam).
2. Ambition to Improve	:	The culture of a healthy organisation will be visible in employees' ambition to continue to work in the same organisation for ones own growth. Win-win culture is practiced in this organisation.
3. Respect for Teamwork and Communication	:	The practice (culture) of open discussion, more open exchange of ideas contributes for the development of team-work which every employee likes. Individually, they

became more open and can give healthy suggestions on an issue. People become active and deveolop positive approach through good communication system and team-work.

4. Quality leadership : A quality top management and with broad outlook and human approach can make an organisation a healthier one. Even the front line and middle managers should have the same outlook and should fully practice the concept of "empathy."

5. Sound Financial Analysis : Every organisation will be aspiring for the growth of financial status. Although there is growth of wealth and position on year on year basis, CFOs and CEOs should assess the genuinety of financial statements by giving an insight into costs and earnings. Inflated or deflated accounting practices will not exhibit real situation.

A bad financial practice will be disastrous. (Enron, Sathyam etc.,) Finance department should find out whether expenses are justified and they really make the company more stronger. Hence, a healthy organisation should adopt sound financial policy.

6. Employee Relationship : A culture which provides an atmosphere to create interpersonal relationship will thrive well. A good understanding between employer and employees can increase productivity through satisfaction of employees. Good employee relationship make employees as team players.

7. External Relationship : A healthy organisation will have good culture of establishing healthy relationship between the company and customers and suppliers. This is very well seen in service organisation. Healthy relationship with outsiders is the capital of service organisations. It is equally essential in other organisations too.

8. Training and Development : Mentoring, training and development of programmers for the growth of employees, positive organisational policies framed and implemented for the all-sided development of personality of workers, are all healthy practices which contribute for developing good culture.

9. Employee Safety : Policies adapted for employee safety prevent employees from having ill will against management and prompts them to develop positive approach towards the organisation.

These elements, when well practiced, can make an organisation a healthier one. A culturally strong organisation will give priority for all these aspects. If these elements are metriculously adopted, the organisation becomes a benchmark organisation for organisational culture. If they are implemented at a low degree and if some of them are absent, such organisation will become sick. Thus, an organisation to be healthier, should practice a high degree of aforesaid elements. This makes the organisation more competitive in its business.

The characteristic features, elements, indicators etc., discussed so far are not all-inclusive of organisational culture. In a social system, most admired and and least admired companies may exist. Considering the 'finance' as a parameter to measure the success of an organisation, a most admired and having a rank–1 in the list of admired companies may be pushed to rank – 3 or 4 after four or five years. Financial policies will have impact on operations of the companies. The change in financial policies are governed by organisational culture.

If the ranking of a company is in an ascending order (like position-3 in one year and acquires the position-2 in next year), besides the sound financial policy, "Retention Policy" (Attraction and retention of talent) also contributes for improving the status of the organisation. When we observe the successful organisations such as century old Tatas and Birlas or even recently established IT giants such as Infosys, TCS etc., besides sound financial management, it is legendary cultures and values that a have made these business houses to be on top. Weak cultural practices make an organisation a weak one.

Weak Culture

Any organisation, cannot have uniform culture. There is no common culture that is practiced in every organisation. All organisations practice their own value systems well within the framework of the society in which they function. All members have to adapt themselves to the perceptions and practices of the organisation. But all do not adopt the practices in the same degree. Many practice dominant culture (core values shared by majority), but some may lag behind and become lethargic. These lethargic people become a group practicing their own culture, which will not conform with core values of the organisation. This becomes a sub-culture. Different groups will have their own sub-culture and they normally will be complementary to the dominant and practiced culture. However, they disturb the normal functioning of the organisation. The weak spots are as follows:

Weak Spots

- **Internal politics:** In many organisations, this will be a major problem than real external problems that companies face.
- **Moral aspects:** People at work will always be grumbling, inspite of all their needs are met by the management. Chronic unhappiness leads to high turnover.
- **Groupism and inconsistency :** Lack of understanding of people behaviour, communication, and perceiving problems and opportunities, give scope for division amongst employees. This leads to inconsistency in operations and gives way for fragmentation (groupism).

- **Development of Sub-cultures:** Groupism gives way for ingrown subculture This occurs due to lack of communication among sub-units. This gives way, for destructive conflict. Warfare starts among sub-cultures. These sub-cultures form "Clubs" with restricted entry. The values of these clubs become more important to members than organisation's values and culture.

These weak spots of an organisation, exist in most of the companies. The adopted culture should be capable of eclipsing the weak spots. Top management will be continuously watching these routine cultural functions and have corrective mechanisms to smoothen the situations. Ultimately, it is the good leadership that overcomes the cultural maladies and make organisations to work with accepted and dominant culture.

Practicing Good Culture

Adopting and maintaining good culture is essential for the organisation. Organisation is like a machine which contains both technology and human resources. Whether an organisation has adopted high degree of good culture, will mainly be decided by rules and regulations followed in such organisation. These rules and regulations are framed by some people and are followed by others. Therefore, if an organisation fails, it is the people who formulated the policies, implemented and monitored are to be blamed and not the organisation. Thus, organisations are composed of concerned human indiviudals, who agree to be as a unit and follow the policies and programmers formulated by human beings only. Hence, the focus of maintaining good culture will be on human factor. In order to maintain socially and morally acceptable practices, organisations have to monitor the process of inducting human factor into the organisation.

The process is as follows:

1. Careful Selection: The selection of people should be such that they humbly and strictly follow the organisational rules and procedures and commit themselves to the tasks assigned to them. Careful selection of people at the entry level goes a long way in practicing good culture.

2. Fixing in the Job: Carefully selected people should be placed in specific jobs and continuously trained to adopt the organisational culture. Some organisations, in the initial stages make new blood to work more than what they can, to test their patience and tolerance and to develop group cohesivenss and humility in them. Some other firms may make the new entrants to work in a relaxed but controlled atmosphere. Placing them in proper manner to understand and commit to the organisational culture in the entry level itself is an essential aspect of maintaining OC.

3. Training and Development: From the beginning, the recruiteees have to be put under continuous training to have control over their assigned tasks. Job mastery is essential for the maintenance of organisational culture. People who learn their jobs, develop organisational identity and commit to the OC. This facilitates the workers to develop a career plan with continuous training and with the passage of time they move from one level to another and understand the work culture. This process makes employees happy and motivate them to work hard to achieve the organisational goals. Thorough socialisation provides them an opportunity to occupy new positions. Hence, continuous training and development of personnel ensures them safety and make them to strongly identify with OC.

4. Evaluation and Rewards: People at work should be subjected to continuous performance appraisal and quality workers should be suitably rewarded. Every organisation adopts performance appraisal programmes which are designed as per its needs and pattern of work. Rewards are given to maintain employee morale. This practice is vital component of good culture. Evaluation and rewarding system focuses on organisational business process and is crucial to corporate values.

5. Practicing Values: Good culture comprises of socially acceptable and organisationally required values. These values have to be practiced by people in the organisation. The personal values that do not suit to the organisational values are to be set aside. Maintaining organisational culture is more important and values oriented towards good OC are to be strictly practiced by employees.

6. Telling Organisational Stories : The founders of organisations will have left memorable legacies and highly cultured practices. There may be many incidents which were critical and management will have taken decisions to up hold the values and ethics of the organisations. They are the moral stories which have to be told to future employees to know about the ethical aspects of the organisation. When heard by employees, these stories will have impact on their behaviour. Past stories of the organisation, when told, make employees to uphold and continue good practices. Repeatedly telling the stories, reinforces the workers to practice established OC.

Besides these aspects, organisations should promote the talented persons to key positions. Recognising the employees and promoting them to coveted positions will add to the value of the organisation. It facilitates the maintenance of good culture. Recognition of people in the organisation is a powerful reinforcer. The successful people can guide new comers to maintain and continue the OC.

Organisational Change and Culture

Organisation is a dynamic entity. Whenever business environment changes, culture of organisations also change. Change is an essential aspect of organisational activity. Hence, OC is also dynamic in character. The change in organisation takes place when the firm undergoes restructuring or when acquisitions and mergers happen or when changes take place in business environment. In all these circumstances, organisational culture changes.

Today, organisational structure is also changing. Network and virtual organisations are becoming prominent. In this context, culture also undergoes drastic change. The culture of new structure will focus mainly on relationship. Companies work with network of offices in different countries and good relationshp between offices will be the real culture of such companies.

This type of relationship organisations have to adopt a culture involving a system to deliver messages accurately to all concerned people in all offices of net work. Employees are to be trained in changed cultural aspects. Employees have to be involved in changing the cultural process. Realistic goals that influence bottom line of the organisational activities are to be framed. Anticipate problems that may crop up in future and formulate solutions to meet such challenges.

In the process of changing culture, the roots and core competence of the organisation have to be preserved. Many organisations which have not preserved their roots in the process of changing the culture, have miserably failed after changed culture. IBM which was the world leader in mainframe had to face challenge when personal computer (PC) was introduced. As it changed the traditional culture, it could successfully face the change and continues to be the world leader. It switched over to new technology quickly and modified its traditional strong research laboratory to manufacture personal computers. This is a fine example of cultural change.

Maintaining valued culture is a challenge for any organisation. Changes in OC are also essential as time and technology advance. But fundamentals, *viz.*, values in operations should not be ignored to be successful.

SUMMARY

1. Human society promoting companionship or friendly interaction with others and contributing for the development of organised communities is called "social system."
2. Organisational culture is the "the collection of expressed or implied beliefs, values, stories, myths and specialised language that foster a feeling of community among organisation members".
3. The quality of culture of an organisation is measured by understanding the values practiced by the organisation, beliefs that has and principles that it follows.
4. Indicators of OC are: (i) values, (ii) selflessness, (iii) faith, (iv) knowledge, (v) problem sharing, (vi) risk taking, (vii) management perspective, (viii) employee satisfaction and (ix) stability.
5. Common features of OC are: (i) collective effort, (ii) historically based, (iii) emotionally charged, (iv) dynamic, (v) exhibition of negative aspects, (vi) dominant values and (vii) norms that guide the organisation.
6. Vital forms of OC are: (i) language which reveals shared jorgans, slogans and humour, (ii) symbols which signify shared objects, values and heroes (personalites), (iii) stories about myths shared and should legends and (iv) practices involving shared rituals, ceremonies and activities.
7. The consequences of the forms of OC will be that they make employees to commit to their takes, bring stability, develop identity for the individual and make organisations to take care of the individuals.
8. Socialisation process of inducting people into organisation involves, recruiting right people, placing them, train them to have job mastery, making them to practice organisational values, telling the stories to reinforce their behaviour rewarding talented people and recognise them.
9. The impact of OC may be positive or negative. The impact of good OC are, increased productivity, stability in operations, attracts fine talent, develops human approach in top brass and workers, energises the whole system, develops organisational identity in workers and employers and avoids laziness. Negative impact is that it ruins the organisation.
10. Healthier organisation possesses the qualities such as enthusiasm in workers to work, respect for team work, motivating leadership, sound financial management, healthy interpersonal relationship amongst members, healthy relationship with suppliers, customers and statutory bodies and looking after employee safety.
11. Weak spots of OC are internal politics, groupism and inconsistency, chronic unhappiness of employees, and development of sub-cultures which hinder the growth of the organisation.
12. As changes in organisation due to restructure, acquisitions and mergers and diversification take place, organisational culture also changes.

STUDY QUESTIONS

1. What is organisational behaviour ? Briefly explain the role of OB in managing a firm.
2. What is a "Social System"? Briefly analyse the features of a social system.
3. What do you mean by "Culture"? What is the meaning of organisational culture? State the importance of 'quality culture' in OB.
4. Give a detailed note on indicators of organisational culture.
5. Briefly explain the common features of organisational culture.
6. Give a note on how organisational culture impacts on organisational effectiveness.
7. What do you mean by sub-culture? Will it disturb organisational operations? What remedial measures you suggest overcome the effect of sub-culture.
8. Give an analytical note on important forms of culture, what they reveal and their consequences.
9. How the culture makes the organisation healthier? Analyse.
10. Give a note on weak culture of an organisation.
11. Analyze the impact of structural change (such as diversification, acquisition and mergers) on culture of the organisation.
12. Give an explanatory note on developing and implementing good culture in an organisation and the disturbances that occur while implementing good culture.

CASE STUDY

OB researchers say "that it is very difficult to change organisational. culture, but it can be changed". Having this statement in backdrop, give a careful reading to the following story.

In your living locality, a big mall is functioning adopting all good business practices. Employees respect the customers and are very humble in their approach. Management people offer after good quality goods at very reasonable price, take back damaged goods even after use, offer other in house facilities such as amusement place for children, resting place and recreation facilities. The mall has created a brand for its excellent service.

In a periodical shuffling of employees (on accepted principle of the organisation), the Managing Director of the mall was transferred. The incoming MD was conservative person and poor in human approach to solve any problem. He introduced new timings which was opposed by the workers. The existing financial policy was modified having a negative impact on employee compensation. These changes had negative impact on workers' behaviour. The situation in the mall turned to worse in two years and reached the point of bankruptcy. You are appointed as turn-around officer to improve the situation.

Questions

1. As turnaround officer, how do you analyse the situation? State the analysing steps.
2. Analyse the weak spots of culture of the mall.
3. What cultural aspects you suggest to turnaround the mall to profitable position?
4. Considering this case, make an analysis of the role of MD as a positive leader.

15

INDIVIDUAL BEHAVIOUR

LEARNING OBJECTIVES

After reading this chapter, you should be able to know:

- Individual Behaviour – The Concept
- Stimuli-Response Model and Indiviudal Behaviour
- Factors influencing behaviour in S-R Model
  (a) Internal factors (b) External factors (c) Perception of the task (d) Ability
  (e) Workplace happenings (f) Biographical character
- The Concept of Corporate Citizenship
- Understanding Behavioural Change-Conditioning
- Knowing about Forms of Behavioural Change
- Individual Behaviour and Creativity

Most of the time, we speak of several good organisations, (be it trade, service or manufacturing) which provide best to the customers. Think of Infosys, Wipro or TCS for information technology, or GE, ITC or TVS for manufacturing, or Indian Hotels Group (Tatas), Oberoi, ITC Group of Hotels for hospitality services, or Corporation Bank for financial services. These and many more companies and individual business units are contributing greatly for customer satisfaction and delight. The quality institutions are identified considering the quality indicators such as quality product or service, quality practices in price fixing, quality promotion practices and quality distribution process. Based on these quality dimensions, we try to identify quality institutions. But these quality aspects are to be implemented in the organisations to be recognised as quality institutions.

Quality organisation is made up of two vital components, *viz*., (i) "quality individuals and (ii) quality dimensions adopted in organisations. Organisation, in this context is considered as "a group of people working together to achieve certain objective". (For more details on organisation, read chapters 6 and 7 of this book). Thus, in an organisation, human factor plays a major role. **The behaviour of the organisation decides whether it is qualitative or not.** Organisational behaviour is mainly decided by two main factors, viz., (i) Individual behaviour and (ii) Group behaviour. In this chapter, we focus on individual behaviour and analyse the aspects connected with it.

Individual Behaviour – The Concept

Behaviour of an individual in an organisation is determined counts to a greater extent by assessing the performance of the task assigned to him/her. Individual behaviour is purely a psychological phenomenon. Management perception of individuals is the focal aspect in this analysis. When a person is to be appointed to perform a task in the organisation, employer considers the behavioural aspects of that person to find out whether he/she fits into situation and perform the assigned task.

Several questions have to be answered to assess the pattern of individual behaviour in the organisation. As people work together in workplaces, the questions that crop up are "What is the impact of individual behaviour on the group in which the person works? What is the group influence on the individual behaviour? Do managers and workers are considered alike or distinguished? What are the responsibilities of each manager and each worker? What is the impact of change that takes place in organisations, on workers and managers? How to get the work done by workers and others in times of turbulence and in times of peace? etc.," All these questions hover around the concepts of "Management Perspectives" and "Behaviour of people at work". These two have to match for the success of "Behaviour of People at Work" and for the success of the organisation.

Organisational Success = Matching Management Perspective and Worker Behaviour

Management perspective will be what management expects. Basically management in business units wants to achieve the business objective of earning profit, by adopting ethical practices. If we observe the growth path of management thought right from Henry Fayol, F.W. Taylor to current day, we understand that management perspective has shifted from maximising productivity focusing on time and motion studies (ignoring human factor) to "Human relations" to "Quantitative approach" to "Contingency approach". All these thoughts focus mainly on "Profit making" which is the main management perspective.

The goal of earning more profit can be achieved if people perform their task as per standards fixed for them and beyond that. Performing task here refers to activity fixed by management which is goal-oriented. Performance of task by workers will not easily take place. Many a time, management perspectives are opposed to worker's behaviour pattern. Unless the **Management perspectives** and **individual behaviour** of workers match with each other, organisations do not succeed.

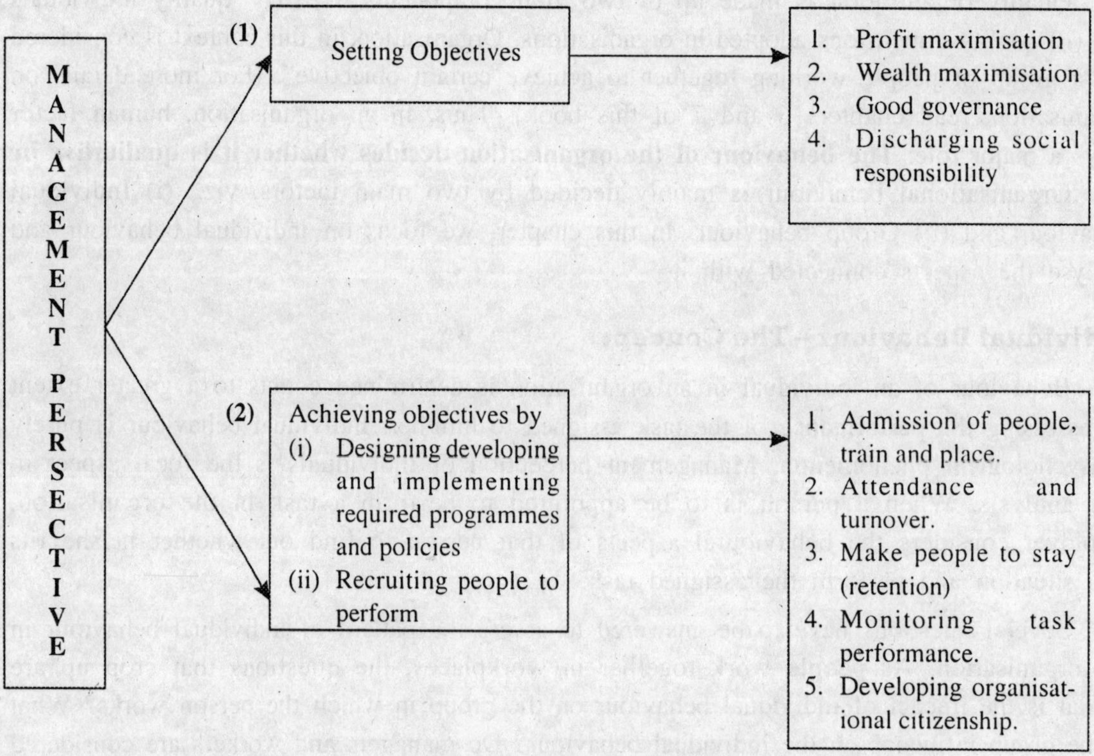

Fig. 15.1. Management Perspectives.

By and large, the essence of Mission Statements of organisations were "Convergence of knowledge, skill and behaviour" of workers to achieve the management perspective of "maximising profit though ethical means." Today, corporate expectation is different. Managements give priority for attitude. Organisations feel that, Mission Statement should be reversed, *i.e.*, "Convergence of Behaviour, skill and knowledge". The reason is very simple. Corporate world has understood that behavioural aspect should be given top priority to run the organisations on sound lines. Skill and knowledge can be acquired through training. But behaviour is basically an inherited feature, which has to be tuned to the needs of the firm. Changing behaviour is a time consuming process. However, individual behaviour in workplaces is a vital factor to achieve organisational goals.

Factors Influencing Individual Behaviour

Individual behaviour comprises of many factors. Psychological/mental factors also known as **internal factors** and **external factors** influence the behaviour. These are the sources of information or otherwise called **"Stimuli".** Other factors, such as **"Biographical features"** of an employee and **"capability to work or ability"** also influence the quality of behaviour.

Stimuli received by individual from different sources prompts him/her to **"Respond."** The response is **"Behaviour."** This is popularly known as **"S-R Model"** (Stimulus – Response Model) of behaviour. Observe the following figure:

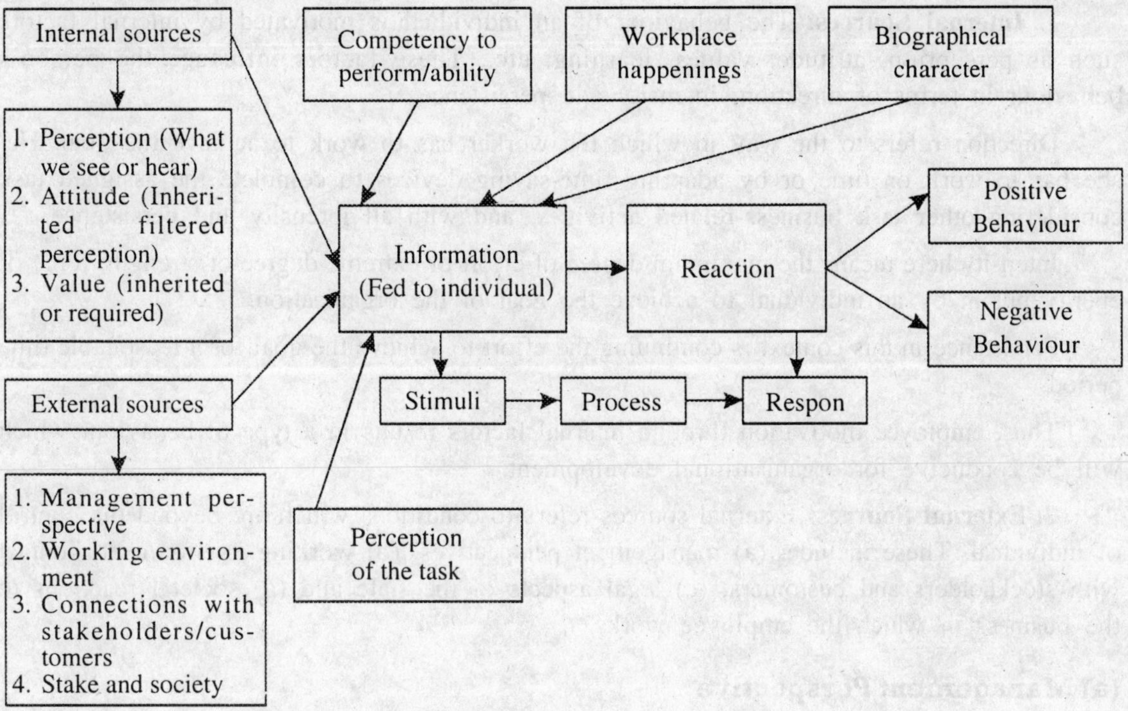

Fig. 15.2. Stimulus-Response Model of Individual Behaviour.

The diagram of S-R model exhibits both internal and external sources of stimuli. When we consider only internal sources, it exhibits pure individual behaviour, *i.e.*, not applicable to any situation. If we consider external sources also it will refer to behaviour of an individual in an organisational setting. Besides these two sources (internal and external), biographical factors, competence of individuals and perception about the task also influence the behaviour. Considering these aspects, a detailed model of individual is developed. Brief analysis of factors influencing behaviour is made in the following paragraphs.

In the diagram showing the behavioural process (S-R Model), it may be observed that "Stimuli" is received by individual from: (i) internal, (ii) external sources, (iii) by one's own ability of the individual and (iv) perception of the tasks to be performed. The stimulus received by individual makes the person to react and reaction/response for stimuli will be the output "Behaviour". The behaviour may be positive or negative. The quality of stimuli will determine the quality of behaviour. Thus, the behaviour of an individual is governed by internal factors of the individual organisations external factors, individual's biographical factors, his/her ability to perform and happenings in workplaces. These factors are analysed in detail.

While processing stimuli, several aspects (as shown in the diagram) influence the output, i.e., 'Behaviour'. Certain sources of stimuli are identified which determine behaviour. They are: (1) Internal sources, (2) External sources, (3) Task perception, (4) Competency/ Ability, (5) Happenings in workplaces and (6) Biographical character of employee.

1. Internal Sources: The behaviour of an individual is motivated by internal factors such as perception, attitude, values, learning, etc., These factors influence the person's behaviour in terms of direction, intensity and persistence.

Direction refers to the way in which the worker has to work to achieve the goal. He/she has to work on time or by adapting time-saving devices to complete the assigned task considering other task business-related activities, and with all intensity and persistence.

Intensity here means the maximum degree of effort or extreme degree of strength, force or energy put in by an individual to achieve the goal of the organisation.

Persistence in this context is continuing the effort to achieve the goal for a reasonable time period.

Thus, employee motivation through internal factors results in a type of behaviour which will be conducive for organisational development.

2. External Sources: External sources refers to conditions which are beyond the control of individual. These include: (a) management perspectives, (b) working environment, contact with stockholders and customers, (c) legal aspects of the state and (d) societal reactions to the business in which the employee works.

(a) Management Perspective

Management Perspectives are task-oriented and work-related factors which will have an impact on the behaviour of the workers. Right, from the point of admission of worker to the point of developing organisational citizenship, worker will have to interact and behave in a befitting manner to contribute to the achievement of the organisational goals. (See Fig.15.1 of this chapter for management perspectives).

Admitting different type of people to different types of tasks is a big challenge for managements. As said earlier, employee motivation plays a major role in attracting talented workers. The behaviour of these talented people has to be tested through different test modules. Though the people with excellent skill and knowledge are available, their behaviour in workplaces should not disturb the working environment. Today, business houses are looking for behavioural aspects at the entry point. Well behaved workers are the real assets of the business houses. Therefore, management prefers to recruit knowledge workers.

(b) Working Environment

Workers always expect congenial working environment. Good ambience, motivating leader, co-operative peers, ergonomics, etc. prompt the employee to work peacefully and the environment contributes for the development of good behaviour.

(c) Connections with Stakeholders

The behaviour of a worker is also influenced by the connections that worker has with suppliers, other departmental workers, shareholders (if necessary), and customers. The interaction with these people also influences the worker behaviour.

(d) State and Society

The government policies, and the activities concerned with society also influence individual behaviour. State legislations enacted in the process of protecting society (regulatory role) have to be strictly followed. Organisations avail **resources from society** and individuals in organisations should work to protect the interest of the society.

3. Perception of the Task

Workers when recruited and placed to perform specific tasks, they have to understand the role that they have to play. Task perception is the belief of the workers that the particular task requires an appropriate behaviour. Behaviour of a worker will not be constant. It changes according to type of task to be accomplished. But the worker should have clear role perception (belief of what task to be accomplished) to adopt a preferred behaviour to discharge the assigned tasks. For example, a worker's job is to lift the finished goods from production point to the godown. If he has the wrong role perception and shifts the goods to a godown, other than the fixed one for those finished goods, it will create chaos.

Wrong role perception leads to inappropriate behaviour which results in waste of worker's effort and adds to pertaining cost of the firm. The reason for wrong perception of task may be that workers do not receive correct information about their assigned task or receive conflicting information. Therefore, correct information of the task to be performed is to be provided through training and development to adopt and exhibit appropriate behaviour required for the specific task.

4. Competency/Ability

Another factor that will have impact and decide the behaviour of a person is his/her competency or ability to perform. Competency or capability or ability to work may be an inherent quality of the worker or it can be acquired though training. Abilites in an individual show his/her work capacity.

Broadly, abilities are classified as: (i) Intellectual abilities and (ii) Physical abilities.

Intellectual abilities which include intellectual power, attitude etc., are natural talents. The natural capabilities make the worker to understand his tasks in the firm very quickly and accordingly his/her behaviour works. For example, a brilliant engineer is asked to design a complicated work-flow chart to produce a product. With his intellectual power, the engineer quickly grasps the manufacturing process and designs the work-flow chart which will reduce the cost of operation. His behaviour in this context is directed by intellectual ability.

Physical abilities are related to individual stamina, dexterity, strength and such other characteristics. Look at the sports persons, particularly football or Hockey or Cricket Players. They need extraordinary stamina and strength to perform. Similarly, police people who work in traffic segments. They, for a long time, work in signal posts, continuously operating their both hands and standing for at least 7 hours. These situations clearly illustrate that behaviour is also governed by physical ability or capability.

On Work Ethic or Ability

Many a time, the work ethic of an individual is measured to rate that person. Work ethic or intrinsic capacity or ability is one of the vital factors, which directs, the behaviour of a person. At times, the ability of an individual worker is over-rated. These workers pose themselves as talented and exhibit an acceptable behaviour. But the reality is that their talent is not fully exhibited in terms of behaviour and is underutilised resulting in under-productivity.

There are very many unsung heroes in the organisations, who do not openly exhibit their ability, but are contributing their full strength to achieve the organisational goals. Their contribution is much more than those who pose themselves are talented. Who are not real achievers. Real contributors are those who work silently to achieve. We praise them for their contribution and success. But there is pain behind success. They honestly put in their effort to fully use their ability.

Managements should recognise able workers, motivate them and direct their behaviour to achieve maximum productivity.

Question: What do you perceive of behaviour from this statement?

Thus, work ethic or ability also governs the behaviour of people. Managements should identify the ability and make the workers to work on their core capabilities to increase productivity. Making the people to work to utilise their ability is a behavioural concept. In the context of considering 'Ability' as a generator of individual behaviour, managements have to: (i) recruit people who can adopt to work or (ii) redesign the work according to ability of the worker or (iii) improve the capability through training.

3. Workplace Events/Contingencies

People at work encounter several types of situations during the course of discharging their duties. Whatever the strength and ability they posses, however they are motivated to work, whatever the perceptions they have to play their role in the workplaces, they face different types of situations or come across contingencies, which are to be handled effectively and efficiently. These situations, sometimes will be beyond their control and such situations are one of the factors that direct the behaviour of workers.

The events or happenings in workplaces may be favourable which smoothens the performance or unfavourable which disturbs the normal working. Essential factors that smoothen the work in organisations are time management, allotment of required money to perform (budget allocation), ambience to work (physical facilities) and group behaviour. These factors are not within the control of the worker. Therefore, these internal controllable aspects of top management which influence the worker's behaviour have to be continuously identified and beefitingly addressed to increase the productivity of the individual. Many organisations do this. Successful firms create grievance cells to continuously identify the disturbing factors including the top management policies and resolve them quickly to see that normal behaviour of employees are not affected.

Workplace happenings also occur, due to consumer behaviour and various economic, social and other general conditions that prevail in the society. These are uncontrollable factors of the firm and the employee. These external situational contingencies will have impact on worker behaviour. If workers become defiadent in times of economic crisis or in other external situations which affect their normal work, managements should encourage workers to work with the things, they can manage. Only incorrigible elements have to be weeded out. The rest may be asked to do the job slowly. Productivity may be decreased. But general behaviour of the worker will be positive and organisational climate will be normal.

4. Biographical Factors

The behaviour of a worker is influenced by biographical factors too. These factors include age, gender, marital status and loyalty with the organisation. The data bank containing personal data of each employee of a firm can provide a base to know the behaviour of the employee.

(i) Age : Age will influence the behaviour of the people. In the business world, we observe, that productivity of a worker is related to age. People of different age groups turnout the work differently, middle aged persons may not work that efficiently as that of younger generation. Similarly, the productivity of aged workers will be less compared to middle aged and young workers. As age advances people lose enthusiasm and zeal due to physiological factors. The stamina, dexterity etc., decrease as age advances and the behaviour of workers also change accordingly. But in executive positions which involve more of intellectual work than physical labour, behaviour will not change that fast and productivity of individuals will not shrink at a faster rate.

Age will have its impact on **job performance, employee turnover, absenteeism, productivity and job satisfaction.** See the following figure for age impact.

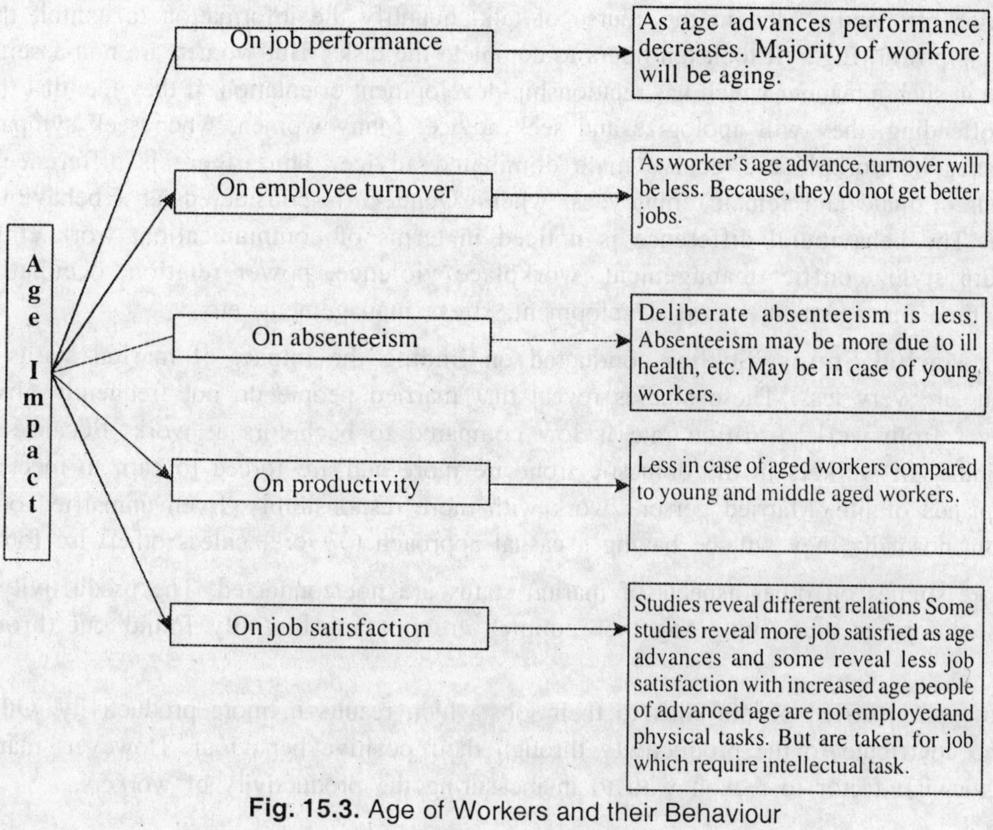

Fig. 15.3. Age of Workers and their Behaviour

(ii) Gender: Many research studies have revealed that gender divide has impact on organisational behaviour. Who is more productive male or female? In the initial stages of organisational development women were restricted/barred from taking jobs. Gradually, the notion changed and they are recognised in workplaces. Although the ratio of male-female is 1 : 0.9 of population, women were not absorbed in workplaces in same proportion. Particularly in manufacturing sector, they were not considered for production activities. Soft jobs in offices were offered, with the growth of service sector and change in quality of life. Today, women are absorbed in workplaces in big number. But they are discriminated (even in advanced countries) in terms of compensation, job type, etc.

Women are turning out quality work and are more loyal to the organisations. Viewing from the behavioural aspect, women are more job-conscious and their productivity is more compared to men. Women are more relationship-oriented, co-operative, nurturing and emotional. They are more suited to leadership positions. Except the hurt and disgruntled women (who are less in number compared to larger section of the society), women by and large involve in work more than their male counterparts.

Gender difference can be observed in communication process. Behaviour in communication process of male and female will be different. Men are more assertive than women, when they communicate. It may be a company meeting or a virtual chat room, men speak in assertive style exhibiting their power in the form of advice. Even the language men use, many a time, will be combative. During conversation with women, men dominate the talk time.

It is always expected that the conversation should be impersonal and should exchange information efficiently. Men in the course of talk, quantify the information to exhibit their dominating power. E.g., "It took ten hours to complete the task". But women are non-assertive and talks in such a manner which has relationship-development orientation. If they feel that their talk is offending, they will apologize and seek advice. Many women, when seek sympathy from males in workplaces, receive male dominated advice. Thus, there is difference in behaviour of male and female employees, when "Gender" is considered as a behavioural variable. The behavioural difference is noticed in terms of communication, work ethics, leadership style, conflict management, workplace violence, power relation, occupation, growth, time management, moral development, stress management, etc.

(ii) Marital Status: Studies conducted on finding the impact of marital status on behaviour are very less. These studies reveal that married people do not frequently absent themselves from work. Attrition rate is low compared to bachelors at work. Because the responsibility of workers in the domestic front are more and are forced to earn to meet the new demands of life. Married persons work with more responsibility. Even unmarried one's work. But normally they will be having a casual approach to work, unless otherwise forced.

More studies on other aspects of marital status are not conducted. The productivity of widows, divorcees and living together couples are not substantially found out through studies.

However, married people stick to their jobs which results in more productivity. Others may also contribute to the productivity through their positive behaviour. However, marital status is a vital factor to reckon with to in measuring the productivity of workers.

(iii) Loyalty: Loyalty is the superlative degree of positive behaviour. If workers of an organisation are loyal to it, top management can achieve any thing that it desires. To achieve loyalty, workers should have "work awareness." This means that they should have the knowledge of work they have to perform. They understand the task to be performed through training and development. Then they should learn the art of "work preference". Work preference refers to listing out of tasks to be discharged on priority basis and perform according to listed priority. This improves the efficiency of workers in terms of time management and producing quality work, with these two processes, workers develop "Organisational Identity" which paves way for organisational loyalty. Thus, workers are developed to become "Truly Loyal" to the organisation through the process of training in work awareness and work preference.

In the days of high turnover of employees, loyalty in workplaces becomes the thing of the past. Job sites (Naukari.com) thrive, because of switching jobs by employees at a faster rate. But the business houses which consider ethics as fundamental principle, strictly implement ethical norms in their operations. They have modified the behaviour of employees and have made them to stay on for a long time in the business.

Companies that expect loyalty from workers, have exhibited loyalty for themselves. These companies are given to exemplary HR practices. Not only they have recruited what they need, but also are not allowing their staff to leave the company through moral persuasion. They voluntarily allow the worker to leave, if he/she gets a better chance for his/her personal growth and support them even after they exit. Disciplined recruiting practices have positive impact on loyalty development and worker behaviour.

> MTR (Mavally Tiffin Room) – The employee loyal firm leading restaurant of Bangalore, did not retrench their employees, when price war took place between Karnataka Government and Hoteliers. MTR was only running a restaurant then. Because of dual price policy administered by GOK, MTR closed the business for some time. But employees were retained. Instead of keeping them idle, MTR started food processing industry. Today, MTR products are branded ones through out the world. It is now taken over and run by a foreign company. As MTR was loyal to their employees in the time of turbulence (price war), Almighty showered on it a big boon.

Understanding employees' behaviour and providing facilites and perquisites can lead the workers to develop loyalty. Even the most unskilled employee can be put to good use. When tough times hit, only perquisites (perks) can be reduced. Executives are the ones, who will be receiving heavy perks. Perks are given for performance. If executives threaten to leave, when perks are reduced, let them leave. Business is run as per organisational objectives and to the way the leaders wish. The leaders should make the employees to feel that they (leaders) are doing all they can to keep the company's members intact. Experience in workplaces reveals that workers will be loyal to the firm if the following aspects are followed:

(i) Placing creative authorities and not bosses who affectionately interact with employees.

(ii) Create "Fun at work" (showing work-reoriented short movies, providing sports facilities etc., during leisure time) which rejuvenate them.

(iii) Building culture and processes that encourage people to share their work-in-progress and support one another as peers.

(iv) Remove the natural barriers that divide the disciplines.

Developing organisational loyalty in workers is a two way track. Top management cannot just ask their employees to perform the way they (management) want. It is a reciprocal activity. Management also should look into the needs of employees and satisfy them. As a behavioural aspect of individuals, loyalty of employer and employees play a major role in the development of the organisation.

Loyalty and Emplyee Behaviour

- Efficiency of employee increases in terms of productivity.
- Employees develop organisational identity.
- They work beyond their assigned task to understand other activities of the firm to develop an integrated approach to work.
- Speak good of the organisation outside to develop image.
- Become immune to firm despite the lucrative offers from outside.
- Give benefit of doubt when some thing goes wrong (opposed to employee safety policy).

Why Employer Loyalty to Employee?

- It costs 10 to 15 times more to recruit and develop a new employee than to keep the existing one.
- A gain in marginal loyalty of workers can lift lifetime profit of the company.
- Substantial (400 to 500%) cost reduction takes place with marginal increase in loyalty.

OTHER ASPECTS

There are other aspects which also influence the worker behaviour: (i) The period of stay (tenure) in the organisation, (ii) attendance, (iii) discharging the assigned tasks and showing organisational citizenship are other factors which influence the behaviour of the workers.

(1) Tenure and Attendance

The period of stay of an employee and on the organisation attendance will have impact on his behaviour and productivity of the worker as well as the organisation. Several studies, have been conducted to find out the relationship between tenure or seniority of employee and productivity. These studies reveal that "there is a positive relationship between tenure and productivity of the individual." Therefore, **"more the people stay in the organisation, more the increase in productivity."**

The period of stay, researches reveal, has negative relationship with **"Absenteeism."**

(2) Absenteeism

Absenteeism consists of two variables viz., frequency of absence and number of days lost at work that are considered for measuring productivity. Good attendance indicates high productivity and *vice versa.*

The period of stay has its influence on rate of turnover of employee. Research findings say that period of stay of an employee in the organisation has a negative impact on turnover. It is strongly indicated that tenure of employee is one of the major parameters to measure the rate of turnover.

Thus, period of stay or tenure is one of the important factors which influences behaviour, productivity and job satisfaction of an employee. Less frequency in absence, low turnover and better job satisfaction strongly indicate that tenure and productivity of the individual worker have positive relationship and worker has a modest behaviour.

(3) Performance

Discharging the assigned task is an individual behavioural aspect which has its impact on productivity. Organisations expect that their workers should work as per standards fixed for the tasks assigned and produce the expected output. Very often, managements expect the performance beyond the prescribed limits. To complete the goal-directed tasks, employee has to blend both his physical and mental abilities and work. Peformance standards can be reached when they possess skill and knowledge of the assigned task. For example: A finance executive should know as to how the finance has to be mobilised for a project. He has to work on sources, cost of capital, effective utilisation of mobilised funds etc. Performance standards are fixed to this job. The productivity and behaviour of this executive is evaluated as per these performance standards.

Developing a worker as a **corporate citizen** is a management perspective. If the worker is converted as a corporate citizen, it indicates that he/she is a full-blown positive employee who turns full work. Corporate citizenship exhibits the behaviour and productivity of worker and beyond that. The worker, besides performing the task, exhibits interest in others' work and tolerance, avoiding conflicts, heartily accepts occupational impositions, involving in other activities of the organisation, working beyond normal work at times of necessity and such other things. These are the "Corporate Citizenship" features.

Corporate citizenship involves a reciprocal discharging of duties, as evidenced in research studies.

On the management side, the organisations have fairness in treating employees. Injustice in the workplace, if any, has to be corrected. Fair distribution of reward has to be done. Employees should be made to feel higher sense of obligation to make an extra walk. Employees have to be involved in all decisions that are concerned to them.

On the employees front, they should practice strong ethical values. They should develop and acquire, if they do not have, social responsibility principles and practice in real time operations. In this context, "Social Responsibility" refers to employee's ethical obligations to co-workers, management and society. Employees having strong moral obligation are more influenced to help others irrespective of any sort of return benefits. The corporate citizenship also demands that employees should not unnecessarily intervene in other's affairs. These positive behaviours learnt though socialisation helps in developing corporate citizenship. Managements, while recruiting, have to look to these values in people to be recruited.

Thus, these aspects, *viz.*, tenure, absenteeism, task performance, corporate citizenship also play a vital role in influencing behaviour of the workers. (Refer chapter on "Behaviour and Relationship" for details on corporate citizenship).

Behavioural Change

It cannot be assumed that all who are recruited in an organisation, behave and engage in their tasks according to organisational norms and standards. Each recruiter's behaviour will be different. This heterogenous type of behaviour needs modification to suit to the organisational requirement.

When workers are appointed and placed in specific jobs, it is expected that these workers have to voluntarily adapt to the new environment and behave in the manner required for performing the assigned task. However, when they enter, they possess a set of behaviour acquired by previous experiences called "Antecedents". Behaviour they possess at the time of entry into the new organisation will not match with the required behaviour of this entity and needs modification. The process of modification of behaviour into organisational needs is called **"Behavioural Change"** or **"Conditioning".**

Although people work for money and other benefits, they learn something while working. People work in variety of challenging environments to learn new things. In the process, they interact with different situations and different people. Each situation requires specific behaviour of the worker. The exhibition of behaviour in a situation might be an acquired one through training or the inherent one which spontaneously outflows. The learning of behaviour in a new environment through training reinforces the worker. He/she becomes conditioned and adopts it for smooth functioning of the task.

Behavioural change acts as testimony to new learning. For example: A worker who is timd and slow in working is given leave for one week and sent for intensive training to acquire the required behaviour. When he returns to work after training, it is observed that he has become smart and works fast. The co-workers and observes feel that he has learnt the art of working smart. Thus, training in behavioural process changes and conditions the behaviour as required. Learning is the key factor in behaviour modification.

All the time, the management cannot expect that learning process of behaviour modification will bring positive result. Sometimes, despite intensive training may not change their behaviour or even if if it is changed, it may be for worse. The effect of behaviour conditoning through training may be positive, negative or constant. The consequences of behaviour modification may result in strengthening required behaviour or maintain the existing behaviour (no change) or weaken the behaviour. Based on these consequences, organisations take further action to retain or retrench the employee.

Conditioning Process

Behaviour conditioning involves two vital aspects: (i) previously acquired behaviour through learning in different settings, which exists in individuals, when they enter a new setting called "Antecedents" and (ii) the resultant behaviour after modification in new setting called **"consequence."** Conditioning refers to the process of changing the existing behaviour to new behaviour. The process of conditioning is called A-B-C model, in which "A" stands of "Antecedents", "B" for "Behaviour" and "C" for "consequence". This is exhibited in the following diagram:

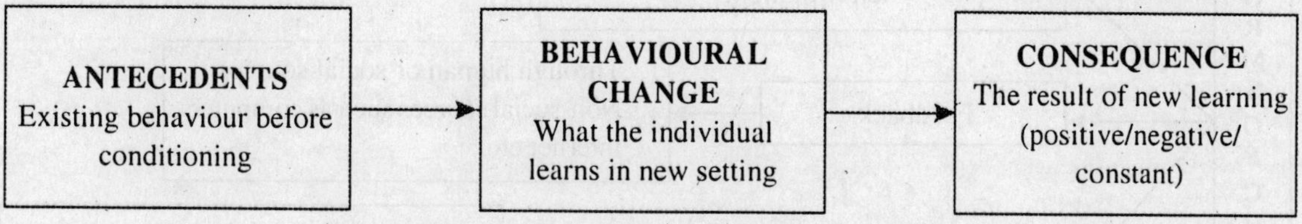

Fig. 15.4. ABC Model of Conditioning.
Source: How to Improve Human Performance?, Harper and Row, 1978.

Innumerable examples can be given to explain A-B-C model of individual behaviour. Supposing the organisation appoints an engineer to work as plant engineer to manufacture X product. He has experience in plant management but not the one on which he has to work in new assignment. Previous work experience is considered as "Antecedent." Now, he has to understand, plant design and work and thus changes his behaviour of working as plant manager by learning new work process, which is termed as **"Behavioural change."** Working as Plant Manager in new setting, the **"consequence"** is that he may work as an excellent Plant Manager (Positive consequence) or becomes neutral in operations and relies on immediate lower engineer (constant consequence) or do not properly perform and production is affected (negative consequence). Researches in behaviour modification reveal different types of consequences. They are as follows:

(i) Positive reinforcement: The consequence is that it increases or maintains the frequency or future probability of behaviour.

(ii) Negative reinforcement: The consequence being discontinuing a negative behaviour which brings good result. For example, a boss criticisess a worker continuously for his negligence in work. In order to rectify this, worker works with consciousness. Then boss stops criticizing.

(iii) Punishment: Consequence being threatening the employee, if the employee does not correct his mistakes committed while performing. Example: threatening the employee that he/she would be dismissed from service. If his/her behaviour is disturbing the normal work in the work place.

(iv) Extinction: Consequence being the behaviour does not continue or stop at the level at which it disturbs the growth of the organisation. Example: If an individual cannot keep pace with the work assigned to him/her, he/she has to remodify the existing behaviour to extinguish the current behaviour. This means, he/she has to improve the speed of work or exit from the situation.

Behavioural conditioning can take place in three forms as shown in the following figure.

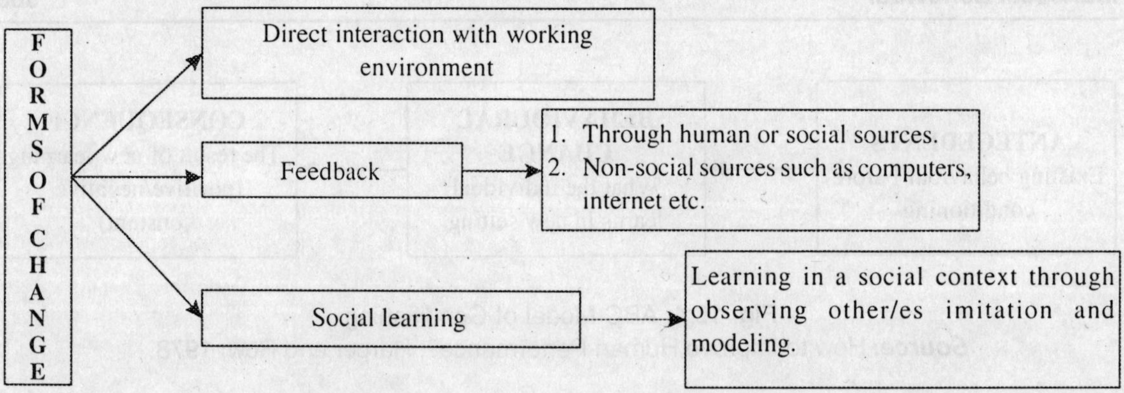

Fig. 15.5. Dimensions of Behavioural Conditioning

Endless research is going on, on behaviour modification in workplaces. Conditioning takes place quickly in case of simple operations or tasks. But, complex tasks, consume more time for conditioning or changing the behaviour. Complex tasks are to be properly structured for easy performance.

Real-time Conditioning

Conditioning the behaviour in real-time operations takes place on a larger scale as a process of learning. Changing the behaviour according to the change in task and keep pace as per task requirement, requires not only the quick perception of task but also the dexterity and mental nimbleness. All psychological (perception, attitude etc.) and physiological factors play a major role in behavioural modification. Conditioning the behaviour in real-time situation has shown improvement in learning and task performance.

Feedback

Feedback is a motivating factor. Employees can improve their behaviour through feedback. Feedback is any information that worker receives about the consequence of his/ her behaviour. Feed back improves competency of worker. It also improves role perception. It makes the worker to understand as to what type of behaviour is required in a particular environment. Performance mistakes are identified by feedback, mistakes can be corrected without much lapse of time through feedback and make the people to increase thier confidence level. This is a 360 degree feed back which enhances the ability and skill of a worker.

Full feedback from customers, co-workers, subordinates and supervisors improves the courage, commitment, confidence, conviction and performance of employees. Several research studies bear testimony to this. Today, the technology has advanced so much that any person in the organisation can get feedback from social (co-workers boss, subordinates, etc.) and non-social sources (computer storage, feedback from internet, e-mail etc.,) to improve his/ her behaviour. Employee performance result also provides feedback. The feedback can be an effective technique to improve the quality of work, if its is timely, credible, specific relevant and more frequent. Feedback sources being very many, employees prefer to get feedback from non-social sources to improve themselves and to suceessfully complete their tasks. Social sources have the limitation of providing poor performance feedback in a positive sense. Because these sources want to avoid confrontations. But it really affects the behaviour of employee and in turn the organisational behaviour.

POSITIVE BEHAVIOUR

Mrs. Parimala, a middle-aged disgruntled lady worker in an office, sits by the side of Mr. Sridhar, a cool, calm and non-intervening person. Parimala does not like the attitude of Sridhar and requests Mrs. Malathi, the office manager to change her workplace.

Mr. Malathi informs her that there is no other place in office, except in boss's PA chamber which is well equipped and fit with air conditioner. Manager, however, said that she would speak to the boss about the problem.

After discussing the problem with the boss, Malathi tells Parimala that there is good news to her and tells that it is most extraordinary to make the kind of change I am asked to do by boss. Given the circumstances, boss felt that Parimala might be uncomfortable with Sridhar and cannot be forced to sit next to him. He has asked me to shift Sridhar's working table to his PA's chamber. Accordingly, Sridhar's workplace is shifted.

(i) What will be the behaviour of Parimala after the decision?
(ii) Give a very small note on boss's behavioural pattern.

Genuine feedback improves the morale and behaviour of an employee. Specific information should be given in the feedback. It should be given at the appropriate time. Accurate feedback has to be given to modify the behaviour of an employee.

Ethical Aspect

Organisations adopt different techniques to monitor employee behaviour and to give feedback. Some use closed circuit TVs some may monitor telephone calls of employees to collect information to give feedback. In this way, many methods are adopted to observe employee behaviour. But the ethical aspect is whether such monitoring devices would encroach on employee's privacy. Many court descions have favoured employee behaviour monitoring though different devices and methods to give a correct feedback to employees to improve their behavioural aspects and the improve product and service quality. By and large, employees also are not opposed to such monitoring of behaviour as it facilitates them to improve their quality of behaviour.

Social Learning

Behavioural conditioning in workplaces, as discussed so far focuses on learning out of interaction with co-workers, customers, bosses, leaders and societal connections. This is a direct conditioning process. Changing the behaviour through interaction with workplace environment is one vital dimension of behaviour modification. Another equally powerful dimension of behavioural conditioning is "learning though observation" or otherwise called **Social Learning.**

People at work, observe others successful activaties and condition their own behaviour. Benchmarking the people who are successful, the workers learn to modify their behaviour. Successful people will be considered as role models. Observing these role models, workers can condition and reinforce their behaviour. While conditioning the behaviours, workers may consider good behaviour of role models and adopt to obtain favourable results. Behaviours of these models which will lead to punishing consequences will be avoided. This is what is called **"Social learning".**

"Social Learning is what is learned, by observation and direct experience."

Learning through observation leads to behaviour modeling. Behaviour modeling means conditioning the behaviour by observing good practices of others and the organisation and adopting them for self-development and conditioning. Example: Genuine workers do not use office time and equipment for personal activities. This is a good practice which can be adapted by others as a behavioural model tool, for their success. This provides a favourable consequence. This is a learning process which enable the workers to acquire knowledge and skill by observation.

Modifying the behaviour by observation or social learning also increases the personal belief of worker that he/she has the competency to complete the task successfully. This is called"self-efficacy". Self-efficacy succeed when expected response gives a reasonable control over the task performance and yields favourable result.

Impact of Social Learning

Learning by observation or social learning takes place through logical thinking. Logical thinking in implementing an observed behaviour exhibits is a consequence which may be positive or negative reinforcement. Reinforcement here we mean the fortification or strengthening of the existing capabilities to perform the task. For example, A co-worker receives a reward for performing the task ahead of schedule. This is observed by other workers and they may try to complete the assigned task, quite ahead of scheduled time to receive a reward.

The negative consequence of observed behaviour may be that the worker may be fined for not completing the tasks on time. Punishment is the consequence. The observer learns that he/she should complete the task on time to avoid punishment.

Another aspect to be understood in social learning is strengthening the self. Self-strengthening or **"Self-reinforcement"** happens when a worker controls a strengthening factor and does not adopt this factor until a self-set objective is completed. For example, A worker decides to complete a task without break. If the task is more time-consuming that leads to monotony, frustration and fatigue the worker may take a break. This break acts as a positive reinforcer to **rejuvenate** the worker to work fast after the break and it is self-induced to strengthen the behaviour to complete the tasks as scheduled. Self-strengthening or self-reinforcement is a vital element of social learning as it improves confidence and morale of the employee. This also does not give room for negative consequence, if the task is not completed as per schedule.

[The different learning modes and their impact on behaviour modification through social learning are discussed in the chapter on "Learning" of this title.]

Every dimension of individual behaviour is briefly analysed in this chapter. Internal factors such as personality, perception, attitude, value, emotion, learning, etc. which influence the individual behaviour are discussed in greater detail in subsequent chapters.

Individual Behaviour and Creativity

Creativity is a factor that plays a vital role in individual's behaviour. Creativity is a process of generation of ideas. It might replace the existing ideas when any new ideas are formed. The creative individuals possess certain attributes that are common in nature. These attributes relate to the cognitive abilities, the personal traits and their past experiences.

The Creative Process

The activities of an individual being innovative are different from that of others. The creative process of an individual involves the processes such as Preparation, Incubation. Insight and Verification.

Preparation – This is the first stage of the creative process. Individual acquire the basic knowledge though various methods. He might go for an intensive training programme or might take up a higher education. He becomes curious about things he sees and develops lot of interest in acquiring knowledge.

Incubation – The second stage of creative process of an individual is incubation. The knowledge acquired in the first state is being analysed rationally. Logic is introduced to the process of thinking. Due to logical thinking, there is discontinuity of thoughts in this stage and idea generation takes place.

Insight – Insight is the stage where it draws all the ideas of the individual. He becomes enlightened at one point. The experience is created as "aha" experience. This illumination of idea generated is called *"insight."*

Verification – Once an illumination to the idea has been formed, the individual moves to the verification of ideas. These verifications might include the empirical evidence, *i.e.*, the scientific results from the ideals, if implemented. It involves the trials of creative ideas.

Creative Behaviour

Creative behaviour takes place irrespective of the cultural difference and the background experiences of an individual. Creativity also includes certain personality traits. Some of the following traits are found in creative individuals:

(a) They are basically independent.

(b) They do not listen to others' idea.

(c) They have high autonomy.

(d) Individuals believe in what they do.

(e) Exhibit high level of self-confidence.

Cognitive Abilites

Cognitive abilities are related to cognition which means the mental act or process of acquiring knowledge that involves the processing of sensory information and includes perception, awareness and judgement.

These abilities are known or perceived as an act or faculty distinct formation and volition. Cognitive abilities include the individual intelligence. This intelligence is found in most of the creative individuals. People who have cognition know more than others in all

These abilities are known or perceived as an act or faculty distinct formation and volition. Cognitive abilities include the individual intelligence. This intelligence is found in most of the creative individuals. People who have cognition know more than others in all aspects. The ability to think divergent or convergent depends upon the views of the person. Divergent thinking is one where different people interpret different meanings to the same situation. On the contrary, convergent thinking helps people to identify the similarities of a situation or objects observed. They tend to have the same line of frequency on their thoughts.

SUMMARY

1. An organisation, being a group of people working together to achieve certain objective, has to work on quality lines.
2. The quality of an organisation is decided by two vital factors, *viz.*, (i) Individual behaviour and (ii) Group behaviour.
3. Individual behaviour plays a vital role in turning out an organisation as a qualitative one. Management perspective should match with worker behaviour for the success of the organisation.
4. Management perspective covers the aspects such as (A) Setting the objectives of the organisation which includes: (i) Profit and wealth maximisation, (ii) Good governance, and (iii) Discharging social responsibility and (B) Achieving objectives (i) by recruiting proper personnel, train and place them in appropriate places, (ii) Managing attendance and turnover of employees, (iii) retention of employees, (iv) Monitoring task performance, and (v) developing organisational citizenship.
5. Individual behaviour is based on a model called "S-R Model" "S" refers to Stimuli. (Information) which will be fed from (i) internal sources, (ii) external sources, (iii) based on ability of the individual, (iv) from workplace happening (contingencies), (v) from biographical characters of the individual and other aspects. "R" is the response or reaction to the stimuli which may be positive or negative.
6. After recruiting the people (employees) for work, their behaviour has to be changed to suit to the requirement of the organisation. Changing behaviour of recruitees or otherwise called behavioural change of new workers involves the process of training of those workers according to organisational needs which is called "Conditioning".
7. Conditioning process is based on a model called "A-B-C Model". Into this, "A" refers to antecedents (existing behaviour), "B" refers to behavioural change (what workers learn) and "C" consequence (the outcome of new learning).
8. Behavioural change takes place in the form of (i) Direct interaction with working environment. (ii) Feedback and (iii) Social learning.
9. Behaviour of the individual is also induced by the creative capacity of that individual. The creative process involves (i) preparation, (ii) incubation and (iii) insight.
10. Creativity takes place beyond cultural differences and includes personality traits such as having high autonomy, believe in what they do, exhibit high level of confidence, very active in nature, not listening to others' ideas and cognitive abilities.
11. Creative people truly behave with the spirit of the organisation and exhibit high level of performance.

STUDY QUESTIONS

1. Briefly explain the concept of individual behaviour in an organisational context. Considering the various dimensions of behaviour.
2. Give an explanatory note on Management perspective having in view the individual behaviour.
3. Breifly explain the S-R Model of individual behaviour.
4. Given an explanatory note on ability which governs individuals behaviour.
5. Give an analytical note on each of the following; which influence the individual behaviour, (i) Internal factors, (ii) External factors, (iii) Contingencies, (iv) Biographical factors, (v) Age, (vi) Gender, (vii) Marital Status, (viii) Loyalty, (ix) Labour turnover, (x) Absenteeism, (xi) Conditioning, and (xii) Cognitive abilities.
6. What is corporate citizenship? Explain the role of both employer and employees in developing the workers as corporate citizen.
7. Give an explanatory note on behavioural change.
8. Breifly explain A-B-C Model of conditioning process.
9. Breifly explain the role of environment in behavioural conditioning.
10. State the role of feedback as a factor of behavioural change.
11. What is social learning? Analyse how social learning can modify the behaviour of employees in an organisation.
12. Give an analytical note on creativity of the individual and its impact on organisational behaviour.

CASE PROBLEMS TO SOLVE

1. Today business houses and other organisations appoint many female workers. As organisations are flat in structure (because of more adaption of information technology), the quantum of work will be more. Absenteeism is also more as workers will have the tendency to utilise leave rights extensively. Particularly female workers, who also have more responsibility to sort out domestic problems inducing kitchen work, avail more leave. High turnover of workers, particularly in flat organisations disturbs operations and productivity.

   Considering the individual behavioural model discussed in this chapter and of your knowledge about absenteeism, analyse the causes for absenteeism and state the solutions to minimise absenteeism.

2. Esteem Ltd., a finance company, has started advancing loans taking gold as security. Some of the senior staff who are identified as honest workers and are not well-versed with the new type of job (handling advances on gold), are promoted and assigned with new task.

   Adopting A-B-C model, explain the process of behaviour modeling which makes the staff adept in performing new task.

3. A company has good number of honest workers. But most of these workers are having inferiority complex. Whenever new programmes are introduced in the organisation, they hesitate to modifty their behaviour to new task, adopting social feedback method and resort to non-social feed back to change themselves. Briefly analyse the reason as to why they resort to non-social feed back method to modify their behaviour suiting to new task.

16

PERSONALITY

LEARNING OBJECTIVES

After reading this chapter you should be able to know;

- The Concept of Personality
- Determinants of Personality
- Characteristics of Personality
- Big-Five Model of Personality
- MBTI Model
- Sixteen Personality Types
- Personality Theories
- Needs/Attributes which Influence Personality Theories
- Tools to Asses Personality
- Personality and Workplace Issues

Personality has a long history. It dates from the time of greek physician Hippocrates (460-377 BC). In order to understand the behaviour of people in the organisational setting, we need to know the basic nature of personality. It is a psycho-social phenomenon, which analyses the cognitive features and presentation of individual in the society.

Personality is made up of the characteristic patterns of thoughts, feelings and behaviour of an individual. These attributes make a person unique. Personality originates within the individual and remains fairly consistent throughout life. Personality exhibits distinctive qualities of a person, especially those distinguishing personal characteristics that make one socially appealing. If a person wins an election on his own, society may say that he/she has won "more on personality than on capability". Personality reveals distinctive traits of mind and behaviour of a person. It is a pattern of collective character which includes behavioural, mental, temperamental, and emotional traits of a person that makes one socially appealing. It exhibits the quality of a person, which is visible and impresses or disturbs others. For example, the statements such as "He has a pleasing personality Raju is a Crude persona" reveal the collective characters of a person which exhibits positive or negative personality.

> "Personality is the supreme realisation of the innate idiosynchrasy, of a living being. It is an act of courage thing in the face of life, the absolute affirmation of all that constitute the individual, the most successful adaptation to the universal, conditions of existence, coupled with the greatest possible freedom of self-determination." — ***C.G. Jung***
>
> "Personality is the relatively stable set of psychological attributes that distinguish one "person from another." — ***Lawerence Ervin***
>
> "Personality refers to the relatively stable pattern of behaviours and consistent internal states that explain a person's behaviour tendencies." — ***RT Hogan.***
>
> "Personality is the sum total of ways in which an individual reacts and interacts with others." — ***Stephen P. Robbins***

The basic components of personality refer to the personality trait. Many researchers have shown interest to know about individual's personality as it is linked with behaviour. If one can predict the behaviour of individuals, modification of behaviour can be done in a smoother way towards achieving the organisational goals. Each personality factor represents a collection of related or cluster of traits. These clusters of traits determine whether the individual is achievement-oriented, dominating, responsible, etc.

Determinants of Personality

As we have read earlier, different theories propose different factors that determine an individual personality. The most popular research work done by Freud deals with the identification of self-concept. Self-concept include things (factor) got by **nature** like gene, *i.e*, heredity and the biological formations and by **nurture,** *i.e* through the social and environmental factors. The major determinants of **personality** are heredity, environment and situation.

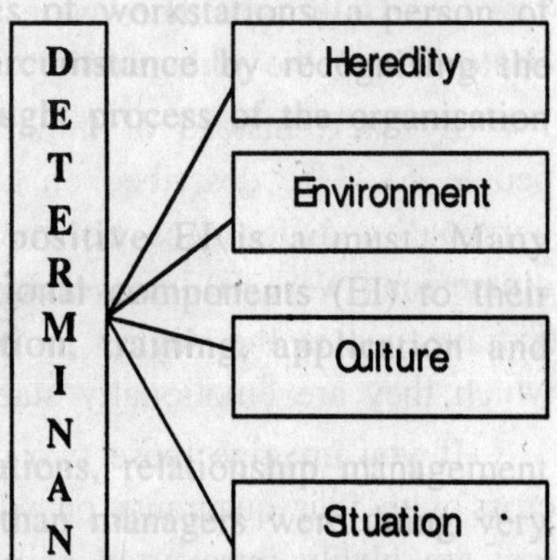

Fig. 16.1. Determinants of Personality

Heredity

Heredity refers to those factors, which predisposes to certain physical, mental and emotional states. It sets the outer parameters of an individual. It also limits the range of development of characters. The arrangement and structure of genes that are located in the chromosomes is passed around 20% to 50% from one generation to another. The studies reveal that twins though brought up in different places exhibit similar characters. Thus, heredity is the transmission of qualities from ancestor to descendent through, a mechanism lying primarily in the genes. There are very many achievers in their own field like Sachin Tendulkar, U.R. Rao, N.R. Narayana Murthy, Former Prime Minister P.V. Narasimha Rao, who gave a new turn to Indian economy and many such others, who are unique in their own, way. These achievers' performance is directed by hereditary factor to certain extent.

Environment

Environment refers to the surroundings in which the individuals are brought up. The environmental factors relating to the formation of personality includes culture, family, society upbrining and experiences. Experiences relate to the confrontation with that of family members, relatives, and friends and to the social groups, which they belong. Culture helps to find the similarity and difference in behaviour.

Family environment refers to the individual's upbringing, the social and economic status the family holds and the size of the family. The society makes an individual to play different roles thus shaping his/her their personality. Environment tends to strengthen or weaken hereditary traits. For example, when an individual interacts with the environment through speech, his speech organs guarantee that he/she is learning to speak.

Situation

Situation has an effect both on environment and heredity. Situation demands certain behaviour. Various psychologists have discovered what personality trait matters to an individual in his or her career. Being successful or unsuccessful depends upon how the individuals control their behaviour in various situations. For example, a candidate attending an interview may exhibit limited traits. The other trait or behaviour is concealed or not exhibited.

Personality or Situation? Analysis of Psychologists

The first is one of the earliest studies in a long line of research by Hansj Eysenck. (1916-97) Eysenck was influenced by Greek philosophy in his search for human personality. The Greeks thought there were four categories of person; the **melancholic**, the **sanguine,** the **choleric** and the **phlegmatic**.

Eysenck, instead of thinking people could be pigeon-holed, has neatly suggested that people could be described on a sliding scale of each of these factors. He had a hunch that personality differences between people could be described in two 'dimensions'. These dimensions were (i) Introversion versus Extraversion and (ii) Neuroticism versus Stability. Extraversion is the degree to which a person is outgoing and neuroticism is the degree to which they are emotionally stable (or not).

If you imagine these two dimensions at right angles to each other then you have a big cross with four quadrants on which everyone's personality falls somewhere. For example, if you are highly introverted and highly neurotic, you are an extremely anxious person.

Eysenck tested this theory by using information form 700 patients at a military hospital. He asked their treating psychiatrists to rate patients on a number of scales which include 'degraded work history', 'sex anomalies' and 'dependent' along with a host of others. From these he used factor analysis (a stastical tool) from which these two dimensions of introversion/

extraversion and neuroticism/stability emerged. When you think about it, Eysenck made an exciting, bold statement: "every human's personality can be classified on just two sliding scales". Since then personality theory has moved on and now theorists have settled on five sliding scales. This scale is going strong and appears to describe some of the systematic ways in which people differ. "Well it would do, if there wasn't one rather large fly in the personality psychologist's ointment: the **situation".**

Mischel and The Situation

In 1968, Walter Mishel droped a bomb on personality theory with his innocuously titled study, 'Personlity and Assessment'. Mischel thought the evidence showed tests such as Eysenck's were almost worthless because they didn't take into account the situation. It is clear, he argued, that people behave quite differently depending on the situation. Imagine you're late for an appointment, you're caught in huge traffic jam. Do you behave the same way as when you're sitting at home, relaxed? It not, then what is a personality test really telling us about a person?

Mischel reviewed a series of studies that attempted to predict people's behaviour from their personality scores. He found there was little consistency in people's behaviour across situations. In fact, he concluded there was as little as 9% of agreement between the way people behaved in different situations, 91% of the differnce behaviour in different situations couldn't be accounted for by personality tests.

Situation versus Personality

The works of both Eysenck and Mischel were crucial in forming what became a massive debate in psychology. Particularly of Michel's, as it made many psychologists ask what was the point of studying personality if it predicted so little. These two studies don't just encapsulate the debate about personality and the situation but also highlight another constant battle in psychology, between the power of internal and external forces, your own thoughts and feelings versus those of society. Eysenck was saying you are what's inside, your personality, and Michel was saying you are what is outside the situation.

It doesn't take a genius to point out they were both right in their own ways. People do seem to be different in certain aspects, for example some people are more sociable than others. But people also show remarkable similarities in certain situations, e.g., their need to conform. The trick is in finding the balance between the two, a problem at which psychology is still working hard. Nevertheless, both Mischel and Eysenck's work gave an important insight into what it means to be human, what it means to be an individual.

What Determines Behaviour of an Individual?

Traits and Situations interact to influence behaviour — how else could it be ? (Its like the genetics *vs.* environment issue, one cannot exist without the other). So, the trait and situations perspectives are too simplistic: reality is more complex. In reality, different situations affect different people in different ways. Some situations allow expression of personality, other situations provoke a narrower range of behaviour. Thus,

Behaviour = personality × interpretation of the situation

It is vital to appreciate that there are individual differences in the personality-situation relationship. High self-monitors display less consistency across situations in their behaviour because they try to adapt more to the situation. Low self-monitors display more consistency in their behaviour across situations because they less to adapt to situations.

Research has shown that a trait will show up only in a situation where it is relevant. So anxiety may show up as a predictor of behaviour some situations, and not others. Also, some situations allow expression of personality, others provoke narrower range of behaviour.

In Summary

- Some individuals show more consistent behaviour.
- Traits may only emerge in some situations; traits do not have a constant influence on behaviour, their influence waxes and wanes.
- Some situations allow expression of personal, whilst others provoke a narrow range of behaviour (e.g., situation is strongly predictive of behaviour of people in ostage during a hijacking of a plane, whereas personality is strongly predictive of behaviour during an exploratory art therapy session).
- People display their traits by all that they do, including choice of situations, e.g., choice of career, choice of relationship, choice of lifestyle etc.

In conclusion, the person-situation debate has lead to more dynamic approach in understanding how personality traits and situation interact to produce a person's behaviour.

In an organizational setting, by observing the individuals behaviour in various situations, both the managers and employees can predict and control each others behaviour.

Characteristics of Personality

If you apply for a job you'ill be asked to list your personal qualities. Employers are assuming that your personality is to an extent fixed and won't change much from one year to the next, Most of us can relate to that idea, but where does our personality come from? Is it in our genes or is it created more by the circumstances of our childhood?

Of course the answer is both. There are bound to be genes which influence our behaviour simply because our brain and the chemicals that operate within it are made by genes. But trying to find any one of the hundreds of genes involved is notoriously difficult. The genetics of behaviour is complex, because personalities are complex. Scientists are only just beginning to have any success in understanding how genes influence behaviour. The box 2 gives an idea about how the emotions could be handled by the individuals in critical situations such as the one when an employee being terminated.

Characteristics of Personality

- Personality is organized and constant
- Personality is psychological, but is used by biological needs and processes.
- Personality causes behaviour to happen.
- Personality is displayed through thoughts, feelings, behaviours and many other ways.

How positive personalities can handle emotions in critical times, is depicted in the following box information.

Handling Emotions in Critical Times

Employee reactions to being terminated can run the full range of human emotion. Here are a few tips for how to handle strong emotions.

Never argue with an employee to justify a termination decision. If you've taken appropriate action in reaching your decision, such as discussing.

The consequences of failing to meet performance criteria, the termination decision should not be a surprised to the employee. Be courteous, confident and firm.

- If an employee asks what they can do to get the decision reversed inform them that the decision is final.
- Employees might respond that the termination will cause hardship to themselves and their families. In the case of an employee terminated for poor performance, you might point out that the employee had ample earning. In any case, you may refer to the benefits for which the employee is eligible.
- If an employee cries, you should allow them ample time to recover, offer a tissue or glass of water, but do not apologize. If an employee shouts or curses, you should state in a normal tone of voice that the meeting will not continue until they calm down. You should never respond in kind.
- If a terminated employee makes a threat of a lawsuit, you should either not respond or make a neutral comment.

But theories evolved though research studies will be relevant at that point of time and when further research is conducted on the topic, the previous opinion (theory) may be disproved or modified. All subjects of humanities face this problem. The study of personality, as suggested above, will have three approaches. But none of them can be taken as definite method of study. In case of all inexact sciences, only contingency approach holds good to adopt a concept.

We are discussing the concept of "Personality" in an organizational setting. Therefore, all the psychological and other factors are discussed in the backdrop of organizational behaviour.

Personality – Traits – "Big Five Model".

There are innumerable personality traits that are identified over the years. The empirical study reveals that hundreds of terms are used to describe personality and its structure. All these traits have been summarized into five main dimensions or factors termed as "Big Five" personality traits.

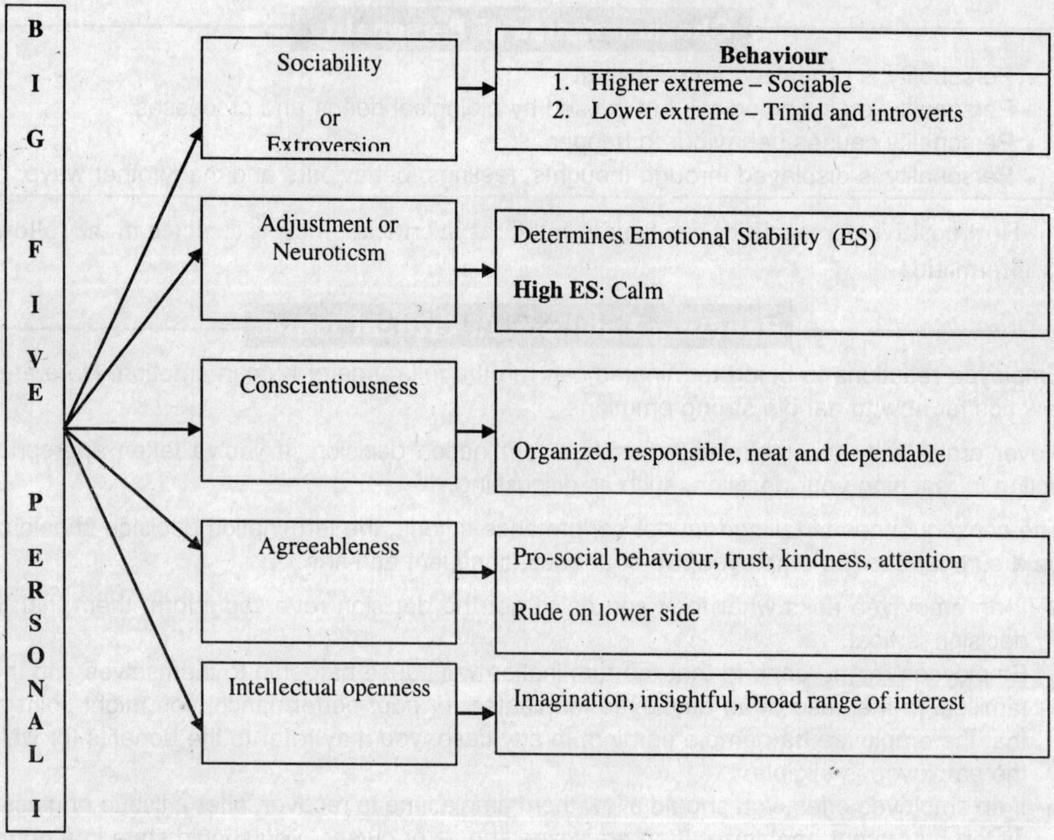

Fig. 16.2. Big-Five personality traits.

Evidence of this theory has been growing over the past 50 years, beginning with research of D.W. Fiske and later expanded upon by other researchers including Norman, Smith, Goldberg, and McCrae & Costa. The "big five" are broad categories of personality traits.

These dimensions are *sociability, adjustment, conscientiousness, agreeableness and intellectual openness.*

These five dimensions identified, explain their extreme nature in detail. For example a person high on the openness is very curious, has imaginative mind and has originality. Let us discuss each of these factors one by one in detail.

Sociability – This factor is otherwise termed as extroversion.

Extroversion – This trait includes characteristics such as excitability, sociability, talkativeness, assertiveness, and high amounts of emotional expressiveness.

It relates to one's degree of comfortness with relationships. Individuals extreme on this factor are sociable and gregarious in nature. Individuals on the lower extreme are termed as being introvert, less sociable, timid and quiet.

Adjustment – The adjustment or **Neuroticism** dimension focuses the emotional stability of an individual. The degree of emotional stability of a person is traced out in this dimension. How far a person is able to withstand anxiety and stress is also determined. People high on the emotional stability remain calm, secure and self-confident. On the other hand, individuals on the lower extreme depict being **anxiety, nervous** and **moody** type.

Conscientiousness – Common features of this dimension include high levels of thoughtfulness, with good impulse control and goal-directed behaviours. Those high in conscientiousness tend to be organised and mindful of details.

An individual's credibility and reliability can be measured with this dimension. It also refers to the focus of an individual towards his goals. People having few goals tend to be organised in nature. Thus, a person holding high on this factor is organised, **responsible, dependable** and **neat.**

Agreeableness – This personality dimension includes attributes such as trust, altruism, kindness, affection, and other pro-social behaviours.

Individual's high on agreeableness tend to be warm, kind and considerate. The lower extreme lists the aspects of being independent, arrogant and rude behaviour.

Intellectual Openness – The trait features such as imagination and insight, and those high in this trait also tend to have a broad range of interests.

These dimensions represent broad areas of personality. Research has demonstrated that these groupings of characteristics tend to occur together in many people. For example, individuals who are sociable tend to be talkative. However, these traits do not always occur all together. Personality is a complex and varied each person may display behaviours across several of these dimensions.

These dimensions otherwise termed as openness to experience points out the individual's range of interests. This dimension depicts the individual's capacity to absorb and thirst for learning. Extremely intellectual openness leads to traits like being anxious, novelty, innovative and original. The other extreme exhibits traits such as being dull, following old patterns (conventional), non-originative and unimaginative.

The big five dimensions of traits help the industry executives to predict the behaviour of employees. From the empirical evidence, one can conclude that a strong relationship can be established between sociability and the organisation-fit behaviour. People with high conscientiousness and agreeableness tend to be more achievement orien.ed. A good example for this is Bill Gates.

Workplace Behaviour and Big Five Model

Workplace behaviour is related to the five-factor model of personality. Interpersonal deviance is negatively correlated with high levels of agreeableness. Organisational deviance is negatively correlated with high levels of conscientiousness and positively correlated with high levels of neuroticism. This implies that indivudals who are emotionally stable and conscientious are less likely to withhold effort or steal, whereas those who are agreeable are less likely to be hostile to their co-workers.

Another entirely different factor to consider is perception of the workplace. Employees who had a positive perception of their workplace were less likely to pursue deviant behaviour. Research indicates that personality acts as moderating factor: workplace deviance was more likely to be endorsed with respect to an individual when the perception of the workplace was negative and emotional stability, conscientiousness or agreeableness were low.

Job absence is very much a part of job performance: employees are not performing effectively if they do not come to work, introverted, conscientious employees are much less likely to be absent form work, as opposed to extroverted employees who are low on conscientiousness. Interestingly enough, neuroticism is not highly correlated with absence.

Often times in the workplace, the ability to be a team player is valued and is critical to job performance. Recent research has suggested that conscientiousness, extroversion, and agreeableness are all related to cooperative behaviour but that they are not related to task performance.

Conscientiousness and extroversion are the two aspects of the give factor model that are always correlated with positive job performance, although conscientiousness is more positively correlated (extroversion is negatively correlated with job performance is that it appears to inspire more absence, but only when combined with low levels of conscientiousness'). Agreeableness is negatively correlated with job performance within a leadership role. Openness to experience, in general, is unrelated. Neuroticism is negatively correlated with job performance.

Cognitive ability may allow an employee to complete a specific task, but the ability to work with others and to stay motivated are aspects of personality. The five-factor model is a valid predictor of workplace performance. Personality is an indispensable consideration for employers looking for quality employees.

Myers-Briggs Type Indicator – MBTI

Another interesting and widely used approach or the personality framework is Myers-Briggs, Type Indicator (MBTI). It was introduced by **Carl Jung** who differentiates people in four dimensions – **thinking, feeling, sensing and intuiting**. Linked with attitudes, such as extroversion and introversion, the two pairs of opposites, **thinking – feeling** (T and F) and **sensation and intuitions** (S and I) stand in compensatory relation to each other.

In addition to this, three are two attitudes that Jung reveals. They are extroversion and introversion (E and I). The introvert is influenced by what he finds within himself. For example, an individual might avoid a social party and get himself engaged in watching television. The extrovert is a kind of person who finds himself with outside world.

There is also another kind of attitude called **"Ambivert".** (Person having both introvert and extrovert features). Ambiverts being introvert or extrovert. Thus the combinations of four dimesions of Karl Jung can exhibit 16 personality types. Thus, a successful manager must use both, mind (thinking) and heart (feeling) to approach his subordinates. Likewise, the management may demand a combination of the sixteen personality traits.

MBTI is a questionnaire that is used to analyse and identify personality types. Many organisations of today adopt this instrument to determine the behaviour of individuals. The instrument has both validity and reliability and it can be easily administered.

Some of the organisations that use the MBTI are 3M, General Electrical, Lucent and Apple Computers.

Other Personality Attributes Influencing OB

Machiavellianism

Niccolo Machiavellian founded this personality trait during the sixteenth century. He initiated the documentation of power and politics in organisations. Machiavellianism refers to the degree of an individual being pragmatic. It is also the maintenance of emotional distance and to what level individuals believe that ends can justify means.

Individuals high on Machiavellians (high-mach) and low Machiavellians (low-mach) exhibit certain behavioural outcomes. For instance, high-mach individuals are more manipulative in nature. They tend to use more power and exhibit high political behaviour. This political behaviour is exhibited during the following situations:

- When the confrontation of the individuals with others that do not take place directly.
- When the rules and regulations to be followed are minimum.
- The emotional involvement is high.

Does this mean that high-mach personalities are great achievers? The answer to this question is 'No'! It once again depends on the performance and type of job performed. There are no such standard behaviours that can be exhibited.

Locus of Control

The extent to which an individual can control the events are referred to as the Locus of Control. Some individuals believe that they are responsible for their own behaviour and actions. These individuals have internal locus of control. They believe that, it is they who control the events happening to them. On the other hand if individual do not take the responsibility for their behaviour and actions, it is referred to as external Locus of Control.

One does not know the expressions of behaviour in the social settings. Individuals with internally locus are less likely to attract and influence others.

Externally locus individuals are open-minded and hence would prefer directive style of leadership. Empirical studies reveal that employees with external locus of control are dissatisfied than internals. For example, if an employee feels that he did not receive his promotion due to politics in the organisation he is high on external locus of control. On the contrary, if the individual blames himself for being incapable of receiving any promotion, the individual is high in internal locus of control.

Chart showing the Locus of Control.

Conditions	*Performance*
Information Processing	
* The work requires complex information processing and complex learning.	* Internals perform better.
* The work is quite simple and easy to learn.	* Internals perform no better than externals.
Initiative	
* The work requires initiative and independent action.	* Internals perform better.
* The work requires compliance and conformity.	* Externals perform better.
Motivation	
* The work requires high motivation and provides valued rewards in return for greater effort, incentive pays for greater productivity.	* Internals perform better.
* The work does not require great effort and contingent rewards are lacking, hourly pay rates determined by collective bargaining.	* Externals perform at least as well as internals.

(*Source:* Don Hellrigel, *et al.*, Organisational Behaviour, South Western, 2001, p. 45)

Dogmatism and Authoritarianism

Dogmatism refers to individuals who have rigidity in their beliefs. People high on this trait are close-minded. They are always dependent and need someone to give them directions. They concentrate on the structure of the groups. Whereas lower extreme on this trait depicts the open mindedness of individuals. The lower extreme on dogmatism does not require any authority to give directions and they are indpendent.

Authoritarianism personalities adhere themselves to conventional values that rare followed for years. They feel that power and authority is a must for organisations and its performance. Individuals high on authoritariansm prefer organised flow of authority and power. Lower extremes reveal that things can be decentralised and that power can be distributed to others to certain extent.

Self-esteem

This trait in individuals reveals the degree of the individual respect and self-worth. Individuals high on self-esteem believe that they posses the capacity and potential to ensure success in whatever they do.

People on lower self-esteem are dependent on others for their happenings. They have low self-worth. They do not believe in the ability and their potential. These individuals have minimum self-respect and seek for others approval in the work they do. They also try to work and please others. Studies reveal that employees on high self-esteem are more satisfied than the lower self-esteemed employees.

Self-monitoring

Self-monitoring is another interesting trait that has emerged in recent days. It refers to the individual's capacity or ability to adjust with environment factors. This trait can also be related to the adjustment factor of the Big Five Model.

Individuals who are high in adjustment tend to perform more than the low adjustment individuals. It reveals the degree of adaptability and adjustability in the workplace or any similar situation. It brings out the relationship between one individual and another. High in self-monitoring reveals that these individuals are highly conscious, sensitive and open to the external stimuli. They monitor others' behaviour very closely. They tend to perform more and receive promotions.

On the other hand, the low self-monitoring individuals have conflict in their own personality and also exhibit contradictions in their behaviour.

Risk Taking

Risk taking refers to the willingness of individuals to take chances. The individuals with high presence of this trait tend to take very rapid decisions with the limited information and they do not give time for the consequences. Depending upon the job demands, the risk-taking factor has to be applied. There is a general notion that high risk taking leads to high performance. On the contrary, in practice moderate risk taking leads to greater performance.

Personality – Types

Earlier researchers have tried to identify different types of personality. Some researchers were trying to classify personality on the basis of temperament and emotions, while others on physique.

Both, the metabolic and chemical changes helps in the formation of personality.

Russian psychologist Ivan Pavlov reviewed, the ancient beliefts with central nervous system. In his research, he discovered that temperaments conform to the four categories of thoughts of the Greeks. Each type had the features as shown in the following table:

The Choleric	The Sanguine	The Phlegmatic	The Melancholic
This temperament emerges out of unbalanced nervous system due to excitement, anxiety, etc., a person's emotions are very easily aroused in this.	A person with high blood red colour, cheerfulness and sturdy temperament confident, optimistic, less emotional compared to choleric, highly cautious, logical and demonstrative.	Exhibits slow and solid, temperament, cool, claim, serene and stable. Experiences an emotion which is not easily arousable.	This temperament is characterized by a very slow feeling and thought which is not expressed. He or she is very slow in making friends.

Fig. 16.3. Temperament Types

Alker Bem, A social-psychologist, introduced the concept that some people may be trait like, and others may be more situational. For example, consider the personality dimensions of high versus low need for social approval. People with a high need for social approval are likely to monitor themselves in many situations in order to maintain in a particular social image. These people will control those behaviours that are under voluntary control, but will not be able to control more autonomic behaviours (example: body posture, sweating, blushing). People with high need for social approval will thus appear to be trait like and continuous in behaviours that are controllable, but will might show within situation cross modal inconsistency.

People with low need for social approval are more sensitive to situational changes. Because they are not monitoring themselves across situations, in order to behave always in socially desirable ways. These people will appear to be more situational, and will also show a within situation consistency across the modalities of their behaviour.

Type "A" and Type "B" Personality

Some personality types based on temperaments – Type A and Type B are discussed in the following paragraphs.

Meyer Friedman and Ray Rosenman, cardiologists, have come out with two types of personalities. They observed people while working and exhibiting certain activities. By close observation, they concluded that there are two different patterns of personality, *viz.*, Type A and Type B.

Type A personality are objective in nature, workaholic and very competitive. They are likely to be impatient and wish to achieve everything at one time. They mess up things and are aggressive.

Type B personality to the contrary, are less objective and less competitive in nature. They never have the urgency of time. They have good interpersonal relationship with other individuals and hence are balanced in their actions. They have a cool approach towards life. A high level of self-confidence can be seen in this type of individuals. They take up another job afer the completion first job. They are focused in their activities.

Classification as Type "A and "B"

Type - A Persons	*Type - B Persons*
* Lose their temper quickly * Talk rapidly * Interrupt others * Highly competitive * Devoted to work * Strong sense for time management * Impatient with idleness.	* Work steadily * Be relaxed * Patient in handling issues * Not having completing tendency * Analyse issues carefully * Not bothered about time. * Do not easily lose temper.

Fig. 16.4. Features of Type-A and Type-B Persons.

16 Personality Types of Carl Jung (For MBTI Model)

ENJF (Extroverted feeling with intuiting): These people are easy speakers. They tend to idealise their friends. They make good parents, but have a tendency to allow themselves to be used. They make good therapists, teachers, executives and salespeople.

ENFP (Extroverted intuiting with feeling): These people love novelty and surprises. They are big on emotions and and expression. They are susceptible to muscle tension and tend to be hyperalert, they tend to feel self-conscious. They are good at sales, advertising, politics and acting.

ENTJ (Extroverted thinking with intuiting): In charge at home, they expect a lot from spouses and kids. They like organisation and structure and tend to make good executives and administrators.

ENTP (Extroverted intuiting with thinking) : These are lively people, not humdrum or orderly. As mates, they are little dangerous, especially economically. They are good at analysis and make good entrepreneurs. They do tend to play one upmanship.

ESFJ (Extroverted feeling with sensing): These people like harmony. They tend to have strong shoulds and should nots. They may be dependent, first on parents and later on spouses. They wear their hearts on their sleeves and excel in service occupations involving personal contact.

ESFP (Extroverted sensing with feeling): Very generous and impulsive, they have a low tolerance for anxiety. They make good performers, they like public relations, and they love the phone. They should avoid scholarly pursuits especially science.

ESTJ (Extroverted thinking with sensing): These are responsible mates and parents and are loyal to the workplace. They are realistic, down-to-earth. Orderly, and love tradition. They often find themselves joining civic clubs!

ESTP (Extroverted sensing with thinking) : These are action-oriented people, often sophisticated, sometimes ruthless—"James Bonds". As mates, they are exciting and charming, but they have trouble with commitment. They make good promoters, entrepreneurs and con-artists.

INFJ (Introverted intuiting with feeling): These are serious students and workers who really want to contribute they are psychic. They make good therapists general practitioners, ministers and so on.

INFP (introverted feeling with intuiting). These people are idealistic, self-sacrificing, and somewhat cool or reserved. They are very family and home oriented, but don't relax well. You find them in psychology, architecture, and religion and never in business.

INTJ (Introverted intuiting with thinking): These are the most independent of all types. They love logic and ideas and are drawn to scientific research. They can be rather single-minded, though.

INTP (introverted thinking with intuiting): Faithful, preoccupied, and forgetful, these are the book worms, They tend to be very precise in their use of language. They are good at logic and math and make good philosophers and theoretical scientists, but not writers or sales people.

ISFJ (Introverted sensing with feeling): These people are service and work oriented. They may suffer from fatigue and tend to be attracted to troublemakers. They are good nurses, teachers, secretaries, general practitioners, librarians and middle managers and housekeepers.

ISFP (Introverted feeling with sensing): They are shy and retiring—are not talkative, but like sensuous action. They like painting, drawing, sculpting, composing, dancing—the arts generally – and they like nature. They are not big on commitment.

ISTJ (Introduced sensing with the thinking) : These are dependable pillars of strength. They often try to reform their mates and other people. They make good bank examiners, auditors, accountants, tax-examiners, supervisors in libraries and hospitals, business, home etc., and physical education teachers, and boy or girl scouts!

ISTP (Introverted thinking with sensing): These people are action-oriented and fearless, and crave excitement. They are impulsive and dangerous to stop. They often like tools, instruments, and weapons, and often become technically experts. They are not interested in communications and are often incorrectly diagnosed as dyslexic or hyperactive. They tend to do badly in school.

Source : Web resource.

Personality Theories

Innumarable theories have been evolved on personality. Each theory exhibits one type of unique personality of an individual. However, following theories are considered to be more prominent among several theories.

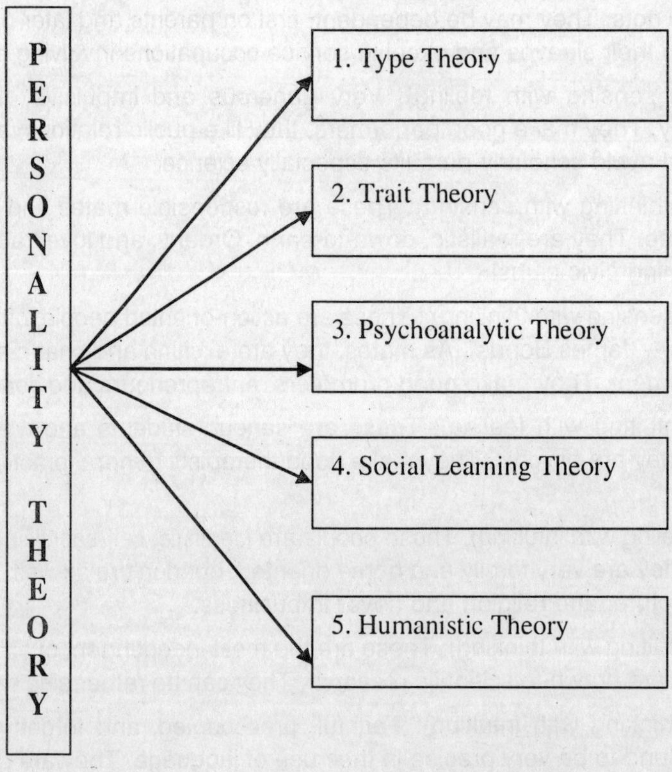

Fig. 16.5. Personality theories which reveal different types of personality

These five theories are briefly explained in the following paragraphs:

1. Type Theory

According to type theories, people are grouped into identifiable categories. One basis for classifying personalities is based on the physique. **Sheldon** proposed type theories and he feels that a relationship is sought to be established between features of body and personality. Thus, a short plump person (endomorph) is said to be sociable, relaxed and even-tempered; a tall, thin person (ectomorph) is characterized as restrained, self-conscious and fond of solitude; a heavy-set muscular individual (mesomorph) is described as noisy, callous, and fond of physical activity.

Classification of personalities on a physical basis is subjective.

1. Alfred Adler's Psychological types

Alfred Adler postulates a single "drive" or motivating force behind all our behaviour and experience. By the time his theory had gelled into its most mature from, he called that motivating force the **striving for perfection.** It is the desire we all have to fulfil our potentials, to come closer and closer to our ideal. It is, as many of you will already see, very similar to the more popular idea of self-actualization.

Striving for perfection was not the first phrase. Adler used to refer to his single motivating force. His earliest phrase was the **aggression drive,** referring to the reaction we have when other drives, such as our need to eat, be sexually satisfied, get things done, or be loved, are frustrated. It might be better called the assertiveness drive, since we tend to think of aggression as physical and negative. But it was Adler's idea of the aggression drive that first caused friction between him and Freud. Freud was afraid that it would detract from the crucial position of the sex drive in psychoanalytic theory. Despite Freud's dislike for the idea, he himself introduced something very similar much later in his life: the death instinct. Thus he came out with the following psychological types in his theory based on the energy level of the individuals.

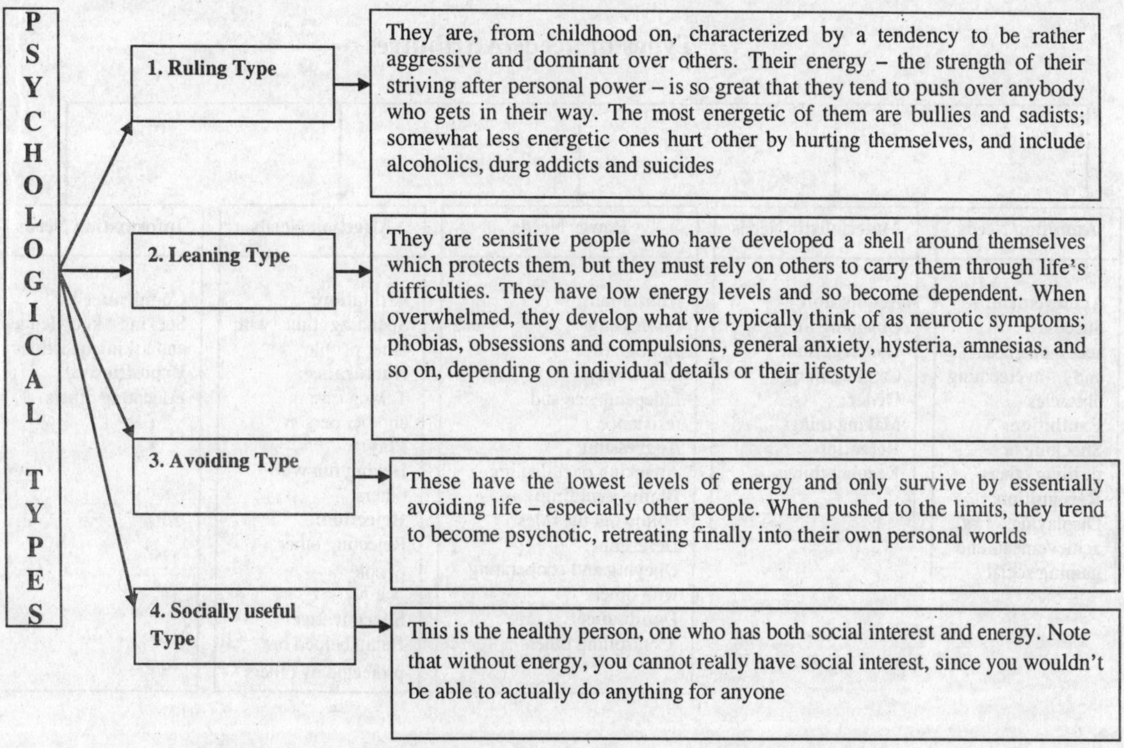

Fig. 16.6. Alfred Adler's Psychological type of personality

2. Henry Murray's Psychogenic Needs

American psychologist Henry Murray developed a theory of personality that was organized in terms of motives, presses, and needs. Murray described needs as a, "potentiality or readiness to respond in a certain way under certain given circumstances".

Theories of personality based upon needs and motives suggest that our personalities are a reflection of behaviours controlled by needs. While some needs are temporary and changing, other needs are more deeply seated in our nature. Accoring to Murray, these psychogenic needs function mostly on the unconscious level, but play a major role in our personality.

Murray's Types of Needs

1. Primary Needs: Primary needs are based upon biological demands, such as the need for oxygen, food, and water.

2. Secondary Needs: Secondary Needs are generally psychological, such as the need for nurturing, independence, and achivement.

Attributes or Needs which influence Personality

There are several attributes suggested by psychologists as parameters to identify a personality. All the people have these needs and on the basis of degree of these needs an individual's personality can be identified. Following chart shows the type of needs and or attributes, which identify personality.

Types of needs/Attributres

Ambition Needs	Materialistic Needs	Power Needs	Affection Needs	Information Needs
Achievement: Success accomplishment and overcoming obstacles **Exhibition:** Shocking or thrilling others **Recognition:** Displaying achievements and gaining social	**Acquisition:** Obtaining things **Construction:** Creating things **Order:** Making things **Retention** Keeping things	**Abasement:** Confessing and apologizing **Autonomy:** Independence and resistance **Aggression:** Attacking or ridiculing **Blame avoiding:** Following the rules **Deference:** Obeying and cooperating with others **Dominance:** Controlling others	**Affiliation:** Spending time with other people **Nurturance:** Taking care of another person **Play:** Having fun with others **Rejection:** Rejecting other people **Succourance** Being helped or protected by others	**Cognizance :** Seeking knowledge and asking questions **Exposition :** Educating others

Fig. 16.7. Need types suggested to identify personality

Influences on Psychogenic Needs

Each need is important of itself. But Murray believed that needs can be interrelated, can support other needs, and can conflict with other needs. For example, the need for dominance may conflict with the need for affiliation when overly controlling behaviour drives away friends, family, and romantic partners. Murray also believed that environmental factors play a role in how these psychogenesis needs are displaed in behaviour. Murray called these environmental forces, "presses."

Thus type theory focuses on needs, health and physical features to identify personality.

2. Trait Theory

Another interesting approach to understand personality is the trait approach. A personality trait is understood as being an enduring attribute of a person that appears consistently in different situations. Each individual trait differs from the other individual in an unique way.

Psychologists working in the area of trait theory are concerned with two processes: (1) determining the basic traits that provide a meaningful description of personality and (2) finding some way to measure them.

There are two ways of assessing personality traits: (i) the person describes himself by answering questions about this attitudes, feelings, and behaviours and (ii) someone else evaluates the person's traits either from what he knows about: the individual/or from direct observations of behaviour. For this, personality inventory or a rating scale is generally used.

3. Psychoanalytic theory

Sigmund Freud developed the first comprehensive personality theory, called psychoanalytic theory.

Freud saw personality as being composed of three elements — id, ego, and super ego.

The Id: The word 'id' is the Latin word for 'it' and refers exclusively to the innate component of personality. The id is the mental agency containing everything inherited, present at birth, and fixed in the individual's constitution, especially instincts. The id, as the original personality system, expresses the primary principle of all human life — the immediate discharge of psychic scenery (libido) produced by animal drives. Immediate tension reduction is called pleasure principle, and the id obeys it, manifesting itself in an impulsive and irrational manner, regardless of the consequences of its actions for others or its own self-preservation. Thus, "Id" is the primitive and unconscious part of the personality that contains instincts.

The Ego: Mental images do not satisfy needs. A man who is starving cannot satisfy his hunger by eating pictures. Reality should be considered. The ego develops out of the id because of the necessity for dealing with the real world. The hungry man must have food if the tension of hungry is to be reduced. Therefore, "The Ego" is the "executive" of the personality that is partly conscious and that meditates between the impulses of the Id, the prohibitions of the super ego and dictates of the reality.

The Super Ego: The super ego is the third part of the personality. It represents the internalized representation of the values and morals or society as taught to the child by and others. The super ego judges whether an action is right or wrong according to the standards of society. Superego is the moral arm of the personality that internalizes the standards and values of society and serves as the person's coscience. These three elements, according to Freud, help an assessor to asses the personality.

4. Social Learning Theory

Many activities of human behaviour is either learnt or modified by learning.

There are two ways of learning. Learning through reinforcement of direct experience, and learning by observing others. An individual can learn by observing the actions of others and this is called **social learning theory.** An interesting story is given in Box to have a deep understanding of what is social learning theory.

The Wooden Bowl

A frail old man went to live with his son, daughter-in-law, and a four year old grandson. The old man's hands trembled, his eyesight was blurred, and his step faltered. The family ate together rightly at the dinner table. But the elderly grandfather's shaky hands and failing sight made eating rather difficult. Peas rolled off his spoon onto the floor. When he grasped the glass often milk spilled on the tablecloth.

The son and daughter-in-law became irritated with the mess, "We must do something about grandfather," said the son. I've had enough of his spilled milk, noisy eating, and food on the floor. So the husband and wife set a small table in the corner. There, grandfather ate alone while the rest of the family enjoyed dinner at the dinner table. Since grandfather had broken a dish or two, his food was served in a wooden bowl. Sometimes when the family glanced in grandfather's direction, he had a tear in his eye as he ate alone. Still, the only words the couple had for him were sharp admonitions when he dropped a fork or spilled food. The four-year-old watched it all in silence.

One evening before supper, the father noticed his son playing with wood scraps on the floor. He asked the child sweetly, "What are you making?" Just as sweetly, the boy responded, "Oh, I am making a little bowl for you and mama to eat food from when I grow up".

The four-year old smiled and went back to work. The words so struck the parents that they are speechless. Then tears started to stream down their cheeks. Though no word was spoken, both knew what must be done. That evening the husband took grandfather's hand and gently led him back to the family table.

For the remaining of his days he ate every meal with the family. And for some reason, neither husband nor wife seemed to care any longer when a fork was dropped, milk spilled, or the tablecloth soiled. Children are remarkably perceptive. Their eyes ever observe, their ears every listen, and their minds ever process the messages they absorb If they see us patiently provide a happy home atomosphere for family members. They will imitate that attitude for the rest of their lives. The wise parent realizes that every day that building blocks are being laid for the child's future.

An individual's action in a given situation depends upon the specific characteristics of a situation, the individual's understanding of the situation, and past behaviour in similar situations.

The social learning theory focuses on behaviour patterns and cognitive activities like :

(a) Competencies;

(b) Developing cognitive Strategies;

(c) Outcome expectations; and

(d) Subjective value outcomes.

It also focuses on self-regulatory systems and plans, where the individual differences have self-imposed goals, rules guiding the individual's behaviour. (More details on social learning theory can be seen in chapter on "learning" of this book).

1. The Humanistic Approach

The humanistic approach share a common emphasis on man's potential for self-direction and freedom of choice. They are concerned with the 'self' and the individual's subjective experiences.

Carl Rogers Self Theory: Carl Roger's approach to personality is described as phenomenological. Phenomenology is the study of the individual's subjective experience, feelings and private concepts as well as his views of the world and self. According to Roger, behaviour is dependent upon how one perceives the world. The theory emphasizes the self and its characteristics.

Thus in Rogers' personality theory, there are two concepts : self and self-actualization. The self consist of all the ideas, perceptions and values that characterized "I' or "me". It includes the awareness 'what I am'? Self-actualization is the basic motivating force presenting the inherent tendency of the organism to develop all its capabilities in ways which serve to maintain or enhance the individual.

Measurement of Personality

There are a number of different techniques that are used in the measurement personality. Each technique has its own strengths and weaknesses. Following are some of the techniques adapted to measure personality.

- **Experimental methods** are those in which the researcher controls and manipulates the variables of interests and takes measures of the results. This is the most scientific form of research, but experimental research can be difficult when studying aspects of personality such as motivations, emotions, and drives. These ideas are internal, abstract, and extremely difficult to measure.
- **Case studies and self-report methods** rely on in-depth analysis of an individual as well as information provided by the individual. Case studies rely heavily on the interpretation of the observer, while self-report methods depend upon the memory of the individual interest. Because of this, these methods tend to be highly subjective and it is difficult to generalize the findings to a larger population.
- **Clinical research** relies upon information gathered from clinical patients over the course of treatment. Many personality theories are based upon this type of research, but because the research subjects are unique and exhibit abnormal behaviour, this research tends to be highly subjective and difficult to generalize.

Tools

Many psychological tests are conducted to measure personality of an individual. These tests may be considred as tools or instruments to measure personality. Many variables and needs of individuals are considred in different settings to measure the personality. Tests such as (i) True or False type question tests,(ii) Pattern tests presenting a series of ambiguous stimuli (e.g., Pictures having different meanings), (iii) Intelligence tests,(iv) Neuropsychological tests (help to recognize normal or abnormal brain functioning) to measure mental and physical talks of the individuals) etc., would facilitate measuring the personality of an individual.

Besides these tests adopted to measure the personality, psychologists have used tools such as: (i) Interview, (ii) Behavioural Assessment, (iii) Remote behavioural sampling,(iv) objective personality scales and self-rating,(v) Projective Tests. All these are basically different forms of psychological tests considered as major tests, amongst many psychological tests adapted for measuring personality. Some of these major tests fall in the categories of tests suggested in the previous paragraph.

Personality and workplace issues

Researchers of social sciences on personality and behaviour of people at work place have made thousands of research studies over the years. But still, the studies do not reveal exact behavioural type that increases the productivity of individual as well as the organization. However, five-factor model of personality has given a direction to assess the individuals, their performance and aspects of job performance such as motivation, deviation, job satisfaction and teamwork. Research has yielded correlation between Five-factor model and aspects of job performance. Job performance and personality (as measured in the five-factor model) are related. It appears that the relation between job performance and the five factors is more a consequence of the social aspects of the workplace than of ability. Research indicates that cognitive ability is more strongly correlated with task performance than any of the five factors are correlated with task performance. The five factors are strongly correlated with cooperating with others and enjoying the overall workplace experience, which are key components of long-term job success. Being absent from work or working as a team are correlated of personality that directly affect whether one will succeed in the workplace, and they are strongly correlated with the Big Five and not with cognitive ability.

It is worth noting that the majority of research has been on sales or other occupations in which interacting with people is required. Is it possible that these studies are skewed? Perhaps researching on individuals in jobs that require very little human interaction would yield different results.

Conscientiousness and extroversion are the two aspects of the give-factor model that are always correlated with positive job performance, although conscientiousness is more positively correlated (extraversion is, negatively correlated with job performance in that it appears to inspire more absence, but only when combined with low levels of conscientiousness). Agreeableness is negatively, correlated with job performance within leadership role. Openness to experience, in general, is unrelated. Neuroticism is negatively correlated with performance. An achronym "OCEAN" is created to remember the components of "Five-factor" model.

Cognitive ability may allow an employee to complete a specific task, but the ability to work with others and to say motivated are aspects of personality. The give-factor model is a valid predictor of workplace performance Personality is an indispensable consideration for employers looking for quality employees.

As said earlier, the give-factor model is only a predictor and cannot be exact model to assess personality. This does not cover the aspects such as important characteristics that definitely cover personality.

Your success at work depends upon what kind of person you are. Researchers have made a comparison between successful and unsuccessful people. In one study the empirical evidence reveals that some defined success in terms of money whereas others in terms of intrinsic happiness. Most successful men were found to be more persistent. They were exhibiting self-confidence, and had high agreeableness. They were open-minded and extroverts. Their sociable nature increased their interpersonal behaviour, which in turn increased their performance.

Generally the essential traits or expected traits of management professionals are persistent and confidence. A congenial job brings self-fulfilment and self-confidence in individuals. Personality is the sum total of our habits, physical, mental and emotional. Individuals in organizations need to improve their personality though their specific habits and behaviour.

Interactive Behaviour

An interactive person is also called extrovert personality. The qualities of an interactive person is simply speaking. They are just opposite to introverts. The people who are interactive are basically friendly, sociable, lively, gregarious, and aggressive and express their feeling and ideas openly. Hence, they are more suitable and successful in the areas/fields, which require continuous and frequent interaction with others. Sales activities, publicity departments, personal relations unit etc., require such people.

So, those people who tend to exhibit the above characteristics and behaviour come under interactive behaviour because there are continuous negotiations between many people. These people tend to work faster, dislike complicated procedure. They usually communicate freely and are often impatient with long slow jobs. They like to have people around them most of the time

SUMMARY

1. Personality is the distinctive and relatively enduring ways of thinking, feeling and acting that characterize a person's responses to life situation. It is a sum total of an individual's interaction with environment and situation.
2. In an organizational context, personality of workers has to be understood as it influences their behaviour as well as different cognitive processes.
3. Factors that determine personality are: (i) Heredity, (ii) Environment, (iii) culture and (iv) situation.
4. There are many types of personalities that exist in any situation. They are identified by the needs, attributes and behaviour of these people.
5. Thousands of personality traits are identified to assess the personality of an individual. All these traits have been summarized into "Big Five" traits. They are (i) Extroversion, (ii) Neuroticism, (iii) Conscientiousness, (iv) Agreeableness, (v) Intellectual openness.

6. Big-Five model is a valid predictor of workplace performance. Personality is an indispensable consideration for employers looking for quality workers.
7. Several theories have been evolved by researchers to identify personality. Important ones are (i) Type theory, (ii) Trait theory, (iii) Psychoanalytic theory, (iv) Social learning theory and (iv) Humanistic theory.
8. Types of personalities are identified by needs and attributes. Basically, there are two types, *viz.*, Type-A and type-B. These two types contain various needs and attributes.
9. Ivan Pavlov, a Russian researcher, analysed four temperaments identified by Greeks recognize personalities such as (i) the choleric, (ii) the sanguine (iii) the phlegmatic and (iv) the melancholic.
10. Alfred Adler's types are (i) Ruling type, (ii) learning type, (iii) Avoiding type and (iv) Socially useful type.
11. Personalities are measured though (i) experimental methods (ii) case studies and self-report methods and (iii) clinical research. Various psychological tests are also conducted to measure personality.
12. In organisational context, extroverts, open-minded, self-confident and of social nature personalities are successful and are more productive. Job type, will also have its impact on the behaviour. A congenial job brings self-fulfilment and confidence in individuals.
13. Understanding personality of workers at organisational level is essential for managers. Because it influences behaviour of people at work as well as different cognitive processes.
14. Personality traits and theories give an input to predict the behaviour of individual and his or her performance.

STUDY QUESTIONS

1 Give a small note on the following terms. Answer for each term carries **four** marks.
(i) Personality, (ii) Heredity, (iii) Environment, (iv) Culture, (v) Melancholic, (vi) Sanguine, (vii) Chaleric, (viii) Phlegmatic, (ix) Extroversion, (x) Introversion, (xi) Neurotism, (xii) Conscientiousness, (xiii) Intellectual openness, (xiv) Agreeableness, (xv) MBTI (xvi) Machiavellianism, (xvii) Locus of control, (xviii) Dogmatism, (xix) Authoritariansim, (xx) Self-esteem, (xxi) self-monitoring, (xxii) Type "A" personality, (xxiii) Type "B" personality, (xxiv) Ambition needs, (axis) Materialistic needs, (xxv) Power needs, (axis) Affection needs, (Xavier) Information needs, (xxvii) Id.(xxix) Ego. (xxx) superego, (xxxi) Interactive Behaviour.
2. Explain the factors that determine the personality.
3. Enumerate the personality traits that shape the personality of the individual.
4. Explain the importance of assessing personality in an organisational setting.
5. Briefly give the meaning of personality. Describe how culture determines personality.
6. Explain the concepts of Locus of control and Machiavellianism.
7. Give a detailed account of various personality types.
8. Briefly explain the role of family in developing the personality of an individual.
9. How self-esteem and self-efficacy facilitate the development of personality?

Personality Dragons

Personality dragons are habits, behaviours and personality traits caused by underlying fears that keep people from being successful. There are seven dragons. When out of control, they become self-fulling prophecies:

Greed – Lose everything you want
Impatience – Slows you down
Arrogance – People judge you.
Stubbornness – Brings authority down on your head.
Self-depreciation – Others put you down.
Martyrdom – Provokes others to hurt you.
Self-destruction – Lose control ultimately.

Exercise: Make a study of the following persons and identify the characteristics of these people which have made them successful.

(1) Mahatma Gandhi (2) N.R. Narayana Murthy (3) JRD Tata (4) Lakshmi Mittal (5) Dhirubhai Ambani (6) Kiran Mujumdar Shah (7) Bharatha Ratna Mokshagundum Vishveswariah.

CASE STUDY

Sumathi and Anitha were great friends in their college days. Sumathi had lot of fun in college. She was an average student. In summer holidays, she was working on hourly basis. Another lady Anitha liked to work fast and she was not satisfied working on hourly basis. After completing her graduation, she took up the job of secretary for an MNC. Work came to her in the form of preparing reports, attending executive calls and being in office from morning 8.30 a.m. to evening 9.00 p.m. This made her to be a real workaholic. Though a highly ambitious lady she could not manage her task. Her things were unorganised. The more she toiled the more was her stress. It was too hard to adjust with non-supportive workers and colleagues.

One fine day, things were getting worse and her boss called up for her. Her boss was an understanding and soft-spoken person. He took her for a cup of coffee and started the conversation slowly. He initially asked her about her parents and later about the job. Anitha busted out. She poured all her pent up emotions to her boss.

Questions

1. What are the signs of Anitha are exhibiting in this case?
2. Could she reconcile with her workers and colleagues. If so how?
3. Suggest a suitable remedy for Anitha to improve her performance.

Skill Exercise

Step 1: With the help of big five personality factors, describe the personality of (i) the individual who is seated next to you, (ii) a person whom you have admired as a role model and (iii) a family member.

Step 2: Identify of the personality factors that is very interesting to you in all these three individuals.

Step 3: After identifying down the factors you discuss the content with your class mates. Refer to the text whenever doubt arises. [Time: 1 hour]

17

PERCEPTION

LEARNING OBJECTIVES

After reading this chapter, you should be able to know:

- Perception — The Concept
- Influencing Factors of Perception
- Perceptual Errors
- Perceptual Process
- Perception Theories
- Perception and Workplace

In an organisation, the productivity is mainly influenced by the behaviour of the people at work. Behaviour is governed by several factors and one such factor is "Perception" of people. The root of behaviour of a person is perception. Perception influences the outlook and actions of each employee, and it has many dimensions. They are: (i) Self-perception of workers, (ii) Perceptions of people around them, (iii) Perception of production components, (iv) Perception of customers and (v) Perception of general public. These dimensions of an individual worker direct the behaviour of that person. Employees have the perception of role that they have to play. Perception is not always accurate and correct. This means, what we perceive about a person or thing may be true or untrue. But the consequence of perception is always true. Observe the following example.

Mr. Raghunath, HRD Manager, Royal Info Systems had two Assistants, *viz.*, Mr. Kiran and Mrs. Ramya. The manager of RIS, had perception that female are more loyal to their work. But much opposed to his perception, he was receiving complaints from female employees that Mrs. Ramya comes to office very late and involves herself more in gossiping rather than doing the job. Ramya, being only one employee in the office to receive complaints from female workers and to listen the grievances of these workers, Raghunath had to do something to address the grievances of female employees. He had to change his perception that all female employees will be loyal to the organisation. Because, Raghunath's perception was not true in this case. Thus, perception may be accurate or incorrect. But the consequences of such perception will be real. Perception is the result of processing an individual's observation and it will guide the individual through its hypothetical thinking.

In our daily life, we all come across various events and objects. Various stimuli is constantly bombarding us in our routine life. To be specific, in practice, while we receive some events and objects, we reject others. Further, we look at the same thing yet perceive it differently. For example, looking at a sculpture some may perceive it as beautiful, and some others as ugly. Why different people perceive the same object and event differently?

The answer is perception, *a cognitive factor of human behaviour.* Strictly speaking perception lies at the base of every human behaviour. There can be no behaviour without perception. In simple terms, perception means perceiving, *i.e.,* **giving meaning to the environment around** us. It is perceiving of objects what we are faced with. We can understand the meaning of perception by certain definitions.

Definitions

1. "Perception can be defined as the process of receiving, selecting, organising, interpreting, checking and reacting to sensory stimuli or data." – ***Udai Pareek and others***
2. "A process by which individuals organise and interpret their sensory impressions in order to give meaning to their environment." – ***Stephen P. Robbins***
3. "Perception is an important mediating cognitive process through which persons make interpretations of the stimulus or situation they are forced with." – ***Fred Luthans***
4. "Perception is the process of receiving information about and making sense of our environment. This includes deciding which information to notice as well as how to categorise and interpret it." – ***Steven L. McShane and Marry Ann Von Glow.***
5. "Perception is a sensory experience in which an individual observes a behaviour, a event or condition forms interpretations of the factor observed; develops attitude; and allows the precessed observation to become a factor influencing his or her behaviour." – ***O. Jeff Harris and others***

These definitions give an idea about perception and explain the perception process. Perception means "a sensory experience in which an individual observes an event of condition and forms interpretations of the factors observed".

In general, perception can be defined as relatively enduring change in behaviour brought about as a consequence of experience. Perception determines how the individuals become aware of the information received from the environment. It is a process that involves seeing, receiving, selecting, organising, interpreting, and giving meaning to the environment. The individual doing the perceiving, the objects of events being perceived, and the environment in which perception occurs influences the functioning of the whole process.

Perception varies between individuals and every person perceive differently about the same situation. Whatever the individuals perceive, they assign different meaning for each of their perceptions. Group perception will also influence the perception of an individual.

Thus, the meaning of perception is the awareness of one's surroundings produced by the operation of the senses. It is the way in which the individual sees, organises and interpret objects, events and persons. Individuals organise and interpret or things based on their past experiences and the important values. Employees tend to behave and act on certain things on the basis of their perception.

There is a famous note by H.M. Tomlinson "We see things not as they are, but as we are". Psychologists consider "perception" as how our brains organise and interpret sensory information and govern our behaviour which is largely a passive and inevitable response to stimuli. But cognitive scientists, however explain perception as an active process in which the brain treats external stmuli as raw material to be shaped and aided by our experience. Therefore, perception will not occur to our brain as it is but emerge as we understand.

NEED

As managers, one need to know which category of information to be received, which information to notice or give importance, etc. One needs to know how can he/she categorise the information, and how to interpret the information the knowledge available with the individual. Our personality influences our perception of others and most of other OB processes. Therefore, there is a great need to understand the concept of perception and the perceptual mechanism.

Need to perceive generally act as the internal factor of an individual. The need to understand the objects, why they are existing, why people are behaving in such a way, etc. Perception is basically a process of receiving information about and making a sense of the world around us. It is a very important process as it helps in understanding, predicting and controlling the behaviour of the individuals.

PERCEPTUAL PROCESS

The perceptual process involves receiving, selecting, organising, interpreting, checking and reacting to stimuli. It is like an "input, throughput and output" process. The *stimuli or the instinct* can be considered as input, *i.e.,* the *selection, organisation and interpretation* as throughput and the ultimate behaviour or response as output. This whole perceptual process is represented in the figure 17.1.

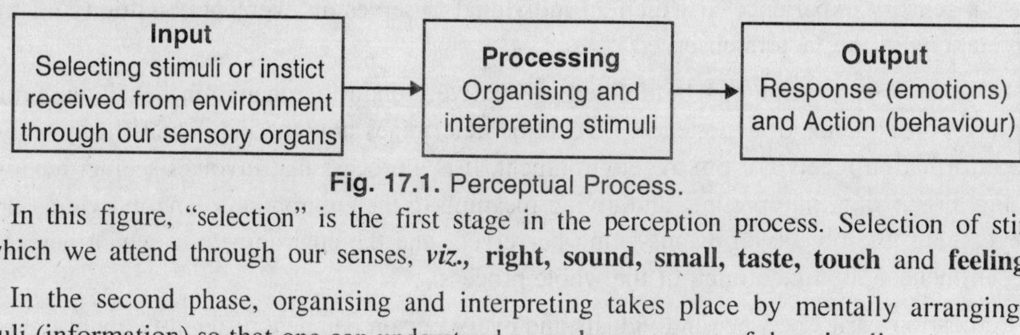

Fig. 17.1. Perceptual Process.

In this figure, "selection" is the first stage in the perception process. Selection of stimuli to which we attend through our senses, *viz.,* **right, sound, small, taste, touch** and **feeling.**

In the second phase, organising and interpreting takes place by mentally arranging the stimuli (information) so that one can understand or make sense out of the stimuli.

In the third phase, response and action by attaching meaning to it. This outcome in the form of emotion and behaviour is subjective and is based on our values, needs, beliefs experiences expectations, involument, self-concept and other personal factors.

These three phases are explained in detail in the following paragraphs:

(a) Receiving stimuli— The perception process starts with the reception of stimulus. Stimuli are things that evoke activity in living beings. The stimuli are received from various sources. Through our sensory organs, we **see, hear, smell, taste feel and touch** things. In this way, the reception of stimuli is a physiological aspect of perception process. Stimuli may be external to us (such as light waves or sound waves) or internal (such as energy generation by muscles). The resulting perception generally influences our emotions and behaviour.

(b) Selection of stimuli – Individuals in their everyday life are bombarded by various stimuli. They cannot assimilate all what they observe or receive from the environment at a time. Hence they select some stimuli for further processing and attach meanings to them. Generally, selection of stimuli depends upon two factors, **internal factors** and **external factors.** While the external factors relate to the intensity of stimuli, its size, movement, repetition familiarity, etc., internal ones relate to the perceiver's age, learning ability, interest etc. Explanations of the internal and external factors are described below for detailed understanding.

(i) External Factors – Larger objects are more likely to be seen than those that are smaller. For example, colourful full-page or half-page advertisements in the newspaper. It is an attempt of the advertiser to draw the attention of potential consumers towards the offer and message of the organisation.

Objects of higher intensity are more visible and therefore more likely to be perceived. For example, bold words on a typeset page stand out, as do backlit billboards. Objects that do not fit with their surroundings or are unexpected are in contrast to their surroundings and therefore more likely to be noticed. Familiarity can help make perception easier. We see easily what we know. Source credibility also affects what is perceived. A source low in credibility is not visible and disturbs our perception.

Fig. 17.2 Figure-Ground Perception Subjective Contours

(ii) Internal Factors – An individual's personality, learning ability, and motivation will influence the perceiver's selection of environmental stimuli. For example, an employee with a strong need for affiliation (the need to be with others) will hear that part of speech of his president's address that focuses on teamwork and how to build strong interpersonal relationship.

Whereas an employee who wants to be a high achiever in his professional life would hear that part which helps him in achieving goals. Therefore employee's internal behavioural factors also influence his perception.

This is a famous picture. What does it look like to you?

Fig. 17.3. A Young Lady or an Old Women?

Some people see a young lady looking away. Others see an old lady looking down. Depending on how you look at it, part of the picture might be the young woman's nose and eyelash, or it might be a wart on the old woman's nose. What is the young woman's ear might be the old woman's eye. What is the young woman's necklace might be the old woman's mouth. The picture hasn't really changed. You just emphasize different parts of it and assign them different meaning.

Look at these two arrows. Which horizontal line is longest?

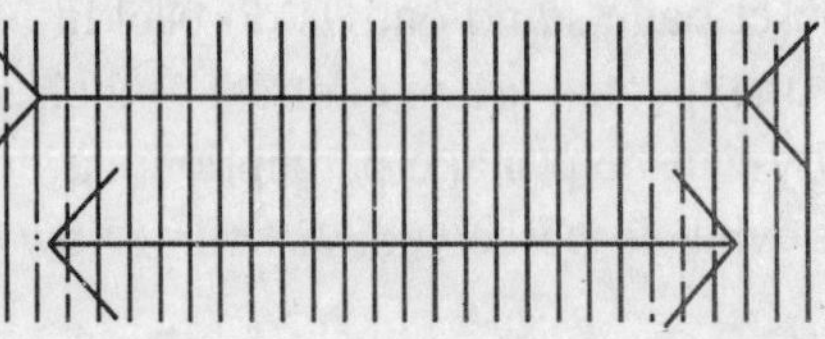

Fig. 17.4. Lines of Different Length?

They are exactly the same size. However, the top one looks longer than the bottom one. It is an optical illusion tricking us into assigning a different meaning to what we see.

We fill in a lot of blanks with our minds. If we have incomplete perceptions, which we practically always do to a certain extent, our minds fill in the rest.

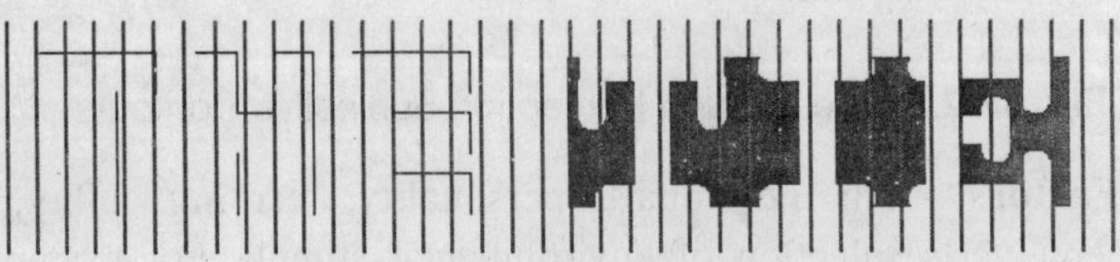

Fig. 17.5. Line or Letters?

Are those letters? Or, are they just lines and blotches on the paper?

The meaning of things or events change when we look at it differently. We can look at anything differently and it will have a different meaning. There is no fixed meaning to anything. We can always change perspectives and change meanings.

(c) Organization of stimuli – After selecting the stimuli, they need to be organized in some form to assign meanings to them. Thus, organizing the bits of information into a meaningful whole is called 'organization'. Generally, there are three ways by which the selected data or the inputs are organized.

(i) **Grouping** – Grouping is based on the similarity or proximity of various stimuli perceived. For example, all the workers having similarity in certain aspects may be perceived to have similar opinion on the basis of proximity. Another that could be cited is if there are twelve oranges and two apples in a basket and if any individual asks for "what are those in the basket?" we tend to answer as "they are oranges or they are fruits " instead of identifying them as twelve oranges and two apples.

(ii) **Closure** – When people face with incomplete information, they tend to fill the gaps themselves to make it more meaningful. They may do it on the basis of their experience, hunches, guess or past data. For example, if there is a phrase with one or two missing alphabetic letters, we tend to complete the phrase with certain message. This is known as closure. Another example cited is also given in Figure.17.6.

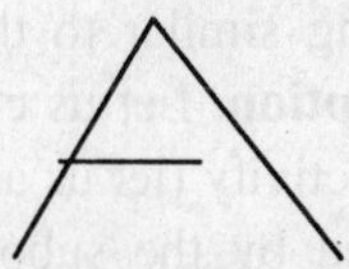

Fig. 17.6. Closure Principle

(iii) **Simplification:** When people find themselves overloaded with information, they try to simplify it to make more meaningful and understandable. In this process, less salient information is subtracted and concentration is given to important data alone.

(iv) **Size Constancy:** Size constancy refers to the fact that our perceptions of the size of objects are relatively constant despite the fact that the size of objects on the retina varies greatly with distance. Assume that there are some pages that show some demonstrations of the power of size constancy. For example, consider that there is a photograph where people are found moving here and there. Look at the photo with great attention. You will find the individuals in the photo are scattered. Especially compare the near and far people in the photograph. They are all of the same size and height, but they might look as small and big. This is called as Size Constancy.

(d) Interpretation – The data collected and organized remain meaningless to the perceiver till meanings are assigned to them. Assigning meanings to data is called 'interpretation'. Thus, interpretation of data forms one of the most important elements in the entire perceptual process. Several factors influence interpretation in organizations. The most important ones are halo effect, attribution, stereotyping, personality, situation, person perceived, i.e., the perceiver.

OUCHI APPARENT MOTION ILLUSION

If you look at the left (black/white) pattern you will probably notice that the vertical pattern in the center appears to move relative to the horizontal pattern in the surround.

Fig. 17.7. Pattern Principle

This diagram was adapted from a design presented by a Japanese artist whose name is Ouchi. If you see relative motion on the right pattern than you can conclude that the illusion also works with color patterns. Perhaps not. It might be that if the luminance of the red and green rectangles were equal then the illusion might not be as strong or perhaps would even disappear.

PERCEPTUAL MECHANISM

The perceptual process is something similar to the perceptual mechanism and it is also discussed **as one of the errors of perception**. Let us consider an example of two employees a supervisor and a subordinate. The work activity (let us assume as a report to be submitted) given by the supervisor may not be completed by the subordinate on time and when the time of submitting nears, the subordinate blames his co-workers for not completing the task (report). He blames for the failure and negligence of his duty on others thinking that his co-workers may not cooperate with him as he does not have good rapport with his subordinates.

Let us understand in detail about the employee's perception from Box 17.1. with respect to employee's compensation.

Box 17.1: Employees' Perception

Compensation is widely acknowledged as an important job composition in the eyes of employees. Health care is a special industry in which compensation among employees differs greatly. The difference in compensation has impact on employees' perception of job equity that may influence the work attitude and the quality of care provided. One study aimed to examine the relationship between hospital employees' perception of compensation equity and their work attitudes. The study also examined the factors that are related to employees' perception of compensation equity and work attitude.

The study of population included 137 regional and higher levels of teaching hospitals in Taiwan. A letter of consent was sent to each hospital asking for participation in the study. The study was conducted at the participating hospitals, where physicians, nurses, pharmacists, medical technicians, and administrative staff were randomly selected. 2,938 individuals from 30 hospitals were included in the sample. The results indicated that hospital employees' perception of compensation equity varies significantly by personal characteristics such as age, and total years of employment. Employees' work attitude differs by age, education and specialty. The design of the compensation system also has effect on employees' perception of compensation equity. Controlling for personal characteristics, and the design of the compensation system, employee' work attitudes were found significantly positively related to their perception of compensation equity.

FACTORS INFLUENCING PERCEPTION

Every individual in some way or the other interacts with other individuals in order to establish relationships with other individuals. This is because of the dependent nature of the individuals. Knowledge of the social behaviour is developed among individuals who are constantly involving in judging others, identifying individual's need and identification of their thoughts and feelings. As per research there are many factors that are identified as influencing perception. Only *three* major factors are considered here.

1. Factors related to the Perceiver

First, let us take the person who perceives the objects, events and environment. The individual factors like the learning process, motivational level and the interest shown to the target act as primary indicators in affecting the perception. The secondary factors are the inner needs and drives of the individual and these constitute the personal factors of an individual.

2. Factors related to the Person/Object/Situation Perceived

Person depends on the cultural background, his/her gestures, how he /she interacts with others, the facial expressions, their voice and appearance matters a lot in the process of perceiving the person/object/the situation is the target here. For the objects, it depends on the colour, size and shape matters and for the situation it depends on the environment in which one could infer.

3. Factors related to the Environment

Environment refers to the social and physical work setting. Some might develop a different perception about a girl who is introvert in the class and who argues loudly with a guy in the supermarket? This is the situation. Individuals tend to make judgements regarding others based on situational factors. Now in the above case the perception of the person who had watched the scene for the first time would be that the girl is assertive. This is due to the current situational factors.

Thus, a person's perception depends on three factors, on the individual himself/herself, the target, *i.e.,* the person or object and the environment in which the events happen.

PERCEPTION MODELS/THEORIES

Basically, perception models/theories can be of two types:

(1) Self-perception model or theory

(2) Perception about others.

In self-perception models/theories, following classifications are observed:

1. Self-esteem or Self-concept Model/Theory.
2. Environmental Reaction Model.
   (a) Positive reaction

(b) Negative reaction

3. Transactional Analysis Model.
4. Mental Storing Approach.

1. Self-esteem Theory

Self-esteem is the outcome of self-perception. It is all an attitude of approval or disapproval an indication of the extent to which the individual believes self to be capable, sufficient and worthy." This statement (of Stanely Coopersmith, a thinker on human psychology of the USA) while writing on the "Antecedents of Self-esteem" tells that self-esteem is an attitude which may be approved or disapproved. But individual thinks that one is capable, worthy and enough to do any work. This is positive understanding one's own self.

When an individual accomplishes something good, one feels happy about such accomplishment and it may be called positive self-esteem. One feels that it is achieved through personal skill and ones own effort. Such positive feeling can give way for good behaviour and develop positive attitude. This will be an incident and consequence of self-esteem.

Therefore, this theory states that the positive self-esteem that emerges out of self-perception enables the people to govern themselves and they need be motivated by others (Employer in case of organisations) to work. People with high self-esteem, utilise the services of their team member without any inhibition and consider it as help. In turn, they are willing to help others in times of necessity. These people identify the help and support extended to them by others and suitably repay or reward them.

On the other hand, low or negative self-esteem persons will be inefficient in their work, do not govern themselves and try to follow others instructions to complete the task, easily exploited and have less confidence and less or no initiative.

Thus, this theory of self-esteem of self-perception considers both high and low of "self" concept of perception and exhibits attitudes and behaviours of both situations, *viz.*, positive and negative. The theory focuses on **"self"** and tells how internal reactions will help or otherwise in a given situations, *i.e.,* about self-perception and resultant behaviour.

2. Environmental Reaction Theory

This theory explains about external and internal influences on perception.

(i) External Environment Theory: This model focuses on individual perception and its interaction with his/her external environment. Interaction may be positive or negative.

(a) Positive Reaction: If positive interaction occurs, the individual (worker in an organisational context) succeeds. This person will be useful to the organisation, his/her, capabilities will be well utilised for organisational success and becomes a recognised person in organisational activities. He/she will be honest dignified, hard-working, sincere to one's duties and meets whatever challenge he/she faces. Thus, if the persons "self" contact with environment is positive following behaviour emerges.

- Individual's reaction with environment is good.
- Perception of self results in success.

- Acceptable attitude of self and towards others occurs.
- Behaviour will be positive.
- Person will be capable of resolving critical situations.
- Possesses innovation and creativity due to positive thinking.
- Has a high degree of empathy and welcomes his team member's opionions and suggestions to solve the problems that may shoot up.

(b) Negative Reaction: If a person has negative interaction towards his surrounding (environment) it will result in the failure of self esteem. Such person feels that he/she is insecured, incapable, unrecognised in a given environment. Low self-esteem persons may turn as: (i) angry people with belligerent attitude and behaviour or (ii) disappear from the given environment in dispair.

They will be under trauma and possess a disturbed behaviour. They may also develop self-pity and feel that they will be rejected. If they are penalised for their wrong doings, they donot take it as a challenge to improve themselves.

Negative reaction of self-esteem results in the following pattern:

- Persons feel that they are a failure.
- They reject themselves or by environment in which they work and develop self-pity.
- These persons are not identified with positive thinking people.
- The attitude and behaviour will be belligrent, aggressive, withdrawal neurotic or psychotic or end in dispair.

  "Johari window" concept and "I am OK, you are OK" model in this context will help us to understand the behaviour and attitude of an individual.

(i) Johari Window: Self-esteem of perception, as analysed so far may be positive or negative. To assess ourselves about our attitude and behaviour, JOHARI WINDOW concept may be adopted. This was developed by Joseph Luft and Harry Ingram. **"JO"** of Joseph and HARRY of Harry Ingram are taken together as "Johari" and as it contains four panes they are together called window. Thus, the concept of "**Johari Window**" was developed to understand more about self-perception of an individual which is very relevant to the organisational functioning. This is a tool which facilitates understanding perception of a person.

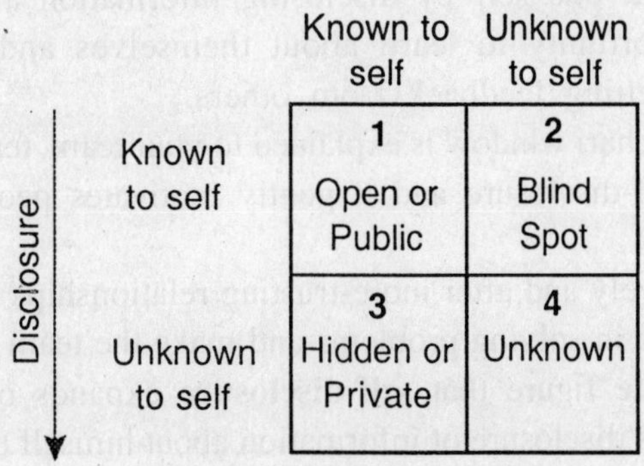

Fig. 17.8. Johari Window

[***Source:*** Joseph Luft, Group Process: Introduction to Group Dynamics, Second Edition (Polo Alto, CA - 1984]

Johari Window concept says that there are four cells/panes in self-perception window, each cell/pane depicting a type of attitude and behaviour. With this window, a person's self-perception can be measured observe the figure 17.8.

Johari Window is a communication model, which analyses perception. It can be adopted to improve understanding between individuals with in a team or in a group setting. JW is a four-square grid. In this grid/window, four compartments/panes are found.

The first pane is an open/public area which tells as to what is known by the person himself/herself as well as by others. For example, you love neat work and professionalism in operation which is known to you as well as your team members. When it is known to others, it is an open or public matter.

The second pane is depicting "Blind" spot which means that an individual does not know about his/her ownself, but others will be knowing. The person is blind about one's own self. For example, an individual is very slow at work or incompetent to discharge a task or unworthy of holding a position. This is not understood by the person himself or herself. But his fellow workers know about it.

The third pane indicates the hidden or private spot. It tells about what the person knows about him/herself that others don not know. Suppose a manager visualises that the market for his company's product slows down in ensuing six months and takes appropriate production decision by scaling down the production. Others concerned with production do not know as to why the production is slowed down. This is a hidden decision, (which others do not know) taken by manager to play safe.

The fourth pane tells that both self and others donot know about one's own self. What is unknown by the person about him/herself and is also unknown by others. For example, a manager for the sake of personal convenience makes some charges in looking hours. Fellow workers also do not seriously take this change. But, it brings amazing result in work culture of the organisation and huge money is saved by this change. This positive occurance is not known either to the manager or to the fellow workers. But a good thing has occured.

Johari window as a tool of understanding self-perception, provides the following:

1. It develops trust about one self by disclosing information about self.
2. It also provides opportunity to learn about themselves and come to terms with personal issues by getting feedback from others.
3. When the concept of Johari window is explained to your team, team member understand the importance of self-disclosure and it gently motivates people to get and accept feedback.
4. If it is adopted sensitively and after more-trusting relationships between members will develop. This will help in solving problems and make the team to work effectively.
5. It is observed from the figure that **self-disclosure** expands open area vertically to hidden area by sender's disclosure of information about himself to the group. **Feedback** process expands this horizontally to blind spot. Here, the individual learns things about him/herself that others can see but the person himself cannot. This indicates

that healthy self-disclosure and sensitive feedback from team members can build a stronger and more effective team.

6. Johari window provides a base to recognise and understand more about our perception. This helps to understand our public and private domains and facilitates to develop positive perceptions which leads to constructive performance. Our negative perceptions can be avoided.

   Thus, JW is a tool to understand and discover individual's perceptions for themselves. From this, we also understand the first pane of the window – "known to self and known to others" – is the acceptable pane for self-perception.

It can be adopted in different ways for self-learning and development. Although, it has several uses, adaptation depends on what we want to achieve. This tool (JW) helps to improve a person's in-depth understanding. It shows the way to optimise the value of people and empowers people to use their thinking in their own way and to incorporate the underlying principles into their future thinking and behaviour. Team members and leaders should always strive to increase their open free areas and reduce their blind, hidden and unknown areas.

The whole analysis is focused on perception of an individual with the self and external environment.

3. Transactional Analysis Model

TA theory was developed as a behavioural theory by Eric Berne in 1955 focusing on the improvement of communication. This theory has roots in **perception.** Individual perception governs behaviour of that person. This theory has undergone several modifications. Several psychologists and researchers have added new concepts to this original theory. New model was published in 2009. Further research is still continued.

The sum and substance of the theory is as follows:

(a) TA exhibits a contractual obligation between two individuals when they speak face-to-face and when the three ego states of an individual (explained in (b) below) have an internal dialogue between themselves which goes unnoticed many a time.

(b) Every individual has three "Ego States," *viz.,* (i) Parent, (ii) Adult and (iii) Child and these three states have their own characteristics.

Parent ego state has the feature of 'advisory' and dictatorial nature. Example: "I am ordering, you follow it" or "Do not do wrong things" etc. It behaves as if the elders behave in normal course. It is a combination of perception or thought, feelings and behaviour acquired from parents or parent's figures. It is a "thought" concept of life.

Adult ego state has the character of perceiving the thoughts and feelings of ours and decide the action ourselves. It is **"thought"** concept of our life. This state of an individual takes best from the past and use it appropriately in the present to **integrate** the positive aspects of both parents and child ego states of this person. "Integrate" here refers to the continuous updating of oneself through one's everyday experiences and using it to inform the person. Whenever clash takes place between parent and child states, adult state resolves it.

For example, the parent ego tells though internal dialogue the child ego state that "you are repeatedly doing wrong things and you are useless". Child ego state reacts to this saying "I am useless because I am not given any right thing by you". This clash will be resolved by the intervention of adult state. Thus, adult state acts as a balancing factor.

Child ego state has the feature of physical movements and verbal expressions.

In terms of physical movements, body movements will be exhibited by sad expressions, despair, whinning voice, rolling eyes, shrugging shoulders, teasing, delight, laughter, raising hand, to speak, speaking behind hand, temper tantrums and such other similar body expressions.

Verbal expression of this state takes by the words such as baby talk, I wish, I don't care, I want oh no, not again, things never go right for me, worst day of my life and many superlative expressions such as biggest, best, etc. These verbal expressions indicate the child ego state of any person.

(c) These two aspects of TA, *viz.,* (i) contractual obligation and (ii) three ego states of an individual are the outcome of self-perception of an individual. TA further states that the perception and feelings of an individual will be converted into behaviour which may be positive or negative. The three ego states of an individual are deciding aspects of pattern of behaviour of an individual.

Transactional Analysis is a very wide topic covering many issues of individual behaviour. Our concern here is, how TA facilitates the understanding of self-perception concept. As already stated, self-perception determines behaviour. TA is accepted as rich dynamic process of self-perception and understanding others. Today, TA is used in organisations, besides in other settings, as a tool of understanding the perceptions of employees through their attitude and behaviour and to know the impact of individual behaviour on fellow workers. This theory states that: (i) people can change by changing their perceptions and (ii) everyone has the right to be in this world and be accepted. Understanding self and self-perception is facilitated by TA theory.

4. Mental Storing Approach/Mental Model

Researches reveal that our perceptions also emerge out of post events recorded in our mind. Every individual looks at the world or perceives his/her environment from the angle of information already stored in his/her mind. We use the stored information in a meaningful way to perceive a thing. For example, when we work in organisations, we will have stored the organisation structure in our mind. We know the levels of authority that is in practice, who is the top boss, his/her mental make-up, who is my immediate authority and how he/she manages us, the type of co-ordination that exists between different departments in the organisation, etc. All these are fixed in our mind. Mental image is already formed about the functioning of our organisation. Our perception emerges from this mental image that guides us to work effectively in the organisation.

The mental model, provides huge information to select suiting to a particular situation which will be mentally processed and used to take an appropriate decision. Storming of our past experiences in our mind is a source of self-perception. The stored knowledge provides different scenarios to perceive an idea to implement. The mental image will help us to observe quickly any deviations that have taken from normal practices. In our example of organisation structure if an employee behaves like a boss, our mental image quickly identifies such discrepancy and demands correction of such deviations.

The mental storing theory of perception will definitely provide us lot of information to know our surroundings. But the limitation of this theory is that it may make us to ignore other equally powerful or better perspectives of the world when surroundings change. Innumerable such situations occur in our life leading to change our stored information. For instance, the introduction of cell phones (mobile) which has stormed the country and created a revolution in communication sector of our country, has pushed back the land line. We had a strong and respectful mental image of wired telephone system (landline) which was automatically passing the information. But today landline is only useful for availing internet facility. In this changed scenario, the mental image about landline becomes obsolete. Thus, the mental models will have to be changed according to our new experiences we have regarding various activities we take up in our life.

Changing mental models as per new experiences is not an ordinary task. We should be continuously storing in our mind the new experiences. With this change, the assumptions we adopt in decision-making will have to be changed to have better perception. Our creative power can assist the process of change to develop new mental models. We can also hire external experts to develop new models to have better perception.

These four models/theories give different dimensions of self-perception. Self-esteem model states the high and low of self which may be positive or negative. External environment theory exposes two aspects, *viz.,* (i) self perception and (ii) perception about environment. TA is also focused on self-perception and exhibits the way in which behaviour of an individual is governed by self-perception. Mental model is also self-perception theory that focuses on understanding are 'self' through our past experiences. Our past experiences are stored in our mind and at times comes out spontaneously which provide a base to take decisions. Mental model/theory is about understanding **self-perception** by digging past experiences stored in our mind.

However, an individual, not only understands one's own self through his/her perception, but also utilises such perceptions to interact with his society and environment. A person cannot live as a saint in a cave. He/she cannot live in an isolated manner, as he/she is a social being. Individuals always associate and identify themselves with the society. In this context, "Social Identity Theory of Perception" was developed. Our perceptions and perceptions of others will be interchanged in a social set-up. In this context, Social Identity Theory is analysed.

Social Identity Theory

This theory of perception is the outcome of several researches made by many experts (Social Identity and Intergroup Relations — H. Tajfel, Cambridge University Press, 1982; Social Identity Theory and Organisation, B.E. Asforth and F. Meol, Academy of Management Review 1989).

This theory explains perceptual process of self-perception and social perception. The concept of self-perception has been explained in previous paragraphs.

Social perception tells as to what we perceive about others and what others perceive about us when we interact with each other. A person, as he/she is a social being live in isolation. He/She is a gregarious animal. Hence, it is inevitable that every individual has to interact with other associates in different settings. In the process of interaction, every individual "develops identity of self and identity with others. Identity with others is called "Social Identity."

Social Identity theory states that "Every individual, through identity of self and social identity, will develop self-perception".

There are three concepts to be understood in this theory: (i) Self or personal identity, (ii) Social identity and (iii) Self-perception.

Self or personal identity can be recognised with different physical characteristic features such as personality traits, unique achievements and physical appearance. For example: the great personality and living legend of Cricket, Sachin Tendulkar. Physically, he is identified as 'Little Master." By personality traits, he is recognised as a cool and humble human being. He is recognised as a top cricketer of the world through his achievement (over 90 centuries, crossing 17,000 runs in ODI, and 13,000 runs in tests). This is an unusual achievement which distinguishes from others in Cricket World. In this manner, every individual with ones characteristic features distinguishes and identities oneself from others. Personal identity gives way for self-perception.

Social identity tells about our belongingness to the society. Exhibiting our belongingness to others through our interactions, we understand them and perceive their behaviour. The interaction we have with others will provide the information to know them. Social identity, therefore, is our self-perception about others when we interact with them. The persons with whom we interact may be our family member or our fellow workers in the organisation. We work as the member of the society in different situations. When we interact with them, we develop our perception of those persons.

Suppose, we interact with a Finance Manager of leading company, who has a management degree from IIM-Ahmedabad, and hails from Karnataka-India. Our self-perception of this person is that he is an Indian, graduated from reputed Business school of the world and he is very intelligent. The perception that "he is intelligent" comes from the fact that he is rolled out as a graduate from the reputed Business School.

Social identity with others is derived from interactions with others becoming member through this theory, we not only have self-perception but also how we recognise and perceive the persons we contact or with whom we interact. This theory also tells us as to how we classify the social groups as **'homogeneous'** or **'heterogeneous'**. This makes us to compare ourselves and perceive to which group we belong to. For example, "I am a management student." This makes me to identify with management subject and with that group of students. The comparative process takes place through our-self perceptions and having perceptions about others, which we get, through interactions with them.

The comparative analysis will have its impact on our perception. We develop a positive perception about homogeneous groups because it has identification with our self-perception and self-image. We also develop positive perception and image of lesser degree with heterogenous groups. This lesser degree perception or image may cause conflict with that groups.

Thus, social identify theory, in an organisational setting, helps to understand our perceptions and perceptions of others, with whom we interact as members of social groups. This will help us to participate in various types of activities. Particularly, in an organisational setting, the theory, provides a base to understand ourselves the wonderful contribution we make to the organisational success. On the other hand, it will also help us to identify the causes of conflicts that may emerge. These causes can provide the solutions to resolve the conflicts . The theory also helps in formulating policies and programmes of an organisation and reformulate them as a corrective measure based on feedback.

Interpersonal Perception

Interpersonal perception is an essential aspect of Social Identity theory. This will tell us the understanding and interpretation process of perceptions of two individuals, *viz.*, self and other member with whom we interact. The other member may be independent individual or belong to a social group of which we may or may not be members. The understanding and interpretation between two individuals will take palce in the following ways:

- To know and perceive others accurately
- To experience situations from other's point of view
- To develop a positive attitude towards other individuals
- Improve one's own self-esteem and self-concept
- To improve the two-way communication process healthy.
- Last mechanism to be included for effective interpersonal perception is *Information Design*. Information Design is the practice of gathering, filtering, and presenting information in accordance with effective design principles in order to understand — and communicate to others — the essence, the meaning of that information.

The box given below provides a clear picture of how interpersonal perception takes place.

The mobile phone story (assumptions, the risks of modern communications)

Several men were in a golf club locker room.

A mobile phone rings.

"Yes I can talk," says the man answering the call, "You're shopping are you? That's nice."

The listening men smile to each other.

"You want to order those new carpets? Okay.. And they'll include the curtains for an extra five thousand? Sure, why not?"

More smiles among the listeners.

"You want to book that week on Necker Island?.. They're holding the price at twenty-two thousand? Sounds a bargain.. You want a fortnight?.. If that's what you want honey, okay by me."

Smiles turn to expressions of mild envy.

"And you want to give the builder the go-ahead for the new conservatory? Seventy-five thousand if we say yes today? Sounds fair.. sure, that's fine."

The listeners exchange glances of amazement.

"Okay sugar, see you later.. Yes, love you too," says the man, ending the call.

He looks at the other men and says, "Whose phone is this anyhow?.."

PERCEPTUAL ERRORS

In the process of self-perception and perceiving others, we may deviate from the general principles of perception. This deviation is called "Perceptual Errors". Generally, following types of deviations (errors) are found in the process of perception.

1. Halo Effect

This is the general error made by most of the managers. They draw a general impression about an individual based on a single trait. For example, if a manager considers that an employee has good skills in analysing a problem, he comes to a conclusion that he can also solve the problem. But solving the problem involves the choosing of the alternatives followed by the decision-making process in which the employee may not be proficient.

The halo effect has to do with judging or evaluating a person, place, or event by a single trait or experience. This overall impression can be good or bad but will prejudice our further involvement with the stimulus. Each of us can remember making a snap judgement about someone based on a first impression. Often, we try to perceive further interaction with the individual based on this first impression, regardless of whether it was positive or negative. If this impression is incorrect, it often takes considerable pressure to concede this fact and break the halo effect.

The halo effect often shows up most conspicuously on performance appraisals where the overall good or bad opinion of the workers interferes with the ability to evaluate weaknesses or strengths accurately on individual job functions.

2. Selective Perception

Normally, people selectively perceive objects or things that interest to them most in a particular situation and avoid others. This is also called 'selective perception' or 'selective attention'. For example, an employee working in the production department, may be concentrating to the skill/work which he is doing and may ignore the sound of machine or the conversation of his co-workers. This process of filtering information is called as selective perception. Selective perception is the personal filtering of what we see and hear so as to suit our own needs. Much of this process is psychological and often unconscious. We only hear what we want to hear. In fact, that is quite true. We simply are bombarded with too much stimuli every day. In order to pay equal attention to everything so we pick and choose according to our own needs, concentrate on only required stumuli and ignore others. The stimulus that are perceived to satisfy our needs are called *selective perceptions.*

3. Stereotyping

It is a process in which the individuals are judged based on the group to which they belong. Walter Lippman introduced this process in the year 1922. There is a general notion that "males have high ego", "women are sensitive", and "Japanese are workaholic", etc. These notions are passed through culture to other individuals which may be false notions in some cases. The false perceptions or incorrect perceptions about others may result in prejudice, employment discrimination and harrasment.

Stereotyping is the assignment of traits and characteristics to an individual based on that person's membership in a larger group. Stereotypes exist for age, sex, culture, socio-economic status, the types of jobs that should be held by various groups in the population, as well as a multitude of other factors. Stereotypes are errors because while they may have some basis of accuracy for a group as a whole they do not necessarily apply to any one individual. For example, we generalise that all employees who work in Infosys are happiest people. But it is not true in case of many individual workers.

4. Perceptual Defense

It is the inability to perceive that is threatening to the perceiver. For example, a person performing poorly at work may be unable to see what is obvious to everyone else and may in fact misinterpret or not hear the warnings about job performance made by the manager. A consequence of perceptual defense is that employees that are fired often express shock and maintain that they were never told about this poor performance.

Expectancy Effects

Expectancy effects result when expectations about someone's behaviour, when communicated to that person, actually cause the behaviour that was expected. This is also known as the Self-Fulfilling Prophecy.

Self-Fulfilling Prophecy

Robert Merton, a 20th century sociologist, coined the term of self-fulfilling prophecy. The self-fulfilling prophecy actually predates its name. Early examples of the self-fulfilling prophecy are the Greek myths surrounding Oedipus. Oedipus fulfills the oracle's prophecy that he will kill his father and marry his mother, by striving to avoid the prophecy. This can be called a self-fulfilling prophecy because it is Oedipus' actions that make the prophecy true. **The Pygmalion Effect** — People tend to live up to what's expected of them and they tend to do better when treated as if they are capable of success. These are the lessons of The Pygmalion Effect. Pygmalion first appeared in Greek mythology as a king of Cyprus who carved and then fell in love with a statue of a woman, which Aphrodite brought to life as Galatea. The Pygmalion Effect has come to mean "you get what you expect." If you expect disaster, your expectations may well be met in a kind of "self-fulfilling prophecy," yet another catch-phrase about the pressure of expectations.

Common sense is the knack of seeing things as they are, and doing things as they ought to be done. — *Harriet Beecher Stowe*

The term "self-fulfilling prophecy" was defined by the American sociologist, William Isaac Thomas (1863-1947) in the dictum: 'If men define situations as real, they are real in their consequences.'

Events tend to turnout as one has hypothesised, not because of some great insight but because one behaves in a manner to achieve this outcome. A large body of evidence exists in various areas of psychology supporting the self-fulfilling prophecy.

This concept explains how a belief or expectation, whether correct or not, affects the outcome of a situation or the way a person (or group) will behave. Thus, for example, labelling someone a criminal, and treating that person as such, may foster criminal behaviour in the person who is subjected to the expectation.

The concept of the self-fulfilling prophecy is based on *four basic principles*:

— We form certain expectations of people or events.

— We communicate those expectations with various cues.

— People tend to respond to these cues by adjusting their behaviour to match them.

— The result is that the original expectation becomes true.

This creates a circle of self-fulfilling prophecies, *i.e.,* **High expectations lead to higher performance; low expectations lead to lower performance.**

6. Primacy Effect

'First impression is the best impression.' Errors based on this type of perception are called as primacy effect. It is the tendency of the individuals to make an opinion based on the first impression. When we confront with an individual who is not sociable and soft-spoken, we conclude he is an introvert.

7. Recency Effect

Individuals tend to remember the recent happenings and based on that, come to a conclusion on a particular event. The recent happenings or incidents remain in our short-term memory and it dominates the other incidents when the perception takes place.

8. Projection

This type of error occurs when we identify ourselves with others. We tend to believe that others posses the same characteristics of what we have.

Errors in perception will influence employer and employee to understand the organisation in his/her own way and will influence attitudes of people. Therefore, goals of the organisation should always be made known to employees through proper training methods so that their perception leads toward the goals of the organisation.

PERCEPTION — APPLICATION IN WORKPLACE

The concept of workplace is normally known as an organisation. Organisation implies a structure where host of individuals work together for achieving the set goals for that enterprise. In order to achieve the goals leaders/managers, perceptions in selecting the workers, performance expectation and appraisal of workers, conflict management, employee's effort and of employee's loyalty are the vital aspects to be analysed. Managers try to evaluate how much effort their workers is putting in their jobs. Thus, the perceptions of managers in these vital issues stated above have effects on organisational work processes and practices. Let us briefly look at few of the more obvious application of perception in organisation.

Employment Interview

Interviewers make perceptual judgements that are often inaccurate. Different interviewers try to see different things in the same candidate. One may give a positive feedback and other a negative on the same candidate. Importantly, interviewers initial impression about the candidate often weighs high in selecting a candidate. To say, information elicited early in the interview carries greater weight then those information elicited later. That is why a good candidate is characterised more by absence of unfavourable characteristics then by the presence of favourable characteristics. It is clear that where interview is an important input for selection, the perceptual factors influence the decision to select a candidate.

Performance Appraisal

An effective performance management process sets the foundation for rewarding excellence:

- By linking individual employee work efforts with the organisation's mission and objectives, the employee and the organisation understand how that job contributes to the organisation.
- By focusing attention on setting clear performance expectations (results + actions and behaviours), it helps the employee know what needs to be done to be successful on the job.
- Through the use of objectives, standards, performance dimensions, and other measures it focuses effort. This helps the department get done what needs to be done and provides a solid rationale for eliminating work that is no longer useful.
- By defining job mastery and career development goals as part of the process, it makes it very clear how the current position supports employee growth and the additional opportunities the employee needs to explore.
- Through regular check-in discussions, which include status updates, coaching, and feedback, it promotes flexibility, allowing you and the employee to identify problems early and change the course of a project or work assignment.

For all these above listed processes, there is a higher need for employees to perceive the other individuals, situation and the objects in such a way that brings excellence both in employee's jobs and in ncreasing the revenue for the company.

Assessment of an employee's performance depends on the perception of the evaluator. In practice, an employee's future is closely tied to his/her performance appraisal. Promotions, pay raises and continuation of job are the most obvious and common outcomes of the employee's performance. Performance appraisal is both objective and subjective. It may be objective when performance can easily be quantified. For example, a salesman's performance can be assessed based on targets he or she achieves during a given period of time. However, employee's job is evaluated in the subjective terms. An impressive amount of evidence demonstrates that subjective measures are by definition and judgemental. Judgementally, as discussed earlier, make one's perception more susceptible to distortions. Thus, subjective approach may influence the appraisal outcome.

Performance Expectation

New employees during their selection process acquire a set of expectations both about the organisation and about the job expecting to achieve. In case, there is a big difference between what they expected and what they actually acquired, it results in increased absenteeism and turnover.

Conflict Management

Employee retention, employee engagement and talent management are the buzzwords in the Human Resources Development and Business Community. We as human beings automatically make observations throughout the day. Some of these observations are good and some are bad. These observations are also known as our perception of a person, place, or situation. The perceptions you have of others even overflow into the workplace and can cause conflicts with other co-workers. When people begin to share their thoughts with other co-workers, they open up the door for their co-workers to spread the gossip. This can cause enormous amounts of animosity amongst co-workers. There is also the issue of people getting involved in other workers lives whether its work related or not. They form opinions, make accusations, and cause drama. All of these problems are due to people forming perceptions of others when they shouldn't. Workers should try to avoid idle gossip and concentrate on the tasks at hand.

Employee Effort

In many organisations, the level of an employee's performance is given high importance. Hence, an employee's future in an organisation depends on his/her effort made for achieving the organisational goals.

Work effort is defined as documents filled in by employees as they complete specific aspects of the work requirements phases. These documents reflect what has already been done in order to calculate the real cost of production, comparing it to the originally planned cost. For every work effort, employees, date, start/finish hours, are introduced. Additionally, it is possible to introduce the accidents or any other issues which may have arisen.

However, assessment of an individual's performance is a subjective judgement and thus, susceptible to perceptual distortions and bias also.

Employee Loyalty

While assessing employees, the managers also make another important decision – employee's loyalty to organisation. Like effort, assessment of loyalty is also a subjective judgement susceptible to perceptual distortions and bias. As an example, an employee looking for greener pastures out side the organisation may be labeled as disloyal to the organisation. As a resultant behaviour, the organisation may cut of his future advancement opportunities. The behaviour is the outcome of perception.

SUMMARY

1. Perception plays a key role in directing the behaviour of people in workplaces.
2. Simple meaning of perception is what we sense or understand about a person with or without personal contact or about a thing.
3. The perception may be true or untrue but consequence is true and will be a fact.

4. Behaviour of individuals is the end result of perception.
5. Perceptual process has three phases, *viz.,* (i) Input (the stimuli or instict we have to select from our environment through our sensory organs, (ii) processing the instinct by organising and interpreting and (iii) availing the end result — response and action in the form of emotions and behaviour.
6. Factors influencing perception are: (i) personal factors of the perceiver, (ii) factors related to object or situation perceived and (iii) factors concerned with environment.
7. Many perception theories are developed by psychologists and thinkers. Mainly, these theories are developed about self-perception and our perception of others.
8. Main theories or models are: (i) Self-esteem theory, (ii) Environmental Reaction theory, (iii) Transactional analysis of perception and (iv) Mental storing approach.
9. In the process of analysing self-esteem model, vital sub-models developed are: (i) Johari Window and (ii) "I am OK – you are OK" concept.
10. Transactional Analysis (TA) model which focuses mainly on behaviour tells how perception wanders and balances in three ego states, *viz.*, (i) Parental, (ii) Adult and (iii) Child states.
11. Social Identity Theory of perceptions states the way in which we perceive self and perceive our social groups.
12. Perceptual errors occur when our perceptions deviate from general principles of perception. The types of errors observed are: (i) Halo effect, (ii) Selective perception, (iii) Sterotyping, (iv) perceptual defense, (v) Expectency effects or Self-fulfilling prophecy, (vi) Recency effect, (vii) primacy effect and (viii) projection.
13. Important application of perception in workplace is concerned with, interviews to select workers, performance expectation and appraisal, conflict management, employee's effort, employee's loyalty, etc.

STUDY QUESTIONS

1. Give the meaning of the following:
   (i) Perception, (ii) Perceptual process, (iii) Transactional Analysis, (iv) Perceptual Defecnce, (v) Closure principle, (vi) Primacy effect, (vii) Recency effect, (viii) Halo effect, (ix) Locus of control, (x) Sterotyping and (xi) Perceptual error.
2. Briefly explain the perceptual process.
3. Analyse the importance of perception in workplace.
4. What is perception? Explain the process involved in perception.
5. Explain the vaious factors influencing perception of an individual.
6. Briefly explain the perceptual errors encountered in an organisational setting.
7. Explain the perceptual mechanism of defence.
8. Give an explanatory note on TA as a tool of understanding perception.
9. Explain the Environmental Reaction Theory of Perception.
10. Give a note of perpetual grouping.
11. Briefly explain the importance of perception in a workplace.
12. Match the following to understand the perception process.

Perception	A. Attending to stimuli.
Selection	B. Attaching meaning to information.
Organisation	C. Process by which you view the world around you.
Interpretation	D. Arranging stimuli in a meaningful way.

18

EMOTION

LEARNING OBJECTIVES

After reading this chapter, you should be able to know:

- Emotion – The Concept
- Factors Determining Emotion
- Emotional Intelligence
- Types of Emotions
- Emotional Labour and Organisation

EMOTION — MEANING

Emotion is the perception of any change in the body. Bodily, change may be, glow and smile of happiness, the pounding heart of anxiety, the clenched first of anger, etc. For example: when we see a snake, we are frightened. Here, the fear is the perception of our body arousing itself for the emergency and moving to escape. Thus, body and mind work together and emotion involves both body and mind.

Emotion is energy-in-motion, a way of expressing ourself in life and how one relates to life.

The term emotion covers wide range of phenomenon. The range is denoted by the terms "Emotion" and "Emotional". Commonly experienced emotion occurs suddenly. We suddenly feel happier when we see a thing which soothens our mind. Similarly, we may feel anger when we look at a person or a thing which is most disliked by us. These feelings fill our inner consciousness. This may be called "Reactive emotion" or simply called "emotion".

Emotion is caused by evaluation of events in relation to what we consider as important. It may be our goals, our concerns or our aspirations. They are the states of immediate readiness to act. Emotional state may remain for seconds, minutes or hours in our mind. It depends upon the event that touches our inner mind. When they lost longer, we may call them "Moods".

"Mood," an emotional state, is long lasting emotional phenomena. Cheerfulness, sadness, irritability, etc. persist for a longer time. It may be for hours or days. For example, when we return from a "Resort" spending a fortnight there, we will be totally different persons with elevated mood. Our mind will be cool and is prepared to do any type of job that we wish to do. Similarly, with the disturbing factors in the workstations, the workers get frustrated and the mood will be down. It will have its impact on the productivity of the individual. Thus, mood may be called an emotional phenomena, which may be elevated or cool or depressed. It can be of an uncertain state which is not focusing on any specific activity to happen.

"Sentiment," another emotional phenomena, remains longer. It is long lasting state of emotion that is related to other people. We like a person who works for us or shows interest in our activities. This is a "Seniment," an emotional state which will be exhibiting positive situation in the form of love or affection. It any person working with us, neglects our work and work for meeting his personal needs, we dislike him or distrust him. This is negative sentiment which lasts long. Sentiments form the central bases of a relationship over many days, months or years.

"EMOTION" may be defined as "thoughts (obsessive thought), which have "happened or might happen next." It is an inner urge to readily act as per our feeling or perceived things.

EMOTION — IMPORTANCE

Emotion assists thinking. Whether it is personal life, living with kith and kins in the house, or work with people in workplaces, our emotions, if effectively used, can solve problems and make us to lead a comfortable life.

The importance of emotion lies in combining heart and head (mind) to avail information to act in a rational way. Many a time, emotions become nagging thoughts. They become unwelcome guests in our lives. The information they provide, if neglected, can cause serious problems. Following aspects suggest the importance of emotions.

- Emotions direct us to fix our boundaries. (Boundary here refers to what can one take and what one cannot endure).
- Emotions serve as our inner moral and ethical compass.
  Emotion, if properly directed by inner mind would provide better communication to make us feel better.
- Emotion communicates to us about our needs.
- Emotions create self-awareness and have the capability to unite and connect us.
  Self-awareness is described as to be aware of what one thinks and feel in the present situation.
- Emotions can be the drivers of our inner moral and ethical aspects.

In a business situation, emotion of a businessman plays a crucial role in running the business effectively. Emotion helps in taking business decisions, which may be good or bad in a particular situation. Similarly, for every individual, emotion directs the person to act as one desires. In an organisation, the behaviour of workers is governed by the individual feelings about the work culture adapted in that organisation. Therefore, emotion in the context of organisational behaviour, can be said as a feeling (positive or negative) of the individual worker about work culture or practice adapted in the organisation and how the individual feeling will have its impact on the work he does.

Our emotions were developed by nature over millions of years of evolution. It has resulted in serving us today or a delicate and internal guidance system. When we do not meet our natural needs, we are alerted by our emotions. For example, when we feel lonely, need for connection arises or need for acceptance occurs when we are rejected or need for safety arises when we are affraid.

Our emotions are a source of information to our brains. We take decisions based on our emotions. If an individual's emotions are disconnected from the brain, one cannot take any decision. The reason is simple. Because one does not know, how one feels about one's choices as the information is not fed to the brain. Thus, emotion helps *"Decision-making."*

In an organisational context, when we feel uncomfortable with other worker's behaviour our emotion alerts us. If we believe our emotion and confident enough to express our feelings, we can let the other person know about our uneasiness about his behaviour. This will facilitate us to fix our limits which are necessary to protect our physical and mental health. Thus, emotion fixes **boundary** to our thinking.

Our facial expressions convey wide range of emotions. Emotions act as means of communication. When we are sad, we communicate through our expression that there is need for help. If we are verbally skilled, we will be able to express more of our emotional needs and thereby have a better chance of filling them. If we are effective listners, we better understand the feelings of others and think helping them. Thus, emotion acts as **communication** tool.

Emotion can bring both happiness and unhappiness. When we are happy, we feel contented and fulfilled. This feeling occurs as our needs are met, particularly emotional needs. Although we procure and enjoy whatever we want, but still feel unhappy. Our emotions and our feelings let us know when we are unhappy and when we are happy.

Human emotion has the capacity to bring together all members of the human species. It has the greatest potential of uniting religious, cultural and political beliefs. But religious, cultural and political beliefs have divided us. The emotions of empathy, comparison, co-operation and forgiveness have the potential to unite human beings as a species. What we understand from this is that **"Beliefs divide us and Emotions Unite us."**

In the context of organisational behaviour (OB), certain terms related to emotion, which will have impact on OB, are explained.

1. Emotional Honesty:

Emotional honesty simply refers to the expression of one's true feelings. First of all, we must be emotionally aware to be emotionally honest. Emotional awareness combined with the necesary learning, practice and experience, gives us the ability to accurately identify our feelings.

If we are more emotionally honest with ourselves, we will get to know our **"True Selves"** on a deeper level. This becomes more self-accepting.

If we are emotionally honest with others, it will encourage others to be more emotionally honest. It will also protect us from working against our conscience.

Openly revealing our feelings establishes credibility.

Emotionally honest people express their true feelings freely and spontaneously. Full emotional honesty simplifies life and offers the opportunity to an individual, a rare sense of integrity, closeness and fulfillment.

2. Emotional Abuse

The meaning of **"Abuse"** says that any behaviour that is designed to control another human being through the use of fear, humiliation, intimidation, guilt, coercion, manipulation, etc. Emotional abuse is any kind of abuse that is emotional rather than physical in nature. It can include anything from verbal abuse and constant criticism to more subtle tactics, such as repeated disapproval or even the refusal to ever be pleased.

Emotional abuse is like brain working. It systematically destroys the self-confidence of an individual. The self-worth, trust in one's own perception, and self-concept wears away by emotional abuse. Many people with negative attitude in organisations influence their co-workers by constant berating, and belittling, by intimidation or under the guise of "guidance," "teaching" or "advice". Eventually, the recipient of abuse, loses all sense of self and remnants of personal value.

EA (Emotional abuse) cuts to the very core of a person, creating scars that may be far deeper and more lasting than physical ones. EA slowly eats away the victim's self-esteem until one is incapable of judging the situation realistically. One becomes so beaten down emotionally that the person has to blame oneself for the abuse.

EA victims can become so convinced that they are worthless. They believe that no one else could want them. They stay in abusive situations. They believe that they have nowhere else to go. Their ultimate tear is being all alone.

In any organisational set-up, EA disturbs the work culture to a greater extent. Abusive expectations of the boss such as unreasonable demands on workers and want them to put everything else aside to tend to their needs, demanding spend all free time with boss, subjecting the workers to constant criticism and constantly berating them as they cannot fulfil all this person's needs and various other abuses such as aggressing, constant chaos, denying, dominating, emotional blackmail, invalidation, unpredictible responses, verbal assaults, etc. put the worker's morale down and the organisational activities hamper resulting in low productivity.

In order to avoid the ill-effects of EA, the organisations have to look into the following needs of workers which develop good relationship and improves productivity.

Basic needs to improve relationship:

- The need for goodwill from others.
- The need for emotional support.
- The need to be heard by the other and to be responded to with respect and acceptance.
- The need to have your own view, even if others have a different view.
- The need to have your feelings and experience acknowledged as real.

- The need to receive a sincere apology for any jokes or actions you find offensive.
- The need for clear, honest and informative answers to questions about what affects you.
- The need for freedom from accusation, interrogation and blame.
- The need to live free from criticism and judgement.
- The need to have your work and your interests respected.
- The need for encouragement.
- The need for freedom from emotional and physical threat.
- The need for freedom from angry outburst and rage.
- The need for freedom from labels which devalue you.
- The need to be respectfully asked rather than ordered.
- The need to have your final decisions accepted.
- The need for privacy at times.

These needs when satisfied, improves the work culture of the organisations and creates a congenial atmosphere inside the organisation.

Empathy

Empathy, simply means identifying yourself with another's feelings. It is putting emotionally yourself in the place of another. Understanding the feeling of others is more important in an organisational set-up. As a manager or as a leader, you have to take the team together to increase the overall productivity of the organisation. Every individual has to experience the happenings and then only you feel about it. If you put your finger in a flame, you will understand the intensity of burning. Otherwise, you cannot undersand as to how the burning creates pain. This holds true for both pleasure and pain. If you have to understand the pain or pleasure of others, you have to first experience such thing. Experiencing the feelings ourselves is called **emotion** and understanding others feeling or stepping into the shoes of others and experience their feelings is called **empathy**. Empathy, solves many organisational problems.

EMOTION — TYPES (OBSERVED IN WORKSTATIONS)

Emotion, as we have now understood is a perceived feeling of an individual about a thing that has occured. This may occur due to several things. The kind or type of emotion that the workers may experience are of the following types. They are the core states of emotion: Joy • Love • Fear • Surprise • Soundness • Anger • Guilt • Disgust

These elements which are the types of emotions are briefly analysed.

Joy:

Joy or state of happiness of an individual happens when an individual experiences an event which brings optimism or relief or pride or contentment or cheerfulness. Example: The employee is promoted to next cadre in the organisation brings happiness.

Love:

This is a state of emotion which exhibits a strong feeling of attachment, tenderness, and protectiveness for another person. It is a state of warm regard. A state of tender and lasting attachment or otherwise called fondness. A state of affection. It lasts longer. Example: The boss has love for his employees. This feeling of boss, definitely encourages the employees to work hard and give their best to the organisation in terms of productivity.

But the lust — strong sexual desire is opposed to the concept of love. Lust is also a state of emotion. When you work with the opposite sex in a workstation, you may develop lust which may end up positively or negatively. If it is a hidden desire and not exhibited apparently, it will have impact on the productivity of the individual and ultimately organisation may suffer. If it works positively, the organisation will be benefitted. However, love, affection, lust, are a group of emotions which will have direct bearing on the productivity of the individual.

Fear:

This is a state of our unpleasant, often strong, emotion caused by anticipation or awareness of danger. This state of emotion of an individual in workplaces will cause disturbed situation. If an individual has the fear to place vital issues and discuss with his or her boss, decisions cannot be taken on time and organisation suffers for want of dynamic worker and quick decisions on vital issues. The individual who has got fear complex will also develop inferiority complex and postpone doing important works. The fear complex in a worker is a dangerous emotional element which may create alraming situtation and create anxiety all over the organisation "Alarm" and "Anxiety" are the subcategories of "Fear" which is a type of emotion experienced in workplaces.

Surprise:

It is a state of emotion or feeling caused by an unexpected event. It is a state of astonishment. It is an amazing situation. It maybe an unexpected joyful or painful situation that occurs instantly to an individual. Example: The employee was taken by surprise on the receipt of promotion order. Or employee was taken by surprise on delivery of transfer order. It is a situation of taking an individual by unawares. This emotional elements will have impact on the productivity of the individual.

Sadness:

This is a kind of emotion which exhibits unhappiness. It is a state of deplorable or regrettable situation. A person will be in a pensive, grave, serious or sorrowful state. This state of person will keep away from normal work. Several negative situations occur due to sadness. In a workplace, worker will be disappointed, may neglect his work, undergoes mute suffering, seeks sympathy and so on. Sadness creates a gloomy atmosphere in workplaces and will have a negative impact on productivity of the individual as well as the organisation. A good leader can control such situation by implementing corrective action plans.

Anger:

A strong feeling of displeasure aroused by real or imagined offence or injustice, usually accompanies by the desire to retaliate. It is a state of disgust, torment, irritation, revenge or exasperation or envy. This keeps the individual in a very disturbed situation and move the person to do only unwanted, useless and unproductive work. This state of mind or feeling will motivate the person to take revenge against a person who causes anger.

'How an angry person behaves in an organisational set-up? If the person is a boss or in the managerial level may penalise the fellow worker who has caused anger. This may have impact on worker's behaviour. He may become slow in his work or postpone doing the work which demands urgency. This ultimately reduces productivity of the organisation.

Guilt:

This is a state of mind which makes one feel of being at fault or to blame. It is a situation of a person who understands the fact of having committed a mistake. In an organisational context, the workers or the managers may deviate from the accepted and directed policies of the organisation to perform some task. This may affect work culture of the organisation. But the employee, when realises his fault, may feel guilt and the damage caused to the business. Guilt is a negative emotional state which will affect the productivity and the work culture of the organisation. The feeling for guilt by the employee may further reduce the productivity of the employee.

Other Types

Besides these core type of emotions felt in the organisational context, following types can also be experienced in an organisation.

(i) Primary and Secondary emotions.

(ii) Positive and Negative emotions

(i) Primary and Secondary Emotions

Primary Emotion: This is a term used to express what we feel first, on experiencing a feeling. It is what we feel first. Suppose you are insulted or cheated or pressurised by somebody which is very intense. The first feeling after insulted or cheated is the state of primary emotion.

Secondary Emotion: This state of emotion is what it leads to. In our example when a person is cheated or insulted, it leads to **anger**. The second state of mind is called secondary emotion. Depression is also a state of secondary emotion. It is caused by the primary emotion of loneliness, landing in a hopless situation, misunderstanding, invalidated, unsupported, etc.

Secondary emotions do not help us much, when it comes to identifying our unmet emotional needs. Secondary emotion tells us as to what is our unmet emotional need or about primary emotional need.

(ii) Positive and Negative Emotions

Emotions of an individual can be broadly classified into two categories.

1. Positive Emotion; and
2. Negative Emotion.

1. Positive Emotion:

This is an expression or an attempt to include a thing or happening which makes us happy. PE is taking the whole into consideration. Working to understand more good aspects, talking intensely with fellow beings to know more good things, enjoying by making things better are all states of positive emotion. Positive emotions are fuelled by an underlying desire for enjoyment and unity. "Interest", "Enthusiasm", "Laughter", "Empathy", "Action", "Curiosity", "Joy", etc. are some of the positive emotions which make the individual to work further. The positive emotions are useful as motivation for moving towards what one does want. In an organisational set-up, positive emotion of an employee contributes to the increase in productivity.

2. Negative Emotion:

Negative emotion is a state of mind which expresses our attempt or expression to exclude a certain thing. It strengthens one's own position at the expense of others. The examples of negative emotions are "Apathy", "Grief", "Fear", "Hatred", "Shame", "Blame", "Regret", "Resentment", "Anger", "Hostility", etc. There are many more.

Negative emotions are generated by underlying fear of the unknown, a fear of actions of others and there is need to control them or stop them to avoid being harmed. NEs are useful or motivation for moving away from what one does not want to do. As negative emotion makes the individual stuck at a point, it gives way for further processing to get the state of mind rectified and move towards positive actions. Processing make people to be more fluid and flexible in terms of emotion. In a third state, person will choose to live mostly in a positive state of mind. But the ultimate aim is to move beyond positive or negative emotional state to achieve integration of situation or ideas.

Avoiding NEs:

Negative emotions are disturbing feelings for a person. If one does not come out of this state of mind, suffering will be substantial. It will not only affect that individual but also disturbs the state of mind of co-workers or persons who transact with him or her in such a state of mind. Negative emotions should be immediately controlled to avoid emerging disturbed situation.

The generally accepted principles to avoid NEs are as follows:

- First identify the type of NE or feeling.
- Put a question to your mind whether it is a healthy feeling.
- Ask what would help you feel better (How do I want to feel?)
- The answers you get will show you the way to get out of the situation.
- Adopt the best one of answers in that situation to get out of NE.

Think that you are the Sectional Head in your firm. While examining the files in your office, you observe, in one of the files, a note put up by your subordinate is against your instruction already given at the time of discussing the file contents with him. Immediately you become furious and warrant him to your chamber. As soon he enters, you hold his tie and raise your hand to slap on his face.

At this point of time, you ask yourself as to what you are feeling as you stared at him to slap. The word which came to your mind was "Destructive" or "Harmful". Then you said to yourself **"that it is not a healthy feeling"**. Immediately you remove your hand on the tie and down your other hand which you have raised to slap. Then you take a deep breath, exhale slowly and express you regret for your action.

This is how one can control negative emotion, even in a serious situation.

DETERMINANTS OF EMOTION

The happening or arousal of an emotion depends upon the meaning of the event for the individual. This also analyses why the emotion that occurs depends upon quite subtle aspects of that meaning. Occurance of an emotion is determined by the interactions between events, the individual's conceptions or expectations as to what constitutes well-being for him or her, the individuals expectations that he or she will be able to deal or cope with the event and, if so, in what manner or how effectively.

Emotional Labour (EL)

A lady sociologist and professor of Sociology in the University of California, Arlie Russell Hochschild, defines EL as **"Management of feeling to create a publicly facial and bodily display"**. Based on this explanation, many interpretations are given to this concept. Without going into all the conceptualisations of others, EL may be understood as "managing emotions, so that they are consistent with organisational or occupational **display rules,** (Display rules means the rules of the organisation regarding the kind of emotion to be expressed) regardless of whether they are discrapant with internal feelings." (Grandy AA)

"Emotional labour is a form of emotional regulation, which makes the employees to exhibit certain emotions as part of their job which facilitates the implementation of organisational goals."

The exhibition of such emotions will have required impact on fellow workers, outsiders having business connections with the organisation and other general public.

EL requires the following actions on the part of workers to regulate emotions.

- To produce a specific emotional state which prompts the contact person to express his/her emotion regarding the work to be completed.
- Workers have to exercise required degree of control over the emotional activities.
- Needs contact with person/s in the form face-to-face or voice-to-voice.

These three actions of workers in an organisational set-up, explains the concept of "Emotional Labour". Any organisation — large, medium or small - for that matter have to interact with people and hence people at work should have "people skills". The basic problems faced in any organisation are common in nature. Managers, for example, often struggle to deal with the interpersonal aspects of management. Similarly, doctors, engineers, lawers, etc. struggle to deal with their interpersonal aspects of their professions.

When employees interact with stakeholders or outsiders for providing services, "service" becomes the heart of such interaction. Whether the service is provided through the talk over the phone or at help desk or through **internet** (mailing) or in the office corridor over a conversation, these encounters render service and determine the quality of service. The service rendered by the employee and the service perceived by customers may or may not match. Because these services are driven by emotions of workers that develop at that point of time. That is the **"Moment of Truth"**. The service quality of the employee is determined by the emotional element that the worker had at that time. The dimensions of service quality — assurance, tangibles, empathy, reliability, adaptability, etc. — are influenced by the emotions. They all are required to connect to the customers and emotional labour.

Contacts with customers and other stakeholders of an organisation is an essential aspect of any business. Lack of connection leads to escalation of bad feeling, as the customer and the organisation fail to understand each other. In order to develop good contacts, we must first, listen to the needs of customers. Good listening to the customer needs will make the organisation to focus on the task and develops good relationship.

As with other emotional needs, the need to be heard is a **survival need.** We are all interdependent. In other words, many of our basic needs depend on the co-operation of others. But first we must know and communicate our needs. For example, if we are a passenger in a car and we feel unsafe, we must communicate our feelings. If the driver ignores us, our lives may literally be threatened. If we are not heard, we cannot communicate our needs. It is understandable, then, that we feel frustrated or worse when we do not feel heard.

By developing our own listening skills, we can model them to others. They in turn will become better listeners and feel heard, understood and respected.

Understanding customer's frustration, anger, or anxiety and showing caring in the face of bad customer behaviour, requires particular effort when the organisation might not feel like being nice. This is emotional labour.

Emotional labour (controlling our emotions and adopt emotions said by the organisation) is a common requirement. When we are interacting with people for a business purpose, the other tasks of the employee have to be balanced with expressing sympathy to the outsiders, making them to feel that organisation is supportive to them. If the customer is stressed, upset or feeling negative about the service for whatever reason of the organisation, a problem can become a complaint and complaint leads to criticism. Particularly in service organisations like transport, healthcare (hospitals) hotels, information technology, telecommunication etc., customers are frequently encountered. Negative feelings may surface in employees at the time of conversation. But the workers, in the interest of the organisation, have to control their emotions and they have to be nice to even rude customers. This is the concept of "Emotional labour."

When you control your negative emotion in the interest of the organisation, it is emotional suppression rather than regulation. Pretending to be happy, ignoring our true concise, will be an exhausting situation and approach to emotional behaviour, which leads to long suffering. Therefore, instead of getting exhausted, we have to think of an alternative approach which does not involve pretending. That is changing our own attitude to a situation.

Changing attitude to the situation by challenging and altering our deeper feelings can only develop good relationship. Emotional regulation make us to remain in a good emotional state. The reappraisal of the situation will ease emotional labour. Surface change never helps. Only deep change, *i.e.,* restructuring our thinking based on cognitive issues such as interacting with rude customers to tame them or summarily dismissing the customer's demand or to be defensive with the customer, etc. will be a good cognitive (related) therapy and this avoids the worker being depressed.

Collective EL

Workers, to regulate their emotions to the organisational needs, can seek the assistance of co-workers. Employees can share their experiences and discuss about the positive approach to regulate emotions which cause untoward happenings in the organisation. The whole process of regulating unwanted emotions and develop good emotions collectively is called **"Collective Emotional Labour".** This collective emotional support takes place in informal way. They discuss about rude customers. They also discuss about their own behaviour of losing cool with the customers. This supportive and informal discussion will help the emotional labour (regulating emotions) of the individual worker.

Most of the time, managers cannot tolerate such informal discussions and they try to suppress such informal thinking and discussion. But the action of managers will be ineffective. They cannot stop such discussions about customers and problems.

Coping with the stress and strains of emotional labour in organisations is better done collectively. Coffee breaks, time away from regular work are critical for getting things in proper perspective, to share problems and develop good service culture.

In a way, there is direct connection between the development of service culture and the individual emotions. Good service culture of an individual will not come naturally and is developed and learned. It requires social focus, self-awareness and sensitivity to others.

EL and Organisations

EL, eversince the term was coined, is focussing on the behavioural aspect of the employee, particularly while interacting with outsiders, who visit the organisation for business purposes. The EL is determined by: (i) the principles adopted in an occupation or in an organisation, (ii) dispositional traits (individual and behaviour as a result caused by internal characteristics that reside in the individual) and inner feelings of the job (expression of emotion in terms of gestures, modulated voice and body movement) and (iii) monitoring display rules (types of emotions to be displayed by workers) by immediate boss (line manager or supervisor). EL which is practiced by workers, will always focus on relationship between customers and other stakeholders on the one hand and the organisation on the other. EL facilitates good relationship management, increases productivity and turnover of the organisation.

Whether the organisation is agro-based or manufacturing or the service ones, EL will have impact and definitely increases productivity of the workers which contributes to the overall increase in productivity of the organisation. If positive EL prevails, productivity increases and it decreases, when negative emotions are displayed by workers.

Experiments show that EL may lead to employee's emotional exhaustion and burn out.

Emotional Intelligence — EI

We always work on our emotions. As understood, emotions are stimulated by past events and present environments. Emotion is again a brain function. Hundreds of researches are going on brain. Intelligence, a brain function, has different forms. EI is one form of brain function on which still the research is going on.

The intelligence distinguish gifted people from others in any walk of life. Intelligence varies in degree from one person to another. Intellectual intelligence is a cognitive (related), innate capacity measured by our intelligence quotient — IQ.

Emotional Intelligence is a part of intelligence and is distinct from Intellectual Intelligence. EI and II emerge from different parts of the brain.

Intellect or thinking or otherwise also called cognition, is a function of 3rd brain which is called in medical term **"Cerebral Cortex".** It is the top layer of the brain. It will think, **strategise**, make plans, reflect, inspire and imagine. Emotions work in the 2nd brain which is called **"Amygdala"** (This is an emotional depository in the brain) which, besides storing emotional memories, compares what is familiar with new incoming infomration.

This brief description says that "Intellectual Intelligence — II" is derived from one part of the brain (3rd brain) and EI is the function of another part of the brain (2nd brain). Intelligence Quotient — IQ and Emotional Quotient — EQ emerge from different layers of the brain. It should also be noted that EQ is complementary to IQ, as it concerns the perception and processing of emotions.

Emotional Intelligence — EI, in this backdrop can be understood as the process of identifying and understanding our emotions and adopt them to better, our life and to develop good relationship with people with whom we work or with people with whom we interact in our life.

Many writers have said that EQ and EI are synonyms and some others have distinguished them as separate concepts. Those who distinguish these two concepts describe it as follows:

1. Each individual was born with a certain potential for *emotional sensitivity, emotional memory, emotional processing and emotional learning* ability. These four components are inborn components and are the core of one's "Emotional Intelligence".
2. These four core components change positively or negatively at later stages depending upon the lessons given by the parents, teachers, and family. The impact of these lessons in the initial stages of childhood and adolescence results in Emotion Quotent — EQ.

"EQ represents a relative measure of a person's healthy or unhealthy development of their innate emotional intelligence."

A comprehensive definition of Peter Solovey and Jhon Mayer of EI published in 1990 is as follows:

"Emotional Intelligence is the subset of social intelligence that involves the ability to monitor one's own and other's feelings and emotions, to discriminate among them and to use this to guide one's thinking and actions."

In 1997, they detailed their "four branch model" of EI which focuses on: (i) Appraisal and expression of emotion, (ii) Facilitation of thinking, (iii) Finding and analysing emotions and employing emotional knowledge and (iv) Regulation of emotion to promote emotional and intellectual growth.

With this discussion, EI may be understood by the following three definitions.

1. "Emotional Intelligence is the innate potential to feel, use, communicate, recognise, remember, describe, identify, learn from, manage, understand and explain emotions."

— S. Hein.

2. "Emotional Intelligence is not just the skill, expertise or potential to feel etc., but it has a new yardstick to measure. The new measure takes for granted having enough intellectual ability and technical know-how to do our jobs; it focuses instead on personal qualities such as empathy, adaptability and persuasiveness."

— Daniel Goleman, Working with Emotional Intelligence

Another definition of Daniel Goleman is as follows:

"Emotional Intelligence refers to the capacity for recognising our own feelings and those of others, for motivating ourselves, and for managing emotions well in ourselves and in our relationships."

While the first one tells about the innate potential of an individual about the type of feelings, the other two focus on other aspects of emotions and how best one can adopt these emotions to better his life, considering empathy, adoptability and persuasiveness.

Daniel Goleman's focus is on:

1. Self-awareness (assess our real ability to take decisions).
2. Self-regulation (controlling and handling our emotions to pursue our goals).
3. Motivation (relegating back our setbacks and frustrations and adopt our deepest preferences to achieve our goals).
4. Empathy (understanding the feelings of others and a good support and attunement to help them out in a possible way).
5. Social Skills (developing skills such as undersanding social situations and networks to smoothly persuade, lead and negotiate to settle disputes with object of developing team work).

If these emotional components are high in any individual, will increase his EI and will be a successful person in any walk of life.

EI is an individual's skill of perceiving, understanding and managing emotions. It is seen in what we do and say each day and how we interact with others. Unlike our IQ, our EQ is a fluid skill that can be greatly improved through awareness and commitment to change. The EI appraisal creates these conditions by delivering constructive feedback and effective strategies for improvement.

EI is one of the most important skills we possess. It is more vital for job performance than IQ, experience or technical ability studies across industries show that EQ predicts job performance 2 to 1 over any other skill.

Key Components of EI: (1) Overall EQ, (2) Self-awareness, (3) Self-management, (4) Social awareness and (5) Relationship management.

EI AND ORGANISATION

EI plays a vital role in an organisational context. Many studies are conducted in advanced countries like USA on EI. The studies have shown that EI has enhanced productivity of the organisations. Results also have shown that in companies where EI of workers and top class is at lower level or otherwise called emotional fallout has resulted in "Self-protective cynicism to anger and even despair".

In an organisation, EI involves the ability to distinguish and monitor one's own and others feelings and emotions and with this understanding, one can work on one's own thinking and action. This leads and develops self-confidence. If every one thinks and works on these lines, morale of the entire organisation raises and the organisation becomes a quality one and brand develops.

The components of EI such as awareness of the self, management of the self, social awareness, management of relationship, help the individual to work better in the organisation.

Modern organisations particularly in India, which are becoming flatter, need persons who have **adaptability** (flexible to face challenges and abstracts), **integrity** (reliability that leads to trust), **achievement** (searching for opportunities for the organisation and seize at the appropriate time), **leveraging diversity** (that is converting threat into opportunity), **Persuasive power** (to influence and control others), **Empathy** (understanding the feeling of others connected with the organisation), **political influence and better relationship temperament.**

These emotional intelligence components, help the worker/manager to succeed in the organisation. EI, as said earlier, has two dimentions — positive and negative.

Positive emotions at the workplace are conducive to the better functioning of the organisation and this leads to achieve better productivity. Organisations having workers and managers with positive EI should be retained.

Negative emotional intelligence will be a disturbing factor for achieving the organisational goals. People possessing negative EI in the organisation should be identified and analyse whether they are really negative in their approach and thinking. The confirmed ones should be dispensed with.

The type of organisation in which a worker works also decides the nature of emotional intelligence required for that organisation. In different types of workstations, a person of flexible nature with positive emotions can adjust to the circumstance by recognising the required emotions of the organisation, adjust them to the thought process of the organisation and control and monitor EI as required.

If any person has to succeeed in an organisation, positive EI is a must. Many organisations provide training on continuous basis on emotional components (EI) to their workers and managers. Training on EI involves, preparation, training, application and evaluation. In this process, EI plays a dominant role.

In the early stages of the development of the organisations, relationship management was lacking. Only such organisations that had good leaders than managers were doing very well. In better managed organisations, people at work were allowed to speak out openly and freely whatever they felt. Top management were open-minded and hear all aspects of a problem expressed by the concerned workers from the bottom line. This all means that successful organisations gave prominance to emotional intelligence. Leaders/management would consider all meaningful suggestions of their employees. This again means those who had positive EI would establish good relationship with the people whom they work. This ultimately enhances the productivity of the individual worker as well as the organisation.

The organisations should value the plain truth, whatever bitter it may be. They should allow the workers to speak freely. They should not be punished, retributed or ridiculed. Then only their positive emotions come out and can be analysed and adopted for the good of the organisations. Where the workers are not allowed to speak out their emotions or feelings and if a nightmarish atmosphere prevails, it becomes an emotional salon and unproductive situation prevails in the organisation.

Daniel Goleman in his book "Working with Emotional Intelligence" says, "In too many organisations, the ground rules that marginalise emotional realities guide our attention away from such emotional static as though it did not matter. These blunders propogate endless problems; decisions that demoralise; difficulty in managing creativity and making decisions; ignoring the crucial value of social skill, the inability to motivate, let alone inspire; hallow mission statements and empty slogans of the day; leadership by the book, lacking zest or energy; drudgery instead of spontaneity; a lack of espirit de corps; teams that do not work". These things have happened or will happen, when the top class and workers never acknowledge their emotions with each other. These negative aspects of EI of employees and bosses bring out following disturbing factors which hinder the increasing productivity of the organisation.

- Work overload
- Lack of autonomy
- Meager rewards
- Loss of connections (increased isolation of workers)
- Unfair treatment to workers in organisation
- Value conflicts (means mismatch between the emotions of workers and tasks assigned to them)

Goleman puts these attributes as "organisational malpractices which breed chronic exhaustion, cynicism and a loss of motivation, enthusiasm and productivity". These malpractices emerge out of negative collective emotions.

In order to overcome these disturbing situations, in any type of organisation, EI emerges to the front line as a soothing factor, organisation has to become a "Learning organisation" and resort to "change management" concept by motivating the employees to develop positive emotions. This leads to collaborative learning through emotional awareness, empathy and building relationship. Isolated islands should be smashed. There should be a constant "back-and-forth" activity. Workers should be made to look at a big picture, *i.e.,* the organisation as a whole. The organisation, when perceived by workers as a whole, one can communicate them the collective intelligence the organisation possesses. This collective organisational intelligence which exhausts relationships, culture and roles within the organisation can solve problems, meet challenges, and create brand for the product or service that organisation produces or provides.

Advantages:

Thus, emotionally intelligent organisations will have the following benefits.

- Organisations grow leaps and bounds with good leadership.
- Understanding employees and adopting empathy concept by each and everyone in the workplace leads to overall productivity of the organisation.
- If the management builds an atmosphere of trust, openness and teamwork, the morale of employees will be on a high pitch.
- Employees commit themselves to a basic work culture of the organisation, by and large voluntarily.
- Top management, when they develop open communication and trust-building practices, can to a greater extent, avoid conflicts and crisis and develop integrity in workers which will be the hallmark of any organisation.
- Developing good relationship with employees and other stakeholders and outsiders provides the competitive advantage to the firm.
- EI helps in having collaboration, support and sharing of resources, which in turn smoothens the organisational operations.
- It develops a **passion** for competition and continual improvement, making the organisation a learning organisation (unlearning old things and learn new things). It provides a firm base for change management.

These advantages reflect EI components such as: (i) building working relationship through developing self-confidence, presence, empathy and good listening, (ii) possessing leadership potential having energy, drive, and sense of urgency which provide results and being an innovative entrepreneur and (iii) possessing qualities of a partner, friend and a colleague having honesty, respecting one's values, motivated, having sense of humour and understanding the firm and its values.

Where is EI Required?

In an organisation in which workers work more for meeting their personal ends and work less for the organisation, EI is required. EI is essential to develop good working conditions through relationship for the survival of the workers as well as the organisation. The immediate task of the management at this point of time is to, identity, assess and upgrade the EI of individuals. Training and development, performance evaluation and attractive compensation management are the important tools to be adopted to complete the task.

In an organisation set-up, human factor is as important as non-human factor such as technology. If the human factor is neglected, the organisation becomes weak. In order to take out the best of the workers, the elements of EI should have a priority.

SUMMARY

1. Emotion is "energy-in-motion" a way of expressing oneself and how one relates to life".
2. Many discussions on emotions cover the following aspects.
   - Emotions are typically conscious phenomena. Inspite of this, they typically involve more pervasive bodily manifestations than other conscious states.
   - Emotions vary along number of dimensions such as intensity, type and range of international objects etc.
   - Emotions play an indispensable role in determining the quality of life. But they are reputed to be antagonists of rationality.
   - Emotions define our ends and priorities. They regulate social life effectively.
3. Mood, an emotional state, is a long-lasting phenomena.
4. Sentiment, another emotional phenomena, remains longer.
5. Emotions help to act in a rational manner by combining body and mind. In the context of business, emotion drives the businessman to be positive and rational in his business deals.
6. Emotion acts as a communicating tool. Our body language, particularly facial expressions convey wide range of emotions. It can bring happiness as well as unhappiness.
7. Emotional honesty means expression of one's true feelings. People with emotional honesty express their true feelings freely. In a business context, EH is essential for those who run business on ethical lines.
8. Emotional abuse is any kind of abuse that is emotional rather than physical in nature. EA tries to control another human being through the use of fear, humiliation, intimidation, guilt, coercion, manupulation, etc. EA is a tool to brainwash another individual.
9. Empathy is a concept which makes us to step into the shoes of others and understanding their feelings. Understanding the feelings of others in an organisational set-up and act is essential for its smooth running.
10. Emotion — The perceived feeling of our individual — has many types which are positive or negative in nature.
11. Positive emotion is a state of mind which makes the individual happy and the PE traits are joy, love, etc.
12. Negative emotion brings unhappiness to the individual and the traits are fear, hatredness, anger, guilt, disgust, etc. These emotions are disturbing factors for the growth of the organisation.

STUDY QUESTIONS

1. Give the meaning of "Emotion", write the importance of emotion in an organisational context.
2. What is emotional honesty and emotional abuse? Briefly analyse how emotional abuse disturbs organisational culture.
3. Briefly explain the types of emotions and their impact on organisational behaviour.
4. Analyse positive and negative emotions.
5. Give on explanatory note on emotional labour. How is it helpful in achieving organisational group?
6. What do you mean by Emotional Intelligence? Briefly explain the impact of EI on organisational activities.
7. Briefly explain the views of Daniel Goleman on EI.

19

ATTITUDE

LEARNING OBJECTIVES

After reading this chapter, you should be able to know:

- Attitude – The Concept
- Attitude – Source of Development
- Attitude – Types
- Attitude – Theories
- Changing Attitude
- Work Related Attitude

You think over any event that happens in our life, in our society or the events occur all over the world, "Attitude" steers the course of these events. Our social thinking involves the attitudes that we hold. Attitude is an important form of social thinking. Attitude helps to define who we are, and it affects the way people judge one another. "An **attitude** is a positive or negative evaluative reaction towards a stimulus, such as a person action object, or concept" (Tesser & Shoffer, 1990). For example: When we exhibit a positive or negative attitude towards a statement of our friend or by anybody, we will be displaying an evaluative reaction. Evaluative reaction towards an event is "Attitude" which guides the behaviour of an individual. Behaviour of an individual in an organisational setting is the focal point of this title. Therefore, all aspects of behaviour are discussed in detail. Attitude is one such aspect of behaviour, which helps to define a person's identity, guide his/her actions and influence how they judge people. The discussion of attitude opens with the following box information.

Box 19.1: The Rose Within

Certain man planted a rose and watered it faithfully and before it blossomed, he examined it.

He saw the bud that would soon blossom, but noticed thorns upon the stem and he thought, "How can any beautiful flower come from a plant burdened with so many sharp thorns? Saddened by this thought, he neglected to water the rose, and just before it was ready to bloom... it died.

So it is with many people. Within every soul there is a rose. The God-like qualities planted in us at birth, grow amid the thorns of our faults. Many of us look at ourselves and see only the thorns, the defects. We despair, thinking that nothing good can possibly come from us. We neglect to water the good within us, and eventually it dies. **We never realise our potential. Only if there is a positive attitude about us, then it helps to find our potential.**

Some people do not see the rose within themselves; someone else must show it to them. Some individuals in their life like their professors, parents and friends show them the path to reach and find their inner qualities. One of the greatest gifts a person can possess is to be able to reach past the thorns of another, and find the rose within them. This is one of the characteristic of love... to look at a person, know their true faults and accepting that person into your life... all the while recognizing the nobility in their soul. Help others to realise they can overcome their faults. If we show them the "rose" within themselves, they will conquer their thorns. Only then will they blossom many times over.

Generally, prospects for an individual's good health and long life are remarkably dependent upon mental habits learned in childhood. These attitudes cause emotional reactions, which strongly affect one's immune system, circulatory system and even one's risk of accidents. The medical profession has grossly underestimated the strength of this correlation between attitudes and health. The above box, clearly depicts what type of attitude is expected about an individual and he should walk towards in reaching success.

ATTITUDE — THE CONCEPT

The concept of attitude is a psychological phenomenon. Analysis of this phenomenon took place in the field of social psychology. Interest and growth in this is necessary to identify the factors contributing to the formation of attitudes. In order to understand this concept, one has to clearly understand the VALUE dimensions, what one has to perceive and adapt in one's own life (value dimensions are explained in a separate chapter of this title).

But it is essential to understand value to understand the ATTITUDE. Till 1920s, most of the attitude researcher's attention was in defining and how to measure the attitude. Later, as the concept started gaining importance in the organisation, researchers started taking factors and the opinions of soldiers regarding war, to give a theoretical framework to this concept. Recently, the researchers have come out with various psychological processes accompanying the attitudes and how it affects the workers and its application in the workplace.

Allport, Gordon W. (1897–1967, an American psychologist) was one of the first psychologists to study personality. Allport researched human attitudes, prejudices, and religious beliefs. His theory of personality, which rejected both Freudian psychology and behaviourism, emphasised the uniqueness of the individual and the need to treat problems in terms of present conditions as opposed to childhood experiences. He wrote *Personality* (1937), *The Individual and His Religion* (1950), and *The Nature of Prejudice* (1954). Most of our behaviours are affected by our attitudes. How we perceive the objects, events, what are the beliefs we hold about others, understanding of certain information, etc. are some of the factors that is influenced by attitudes. ***Attitudes are the set or cluster of beliefs towards objects, events and situation.*** They are the basic intentions of individuals. These intentions might be right or wrong. The happiness that we receive from a promotion is called as *emotion*. By framing different emotions, our attitudes are formed.

"Say nothing good of yourself, you will be distrusted; say nothing bad of yourself, you will be taken at your word." — Joseph Roux

Values and Beliefs

"Values and beliefs give a direction to attitude." The foundation of each organisation is the values and beliefs that employees possess. The leaders of each organisation shape the values and beliefs of the employees in the organisation. This value is a force, energy, and fuel for action towards excellence in the accomplishments of the objectives of the organisation. A leader with vision who cannot articulate beliefs and values in the employees is a dreamer, not a leader. The values and beliefs have been the foundation of what our country stands for, and these two factors will continue to play very critical roles in maintaining the strength of our nation.

The great leaders of each organisation impart their own values and beliefs to the organisation they created or directed. As a result, each organisation has its own unique set of values and beliefs which shape the character of the organisation. Some of the common values and beliefs are, belief in the importance of employee as individual, belief in superior service and quality, belief in leaders' good intentions in the decision-making, belief in the sharing ideas and being innovator, and belief in mission of the organisation.

Definitions

Attitudes are generally defined in two different ways – ***conceptual basis and operational basis***. Now let us look at some of the definitions from **conceptual** point of view. Most of the scholars have defined the term attitude in two major dimensions: set and readiness and effect and evaluation. It was Gordon Allport who found that most of the definitions contained the words 'readiness' 'set-otherwise termed as tendency to respond' and 'effect'. Attitudes are derived from the action of stimuli in the environment. The general definitions that were given in the early days were –

"Attitudes are defined as a tendency, set or readiness to respond to some social object."

"Evaluative statements or judgements concerning objects, people, or events."

"Attitude is defined as a mental and neural state of readiness, organised through experience, exerting a directive or dynamic influence upon the individual's response to all objects and situations with which it is related." – ***Gordon Allport***

"Attitude represent the cluster of beliefs, assessed feelings, and behavioural intentions toward an object." – ***P.R. Lawrence***

"Attitudes are learned predispositions towards aspects of our environment. They are positively or negatively directed towards certain people, service or institutions". – ***Munn***

"An attitude is any cognitive representation that summarises our evaluation of an object, which may be the self, other people, things, actions, events, or ideas." – ***Smith & Mackie***

The stories/explanations that have come up with, to account for the world around us are nothing more than attitudes. Evaluating the inherent characteristics of attitudes will allow us to gain insight into new and more useful ways of thinking about persuasion, *i.e.,* "the process by which attitudes are developed, reinforced, or changed by communications", thereby allowing us to further understand why conflicting stories, specifically the stories of creationism vs. evolution, can be perceived as tremendously threatening.

Apart from the conceptualised view, there is an operationalised view of defining attitude. Operationalised in the sense taking only the evaluative part of attitude, and identifying the factors for measuring attitude, and from these points of view definitions were given. From the **operational** point of view, let us read a definition: "Attitude is often used in a generic sense to any reports of what people think or feel or the ways in which they intend to act".

Difference between Attitude and Belief

As beliefs are commonly used with attitudes let us differentiate between the two. Attitudes are predisposition to react in some way towards the objects or concepts and the measurement of attitudes is generally based on the expressions of opinions. On the other hand, a belief is an enduring organisation of perceptions and cognitions about some aspects of individual's world. Thus, belief is just a hypothesis concerning the nature of objects, especially concerning individual's judgement of the probability regarding their nature.

Judgements of Alternative Positions on an Issue

On any given persuasive issue, there are likely to be a number of different positions or points of view available. Consider, for example, some different possible stands on an issue such as legalising marijuana: One might think that all marijuana use should be illegal, or that its use should only be permitted for medical reasons, or marijuana should be legalised for everyday use.

A person is likely to have varying beliefs of these different positions – a person will likely find some of the positions acceptable, some of the positions objectionable, and some neither particularly acceptable nor unacceptable. From a social judgement theory point of view, the person's reaction to persuasive communication on this topic will depend on the person's judgement of the position that the message advocates. It is important to assess persons' judgements of the various possible positions. The assessment procedure offered by social judgement theory is known as the Ordered Alternatives Questionnaire.

Generally attitudes are formed by two ways: (i) Direct Experience and (ii) Social Learning.

(i) Direct Experience: For example, if an individual happens to go in a bike and meets with accident, he/she may get an attitude formation that going in bike in future may cause accidents. This is called as attitude formation through direct experience.

(ii) Social Learning: Attitudes may also be formed through social learning *i.e.*, by way of observing other individual's actions or opinions. It may be favourable or unfavourable. For example; if Kapil Dev expresses his opinion for the energy drink 'Boost', the individual watching or observing may form an attitude towards the drink similar to that of the celebrity. This is viewed as *'Social Learning'*.

Sources of Attitude Formation

Attitude emerges from our emotional experiences and our perceptual process.

Emotions are felt and stay temporarily or for long. It is a feeling state.

Perceptual process starts when our sensory organs receive stimuli from environment.

Both are the sources of attitude. As understood, attitudes are learnt from this point of view, following factors also contribute for attitude formation.

I. Group Factors

(a) Family
(b) Influence or Reference Groups
(c) Society

II. Personality Factors

We analyse briefly both the factor.

(a) Family: In the group factors, the first thing that is considered is family. Because family plays an important role in socialisation of an individual. During the process of socialisation, the individual forms different attitudes. Families may be of two kinds, either nuclear family or joint family. The individuals brought up in these two families will have different set of attitudes. The mother and father form the basis for the formation of attitudes. Later, the relatives join in, developing different set of attitudes, as there are different personalities playing different roles.

(b) Influence or Reference Groups: A reference or influence group is one where lot of interactions take place. These interactions affect the individual's behaviour.

(c) Society: Society plays a major role in shaping the attitude of the individual. The norms, values and beliefs of the society gets closely attached and attracted by the individual. For example, if a particular society is against following rituals and celebrations, the individual brought up in the society, develops same attitude towards the rituals and celebrations followed by others.

Precisely, attitudes, like value are acquired from parents, teachers and peer group members. It is generally derived and developed from two important sources: (i) Our own experiences and (ii) our perception towards the object, person or events.

"Things are the way you think they are, because you think they are that way." Keep Smiling (*Anonymous*)

When an individual confronts with any objects or events a series of emotions are followed, and by coming to a conclusion one decides that this as an experience. The other source is that the individual's perception towards objects and events – the way the individuals selects, organises and interpret the stimuli and giving a meaning to objects or events. In contrast to values, attitudes are less stable, and in organisations, attitudes are important because they affect job behaviour. Job behaviour is a concept important in organisational behaviour as it directly correlates to the performance of the job by an employee.

ATTITUDES AND BEHAVIOUR

Perception exhibits the relationship between stimulus-response and shows how it affects the individual's behaviour. In this chapter, let us find out how attitudes affect the individual's behaviour. Generally, the individuals working in an organisation are affected by the different attitudes of co-workers, management and customers/clients. Interpretation of the situation should be well understood by an individual in order to develop a right attitude.

Why attitude?

People form attitudes/create stories because they are useful in mastering the social environment and in establishing important connections with others. It is a well-known fact in psychology that once an attitude is formed, it becomes very closely linked to the representation of the object to which that attitude has been ascribed.

This cognitive connection helps us to negotiate our interactions with these attitude objects in two ways: through the "object appraisal or knowledge function" and/or the "instrumental or utilitarian function". The object appraisal function refers to the ways in which attitudes/stories help us to organise and simplify our experience, thus allowing us to "deal with it efficiently". The instrumental explanation of the usefulness and function of stories, events and things perceived serves to orient us "towards objects that will help maximise our rewards and reach desired goals while avoiding undesirable situations or events". Box 19.2 gives a clear picture of how to increase and strengthen the attitude and behaviour relationship.

Box 19.2 Increasing the Attitude-Behaviour Relationship

The Theory of Planned Behaviour: Fishbein and Ajzen (1980) proposed that the best predictor of behaviour is one's intentions.

1. Whether a person behaves in an attitude consistent way or not depends on the nature of the behaviour intention formed.
2. Behavior intentions are influenced by three factors:
   - Attitude toward the behaviour: **How does the person feel about the behaviour in question?**
   - Subjective norms: **What others are doing?**
   - Perceived behaviour control: **How easy or hard is the behaviour and what will the outcome of the behaviour be?**
3. Accuracy of behaviour intentions is supported by Gallup polls taken before presidential elections.

Functions of Attitude

Attitudes have basically ***four functions*** in order to affect the behaviour. They are:

(a) Instrumental or Utilitarian: Generally, attitude functions like achieving means towards a desired set of goals or objectives. It acts as an instrument to reach the terminal goals and the terminal goals may be favourable or unfavourable feelings that would be aroused along with the activation of a need or cues.

(b) Ego-defensive: The acknowledgement of the psychological thought is the function of ego-defensive. Attitudes here are required in order to protect one from threats and becoming aware of the things happening in the outside world. The internal threats or external threats are the frustrating events, arouses to form the ego-defensive attitudes. Attitudes protect us from our fears and rejections.

For Example: A boss asks his subordinate to perform a task taking timely decision. Subordinate may be ineffective in taking decision and slowly works on the assigned task. But subordinate worker does not accept his weakness and blames boss and will have negative attitude towards boss. This negative attitude of subordinate makes him to stick to his action and his ego is protected.

(c) Value Oriented, Value Expressive: As mentioned in the earlier paragraphs attitudes and values go hand in hand. The value-orientation function considers attitudes that are held, as these attitudes express an individual's values or showing his/her self/identity. One must be aware of his/herself (Self-concept is where the individual is aware of oneself, his/her strengths, weaknesses, threats and opportunities) in order that the value-orientation function takes place in an attitude. When there is a threat in the self-concept, self-image etc., the attitudes are formed with value-orientation. Supposing an organisation tells its new recruits that "time management" and "hard work" are the core strength of their organisation and it shoule be strictly followed. In this, value of the organisation is expressed, *i.e.,* "Time management" and "Hard work".

(d) Function of Knowledge and Economy: This is another function of attitudes. The knowledge part is nothing but the individual's need to maintain a stable, organised and meaningful structure of the events, situation, objects and people around the world. Attitudes allow us to categorise information about objects and more easily, manage our world.

Finally, attitudes help to define us and make up-front statements about who we are and what we believe.

An individual's behaviour is affected by these functions of attitudes. It involves the interpretation of the ideas and information acquired by the individual. In the organisational setting the work itself and co-workers intervention with each other results in job satisfaction, This job satisfaction is identified as a type of work attitude. If an individual has a right attitude towards his job then he is successful in his job and in turn the individual and the organisational productivity is increased.

Attitude Change

Different individuals have different attitudes. In this uncertain and changing world, an individual need to keep changing their attitudes according to situation. The requirement of attitude change is the most important because attitudes affect the behaviour and this behaviour must be generally be desirable. Whenever the need arises to change the attitude, one or the other following methods can be adotped.

- Wooing the person to change his attitude by providing necessary information.
- Making necessary alternations in work practices, if possible, and thus solving this disturbing factors that are on his way to change.
- By threatening or through fear.
- By applying pressure by his co-workers or by his higher-ups (Peer pressure).
- By putting the person in a situation which needs change and make the person to work along with other workers who have changed their attitude.

Formation and change of attitude are not two separate things. They are interwoven. People are always adopting, modifying, and relinquishing attitudes to fit their ever-changing needs and interests. Attitude cannot be changed by simple education. Acceptance of new attitudes depends on who is presenting the knowledge, how it is presented, how the person is perceived, the credibility of the communicator, and the conditions by which the knowledge was received.

Attitudes change when:

1. A person receives new information from others or media – *Cognitive change.*
2. Through direct experience with the attitude object – *Affective change.*
3. Force a person to behave in a way different than normal – *Behavioural change.*

Attitude can be changed by a number of sources including other people, family, media, church, or the object itself. In 1968, McGuire developed steps to change an attitude. The steps are attention, comprehension, yielding, retention, and action. Attitude will be changed based on how a person sees the communication and the communicator. Less committed people will change ideas more frequently. Attitude change also has to do with other personality characteristics such as susceptibility to persuasion, intelligence, readiness to accept change, etc. We are more likely to accept information if we feel the communicator has no intent to change their attitudes and opinions.

The change in attitudes could be understood in detail only if the individual understands these three factors, which play a major role in the attitude change. They are: (1) Characteristics of Attitude, (2) Personality and (3) Group Affiliation.

1. Characteristics of Attitude

This is a most important element in understanding the attitude change. There are various characteristics identified in the theories of attitudes. Some of them are as follows:

1. Multiplicity
2. Consistency
3. Interconnectedness
4. Cognitive dissonance
5. Consonance of the attitude
6. The number of needs
7. The strength of the needs
8. The centrality of the related values
9. The extremeness of the attitude
10. Simplicity

Simplicity is the most important characteristic of an attitude. If an attitude is simple, then it is easy to change. If the degree of **interconnectedness** is high then there is the possibility of change in the existing attitude. **Cognitive dissonance** refers to a paradoxical nature between two attitudes. For example, a person is a chain smoker and if he is a regular yoga practicising person then there is cognitive dissonance in his attitudes. In this case, the change may not be effective.

Based on these characteristics, there are two different types of attitude change that could be brought within the individuals. They are:

(a) Congruent Change: This involves an increase in the strength of an existing attitude. It may be for making a positive attitude more favourable or to make a negative attitude more unfavourable.

For example, when an employee, Mr. Ram has an aversive attitude towards Mr. Raghu, and if the situation is also unfavourable, then the attitude of Mr. Ram would be strengthened because of the situation.

(b) Incongruent Change: An incongruent change is one in which the direction of change is opposite to the originally held attitude. For example, if the employees are confident that their jobs would not be changed (job security) and all on a sudden if the management is bringing in the technological change, there is fear of unknown in the minds of the employees, which in turn brings a different direction in the change in their attitude. Generally, the congruent attitude change is much easier than to bring a change in incongruent change.

2. Personality of Attitude Holder

As individuals are different, each individual may be persuaded or influenced to different degrees. This is due to the individual's personality differences. As attitudes have the subjective qualities, it depends on the individual's level of acceptance to bring about a change in his/her attitude. Several empirical studies reveal that value and personality factors influence the formation of attitudes.

It is not possible to change an individual's attitude that has the characteristic of being consistent and distinctive in their behaviour. It may be possible for a case that has the intellectual ability and if the personality is identified as a person who is open to experience then the change in attitude is possible.

3. Group Affiliation

Generally, as individuals, we often express our attitudes in terms of group. Certain types of action are thus determined, and others inhibited, at the start by the group to which we

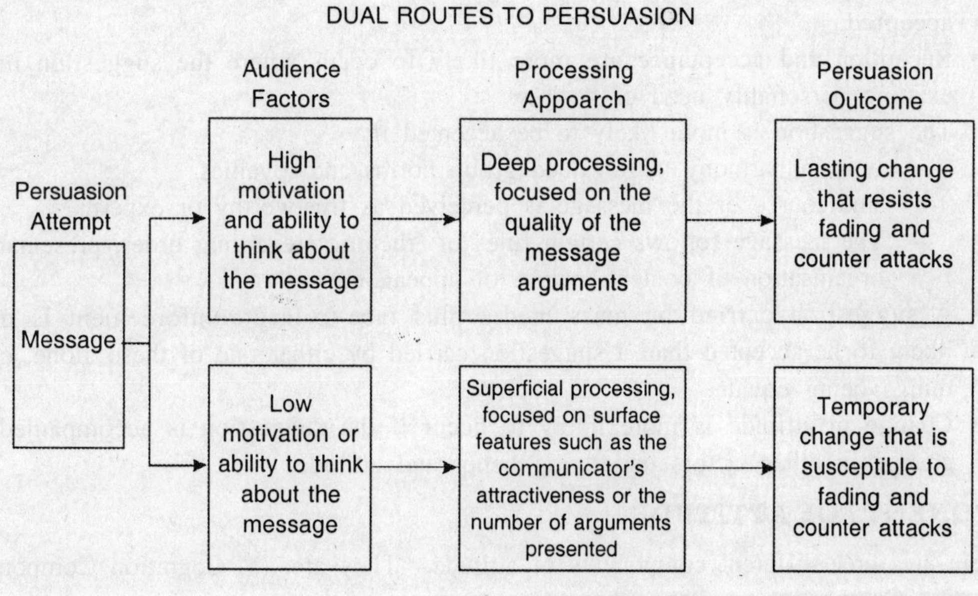

Fig. 19.1. Attitude Change Process
(Chart Source from http://chiron.valdosta.edu/mawhately/767/attitude.htm)

belong. We are set, for example, to conform in our reactions to the conduct of the others. In thinking, we expand our range of associations to objects about us; and we tend to impress others with our conclusions, rather than prove them in a logical fashion.

Less extreme attitudes (see characteristics of attitudes) may be expressed in terms of group because membership in the groups prevents existing attitudes from being disturbed by filtering the information. We set ourselves for rivalry, auto-competition, or co-operation, and are affected accordingly in our, work. We even assume an attitude to react *as if* certain imagined social stimulations are present. In all these instances, the attitude, or preparation in advance of the actual response constitutes an important determinant of the ensuing social behaviour.

Upon entering the presence of various groups, we assume specific attitudes, which control our responses in appropriate ways. There is a fairly universal readiness to communicate to other's thoughts or feelings, which we regard as significant. We are usually aware that the information will produce a sensation, create a laugh, impress the hearer with our own importance, or otherwise control the reactions. We have so far discussed the one side of the attitudinal relations of individuals. It must not be forgotten that in social life the response to call of others, forms a stimulus to which they in turn respond. Consequently, each person toward whom the individual has prepared responses has also definite attitudes toward him. It makes a great deal of difference to us. Moreover, what sort of attitudes our fellows assume. We strive to build up in them those settings which we have about us. Furthermore, when such attitudes are established we strive to keep them as they are. We are hemmed in our behaviour by the manner in which others expect us to behave.

What can we do to change attitudes?

- In order to produce change, a suggestion for change must be reviewed and accepted.
- Reception and acceptance are more likely to occur where the suggestion meets existing personality need or desires.
- The suggestion is more likely to be accepted if:
  - — It is in harmony with valued group norms and loyalties.
  - — The source of the message is perceived as trustworthy or expert.
  - — The message follows certain rules of 'rhetoric' regarding order, presentation, organisation of content, nature of appeal, etc.
- A suggestion carried by mass media plus face-to-face reinforcement is more likely to be accepted than a suggestion carried by either one of these alone, other things being equal.
- Change in attitude is more likely to occur if the suggestion is accompanied by change in other factors underlying belief and attitude.

COMPONENTS OF ATTITUDE

There are three different components of attitude. They are: (a) Cognition Component, (b) Affective Component (c) Behavioural Component.

These components play a major role in every individual's life.

The word cognition literally means '*knowing*'. Knowingly if an attitude is formed, then we call it as cognitive attitude.

Cognition – Opinion or belief segment of an attitude, *i.e.*, knowing something and arriving at a conclusion.

Affect – Emotion or feeling segments of an attitude.

Behaviour – Intention to behave in a certain way towards someone or something, *i.e.*, basic response to a stimuli.

These are the three "building blocks" of attitudes cognitive information, affective information and behavioural information. Each of these building blocks serves to solidify ones own attitudes about the stories we tell, as well as inhibit the possibility for the blending/reconciliation of different stories regarding the same attitude object (*e.g.*, Creation). Take for example, the following schematic representation of the attitude/story of creationism:

(a) Cognitive Information = Vision statement of the organisation = ***"To render best service to customer".***

(b) Affective Information = ***"Employees feel comfortable with the internal policies and procedures".***

(c) Behavioural Information = ***"Employees are on time at the workplace everday".*** These three components in combination state the attitude of employees in workplace.

Components of an Attitude
• An attitude comprises three parts: — The AFFECTIVE component is the emotional (like-dislike) component of an attitude. — The BEHAVIOURAL component is the overt behaviour attached to our internal attitudes. — The COGNITIVE component is the storage component where we organise information about an attitude object. Together, these make up the ABCs of attitudes.
• The affective component makes an attitude different from categorisation
• A fourth component, the BEHAVIOUR INTENTION, was later added to increase the attitude-behaviour predictive relationship.

Herein, lies a fundamental problem regarding the reconciliation of different versions of a story: cognitive information can be shared/learned and behavioural information can be altered/adapted, but affective information is not so easily modified.

TYPES OF ATTITUDES

There are many different types of attitudes. We would discuss mainly the work-related attitudes, as it is more relevant to our understanding of human attitudes in the workplace.

The job related attitudes are, Job Involvement, Organisational Commitment and Job Satisfaction.

Job Involvement

Job involvement measures the degree to which a person identifies himself psychologically with his job and considers his perceived performance level important to self-worth. The level of the involvement of the worker towards his job should be kept at high. If it is low, the reasons for not involving in the job have to be analysed and necessary corrections are to be done to maintain a high involvement. Some employees feel exhausted regarding routine activities, unchallenging job nature, etc. Performance of the employees is directly related to amount of job involvement.

Organisational Commitment

Organisational commitment is defined as a state in which an employee identifies with a particular organisation and its goals, and wishes to maintain membership in the organisation. It depicts the level of attachment of the individual towards the organisation. People who are less committed to the organisation feel that they are like the outsiders. Individuals who are more committed have a "we" feeling and they consider themselves as the partners of the company.

Organisations that have employees who are more committed have greater productivity. Research works suggest that Japanese workers are more committed than the US workers.

Job Satisfaction

What is job satisfaction? There are various questions raised by individuals, when diverse concepts regarding attitudes have to be discussed. Job satisfaction is a type of work attitude. Basically, it is the individual's general attitude toward one's job. The level of the satisfaction differs from one job to another and also form one individual to other.

Job Satisfaction refers to individuals general attitudes towards his or her job. A person with high level of job satisfaction holds positive attitude towards the job, and a person dissatisfied with his or her job holds negative attitude about the job. Individual's needs and desires differ form person to person. Their relationships with the co-workers also differ and interpersonal behaviour also differs from one individual to another. Difference in the needs, compensation and working conditions also matters. These factors determine whether the employees are satisfied or dissatisfied depending upon the fulfillment of the requirements.

Determinants of Job Satisfaction

There are certain factors that contribute to the job satisfaction.

Factors that determine employee job satisfaction are, equitable rewards, challenging work, good working conditions, favourable organisational climate, supportive colleagues and person's perception.

Equitable Rewards

In any organisation, irrespective of whether it is a manufacturing unit or a service sector, 80% of the employees are bothered about their compensation and rewards.

Reward system of any organisation should adopt understandable norms. The pay given to the employees must be fair and the policies clearly stated. Employees should be aware of the promotion policies, their performance level and feedback on their ability to meet the company standards.

Challenging Work

Employees prefer that they should be given the opportunities to prove their skills. Jobs that do not provide different feelings give a poor look to the job itself. The routine jobs might create boredom and fatigue for the employees. Design of the job should be done in an appropriate way so that the employee finds a challenge to meet his job requirements.

Good Working Conditions

Good working conditions like proper ventilation and lighting should be provided to the workers. Individuals should feel comfortable in the working environment. Creating good ambience is necessary. Congenial work environment psychologically pulls up the employee and his morale. The workers are motivated to give a better performance, if they are made to work in a conducive environment. Conducive environment includes all the hygiene factors of the workplace. It also includes the cordial relationship among the workers.

Favourable Organisational Climate

An individual working in an organisation comes from different backgrounds. The diversity faced in the working situation must be favourable to everyone. Climate refers to the shared views of the employees. It must be flexible favouring good communication and must facilitate high interpersonal relationship.

Supportive Colleagues

Certain employees do not concentrate only on the monetary benefits, but, also on the favourable relationship created by the co-workers. Conflicts aroused among the employees should be resolved immediately than being carried to create an unfriendly situation.

Person's Perception

Finally, the person's perception and their own personality play a very important role in the individual's job satisfaction. People with the positive attitude towards their job are tended to be highly satisfied with their job.

Bavendam's Job Satisfaction Factors

Bavendam's research identified six factors that influenced job satisfaction. When these six factors are high, job satisfaction is high. When the six factors are low, job satisfaction is low.

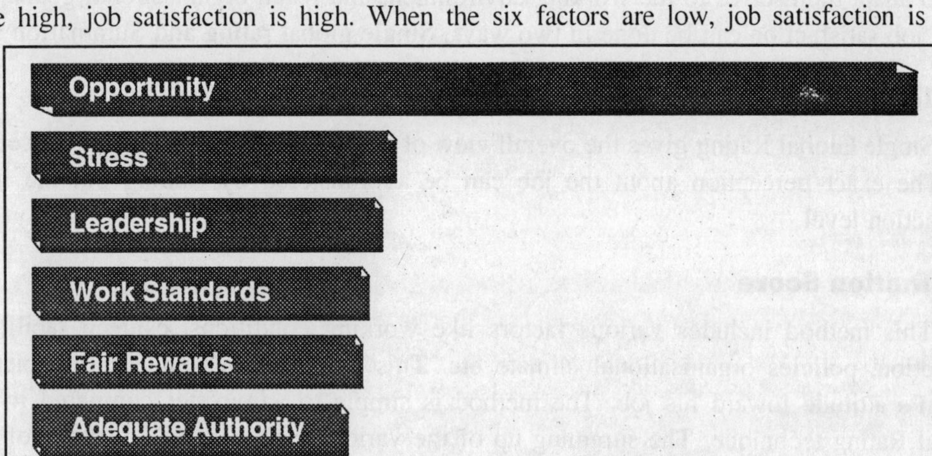

Fig. 19.2. Bavendam's Job Satisfaction Factors

Opportunity – Employees are more satisfied when they have challenging opportunities at work. This includes chances to participate in interesting projects, jobs with a satisfying degree of challenge and opportunities for increased responsibility. Importantly, this is not simply "promotional opportunity." As organisations have become flatter, promotions can be rare. People have found challenge through projects, team leadership, special assignments as well as promotions.

Stress – When negative stress is continuously high, job satisfaction is low. Jobs are more stressful if they interfere with employee's personal lives or are a continuing source of worry or concern.

Leadership – Employees are more satisfied when their managers are good leaders. This includes motivating employees to do a good job, striving for excellence or just taking action. Generally, democratic or participative type of leadership style is preferred by the employees.

Work Standards – Standards are nothing but optimum limits set by the organisation. It is set in such a way that it is achievable by the employees with increase in their performance levels. Employees are more satisfied when their entire workgroup takes pride in the quality of its work. Encouraging communication between employees and customers, developing meaningful measures of quality and celebrating achievements in quality are few of the scopes to increase work standards.

Fair Rewards – Employees are more satisfied when they feel they are rewarded fairly for the work they do. Considering employee responsibilities, the effort they have put forth, the work they have done, and rewarding systems should encourage meeting the demands of their jobs. Rewards should be for genuine contributions to the organisation and consistency in your reward policies should be maintained.

Adequate Authority – Employees are more satisfied when they have adequate freedom and authority to do their jobs. They should be given enough responsibility and the decision-making powers.

Measuring Job Satisfaction

Any job, a bus driver or a software engineer, the ultimate searching is individual's job satisfaction. Individual's working in an organisation are expected to give higher performance, able to adapt themselves to the working environment and reach organisational goals. Measuring of the job satisfaction can be done in two ways, Single global rating and Summation score.

Single Global Rating

Single Global Rating gives the overall view of the job and the individual's perception of the job. The exact perception about the job can be administered by finding out the individual's satisfaction level.

Summation Score

This method includes various factors like working conditions, canteen facilities, salary, promotion, policies organisational climate, etc. This method gives an accurate picture of the person's attitude toward his job. The method is simple to administer compared to the Single Global Rating technique. The summing up of the various responses to a number of job factors would achieve a more accurate rating about the individual's job.

A conflict between two attitudes of an individual is called as *cognitive dissonance*. For example, a person practicing yoga regularly might also be a chain smoker. There is a contradictory in the views of the individual. His main aim to practice yoga is to maintain his health. Unfortunately he has the practice of smoking regularly.

The same happens in the workplace situation. A person who is dissatisfied with his job might stay in the job for various other reasons. Job satisfaction has a very good impact on the employee's performance. It affects the employee's productivity, increases absenteeism rate and the labor turnover.

Job Dissatisfaction

Job dissatisfaction is the negative attitude of an individual towards one's job. It can be either expressed or can be suppressed. Many of the activities of the organisation are moving towards the transformation mode, people are expected to express their dissatisfaction through the following ways.

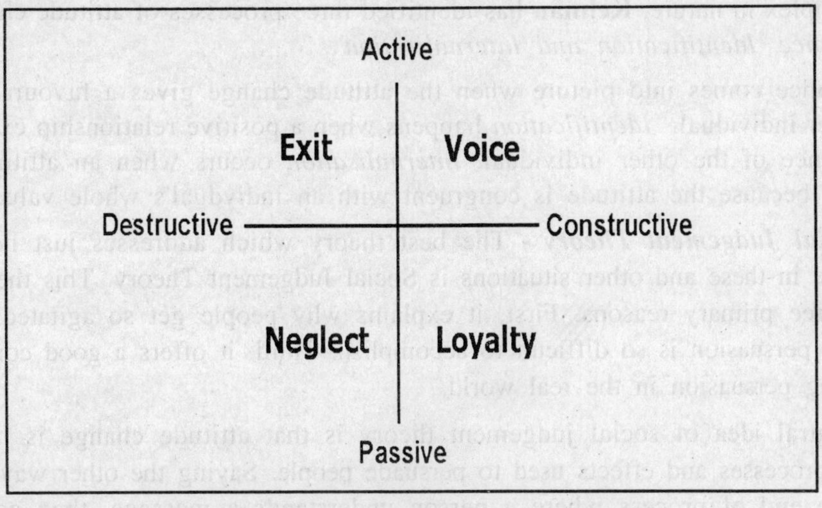

Fig. 19.3. Responses to Job Dissatisfaction

Theories of Attitude

An individual's performance in a workplace is affected by many attitudes. It is not just a stimulus-response relationship. There are a great number of theories formed to explain how the attitudes are formed. Let us look into a few of the theories. The theories are classified into three main categories. They are:

(*a*) *Cognitive-Consistency Theory*
(*b*) *Functional Theory*
(*c*) *Social Judgement Theory*

(a) Cognitive-Consistency Theory - This theory explains that attitudes do not exist or formed in isolation. Attitudes are concerned with the consistencies and inconsistencies with respect to various beliefs or evaluations.

Let us look into one major theory under this classification of cognitive consistency. It is *'Cognitive Dissonance Theory'*. The word cognition simply means "knowing". This theory was developed by **Festinger.** An individual instead of having one idea for a particular belief may have two ideas. Cognitions are consonance when one belief's idea follows the other. But the cognitions become disonant (dissonance) when the idea of one belief is different from that of another idea about the same belief. For example, a person may believe that practising yoga may maintain your health. It may keep your health in good condition. But to the contrary, the same individual is a smoker. Then there is inconsistency with the ideas regarding the belief about health. This is called as "Cognitive Dissonance".

(b) Functional Theory - The relationship between attitudes and efforts are considered in this theory. It also concentrates on the motivational structure of an individual. There are some important functions performed by attitudes.

For the functions, please refer the paras containing four functions. Depending on these four functions, there might be a change in the attitude. This must be considered as crucial for the reason that the four functions of attitudes are cognitive processes and the functions are quite complex in nature. **Kelman** has identified three processes of attitude change. They are '*Compliance, Identification and Internalisation*'.

Compliance comes into picture when the attitude change gives a favourable reaction from the other individual. *Identification* happens when a positive relationship exists because of the influence of the other individual. *Internalisation* occurs when an attitude is being adopted, and because the attitude is congruent with an indivdual's whole value systems.

(c) Social Judgement Theory - The best theory which addresses just how difficult people can be in these and other situations is Social Judgement Theory. This theory is quite useful for three primary reasons. First, it explains why people get so agitated. Second, it explains why persuasion is so difficult to accomplish. Third, it offers a good common sense plan for doing persuasion in the real world.

The central idea of social judgement theory is that attitude change is mediated by judgemental processes and effects used to persuade people. Saying the other way, persuasion occurs at the end of process where a person understands a message, then compares the position it advocates to the person's position on that issue.

A person's position depends upon:

(i) Ones most preferred position.

(ii) Person's judgement of various alternatives such as judgement, rejection and non-commitment.

(iii) The person's level of ego-involvement with the issue.

According to social judgement theory, mental representation of attitudes is not a single point like "This is where I am", but one need to know the range of acceptable options and what is objectionable.

This theory was proposed by **Sherif** and **Hoveland**. When an attitude is formed, it produces lot of distortions. The initial attitude which is formed may be changed or altered when this attitude is compared with different opinions about the same attitude.

Attitude Measurement

There are five major approaches to collecting attitude data:

- Records - These include observed behaviour such as attendance records, anecdotal records, incidents, and interviews.
- Self Reports - Such as inventories of employees reporting directly about their own attitudes.
- Report of Others - These include information, rating scales, and interview results of others reporting about the attitude of an employee or team.
- Sociometric Techniques - Such as sociograms and social distance scales in which members of a group report about their attitudes towards one another.
- Projective Technique - Picture presentations and sentence completion in which the learner supplies a response to the stimulus.

Precautions in Attitude Measurement:

- Attitudes are impossible to measure directly. The evaluator is relying on inference.
- Behaviours, beliefs, and feelings, are not consistent, even when we assume they reflect a single attitude. The pattern of behaviour may be very complex and be a manifestation of more that one attitude.
- Attitudes do not stand still long enough for a one time snap shot measurement. Frequent measurements at selected intervals will reflect a more accurate representation of a consistent attitude.
- Certain attitudes do not have a universal agreement on their nature or what the correct behavioural display is.
- Collection of certain types of personal data about learners may lead to legal complications involving their rights to privacy.

ATTITUDE — CHANGE TO SKILLS

Attitude is discussed in this chapter focusing on the productivity of individuals who work in different organisations. Workers should possess necessary attitude to develop skills required by the organisations. In the organisational setting, each worker will have one's own personal beliefs and values, their own perspective of the community where they live and their quality of life. The roles the governments should play workers attitudes about economic development and attitude towards their organisation are also necessary to develop skills.

Many a time, the perception and attitude of people selected for jobs in organisations mismatch with the skillls required by the organisation. Therefore, their attitude should be directed towards learning skills required to increase productivity of the organisation. Workers also feel and will be prepared to change their attitude to learn new skills or enhance existing skills. Hence, workers seek for training programmes with the expectation that this will lead them to better jobs and higher standard of living.

The attitude of people at work is also changing. Historically, our economy was not fully exposed to technological advancement. To a greater extent, economy was stable, irrespective of earning of the individuals and nation. India labelled as a poor country and people are adjusted to this type of living. Only recently (1991 onwards), the economy is exposed to change, and workers are also aspiring to gain knowledge and skill in new areas. Now, most employees recognise that even if they do not change jobs, they are likely to have and accept changes in the type of work they perform.

Changing the present attitude to acquire new skills through training requires willingness to learn and change over to new skills. Change over of attitude can be impeded by practical obstacles such as mental mood of the employee, the length of training time, the cost of the training, the loss of income during training period, the time and expense of training, etc.

However, the employees are prepared to change their attitude to acquire new skills if new skills would definitely increase their standard of living. Therefore, the motivating factor for changing or converting the current attitude to required skills of the organisation through training and development is improved status to employees and improved overall productivity to the organisation.

People without flexibility in thinking, perception and attitude cannot survive. Because, employers in a competitive market, search for talented and dynamic people who can steer their organisation. People who are not ready to change their attitude or change over to changing times cannot better their future life. Therefore, the attitude to adopt to changing environment and acquiring new skills by the workers become inevitable, irrespective of various constraints they will have.

Work-Related Attitudes

Previous paragraphs throw light on this aspect. Attitude is a general psychological term. But it is identified differently in different settings. What attitude of workers is required in an organisational context? The question is answered by saying that each worker should have attitude to increase productivity of the organisation within the framework set by the top management. In the initial stages of worker's entry into organisation there will be conflict between the attitude of worker and organisational, work culture.

The solution to this is that the worker has to be finetuned to the organisational culture. Adjusting to the work culture of the organisation will take place through training and development. Gradually, the worker adopts to the organisational attitude, *viz.,* identifying oneself with the principles and practices of the organisation to achieve the set objective. The attitude of worker should blend with the attitude of the organisation. General attitude of the organisation is to maximise productivity through positive attitude of the worker. Bad attitude of worker may destroy to some extent the organisational attitude. Therefore, the manager/top management should create an environment allowing the worker to focus his/her attitude for a more productive and positive effort.

Many aspects are identified with the work-related attitudes. They are as follows.

- Job performance
- Meeting quality standards
- Sales potential

- Customer service and support
- Team spirit
- Boss/employee relationship
- Co-worker's support
- Stakeholder's expectations

Besides these main aspects, many more issues are concerned with organisational or work-related attitudes. These aspects or attitudes of the organisation have to be blended with the workers attitude. The blending process is as follows.

- Understanding attitude of both employer and employee.
- Recognise the importance of blending.
- Design work procedure which directs both towards positive attitude required for success.
- The procedure should contain vital issues such as customer relationship enhancement, developing customer loyalty, improving team effort, goal achievement, etc.
- Implement the procedure, monitor and adopt corrective measures continuously when deviations take place.
- Standardise the procedure.
- Develop "Yes I can" attitude in workers by identifying attitude origins and tuning it into "self-confidence" of the worker.
- Do not let fear stop your success, take responsibility for your attitude and actions and result.
- Invite participation, radiate optimism in workers and recognise achievement.
- If need be, develop individual action plan to wipe out negative attitude of a worker.

Implementing successfully the work-related attitudes is a challenging task, It will not automatically happen. Creating great workplace attitude is everyone's job involved in work process.

SUMMARY

1. The concept of "Attitude" is a psychological phenomenon applied to organisational behaviour to analyse the behaviour of individuals in the organisations.
2. Attitude is defined in two ways, *viz.,* (i) conceptual and (ii) operational.
3. Conceptual definition states attitude as "a mental and neutral state of readiness, organised through experience, experting a directive or dynamic influence upon the individual response to all objects and situations with which it is related".
4. Operational definition focuses on evaluative part of attitude. Accordingly, "Attitude is often used in a generic sense to any reports of what people think or feel or the way in which they intend to act".
5. Regarding sources of attitude, it emerges from our emotional experiences and our perceptual process.
6. Attitude is formulated to master the social environment and to establish vital connections with others.
7. The functions of attitude are: (i) Instrumental or Utilitarian, (ii) Ego-defensive and (iii) Value-oriented, value expressive and the function of knowledge and economy.

8. Change of attitude is required in a dynamic world to have a desirable behaviour.
9. **Cognative change, affective** change and **behavioural** change takes place in each individual. These are the three components of attitude.
10. Change in attitude can be experienced, if an individual understands: (i) characteristics of attitude (ii) personality of attitude holder, and (ii) group affiliation.
11. The types of work-related attitude are: (i) Job involvement (ii) Organisational commitment and (iii) Job satisfaction.
12. Main theories of attitude are (i) Cognative-consistancy theory, (ii) Functional theory and (iii) Social Judgement theory.
13. The attitudes of workers and employees are to be blended to achieve organisational success.

STUDY QUESTIONS

1. What is attitude? Analyse how attitudes are formed.
2. Analyse the various types of attitude you find in workplaces.
3. Give an explanatory note on job satisfaction.
4. Write a brief note on: (i) job involvement and (ii) job enrichment.
5. Briefly explain the different sources of attitude.
6. Explain how attitudes are formed with organisational examples.
7. Give an explanatory note on: (i) job enrichment, (ii) job rotation (iii) job enlargement.
8. Briefly explain the theories of attitude.
9. Give an explanatory note on functions of attitude.
10. Explain the aspects of attitude change.
11. Explain the various types of attitudes.
12. How the attitude can be measured? Explain.
13. Write a note on motivating factors which change the attitude to skills required by an organisation.

CASE STUDY

Bhaskar runs a small manufacturing unit, employing 50 persons. After his graduation, he took to this activity. His father had very meagre resources and could not support Bhaskar with necessary funds. Bhaskar, after sometime of commencing the business, changed the work culture of his unit, giving more freedom to workers to improve production. They were asked to design innovative work practices themselves and implement them. He also provided necessary funds to change the practices; workers were also given better emoluments to work with vigour. However, employees could not perform to the expectation of Bhaskar. Frustrated Bhaskar became rude and introduced strict work norms, which were opposed by employees. There was lot of commotion. Employees did not work to the norms. production failed. Finally, Bhaskar announced that wages will be cut for those who fail to reach their productivity standards.

Questions:

1. If you are an entrepreneur, what would you do in this situation?
2. Explain the different attitudes you find in this case?
3. Suggest a possible solution to correct the situation of the case.

Skill Exercise

Step 1 : Select and identify a strong attitude that you and your friend hold.

Step 2 : Describe the attitude in terms of the components of an attitude.

Step 3 : Discuss as a team of two members and share your attitudes of a particular situation.

[Time: 45 minutes]

AVOIDING PITFALLS

Pitfalls

1. A meeting for international students has been scheduled, and you wish to invite international students to attend. You go door-to-door to pass out invitations. There are only a few people on your team, but you hope to invite as many as possible of the many internationals living there. After a short time, a student who has come for tea invites you. What do you say?
2. Imagine you've invited some students from the Philippines to your place for dinner. They arrive; you greet them, invite them in, and offer them chairs. But before your guests sit down, each takes a handkerchief from his pocket, wipes the chair and then spreads the cloth on the chair. Before the meal, your guests take the table napkins, and wipe the plates and silverware. What are you thinking as they do this?

Probable Answer to Questions

1. If you refuse the invitation because of time, you've just missed an opportunity to get to know someone who might have come to your meeting with you, and instead you've passed out many almost worthless invitations. Most international students won't come based on an invitation from a total stranger, but after a personal conversation the probability of attending is higher. You must plan, at the minimum, half an hour's visit for such an invitation.

20

VALUE

LEARNING OBJECTIVES

After reading this chapter you should be able to know;

- Value – The Concept
- Importance of Value
- Sources of Value Systems
- Types of Value
- Loyalty
- Ethical Behaviour

Values represent basic convictions. Values are the basic beliefs of individuals. Attitudes are patterns of the individual's feeling and beliefs. It is a set of behavioural tedencies shown towards certain individuals, objects and events.

Individuals have a basic set of general beliefs passed on from one generation to another. These beliefs are in an hierarchical order depending on how much importance is given to each belief. In managerial decision-making, manager's personal values play a significant role. But it is unfortunate that managers, many a time, do not consider ethical value such as honesty, while making decisions. Basic values such as trust, commitment, integrity etc. are to be considered as more important in business decisions. Values are only abstract ideals. These ideals make an individual to think and behave appropriately before taking any decision or perform any task.

CONCEPT OF VALUES

Value system is a hierarchy, based on the ranking of an individual's value in terms of their intensity such as freedom, pleasure, self-respect, honesty, obedience and equality. These values are stable and consistent for a period of time. At times depending on their importance, some values last long. Values to help the individuals to define and identify what is good and bad in the environment. Values as a whole influence the attitudes.

Value theory is a concept concerned with the value or worth of people or things. Worth may be considered in terms of usefulness or economic value. Value theory can also involve legal, moral, aesthetic, or quantitative value. It can involve just one type of value, or a combination of different types.

> Value may be defined as "Important and enduring beliefs or ideals shared by the members of a culture about what is good or desirable and what is not."

It is generally accepted that values are at the root of all types of behaviour, including those that are morally, politically, or economically motivated. Values may be held individually, socially, or both. However, in some cases, individual values may seem worthless without social understanding and acceptance. Value theory deals with examining the individual and social repercussions of values.

In psychological terms, value theory concerns the examination of the development and assertion of human values. It also concerns the study of ways in which human beings act on values or fail to act on them. Psychology related value theory focuses on determining the reasons behind human preferences and choices in relation to values. Studying value theory also includes attempting to develop plausible explanations for the ways in which values may or may not govern behaviour.

Values and Organisations

Values are internal to a personal and are psychological constructs. Organisations as such do not have values. But, because they are composed of human beings, their cultures are shaped by values. These values of persons shape organisational behaviour and direction taken by organisations. These values are shared in the organisation amongst members for organisational success. Without sharing values, organisations cannot succeed. Therefore, understanding individual values, team and organisational values is crucial to the effectiveness of all organisational development.

In sociological terms, value theory deals with the types of personal values that are commonly held within a community. It also examines ways in which certain conditions or situations may change those values. Additionally, sociological value theory is concerned with how different groups of people may believe in and prioritize values that influence how they behave in social situations.

IMPORTANCE OF VALUES

Organisation cannot function without values. They are the glue for an organisation's system, structure and process. Valueless organisations are like robotic machines which work mechanically and without regard to human factor and their attitudes. Attitudes are governed and shaped by values, the organisations hold.

Values are important for organisations. Because they are the core strength of the organisation. Good values direct the organisations to perform better. Values make the people at work behave cohesively and develop team spirit in workers.

From the period of Industrial Revolution (18th century) to this date, many organisations are under bureaucratic control. Humanistic values are grounded in these organisations. But parallel to this, in the process of organisational development, a thinking emerged that people at work should have opportunities to develop their full potential. Basic value to extract full potential for organisational development is "**Choice**". Gradually, it was considered that organisations should strike a healthier balance between the needs of organisations and needs of individuals. To achieve this balance, bureaucratic model should be changed and focus should be on human values. Human values are important in organisations as they (i) generally influence attitude and behaviour and (ii) they lay the foundation for the understanding of motivation and their influence on perceptions of people.

Values are necessary and explicit in organisations for the following reasons.

- **Human Development:** People in organisations should have opportunities to learn to grow.
- **Fairness:** People should be treated equally, with dignity and without discrimination.
- **Openness:** People should freely communicate honestly with each other.
- **Choice:** People at work should not be subjected to coercion and the arbitrary use of power and authority.
- **Balance of Autonomy and Constraint:** People should have freedom to work as they see good for the organisation and support the organisational practices and procedures set for the success of the organisation.

SOURCES OF VALUES

Values originate from different sources. Some values are instilled in childhood of an individual which is held for long. Certain values are learnt from experiences. Certain values are acquired through the religious organisations also. Thus, the sources of values are as follows:

- National culture
- Parental dictates
- Teachers
- Friends
- Similar environmental influences that serve as sources.

Significant portion of the value we hold are established in our early years from parents, teachers, friends and others.

Personal values such as honesty, integrity sincerity etc. are the ones that are essentially required for organisational success. These value sources are either inherent in workers or acquired in the process of learning organisational culture. As personal values play a vital role in decision-making, these are to be practiced by managers. Many managers and managements, in the process of developing business, have turned their backs on ethical values. However, successful companies and business houses have considered "values" as basic mantra for their success. Fundamental values such as commitment, dignity respect, trust, accountability etc. that are required for individuals to succeed in any organisational or other settings, will be acquired by them, if they do not possess them through their family heritage. Thus, the sources stated above will provide the people, the required values which are abstract, to shape their thinking and behaviour.

TYPES OF VALUES

One of the earliest efforts to categorise the values was made by Allport and his associates. They identified six types of values from their research studies.

- Theoretical – places of high importance on the discovery of truth through a critical and rational approach.
- Economic – emphasise the useful and practical.
- Aesthetic – places the highest value on form and harmony.
- Social – assigns the highest value to the love of the people.
- Religious – is concerned with the unity of experience and understanding of the outer space as a whole.

Interestingly values are relatively stable and enduring. This has been explained as a result of both their genetic component and the way in which they are learned. The values which parents give importance may be taken as important by their children too. There are two types of values, *Instrumental and Terminal values.*

Terminal values represent the end **state** of existance for which an individual desires to be. It also depends on how much importance is attached to that particular terminal value. For example: "success by earning thirty per cent more profit over last year's profit has been achieved". Here, the "success" is the terminal value. "Terminal" means the end or final state of an activity. These values focus on the question "what"?

Instrumental values pave way to achieve terminal values. These values focus on means to achieve. "How" question is answered by these values. They act as tools or instruments to gain something. In our example, "success by earning thirty per cent more profit over last year's is achieved by adopting a **new strategy"**. Here, "New strategy" is an instrumental value.

Thus, "Success" is a terminal value and "New strategy" is an instrumental value.

Terminal Values	***Rank***	***Instrumental Values***	***Rank***
1. Comfortable life (Prosperous)	....	1. Aspiring (Ambitious, hard work)	
2. Equality (brotherhood)	....	2. Broad minded (open)	
3. Exciting life (Stimulative life)	....	3. Competence (Capable)	
4. Family Security	....	4. Cheerful (Joyful)	
5. Freedom (Free Choice)		5. Clean (Neat, tidy)	
6. Happiness (Contented)		6. Courage (Uphold your belief)	
7. Inner Harmony		7. Forgive (Pardon others)	
8. Mature Love (Spiritual Intimacy)		8. Helpfulness (Work for other's welfare)	
9. National Security		9. Honesty	
10. Pleasure (Enjoyable)		10. Imaginative (Dare)	
11. Salvation (Saved)		11. Independent	
12. Self-respect		12. Intelligence (Reflective)	
13. Social recognition (admiration)		13. Rational (Logical)	
14. True friendship (close companionship)		14. Obedient (Dutiful)	
15. Wisdom matured understanding)		15. Politeness (Curtiousness)	
16. World at peace		16. Loving (Tender)	
17. World of beauty (Beauty of nature)		17. Responsible (Dependable)	
18. Sense of accomplishment		18. Self-control (Restrain)	

Source: Adapted from Milton Rokeach: The Free Press,New York, 1973.

Milton Rokeach gives the list of both Terminal values and Instrumental values. These values are to be ranked according to your order of preference (Rank 1 for most important and rank - 18 for least important).

Using this table, we can identify our own values and also find out how best our values fit into organisational values which we have to respect and adopt when we serve an organisation.

Terminal values represent the end state of existence for which an individual desires to be. It also depends on how much importance is attached to that particular terminal value. On the contrary, instrumental value paves way to achieve terminal value. The terminal value such as 'happiness' can be reached by following the instrumental value, like being 'cheerful'. In the workplace the employees have values that help them to take decision. Employees have an hierarchical order of values that improve their performace.

Some empirical studies have revealed that managers who were interviewed, ranked their first five terminal values as: (i) self-respect, (ii) family security, (iii) freedom, (iv) a sense of accomplishment and (v) happiness and first five Instrumental values ranked were, (i) honest, (ii) responsible, (iii) capable, (iv) ambitious and (v) independent. These research-based values need not necessarily be taken as standard rankings and priorities of values we find in managers. They are only indicators of how managers perceive values in the organisational context.

The following paragraphs help us to understand the working style of today's individuals and let us try to ponder where their (employee's) **value lie.**

The 40-hour work week is dead. But people are not just working longer hours. They're holding down **extreme jobs** — logging 60-plus hours a week and enduring 24/7 client demand, tighter-than-ever deadlines, and unpredictable work flows.

Yet strangely, many extreme workers don't feel exploited — they feel exalted. Some love the intellectual challenge and the thrill of achieving something big. Others relish the oversize compensation packages and status that come with the territory.

Extreme jobs fuel worker's adrenalin highs and beef up entire nations competitive prowess–popping up in industries as diverse as financial services, consulting, medicine, law, and manufacturing.

Hewlett sees hints of dangers a foot: health problems will be more increase and family woes increase for extreme workers, along with eroded corporate productivity, when extreme job holders suffer the inevitable burnout or defect for less demanding waters.

Extreme jobs may enrich your company in the short run. But can it live with the costs in the *long* run?

Value analysis in this context is as follows:

Value as understood, is belief. Workers donot believe that they are exploited, but believe that they are offered unique jobs to grow. In terms of money, they get more.

Extreme works in industries, increases competitive power of the economy.

But, on the other hand, the additional work of workers make them exhausted.

How Extreme Are Your Company's Jobs?

In addition to 60-plus-hour weeks, 24/7 client demands, unpredictable work flows, and tight deadlines, many extreme jobs have these characteristics :

- Inordinate scope of responsibility
- Work-related events outside regular work hours
- Responsibility for profit/loss
- Responsibility for mentoring/recruiting
- Large amount of travel
- Large number of direct reports
- Physical presence in the workplace – 10-plus hours a day

Why the rise in Extreme Jobs?

Powerful interesting trends have driven the proliferation of extreme jobs.

(i) Competitive Pressures: Executive positions in any organisation/company are less in number. In case of acquisitions and mergers, the officer positions will be further reduced. Simultaneously, new aspirants, with diversified talent will be added. All these happenings increase the available number of executives and the positions remain the same. This situation intensifies competition. People are strongly motivated to work more than their rivals to win plum rules.

(ii) The "extreme" ethos: Many people (workers) will be interested in taking jobs of "extreme" ethos (exclusive nature) like thrill-seeking sports and stunt-based reality. TV shows, which are pervaded in an economy. The ethos (exclusive features) has been blended with business to make extreme jobs look glamourous and desirable. The value concept is that they feel elated when they accept these extreme jobs.

(iii) Communication Technologies: Technology has prompted a shift in people's expectations and behaviour. Instead of fixing boundaries around their workday, they are constantly glued to their cell phones and other tech-based gadgets and are willing to work more. Because such jobs instill more joy and make it enjoyable. This is only their belief or value they attach.

(iv) Workplace as a Social Centre: Workplace provides the workers with best friends and most stimulating encounters. People are ready to work late in the night. Their family and personal life has become atropy (decrease in interest or the interest in family degenerates). Work station becomes an admirable place. People think that they are respected there. This is the value they attach to the work places and consider this place as a social centre where they will be recognised.

(v) More Knowledge-based Work: Workers today are filled with vigour and knowledge. These talented workers are more in corporate world who use their brains for company's growth as well as their personal growth in terms of skill acquisition. They enjoy exchanging ideas with their peers. They feel that their workplaces are more stimulating and not painful. This is the value they attach to their working environment.

(vi) Globalisation: As companies expand their operations to global markets, Time zones expand, managers are forced to travel more and their working hours increase. It will be a thrill to accept such jobs abroad for managers and workers. They attach too much value except those who have sufficiently worked in this line and are exhaused.

These extreme jobs, although bit difficult to discharge, motivate employees to accept them more willingly. These type of jobs make them to enjoy and productivity improves. These type of jobs are hard in nature. But more **value** (belief) is attached to them.

LOYALTY AND ETHICAL BEHAVIOUR

Loyalty is a term which depicts unswerving support to a person or to an organisation. Loyalty is a real, important value to any individual or organisations. Loyalty, being a value component, every organisation expects that their workers should be loyal to it. All loyal workers are put together and a network of loyal workers is created. This network plays a key role in increasing productivity of the organisation and creating value and image to that business unit. The features of loyalty network are;

(i) no worker intentionally commits any mistake;
(ii) no worker opposes the orders of the organisation;
(iii) every employee sticks to his/her job;
(iv) they do not bother about someone's fault. But try to put it to order.

Many a time, loyalty in organisations is more important than truth. The truth-seekers revolt against certain policies and programmes of the organisation. They feel that certain policies are opposed to the growth of really talented and hard workers. These frustrated employees join together and fight for modification of the policy.

For loyal workers, truth-seeking (modification of the policy) is not as important as that of being loyal to the organisation. Loyalty makes them blind and simply accept the programmes and work practices which are hard and not conducive for growth. But sensible managements do look into such practices which hinder the growth of loyal workers and modify the practices suiting to the needs of workers. The truth-seekers or stand fasters (otherwise called) are also benefited in the process and develop a positive approach towards the organisation.

Loyalty concept does not strictly oppose the policies and programmes which are opposed by value systems. Although loyalty is one of the essential components of "value", loyal workers give unswerving support to the management when certain decisions are adopted which are opposed to the public policy. Loyalists feel that a decision taken by the management is supportive to the overall development of the organisation and implicity accept such decisions.

Any non-value decision of management is opposed by ethics of business. But loyalists blindly follow. They may or may not be knowing that the following of non-value decisions would hinder the growth of the organisation and is unethical.

ETHICAL PRINCIPLES

Like various social institutions (family, etc.), business units of a society are also the organs of such social institutions. These social institutions are run on certain value system and ethics. Following are the ethical principles generally adopted but not stated explicitly by business units. These principles which are visible or invisible are shaped by family and friends, the media, culture, schooling, religious instructions and general life experiences. These are value-based ethical principles.

1. Do not take actions which serves self-interest of the individual worker or the organisation.
2. Dishonest, closed and untruthful practices should not be adopted and publicised.
3. Any dictum that is opposed to humanitarian practice which will be detrimental to the growth and team-building activities of the organisation, should not be adopted.
4. Do not oppose or violate government policies as they are the minimal moral standards of the society. They have to be accepted by the organisations.
5. Policies and programmes of the organisation should be oriented towards greater benefit and should be least or no harmful to the society.
6. Rules should be universally applicable. In other words, there should not be biased rules which places some workers in predicament.
7. The actions of the firm should not encroach upon the individual rights.
8. The efficiency of the firm has to be exhibited by economic parameter such as increase in profit on year on year (y_0 y) basis. While increasing the profit, ethical issues are to be strictly followed. Legal and market constraints have to be considered. **Profit making** should be the motto and not **Profiteering**.
9. The principle of "Distributive Justice" has to be followed. Fortunate and least fortunate are to be treated equally.
10. The Management/Managers/Workers amongst themselves should not interface with the right of self-development and self-fulfillment of individuals employed in the firm.

These ethical aspects have to be practiced by organisations to create value. Simply preaching these ethical norms in workplaces do not create value. They have to be enforced by adopting methods such as conducting **ethical training** to all people [managers and workers], developing and implementing **code of ethics, monitoring** ethical practices adopted in the organisation, and **whistle-blowing**.

"Whistle-blowing" is a term which denotes the announcement of unethical practices of the organisation to make such practices public by inside people, who are bold enough to face any consequence. Whistle-blowing can take place through media, government agencies, and by any public interest groups.

Whistle-blowing is a debtable and a controversial issue. The loyal workers prefer to suffer with unethical practices, rather than blowing the whistle. But certain people are dare enough to blow the whistle as they get monetary benefit. This means that whistle-blowers are motivated by revenge and blow the whistle, *i.e.*, reveal the unethical practice of an organisation. In turn, when firm pays compensation for violating agreed ethical norms to concerned aggrieved persons, a portion of compensation is payable to whistle-blower. In USA, False Claims Act provides for this.

Many organisations, in the process of value creation, motivate their employees to be loyal to the organisation. Even employees also cherish to be loyal as it provides peace to them. Whistle-blowing is considered as a disloyal behaviour of an employee. Hence, it is taken a last line of defense by employees to protect themselves of the organisational onslaughts.

Every organisation prefers an organisational climate, in which whistle-blowing should be very minimal. Value for the organisation can be created by adopting following practices.

- Conduct open meetings with employees frequently to discuss controversial and dissenting issues and try to get acceptable solutions.
- Grievance cell of the firm should be activated to analyse grievance employees as and when they crop up. Restructure the cell, if need be.
- Develop a positive feeling in employees that the "Management supports their genuine demand and satisfy such demands as quickly as possible".

The bottomline is to make employees happier and create value for the organisation. No doubt that there are very many financial and other constraints. The beauty of managers and organisation lies in balancing these constraints intelligently and create a good image for the organisation.

Value creation process for an organisation involves the following aspects:

1. Consider every worker as human being and treat them equally.
2. Consider customers of the firm as our brand ambassadors. Delight them by providing quality goods and services. Meet their desires, needs and expectations. Charge a fair price.
3. Reduce cost of production by avoiding unwanted purchases and having optimum labour.
4. Develop an integrated and holistic approach and implement to successfully manage.
5. Encourage self-management and self-development of employees.
6. Care for societal needs and needs of communities with which the organisation works. The focal areas are: (i) prompt payment of correct taxes, (ii) associating with healthcare and educational programmes of the society, (iii) environmental protection and (iv) balanced use of natural resources.

These practices undoubtedly create value for an organisation. Majority of people at work in such organisations will be humble, positive, more humanistic in approach, loyal and contribute their best to increase the productivity of the organisation.

Value-based organisations have not failed. They try and adapt all the six main aspects stated above to be an organisation well cherished by public and people at work. Greedy organisations cannot create value. In valueless firms, social violence will be in a prime place, criminal activities are on top, and exploitation and other vices are deep rooted and finally such organisations will have a natural death at the earliest.

QUOTES ON VALUE

1. "We do not act rightly because we have virtue or excellence, but we rather have those because we have acted rightly."

— Aristotle, 384 B.C.–322 B.C., Greek Philosopher and Scientist.

2. "Capital must be propelled by self-interest; It cannot be enticed by benevolence."
— Walter Bagehot, 1826-77, English Monetary Economist.

3. "There are two levers to set a man in motion, fear and self-interest."
— Nepoleon Bonaparte, 1769-1821, French Emperor.

4. "Price is what you pay. Value is what you get."
— Warren Buffet, 1930, American Investment Entrepreneur.

5. "In God we trust, all others bring data."
— Edward Deming, 1900-1993, American Statistician.

6. "It is not hard to make decisions, when you know what your values are."
— Roy Disney, American Film Writer.

7. "Try not to become a man of success but rather try to become a man of value."
— Albert Einstein, 1879-1955, German born American Theoretical Physicist.

8. "Management is doing things right; Leadership is doing the right thing."
— Peter F. Drucker, American Management Guru.

9. "True value of a human being can be found in the degree to which he has attained liberation from the self."
— Albert Einstein.

10. "Earth provides enough the satisfy every man's need, but not everyman's greed."
— Mahatma Gandhi, 1869-1948.

11. "Happiness is the state of consciousness which proceeds from the achievements of one's values".
— Ayn Rand, 1905-1982, US Novelist.

12. "People exaggerate the value of things they haven't got: Everybody workships truth and unselfishness because they have no experience with them."
– G.B. Shaw, 1856-1950, Irish Critic and Poet.

SUMMARY

1. Value may be defined as "important and enduring beliefs or ideas shared by the members of a culture about what is good or desirable and what is not.
2. Organisation as such do not have value. But people in organisation have values and they are reflected in the organisations. Good values direct the organisation to perform better.
3. Sources of values are national culture, parental dictates, teachers, friends and other environmental influences.
4. The values are of different types. It may be theoretical, economics, aesthetic, social and religious. Terminal and Instrumental types of values are also recognised.
5. Loyalty, is a value component which depicts unswerving support to an individual or organisation. Loyalty is more important than truth in certain situations. Loyalty workers blindly accept hard jobs that are not conducive for growth.
6. Ethical principles are practiced to create value for the organisation.
7. Whistle-blowing is an extreme type of value. It is value aspect for society as the malpractices of the organisation are disclosed to the society by any member of the organisation who cannot tolerate any more such malpractices.
8. Valued organisations possess a brand in the market and society.

STUDY QUESTIONS

1. Give the meaning of the term value. Write a note on different types of values.
2. Analyse the sources of values. Give a note on terminal values which provide base for taking sound managerial decisions by managers.
3. Distinguish between 'Loyalty" and "Value". Give a note on loyalty and ethical behaviour.
4. Briefly explain the impact of Whistle-blowing on value system of an organisation.

21

LEARNING

LEARNING OBJECTIVES

After reading this chapter, you should be able to know:

- The Concept of "Learning"
- Factors Influencing Learning
- Principles of Learning:
  (1) Reinforcement,
  (2) Punishment
- Learning Theories:
  (1) Classical Conditioning,
  (2) Operant Conditioning,
  (3) Cognitive Theory,
  (4) Social Learning Theory.
- Environment Reinforcing
- Learning Process and Change in Behaviour
- Trends in Individual's Learning
- Learning and Organisational Applications.

Learning is one of the most common words in our daily life. What is learning? In simple terms, learning is a change in behaviour as a result of experience. Learning is the central topic in the study of human behaviour. Learning means all changes in behaviour that result from prior experience and behaviour in similar situations. Learning is the product of reasoning, thinking, information processing and perception. Different psychologists and behavioural scientists have defined learning differently.

Managers including employees must take responsibility for their own learning. Many companies may promise a new employee lifelong employment and a predictable career path. Today, very few companies can make that promise. Even when any company has a formal training department and offers catalog full of courses for employees, no one knows better than it's employee and his or her manager what needs to be learned and how that learning can be applied to the job to make a positive difference in individual and group. One must take responsibility for one's own career path, whether with their current employer or though a series of employers. And the way to build his/her career is to keep learning throughout one's career.

Many companies promise that every employee will receive one week of training per year. But forward-looking managers know that one week of training is not enough to create better performance and new opportunities for the future. They know that they and their employees must be in a continuous learning mode-learning every month, every week, every day.

Learning – Your Role in Continuous Improvement

Employees must make learning a part of their work life. They need to share learning with their colleagues and supervisor to foster growth and effectiveness. More specifically, they have to help develop a learning strategy that will assist them, the unit and the organisation in providing continuously improved quality products and service delivery.

ELEMENTS OF LEARNING

Main features of learning are as follows:

(i) **Change:** This means that a learner acquires new things or modifies his/her existing behaviour or work style.

(ii) **Long Lasting:** The change or modification should stay in the learner for a long time. Supposing a work pattern is modified, and if a person does not remember till it is further changed, it cannot be called learning.

(iii) **Focus:** The focus of learning will be on behaviour, effect and cognition or any combination of these three.

(iv) Individual's interaction with the environment.

Their role in the coaching relationship includes:

- Assessing their current level of performance in relation to competencies required to perform their job.
- Clarifying their learning requirements and ensuring that their learning goals and aspirations are made clear.
- Being open to try new ways of doing things, develop new skills and address identified performance deficiencies.
- Ensuring that they have access to the people and the resources available to further their developmental goals.
- Advising their supervisor/manager when they are overwhelmed or when efforts to improve are not succeeding.

Coaching is one of several ways to ensure that learning takes place. However, successful learning also requires employees to take responsibility for a good deal of the learning necessary for continuous improvement. Self-directed learning is key to enhance knowledge though reading, interviews and discussions with unit employees, colleagues, community leaders and citizens, etc., Also important are on-the-job assignments, special projects, assignments, second meets and other such arrangements. Formal training opportunities should be arranged when warranted. Formal training refers to classroom training, workshops and self-study modules (computer-based or text).

Definition:

1. Learning can be defined as "relatively permanent change in behaviour the potentiality that results from reinforced practice or experience." ***— Steers and Porter***
2. "Learning is any relatively permanent change in behaviour that occurs as a result of experience." ***— Stephen P. Robbins***
3. "Learning is a relatively permanent change in the frequency of occurrences of a specific individual behaviour." ***— Kanber. R.***
4. Driscoll defines learning as "a persisting change in human performance or performance potential.. (which) must come about as a result of the learner's experience and interaction with the world". This definition encompasses many of the attributes commonly associated with behaviourism cognitive, and constructivism – namely, learning as a lasting change state (emotional, mental, physiological (*i.e.*, skills) brought about as a result of experiences and interactions with content or other people.

Driscoll explores some of the complexities of defining learning. Debate centers on:

- ***Valid sources of knowledge*** – Do we gain, knowledge though experiences? Is it innate (present at birth)? Do we acquire it through thinking and reasoning?
- ***Content of knowledge*** – Is knowledge actually knowable? Is it directly knowable though human experience?
- The final consideration focuses on **three epistemological traditions** in relation to learning: **Objectivism, Pragmatism, and Interpretivism.**
  - — Objectivism, (similar to behaviourism) states that reality is external and is objective, and knowledge is gained through experiences.
  - — Pragmatism (similar to cognitivism) states that reality is interpreted, and knowledge is negotiated though experience and thinking.
  - — Interpretivism (similar to constructivism) states that reality is internal, and knowledge is constructed.

The learning theories hold the notion that knowledge is an objective (or a state) that is attainable though either reasoning or experiences.

Behaviourism, cognitivism, and constructivism (built on the epistemological traditions) attempts to address how it is that a person learns. Let us try to understand this in detail.

Behaviourism: states that learning is largely unknowable, that is, we can't possibly understand what goes on inside a person (the "black box theory"). Gredler expresses behaviourism as being comprised of several theories that make three assumptions about learning:

1. Observable behaviour is more important than understanding internal activities.
2. Behaviour should be focused on simple elements: specific stimuli and responses.
3. Learning is about behaviour change.

Cognitivism: Often takes a computer information processing model, Learning is viewed as a process of inputs, managed in short term memory, and coded for long-term recall. Cindy Bell details this process: "In cognitive theories, knowledge is viewed as symbolic mental constructs in details this process: "In cognitive theories, knowledge is viewed as symbolic mental constructs in the learner's mind, and the learning process is the means by which these symbolic representations are committed to memory".

Constructivism suggests that learners create knowledge as they attempt to understand their experiences. Behaviourism and cognitivism view knowledge as external to the learner and the learning process as the act of internalizing knowledge. Constructivism, assumes that learners are not empty vessels to be filled with knowledge. Instead, learners are actively attempting to create meaning. Learners often select and pursue their own learning. Constructivist principles acknowledge that real-life learning is messy and complex. Classrooms which emulate the "fuzziness" of this learning will be more effective in preparing learners for life-long learning.

In simple terms, learning can be defined as **"a change in behaviour acquired though experience".** The above definitions of learning reveal several components that deserve clarification.

First, learning involves change, it may be good or bad. For example a person is attracted towards the fragrance of perfume (stimuli) and he wishes to purchase (drive) and accordingly if he is satisfied with the cost and other factors (positive reinforcement), he purchases it. He learns to link the stimuli and response to the environment and consequently learning has taken place.

Second, the change in behaviour must be relatively permanent. A temporary change in behaviour as a result of fatigue or temporary adoptions are not considered as learning.

Third, change in behavior acquired though experience is considered as learning. A change in individuals through process or attitudes accompanied by no change in behaviour will not be learning.

Fourth, experience in some form is necessary for learning. Experience may be acquired directly though practice or observation or through reading.

Finally, learning is a continuous process. It has the ability to resound adequately to a situation that may or may not have been encountered. Learning is not restricted to the schooldays but it is a lifelong process.

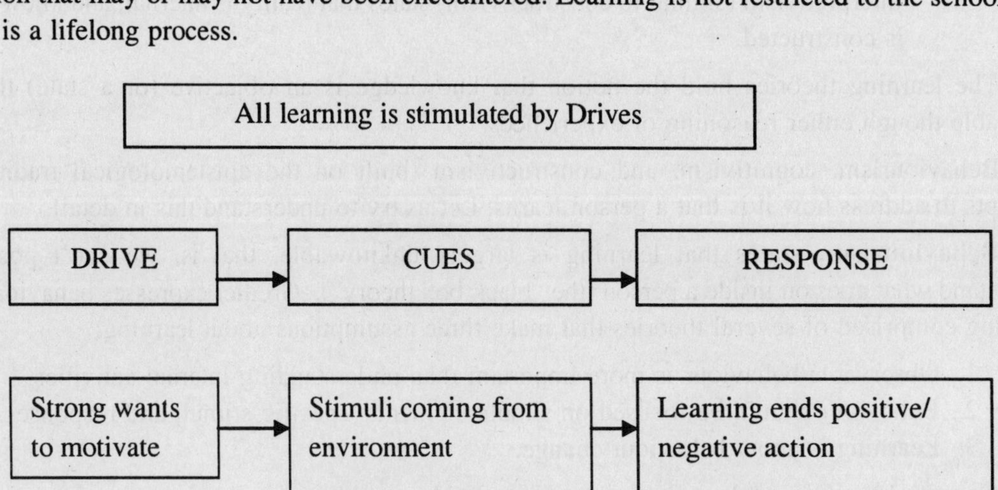

Fig. 21.1. Learning Process

Considering these definitions and learning process, we understand that learning is not visible and can be observed through the behaviour of an individual. If an individual behaves rudely when we contact him for the first time and behaves nicely when contacted for the second time, change in behaviour is presumed to have taken place due to learning. In an organisational context, when an employee is assigned with a well-defined task to perform, his behaviour towards task exhibits whether he needs more learning to perform to the set standards. Learning being invisible and happens by inner urge, comparison of standards set to perform and behaviour of individual towards set work can tell whether the person needs further learning or not.

Further, learning is a continuous activity in one's life. Even in an organisational setting, the workers will have to be continuously learning as and when new works have to be executed. The work of employees, although look like routine, when they are shifted from one department to another related department, the task will be different and one has to learn about new task to perform.

FACTORS THAT INFLUENCE LEARNING

Learning is the outcome of various related factors. The important factors that determine learning are motive, stimuli, response, reinforcement, and retention.

1. Motive or Drive

Motives refer to certain goals that the individual attempts to achieve. They are primary energisers of behaviour. Motives prompt people to action. They are largely subjective and represent the mental feelings of human beings. They are the ways of behaviour and main springs of action. Motive arises continuously and determines the general direction of an individual's behaviour.

2. Stimuli

Stimuli exist in the environment in which a person lives. Stimuli increase the probability of extracting a specific response from a person. Viewed from this point, stimuli may be of two types, generalisation and discrimination.

(a) Generalisation – Generalisation takes place when the similar stimulus repeats in the environment. When two stimuli are exactly same, they will have the probability to extract a specific response. It makes possible for a manager to predict human behaviour when stimuli are exactly alike. But, the negative implication of generalisation is that any manager may make false inferences and conclusions based on the principle of generalisation.

(b) Discrimination – In discrimination, responses of the individuals vary according to different stimuli. Discrimination has wide applications in organisational behaviour in view of individual differences. For example, a supervisor may respond to a high producing worker in a positive manner, but in a different manner to one producing very less.

3. Response

The stimulus generates response. The response may be in the physical form or in terms of attitudes or perception. However, the responses need to be operationally defined and preferably physically observable. The response of the individuals is termed as 'behaviour'. The response may be either positive or negative.

4. Reinforcement

Reinforcement is a primary condition of learning. Reinforcement is anything that increases the strength of response and tends to induce repetitions of the behaviour that precede the reinforcement. Without reinforcement, no quantifiable alteration of behaviour will take place. Reinforcement helps in the repetition of any behaviour. For example, if an employee is rewarded for his hard work, he repeats his behaviour, *i.e.*, he works much harder to get the reward again.

5. Retention

The learned behaviour should be retrieved according to the needs. Retention means remembrance of learned behaviour over time. Learning which is forgotten over time is called **'extinction'**. When response behaviour returns without any intervening reinforcement, it is called **'spontaneous recovery'**.

Dr. Daniel R. Tobin in his article "Corporate Learning Strategies" feels that employees and employers must develop the learning contract and then brings out clearly of what should be included in the learning agreement/contract.

PRINCIPLES OF LEARNING

There are two most important principles of learning.

1. Reinforcement.
2. Punishment.

1. Reinforcement

Reinforcement is an attempt to develop a desirable behaviour by either imparting positive consequences or negative consequences. Reinforcement may be defined as "anything that increases both the strength of response and tends to induce repetitions of the behaviour that precedes the reinforcement". Basically, there are two types of reinforcement. They are **positive reinforcement** and **negative reinforcement.**

Positive reinforcement occurs from the application of a positive consequence following a desirable behaviour. Rewards given after successful completion of a task is an example of positive reinforcement.

Negative reinforcement: results from withholding or threatening negative consequence when an undesirable behaviour occurs. Holding back the incentive for not achieving the sales target can be example of negative reinforcement.

Behaviour can be modified and strengthened by keeping the negative result at bay. An employee may be trying to avoid the workplace simply because he does not deal with ease and comfort with the colleagues in the office. In such a case,merely a change in his workplace may help regain the enthusiasm. Similarly, taking away a positive consequence can serve as a source of negative reinforcement. A reduction in pay would serve as a negative consequence or punishment. Fig. 21.2 explains in brief both the positive and negative reinforcement.

Schedules of Reinforcement

Reinforcements should be scheduled and implemented in a controlled way to get better results. The managers should be aware of when and where the reinforcements can be applied. Following are some of the types of reinforcement schedules.

(a) Continuous Reinforcement: In continuous reinforcement, a preferred behaviour is reinforced each and every time. For example, if an employee always arrives early to the work, the manager instead of taking negative action might compliment him on his desirable behaviour.

(b) Intermittent Reinforcement: In intermittent reinforcement schedule, a desired behaviour is reinforced often enough to make the behaviour worth repeating but not every time it is demonstrated. Following are the four methods adopted for reinforcement in the organisations.

Fixed Ratio: Fixed ratio schedule rewards are limited after a fixed or constant number of responses. A good example for fixed ratio schedule is garment export industry. Every time a fixed number of completed dresses are handed over, then the fixed reward is given.

(ii) Variable Ratio: A variable ratio schedule exhibits that the reward varies relative to the behaviour of the individual. Examples of such reinforcement schedule are salesmen who are rewarded with commission for achieving targets.

(iii) Fixed Interval: In fixed interval, rewards are given at uniform time intervals. The critical variable is time, and it is held fixed or constant. The monthly payment of fixed salary to executives is a good example.

(iv) Variable Interval: In case of variable interval, rewards are distributed without any control over time. This happens when employees achieve success and rewards are given instantly. For example, bonus and awards are given at variable intervals depending on company's revenue/profit (See Fig. 21.2 Principles of Learning).

Changes in Consequence	Changes in Behaviour: Increase in Behaviour ↓	Changes in Behaviour: Decrease in Behaviour ↓
Introducing Consequence	**Positive reinforcement** Employee receiving incentive for achieving targets.	**Punishment** Employees are threatened of cutting pay, if the report is not submitted on time.
No Consequence		**Extinction** Employee not recognised for his hard work.
Removal of Consequence	**Negative reinforcement** Sarcastic comments of the boss is reduced and the employees satisfaction increases.	**Punishment** The expected portion of employee X is given to employee Y.

Fig. 21.2. Principles of Learning

2. Punishment

Punishment occurs when a decrease in the consequence or unfavourable consequence is noticed. When the expected behaviour decreases, it results in punishment. For example, an employee may be given demotion or transfer for ill-treating his co-worker. Here, ill-treating the co-worker is an unexpected or unfavourable consequence.

As with reinforcement, there are two classes or events that fall in the category of punishment. Positive Punishment refers to the on set of an aversive event, such as giving higher target to the salesman as he is nearing to the actual target given. Negative Punishment refers to the withdrawal of an emotionally positive event, such as the taking of the promotional opportunity. In the latter case, we are talking about withdrawing a positive event that is actually present. Not giving a customary reward constitutes extinction rather than punishment.

Positive punishment is, by all odds, the most common procure in the aversive control of behaviour. As expected, the effectiveness of punishment increases greatly in its intensity. Strong shocks are more effective than weak shocks. The greater the amount of reinforcement that has been given for making a response, the stronger the punishment must be in order to suppress it. The effectiveness of punishment also depends on what the aversive event causes the individual to do. Punishment is most effective when it leads to the making of responses that are incompatible with the reinforced response.

Let us understand this from a corporate story. See the following box for the new learning. (A story of SISCO systems IT Company).

Box 21.1: The Situation Leading to Learning: Cisco Systems
I. The high-tech economy has taken a "downturn". A. Cisco Systems eliminated 6,000 jobs. B. That was a reduction of 15% of its workforce. II. The company offered its employees a special exit package. Employees were offered one-third of their regular salary plus benefits for one year. Employees would volunteer their services in community non-profit organisations and many Cisco workers took the offer. Patrick Leaner one of the employees of Cisco Systems now works on inventory data programs at Second Harvest, a food bank, Tam Do another employee of Cisco now works at Inn Vision, which provides services to the homeless. Leaner says, "This is an opportunity to really do something that helps people in the community that are in real need of food. Tam Do says, "I like to do something I like. I wanted to do something different".

From the above story of learning, it is inferred that the individuals must take the positive aspects of any situation and continue their learning process. Many psychologists are concerned about the high frequency of using punishment in the control of behaviour. This is because, fear is not only conditioned to the response-produced or the undesirable behaviour itself but fear also becomes associated with all of the contextual environmental indication at the time punishment is given.

Extinction or Omission

Extinction or Omission is a type of behaviour which occurs when there is no consequence to follow up the behaviour. For instance, when due recognition is not given to an hardworking employee, the behaviour of putting more effort decreases. No reinforcement follows his behaviour. This phase of recreate in the expected behaviour is termed as extinction. The extinction principle is included in the reinforcement. It could also, be used by managers when an undesirable behaviour is elicited by a subordinate as omission of a reward may decrease the undesirable behaviour.

LEARNING THEORIES

Psychologists and behavioural scientists have attempted to develop various theories of learning. To date, the most widely recognised theories of learning are – *Classical conditioning, Operant conditioning, Cognitive and Social learning theories.*

Classical Conditioning Theory

"Classical conditioning" describes a type of associative learning in which there is no contingency between responses and reinforces. Ivan Pavlov, a Russian psychologist developed classical conditioning theory based on his experiments to teach a dog to salivate in response to the ringing of a bell. In the experiments, the dog initially shows weak or no response to a conditioned stimulus (CS) *i.e.*, the bell sound. But a measurable unconditioned response (UR) *i.e.*, saliva production, to unconditioned stimulus (US) *i.e.*, food was noticed. When Pavlov presented meat to the dog, he noticed a great deal of salivation. When merely the bell was rung; no salivation was noticed in the dog.

Later in the course of the training, the conditioned stimulus (CS) is repeatedly presented together with the unconditioned (US stimuli). Eventually, the dog forms an association between the unconditioned (US) and the conditioned stimulus (CS).

In a subsequent test phase, the dog showed the conditioned response (CR), saliva production to the conditioned stimulus (CS) alone. If such an association has been established and memorised, the dog would salivate mercy at the sound of the bell, even if no meat was presented.

Though the above-cited example is logical, yet classical conditioning has real limitations in its applicability to human behaviour in organisations.

Phenomena in Classical Conditioning

There are a number of different phenomena that impact classical conditioning. These factors can impact how quickly a behaviour is acquired and the strength of that association. For example, a process known as extinction occurs when an association disappears; this causes the behaviour to gradually disappear.

Human beings are more complex than animals but less amenable to simple cause. The behavioural environment in organisations is more complex. Human decision-making process being complex in nature makes it possible to override simple classical conditioning.

The theory of classical conditioning is very relevant in OB. Both employers and employees understand several types of behaviours in any organisation.

Supposing an Ambulance is carrying a patient, the light on top of the ambulance will be on and makes a peculiar noice to clear the way for fast movement. This is a case of classical conditioning. Similarily, when advertisement is made by the companies, the purpose is to motivate the prospects to buy their product. It is "S-R" (Stimulus-Response) situation created to stimulate the buyer behaviour. You might have observed an advertisement of FEVICOL which used an elephant to depict the strength of Fevicol. Thus, in organisational activities, classical conditioning theory works positively to make people work motivate prospects to modify their buying behaviour. In sales activities, this theory works well.

Operant Learning

Classical conditioning forms an association between two stimuli. Whereas operant conditioning forms an association between a behaviour and a consequence. It is also called *response-stimulus conditioning* because it forms an association between the animal's response, *i.e.*, behaviour, and the stimulus that follows, *i.e.*, consequence. Antecedents are the events that happen before the behaviour takes place. It may be a stimuli or instinct in the form of sound, light or any signal which is noticeable. Antecedents as such do not cause behaviour. Only when they are confronted with the environment the behaviour takes place. The behaviour that is exhibited depends on the consequences.

Consequences are the events that follow the occurrence of the behaviour. If the consequence is favourable, then there is repetition of the behaviour. Otherwise the behaviour decreases or extinguishes.

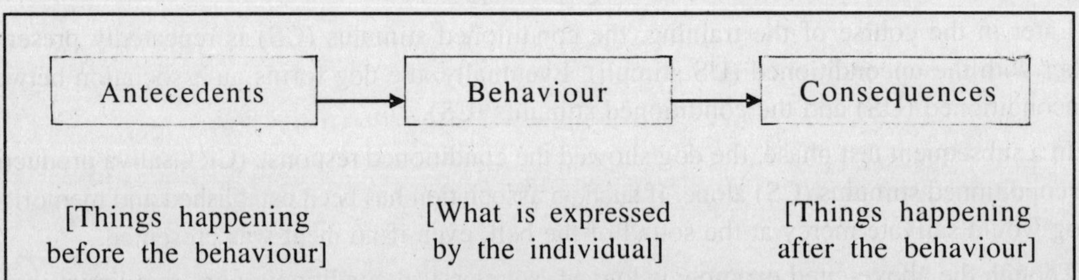

Fig. 21.3. Behaviour Modification Process

Learning can Occur Through Reward and Punishment

In addition to conditioning natural responses through association, behaviourist B.F. Skinner described a process in which learning could occur through reinforcement and punishment. This process, known as **operant conditioning** functions by forming an association between a behaviour and the consequences of the behaviour. Operant is applied in the context of voluntary behaviour.

Reinforcement Schedules are Important

At first glance, the operant conditioning process seems fairly straightforward. Simply observe a behaviour and then offer a reward or punishment. However, B.F. Skinner discovered that the timing of these rewards and punishments have an important influence on how quickly a new behaviour is acquired and on the strength of the response.

Behaviour modification – Often referred to as **b-mod** — is the therapy technique based on Skinner's work. It is very straight forward: Extinguish an undesirable behaviour (by removing the reinforcer) and replace it with a desirable behaviour by reinforcement. It has been used on all sorts of psychological problems — addictions, neuroses, shyness, autism, even schizophrenia — and works particularly well with children. There are examples of backward psychotics who haven't communicated with others for years who have been conditioned to behave themselves in fairly normal ways, such as eating with a knife and fork, taking care of their own hygiene needs, dressing themselves, and so on.

Skinner's operant condtioning is based on the notion that behaviour is a function of its consequence, which may be either positive or negative.

In organisational setting, we use the term **"learning organisation"**. This term was popularised by Peter Singe. The concept says that the organisation will be ever learning with the changes that take place due to new policies and programmes introduced as a result of innovations in work practices and adaptation of new technology. Organisations provide all facilities to employees to increase productivity, by learning new techniques and adopting to changes. How they learn and change themselves depends upon their capacity to learn. If they learn to adapt to change, it is the consequence of the behaviour. Any work behaviour exhibited by employees is operant behaviour. When they learn new things and adopt it for organisational learning, results in organisational improvement and productivity. (Read Chapter 4 of this title for more information on Learning Organisation).

This theory is based on the law of effect. The law of effect states that there is probability of repetition of the operant behaviour and this behaviour entirely depends on the consequences.

Thus, operant conditioning is the process of modifying behaviours through the use of positive or negative consequences following specific behaviours.

Cognitive Theory

A general approach that views learning as an active mental process of acquiring, remembering, and using knowledge. Learning is evidenced by a change in knowledge that makes a change in behaviour possible.

The cognitive theory defines human behaviour as a dynamic and reciprocal interaction of personal factors, behaviour, and the environment. According to this theory, an individual's behaviour is uniquely determined by each of these three factors. While the cognitive theory upholds the behaviourist's notion that response and consequences mediate behaviour, it contends that behaviour is largely regulated though cognitive process. Therefore, response or consequences of behaviour are used to form expectations of behavioural outcomes. It is the ability to form these expectations that give human the capability to predict the outcomes of their behaviour, before the behaviour is performed.

The cognitive theory strongly emphasises on one's cognitions. Cognition refes to the power and ability of knowing. It suggests that the mind is an active force that constructs one's reality, selectively encodes information, performs behaviour on the basis of values and expectations, and imposes structure on its won actions. Through feedback and reciprocity, a person's own reality is formed by the interaction of the environment and one's conditions.

In addition, cognitions change over time as a function of maturation and experience, *i.e.*, attention span, memory, ability to form symbols, reasoning skills. It is through an understanding of the processes involved in one's construction of reality that enables human behaviour to be understood, predicted, and changed.

Cognitive Learning Process (A Psychological Model)

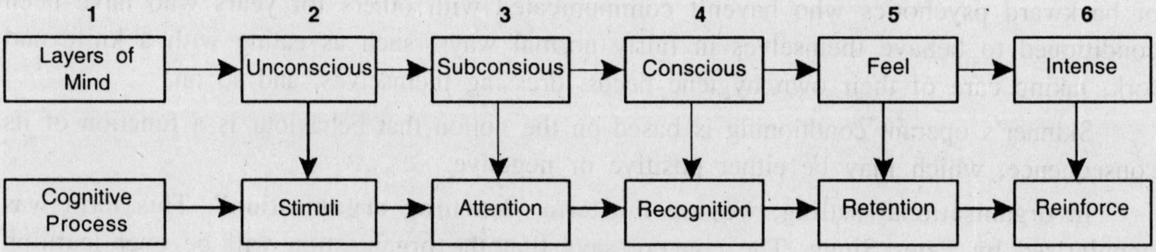

Fig. 21.4. Cognitive Learning Process

As per this cognitive process, learning commences and closes in different layers of mind. Commencing from the **unconscious** (which is the layer one) and ends in layer five **Intensive.** Intense layer is the heart of learning where repeated learning takes place to reinforce and it changes the behaviour to action. See the following figure:

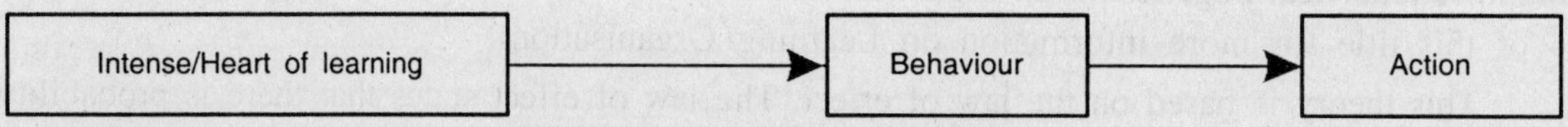

Fig. 21.5. Reinforcing Behaviour

Cognitive – The Concept: Related to mental act or process of acquiring knowledge that involves processing of the sensory information and includes perception, awareness and judgement.

Cognitive Learning process can be well understood with an example — Salesperson of a Pharmaceautical company. Salesperson gets stimuli from training, knows his job with rapt **attention, recognises** the importance of the job, **retains** the job in mind as to what is to be done, **reinforces the job** with repeated memorising, **behaves**, *i.e.*, moves into action and **acts,** *i.e.*, meeting the prospects and convert them to become purchasers. Cognitive process to stops at **"Action"** point. The "Response" of other person (*i.e.*, buyer) is guided by cognitive process of that person, *i.e.*, to purchase (positive response) or not to purchase (negative response).

In an organisational context, the cognitive aspect provides a situation wherein employees understand the importance of change of behaviour to improve the quality and image of the organisation.

Social Learning Theory

Social learning theory focuses on the learning that occurs within a social context. It considers that people learn from one another, including such concepts as observational learning, imitation, and modeling. Among others, Albert Bandura is considered as the leading proponent of this theory.

Social Learning theory states that "Learning mainly occurs by observing others and then modeling the behaviours that lead to favourable outcomes and avoiding behaviours that lead to punishing consequences".

General Principles of Social Learning Theory

(a) People can learn by observing the behaviour of others and the outcomes of those behaviours.

(b) Learning can occur without a change in behaviour. Behaviourists say that learning has to be represented by a permanent change in behaviour, in contrast social learning theorists say that because people can learn through observation alone, their learning may not necessarily be shown in their performance. Learning may or may not result in a behaviour change.

(c) Cognition plays a role in learning. Over the last 40 years, social learning theory has become increasingly cognitive in its interpretation of human learning. Awareness and expectations of future reinforcements or punishments can have a major effect on the behaviours that people exhibit.

(d) Social learning theory can be considered as a bridge or a transition between behaviourists' learning theories and cognitive learning theories.

Social learning theory has related features which make the learner to understand and adopt them for his/her growth. They are: (i) Behaviour modeling, (ii) learning behaviour consequences and (iii) Self-reinforcement.

(i) Behavioural modeling: This provides the learner a role model to follow precisely the actions of that role model to perform a task successfully. The action of role model would change the behaviour of learner to be successful. Behavioural model suits well, if it leads to favourable consequences. For Example: A newly appointed employee in a particular department can strictly follow the behaviour of the existing worker who is successful in his work in discharging the similar task. Considering the successful employee as role model by the new employee is a behaviour modeling concept. It is a form of learning process. This increases the "Self-efficacy" of the learner.

Self-efficacy

Self-efficacy is a concept that tells about the competancy of an employee to complete the assigned task successfully. Employee firmly believes that he/she has the potentiality to complete the task without any problem. Behaviour modeling increases self-efficacy.

The performance of a person working in an organisation depends on his technical competence, his managerial experience, etc., as well as how the role is performed in a given situation. It is the integration of the person and the role he/she plays. Integration ensures the person's effectiveness in the organisation. Unless the person has the requisite knowledge, technical competence and the skills required for the role, he/she cannot be effective.

The integration of the person and the role comes about when the role is able to fulfil the needs of the individuals and when the individual is able to contribute to the evaluation of the role. The more we move from **role taking** (responding to the expectation by various other persons) to **role making** (taking initiative in designing the role more creatively in a way that the various expectations from others as well as of the role occupant integrated), the role is more likely to be effective.

Self-efficacy increases the confidence of an individual after observing the behavioural model rather than hearing about a role model. By observing the model, the individual tries to identify with the role and gains self-confidence to perform the tasks.

In the initial stages of adoption of behavioural modeling, self-efficacy may be affected. But gradually the expected response will emerge and can predict the result by following the particular behavioural model.

(ii) Learning Behaviour Consequences: Another aspect of social learning theory is that consequences of behaviour can also be understood in the forms other than direct experience. Logical thinking can provide consequences of our actions. For example, if an employee thinks in a negative way while performing a task the consequent result will be punishment for wrong doing. Consequences can also be learnt by observing others.

(iii) Self-reinforcement is another aspect of social learning theory. This takes place when an employee can control his actions. Supposing an employee is performing a task, *i.e.*, finalising a project. Due to continuous work, he gets exhausted and needs a break and avails it and visits coffee house for ten-fifteen minutes. After coming back, he sticks to his job and finishes successfully. Here, the employee has the control over his task. But he takes a break to reinforce the finishing of the assigned task. Any number of consequences can be thought of and used in self-reinforcement. Self-reinforcement has become a vital activity to keep employees more relaxed to perform the task effectively. In this case, supervision and monitoring are lessened or not required at times.

Thus, social learning theory explains that more of learning takes place by observing others and then convert those observations into behavioural models and adopt them to perform tasks. Behaviours that can give good or positive results have to be adopted and behaviours that lead to punishing consequences have to be avoided.

Learning can also be made through experience. It is not only the acquisition of knowledge through books or an instructor that helps in learning, but also employees learn by discovering new knowledge through direct experience and experimentation in a fast changing organisational and social environment. It is called "Implicit".

"Learning", it is so called because, the information is acquired by us without our knowledge and without any conscious efforts.

Environment Reinforces Modeling

People are often reinforced for modeling the behaviour of others. Bandura suggested that the environment also reinforces modeling.

(a) The observer is reinforced by the model. For example, a student who changes his dressing style to fit in which a certain group of students has strong likelihood of being accepted and thus reinforced by that group.

(b) **The observer is reinforced by a third person.** The observer might be modeling actions of some one else. For example, an outstanding class leader or student. The teacher notice this and compliments and praises the observer for modeling such behaviour, thus reinforcing that behaviour.

(c) **The imitated behaviour itself leads to reinforcing consequences.** Many behaviours that we learn from others produce satisfying or reinforcing results. For example, a student in a class could observe how the extra work a classmate does. This student in turn would do the same extra work and also receive enjoyment.

(d) **Consequences of the model's behaviour affect the observer's behaviour vicariously.** This is known as **vicarious reinforcement.** In this model is reinforced for a response and then the observer shows an increase in that same response. Bandura illustrated this by having students watch a film of a model hitting an inflated clown doll. One group of children saw the model being praised for such action. Without being reinforced, the group of children also began to, hit the doll.

To conclude, if there is a reward accompanied by the favourable response, then the behaviour is repeated. Else the behaviour comes to extiniction.

The box below gives guidelines for supervisors to enhance their employee's growth and learning process.

Box 21.2: Guidelines for Employees' Growth

Supervisors are there to provide employees with the guidance, tools and leadership to foster learning, growth and effectiveness by:

- **Clarifying:** eliciting descriptions of problems and contributing factors; providing technical and organisational insight; encouraging venting of strong feelings and exploring instincts into feelings and behaviour; and encouraging consideration of the advantages and disadvantages of alternative learning approaches.
- **Mentoring:** demonstrating commitment to organisational goals and values; sensitising individuals to the organisation's culture; developing an awareness of informal and formal organisation; encouraging personal networking; sensitising individuals to unit and organisational priorities and expectations; and encouraging pro-activity in bringing about change.
- **Tutoring:** demonstrating technical skills; developing technical understanding; monitoring learning pace and adjusting tasks to suit; providing opportunities to demonstrate skills and provide feedback; and encouraging continuous learning.
- **Confronting:** clarifying performance expectations; identifying performance deficits; providing tasks at increasing levels of difficulty; and encouraging continuous improvement.

The role of a supervisor as a coach is to help reinforce that learning is a part of the employees' work life and sharing learning is essential to organisational growth and renewal.

Latest Trends in Individual's Learning Process

Behaviourism, cognitive, and constructivism are the three broad learning theories most often utilised in the creation of instructional environments. These theories, however were developed in a time when learning was not impacted through techonology. Over the last twenty years, technology has reorganised how we live, how we communicate, and how we learn. Learning needs and theories that describe learning principles and processes should be reflective of underlying social environments. Vaill in the year 1996, emphasises that "learning must be a way of being — an on going set of attitudes and actions by individuals and groups that they to try to keep abreast of the surprising, nove, messy, obtrusive, recurring events."

Learners in the formative stages would complete the required schooling and enter a career that would often last lifetime. Previously information development was slow. The life of knowledge was measured in decades. Today, these foundational principles have been altered. Knowledge is growing exponentially. In many fields, the life of knowledge is now measured in months and years.

Gozalez describes the challenges of rapidly diminishing knowledge life: One of the most persuasive factors is the shrinking half-life of knowledge. The "half-life of knowledge" is the time span from when knowledge is gained to when it becomes obsolete. Half of that is known today was not known 20 years ago. The amount of knowledge in the world has doubled the past 10 years and is doubling every 18 months according to the American Society of Training and Documentation (ASTD). To combat the shrinking half-life of knowledge, organisations have been forced to develop new methods of deploying instruction.

Some Significant Trends in Today's Learning

- Many learners will move into a variety of different, possibly unrelated fields over the course of their lifetime.
- Informal learning is a significant aspect of our learning experience. Formal education no longer comprises the majority of our learning. Learning now occurs in a variety of ways – through communities of practice, personal networks, and through completion of work-related tasks.
- Learning is a continual process, lasting for a lifetime. Learning and work-related activities are no longer separate. In many situations, they are the same.
- Technology is altering our brains. The tools we use define and sharper our thinking.
- The organisation and the individual are both learning organisms.
- Increased attention to knowledge management highlights the need for a theory a that attempts to explain the link between individual and organisational learning.
- Many of the processes previously handled by learning theories can now be off-loaded to, or supported by technology.
- Know-how and know-what is being supplemented with know-where (the understanding or where to find knowledge needed).

Learning activities including technology and forming connection begin to move push learning theories into a digital age. We can no longer personally experience and acquire learning that we need to act. We derive our competence from forming connections. Karen Stephenson states:

"Experience has long been considered the best teacher of knowledge. Since we cannot experience everything, other people's experiences, and hence other people, become the surrogate for knowledge. 'I store my knowledge in my frineds' is an axiom for collecting knowledge through collecting people (undated)."

Chaos and Learning

Chaos is a new reality for knowledge workers. Science Week, 2004 quoted that Nigel Calder's definition that chaos is 'cryptic form of order". Chaos is the breakdown of predictablility, evidenced in complicated arrangements that initially defy order. Unlike constructivism, which states that learners attempt to foster understanding by meaning making tasks, chaos states that the meaning exists – the learner's challenge is to recognise the patterns which appear to be hidden. Meaning-making and forming connections between specialised communities are important activities, in chaotic conditions.

Chaos, as a science, recognises the connection of everything to everything. Gerick states: "in weather, for example, this translates into what is only half-jokingly known as the Butterfly Effect – the notion that a butterfly stirring the air today in speaking can transform storm systems next month in New York". This analogy highlights a real challenge: "sensitive dependence on initial conditions" profoundly impacts what we learn and how we act based on our learning". Decision-making is indicative of this. If the underlying conditions used to make decisions change, the decision itself is no longer correct as it was at the time it was made. The ability to recognise and adjust to patterns is a key learning task Chaos leads to self-organisation.

Self-organisation

Luis Mates Rocha defines self-organisation as the "spontaneous formation of well organised structure, patterns, or behaviours, from random initial conditions. "Learning, as a self-organising process require that the system "be informational open, that is, for it to be able to classify its own interaction with an environment. It must be able to change its structure".

Wiley and Edwards acknowledge the importance of self-organisation as a learning process. They argues that "Jacobs argues that communities self-organise in a manner similar to social insects: instead of thousands of ants crossing each other's performance traits and changing their behaviour, accordingly, thousands of humans pass each other on the sidewalk and change their behaviour accordingly. "Self-organisation on a personal level is a micro-process of the larger self-organising knowledge domain, created within corporate or institutional environments. The capacity to form connections between sources of information, and thereby create useful information patterns, is required to learn in our knowledge economy.

Action Learning

The best performing companies adopt "Action learning". It is a form of experiment-based learning. This involves the formation of cross-functional teams for the purpose of investigating the problems of the organisation or to cease an opportunity that has come on its way. The team examines the problem or opportunity, comes out with its findings and discuses those findings with concerned senior executives and adopt it to solve the problem.

In a setting of organisational change, management process adopted to have continuous learning, "Action plan" looks like a new business development proposed rather than an educational programme. In the learning process", "employees participate in new ventures and develop innovative solutions to unique problems".

Knowledge gets value only when it is converted into action. In "Action learning, employees involve in experimental learning, enter into new situations, learn from their mistakes in controlled setting and rethink about the ongoing work practices. The result obtained through this refined process adds value to the organisation in terms of better work processes.

***Source**: Organisational Behaviour:* Steven L.MC's chane and Others, TMH,p.54

LEARNING AND ORGANISATIONAL APPLICATIONS

We have discussed several dimensions of learning, mainly from the point of psychological attributes. As understood so far, learning changes the behaviour of an individual. Learning is invisible and can be understood through the change in behaviour of an individual. Only by continuous observation we can say that an individual has learnt some new things and it is exhibited in the form of changed behaviour.

In an organisational setting, changes will be having place. Because, organisation has to be dynamic to be in the growth path. There will be many disturbing factors which hinder the growth. To weed out these disturbances, the management should immediately take decisions,. Implementing the decision itself is 'learning process', as the process modifies the behaviour of the people who are involved in that process. In the process of implementing decisions, behaviour modification through learning can be viewed from two angles, *viz.*, (i) from the angle of employer and (ii) from the angle of employees.

(i) Behaviour modification of employer: Employer, performing the role of decision-maker has to take several decisions on routine matters and on special issues. Each issue, irrespective of the category is to be sorted out and the sorting process is a **"Learning activity".** Decision that emerges out of this learning has to be implemented and when implemented, it becomes a "Behaviour modification".

Supposing in a shop floor, the conveyance of raw material to the plant involves 3 or 4 activities. With the introduction of new technology, it can be reduced to 2 activities. Management takes a decision to implement the new procedure of a conveyance as a measure of cost cutting. When implemented, it amounts to behaviour modification through learning a new procedure. Several such activities take place in an organisation and each change involves decision-making, learning and behaviour modificaiton on the part of employer.

(ii) Behaviour modification of employees: When the employer takes a decision to change a procedure as a matter of cost saving device, they have to train employees to adapt themselves to new procedure. Management has to design the learning process of new procedure which will be as follows.

New Procedure and Adaptation

1. Identify the required behaviour that makes the employees to adapt to the required change.

2. While identifying the required new behavioural mode, prepare a faultless model which paves way for implementation without any disturbance.

3. Empower the employees with technical and other skills (give proper training) required for adopting to new procedure.

4. Create a congenial situation so that employees learn new procedure at a faster rate and quickly adopt to a new situation.

5. Provide for incentives such as promotion, bonus, etc., as positive consequences for these employees who reach the expected new standards.

6. Standardise these new practices to maintain them till such time the new practices are further processed.

This learning process will be adopted to change the behaviour of employes wherever a change in activity takes place. It may be expansion, diversification or may change in office procedure or change due to consolidation of activities or adaptation of new technology, etc., Any change that takes place needs learning the new order to modify the behaviour.

SUMMARY

1. According to Steers and Porter, "Learning can be defined as relatively permanent change in behaviour potentiality that results from reinforced practice or experience". The important factors that determine learning are motive, stimuli, response, reinforcement, and retention.
2. Reinforcement is an attempt to develop desirable behaviour by either imparting positive consequences or with negative consequences. Positive punishment refers to the onset of an aversive event, such as giving higher target to the saleman as he is nearing to the actual target given. Negative punishment refers to the withdrawal of an emotionally positive event, such as the taking of the proposed commission on targets.
3. "Classical conditioning" describes a type of associative learning in which there is no contingency between responses and reinforces.
4. Operant conditioning forms an association between a behaviour and a consequence.
5. The cognitive theory defines human behaviour as a dynamical and reciprocal interaction of personal factors, behaviour, and the environment.
6. Social learning theory focuses on the learning that occurs within a social context. It considers that people learn from one another, including such concepts as observational learning, limitation, and modeling.

STUDY QUESTIONS

1. What do you mean by learning? As a manager of an organisation, what aspects of learning you should know? Explain.
2. Sate how behaviourism, cognitive and constructivism helps in undertstanding learning process of an individual.
3. Briefly explain the learning process of an individual.
4. Explain the factors that influence learning.
5. Briefly explain the principles of learning.

6. Briefly explain "classical conditioning" theory of learning
7. Given an analytical note on operant conditioning theory
8. Explain cognitive and social learning theory
9. Give a brief note on each of the following:
(i) Behaviour modeling, (ii) Self-efficacy, (iii) Self-reinforcement, (iv) Mentoring, (v) Action learning, (vi) Reinforcement, (vii) Conditioning, (viii) Shaping the behaviour.
10. Given an explanatory a note on applications of learning process in organisational settings.
11. Briefly explain the Organisational Behaviour modification.
12. Briefly explain how behaviour of an individual is directed by reinforcement and conditioning.

Problem-solving Cases

1. The organisation in which you work has adopted continuous training process with more frequency as a measure of developing employees on quality lines. As an employee of the organisation, analyse whether this programme is effective or ineffective to develop the "Organisational identity" in the workers.
2. You are an executive of a company in HR department. Your organisation is contemplating to adopt "Action learning" to develop its other executives to hold top executive positions in upcoming projects. As a HR executive of the firm, you express that action learning is a time consuming process and suggest that short-term course can be conducted with the help of experts having knowledge in the proposed project.
In this backdrop, discuss the pros and cons of action learning.
3. Identify any one of the Indian Management Guru's characteristics and achievements. State also how you would learn adopting social learning theory. Do you require any reinforcement to apply the theory?

22

BEHAVIOUR AND RELATIONSHIP

LEARNING OBJECTIVES

After reading this chapter, you should be able to know:

- Factors affecting relationship
  (i) Encroachment on the Rights of Privacy of Employees by Management
  (ii) Obligation to Improve Quality of Work life.
  (iii) Conformity Issue
  (iv) Not providing Job Enrichment Opportunities
  (v) Undue Control of Employees.
- Role of Employees
  (i) Become Good Organisational Citizens, (ii) Exhibit Mutual Trust, (iii) Adapt Ethical Practices and Avoiding Unethical Practices such as Insider Trading and Whistle-blowing.

Behaviour of people, both employer and employee, in the organisation is mainly guided by individual perception, attitude, learning, etc. These aspects are fully discussed in separate chapters of this book. However, certain issues other than personal traits also influence the behaviour of the individuals. The issues are between organisations and individuals between groups of the organisation and individuals and group. Understanding these issues are essential to develop and practice healthy relationship amongst members of the organisation. Healthy relationship contributes greatly for the success of the organisation. Better image can be created thorough good understanding between workers and management. Misunderstanding between the people and organisation leads to conflict. The issues that lead to conflict are: (i) encroachment on rights of privacy of people who work in the organisation, (ii) obligation of the organisation to improve the quality of work life (QWL), (iii) conformity issue, (iv) failure on the part of the organisation to provide job enrichment opportunities, (v) discipline and (vi) undue control of employee's activities and choices. These issues are examined in detail in the following paragraphs.

I. Privacy Policy

Privacy Policy is a policy formulated by the individuals or by organisations expressing therein the areas which are not to be encroached upon by outsiders. There are certain rights of the individuals or organisations which are purely private in nature. People dealing with organisations or individuals in organisations should not spy on the private aspects. The **right to privacy** has to be left alone. Privacy policy insists that an individual's or organisational private aspects have freedom from undesirable intrusions. Hence, **Privacy Policy** or **Right to Privacy** can be defined as follows:

"A policy or right of persons to decide how much information, what information and what information about themselves have to be disclosed to others".

This definition implies that only essential information of individuals or of the organisations have to be disseminated to others in completing an agreement or task. Unnecessarily, all private information should not be disclosed.

Privacy Policy – Why?

Privacy Policy is essential for every one for the following reasons.

- The individual/firm is protected from shame, ridicule, embarrassment, black mail (if personal) information is given to outsiders).
- The plans and actions prepared on the basis of our culture and values are to be protected from being copied.
- There are certain private information which should not be disclosed to any body including the persons who like us most. When disclosed will hurt those who like us. Hence Privacy Policy.
- Privacy Policy protects the image of self. Individual's reputation will not be tarnished.

Privacy will be of two types, viz.,

(i) Psychological and (ii) Physical

Psychological Privacy is concerned with an individual's inner urges and thoughts. Personal belief, plans, values, feelings and desires of the individual are considered to be psychological privacy aspects.

Physical privacy relates to individual's physical activities. The psychological privacy or the inner urge of an individual will be revealed by physical expressions. These expressions are essential to protect psychological privacy. Physical Privacy is governed by ones own culture. For example, one cannot perform an abscence function in public. Hence, physical privacy is respected for its own sake.

Advantages

The right to privacy protects the personal interest of individual. The activities that are private in nature and to be protected are as follows:

- Certain personal information when disclosed causes harm to an individual. He may be embarrassed, or put into shame, or ridiculed or blackmail him. Such privacy aspect has to be protected. Privacy right ensures that others cannot access to such information.
- Privacy rights protect our personal activities. These activities may not cause any harm to any body. But we feel that it should not be disclosed to others as they do not consider such activities with same intensity as we consider, privacy policy holds others from intervention and allow us to enjoy freedom in our private plans.
- In case of people for whom we have affection, their good feeling about us should not be shaken by disclosing certain things about us which are not palatable to them. Privacy rights prevent such disclosures.
- Private rights protect the individuals from self-incrimination (guilty of wrong doing).

Privacy Policy — Importance

Privacy policy not only protects an individual, but also enables the person in doing good things. Following are the reasons as to why privacy policy has to be adopted.

(i) It develops intimacy with others leading to friendship, affection and trust. This intimacy makes an individual to share personal information with intimates and with everyone.

(ii) There are certain activities carried out by individuals whom they feel are not to be published. They are mainly concerned with professional relationship. For example, a doctor should not reveal his patient's disease to others. Similarly, an advocate should not reveal his client's problems to others. A psychiatrist should not disclose depression or any other mental disorder of his patient to others. An employee should not reveal the management's secret policies to outsiders. Registered patients should not be disclosed to outsiders. Thus, privacy policy protects such functions.

(iii) Privacy policy protects a person who is carrying out distinct social roles. One can involve freely in activities as a citizen rather than an employee in an organisation. One can perform other duties along with the one he holds in the organisation. Privacy policy provides scope for this.

(iv) Privacy Policy helps individuals in presenting themselves to the society and make society to think and understand him in the way in which the individual wants. Privacy Policy protects the interest of everybody. Not only of the employees. It will protect consumers, business people and individuals at large in the society. But the focal point is that it protects every one from disclosing unwanted information to others and develops healthy relationship between individuals.

Certain conditions are followed while framing the privacy policy.

(a) Relevance

The information collected for framing privacy policy should be relevant and informed to concerned. Organisations collecting information should reveal to the concerned individuals as to why and for what purpose it is collected. This disclosure will prevent employees from indulging in such activities. For example: Information about the activities of an employee off the working hours will be collected which is relevant for smooth running of the organisation. This information also gives caution to employee that he/she should not involve in any activity after duty hours which hampers the organisational interest. Thus, relevant information concerning privacy should be collected to use it when employee trespasses.

(b) Consent

The concerned person from whom the private information is to be collected has to express his/her **acceptance** for such collection. Person at the time of giving acceptance to collect information can do so only after confirming that the information will be used for the purpose for which it is collected. Supposing the employees are provided certain facility such as becoming a member of a social club. The club, on admission, collects some private information of the person. Such information should not be misused by the club after the person accepts membership. Similarly, the member should not indulge in activities mentioned in private information, that is collected at the time of admission.

(c) Genuine Purpose

The information collected should have some **purpose** and it should have **legitimacy.** The information so collected should provide some benefits to the person who provides information. Bank loan or insurance is the best example. When a person avails loan enjoys benefit out of it. Bank also collects information with the purpose of using it when the client defaults. Similarly, an employee may get additional incentive on disclosing some secret personal traits to top management.

(d) Truth

Whatever the information collected should be accurate. Inaccurate information should not be collected. If collected, it has to be processed and rectified. Persons from whom the inaccurate information is collected has to be made known to that person before it is rectified.

(e) Protection

Information collected should be fully **secured** by the organisation. Others in the organisation should not know about the private information of individuals collected by the organisation. In times of acquisitions and mergers, personal information of employees should not be revealed to new employer without the consent of employees who continue to work in the new firm.

Thus, privacy policy is a two-way approach. In all activities of the organisation, privacy policy plays a major role. Secured privacy policy facilitates to develop healthy relationship amongst members and between employees and employer. Encroachment of privacy policy leads to conflict.

II. Quality of Work Life – QWL

The organisation has the primary responsibility to improve the quality of work on a sustainable note. Work life here refers to the time period that employees spends in an organisation. Quality means that whatever the work done in an organisation by a worker should match to the standard fixed by management and the management has to provide everything to employees to maintain quality in service rendered. Ensuring service quality by both employees and management is an overwhelming task. Though maintaining quality of work life is formidable, certain guidelines can make the task more achievable. In this direction, contributors on management thought such as Edward Deming, Philip. B. Crosby, Joseph. M. Juran have given certain guidelines to achieve quality in all activities of the organisation including the working pattern of employees. (Read, the chapter on "Development of Management Thought" of this book).

Deming gives 14 principles to achieve quality. He advocates continuous improvement. Crosby who is considered as pioneer of quality movement in the USA says, that quality can be achieved through the adaptation of integrity, systems, communication, operations and policies. Joseph. M. Juran emphasises that management has to adopt quality improvement programmes at two levels: (i) the organisation as a whole to achieve and maintain quality and (ii) the strategic planning by individual departments to control and maintain quality and linking this plan to organisational strategic planning.

Many organisations have adopted the quality guidelines of experts to improve and maintain quality of their products and services. This has improved and is improving the relationship between customers and the organisation.

What is Quality of Work Life ?

Modern generation of workers are more enthusiastic in workplaces, as HRM programmes of the organisations induce them to work. Workers always look for quality improvement in their operations and they have to freedom to work. This is what "quality of work life" insists.

"Quality of work life is the degree of opportunity of workers to make decisions that influence their work situation. The greater the opportunity of workers to make such decisions, the higher the quality of work life is said to be". (Tom Lupton, "Efficiency and the Quality of Life", Organisational Dynamics).

This meaning of quality of work life prompts the workers to take the decisions that lead to the following:

1. Job for them will be challenging, interesting and make them to be more responsible.
2. They are recognised in workplace and rewarded suitably through fair wages and other incentives.
3. Work stations will be very congenial, safe and bright.
4. Organisations look after their employees in befitting manner.
5. Supervision of workers will be at minimal.
6. Jobs for employees are more secured.
7. Friendly relationship exists between co-workers and between various departments of the organisations.
8. Service quality of workers will be on a higher side as the whole atmosphere is filled with high morale.

Thus, quality of work life in organisations leads to the development of quality relationship with stakeholders. QWL motivate employees to work hard to increase productivity. Managements also, in turn, work for the welfare of employees and develop healthy relationship and deal fairly with all their stakeholders. They work for improving the general quality of life and build competitive organisation.

III. Conformity Issue

Conformity here refers to the performance of tasks by the employees as per the standards fixed by the employer. Similarly, the employer should deliver or fulfil the terms and conditions agreed upon at the time of appointment of an employee. Conformity aspect mainly refers here to relationship management and behaviour. Conformity issue in an organisational backdrop involves developing attitudes, opinions and behaviours to match the attitude of the group in which the individual works or the expectations of the organisation. Every employee normally conform to the standard values or norms of the organisation to have a good relationship with co-workers and organisation.

Some degree of conformity is essential for organisations to function. Imbalance in conformity leads to conflict between employer and employees. Hence, while fixing standards of work, employer has to consider workable norms. Too much expectation leads to confrontation and develops unhealthy relationship.

Different organisations fix different values on conformity. This depends on size and structure of the organisation. Inspite of fixing practicable norms or values, some individuals will be non-conformists and disturb the working of the organisation. Non-conformity to some extent is common in every organisation. There are organisations which fix higher values and norms to be followed by their employees. For example, military organisations expect a high level of conformity in the behaviour of their members. They are very strict regarding non-conformists and ruthlessly punish those who do not conform to their standards.

Non-conformists in organisations have to face problems. They are not liked by co-workers. Even the organisation will place such people in the last line as far as awarding incentives and special benefits. They are distinguished from conformists.

Conformity leads to loyalty and obedience. Loyalists implicitly follow the values and norms. Many a time, they have to work against their conscience. Obedience is a requirement in an organisation, and those who obey achieve strength and are liked by all. They become the trusted employees of the organisation.

Thus, conformity aspect tells that those who conform to the organisational norms develop a required behaviour and contribute for developing normal relationship.

IV. Job Enrichment

Sound relationship exists between employees and management, when the managements motivate their employees to do better job. Paying salary for the job done by employee is a routine affair and it does not motivate employees to perform better. When additional motivators are incorporated into the job, employees are further motivated and perform the task to the organisation's expectations. The process of introducing additional motivators into jobs to get better performance is called **"Job Enrichment".** It makes an employee satisfied one.

> "Job enrichment involves redesigning work to give employees more authority in planning their tasks, deciding how to complete their work and allowing them to learn related skills or to trade jobs with theirs".

Many organisations have succeeded in achieving the organisational goals, after adopting job enrichment programmes. Job enrichment keeps employees happier and make them to stick on to the organisation for a long time. This also contributes for the maintenance of sound relationship between employer and employees. Following Table 22.1 shows the job enrichment aspects and the corresponding changes that are expected to derive.

TABLE 22.1: Job Enrichment Activities and Corresponding Changes Expected

Activities those leading to Job Enrichment	*Expected Result*
1. Lifting restrictions and having only accountablity.	Responsibility increases. achievement follows.
2. Demanding more accountability for an individual's work.	Recognition for individual's work and oncreased responsibility.
3. Placing an individual in charge of one full unit or division or one module and giving more job freedom in his work.	Increases responsibility, recognition and achievement.
4. Giving periodical reports to employees directly instead of giving it to supervisors.	Increases employee confidence and he/she is internally recognised.
5. Assigning new difficult tasks on which the employee has not previously worked.	Employee learns new things and personally grows.
6. Assigning such tasks which make employees to become proficient.	Employee's responsibility increases and he/she grows and have career advancement.

Thus, the organisations have to provide opportunities for job enrichment, to keep the workers happier. This enables the organisation to have a sound relationship with employees.

V. Discipline

Discipline means training of the mind and character designed to produce obedience and self-control. Organisational discipline expects that the employee should have self-control about the adaptation of organisational norms. Any deviation from the norms or set procedure will attract punishment according to the degree of mistakes committed.

The focal aspect here is that employees when disciplined regarding work, will automatically gain the confidence of the management and it paves way for sustainable and good relationship. Employees are essentially pure and unpolluted. A teacher-student relationship exists in organisations. Organisation behaves in the manner a teacher behaves. A teacher monitors has/her wards to see that wards learn the prescribed lessons. In an organisational set-up, the manager (teacher) supervises the activities of his team members (students). Employees (Students) have to strictly follow the rules, regulations and work order (Job description) to produce the target work. The effectiveness and efficiency of work done depends on the degree of discipline (set work procedure) maintained by worker and managers.

Discipline plays a vital role in organisational development and growth. Employees have to be self-disciplined as far as work is concerned. Then only they can have identity with the work and grow fast.

Discipline also contributes for personal growth of the employee as well as the organisation. Disciplined workers become more work-oriented and develop a healthy relationship with other employees and management. Every successful organisation will have disciplined approach to the work.

Organisational discipline means the behaviour of workers and management. Every piece of work is proficiently carried out. Customers would like to have continuous contact with the organisation and this leads to brand creation. Thus, discipline creates healthy relationship with each and every individual connected with the organisation.

VI. Undue Control

Employees have to work in an organisation as per the set standards, rules and procedure. But undue control of employee's activities and choices leads to stiff atmosphere. Supervisors may unnecessarily harass workers. There may not be any valid reason. Such unreasonable harassment prevents employees from having unhealthy relationship. The forms of undue control are: (i) Make employee to work on unwanted jobs, (ii) Job discrimination, (iii) Preventing employee to get normal benefits, etc.

Unwanted Job

Supposing an employee is transferred without reason from the unit he/she is working happily to another unit where she cannot enjoy. While performing the new task. Similarly, encroaching on privacy of employees is an act of undue control.

Job Discrimination

Job discrimination not on the basis of merit but on the basis of prejudice, is an act of harassment to control the employee. It is an adverse decision against an employee for an unacceptable reason. It may be racial or sexual or false stereotype (a generalized belief that one's behaviour will confirm negative activity). This unethical decision will have a negative impact on the interest of the employee.

Prevention of Natural Rights

Employees will have wage, certain incentives and benefits which go along with the job. Wage is the main means for an employee to satisfy his needs. Incentives such as health care benefits, educational facility to the children of employees and such other benefits are extended to employees. These are all natural rights acquired though contract of employment. Although employer acting as principal and employee as agent, they will have mutual respect. Otherwise, organisation does not function in an harmoneous way. Supposing an employee, who is honest and dedicated, is prevented from getting his wage and other incentives as a penalty for doing the job in his own way. The deviation of employee in doing the job may not be unethical. But his supervisor or manager may not appreciate the quality of work he does and finding a clumsy reason may penalise him. This undue control of manager of his team members will develop unhealthy situation and relationship between the boss and employee will not be good. Estrangement develops leading to conflict.

Thus, employer has the responsibility of looking after the welfare of his employees to have a harmonious relationship. He has to discharge his obligations such as payment of wages, creating good organisational climate, providing fair working conditions through studying and eliminating job risks, compensating for risk, informing workers of known risks, insuring workers against unknown risks, etc.

In the USA, Occupational Safety and Health Administration (OSHA) was established to look after wellness programmes of employees. In India, many legislations have been enacted to protect the interest of employees.

It is not enough that only employer should provide benefits to have good relationship. It is not a one-way approach. Employees also have to equally contribute to have a congenial atmosphere in workstations. Employee role is analysed in the following paragraphs.

Role of Employees

Employees of an organisation have a contractual obligation to the firm and their owners. The primary duty is to exercise their authority and judgement to achieve the goals of the organisation. They have to avoid any activity that harms the organisation and gives personal benefit. Indulging in unethical activity creates conflict.

In order to avoid the conflict, understanding between employees and organisation is essential. The social relationship (between employer and employees) of employment is a two-way approach with mutual responsibilities for the individual and organisation. Individuals responsibilities to the organisation will be:

(1) To be a good organisational citizen

(2) Adopting ethical practices

(3) Exhibiting mutual trust

(4) Resorting to whistle-blowing, if necessary.

Organisations, in order to accomplish their goals and to influence employees discharge their responsibilities to the organisations adopt both preventive and corrective measures. Now, we will examine the issues cited above which make employees to discharge their responsibilities and adopt positive approach towards their duties.

1. Organisational Citizen

Conscientious employee is the true citizen of the organisation. Conscientiousness, extroversion, agreeableness, openness to experience and emotional stability – the big five personality traits are the ones which make a worker a good organisational citizen. The big five traits make an employee as dependable, hardworking, responsible preserving and achiever. The worker, possessing all these qualities will be considered as an effective and high performance worker. This is what organisational citizenship considers.

An organisational citizenship is an exemplary behavioural aspect which creates a special status to an employee and will develop a strong and special relationship between such worker and the organisation. Besides performing assigned tasks effectively, the worker-organisational citizen — involves in helping others, silently suffers and never contests the impositions, participates in other activities of the organisation and many a time works beyond assigned tasks.

The worker considered as a good organisational citizen submerges one's identity for the good of the organisation. Puts in all one's best to the organisational development. One does not pretend that he/she knows the job. The real worker frankly submits one's own limitations and thus contributes for the good of the organisation avoiding the tasks that he/she does not know.

While performing the job, a corporate citizen becomes boss for oneself. This means he/she decides what is best in performing the task and does accordingly within the preview of the organisation framework. The extra work that a worker discharges will be discretionary or voluntary in nature and these extra works may be rewarded or not.

Thus, organisational citizenship involves the following features or activities.

- Assisting the co-worker when that person is involved in complex tasks or cannot attend to his/her duties in extraneous circumstances.
- Working beyond stipulated time of the organistion to finish the work in demanding situations.
- Volunteering oneself to participate in organisation-sponsored societal programmes.
- Simply accepting the mistakes one commits while performing the job and understanding the intensity of loss caused to the organisation by such mistake.
- Be humble and courteous to others while performing the tasks.

These features constitute the organisational citizenship and the employee who possess these traits can develop a healthy relationship with the organisation.

2. Adopting Ethical Practices

Conventional organisations have a formal structure, coordinating rationally the activities of many people functioning at different levels, to achieve some common clear-cut goals through division of labour and with responsibility. Normally, three levels will be in line of management exhibiting the hierarchy of authority. The top management, middle managements and operating level, which show the relationship of employees and their nature of work.

The modern structures are heading towards network structures which are flat in nature having less human resources.

In both conventional and network structures, formal relationship exists between the higher ups and individuals. It is type of contractual relationship that exists between employer and employees like that of "Law of Agency". In this law, there are two parties, *viz.*, (i) The principal and (ii) Agent. There will be a contractual obligation between the two to perform some pre-determined task. As per law, the agent has to act solely for the benefit of the principal. He/she gets consideration in the form of money and other incentives. In an organisational set-up employer assumes the position of principal and employees perform like agents. Both should adopt ethical practices while performing and should not indulge in activities leading to conflict of interest.

Conflict of Interest

In an organisation, an employee has to work for the achievement of organisational goals as in case of law of agency. The **"Ethical Aspect"** is that an employee should not do anything that conflicts with the operational norms set to achieve the organisational goals. Operational norms will be both explict and implied. Conflict arises when an employee misuses this position in the organisation or steal something from the firm or get some illicit benefits from others through extortion or commercial bribery, or will be slow or inactive in performing the organisational tasks. These extra acts of an employee leads to **"conflict of interest".**

"Conflict of interest" occurs when an employee gets some personal benefit (in any form) or have "interest" in a job that might benefit him/her, but such job is not required in the best interest of the firm. When he/she performs on such unwanted task "conflict of interest" arises. The "interests" stated in previous paragraph motivate employees to perform tasks which have some personal interests (financial or non-financial). Even an employee influences ones boss to take a decision or judge an issue which favours an employees personal interest will be the conflict of interest. There are many forms of conflict of interest which are shown in the following diagram.

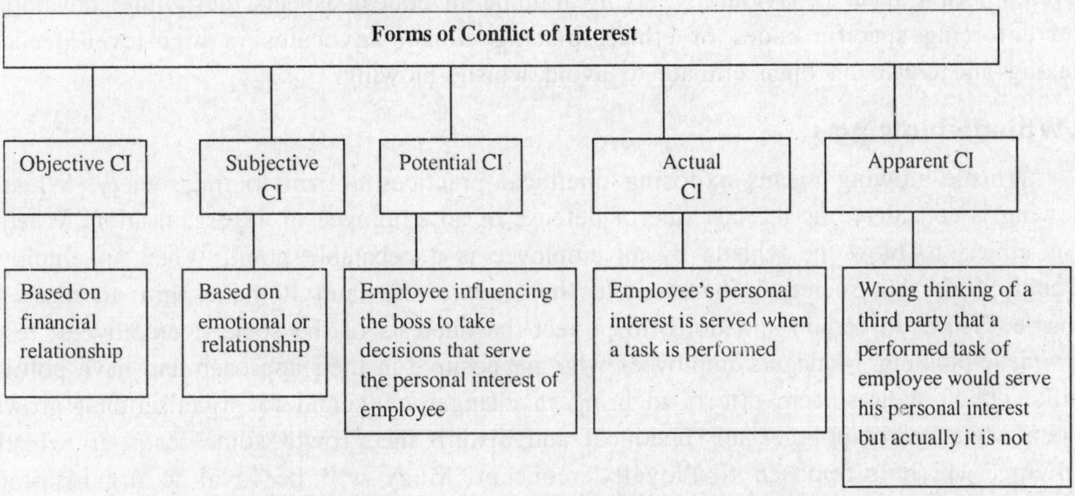

Fig. 22.1. Different Types of Conflict of Interest

Thus, conflict of interest emerges from unethical practices of employees as well as employers. Demanding some consideration from outsiders to deal favourably with them, (extortion and bribery), using organisational resources for personal benefits, leaking out trade secrets relating to technology adopted in firms to outsiders disclosing future plans of the organisations, and giving secret documents to outsiders, are all unethical practices leading to conflict of interest.

Insider Trading – Unethical

Insider trading refers to buying of shares of a company by the employees of that company at the existing market price, anticipating higher price at a future date, by knowing the information from the top class which is not available to the public. Supposing a worker in a company gets the information that his company adopts a policy which influences the share price. As an insider, he knows the information in advance acquires as much share as he can (or sells) quite ahead of the outsiders come to know of it. Purchase or sell the share of his company for his personal benefit, much before public learns about the policy which influences the share price is called "Insider Trading". Many say that insider trading is an unethical practice of the employee.

Who are in favour of this, argue that insider trading does not harm any body as the price of share more would go up and favours outside holders of this share. The opinion is that insider traders bring the proprietary information to the market which makes that share to move in the market according to its real worth.

Whatever may be the argument, insider trading is an unethical practice. Workers should refrain from using company information for personal benefits. The proprietary information should be used only for the benefit of owners (shareholders) of that company. Insider trading not only violates the rights of shareholders, it harms the society's overall utility as well. Law is firm in this regard and has punished many insider traders.

Thus, employees should not indulge in any form of unethical practice which disturbs the growth of the organisation. Employee of any organisation has the moral obligation to protect the interest of the firm in which he works. Management can motivate employees to develop their ethical behaviour by giving training in ethical aspects, designing, developing and enforcing specific codes of ethics, placing ethical advocates in high-level decision-making and create on open climate to avoid whistle-blowing.

3. Whistle-blowing

Whistle-blowing means exposing unethical practices a firm to the society. Whistle-blowing is considered as the last line of defense of an employee in an organisation. Whether it is ethical to blow the whistle by an employee is a debatable point. When an employee strongly feels that society is harassed to the core for no fault it makes him to blow the whistle. Hence, in certain situations, to protect the interests of the society, employees, resort to whistle-blowing. Managers/employees who are positive in their approach and have political skills, put in their sincere efforts to bring in changes congenial to organisational growth. When management policies are unethical and disturb the growth some resort to whistle-blowing, which is opposed to "loyalty" concept. Many will be loyal to organisations, fearing that they may caught in the organisational politics. They implicitly follow the orders of higher-ups. But some will be dare enough to expose unethical practices of management.

Whistle-blowing is a term which explains "the disclosing of perceived unethical organisational practices to outsiders by the inside people". Whistle-blowing is deemed to be the epitome of disloyalty. When the rights of employees are encroached by the top management, on the advice of managers, many workers bear the brunt of this encroachment and suffer silently. Whereas some workers who cannot tolerate the suppression, revolt against the organisation, in the form of whistle-blowing. But whistle blowing should not happen for the personal benefit of the employees.

Whistle-blowing is not good for the organisation. In US, legislation has been enacted to reduce whistle-blowing. In India and in other countries of the world, whistle-blowers are protected through law. Only legitimate whistle-blowing is protected.

Legitimate whistle-blowing

Whistle-blowing is considered as legitimate when the following aspects are satisfied.

(i) The objective of WB should be in the public interest and not for personal benefits of the individuals.

(ii) The purpose should be specific and matter should be serious.

(iii) All other avenues to correct unethical practice in the organisation are closed and it should be a final resort.

(iv) Whistle-blower should not gain anything personally.

Whistle-blowing hinders the growth of the organisation. Many organisations are penalised and are asked to change such policies and practices which harm the interest of the society. Whistle-blowers are also penalised by the management. An IIM (MBA) degree holder an honest employee of ONGC was hackled to death by a petrol bunk people in Uttar Pradesh. As he exposed the illegal activities of that bunk, he was ruthlessly handled by that organisation.

It may be true in certain cases that an employee to gain fame or to advance his careers; resort to whistle-blowing. He may or may not be benefited from this activity.

A book published by Ralph Nadir on whistle-blowing in 1972 says that "the willingness and ability of insiders to blow the whistle is the last line of defense, ordinary citizens have, against the denial of their rights and destruction of their interests by secretive and powerful institutions". Whatever may be the inference drawn (WB is in the interest of the society or for personal benefit of the employee) of whistle-blowing, the managements should create a good organisational climate which will not make employees to resort to whistle-blowing. The preventive measures can be implemented to hold this.

Preventive Measures

- Employees have to be encouraged to express their free opinion about controversial and dissenting issues.
- Grievance cell of the organisation should be more methodic and fast to address the grievance of employees.
- Adopt social responsibility policies incorporating genuine views of employees.
- Management should create a feeling in the employees that they and their opinions are considered.
- Managements have to understand that treating the whistle-blower severely will gain adverse public opinion.

Thus, whistle-blowing may be ethical or unethical, continues by dare employees to protect the interest of the society.

4. Mutual Trust

Developing mutual trust (between employer and employees) is essential for organisational growth and to maintain healthy, clean atmosphere in the organisation. It develops healthy relationship. "Mistrust" or otherwise called "organisational infidelity" reduces commitment to organisational activities by employees. Suspicion hoovers round the organisation and healthy relationship between employees and employer evaporates. Distrust leads to disruptive activities and organisational growth becomes slow. Therefore, mutual trust is vital factor and proves as a powerful tool in establishing healthy relationship between employer and employees.

Mutual trust empowers employer, employees and organisation on as a whole. In fact, mutual trust is one of the principles of empowerment. Mutual trust builds healthy relationship which develops ability of employees as well as employer to share innovative ideas and information as quickly as possible. This motivates people in organisations to introduce innovative practices and always makes employees to be on their toes to create something new for organisational growth.

Shared mind-set, the outcome of mutual trust, induces workforce to be honest and sincere to their duties and develops **organisational identity.** It strongly commits employees to work with zeal to increase productivity of both organisation and themselves. The intensity of mutual trust also determines the degree of involvement of employer in taking out the best of each employee to develop the organisation.

Trust, for individual employee, develops **sustainable creditworthiness** and credibility. People having credibility are honoured more and maintain a special status in the organisations. Their words are respected. They create a feeling amongst peers and top management that whatever they say has to be respected and emulated. For example, a good teacher or a good sports coach or an expert consultancy firm command credibility. Because they have made the people to believe that their performance or guidance will do good for concerned people. A good teacher turns his wards as honest and trustworthy citizens. An expert consultant make his client believe that his expert opinion and action plan will turn around the organisation. Thus, mutual trust creates relevant actions on the part of employees.

Mutual trust provides a strong base for **interdependence** in work places. In every organisation, all workers and management have to depend on each other to execute tasks. Interdependence with mutual trust will help the management to improve productivity and facilitate employees to get better emoluments. Thus, the trust enhances the relationships.

In general, mutual trust is an invisible power of any organisation. This facilitates employees to share their innovative ideas, gives scope for implementing quality circles, and combine efforts of individuals and groups to achieve the organisational goals. It also helps in enhancing the creativity of individuals which in turn makes the organisation to become strong in future. Mutual trust makes people to be more productive than expecting more money and fringe benefits. Organisations run on mutual trust develops strong loyalty amongst workers to the organisation. Employee turnover will be minimal. Recent researchers reveal that organisations having trust in their employees have good image in the society and possess brand. They are easily accessible by the public and employees are more friendly to the society. Distrust organisations will cause much hardship to society like Enron or sthyams. Trustworthy organisations will care for their employees and society.

Employee has the primary responsibility of performing the tasks as per the expectations of the employer. Performance is both ethical and legal. Ethical aspect is that the employee has to work to achieve the goals of the firm. He/she should not deviate from the set standards of the firm or resort to such actions which might harm the achievement of organisational goals. Legal aspect is that an individual has become the employee of the organisation under a contract.

Thus, in order to exhibit a healthy behaviour, employee has to be pro-active and be ethical in his operations. This behaviour contributes for the development of healthy relationship between employee and employer.

Behaviour of state, individuals, groups and organisation will decide whether the organisation is strong or not. Good behaviour of all these four components determines the relationship type between individual and group, between individual and employer and between group and the organisation. Both employer and employees work together for establishing as sound and harmonious relationship. Certain incidents which have occurred in the country can destroy even the best organisations.

Maintaining relationship is not a simple task. It includes functional interdependencies, involving historical, economical, social and psychological aspects. Inspite of clear definitions of roles of employer and employees and statutory stipulations by the State to support employees, particularly the weaker ones, people at work in workstations ignore their duties and indulge in activities which hamper the growth of the organisation. Following incidents are cited here which bear testimoney to this.

Davanagere Cotton Mills (DCM) ((Karnataka-India) was a famous and quality organisation which produced, cotton voil sarees which were one of the best sarees produced ever. It played the role of "status symbol" in elite class. "The relationship management" of DCM was good. Still the employees were not happy with compensation management. Labour union of DCM was agitating to improve the monetary benefits. As Management did not heed to the full demand, the General Manager was hacked to death by employees. This was a major blow and the mill was closed.

Many such incidents have occurred. The great "Bombay Textile Industry Strike" lead by Datta Samanth made textile industry to come to a grinding halt and all labour class came to street.

Therefore, in the current day economy which is driven by technology and organisational structure becoming virtual, the state laws are to be suitably amended or repealed to avoid unhappy incidents in the organisations and make people more productive. Besides the changes made in labour legislations, employers have to take care of employees and employees in turn work for reaching optimal production. A culture of trust and confidence has to be created for having harmonious relationship.

SUMMARY

1. Creating sound relationship amongst employees and top management is the key factor and focal aspect of organisational behaviour. Healthy relationship builds a sound organisations.
2. The contribution of both employer and employees for the development of organisation is required. Mutual respect brings harmony and both should honour organisational values and norms.
3. Managements should not encroach on rights of privacy of people. They should assist employees to improve the quality of work life and look into conformity issue. Job enrichment opportunities have to be extended. Employees should not be unduly controlled and organisational discipline has to be maintained. All these contribute for the healthy maintenance of harmonious relationship throughout the organisation.
4. Employees have equal responsibility. They should not indulge in any activity that hampers the growth of the organisation. They should become good organisational citizens, exhibit mutual trust adopt, ethical practices and rarely resort to whistle-blowing in the interest of the society.
5. If any one does not perform as per accepted norms, it results in conflict of interest. The key deviations from normal practices or the important aspects that contribute for conflict of interest are: (i) Insider trading, (ii) whistle-blowing and (iii) casual approach to perform the assigned tasks, etc. These unhealthy practices are to be avoided to have harmonious relationship.

STUDY QUESTIONS

1. What is Privacy Policy? Write an explanatory note on right to privacy and its impact on employee behaviour.
2. State and explain the objectives and features of a sound privacy policy.
3. Give the meaning of Quality of Work Life (QWL). Explain how QWL improves the relationship between employee and employer.
4. What do you mean by conformity issue? Explain the various aspects of conformity issue in the backdrop of relationship management.
5. What is "Job Enrichment"? Explain the activities that lead to job enrichment and the end result of each activity.
6. What is "organisational discipline"? Briefly explain the role of discipline in developing healthy relationship between co-workers and the employer.
7. Briefly explain how undue control of employees' activities and choices lead to unhealthy relationship between employer and employees.
8. Briefly explain vital elements that develop a healthy relationship between employer and employees.
9. Give the meaning of "Organisational citizenship". Explain how organisational citizenship makes an employee dedicated one.
10. Write a detailed note on ethical practices that an employee has to adapt to become an identified employee.
11. What is "conflict of Interest"? Explain the types of conflict of interest.
12. Explain the impact of whistle-blowing and insider trading on the relationship between employer and employee. Suggest remedial measures to prevent these unethical practices.
13. Write an explanatory note on "Mutual Trust". Analyse, how it empowers employer and employees.
14. Briefly explain, the various unethical practices that estrange the relationship between employer and employees.

23

CONFLICT MANAGEMENT

LEARNING OBJECTIVES

After reading this chapter, you should be able to know:

- Conflict — The Concept
- Levels of Conflict
- Nature of Conflicts
- Conflict Resolution

People at work vary in their ideas, skills and thinking. These differences may lead to individual and group differences. Such differences are the basis of organizational conflict. Conflict is inevitable in an organisation. In any business or personal relationship of any depth, conflict will occur at times. The seriousness of the conflict is dependent on the nature of conflict. Not all workplace conflicts are bad. Conflict has three elements. The first element of conflict is the existence of a struggle of some type. Secondly, the involved parties must have, or think they have, incompatible goals. Lastly, there must be some degree of interdependence between the people who are involved.

Conflict can be constructive, and it can be destructive. The distinction is based on how the conflict is managed. Conflict cannot always be avoided. Many positive outcomes can result from working through conflict. Properly managed conflict can help in bringing constructive change.

CONFLICT – THE CONCEPT

Organizations have people with different interests, perceptions, personalities, attitudes, values and views. This leads to difference of opinion in the organization. Disagreement is the basis of conflicts in the organisation. This happens mainly because of the conflicting interests of the individuals or groups.

Conflict is any situation in which two or more parties feel themselves in opposition. It is an interpersonal process that arises from disagreements over the goals or the methods to accomplish those goals. Therefore, conflict may be defined as an expressed struggle between at least two interdependent parties who perceive incompatible goals, scarce resources, and interference from the other party in achieving their goals.

NATURE OF CONFLICT

1. Conflict occurs when two or more parties have incomputable interest or goals.
2. Conflict arises mainly because of different perceptions of individuals.
3. Conflict is a deliberate behaviour.
4. Conflict differs from competition.

LEVELS OF CONFLICT

There are basically three levels of conflict.

1. Individual Level Conflict.
2. Group Level Conflict.
3. Organisation Level Conflict.

1. Individual Level Conflict: Conflict may arise with an individual or between two different individuals. If the conflict is with an individual, the conflict is referred to as *intra-individual* conflict. If the conflict is between individuals, the conflict is referred to as *interpersonal* conflict.

Intra-individual Conflict

Intra-individual conflict can be further divided into: (a) Goal Conflict and (b) Role Conflict.

(a) Goal Conflict: Goal conflict arises when two or more competing goals exist. Goal conflict may also arise when the intended goal as both positive and negative features. Different goals demand different expectations, leading to goal conflict.

(b) Role Conflict: Individuals play multiple roles simultaneously in his daily life. If he finds inadequate time and resources to accomplish these roles, causes role conflict.

Interpersonal Conflict

Interpersonal conflict occurs when two or more individuals who must work together fail to share the same views, and have different interests or goals. Interpersonal conflict can be defined by the focus and source of the conflict.

People-Focused vs. Issue-Focused

People-focused conflicts are based on emotions and feelings, and are more of a personal attack. Issue-focused conflicts are centered on issues and events, and are more representative of a calm negotiation.

Personal Differences

A common source of interpersonal conflict is personal differences, because every person brings a unique (and often incompatible) set of values, perceptions and expectations into to the organisation.

Informational Deficiencies

Another source of interpersonal conflict is informational deficiencies. Communications are not always received, may be misinterpreted or different conclusions may be drawn based on past experiences.

Role Incompatibility

Role incompatibility may be a cause of interpersonal conflict because of differences between the goals and responsibilities assigned to an individual and what the individual would rather be doing.

Environmental Stress

A stressful environment is another source of interpersonal conflict. Uncertainty of future events and scarcity of resources, such as food or money, can lead to disputes among otherwise friendly individuals.

2. Group Level Conflict: A group consists of two or more persons. It individual differs in their approach, behaviour, thinking, temperament and so on. This causes difference of opinion among the members of the group leading to conflict. The following are the reasons was to why group conflict may arise: (a) incompatible goals, (b) Resource allocation, (c) Reward System, (d) Line and staff conflict, (e) difference in values or perception and (f) Communication distortions and so on.

3. Organizational level Conflict: Individual and group level conflicts are the part of organisational conflict. Infact, they are the part of intra-organisational conflict. There can be inter-organisational conflict also. Inter- organisational conflict arises where the conflict exists between two organisations. Inter-organisational conflict may arise between a government agency and the organisation, one organisation and the other.

CONFLICT RESOLUTION

There are five different ways in which conflict is resolved as shown in the following picture.

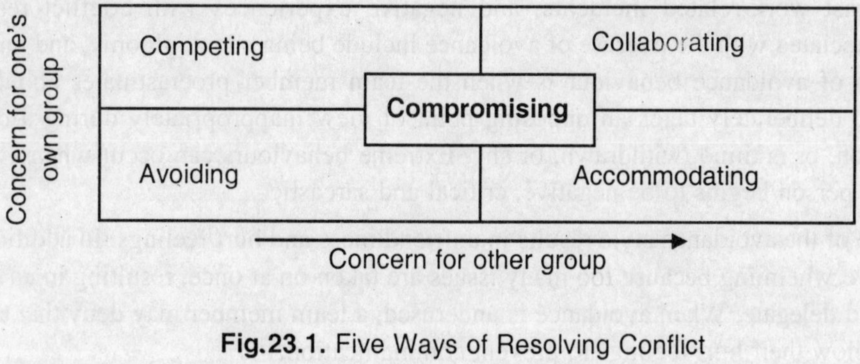

Fig.23.1. Five Ways of Resolving Conflict

The Competing Style

The competing style is used when a person has to take quick action, make unpopular decisions, handle vital issues, or when one needs protection in a situation where non-competitive behaviour can be exploited. To develop this style, one must develop the ability to argue and debate, use his rank or position, assert his opinions and feelings, and learn to state his position and stand his ground.

Overuse of this style can lead to lack of feedback, reduced learning, and low empowerment. This can result in being surrounded by "Yes-Men". People who overuse the competing style often use inflammatory statements due to lack of training on interpersonal skills. When overuse is taken to an extreme, the person will create errors in the implementation of the task by withholding needed information, talking behind another person's back (or "back-stabbing"), using eye motions and gestures designed to express disapproval, and creating distractions by fiddling or interrupting. Overuse of this style can be exhibited through constant tension or anger and occasional outbursts of violent temper.

Under use of the competing style leads to a lowered level of influence, indecisiveness, slow action, and withheld contributions.

The Avoiding Style

This style is used when you do not satisfy your concerns or the concerns of the other person. This style is low assertiveness and low co-operativeness. The goal is to delay. It is appropriate to use this style when there are issues of low importance, to reduce tensions, or to buy time. Avoidance is also appropriate when you are in a low power position and have little control over the situation, when you need to allow others to deal with the conflict, or when the problem is symptomatic of a much larger issue and you need to work on the core issue.

Overuse of the avoidance style can result in a low level of input, decision-making by default, and allowing issues to fester, which can produce a breakdown in communication between team members. This can inhibit brainstorming sessions from being productive and can prevent the team from functioning. People who overuse avoidance, feel they cannot speak frankly without fear of repercussions. The overuse of conflict avoidance can often be a result of childhood experiences, past work-related incidents, and negative experiences with conflict resolution. Behaviours associated with the overuse of avoidance include being silent, gloomy, and untruthful. A milder form of avoidance behaviour is when the team member procrastinates about getting work done and deliberately takes an opposing point of view inappropriately during a decision-making situation, or is timid, withdrawn, or shy. Extreme behaviours can occur when avoidance is overused. A person begins to be negative, critical and sarcastic.

Underuse of the avoidance style results in unfriendliness and hurt feelings. In addition, work can become overwhelming because too many issues are taken on at once, resulting in an inability to prioritize and delegate. When avoidance is underused, a team member may deny that there is a problem and allow their hurt feelings to prevent communication.

The Compromising Style

This style is moderately assertive and moderately co-operative. The compromising style is used with issues of moderate importance, when both parties are equally powerful and equally committed to opposing views. This style produces temporary solutions and is appropriate when time is a concern, and as a back up for the competing and collaborating styles when they are unsuccessful in resolving the situation. Compromising skills include the ability to communicate and keep the dialogue open, the ability to find an answer that is fair to both parties, the ability to give up part of what you want, and the ability to assign value to all aspects of the issue.

Overuse of the compromising style leads to loss of long-term goals, lack of trust, creation of a cynical environment, and being viewed as having no firm values. Overuse of compromise can result in making concessions to keep people happy without resolving the original conflict.

Underuse leads to unnecessary confrontations, frequent power struggles, and ineffective negotiation.

The Collaborating Style

The Collaborating Style is when the concern is to satisfy both sides. It is highly assertive and highly co-operative. The goal is to find a "win/win" solution. Appropriate uses of the collaborating style include integrating solutions, learning, merging perspectives, gaining commitment, and improving relationships. Using this style can support open discussion of issues, task proficiency, equal distribution of work amongst the team members, better brainstorming, and development of creative problem-solving. This style is appropriate to use frequently in a team environment. Collaborating skills include the ability to use active or effective listening, confront situations in a non-threatening way, analyse input, and identify underlying concerns.

Overuse of the collaborating style can lead to spending too much time on minor matters, diffusion of responsibility, being taken advantage of, and being overloaded with work.

Underuse can result in using quick fix solutions, lack of commitment by other team members, disempowerment, and loss of innovation.

The Accommodating Style

The Accommodating Style is foregoing your concerns in order to satisfy the concerns of others. This style is low assertiveness and high co-operativeness. The goal is to yield. The accommodating style is appropriate to use in situations when you want to show that you are reasonable, develop performance, create goodwill, keep peace, retreat, or for issues of low importance. Accommodating skills include the ability to sacrifice, the ability to be selfless, the ability to obey orders, and the ability to yield.

Overuse of the accommodating style results in ideas getting little attention, restricted influence, loss of contribution, and chaos. People who overuse the accommodating style exhibit a lack of desire to change and usually demonstrate anxiety over future uncertainties.

Underuse of the accommodating style can result in lack of rapport, low morale, and an inability to yield. When the accommodating style is underused, a person may display indifference as a way of not addressing the anger or hurt.

EXHIBIT: When to use a specific strategy

A. COMPETING

Uses:

1. When quick, decisive action is vital, e.g., emergencies.
2. On important issues where unpopular courses of action need to be implemented, e.g., cost cutting, enforcing unpopular rules, discipline.
3. On issues vital to company welfare when you know you are right.
4. To protect yourself against people who take advantage of non-competitive behaviour.

B. COLLABORATING

Uses:

1. To find an integrative solution when both sets of concerns are too important to be compromised.
2. When your objective is to learn, e.g., testing your own assumptions, understanding the views of others.
3. To merge insights from people with different perspectives on a problem.
4. To gain commitment by incorporating other's concerns into a consensual decision.
5. To work through hard feelings which have been interfering with an interpersonal relationship.

C. COMPROMISING

Uses:

1. When goals are moderately important, but not worth the effort or potential disruption of more assertive modes.
2. When two opponents with equal power are strongly committed to mutually exclusive goals – e.g., as in labour-management bargaining.
3. To achieve temporary settlements to complex issues.
4. To arrive at expedient solutions under time pressure.
5. As a backup mode when collaboration or competition fails to be successful.

D. AVOIDING

Uses:

1. When an issue is trivial, of only passing importance, or when other more important issues are pressing.
2. When you perceive no chance of satisfying your concerns – e.g., when you have low power or you are frustrated by something which would be very difficult to change (national policies, someone's personality structure, etc.)
3. When the potential damage of confronting a conflict outweighs the benefits of its resolution.
4. To let people cool down – to reduce tensions to a productive level and to regain perspective and composure.
5. When gathering more information outweighs the advantages of an immediate decision.
6. When others can resolve the conflict more effectively.
7. When the issue seems tangential or symptomatic of another more basic issue.

E. ACCOMMODATING

Uses:

1. When you realise that you are wrong (or less experienced or knowledgeable) — to allow a better position to be heard, to from others, and to show that you are reasonable.

2. When the issue is much more important to the other person than to yourself — to satisfy the needs of others, and as a goodwill gesture to help maintain a co-operative relationship.
3. To build up social credits for later issues which are important to you.
4. When continued competition would only damage your cause — when you are outmatched and losing.
5. When preserving harmony and avoiding disruption are especially important.
6. To aid in the managerial development of subordinates by allowing them to experiment and learn from their own mistakes.

SUMMARY

1. Difference of opinion is common and inevitable in an organisation. This causes conflict in the organisation. Conflict may be within an individual, between the individuals and between the groups. The commons reasons for conflict are scarcity of resources (finance, equipment, facilities, etc.), different attitudes, values or perceptions, disagreements about needs, goals, priorities and interests, poor communication, poor or inadequate organisational structure, lack of teamwork, lack of clarity in roles and responsibilities
2. For any organisation to be effective and efficient in achieving its goals, the people in the organisation need to have a shared vision of what they are striving to achieve, as well as clear objectives for each team/department and individual.
3. A manager can select Accommodating, Collaborating, Competing or Avoiding strategies to resolve the conflict depending upon the situation.
4. Conflict need not be viewed as negative phenomena. The functional view of organisational conflict sees conflict as a productive force. One can think that the conflict can stimulate members of the organisation to increase their knowledge and skills, and their contribution to organisational innovation and productivity. Therefore, conflict can be directed and managed so that it causes both people and organisations to grow, innovate and improve.

STUDY QUESTIONS

1. Explain the concept of Conflict.
2. Explain the nature of Conflict in detail.
3. Write a note on individual level conflict.
4. Write an explanatory note on group level conflict and organisational level conflict.
5. Explain the conflict resolution techniques in detail.

CASE STUDY

Mr. Arun and Mr. Sharan are working for Well Done Ltd., a manufacturing company. They are sincere and loyal to the company. Both of them have conflicting view regarding their roles in the organisation.

The contention of Mr. Arun is "I have been in this organisation for three years. Nobody has made an effort to get to know me. In fact, even my boss is not totally aware of the work that I do. I think I am wasting my life even though I am contributing to the organisation".

The contention of Mr. Sharan is "I am a chemical engineer but all the work related to my area is given to a mechanical engineer. This person is a big show off and most of the time is talking about his own work. He has more friends than I have, but as far as the quality of work is concerned, I think I am superior."

Considering the statements of Mr. Arun and Mr. Sharan:

(a) Analyze the seriousness of the situation.

(b) What steps are needed resolve the above issue?

(c) Would you suggest any structural change to resolve the issue?

24

STRESS MANAGEMENT

LEARNING OBJECTIVES

After reading this chapter, you should be able to know:

- Stress—The Concept
- Factors Influencing Stress
- Implications of Stress
- Symptoms of Stress
- Measures to Reduce Stress

People working in organisations and elsewhere feel the stress after day's work. In global business environment a change over is taking place from old order to new order. Very many routine and special operations in the organisations make people work beyond limit for existence and it has the impact on mind and body of every human being that works in any place. More so in organisations workers have lost privacy. Personal contact has become minimal due to advancement of technology. People have to continuously learn several new methods and procedure and are made to over-work. Research studies reveal that job related stress is increasing for the afore said reasons. Although working hours are stipulated statutorily, people are not prepared to enjoy the holidays for economic reasons. Many a time the stress is a self-imposed one and deliberately it is caused to complete the tasks on time.

STRESS – THE CONCEPT

Modern life style is characterized by too many obligations, accepting too many responsibilities, long traveling distance between office and the residence and too much of thinking about the future. This has made them to feel that there is no time for rest and leisure. This feel of unrest and shortage of time has become the source of stress in modern day's life. Stress can often be called a modern acquired disease. Stress at work is a relatively new phenomenon of modern lifestyles. The nature of work has gone through drastic changes over the last century and it is still changing at rapid speed. The stress has touched almost all professions.

Meaning of Stress

Stress is the emotional and physical strain caused by our response to pressure from the outside world. It can be caused by both good and bad experiences. Stress can affect both our body and mind. People under large amounts of stress can become tired, sick, and unable to concentrate or think clearly. Sometimes, they even suffer mental breakdowns. Common stress reactions include tension, irritability, inability to concentrate, and a variety of physical symptoms that include headache and a fast heartbeat. Job stress is one of the major problems that the corporate world is facing today. Job stress is a chronic disease caused by conditions in the workplace that negatively affect an individual's performance and overall well-being of his body and mind. When under severe stress, an individual fails to take clear-cut decisions, reevaluate and reassess the priorities and lifestyles.

Individuals differ in their capacity to accept and perform different activities. If the expectation is more than the capacity of an individual, stress begins to influence him. In a way, stress is the reaction people have to excessive demands or pressures. But we need certain amount of stress in our lives in order to function properly. Stress is what makes us perform at our best.

Therefore, stress can be defined as follows **"state that we are in when the demands that are made upon us exceed our ability to perform"**.

This definition clearly states that stress is caused by excess of work to be performed which exceeds the actual ability or capacity to perform in a given period of time. The stress so caused will be revealed in two forms, viz., (i) mental and (ii) physical.

Mental stress is caused by tension, irritability, inability to concentrate, feeling excessively tired and disturbed sleeping. These symptoms and expressions exhibit mental stress.

Physical stress is caused by variations in human body and is expressed in different ways symptoms are, dry mouth, pounding heart, difficulty in breathing, stomach upset etc. (see the box for symptoms).

EXHIBIT: Symptoms of stress

The mental symptoms of stress include:

- Tension
- Irritability
- Inability to concentrate
- Feeling excessively tired
- Troubled sleeping

The physical symptoms of stress include:

- Dry mouth
- A pounding heart
- Difficulty in breathing
- Stomach upset
- Frequent urination
- Sweating palms
- Tight muscles that may cause pain and trembling

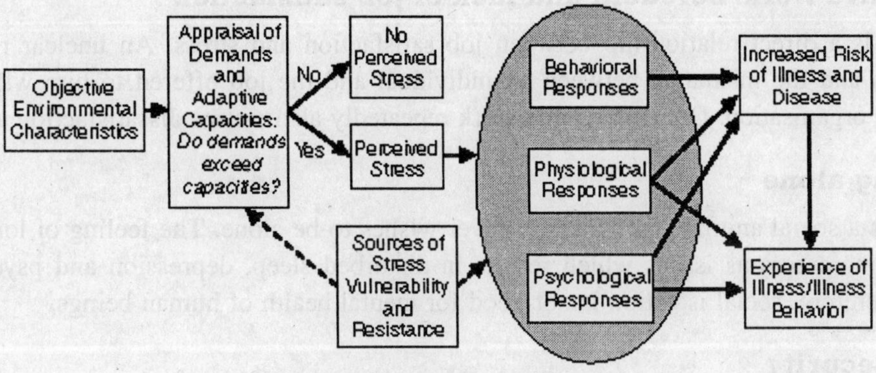

Fig. 24.1. Model of stress

FACTORS AFFECTING STRESS

There are many factors which creates stress in a workplace. Following are the important factors affecting stress in a workplace.

1. Bad relations with other colleagues

In a workplace, people are interdependent. Therefore, understanding each other and to build good interpersonal relationship is vital for the success of personal and professional life. It causes stress when it is difficult to establish a relationship with a person who cannot be easily socialized. Stress also causes when people start taking advantages of each other's weaknesses. Stress also causes when an employee does something which is not in favour of his colleague. Lack of support from other co-workers is a common source of stress.

In a workplace, negative stress responses are so powerful that they weaken our characters and damage even the strongest and most solid work relationships. It affects not just the professional aspect but our personal relationships with those who are close to us. Therefore, it is necessary for us to be calm and judgemental in our workplace.

2. Long and or irregular hours

Long and irregular working hours will also cause stress for an employee. On the one hand, organisations are reducing manpower and on the other hand they are aiming to increase productivity. These made employees to work for longer hours creating higher stress to them. In today's competitive world, working for longer hours has become a necessity. Therefore, one should manage his work schedule to reduce work-related stress.

3. Too little work – or too much

Amount of work assigned to a worker is also a source of stress. Work assigned may be too much to handle or it may be too little. Too much of work makes people feel hurried, defeated and hectic. Too little work makes people feel that the work is unchallenging.

4. Repetitive work/boredom and lack of job satisfaction

There is a direct relationship between job satisfaction and stress. An unclear role in the organisation and the mismatch between an individual and the job offered to him will increase stress in the organisation. Doing the same work repeatedly also causes dissatisfaction and stress.

5. Working alone

Man is a social animal and hence he never wishes to be alone. The feeling of loneliness is one of the more serious issues which results in disturbed sleep, depression and psychological distress. Therefore, social isolation is not good for mental health of human beings.

6. Job insecurity

The rapid development and use of technology are increasingly substituting human work. This has created lot of competition in the employment market. No one feels secure in his or her job, as they can be replaced any moment either with the technology or a younger and more efficient person willing to work for lower salary. This insecure feeling about their job is a source of stress for many employees in organizations.

7. Incompatible managers

Most workers are stressed out because of their managers. If the superior fails to appreciative the efforts of the employees, and if he has little understanding of the working methods, then it can cause lot of unnecessary job stress. Some managers are known for fearful approach and they continuously pressurize their staff asking for frequent updates and setting non-attainable deadlines.

8. Job or organizational change

Organizational change is the process whereby an organization moves from an existing state to an expected future state in order to increase its effectiveness. Due to the change in the organisation, there may be change in the position of employees or technology. When employees cannot make necessary technical adjustments, a sense of uncertainty arises about the future, which, in turn, creates stress. This uncertainty can affect employees' job commitment and job satisfaction.

9. Low pay

Work is the only source of income for many people. Any insecurity at the financial level will directly increase the work stress. Several employee works in resentment because they believe their pay package is too low for their position. Such thoughts and feelings leads to increased job stress.

10. Jobs with heavy emotional demands

Emotion regulation refers to the process of modifying one's own emotions and expressions to adjust to the needs of the situation. It is most common in hospitality industry. In such industries, it has become an integral part of occupational display rules. To maintain desired emotion may not be possible, which in turn, causes stress to those employees.

11. Harassment

Harassment refers to repeated, unreasonable behaviour directed towards an employee, or group of employees. It aims at victimising, humiliating, undermining or threatening harassed person or persons. It can involve both verbal and physical attacks, as well as more delicate acts such as social isolation. A person dignity, professional capability, private life, physical features, race, gender or sexual orientation can be the subject of harassment. Harassment at work causes considerable stress to the victims, their colleagues, families and friends. In some cases, individuals are unable to function normally at work and at home. Harassment can lead to post-traumatic stress disorder, loss of self-esteem, anxiety, depression, apathy, irritability, memory disorders, sleep disorders and problems with digestion, and even suicide.

12. Poor working environment

Poor working conditions such as excessive noise, the presence of dangerous materials, over-crowding, poor facilities, or extreme temperatures or humidity loud music or conversation, poor lighting, uncomfortable chairs and equipment that constantly breaks, new staff, new boss, new procedures for accomplishing goals and so on leads to more stress in the work environment.

13. Increased accessibility

With the rapid change in technology, it has become very easy to access anybody in any corner of the world. Using mobile phones and e-mails, the officials can always pressurise employees to complete the target way ahead of the scheduled time. This pressure leads to stress among employees.

14. Discrimination at workplace

There may be cases of racial, cultural or gender discrimination in any office. Any employee who feels victimised by discrimination is bound to feel stressed at workplace. Such a person looses interest in work and may become indifferent also.

15. Job-related travel

Traveling has become an integral part of modern day's job. Work-related traveling as source of stress is quite common in most marketing jobs. Excessive travelling affects a person's body, mind, and ability to perform the assigned job.

16. Lack of employee participation

Most employees are dissatisfied with their jobs, usually because it does not allow them to express their inherent potential or creativity. An active employee desires to work on a challenging job always. A dull job usually does not meet this criterion. This causes workplace stress among employees.

17. The stress of survival

Change is the only permanent phenomena on this earth. As a result of this, stress has become a common byproduct of today's society. These changes will have direct impact on physical and mental performance of individuals.

18. External pressures

External pressures such as financial worries and family problems are always stressful. Financial stress causes due to contestant increase in the cost essential commodities. Noncooperation and misunderstanding between family members and too much of expectation from the members of the family, especially, growing children are the main sources of family stress.

Factors influencing stress tolerance level

- **Supporting Network –** A strong network of supportive friends and family members is an enormous power to reduce the effect of stressors. On the contrary, loneliness and isolation exposes an individual to stress.
- **Sense of control** – If we have confidence in us it is easy to take stress without much disturbance. People who are exposed to stress tend to feel that things are out of their control.
- **Attitude and outlook –** Stress-hardy people have an optimistic attitude and they believe in control commitment and challenge. They tend to welcome challenges, have a strong sense of humour, accept that change is a part of life, and believe in a higher power or purpose.
- **Ability to deal with emotions**. The ability to maintain balanced emotions helps us to fight with adverse situations.
- **Knowledge and preparation –** The more we know about a stressful situation, including how long it will last and what to expect, the easier it is to cope. Knowing stress in advance helps us to be prepared to face such situations.

FORMS OF STRESS

Most people think that stress is always bad. But a little stress is absolutely necessary for our survival in this highly competitive world. The effect of stress depends on the nature of stress one is undergoing. Basically stress can be classified into good and bad.

1. Good Stress (Eustress)
2. Bad Stress (Distress)

Eustress

Stress need not be bad all the time. But stress affects us positively also. Eustress is a positive stress. It is basically a desirable form of stress which is healthful and gives a feeling of satisfaction. It keeps us excited about life. It brings extra energy and creativity. Eustress positively affect our activities. It is a type of short-term stress that increases our primary strength. Eustress arises at points of increased physical activity, enthusiasm, and creativity. Eustress is a positive stress that arises when motivation and inspiration are needed. It helps us to be enthusiastic about personal and professional life.

The effects of eustress are many. They range from short-term to long-term benefits. In the short-term, eustress provides motivation to keep moving forward with an activity or project, even though it may be difficult. In the long-term, good stress helps to promote emotional balance, confidence, and a general feeling of being in harmony with others. All these positive benefits help to minimize the chances of a number of physical and mental disorders.

Distress

Distress is one of the negative types of stress. This arises when the normal routine is constantly adjusted and altered. Distress creates feelings of discomfort and unfamiliarity. When distress is experienced, the mind will not feel comfortable with this routine, and constantly asks for the familiarity of a common routine which existed earlier. Distress weakens our body and mind makes us exposed to fatigue and illness. Distress can be further classified into:

(a) Acute Stress
(b) Chronic Stress

Acute stress is a type of stress that comes immediately with a change of routine. It is an intense type of stress, but it passes quickly.

Chronic stress is a prolonged stress that exists for weeks, months, or even years. This type of stress is usually experienced by those who constantly relocating from one place to another or changing jobs frequently.

Hyperstress

Hyperstress occurs when an individual is asked to do something which is beyond his or her capacity. Overloaded or overwork are the reasons for hyperstress.

Hypostress

Hypostress is the opposite of hyperstress. Hypostress occurs when an individual feels that the job is boring or unchallenging. People who experience hypostress are often restless and uninspired. A factory worker who performs repetitive tasks might experience hypostress.

Stress and performance level

Each one of us have certain abilities to perform a given task. If demand for work is more than the capacity of an individual, he experiences stress. Our ability to perform increases up to a certain level of stress arousal. This is the healthy tension or eustress. But if this stress continues further without any control, a fatigue point is reached. Any further stress arousal will take the performance level down, ultimately leading to exhaustion, ill-health and, finally breakdown. If stress management techniques are properly applied regularly before the fatigue point is reached, the stress performance curve can be straightened. Observe the fig. 24.2.

IMPLICATIONS OF STRESS

As stated earlier, stress occurs when a person finds that he is incapable of mobilizing his intellectual, physical and social resources to meet the demands of a situation. Most stress is generated from: work overload, competing priorities, conflict with colleagues, an unhappy work environment, strange values and over demanding deadlines. The effects of stress could either be good or bad, depending entirely on how we handle it. Stress when handled positively is beneficial to us. It helps keep us alert, active, and more energetic. If stress goes beyond our control, it turns into distress. If we handle it in a negative manner, it begins having an affect on us physically, mentally, and emotionally. This is really bad for us because it can strain our relations with everyone around us and deteriorate our physical and mental condition.

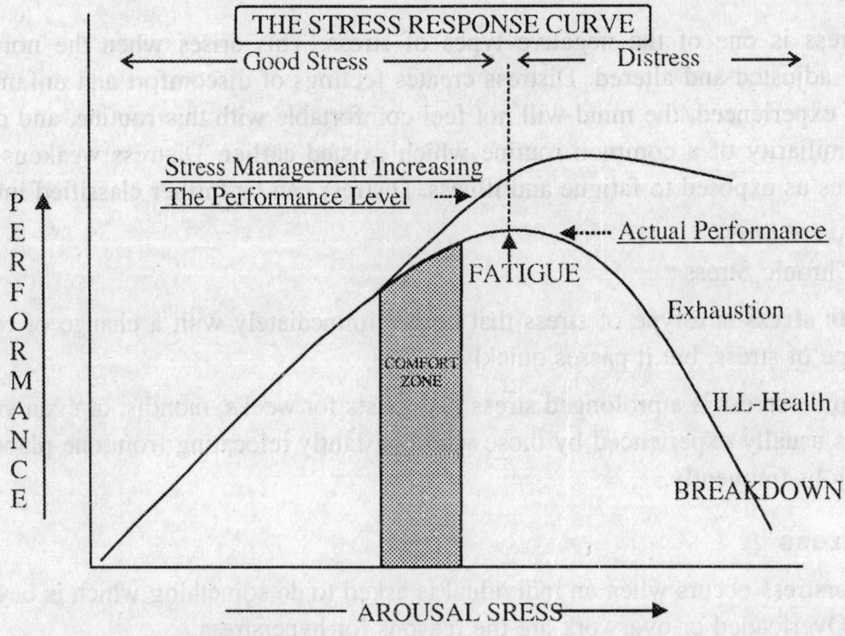

Fig. 24.2. Stress and Job Performance

Long-term exposure to stress can lead to serious health problems. Chronic stress disrupts nearly every system in your body. It can raise blood pressure, suppress the immune system, increase the risk of heart attack and stroke, contribute to infertility, and speed up the aging process. It can also expose an individual to anxiety and depression. Following are the effects of negative stress on individuals:

- Hair loss or early graying of hair
- Problem remembering things
- Poor concentration
- Poor judgement
- Hypersensitive and extremely moody
- Able to see only the negative side of things
- Confused mind
- An urge to get away (isolate) from everyone/everything
- Sudden and unwarranted anger
- Getting irritated for the smallest of reasons
- Overreacting to any situation
- Loss of confidence
- Eating too much or too little
- Sleeping too much or too little
- Sharp increase in alcohol/tobacco consumption

- Disturbed sleep, leading to a host of other problems
- Constant headache
- Severe digestive problems (constipation, diarrhea)
- High blood pressure
- Breathing problems
- Feeling tired constantly (even when you wake up in the morning)
- Irregular heartbeats
- Muscle tension and severe muscle pain

APPROACHES TO STRESS MANAGEMENT

Following are the some of the was in which stress can be reduced:

1. Time Management

One should manage his time properly. He should avoid setting unrealistic goals. Preparation of to do list helps managing time effectively. One should also note that he should not accept responsibilities over and above his capacity.

2. Prioritize tasks

Make a list of tasks you have to do, and, tackle them in order of importance. Do the high priority items first. This helps in completing the work more pleasantly.

3. Relax and breathe deeply

Our body cannot maintain the same level of energy without that extra oxygen. Therefore, it is necessary to breathe deeply to get extra oxygen. This releases considerable amount of stress.

4. Take more breaks from your work

Working continuously, without break causes monotony, boredom and stress. Therefore, taking break in between helps us to relax, break monotony and reduce stress. One should get away from the desk and move out for few minutes and resume work.

5. Delegate responsibility

Management is all about getting things done by others. One should learn the art of delegation of responsibilities to others. If the task is properly distributed to the capable persons in the organisation, the considerable amount of stress can be reduced.

6. Get more sleep

Stress causes due to lack of sleep also. One should take enough sleep in order to stay fresh and fit to work the next day. Taking proper sleep increases energy level and ability to concentrate.

7. Spend more time with optimistic people

It is necessary to have a company of people with positive attitude. Negative people will create negative thoughts, leading to a stressful situation. One should always think positively to gain positive energies. Business is not always smooth. It may face ups and down. Keeping our mind calm and cool is essential during such situations. To be cool and calm, it requires that one should practice positive attitude.

8. Practice effective communication

Communication is essential for preventing tensions. One should communicate in the language of the receiver. He should be good in both verbal and non-verbal communication. He should also pay attention to co-workers' gestures, tone of voice and posture.

9. Develop good working relationships

Trust, respect, understanding and compassion are necessary in any relationship. Co-workers have to function as a team and reach a common goal. But they often focus all their attention on their tasks and very little on how they treat each other. Good work relationships will relieve stress. One should spend little time with co-workers to improve interpersonal relationship.

10. Exercise regularly

Aerobic exercise, such as walking and swimming, produces brain chemicals that uplift your mood and mental well-being. Exercise also improves sleep and gives you time to think and focus on other things.

11. Eat healthy foods

One should have proper food at specified intervals. He should never skip meals. It is necessary to take time out for lunch no matter how busy he is.

STRESS AND BEHAVIOUR

Stress is caused by variety of reasons discussed earlier. Remedial measures are also suggested. But what will happen in work stations, when the employees are under stress? The psychological problems that cause stress such as anxiety, anger, tension, irritation etc. result in poor job performance, losing concentration, fail to supervise properly, and wrong decisions. The psychological problems may lead to behavioural problems such as sleeplessness, under rating or over rating the work, becoming more alcoholic, and addict to drugs. Such behavioural problems result in low productivity of the worker, increased absenteeism and high turnover.

Many types of remedial measures are suggested to control the behavioural problems. But one remedial measure that can give far reaching remedy is "negotiation". Both employers and employees sit across the table and sort out the specific problems that are causing stress and bad impact of it on work. Find out mutually agreeable solution and implement the decision. In most of the situations, negations, do miracles. "Destructive bargaining" (who will (employer or employees) get more slice in a pie in negotiations will have effectiveness.

Besides negotiations, which involve traditional and modern negotiating skill, practical aspects considered are (i) flattery, (ii) solving the easy problems first, (iii) keeping silence over the problem and not provoking the opponent and (iv) showing sympathy. These also play some role at times to release stress.

SUMMARY

1. As business worked expanding its operations, workload, irrespective of type and pattern, is increasing. Associated with this increased workload are: (i) pressure to perform, (ii) job insecurity, (iii) working beyond stipulated time, etc.
2. These problems have caused stress and fatigue in different degrees, depending upon the intensity of stress.
3. Stress of different types and degrees have a negative impact on organisational behaviour and resulted in low productivity, high turnover of labour, absenteeism and casual approach to work. Every worker suffers one type or the other of stress. Managers become indecisive due to stress.
4. Health problems are also increasing due to stress. Heart disease, accidents, work-related injuries are the common outcomes of stress. Mental disorders and family social problems are on the increase due to job-related stress.
5. The stress can be and or controlled by adapting measures such as consuming good food, better time management, relaxing, giving time for family meetings, positive thinking, participating in sports activities, etc.
6. Organisations also provide supportive measures such as creating good working environment, adopting variety of employee welfare programmes (both monetary and non-monetary), designing jobs to reduce stress and role conflict etc.

STUDY QUESTIONS

1. Give the meaning of stress. Is it good for an individual in an organizational setting? Explain the good and bad effects of stress.
2. State and explain the different job-related stressors with examples.
3. Give the meaning of frustration. Briefly explain the features of stress and its impact on organistional behaviour.
4. Briefly explain the psychological, physiological and behavioural effects of stress with examples.
5. Give the meaning of (i) Eustress and (ii) Distress. Explain their consequences on OB.

CASE STUDY

Much legislations have been enacted in the country directing the business houses to adopt measures to reduce job related stress. Accordingly, majority of the corporate houses have implemented for reaching programmes to reduce stress.

There are thousands of sympathetic stress cases of managements to address such cases. Of these cases, psychiatric cases (mental disorder due to stress) are increasing according to one report. Employees are in a dilemma to handle such cases. Neither they can be discharged from services nor they may be allowed to continue for long.

If they are allowed to continue as per statutes, the companies suffer in terms of productivity. Business houses cannot compromise with work standards, tolerate low productivity due to absence of employees or provide jobs to others to compete the tasks which are on priority list. Employers cannot also find out light duty jobs for mentally retarded workers.

Considering the inabilities faced by the employers, answer the following questions to reduce the stress of employer.

1. What employers have to do maintain standard productivity of the organisations, having psychotic cases on the roll? Do you feel that statutory provisions have to be amended to facilitate both employers and employees?
2. State the types of jobs that can be created for psychotic employees.
3. What are the general principles that can be deduced to help the mentally retarded employees that can be adapted to reduce stress to employees?

25

GROUP DYNAMICS

LEARNING OBJECTIVES

After reading this chapter, you should be able to know:

- Group — The Concept
- Group Effectiveness
- Stages of Group Formation
- Types of Group and their Function
- Group Norms and their Impact on Organisation
- Factors Influencing Group Success

Consider any organisation and watch its functioning. There are several people working in that organisation like that of a machine in which multiple components are fixed in appropriate places, each component discharging its own function. When all components work together, the machine will have value. If any one component fails to discharge its duty, smooth functioning of machine does not take place. Machine fails to give the required output. Similarly every human being working in an organisation (right from CEO to last person doing the cleaning work and security at the gate) has to be valued. Then only everyone cooperates. No person has to be taken for granted. If a cleaner does not clean the machine as per schedule, machine fails to work and the whole organisational work is paralysed. Similarly, all human resources of an organisation are valued ones and anybody cannot be ignored.

People working in an organisation are like members working in a team sports such as football or volley-ball or kho-kho or basket-ball. In each of these games, every individual is great as far as his play is concerned. Batsman should bat well to score and Bowler should bowl well to take wickets. The end result in the process is that "team wins." Thus, in a successful organisation top members — Chairman, Directors, CEO — have to work together to sort out the organisational work and make a best management team. They keep in mind the organisational vision, mission and objectives in mind and together formulate policies and programmes for the success of the organisation.

The top class and rest of the people working in different functional wings of the organisation have to know the concept of "success" and work towards that in a team. Each functional department (production, finance, marketing, HRD, etc.) should clearly understand its nature of work. Every one in the team should understand the meaning of success and work in that direction. Each functional department has its own meaning of success. If finance department works for managing the funds at low cost every year, the meaning of success will be in achieving it. For HRD department, increasing productivity of employee through employee welfare activities is the success. Marketing department finds its success in increasing turnover and market share for the product. Production department focuses on producing quality product at low cost to succeed. The total success of the organisation of maximising wealth and profit is achieved by the co-operation and co-ordination of each functional team. Cohesive teamwork opens the door to achieve organisational objectives.

The success of the organisation lies in maintaining employees on a permanent basis. They should be made to stay for long in the organisation and make them to work in a team. People in the organisation should also know as to what is happening in the organisation. Every one should be posted with operational information. In house, circulars and news letters have to be released on a weekly or fortnightly or monthly basis. When every worker is posted with information about the organisation, employees understand the organisation in proper perspective. Besides this, when various groups working in the organisation conduct cross-functional interactive meetings to solve day-to-day problems, a healthy and serene atmosphere prevails in the organisation.

People working at different levels of organisation in different capacities, can work in teams and groups ignoring hierarchy to achive organisational goals.

In this backdrop, this chapter focuses on group behaviour in organisations. A detailed analysis of 'team' concept provides a base to design "group behaviour practice" for an organisation and the benefits enjoyed by group. Explanation of "group" concept, type of group (Formal and informal), their thinking and impact on organisation, role of self-managed and cross-functional teams are briefly analysed.

Human beings are sociable in nature, spending much of their time in groups. There are various reasons for individuals to join groups. Individuals get themselves associated with groups for status, security or for any personal interest. The success of any organisation is determined by the 'team' — its people, their potential and attitude to give higher performance. It seems axiomatic that groups have a life of their own and that they influence the individuals within them, and *vice versa*. But that idea, along with the very phrase "group dynamics," was the contribution of a singular psychologist, Kurt Lewin who emigrated to the US from Germany in the 1930s. Kurt Lewin permanently widened the lends of psychology, demonstrating that human behaviour is the product not simply of personal characteristics, instincts and other forces within but also the inclusion of individuals in a group and organisation.

DEFINITION AND MEANING

Every individual is facing a challenge everyday to resolve the conflict between the demands of individuality and society. Even in workstations or offices, the managers should have the working knowledge of their domains. Particularly, they should know the social forces that constantly shape and redirect working lives, because, managerial roles are fundamentally social in nature. The manager, laughs, fights, interacts, imposes and weeps with social group only. Therefore, the person at the helm of affairs in an enterprise-manager should properly understand his social group.

Look at this statement. "All groups may be collections of individuals, but all collections of individuals are not groups." This is not a statement made to play on words (punning). The inner meaning of this statement is more than what it appears to be. Mere collection of individuals does not form a group. Take for example, students belonging to same college studying different courses, residing in a particular locality, commute to the college by different modes of transport. As time passes they come to know each other and exchange pleasantries. Then they decide to have transport system of their own by hiring a vehicle to commute to college everyday. Thus they form a vehicle pool In this example, group was technically formed when vehicle pool was formed. This really makes us to understand the term "GROUP."

As we are looking this concept from sociological angle, "a group is a composition of two or more freely interacting individuals who share a common identity and purpose." (Joseph A. Litterer – The Analysis of Organisations, Wiley, 1973).

A group may be defined as some people getting together for a common ideology.

A group is an aggregation of people interacting and interdependent and are aware of one another.

These definitions identify four features of a group and is presented in the following picture:

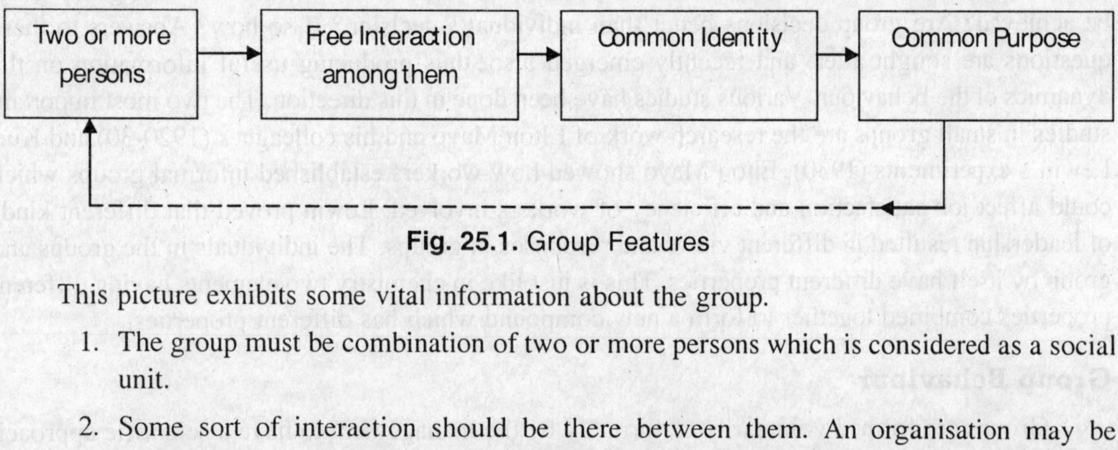

Fig. 25.1. Group Features

This picture exhibits some vital information about the group.

1. The group must be combination of two or more persons which is considered as a social unit.

2. Some sort of interaction should be there between them. An organisation may be considered as a social group, if the authorities allow the members to interact freely with each other. The organisation should be small enough to provide scope for interaction. However, in large organisations with bureaucratic tendencies many overlapping groups can be observed.

3. The group members shall interact to share a common identity. That means each one in the group should recognise one self as a member of the group.

4. Interacting members with common identity should also have common purpose. At least they should have an idea as to why group is formed or exists.

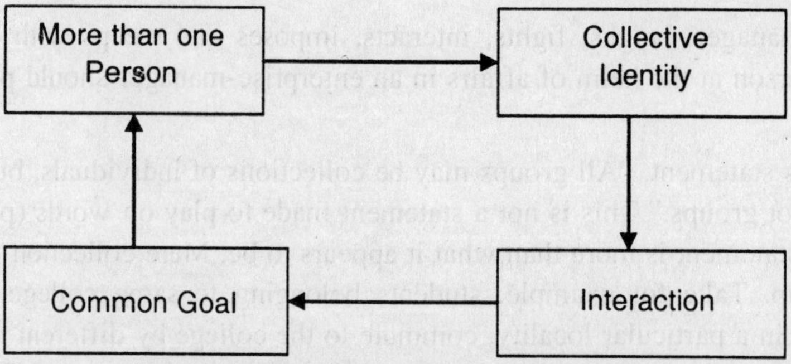

Fig. 25.2. Vital Information of the Group

> A group is any number of people who: (1) interact with one another, (2) are psychologically aware of one another, and (3) perceive themselves to be a group. — ***Samuel C. Certo.***

Group Dynamics

The social process by which people interact with each other in small groups is called group dynamics. Group dynamics is the study of forces operating within a group.

Small groups like family have functioned from yesteryears. In modern times, researchers have studied the process by which groups evolve and work. The usual questions which comes to the mind are — How does a group perform? How does it operate? Who is the leader? What role does he play? Does the role of the leader vary if objectives are different? How can the group goals be achieved? Are group decisions better than individual's decision? If so how? Answers to these questions are sought after, and recently emerged also, thus producing useful information on the dynamics of the behaviour. Various studies have been done in this direction. The two most important studies in small groups are the research work of Elton Mayo and his colleagues (1920-30) and Kurt Lewin's experiments (1930), Elton Mayo showed how workers established informal groups which could affect job satisfaction and efficiency of workers involved. Lewin proved that different kinds of leadership resulted in different views and responses in groups. The individuals in the groups and group by itself have different properties. This is just like in chemistry two elements having different properties combined together to form a new compound which has different properties.

Group Behaviour

Groups are formed voluntarily or formally by the management to have a scientific approach for problem solving. Individuals who join the group have to adapt themselves to the situation that group demands. Adaptablility of an individual to the group is a big challenge. Because group norms will be different and are prepared for the smooth follow of the group work. Individuals may not or cannot easily adapt as they have to work much against their conscience at times. Sometimes non-adaptablity causes either conflict or stress. Conflict zooms if the individual comes out openly expresses his dissatisfaction of the norms to be followed. Or stress is caused if the group member is introvert. The person suffers silently. The group behaviour, this, differs from individual behaviour. As the group norms demand a type of behaviour different from individual behaviour, management expects the following from the individual to work in a group:

(i) When individuals form into group, in the initial stages there will be mistrust amongst them and this mistrust has to be vanished and mutual trust should emerge. Members should have good understanding.

(ii) When mutual trust exists, it gives way for free communication amongst members and the base will be created for group decision-making.

(iii) Further, group cohesiveness emerges and every one co-operates with each other. Group solidarity naturally takes place and this results in group control, this means group members have flexibility in operations.

Simply enforcing government regulations will not get one to be the best. To obtain the fullest competitive edge, one need to create great teams by using the full potential of every individual. Teams are much more than a group. A group is collection of individuals where each person is working towards his or her own personal goal or agenda, whereas a team is a collection of individuals working towards a common goal or vision. This creates a synergy effect within the team — one plus on equals much more than one.

An individual, acting alone, can accomplish much; but a group of people acting together in a unified force can accomplish great wonders. This is because team members understand each other and support each other. Their main goal is to see the team accomplish its mission.

By using the synergy effect of teams to create a competitive advantage over other organisations who are using individuals acting alone. If team members do not accept others for what they are, they will be unable to use the abilities of each team member to fill in their own weak areas. Hence, the team effort develops knowledge and skill gaps that often lead to failure. Their only goal becomes the ones on their personal agendas....to make them as an individual look good while ignoring the needs of the team and the organisation.

Embracing diversity is the first item for building teams. Almost every team building theory states that to build a great team, there must be a diverse group of people on the team, that is, one must avoid choosing people who are like them. Choosing people like themselves to be on teams is similar to inbreeding — it multiplies the flaws. Compare this to the other end of the continuum having an assorted group of individuals which diminishes the flaws of others.

Diversity — An Organisation's Greatest Challenge?

Individuals' bias and prejudice are deeply rooted within themselves. From the moment an individual is born, he/she learn about himself/herself, environment, and the world. Families, friends, peers, books, teachers, idols, and others influence them on what is right and what is wrong. These early learnings are deeply rooted within these individuals and shape their perceptions about how they view things and how they respond to them. What an individual learn and experience gives him/her subjective point of view known as bias. Their biases serve as filtering devices that allow the individuals to make sense of new information and experiences based on what they already know.

Embracing diversity is more than tolerating people who are different. It means actively welcoming and involving them by:

- Developing an atmosphere in which it is safe for all employees to ask for help. People should not be viewed as weak if they ask for help. This is what helps to build great teams — joining weakness with strengths to get a goal or objective accomplished.

- Actively seeking information from people from a variety of backgrounds and cultures in order to develop a broad picture. Also, including everyone on the problem solving and decision-making process.

Including people who are different than you in informal gatherings such as lunch, coffee breaks, and spur of the moment meetings.

Organisations cannot function successfully without groups. The behaviour of an individuals take decisions on consensus bais. Each group varies with another depending on the size, position and the flow of authority. Box. 25.1 explains the necessity for organising teams in a workplace.

BOX 25.1. Need for Teams

- Managerial interest in group-working arrangement has increased dramatically in recent years.
- Collective working arrangements at work is now commonplace–the production team, the quality circle, etc.
- Managements increasingly use teams to carry out the work around; this is done in the expectation that teams deliver more than individuals.
- The current team and team working has its origin in Hawthorne Studies, carried out in Chicago between the late 1920s and to the early 1940s.

Why do individuals join groups?

The members of the group are basically individuals. Individual's performance affects the group performance. The success of a group depends on the individual's contribution towards the group task. Two main factors that determine the success of groups are:

(a) Traits/personality of the member.

(b) Member's ability.

Enough research is being done in the field of group behaviour. The early studies reveal a direct relationship between the member's behaviour and his/her personality. Individuals who are satisfied and yield productivity have certain characteristics in common like openness, self-confidence and independent. They have a positive attitude towards organisation. Employees who are autocratic and dominant in nature tend to exhibit a non-cooperative behaviour. Non-cooperation lessons the group productivity. One cannot depend on group's potential based on personality alone. It also depends on the individual's ability.

1. Ability of the group member includes the intellectual and physical strengths of members (**synergistic effect**). Individuals who have strong ability are found to be more attached to group. Strong ability in all dimensions will make the group performance a successful one.
2. As the groups provide the **security and safety,** people tend to join groups. They join the associations and trade unions so that their needs may be fulfilled due to the strength of the members.
3. Some individuals join the groups for mere **praising and recognition** from the other individuals. This brings the individuals who join the group to have and acquire sense of self-esteem.

4. Individuals join in groups mainly due to **power** acquisition. When joined in a group, some individuals become dominant and want to lead the other group members. Employees acquire a great deal of power when joined in a recognised group or association. For example, becoming a member in INTUC, gives an employee a formal recognition.

Work Group Effectiveness

Work group effectiveness is composed of three parts. The **first** is the performance of the group as rated by the team itself and by the outsiders who receive the team's output.

The **second** is the team's viability in the future. Viability is the team's long-term effectiveness, its ability to work together, and its ability to adapt to changing organisational and environmental conditions.

The **third** part of work group effectiveness is the satisfaction of the members of work group. The relative importance of these three effectiveness components is certain to vary for specific teams in their unique circumstances. There is no one best way to weigh the three group effectiveness factors. Their relative importance will change from one group to another group and over time, depending on the organisation and the group itself. Box 25.2 gives information about the features of effective group.

BOX 25.2. An Effective Group

- **An Effective Group** has a clear understanding of its goals: overall and immediate.
- Is flexible in selecting its procedure as it works towards its goals.
- Has achieved a high degree of communication and understanding among its members. Communication of personal feelings and attitudes as well as ideas occurs in direct and open fashion because it is considered important to the work of the group.
- Is able to initiate and carry out an effective decision-making, carefully considering minority viewpoints and securing the commitment of all members to important decisions.
- Achieves an appropriate balance between group productivity and the satisfaction of individual needs.
- Provides for sharing of leadership responsibilities.
- Has a high degree of cohesiveness (attractiveness to its members).
- Makes intelligent use of the differing abilities of its members.
- Can be objective about reviewing its own processes.
- Can face problems and adjust to needed modification.
- Maintains a balance between emotional and rational behaviour, channeling emotionally into productive group effort.

Group Formation – Stages

Individuals having similar likings tend to form a group. As a new group comes together, its members are faced with a dilemma. People want to belong to groups. The group's common goal provides a sense of purpose, and self-selection homogenizes membership. At the same time, individuals also want to maintain their independent identities. The interpersonal and work-related behaviour are exhibited and analysed during the stages of group development.

Two main assumptions for the basis for group formation have been put forward:

Functional: Such as joint action on a task; face-to-face interaction or mutually dependant relationships.

Psychological: The perception of a shared identity.

Most groups, according to research do not follow a standardised form of creation. It differs from one organisation to another. It also depends upon the number of members of the group, its structure and communication. The process of group formation can be depicted by five stages.

1. Forming: This is the first stage of group formation. During the initial stage, the members of the group do not have any clear idea. This first stage is characterised by a sense of uncertainty and awkwardness and perhaps anxiety. Participants may be unsure of what to do and how to do it, The "rules of the road"–group norms and standards have yet to be defined and participants are eagerly looking to find out what is okay and not okay. This phase often shows as tentativeness or even some anxiety on the part of the participants. Leaders need to set the tone for group behaviour, activities, and interactions High level of ambiguity is prevailing in the process. When members think about each other the process moves on to the next stage.

Most people are polite as they try to put their "best foot forward." The result is a superficial level of harmony and co-operation. This serves the purpose of getting the group started and off the ground in terms of motivation and commitment. Members may tend to verbalise how close they feel to each other, and may develop quite a group spirit due to successful task accomplishment. Leadership at this point should be a combination of High Task/Low Relationship (Telling) in terms of teaching skills and establishing norms moving to High Task/High Relationship (Selling) to get everyone involved and interacting in the group. This stage is otherwise termed as the phase of the members "getting acquainted".

2. Storming: This is the second stage of group forming. It is characterised by individual assertive behaviour, which may result in some group instability. Participants have begun to feel comfortable enough with their new environment to take some risks in revealing more of their personalities. Each person wants to get a sense of individual importance and influence on the group — "finding a niche." This becomes more evident as increasing responsibility is shifted to the group as they move into moderate levels of maturity. It involves conflict of the member's ideas.

One of the members assuming the leadership role tries to direct the group by bringing the members of the group together. The leadership style which may be most effective, are High Task/ High Relationship (Selling). Leaders should not be surprised if some conflicts develop in the group at this stage. This is a part of the natural process of the group becoming self-outstanding. This stage is otherwise called as the phase of "struggling forward."

3. Norming – This phase is otherwise called as "becoming personal". Norming is the stage where the group is **formed and structured completely.** A growth of affection and establishment of personal relationships characterise this phase. Participants will begin to take responsibility for resolving conflicts and strengthening friendships. Group cohesiveness exists in this stage.

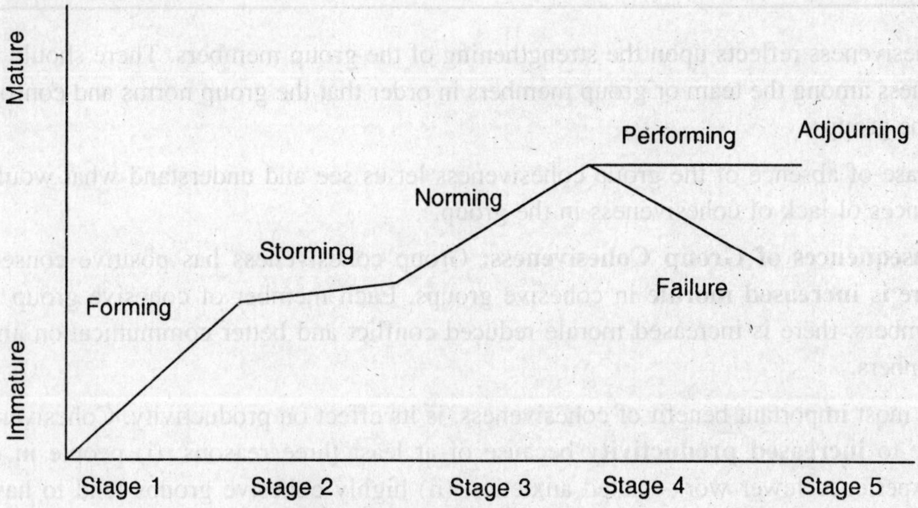

Fig. 25.3. Formation of Group

Cohesiveness relates to the togetherness of the members of the group. Each member realises his role and job to perform. The Leadership style, which may be most effective, is Low Task/ High Relationship (Participating) since the group is competent regarding tasks but needs assistance and support in terms of relationships.

4. Performing – When the group has adapted itself to the group environment, performance takes place. This phase is termed otherwise as "working together". The functional activities of the group are stated and members hold high co-ordination. The members try to pool their potential and give high productivity. This phase is characterised by harmony among group members. Participants look outwards to see how other people in the group are doing to make sure all are supported. Decision-making and problem-solving will be shared within the group.

At this stage, the group is mature enough to attend to its own needs both in terms of task and relationship matters. The leadership style, which would be most effective, would be Low Task/Low Relationship. Higher performance is achieved due to high interpersonal behaviour exhibited by the individuals.

5. Adjourning – If the groups are formed temporarily, then another stage follows, called as **Adjourning.**

It is otherwise termed as transference. In adjourning stage, the group disperses after the group activity is completed. Here, priority is given to wrapping up of the activities rather than increasing performance. This final part of the group process is essential in making sure that the trip is not remembered as "just a fun couple days in the woods." It is important that participants be able to transfer the things which they have learned about themselves and being in a group back to their regular lives. This is accomplished through the debriefing process (discussed in Transferring the Experience.) In the permanent groups, the performances of the group members are high compared to the temporary group.

Group Cohesiveness

Group Cohesiveness means the extent to which the members are attached towards each other. It response to the amount of motivation to remain the group.

Cohesiveness reflects upon the strengthening of the group members. There should be lot of cohesiveness among the team or group members in order that the group norms and conformity do exist in the groups.

In case of absence of the group cohesiveness let us see and understand what would be the consequences of lack of cohesiveness in the group.

Consequences of Group Cohesiveness: Group cohesiveness has positive consequences. First, there **is increased morale** in cohesive groups. Each member of cohesive group likes the other members, there is increased morale reduced conflict and better communication among the team members.

The most important benefit of cohesiveness, is its effect on productivity. Cohesiveness may contribute to **increased productivity** because of at least three reasons: (i) people in cohesive groups experience fewer work-related anxieties, (ii) highly cohesive groups tend to have lower absenteeism and turnover, and (iii) cohesiveness decreases productivity differences among groups.

Members of cohesive groups communicate with each other more than members of non-cohesive groups do. Sharing common ideologies, goals, backgrounds, or attitudes gives cohesive groups a lot to talk about, and such discussion is usually reinforcing. **Effective Communication** emerges from group cohesiveness.

The three points mentioned above speak about the benefits of groups to members generally. But the critical remaining question is whether or not cohesive work groups are good for their host organisations. Effect of cohesiveness depends on performance norms. A basic rule of group dynamics is that, the more cohesive the group, the greater the conformity of members to group norms. When the performance norm is positive, high conformity has a very beneficial effect. However, substantial undesirable result can occur when conformity is high.

Drexler Sibbet's Team Performance Model

A model of seven stages of work team performance is the Drexler Sibee Team Performance Model. At six of the stages, there is a primary question that must be addressed. If these questions are resolved well, then the team/group is prepared to deal effectively with the next stage. Unresolved behaviours indicate the question at that stage has not been well answered. More work is necessary for the team at that stage.

- **Orientation Stage:** Why am I here? People wonder whether or not they will fit in and be accepted by others. They need an answer to continue on with the team.
- **Trust Building Stage:** Who are you? People want to know about others who they will work with. What do they expect? What are they good at? What do they want from the group? Sharing information builds trust and free exchange in the group.
- **Goal/Role Clarification Stage:** What are we doing? What are the team's goals and what is each member's role in accomplishing those goals? People in the team want assumptions made explicit.
- **Commitment Stage:** How will we do it? At this stage, the team moves from discussing what to do to discussing exactly how to do. Resources, people, and time must be allocated.

- **Implementation Stage:** Who does what, when, where? Teams at this stage start doing their work. Timing, scheduling, and execution of tasks are predominant.
- **High Performance Stage:** A team that masters its methods of operating can become more flexible in responding to the environment. Goals can change as the team adapts as required.
- **Renewal Stage:** Why continue? People can get tired, group members change and continuing to perform the task can lose its appeal. Team members confront the question of why the group should continue as it has.

Some Roles Commonly Played by Group Members

Task-oriented Roles	*Relations-oriented Roles*	*Self-oriented Roles*
Initiator-Contributors Recommend new solutions to group members.	**Harmonisers** Mediate group conflicts	**Blockers** Act stubborn and resistant to the group.
Information Seekers Attempt to obtain the necessary facts	**Compromisers** Shift opinions to create group harmony.	**Recognition Seekers** Call attention to their own achievements.
Opinion givers Share own opinion with others.	**Encouragers** Praise and encourage others	**Dominators** Assert authority by manipulating the group.
Energisers Stimulate the group into Action whenever interest drops.	**Expediters** Suggest ways the groups can operate more smoothly	**Avoiders** Maintain distance,isolate themselves from fellow group members.

(***Source:*** J. Greenberg and B.A. Baron, Behaviour in Organisation, PHI, 1995, p. 292)

Theories of Group Dynamics

Many theories have been developed by different psychologists on group dynamics. The basic theory developed by George Homans, besides telling about "Propinquity" also speaks of activities, interaction and sentiments for forming the group. This means that persons join and form groups as they work closely with each other. It may be of geographical or spatial proximity. Supposing individuals work in an office or in a department become close and form the group. This may be formal or informal. They interact with each other on a specific task and gradually develop sentiment. Thus, the group is formed. Though the propinquity theory has many advantages to tell as to why the group is formed, the main limitation is that it is not analytical. It cannot consider many complex aspects of information technology. Today's organisational structure being more of network or virtual, propinquity cannot fully answer the complex aspects of group formation in this new structure.

Balance Theory

Many other theories are put forward regarding group formation. But they tell one or two dimensions of group formation. The theory, of these many theories, considered to be comprehensive is "**Balance Theory**" developed by Theodre Newcomb. This theory states that "two or more individuals interact with each other as they have common attitudes and values. These include, authority politics, work, religion, lifestyle and marriage." The theory further states that individuals who form the group try to maintain balance between attitudes and values through interaction and propinquity and if they cannot maintain balance, they back out resulting in disconnection of relationship.

Exchange Theory

This is a socio-psychological theory. In this theory, cost-benefit aspect is considered. Here, the "Cost" refers to anxiety, frustration, embarrassment and fatigue that occurs due to participation in a group. Benefit refers to satisfaction of personal needs. If reward is more than the cost, people join the group. The attributes such as attitude, propinquity, interaction are all key factors that facilitate the formation or disintegrate the group.

Thus, benefits and rewards are exchanged for costs (anxiety, frustration, etc.) and if rewards and benefits are more, the group is formed and developed.

Practical Aspects

Though the theories tell about the various reasons and contexts for group formation in workplaces, certain real and practical aspects prompt the people to from the group. The vital reasons for group formation are: (i) security, (ii) social and (iii) economic reasons.

Security reason implies that when an individual is harassed in a workplace and if such person does not have any type of support from any corner, he suffers. On the other hand, if he is a member of a group, his grievance can be easily addressed. Therefore, individuals wish to be group members for security reason.

Satisfaction of social needs is another practical reason as to why workers wish to affiliate to a group. Human relations approach to management thought has clearly indicated this. It is proved in many empirical studies that the workers would like to be group members to fulfil their social needs.

Economic reason is perhaps the most powerful practical reason that prompts individuals to join the group. Demanding higher wages or asking for better monetary incentives will have strong impact when fought for them unitedly. Trade unions for that matter can shake the organisation when genuine demands are not met. But an individual cannot influence the management so powerfully as the group does. Thus, in reality, economic factor strongly motivates the workers to become members of a recognised group.

Types of Groups

In an organisational work setting, there might be different groups. Generally, groups differ on the size, the flow of authority and communication. The major classification of groups are given below.

Much of the confusion about teams in the workplace has to do with loose definitions of terms. Let's start off on the right foot by specifying what a few keywords and phrases mean.

Work Group: A group of people working together (Example – the mechanics in an Auto Center).

Team: A group of people working together toward a common goal (Example – The quality circle group working in a manufacturing unit).

(a) Formal Group: The line of authority forms the members of this group formally. They are formed for specific purpose. The purpose or objective of forming is given by the management.

(b) Informal Group: Members of this group belong to various divisions or sections irrespective of their jobs. These groups are formed for the purpose of solving any serious problems, or generally for sharing their ideas about any matter related or unrelated to the organisation. Grapewine (rumours) is followed in these types of groups. Informal groups might positively or negatively affect the performance of the organisation.

(c) Reference Group: The members of this group act as a comparison or reference for other individuals. Individuals outside the reference groups form their attitudes and frame their personality by referring or identifying themselves with reference groups. Thus, these reference groups may directly or indirectly affect the individual's attitude who may or may not be the member of the reference groups. The reference groups have power and attractiveness compared to other groups.

Depending on the number of members and the size of the groups, the groups can be further classified as small groups, medium-sized groups and larger groups.

(d) Small Groups are highly effective for short-term decision-making process. Here the number of group members are restricted up to 5. The decision-making process is much facilitated in the medium-sized groups. Here, the number of members are limited. The humber of members may vary from 7 to 12. The communications among the members are fast.

In larger group, the decision-making is conventional as the number of members are large. Communication is difficult.

(e) Friendship groups: Another type of group formed is called as friendship group. They are a type of informal groups. These groups are basically formed to satisfy the needs of belongingness and security.

(f) Task groups: The management might form task groups in order to accomplish some of the organisational goals.

(g) Focus groups are a powerful means to evaluate services or test new ideas. Basically, focus groups concentrate on an issue to sort out the problem are to execute a work. Focus Groups work in-depth on issue and give results. One can get a great deal of information during a focus group session.

Focus groups uniquely expose and accentuate both the similarities and the differences between *distinct types* of people. By seeing how these different types of people interact, one gets complete information that can be achieved. Focus groups spark more new ideas and identify more unexpected information than any other method of marketing research.

(h) Self-managed Team: A group of people working together in their own ways toward a common goal which is defined outside the team (Example – In XYZ company, there is a team named BETA. They manufacture cardboard boxes as defined by executive leadership. Team does their own work scheduling, training, rewards and recognition, etc.)

(i) Self-directed Team: A group of people working together in their own ways towards a common goal which the team defines (as above, but team also handles compensation, discipline and acts as a profit centre by defining its own feature).

The different types of the groups are given in the diagram below:

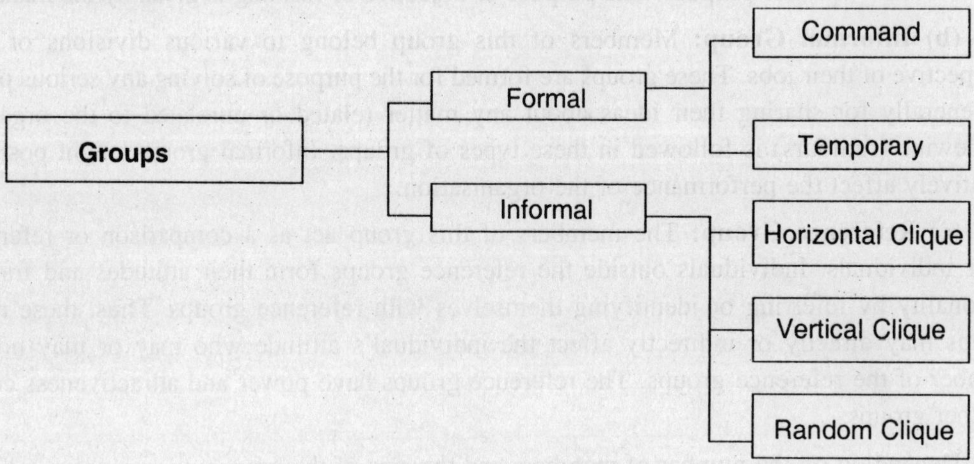

Fig. 25.4. Types of Different Groups

Note on Informal Group

Although informal group in an organisation does not have specific goals fixed officially as in case of formal ones, this group plays a major role in organisational activities. Both formal and informal groups are inseparables in any organisation. But informal groups can deviate from formal structures.

Meaning

Informal groups are not recognised by the top management. The group is an association of like-minded people who share their feelings themselves freely about the organisation. This may be defined as "collection of individuals whose common work experiences result in the development of a system of interpersonal relations that extend beyond these established by management". (Raef T. Hussein, "Informal Groups, Leadership and Productivity", OD Journal).

This definition provides information about informal groups. Its features are as follows:

1. Infomal groups deviate significantly from formal groups.
2. An organisational member can become a member of any number of informal groups.
3. It is not structured.
4. Each member has his/her own issue.
5. Group is formed to address certain issues that are not solved by formal groups and will be dissolved after the problem is solved or member server his connection from the group after his issue is solved.
6. Informal groups work to satisfy the needs of its members and provide opportunities for the growth of their members.

Infomal group will be in two forms.

(1) Interest groups are those that work to satisfy special issues of membes. For example : A group that functions to demand better working condition. After the satisfaction of social issue, the group dissolves.

(2) Friendship groups that are formed on the basis of race, religion gender, etc., to have personal affiliation with one another.

Benefits

Informal groups enjoy certain benefits which members of organised group does not.

(i) Availing social and cultural benefits that formal group members cannot get. The group also perpetuates cultural values that group members want.

(ii) The members of informal group enjoy certain status in the organisational which other cannot.

(iii) Communication amongst group members will be very fast. Sometimes, information created by informal group becomes a reality and the benefits are enjoyed by all.

(iv) Informal group will be complementary to formal group in many of the organisations and positive overall work environment is created.

The members of informal group would like to work in same shifts to have work cohesiveness.

Before anyone would try to implement something as aggressive as a self-managed (and subsequently self-directed) team, they should know and be able to articulate the expected benefits. A mature self-managed team, when compared to typical hierarchical management, would have measured results showing:

More	*Less*
Enthusiasm	Individual opinion about what's important
Learning from peers	Reliance on individual abilities
Comfort knowing help is there	Panic when workload peaks
Camaraderie	Backbiting
Shared responsibility	Protecting information
Focus on the organisation	What's in it for me?
Responsibility for the team	Stress on the "supervisor"
Simple, visible measurement	Feeling unaccomplished

The figure 25.5 brings out the factors responsible for group formation.

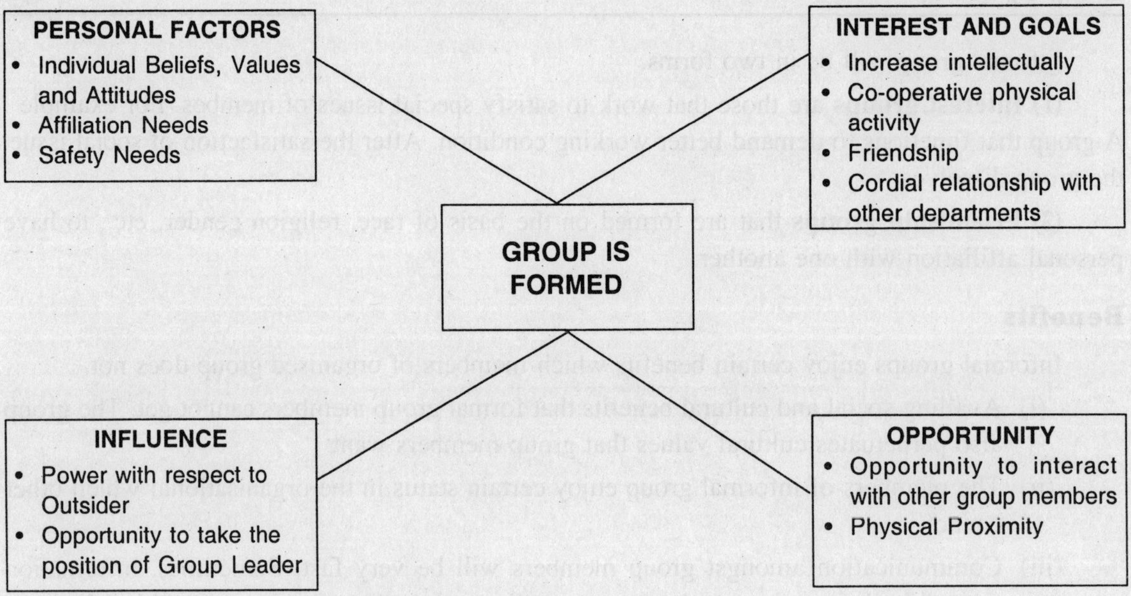

Fig. 25.5. Factors in Group Formation

FACTORS DETERMINING GROUP SUCCESS

According to the needs of the organisation, groups are formed to accomplish certain tasks. Many of the turnkey projects are made successful due to better teamwork. There is an effect called **'synergy'** in groups. Synergy says that the total effort of the group is greater than the individual efforts. It is generally stated as 2 + 2 = 5, *i.e.*, the sum total of group is greater than individual numbers. The successful completion of a group task depends on the following factors.

1. Organisation Structure: Work groups forms a part of the larger organisation. They are therefore affected by its design, culture, and systems. These organisational context factors are likely to have strong effects especially on newly formed groups because new group members are open to outside influences as they begin to create their team's processes.

2. Organisational Culture: The cultural profile of a company will affect how groups operate in that culture. For example, an organisation with a Tough-Guy culture will be probably have cohesive groups that interact a great deal. People in these kinds of organisations need social support that can best be provided by a closely-knit team. An example is the Indian Navy.

3. Task Design and Technology: The methods and machines used to perform the group's task will affect how the group is designed, how it functions, and its ultimate effectiveness. The performance of a team can be directly affected by charging the tools, design and introducing new technology.

4. Mission Clarity – The more clear the mission at the orgnisational leve, the clearer are the group taks and goals. The organisation's mission must be communicated down to the group level. Ambiguity of the mission leads to lower productivity of the group.

5. Autonomy Given to Work Groups – Autonomy refers to the certain independent powers given to the groups. More autonomous groups are able to design their own work, provide their own internal group leadership. The group determines how the group's task is to be divided among the group members. In order to meet the market demands for greater variety of goods and of high quality, a new technique called '*cell manufacturing*' is being adopted. Employees are grouped into different teams. Each team has all the equipment and parts it needs to make and check an entire piece or major component. Employees in cells see their products from start to finish. They deal with problems as they come up and are responsible for the quality of their product.

6. Performance Feedback – More feedback to the group about its performance allows the groups to adjust its design and its processes in order to be more effective.

7. Rewards and Recongition Given to the Group – The rewards and recognitions given to the groups are more effective and strengthen the identification of its members. An individualistic organisation will find it difficult to have effective groups due to its reward structure.

8. Training and Consultation – Groups in organisations need training and consultation to help them improve their group processes. Group members need to learn both technical job requirements and how to work with together. People cannot simply be put into a group and expcted to perform well. Working on a group presents its own challenges and opportunities. Training is required to help group members to accept the challenges and seek opportunities.

9. Physical Environment – Groups can be possessive of their physical space. By establishing a territory and defending it against outsiders, the group can protect valuable resources, improve its own living and working conditions, gain a sense of privacy, control social interactions, become more cohesive, and express its social identity. The organisation can therefore have a direct effect on a group by controlling the group's work area. The organisational control of where the group works also affects its performance.

10. The Degree of Change in the Organisation – High rates of organisational change can cause instability within work groups due to changes in organisational policies and personnel.

Box 25.3 brings out the mistakes in handling teams.

BOX 25.3. The Greatest Management Mistake in Handling Teams

Preparing and cooking ice-cream in the same manner as a hamburger would obviously result in failure. One can't treat all ingredients and meals as the same thing — they are all different, requiring different methods and techniques to achive their particular result.

The greatest management mistake should becoming painfully clear. Many managers treat all employees as the same assortment of ingredients, trying to motivate them toward greater success, using one cookie-cutter approach.

Just as failure results from throwing ice-cream on a grill, so too will a manager fail in inspiring his people if he attempts to do so using a single method.The people on your team are as different as baked beans and apple pie. They each work from an unique set of motivators, responding to some with excited action and others with boredom or even anger. It's up to one to discover what drives each one of your team members. What elements excite them? What elements turn them off? It may take a little time and concreted effort on one part, but uncovering the powerful motivators that drive your people will be best thing one can do for you and your team.

Remember, one may respond to financial rewards or incentives, but that doesn't mean everyone in your team will share your sentiments. Listen to your people. Recognise and utilise their motivators. You are dealing with a wide assortment of ingredients, and following this principle will allow one to prepare each one with amazing success.

Some of the lessons that are to be learned in implementing teams are summarised below:

1. To create a team. A demand for performance is more important than team-building exercises. You can get a group together and train them in teamwork for weeks but they won't be a team until they have a common understanding of the need to perform. First comes the strategic plan, then the tasks needed to carry out the plan. Finally, teams are formed to do the tasks.
2. Team basics are often overlooked. Team basics are: size, purpose, goals, skills, approach, and accountability.
3. Teams at the top are the most difficult. Executives have complex, long-term challenges, heavy demands on their time, and they got where they are by being John Waynes.
4. There's no need to throw out the hierarchy. Teams are the best way to integrate across structural boundaries. They are the best way to design and energise core processes.
5. Teams permit performance and learning at the same time. There is no better way to become a learning organisation than to have a team-based structure, which thrives on people learning from peers. The learning endures.

Group Meetings and Decisions

Groups are formed in an organisation for a specific purpose. During the formation of the group the members exchange various ideas. Organisation members and leaders make decisions in the group. The decision-making process can be stressful because each individual's perception about the problem is viewed differently. For example, some people see it as a form of poor struggle, some people cannot bear the idea of losing an argument, and some people simply do not like to make decisions.

For example, during the course of a trip, there are a number of decisions that will need to be made by the whole group. These might include things like where to camp, which route to take, whether to rest for the afternoon or do a side hike, etc. Group decision-making can be a powerful learning and growth tool for the group. It can also be a place for conflict to develop. The first thing to determine is whether it is a decision that can and should be made by the group, or with input from the group, or is it a decsion to be made solely by the leaders.

The leaders will make obviously some issue, such as those that involve safety. To present such a decision to the group suggest that they have authority to make the decision, and if the leaders disagree, they must countermand the group's decision. Also some decision-making can lead to splintering the group. Both of these can lead to bad feelings by the group members and damage the positive group spirit. Avoid this problem by thinking ahead and determining what decisions are appropriate for the group to make. It may be better for the leaders to make decision from their status as authorities, that to give the decision to the group and have the process lead to negative outcomes.

Let us examine the steps in the Group Decision-making Process.

1. Set goal(s) and prioritize them.
2. Brainstorm options for achieving goals.
3. Evaluate the different options and examine how the options meet the goal(s).
4. Determine the decision-making strategy to be used.

- Best serves highest priority goals
- Best serves all goals
- Serves goals without creating any negative outcomes
- Creates the least negative outcomes

Leaders will also need to decide if they should be involved in the decision process, or "sit it out." Sometimes, the presence and perceived authority of the leaders can slant the decision-making process. However, in certain situations, this can work to your advantage as a leader. Making good group decisions involves a process, which the leaders may have to state or model as a norm for the group to follow.

Making decisions is an important part of group life. There are several types of group decisions.

(a) Unilateral: These are the decisions made by one person, often the leader, without other group members. At times, it can be appropriate. For example, a minor decision that needs to be made right away. If the decision-making is repetitive in nature and of less importance, there will be a very low group commitment.

(b) Handclasp: Decisions are made by two members. One suggests, the other endorses and carries it through without adequate discussion or group consideration. This has high commitment for the two who made it, but generally not for the others.

(c) Clique: This method is similar to the Handclasp but with a small set of group members involvement. This usually occurs when a close sub-group decides what is good for the rest of group. Repeated clique decisions cause splintering of the group and low commitment.

(d) Majortiy Rule: This is the most popular way of making decisions. The opinions are collected through secret ballot vote. In this case members of the group are polled and the option that receives support from the greatest number in the group is chosen. This strategy works well if everyone agrees to be bound by it, and if everyone feels they have a chance to express their view points and needs. However, it can lead to splitting of the group. Once again leaders whould evaluate if this method will be a positive or negative experience for the group. However, a sizeable segment of the group may feel devalued and decrease their commitment to the decisions in which they "lose" to the majority vote.

(e) Consensus: This is the most effective method of making a group decision in terms of members feeling included. Consensus decision-making means reaching a decision that all members of the group are willing to support at some level. In order to reach this point, everyone in the group must be given ample time to express their view and time to express their disagreement with other's views. *This method* is similar to Majority Rule, but the individuals know that what they think and the entire group considers value. Each person will agree with the decision, under the circumstances, which may not be ideal.

Any method may prove effective under a given set of circumstances. However, it is apparent that the first three approaches are likely to reinforce the power in the group and create tension. Morale and commitment can be lowered if these are the usual methods of making organisational decisions.

As members posess the fundamental ingredients for solutions to all problems, group decisions should be based on all member's input. If there are decisions that take a few people to make, it may not be necessary to involve the entire group.

Advantages of Group Consensus Approach

- **Greater number of approaches to a problem.**
- **Participation in problem-solving increases acceptance level:** A lower quality solution that has wide acceptance can be more effective than a higher quality solution that lacks acceptance.
- **Better understanding of the decision:** Communication failures are greatly reduced when the individuals who must work together in executing the decision have participated in making it.
- **Exchange of more knowledge and information.**
- **High level of commitment by the members to the decision.**

Disadvantages of Group Consensus Approach

- **Social Pressure:** Minority opinions in groups can have very little influence on the solutions even when their opinions are correct ones.
- **Individual Domination:** Generally, dominant individuals emerge and capture more than their share of influence on the outcome.
- **Conflicting Secondary Goal:** Individuals tend to aim at winning the argument at the cost of finding the best answer.
- **Time:** Listening and considering all points of view in order to arrive at the best solution takes time.

Effectiveness in communication is of paramount importance in the decision-making process. The leader plays an important role in group decision-making. In all of these strategies, it is important for leaders to model good listening and communication skills. Leaders may need to act as facilitators for effective communication through such things as asking people not to interrupt others, quieting dominant members of the group, and asking silent members to speak up. The leader must cease to contribute, avoid evaluation, and withhold from thinking about solutions. Instead he/she must concentrate on the group process by assuming responsibility for accurate communication between members.

The way decisions are made shows the degree of effectiveness of a group. An effective group generates more ideas than individuals generate independently. They have a high level of participation and are task-oriented.

NORMS

A norm is a set of expected attitudes, beliefs, and behaviours that define how a group member is expected to think or act. Descriptive norms identify what most people do in a given situation. Injunctive norm indicate what behaviour is generally approved of in the society. To be considered a norm, these expectations should be held by most group members and should be enforced. When a person deviates from the norm, there is a punishment.

Norms are common to most groups deal with sharing the rewards or costs of group membership, preventing conflicts among group members, regulating contacts with outsiders, and expressing a group's core values.

Commitment to the group's tasks is increased when the act of committing to the group and its task is clearly stated, cannot be changed, is made in public, and is done freely. Violation of group norms will lead to conflict with the norm violator. However, the consequences of norm violation do depend on the violator's level in the organisational hierarchy. A group's leader is allowed more flexibility to violate group norms.

Peripheral norms in a group are less central and less important to group survival. They may be violated with fewer penalties than central norms. Finally, the consequences of norm violation depend on the member's previous behaviour in the group. Those who have accepted the group's norms and acted in accordance with them have credit with the group. This credit is used up as more norms violation occurs.

Development of Group Norms

Group norms generally develop from the following:

- Explicit statements by supervisors or co-workers about expected behaviour.
- Critical events in the group's history helps to establish precedents about expected behaviour.
- Primacy – The first behaviour pattern that emerges in a group often becomes a group norm about expected behaviour.
- Carry-over behaviours from past situations – Individuals bring norms with them from their other work groups, organisations or cultures.

Reasons for Enforcement of Norms

Group norms are enforced for the following four reasons:

- They facilitate group survival, keeping the group together and protecting it from other groups. Behaviour that threatens the group is punished.
- They simplify and make predictable what behaviour is expected of group members. Norms help group members to predict and anticipate the actions of other group members.
- They help the group avoid embarassing interpersonal problems. Norms of behaviour help to make sure no one's self-image is damaged.
- They express the central values of the group and clarify what is distinctive about the group's identifity.

Norms about a sequence of behaviours can be called a script. For example, when meeting a business colleague, the script is to shake hands, exhange names, conduct business, then depart. In many countries, the scripts for normal business interaction can be quite different form that of ours. For example, the occupant of an Arab office will sit on the floor in the center of the room surrounded by people who have come to see him. The same may not be followed elsewhere!

SUMMARY

1. Organisations cannot function successfully without groups. The behaviour of an individual is totally different when he is single and in a group. The success of the group depends on the individual's contribution towards the group task.
2. The group's common goal provides a sense of purpose, and self-selection homogenises membership. But people also want to maintain their independent identities. Groups are formed

by four stages, forming, storming, norming and performing. The life of a group depends upon the difference in the various stages of the groups.

3. Factors such as, organisation structure, organisational culture, task design and technology, autonomy given to work groups, rewards and recongition, training and consultation, etc., determine group success.
4. Group behaviour is determined by several factors such as organisational resources, the working condtions, *i.e,*, conducive environments and the culture of the organisation.
5. There are a variety of methods in group decision-making.

   Majority of the methods are most popular methods for making decisions. The opinions are collected through secret ballot vote. Consensus, a similar method of decision-making as majority rule, but the individuals know that what they think and value is considered by the entire group.
6. A norm is a set of expected attitudes, beliefs, and behaviours that defined how a group member is expected to think or act. Descriptive norms identify what most people do in a given situation.

STUDY QUESTIONS

1. What is a group?
2. What is a group cohesiveness?
3. Define team?
4. Define Role identity?
5. Define conformity?
6. What is group think?
7. Why are groups formed?
8. What are group norms? How are they developed? When are group endorsed?
9. Explain the various stages of group development?
10. Why people join groups?
11. How are group decisions made? What are the types of group decisions?
12. Discuss different types of groups.
13. Write note on:
    (a) Informal Group
    (b) Group Cohesion
    (c) Quality Circle
    (d) Group Conflict
14. What is group dynamics? What are the different types of groups? Explain.
15. Discuss in what way the group behaviour affects the productivity of an organisation?
16. Explain in detail the function of small groups?
17. Does group size and status has an effect on productivity?

CASE STUDY

CASE 1: GROUP BEHAVIOUR

Prasad is the Deputy Director of the Municipal Corporation, of a city and he reports directly to the Chief Director, South. If the Zone is divided into different divisions then the work can be done in a better way. It will be easy to manage. Manager of the particular divisions were given in charge of certain duties. Like maintenance and control of their subordinates and the activities.

David was given the major responsibilities of maintaining the key projects. He was also provided with the resources.

For the next six months, he was told by his Chief Director, that he would be receiving Rs. 60 croses He was also instructed to undertake 4 projects. He has allotted 4 teams each under the head of Adithya, Lakhsmi, Rajani and Bhaskara. He also divided the work of planning which is to be done by Kilman and team. The research for the project will be done by Agnes and team.

The last two teams were given in charge of carrying out the projects successfully. The key projects were involved of purchasing imported machines and equipment for cleaning process. Employees training and development programme for all the employees within the corporation, etc. Every week, Prasad calls for group discussion to share the views of all heads. In the beginning, everything went on well. But later, Prasad found some difficulties in getting the heads together. The overall performances of the teams were slow. The projects bring to a consensus of all the heads. He tries best to remind them of the main objectives of the projects. Some heads like Bhaskara and Rajani just provide the information with a material to support.

Rajani is highly objective in nature and Lakshmi is mostly plunged into her own thoughts. Adithya co-operates only if each time benefits are shown. Prasad tries to overcome all these difficulties and tries to achieve the success in all the four projects.

Case Questions:

1. Why did Prasad prefer to have group decision-making rather than individual decision-making?
2. What type of group decision-making can be applied in this case?
3. What can be done to make higher team performance?

CASE 2: THE MANAGER'S MEMO

Following is the letter authored by the Vice President, Consumer Electronics Division and addressed to the Production Manager. The issue raised in the letter relates to Quality First Programme.

"I think it's time to look at a new approach to our Quality First Programme. We've had the suggestion box out for a year and so far we have received only two suggestions for quality improvements, of which only one made sense.

"Let's try a group approach. We can divide the employees into groups that can meet to come up with ideas for improving the quality of our products and production process".

"I'd like you to prepare a plan for these groups. How should they operate? How often should they meet? What should be the size of each group? Should we divide the groups into engineers, production workers, maintenance personnel and so on, or should we put a variety of workers into each group? What problems can we anticipate with group format, and how can we solve them? These questions are meant as starting point. If you have other ideas or concerns, please include them in your plan."

Case Questions:

Assume you are production manager and respond to Vice President's letter with a memo outlining the plan requested. Be sure to respond to specific questions. Use as many of the concepts in the chapter as you can develop a complete plan that minimises the pitfalls of group dynamics.

(***Source:*** Adapted from *Organisational Behaviour* by Gregory B. Northaraft and Maggaret A. Neole, The Dryden Press, 1990, p. 321)

REFERENCES

1. Allen. L.A., Management and Organisation (N.Y.: McGraw-Hill, 1958).
2. Anthony, Robert N., and John Dearden, Management Control Systems (Homewood, III: Irwin, 1976).
3. Argyris, Chris, Personality and Organisation (N.Y.: Harper and Row, 1957).
4. Bedeian, Arthur G., Organisations – Theory and Analysis (N.Y.: The Dryden Press, 1984).
5. Beesley, Michael and Tom Evans, Corporate Social Responsibility (London: Croomhelm, 1978).
6. Berne, Eric, Priniciples of Group Treatment (N.Y.: Oxford University Press, 1964).
7. Brech, E.F.L., Principles and Practice of Management (London: Pitman, 1972).
8. Brown. A., Organisation of Industry (Englewood Cliffs, N.J.:Prentice-Hall, 1947).
9. Davis, Keith A., and John W. Newstrom, Human Behaviour at Work: Organisational Behaviour, 8th edn.
10. Ernest Dale, Organisation (N.Y.:AMA, 1967)
11. Ernest Dale, Planning and Developing the Company Organisation Structure, Research Report No. 20 (N.Y.:AMA, 1952).
12. Fiedler, Fred E., A Theory of Leadership Effectiveness (N.Y.:McGraw-Hill, 1957).
13. Gallerman, Saul, Motivation and Productivity (N.Y.: AMA, 1953).
14. George Claude S., Jr., The History of Management Thought (New Delhi: Prentice-Hall, 1978).
15. Gorwala, A.D., Report on the Efficient Conduct of State Enterprises, 1951.

16. Hiller, Frederick S. and Gerald J. Lieberman, Operations Research, 2nd edn, (San Francisco: Holden Day).
17. James D. Mooney, Priniciples of Organisation (N.Y.: Harper and Row, 1947).
18. Koontz, Harold D. and Cyril J. O'Donnell, Principles of Management: An Analysis of Managerial Functions (Tokyo:McGraw-Hill Kogakusha, 1972).
19. Likert, Rensis, Motivation: The Core of Management (N.Y.: AMA, 1953).
20. Likert, Rensis, New Patterns of Management (N.Y.: McGraw-Hill, 1951).
21. Lynton, R.F. and Udai Pareek, Training for Development (Bombay: Taraporevala, 1973).
22. Maslow, A.H., Motivation and Personality (N.Y.: Harper and Bros., 1954).
23. Miner, Joh B., The Practice of Management (Columbus: Charles E.Merrill Publishing Co., 1985).
24. Mockler, Robert J., Readings in Business Planning and Policy Formulation (Englewood Cliffs, N.J.: Prentice-Hall, 1972).
25. Monappa, A. and M.S. Saiyadain, Psychological Tests for Executive Selection (Ahmedabad: IIM, 1977).
26. Robey Daniel, Designing Organisations (Homewood, Ill: Richard D. Irwin, 1986).
27. Terry, George R., Principles of Management (Homewood, III., Richard D.Irwin, 1961)
28. Vroom, Victor H., Work and Motivation (N.Y.: Wiley, 1954).